CHAOTIC SYSTEMS

Edited by **Esteban Tlelo-Cuautle**

Chaotic Systems
Edited by Esteban Tlelo-Cuautle

Published by InTech
Janeza Trdine 9, 51000 Rijeka, Croatia

Publishing Process Manager Katarina Lovrecic

Technical Editor Teodora Smiljanic

Cover Designer InTech Design Team

Additional hard copies can be obtained from orders@intechopen.com

Chaotic Systems, Edited by Esteban Tlelo-Cuautle
p. cm.
ISBN 978-953-307-564-8

For EU product safety concerns:
IN TECH d.o.o., Prolaz Marije Krucifikse Kozulić 3, 51000 Rijeka, Croatia,
info@intechopen.com or visit our website at intechopen.com.

Meet the editor

Esteban Tlelo-Cuautle received a B.Sc. degree from Instituto Tecnológico de Puebla in 1993. He then received both M.Sc. and Ph.D. degrees from Instituto Nacional de Astrofísica, Óptica y Electrónica (INAOE), in 1995 and 2000, respectively. In 2001 he was appointed as professor-researcher at INAOE. From 2009-2010, he served as a Visiting Researcher in the department of electrical engineering at the University of California Riverside, USA. He has authored four books, ten book chapters, 46 journal articles and around 100 conference papers. He is an IEEE Senior Member, IEICE Member, and a member of the National System for Researchers (SNI-México). He serves in the editorial board of Nonlinear Science Letters B: Chaos, Fractal and Synchronization; Trends in Applied Sciences Research; and Journal of Applied Sciences. He regularly serves as a reviewer in about 22 journals and 15 international conferences. His research interests include systematic synthesis and behavioral modeling and simulation of linear and nonlinear circuits and systems, chaotic oscillators, symbolic analysis, multi-objective evolutionary algorithms, and analog/RF and mixed-signal design automation tools.

Contents

Preface XI

Part 1 Chaotic Systems 1

Chapter 1 **Short-Term Chaotic Time Series Forecast 3**
Jiin-Po Yeh

Chapter 2 **Predicting Chaos with Lyapunov Exponents: Zero Plays no Role in Forecasting Chaotic Systems 25**
Dominique Guégan and Justin Leroux

Chapter 3 **Relationship between the Predictability Limit and Initial Error in Chaotic Systems 39**
Jianping Li and Ruiqiang Ding

Chapter 4 **Microscopic Theory of Transport Phenomenon in Hamiltonian Chaotic Systems 51**
Shiwei Yan

Part 2 Chaos Control 117

Chapter 5 **Chaos Analysis and Control in AFM and MEMS Resonators 119**
Amir Hossein Davaie-Markazi and Hossein Sohanian-Haghighi

Chapter 6 **Control and Identification of Chaotic Systems by Altering the Oscillation Energy 135**
Valery Tereshko

Chapter 7 **Adaptive Control of Chaos 161**
Hassan Salarieh and Mohammad Shahrokhi

Part 3 Synchronization 185

Chapter 8 **Chaotic Clustering: Fragmentary Synchronization of Fractal Waves 187**
Elena N. Benderskaya and Sofya V. Zhukova

Chapter 9 **Coexistence of Synchronization and Anti-Synchronization for Chaotic Systems via Feedback Control 203**
Hammami Sonia and Benrejeb Mohamed

Part 4 Applications 225

Chapter 10 **Design and Applications of Continuous-Time Chaos Generators 227**
Carlos Sánchez-López, JesusManuel Muñoz-Pacheco, Victor Hugo Carbajal-Gómez, Rodolfo Trejo-Guerra, Cristopher Ramírez-Soto, Oscar S. Echeverria-Solis and Esteban Tlelo-Cuautle

Chapter 11 **Applying Estimation Techniques to Chaos-based Digital Communications 255**
Marcio Eisencraft and Luiz Antonio Baccalá

Chapter 12 **Emergence of Matured Chaos During, Network Growth, Place for Adaptive Evolution and More of Equally Probable Signal Variants as an Alternative to Bias p 281**
Andrzej Gecow

Preface

This book represents a collection of major developments in the area of Chaotic Systems. Researchers from around the world summarize key guidelines on modeling, simulation, control synchronization, and applications of these systems. The organization of the book includes twelve chapters covering a wide variety of engineering areas regarding basic scientific research and technological development.

The first chapter presents a time series technique to forecast future events. The second chapter analyzes forecasting chaos, providing a deep insight on the meaning of Lyapunov exponents locally. The predictability of chaotic events considering initial error in chaotic systems is presented in chapter three. The fourth chapter introduces a microscopic theory of transport phenomena which is supported by applying Hamiltonian forms. These four chapters motivate the reader to look for approaches to control and synchronization of chaotic systems. Furthermore, chapters five, six and seven focus on controlling the chaos phenomenon. For instance, micro-electromechanical systems like resonators might present chaotic behavior, the prediction and control of chaos is then presented in chapter five. Chaotic systems can be perturbed, and control and identification approaches can be applied as shown in chapter six. Among all techniques for controlling chaos the adaptive one is very useful, as described in chapter seven. Chaos systems can be synchronized as shown in chapters eight and nine. In chapter nine a technique for chaos control called feedback control, is also presented. Some realizations of chaotic oscillators with electronic circuits are presented in chapter ten. In this chapter two chaos systems are synchronized by Hamiltonian forms and observer approach, to realize a secure communication system. Chapter eleven introduces estimation techniques for chaos systems to develop digital communications. Some open research problems can be identified in these eleven chapters, as well as in the final chapter devoted to the emergence of matured chaos during network growth.

This book includes recent advances in science and engineering applications. However, as highlighted in the majority of chapters, still many research and applications are very much in need of further development. In this way, the book is a good source for identifying basics on chaotic systems, techniques to control and synchronize them, and to acquire recent knowledge and ideas for future research in this area. Some applications to engineering motivate the reader to develop experiments applied to real life problems. This book is intended for students, academia and industry since the collected chapters provide a rich cocktail while balancing theory and applications.

Enjoy the book!

Esteban Tlelo-Cuautle
INAOE
Department of Electronics
Mexico

Part 1

Chaotic Systems

1

Short-Term Chaotic Time Series Forecast

Jiin-Po Yeh
I-Shou University
Taiwan

1. Introduction

The neural network was initiated by McCulloch and Pitts (1943), who claimed that neurons with binary inputs and a step-threshold activation function were analogous to first order systems. Hebb (1949) revolutionized the perception of artificial neurons. Rosenblatt (1958), using the McCulloch-Pitts neuron and the findings of Hebb, developed the first perception model of the neuron, which is still widely accepted today. Hopfield (1982) and Hopfield et al. (1983) demonstrated from work on the neuronal structure of the common garden slug that ANNs (artificial neural networks) can solve non-separable problems by placing a hidden layer between the input and output layers. Rumelhart and McClelland (1986) developed the most famous learning algorithm in ANN-backpropagation, which used a gradient descent technique to propagate error through a network to adjust the weights in an attempt to find the global error minimum, marking a milestone in the current artificial neural networks. Since then, a huge proliferation in the ANN methodologies has come about.

Many physical systems in the real world, such as rainfall systems (Hense, 1987), chemical reactions (Argoul et al., 1987), biological systems (Glass et al., 1983) and traffic flow systems (Dendrinos, 1994), have complicated dynamical behaviors and their mathematical models are usually difficult to derive. If the system has only one measurement available, to obtain knowledge about its dynamical behaviors, one usual method is to reconstruct the state space by using delay coordinates: $\{x(t), x(t-\tau), x(t-2\tau), \ldots, x(t-(q-1)\tau)\}$, where $x(t)$ is time series of the measurement, q is the dimension of the reconstructed state space and τ is the time delay (Moon, 1992; Alligood et al., 1997). By gradually increasing the dimension of the state space, the fractal dimension of the chaotic attractor (Moon, 1992; Grassberger and Proccacia, 1983) will approach an asymptote. This asymptote is often considered to be the chaotic attractor dimension of the dynamical system. According to Takens (1981), the embedding dimension of the chaotic attractor, or the dimension required to reconstruct the state space, must be at least twice larger than the chaotic attractor dimension so that the generic delay plots could be obtained.

That chaotic behaviors exist in the traffic flow system has been known for decades. Gazis et al. (1961) developed a generalized car-following model, known as the GHR (Gazis-Herman-Rothery) model, whose discontinuous behavior and nonlinearity suggested chaotic solutions for a certain range of input parameters. Traffic systems without signals, bottlenecks, intersections, etc. or with a coordinate signal network, modeled by the traditional GHR traffic-flow equation, were tested for presence of chaotic behaviors (Disbro and Frame, 1989; Fu et al., 2005). Chaos was also observed in a platoon of vehicles described by the traditional GHR model with a nonlinear inter-vehicle separation dependent term added (Addison and Low, 1996).

Up to the present, there have been a variety of methodologies devoted to short-term chaotic time series prediction, including local linear models (Farmer and Sidorowich, 1987), polynomial models (Acquirre and Billings, 1994) and neural network-based black-box models (Principe et al., 1992; Albano et al., 1992; Deco and Schurmann, 1994; Bakker et al., 1996), just to name a few. However, this chapter will only focus on two easy-to-implement methods: (i) the feedforward backpropagation neural network and (ii) the multiple linear regression.

2. Embedding dimension

To get the right dimension of the reconstructed state space to embed the attractor (chaotic or periodic), the dimension of the attractor must first be found. There are a number of ways to measure the attractor dimension (Moon, 1992; Grassberger and Proccacia, 1983). Among them, this chapter only demonstrates two measures easily processed with the aid of the computer: (i) the pointwise dimension; (ii) the correlation dimension.

2.1 Pointwise dimension

A long-time trajectory in the state space is considered, as shown in Fig. 1, where a sphere of radius r is placed at some point on the orbit. The probability of finding a point inside the sphere is (Moon, 1992)

$$P(r) = \frac{N(r)}{N_0} \tag{1}$$

where $N(r)$ is the number of points within the sphere and N_0 the total number of points in the orbit. When the radius r becomes smaller, and $N_0 \rightarrow \infty$, there exists a relationship between $\ln P(r)$ and $\ln r$, which can be expressed as (Moon, 1992):

$$\tilde{d}_p = \lim_{r \rightarrow 0} \frac{\ln P(r)}{\ln r} \tag{2}$$

In order to have better results, the averaged pointwise dimension is usually used; that is

$$d_P = \lim_{r \rightarrow 0} \frac{\ln\left[(1/M)\Sigma P(r)\right]}{\ln(r)} \tag{3}$$

where M is the number of randomly selected points on the orbit. In practice, M is approximately one tenth of the total number of points on the orbit.

2.2 Correlation dimension

As in the definition of pointwise dimension, the orbit is discretized to a set of points in the state space. A sphere of radius r is first placed at each and every point of the orbit and then the Euclidean distances between pairs of points are calculated. A correlation function is defined as (Moon, 1992; Grassberger and Proccacia, 1983)

$$C(r) = \lim_{n \rightarrow \infty} \frac{1}{N(N-1)} \sum_i \sum_j \mathrm{u}(r - |\mathbf{x}_i - \mathbf{x}_j|) \qquad (i \neq j) \tag{4}$$

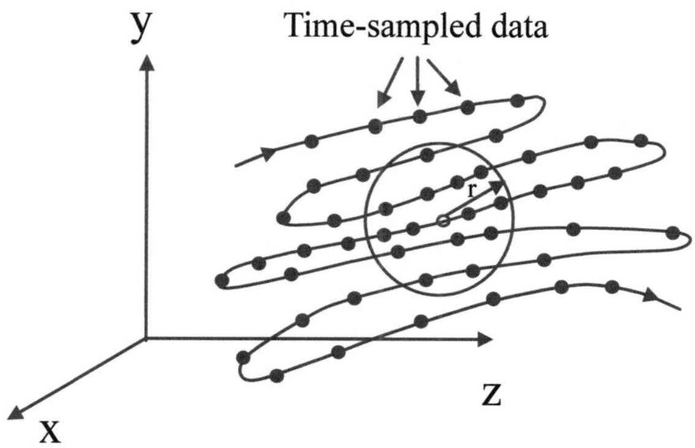

Fig. 1. A trajectory in the state space.

where $\left|\mathbf{x}_i - \mathbf{x}_j\right|$ is the Euclidean distance between points $\boldsymbol{x}_i$ and $\boldsymbol{x}_j$ of the orbit and $\boldsymbol{u}$ is the unit step function. For a lot of attractors, this function $C(r)$ exhibits a power law dependence on r, as $r \to 0$; that is

$$\lim_{r \to 0} C(r) = ar^d \tag{5}$$

Based on the above relationship, a correlation dimension is defined by the expression

$$d_c = \lim_{r \to 0} \frac{\ln C(r)}{\ln r} \tag{6}$$

The dimension of the attractor found by Eq. (3) or (6) will approach an asymptote d with the conjectured dimension of the reconstructed state space gradually increasing. To represent the attractor one to one without causing self-intersection, the embedding dimension of the attractor must be at least $2d+1$ (Takens, 1981). For a chaotic attractor, the dimension d is always fractal, not an integer. Therefore, the appropriate dimension for the reconstructed state space will be the smallest integer greater than or equal to $2d+1$.

3. Forecasting models

3.1 Neural networks

The first forecasting model introduced in this chapter is a two-layer feedforward neural network with the backpropagation training algorithm, as shown in Fig. 2. The transfer function used in the single hidden layer is the tan-sigmoid function for mapping the input to the interval [-1, 1] of the following form

$$a_i = f(n_i) = \frac{1 - e^{-n_i}}{1 + e^{-n_i}} \quad , \quad i = 1,2,3,\ldots,s \tag{7}$$

where $n_i = w_{i1}x_1 + w_{i2}x_2 + \ldots + w_{iR}x_R + b_i$, $x_1, x_2, \ldots, x_R$ are the inputs, s is the number of neurons, w_{i1}, $w_{i2}, \ldots, w_{iR}$ are the weights connecting the input vector and the ith neuron of the hidden layer, and b_i is its bias. The output layer with a single neuron uses the linear transfer function

$$a = f(n) = n \tag{8}$$

where $n=W_{11}a_1+ W_{12}a_2+......+W_{is}a_s+ b$, $W_{11},W_{12},...,W_{is}$ are the weights connecting the neurons of the hidden layer and the neuron of the output layer, and b is the bias of the output neuron.

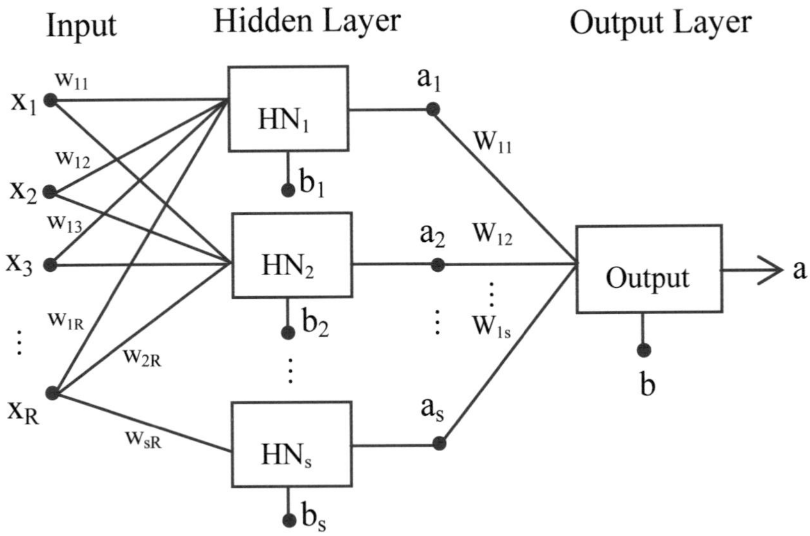

Fig. 2. The feedforward neural network with two layers

There are many variations of the backpropagation algorithm, which is aimed at minimizing the network performance function, i.e., the mean square error between the network outputs and the target outputs, which is

$$MSE = \frac{1}{m}\sum_{j=1}^{m} (t_j - a_j)^2 \tag{9}$$

where t_j and a_j are the jth target output and network output, respectively. The Levenberg-Marquardt algorithm (Hagan and Menhaj, 1994; Levenberg, 1944; Marquardt, 1963) is selected as the training function to minimize the network performance function. This algorithm interpolates between the Newton's algorithm and the gradient descent method. If a tentative step increases the performance function, this algorithm will act like the gradient descent method, while it shifts toward Newton's method if the reduction of the performance function is successful. In this way, the performance function will always be reduced at each iteration of the algorithm. To make the neural networks more efficient, it is quite beneficial to scale inputs and targets so that they will fall within a specific range. For example, the following formula

$$k' = 2\left(\frac{k - min}{max - min}\right) - 1 \tag{10}$$

is often used to scale both inputs and targets, where k is the original value, k' is the scaled value, and max and min are the maximum and minimum of the inputs or targets,

respectively. Eq. (10) produces inputs and targets in the range [-1, 1]; the scaled outputs of the trained networks will be usually converted back to the original units.
There are two methods to improve the network generalization: Bayesian regularization (MacKay, 1992) and early stopping. The Bayesian regularization provides a measure of how many network parameters (weights and biases) are being effectively used by the network. From this effective number of parameters, the number of neurons required in the hidden layer of the two-layer neural network can be derived by the following equation

$$(Rs+s)+(s+1)=P \tag{11}$$

where R is the number of elements in the input vector, s is the number of neurons in the hidden layer, and P is the effective number of parameters found by the Bayesian regularization. With the strategy of early stopping incorporated into the neural network, the error on the validation set is monitored during the training process. When the network begins to overfit the training data, the error on the validation set typically also begins to rise. Once the validation error increases for a specified number of iterations, the training stops and the weights and biases at the minimum of validation error are returned. To evaluate the performance of the trained network, the regression analysis between the network outputs and the corresponding targets is frequently adopted, and the result is usually displayed by the scatter plot or correlation coefficient (Mendenhall et al., 1986).

3.2 The multiple linear regression

Because nearby states in the state space have analogous behaviors (Alligood et al. 1997; Farmer and Sidorowich, 1987), as shown in Fig. 3, a multiple linear regression model (Mendenhall et al., 1986), fitted to the delay coordinates of nearby states in the reconstructed state space is another good choice to forecast the short-term behavior of the chaotic dynamical system. Assuming that q is the appropriate embedding dimension of the strange attractor, the multiple linear regression to predict the future behaviors of a trajectory has the following form

$$\hat{y}_i = \beta_0 + \beta_1 x_{i1} + \beta_2 x_{i2} + \cdots + \beta_q x_{iq}, \quad i = 1,\dots,p \tag{12}$$

where $\hat{y}_i$ is the predicted value of the observed response y_i, which corresponds to the first delay coordinate of the ith nearest state some time units later, the independent variables $x_{i1}, x_{i2},\dots,x_{iq}$ correspond to the delay coordinates of the ith nearest state: $\{x(t), x(t-\tau), x(t-2\tau),\dots, x(t-(q-1)\tau)\}$, respectively, p is the total number of data, and $\beta_0, \beta_1, \beta_2,\dots, \beta_q$ are unknown parameters to be decided by the method of least squares (Mendenhall et al., 1986).

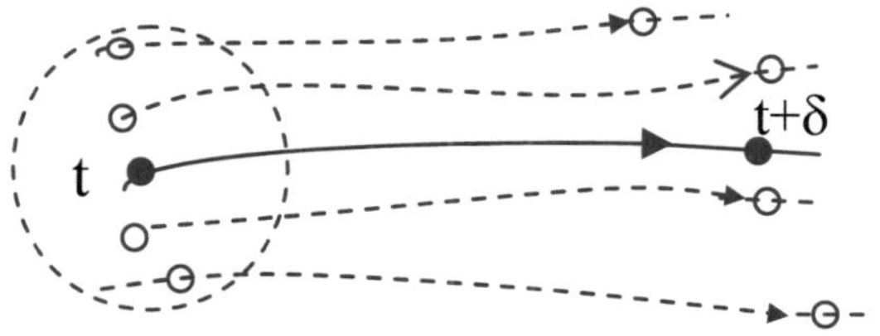

Fig. 3. Analogues of nearby trajectories in a short period of time.

4. Numerical results

Examples chosen for demonstration are the westbound passing traffic volume at the intersection of Xingai Road and Guanfu S. Road, Taipei City, Taiwan. The data were collected by the vehicle traffic counter from August 22, 2005 to September 2, 2005, totaling 10 weekdays excluding the weekend. There are three time scales involved: 5-min, 10-min, and 15-min.

4.1 Reconstruction of the traffic flow system

Time series of the three different time intervals show no repeat of themselves and have the tendency to be aperiodic. For example, Fig. 4 shows time series of the 5- min traffic volume for the training set (first 7 days totaling 2016 observations). The state-space dimension n for the delay coordinate reconstruction of the traffic flow system is increased gradually from 3 to 22. For each reconstruction, both the pointwise dimension and correlation dimension of the strange attractor are found for comparison. Fig. 5(a) shows the limiting behavior of the function $\ln\left[(\Sigma P(r))/M\right]$ as $r \to 0$ for different state-space dimension n with time delay τ fixed at 20, and Fig. 5(b) shows the pointwise dimension approaching an asymptote of 6.449. Fig. 6(a) shows the limiting behavior of the function $\ln C(r)$ as $r \to 0$ for different state-space dimension n with time delay τ fixed at 20, and Fig. 6(b) shows the correlation dimension approaching an asymptote of 6.427. The results shown in Figs. 5 and 6

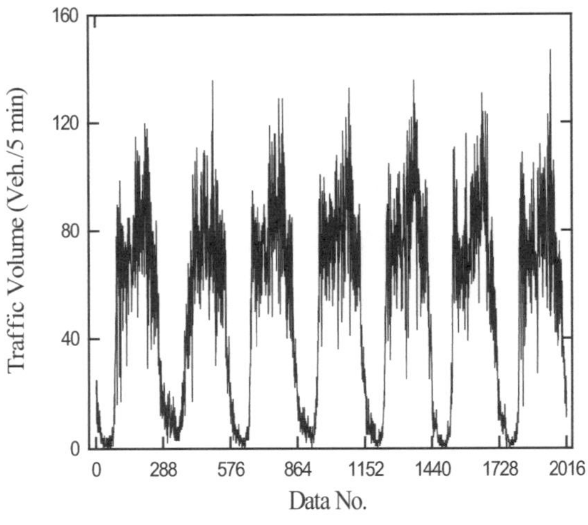

Fig. 4. Time series of the 5-min traffic volume.

are valid only for the 5-min traffic volume and time delay τ = 20. The asymptotes of the pointwise dimension and correlation dimension for a variety of different time intervals and time delays are presented in Tables 1 and 2, respectively, where the limiting dimension of the chaotic attractor ranges from 6.307 to 6.462. Different time intervals and time delays lead to almost the same fractal dimension. According to Takens (1981), the embedding dimension of chaotic attractors of the traffic flow system is therefore found to be at least 14. Because different time delays result in almost identical limiting fractal dimension of the chaotic attractor, the choice of time delay in fact is actually not decisive, except to avoid the natural period of the system.

Time Interval \ Time Delay	τ=10	τ=20	τ=30	τ=40	τ=50	τ=60	τ=70
5-min	6.445	6.449	6.449	6.429	6.434	6.431	6.449
10-min	6.435	6.432	6.331	6.307			
15-min	6.445	6.427	6.454				

Table 1. Asymptotes of pointwise dimension for different time intervals and delays.

Time Interval \ Time Delay	τ=10	τ=20	τ=30	τ=40	τ=50	τ=60	τ=70
5-min	6.408	6.427	6.447	6.433	6.432	6.462	6.440
10-min	6.423	6.415	6.416	6.419			
15-min	6.444	6.443	6.430				

Table 2. Asymptotes of correlation dimension for diferent time intervals and delays.

4.2 Neural networks

The neural network toolbox of MATLAB (Demuth et al., 2010) software is used to build up neural networks and perform the training. The elements of the input vector are composed of 14-dimensional delay coordinates: $x(i)$, $x(i-\tau)$, $x(i-2\tau)$,..., $x(i-13\tau)$, where $x(i)$ is the ith observation of the time series of traffic volume, and τ is the time delay, which is chosen to be 20, 10 and 5 for 5-min, 10-min, and 15-min traffic volumes, respectively. The network target corresponding to this input is $x(i+1)$. All forecasts are only one time interval ahead of occurrence, i.e., 5-min, 10-min or 15-min ahead of time. When using the strategy "early stopping" to monitor the training process, the allowed number of iterations for the validation error to increase is set to be 5. The data collected is divided into three sets: the training set (the first 7 days), the validation set (the 8th and 9th days), and the prediction set (the 10th day).

4.2.1 5-min traffic volume

First of all, a feedforward backpropogation neural network with the Bayesian regularization is creasted to get the effective number of network parameters. The network inputs and targets are imported from the 14-dimensional delay coordinates: $x(i)$, $x(i-20)$, $x(i-40)$,..., $x(i-260)$, and $x(i+1)$, respectively. The results are shown in Fig. 7, which indicates only approximately 216 effective parameters are required in this network; therefore, the appropriate number of neurons in the hidden layer is found by Eq. (11) to be 14 (equal to the number of elements in the input vector). Then, replace the number of neurons in the hidden layer with 14 and train the network again by the Levenberg-Marquardt algorithm coupled with the strategy "early stopping." The training process stops at 10 epochs because the validation error already has increased for 5 iterations. Fig. 8 shows the scatter plot for the training set with correlation coefficient ρ=0.90249. Lastly, simulate the trained network with the prediction set. Fig. 9 shows the scatter plot for the prediction set with the correlation coefficient ρ=0.83086. Time series of the observed value (network targets) and the predicted

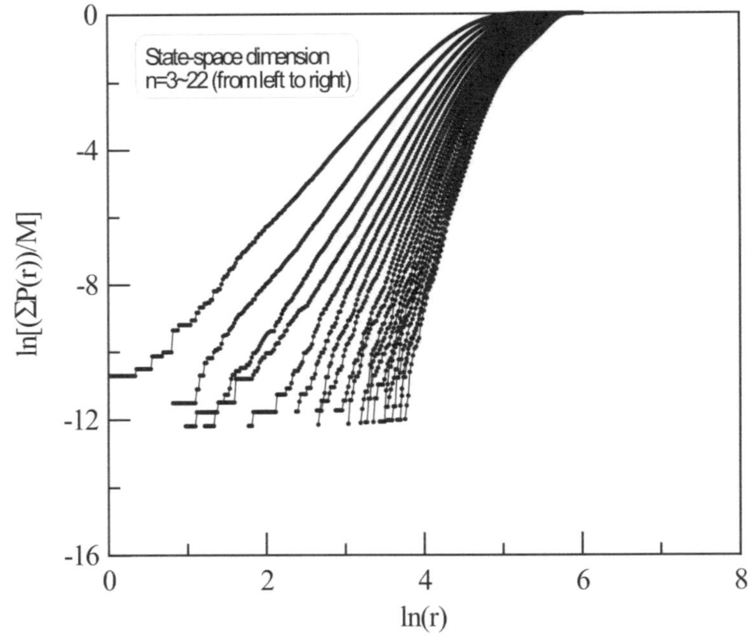

(a)

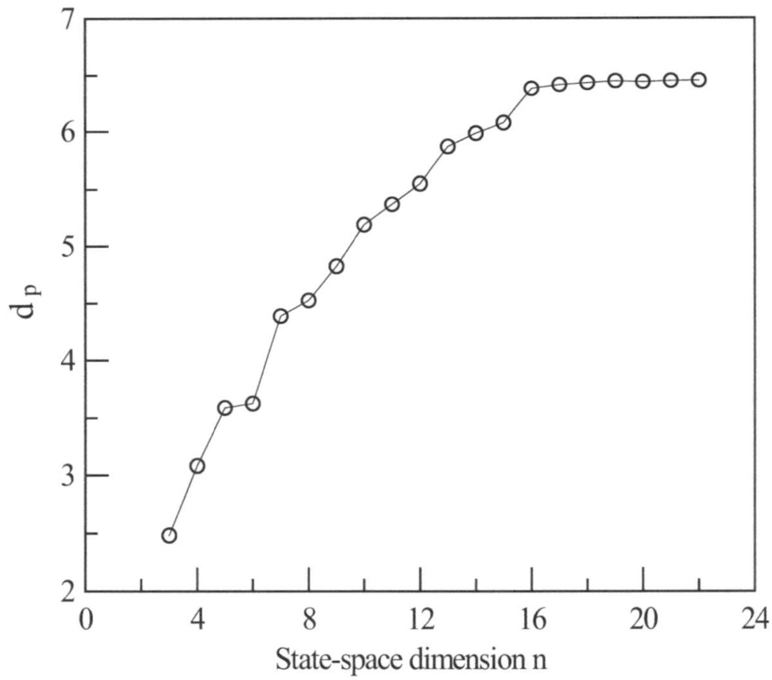

(b)

Fig. 5. (a) Limiting behavior of the function $\ln\left[(\sum P(r))/M\right]$ as $r \to 0$ for time delay $\tau = 20$ and (b) the asymptote of pointwise dimension, with the state-space dimension n increasing from 3 to 22 for the 5-min traffic volume.

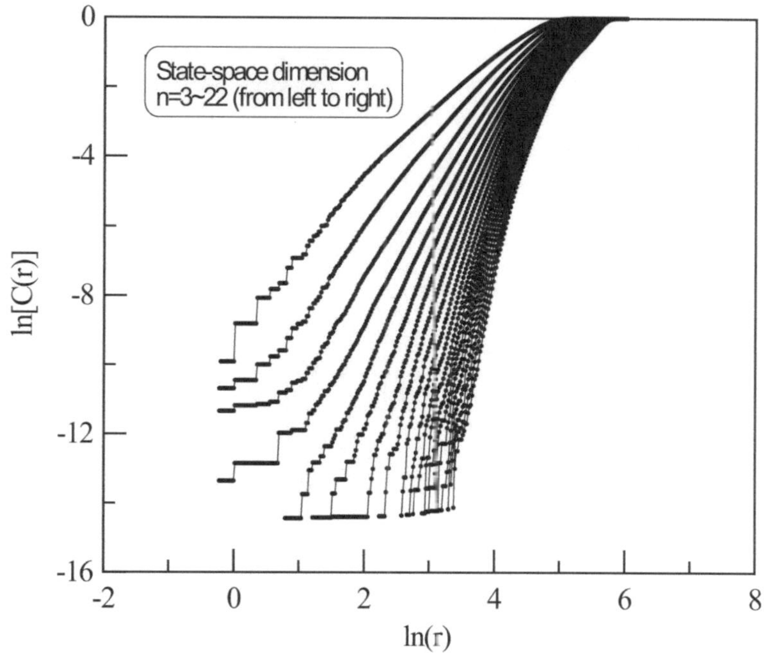

(a)

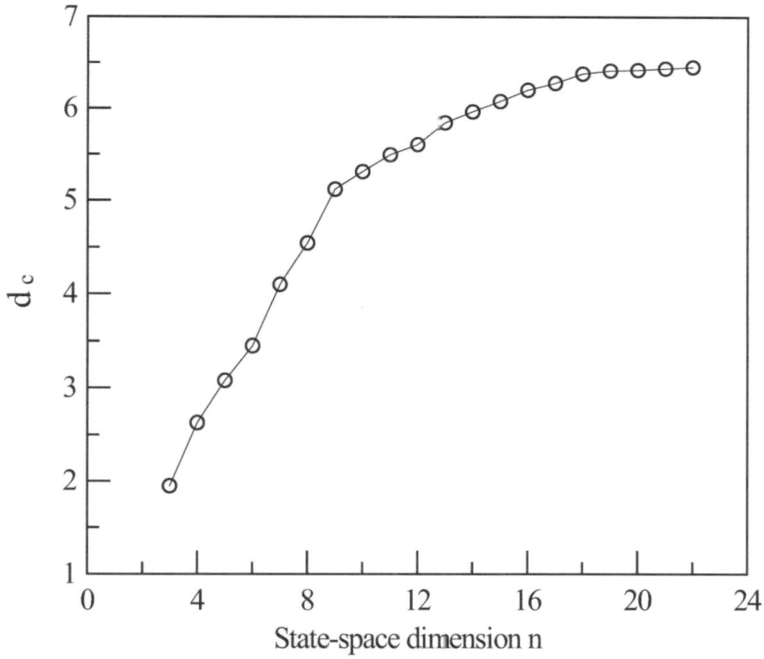

(b)

Fig. 6. (a) Limiting behavior of the function $\ln C(r)$ as $r \to 0$ for time delay $\tau = 20$ and (b) the asymptote of correlation dimension, with the state-space dimension n increasing from 3 to 22 for the 5-min traffic volume.

value (network outputs) are shown in Fig. 10. If the strategy "early stopping" is disregarded and 100 epochs is chosen for the training process, the trained network performance indeed improves for the training set, but gets worse for the validation and prediction sets. If the number of neurons in the hidden layer is increased to 28 and 42, the performance of the network for the training set tends to improve, but does not have the tendency to significantly improve for the validation and prediction sets, as listed in Table 3.

Data \ No. of Neurons	14	28	42
Training Set	0.90249	0.90593	0.94371
Validation Set	0.86535	0.86614	0.86757
Prediction Set	0.83086	0.85049	0.82901

Table 3. Correlation coefficients for training, validation and prediction data sets with the number of neurons in the hidden layer increasing (5-min traffic volume).

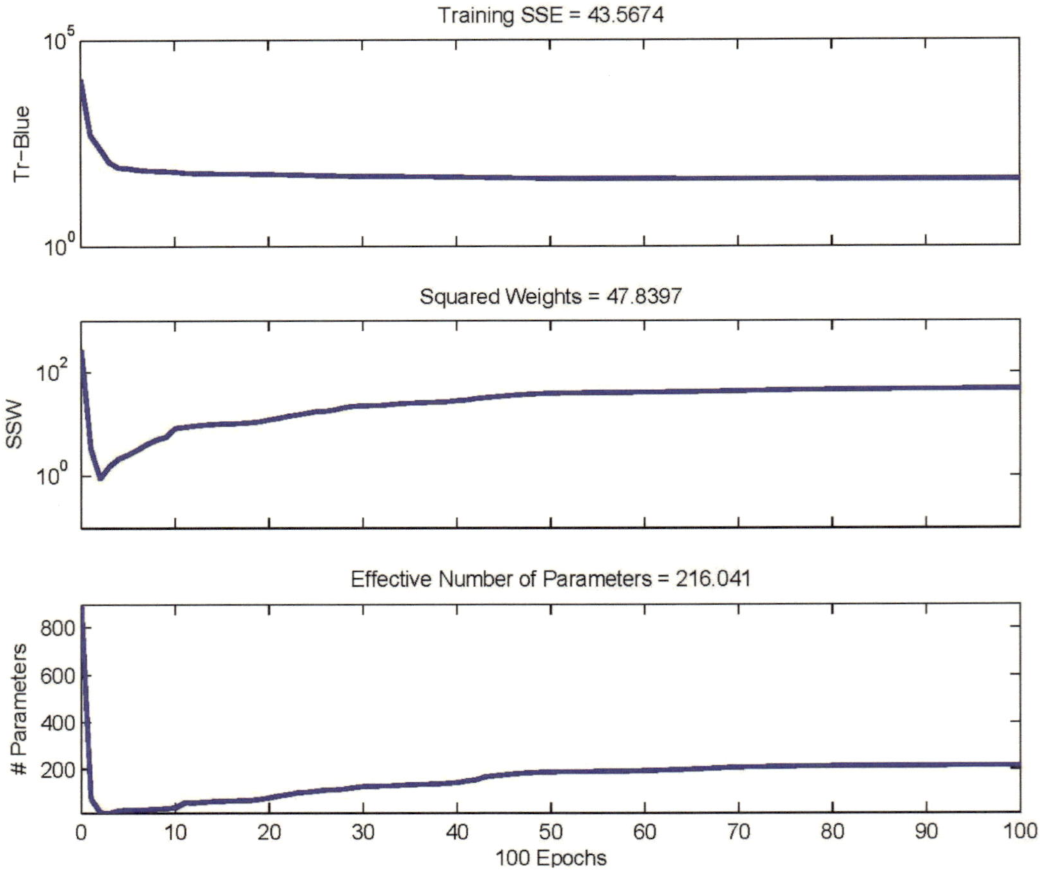

Fig. 7. The convergence process to find effective number of parameters used by the network for the 5-min traffic volume

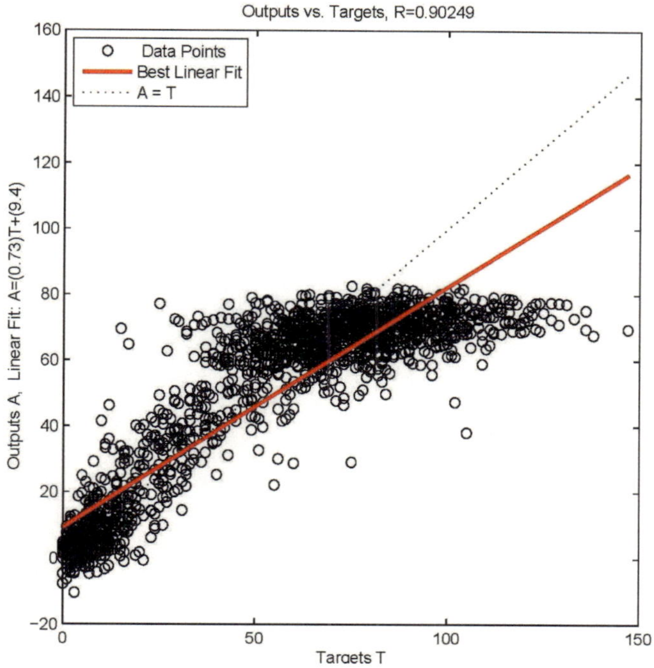

Fig. 8. The scatter plot of the network outputs and targets for the training set of the 5-min traffic volume.

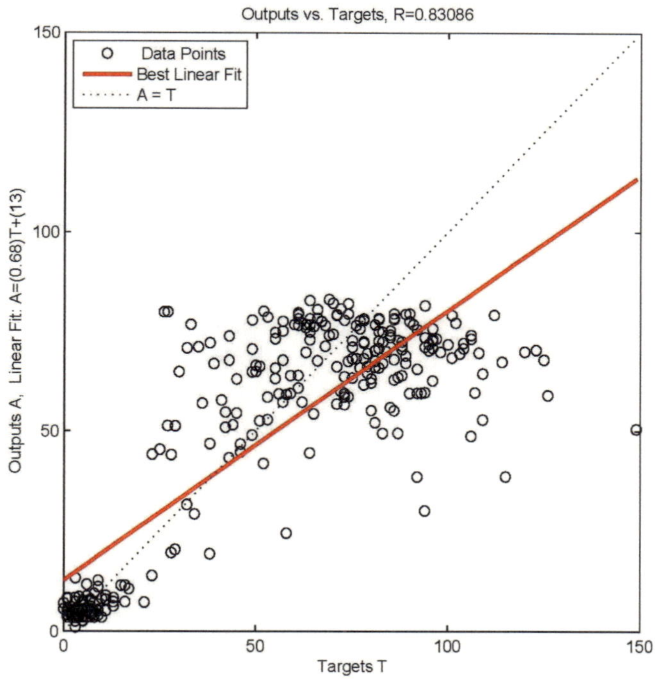

Fig. 9. The scatter plot of the network outputs and targets for the prediction set of the 5-min traffic volume.

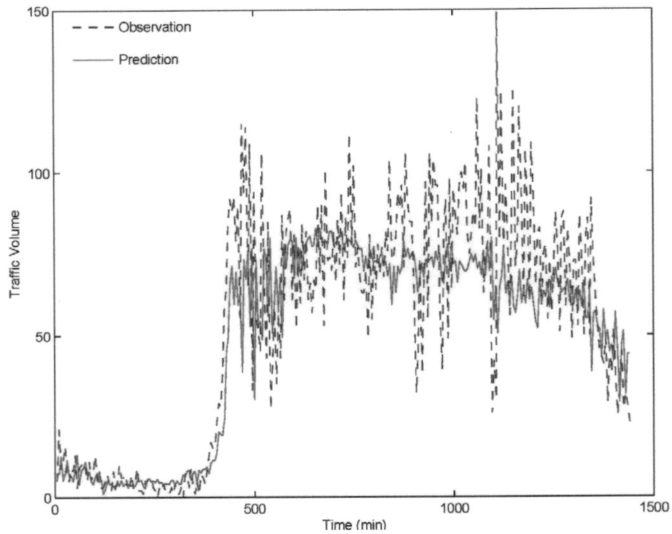

Fig. 10. Time series of the observed value (network targets) and the predicted value (network outputs) for the 5-min traffic volume.

4.2.2 10-min traffic volume

The network inputs and targets are the 14-dimensional delay coordinates: $x(i)$, $x(i\text{-}10)$, $x(i\text{-}20)$,…, $x(i\text{-}130)$, and $x(i\text{+}1)$, respectively. Similarly, by using Bayesian regularization, the effective number of parameters is first found to be 108, as shown in Fig. 11; therefore, the appropriate number of neurons in the hidden layer is 7 (one half of the number of elements in the input vector). Replace the number of neurons in the hidden layer with 7 and train the network again. The training process stops at 11 epochs because the validation error has increased for 5 iterations. Fig. 12 shows the scatter plot for the training set with correlation coefficient ρ=0.93874. Simulate the trained network with the prediction set. Fig. 13 shows the scatter plot for the prediction set with the correlation coefficient ρ=0.91976. Time series of the observed value (network targets) and the predicted value (network outputs) are shown in Fig. 14. If the strategy "early stopping" is disregarded and 100 epochs is chosen for the training process, the performance of the network improves for the training set, but gets worse for the validation and prediction sets. If the number of neurons in the hidden layer is increased to 14 and 28, the performance of the network for the training set tends to improve, but does not have the tendency to improve for the validation and prediction sets, as listed in Table 4.

Data \ No. of Neurons	7	14	28
Training Set	0.93874	0.95814	0.96486
Validation Set	0.92477	0.87930	0.88337
Prediction Set	0.91976	0.90587	0.91352

Table 4. Correlation coefficients for training, validation and prediction data sets with the number of neurons in the hidden layer increasing (10-min traffic volume).

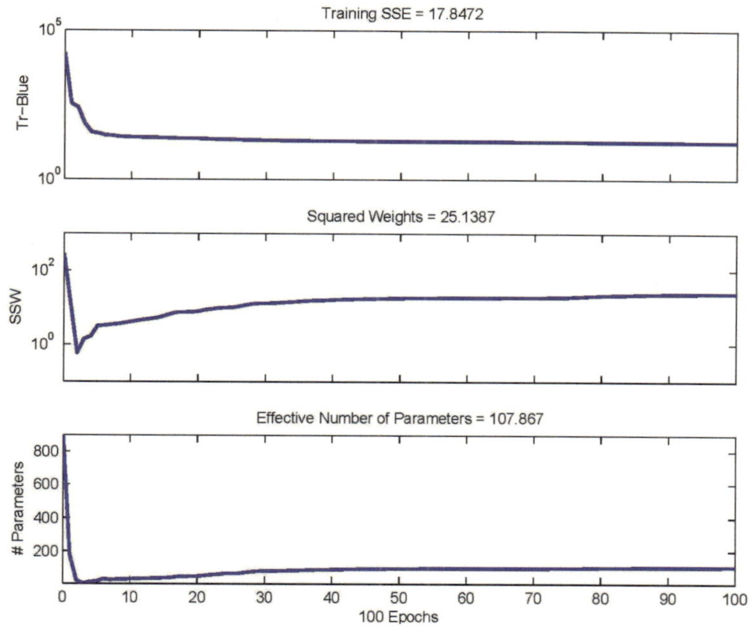

Fig. 11. The convergence process to find effective number of parameters used by the network for the 10-min traffic volume.

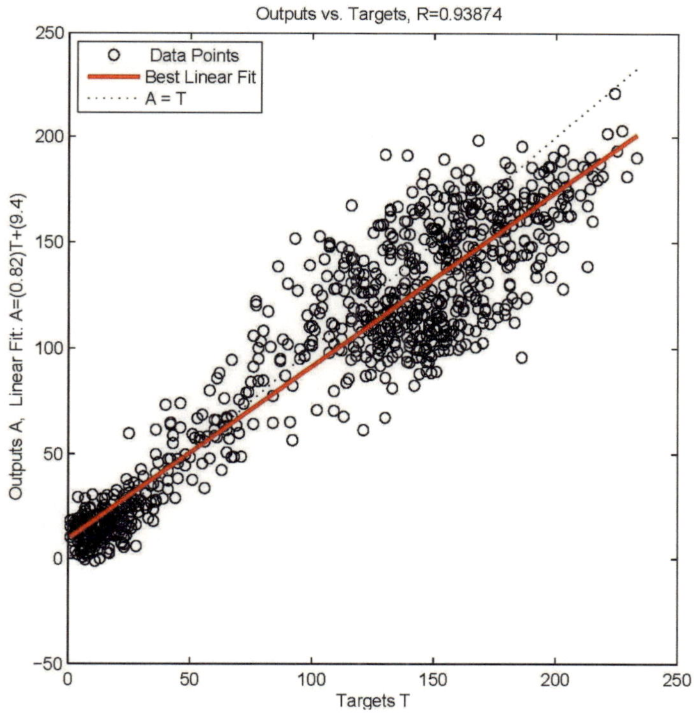

Fig. 12. The scatter plot of the network outputs and targets for the training set of the 10-min traffic volume.

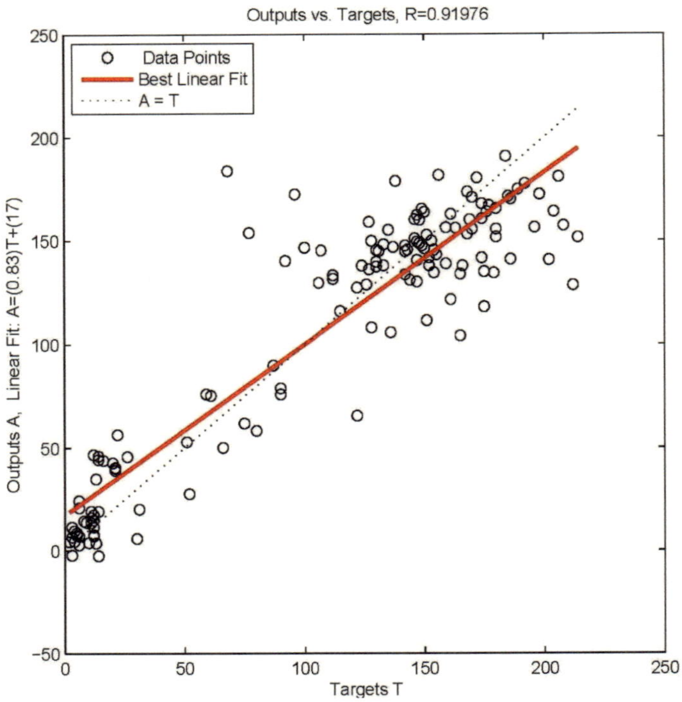

Fig. 13. The scatter plot of the network outputs and targets for the prediction set of the 10-min traffic volume.

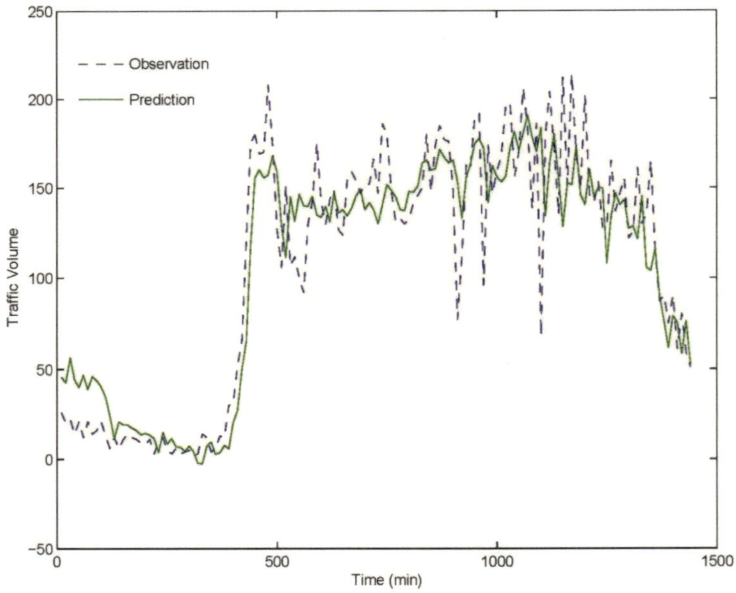

Fig. 14. Time series of the observed value (network targets) and the predicted value (network outputs) for the 10-min traffic volume.

4.2.3 15-min traffic volume

The network inputs and targets are the 14-dimensional delay coordinates: $x(i)$, $x(i\text{-}5)$, $x(i\text{-}10),\ldots,$ $x(i\text{-}65)$, and $x(i+1)$, respectively. In a similar way, the effective number of parameters is found to be 88 from the results of Bayesian regularization, as shown in Fig. 15. Instead of using 6 neurons obtained by Eq. (11), 7 neurons (one half of the number of elements in the input vector), are used in the hidden layer for consistence. Replace the number of neurons in the hidden layer with 7 and train the network again. The training process stops at 11 epochs because the validation error has increased for 5 iterations. Fig. 16 shows the scatter plot for the training set with correlation coefficient ρ=0.95113. Simulate the trained network with the prediction set. Fig. 17 shows the scatter plot for the prediction set with the correlation coefficient ρ=0.93333. Time series of the observed value (network targets) and the predicted value (network outputs) are shown in Fig. 18. If the strategy "early stopping" is disregarded and 100 epochs is chosen for the training process, the performance of the network gets better for the training set, but gets worse for the validation and prediction sets. If the number of neurons in the hidden layer is increased to 14 and 28, the performance of the network for the training set tends to improve, but does not have the tendency to significantly improve for the validation and prediction sets, as listed in Table 5.

No. of Neurons / Data	7	14	28
Training Set	0.95113	0.96970	0.97013
Validation Set	0.88594	0.93893	0.92177
Prediction Set	0.93333	0.94151	0.94915

Table 5. Correlation coefficients for training, validation and prediction data sets with the number of neurons in the hidden layer increasing (15-min traffic volume).

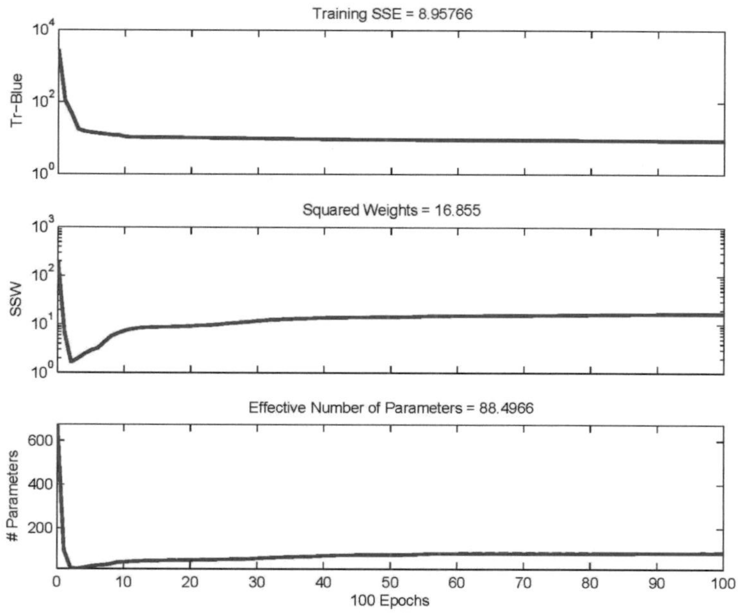

Fig. 15. The convergence process to find effective number of parameters used by the network for the 15-min traffic volume.

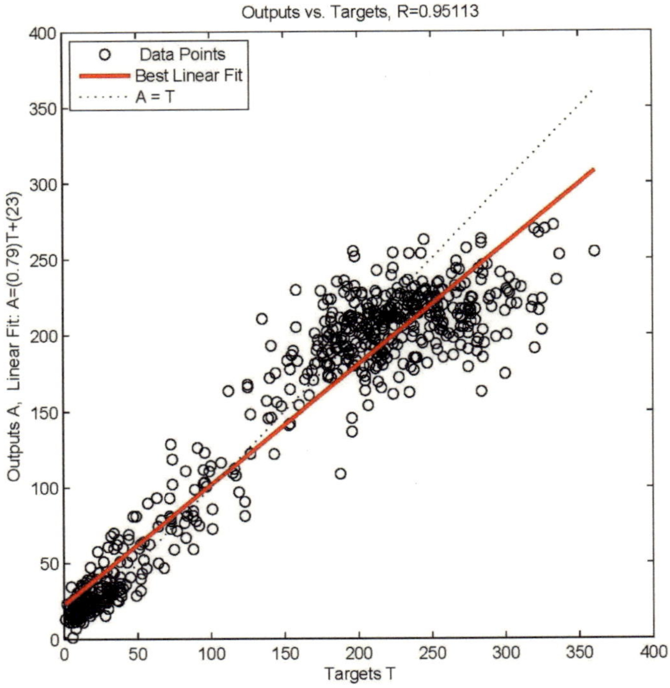

Fig. 16. The scatter plot of the network outputs and targets for the training set of the 15-min traffic volume.

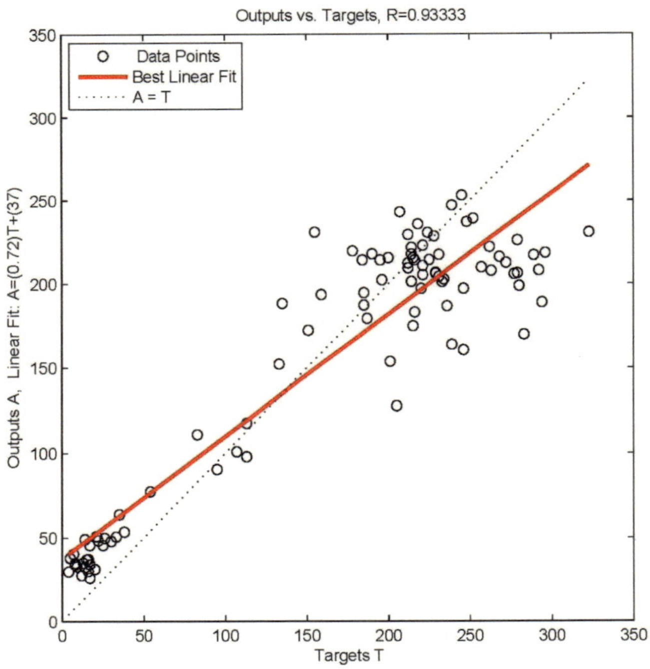

Fig. 17. The scatter plot of the network outputs and targets for the prediction set of the 15-min traffic volume.

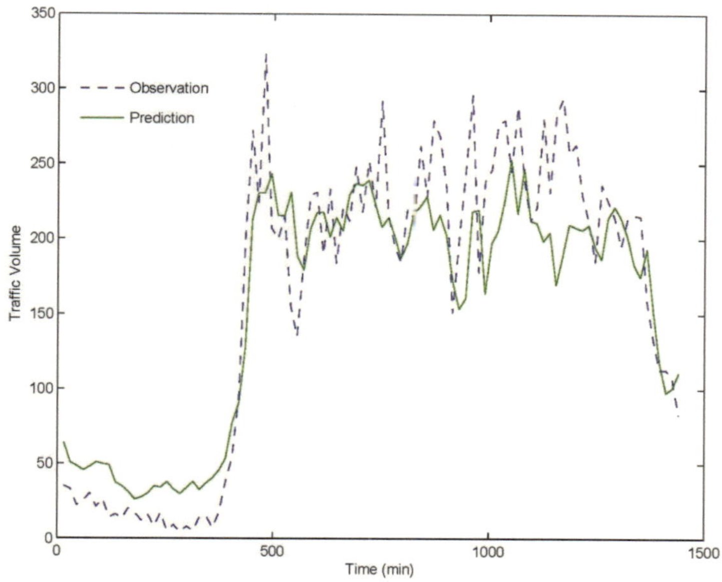

Fig. 18. Time series of the observed value (network targets) and the predicted value (network outputs) for the 15-min traffic volume.

4.3 The multiple linear regression

Data collected for the first nine days are used to build the prediction model, and data collected for the tenth day to test the prediction model. To forecast the near future behavior of a trajectory in the reconstructed 14-dimensional state space with time delay τ= 20, the number of 200 nearest states of the trajectory, after a few trials, is found appropriate for building the multiple linear regression model. Figs. 19-21 show time series of the predicted and observed volume for 5-min, 10-min, and 15-min intervals whose correlation coefficients ρ's are 0.850, 0.932 and 0.951, respectively. All forecasts are all one time interval ahead of occurrence, i.e., 5-min, 10-min and 15-min ahead of time. These three figures indicate that the larger the time interval, the better the performance of the prediction mode. To study the effects of the number K of the nearest states on the performance of the prediction model, a number of K's are tested for different time intervals. Figs. 22-24 show the limiting behavior of the correlation coefficient ρ for the three time intervals. These three figures reveal that the larger the number K, the better the performance of the prediction mode, but after a certain number, the correlation coefficient ρ does not increase significantly.

5. Conclusions

Numerical experiments have shown the effectiveness of the techniques introduced in this chapter to predict short-term chaotic time series. The dimension of the chaotic attractor in the delay plot increases with the dimension of the reconstructed state space and finally reaches an asymptote, which is fractal. A number of time delays have been tried to find the limiting dimension of the chaotic attractor, and the results are almost identical, which indicates the choice of time delay is not decisive, when the state space of the chaotic time series is being reconstructed. The effective number of neurons in the hidden layer of neural networks can be derived with the aid of the Bayesian regularization instead of using the trial and error.

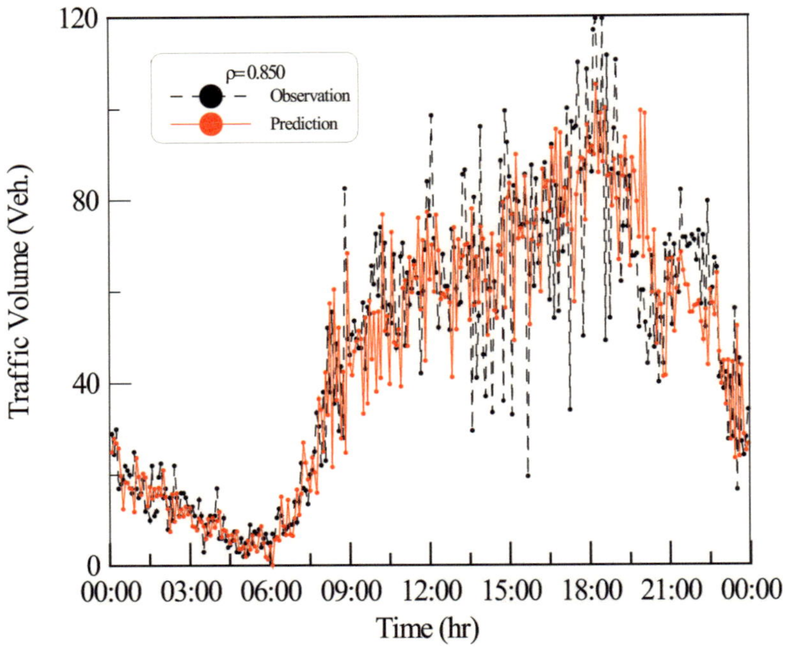

Fig. 19. Time series of the predicted and observed 5-min traffic volumes.

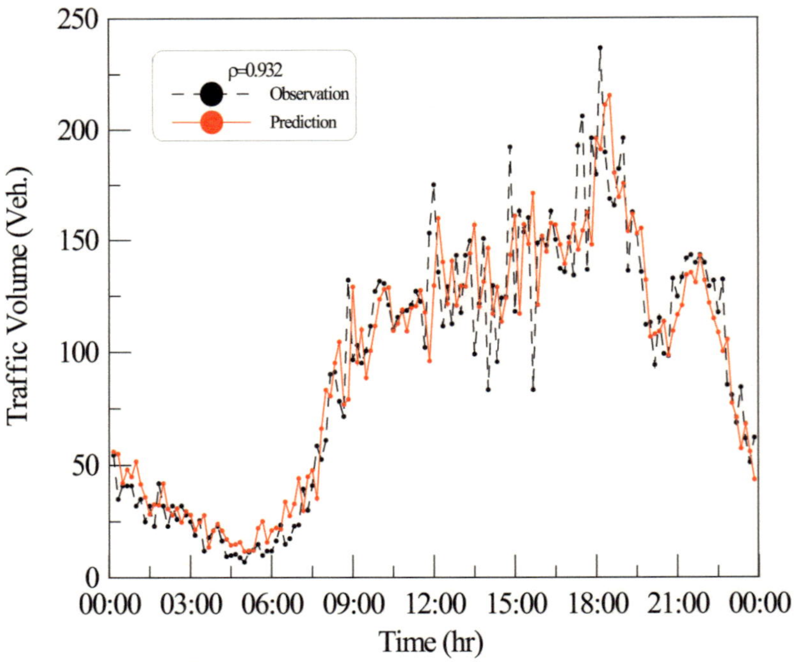

Fig. 20. Time series of the predicted and observed 10-min traffic volumes.

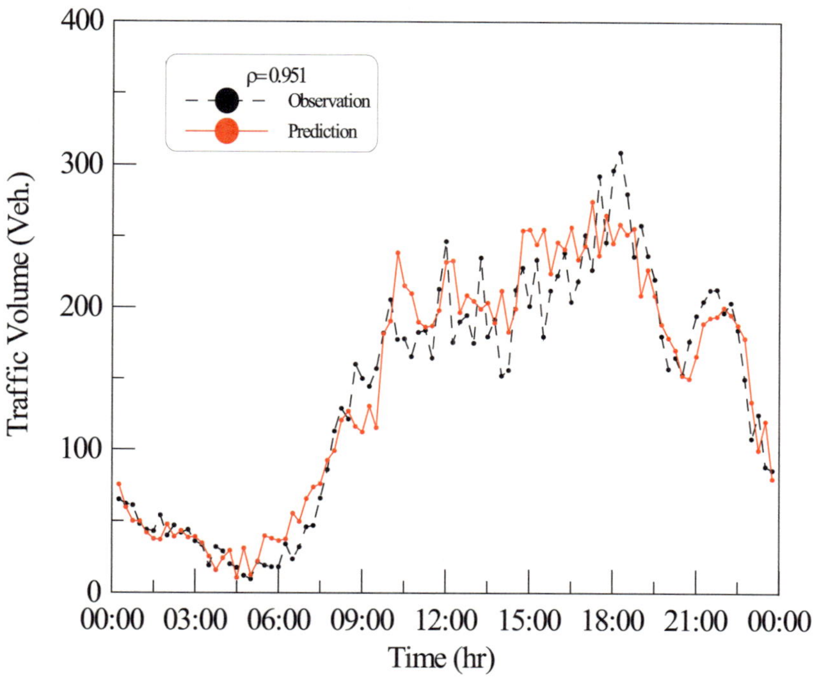

Fig. 21. Time series of the predicted and observed 15-min traffic volumes.

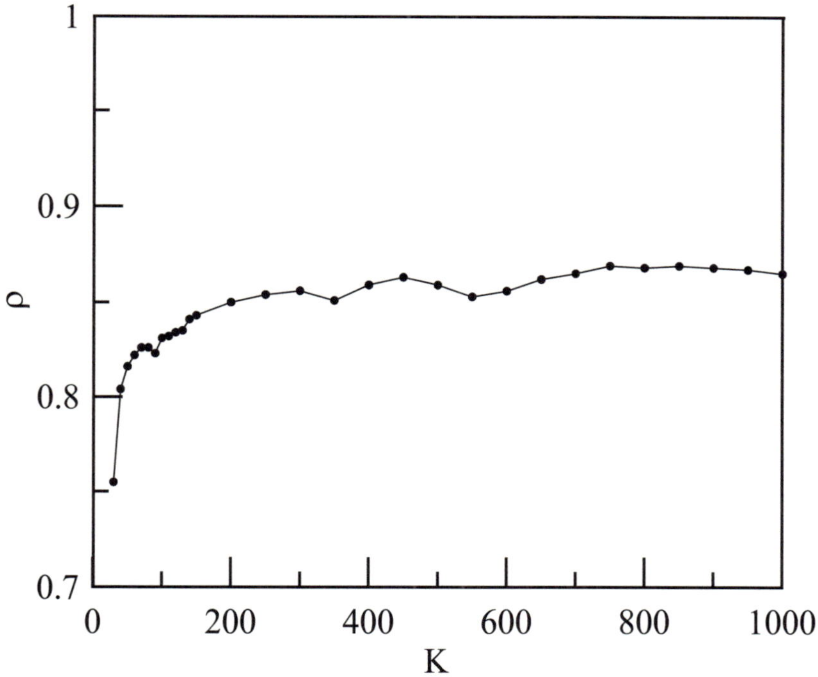

Fig. 22. The limiting behavior of the correlation coefficient ρ with K increasing for the 5-min traffic volume.

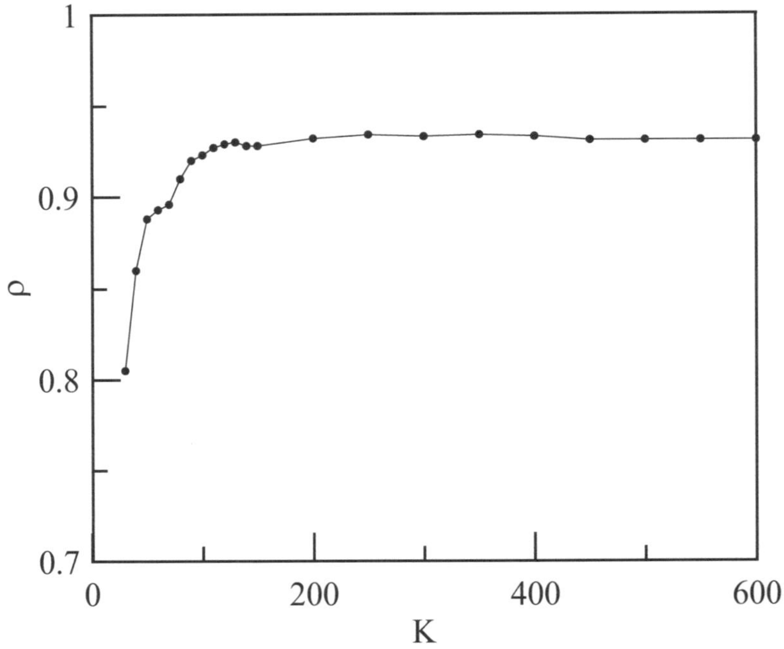

Fig. 23. The limiting behavior of the correlation coefficient ρ with K increasing for the 10-min traffic volume.

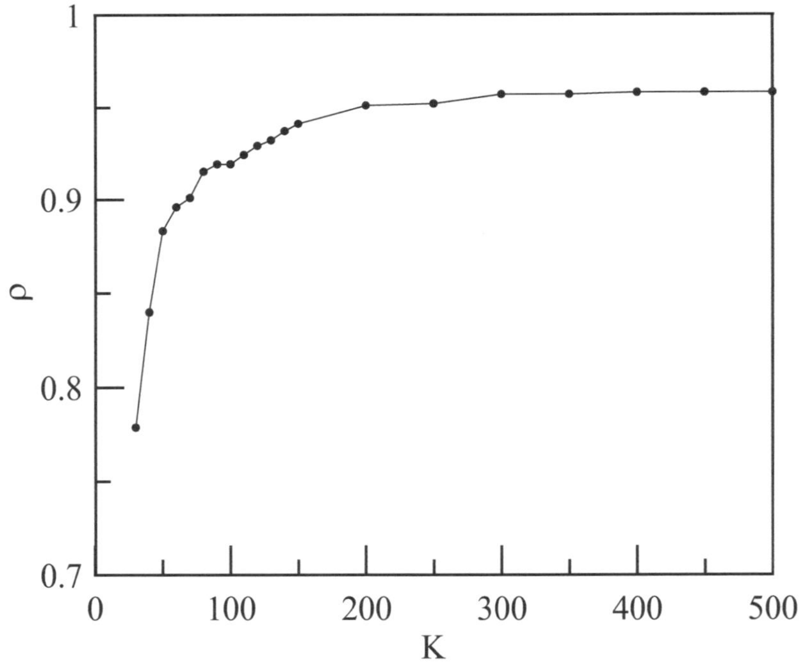

Fig. 24. The limiting behavior of correlation coefficient ρ with K increasing for the 15-min traffic volume.

Using neurons in the hidden layer more than the number decided by the Bayesian regularization can indeed improve the performance of neural networks for the training set, but does not necessarily better the performance for the validation and prediction sets. Although disregarding the strategy "early stopping" can improve the network performance for the training set, it causes worse performance for the validation and prediction sets. Increasing the number of nearest states to fit the multiple linear regression forecast model can indeed enhance the performance of the prediction, but after the nearest states reach a certain number, the performance does not improve significantly. Numerical results from these two forecast models also show that the multiple linear regression is superior to neural networks, as far as the prediction accuracy is concerned. In addition, the longer the traffic volume scales are, the better the prediction of the traffic flow becomes.

6. References

Addison, P. S. and Low, D. J. (1996). Order and Chaos in the Dynamics of Vehicle Platoons, *Traffic Engineering and Control*, July/August, pp. 456-459, ISSN 0041-0683.

Albano, A. M., Passamante, A., Hediger, T. and Farrell, M. E. (1992). Using Neural Nets to Look for Chaos, *Physica D*, Vol. 58, pp. 1-9, ISSN 0167-2789.

Alligood, K. T., Sauer, T. D., and Yorke, J. A. (1997). *Chaos: An Introduction to Dynamical Systems*, Springer-Verlag, ISBN 3-540-78036-x, New York.

Aquirre, L. A. and Billings, S. A. (1994). Validating Identified Nonlinear Models with Chaotic Dynamics, *International Journal of Bifurcation and Chaos in Applied Sciences and Engineering*, Vol.4, No. 1, pp. 109-125, ISSN 0218-1274.

Argoul, F., Arnedo, A., and Richetti, P. (1987). Experimental Evidence for Homoclinic Chaos in Belousov-Ehabotinski Reaction, *Physics Letters*, Section A, Vol. 120, No. 6, pp.269-275, ISSN 0375-9601.

Bakker, R., Schouten, J. C., Takens, F. and van den Bleek, C. M. (1996). Neural Network Model to Control an Experimental Chaotic Pendulum, *Physical Review E*, 54A, pp. 3545-3552, ISSN 1539-3755.

Deco, G. and Schurmann, B. (1994). Neural Learning of Chaotic System Behavior, *IEICE Transactions Fundamentals*, Vol. E77-A, No. 11, pp.1840-1845, ISSN 0916-8508.

Demuth, H., Beale, M., and Hagan, M. (2010). Neural Network Toolbox User's Guide, The MathWorks, Inc., ISBN 0-9717321-0-8, Natick, Massachusetts.

Dendrinos, D. S. (1994). Traffic-Flow Dynamics: A Search for Chaos, *Chaos, Solitons, & Fractals*, Vol. 4, No. 4, pp. 605-617, ISSN 0960-0779.

Disbro, J. E. and Frame, M. (1989). Traffic Flow Theory and Chaotic Behavior, *Transportation Research Record* 1225, pp. 109-115. ISSN: 0361-1981

Farmer, J. D. and Sidorowich, J. J. (1987). Predicting Chaotic Time Series, *Physical Review Letters*, Vol. 59, pp. 845-848, ISSN 0031-9007.

Fu, H., Xu, J. and Xu, L. (2005). Traffic Chaos and Its Prediction Based on a Nonlinear Car-Following Model, *Journal of Control Theory and Applications*, Vol. 3, No. 3, pp. 302-307, ISSN 1672-6340.

Gazis, D. C., Herman, R., and Rothery, R. W. (1961). Nonlinear Follow-The-Leader Models of Traffic Flow, *Operations Research*, Vol. 9, No. 4, pp. 545-567, ISSN 0030-364X.

Glass, L., Guevau, X., and Shrier, A. (1983). Bifurcation and Chaos in Periodically Stimulated Cardiac Oscillator, *Physica 7D*, pp. 89-101, ISSN 0167-2789.

Grassberger, P. and Proccacia, I. (1983). Characterization of Strange Attractors, *Physical Review Letters*, No. 50, pp. 346-349, ISSN 0031-9007.

Hagan, M. T. and Menhaj, M. (1994). Training Feedforeword Networks with the Marquardt Algorithm, IEEE Transactions on Neural Networks, Vol.5, No.6, pp. 989-903, ISSN 1045-9227.

Hebb, D. O. (1949). The Organization of Behavior, John Wiley & Sons, ISBN 0-8058-4300-0, New York.

Hense, A. (1987). On the Possible Existence of a Strange Attractor for the Southern Oscillation, *Beitr Physical Atmosphere*, Vol. 60, No. 1, pp. 34-47, ISSN 0005-8173.

Hopfield, J. J. (1982). Neural Networks and Physical Systems with Emergent Collective Computational Abilities, Proceedings of the National Academy of Sciences of the USA, Vol. 79, No. 8, pp. 2554-2558,ISSN 0027-8424.

Hopfield, J. J., Feinstein D. I. and Palmers, R. G. (1983). Unlearning Has a Stabilizing Effect in Collective Memories, Nature, Vol. 304, pp. 158-159, ISSN 0028-0836.

Levenberg, K. (1944). A Method for the Solution of Certain Problems in Least Squares, *Quarterly of Applied Mathematics*, No.2, pp.164-168, ISSN 0033-569X.

MacKay, D. J. C. (1992). Bayesian Interpolation, *Neural Computation*, Vol. 4, No. 3, pp. 415-447, ISSN 0899-7667.

Marquardt, D. (1963). An Algorithm for Least Squares Estimation of Nonlinear Parameters, *SIAM Journal on Applied Mathematics*, Vol.11, pp.431-441, ISSN 0036-1399.

McCulloch, W. S. and Pitts, W. (1943). A Logical Calculus of Ideas Immanent in Nervous Activity, Bulletin of Mathematical Biophysics, Vol. 5, pp. 115-133, ISSN 0007-4985.

Mendenhall, W., Scheaffer, R. L., and Wackerly, D. D. (1986). *Mathematical Statistics with Application*, Third Edition, Duxbury Press, ISBN 0-87150-939-3, Boston, Massachusetts.

Moon, F. C. (1992). *Chaotic and Fractal Dynamics: An Introduction for Applied Scientists and Engineer*, John-Wiley and Sons, ISBN 0-471-54571-6, New York.

Principe, J. C., Rathie, A. and Kuo, J. M. (1992). Prediction of Chaotic Time Series with Neural Networks and the Issue of Dynamic Modeling, *International Journal of Bifurcation and Chaos in Applied Sciences and Engineering*, Vol.2, pp. 989-996, ISSN 0218-1274.

Rosenblatt, F. (1958). The Perception: A Probabilistic Model for Information Storage and Organization in the Brain, Psychological Review, Vol. 65, No. 6, pp. 386-408, ISSN 0033-295X.

Rumelhart, D. E. and McClelland, J. L. (1986). Parallel Distributed Processing: Explorations in the Microstructure of Cognition, Volume 1 (Foundations), The MIT Press, ISBN 0-262-68053-x, Cambridge, Massachusetts.

Takens, F. (1981). *Detecting Strange Attractors in Turbulence*, Lecture Notes in Mathematics, No. 898, pp. 366-381.

2

Predicting Chaos with Lyapunov Exponents: Zero Plays no Role in Forecasting Chaotic Systems

Dominique Guégan[1] and Justin Leroux[2]
[1]*Université Paris1 Panthéon-Sorbonne, 106-112 boulevard de l'Hôpital, 75013 Paris*
[2]*Institute for Applied Economics, HEC Montréal, CIRANO and CIRPÉE, 3000 chemin de la Côte-Ste-Catherine, Montréal, QC H3T 2A7*
[1]*France*
[2]*Canada*

1. Introduction

When taking a deterministic approach to predicting the future of a system, the main premise is that future states can be fully inferred from the current state. Hence, deterministic systems should in principle be easy to predict. Yet, some systems can be difficult to forecast accurately: such chaotic systems are extremely sensitive to initial conditions, so that a slight deviation from a trajectory in the state space can lead to dramatic changes in future behavior.
We propose a novel methodology for forecasting deterministic systems using information on the local chaoticity of the system via the so-called local Lyapunov exponent (LLE). To the best of our knowledge, while several works exist on the forecasting of chaotic systems (see, e.g., Murray, 1993; and Doerner et al, 1991) as well as on LLEs (e.g., Abarbanel, 1992; Wolff, 1992; Eckhardt & Yao, Bailey, 1997), none exploit the information contained in the LLE to forecasting. The general intuition behind our methodology can be viewed as a complement to existing forecasting methods, and can be extended to chaotic time series.
In this chapter, we start by illustrating the fact that chaoticity generally is not uniform on the orbit of a chaotic system, and that it may have considerable consequences in terms of the prediction accuracy of existing methods. For illustrative purposes, we describe how our methodology can be used to improve upon the well-known nearest-neighbor predictor on three deterministic systems: the Rössler, Lorenz and Chua attractors. We analyse the sensitivity of our methodology to changes in the prediction horizon and in the number of neighbors considered, and compare it to that of the nearest-neighbor predictor.
The nearest-neighbor predictor has proved to be a simple yet useful tool for forecasting chaotic systems (see Farmer & Sidorowich, 1987). In the case of a one-neighbor predictor, it takes the observation in the past which most resembles today's state and returns that observation's successor as a predictor of tomorrow's state. The rationale behind the nearest-neighbor predictor is quite simple: given that the system is assumed to be deterministic and ergodic, one obtains a sensible prediction of the variable's future by looking back at its evolution from a similar, past situation. For predictions more than one step ahead, the procedure is iterated by successively merging the predicted values with the observed data.

The nearest-neighbor predictor performs reasonably well in the short run (Ziehmann et al, 2000; Guégan, 2003). Nevertheless, by construction it can *never* produce an exact prediction because the nearest neighbor on which predictions are based can never exactly coincide with today's state—or else the underlying process, being deterministic, would also be periodic and trivially predicted. The same argument applies to other non-parametric predictors, like kernel methods, radial functions, etc. (see, e.g., Shintani & Linton, 2004; Guégan & Mercier, 1998). Hence, we argue that these predictors can be improved upon by correcting this inherent shortcoming.

Our methodology aims at correcting the above shortcoming by incorporating information carried by the system's LLE into the prediction. The methodology yields two possible candidates, potentially leading to significant improvements over the nearest neighbor predictor, provided one manages to solve the selection problem, which is an issue we address here. We develop a systematic method for solving the candidate selection problem and show, on three known chaotic systems, that it yields statisfactory results (close to a 100% success rate in selecting the "right" candidate).

The rest of the paper is organized as follows. In Section 2, we present our methodology on the use of LLEs in forecasting and introduce the candidate selection problem. In Section 3, we solve the selection problem and show using simulated chaotic systems that the size of the LLEs plays no role in the optimality of the selection procedure. However, the size of the LLEs does matter for the success rate of our selection algorithm and has an impact on the size of errors. These findings, as well as the sensitivity analysis of our methodology to the prediciton horizon and the number of neighbors, are presented in Section 4. Section 5 concludes.

2. Chaoticity depends on where you are

Consider a one-dimensional series of T observations from a chaotic system, $(x_1, ...x_T)$, whose future values we wish to forecast. Here, we consider that a chaotic system is characterized by the existence of an attractor in a d-dimensional phase space (Eckmann & Ruelle, 1985), where $d > 1$ is the embedding dimension.[1] A possible embedding method involves building a d-dimensional orbit, (X_t), with $X_t = (x_t, x_{t-\tau}, ..., x_{t-(d-1)\tau})$.[2] For the sake of exposition, we shall assume $\tau = 1$ in the remainder of the paper.

By definition, the local Lyapunov exponent (LLE) of a dynamical system characterizes the rate of separation of points infinitesimally close on an orbit. Formally, two neighboring points in phase space with initial separation δX_0 are separated, t periods later, by the distance:

$$\delta X = \delta X_0 e^{\lambda_0 t},$$

where λ_0 is the (largest) LLE of the system in the vicinity of the initial points. Typically, this local rate of divergence (or convergence, if $\lambda_0 < 0$) depends on the orientation of the initial vector δX_0. Thus, strictly speaking, a whole spectrum of local Lyapunov exponents exists, one per dimension of the state space. A dynamic system is considered to be (locally) chaotic if $\lambda_0 > 0$, and (locally) stable if $\lambda_0 < 0$. (see, e.g., Bailey, 1997)

We develop a methodology which exploits the local information carried by the LLE to improve upon existing methods of reconstruction and prediction. Our methodology utilizes the

[1] The choice of the embedding dimension has been the object of much work (see Takens, 1996, for a survey) and is beyond the scope of this work.

[2] Throughout the paper, capital letters will be used to denote vectors (e.g., X) while small caps letters denote real values (e.g., x).

(estimated) value of the LLE to measure the intrinsic prediction error of existing predictors and corrects these predictors accordingly. Note that this methodology applies regardless of the sign of λ_i; i.e., regardless of whether the system is locally chaotic or locally stable. The only drawback of our approach is that it generates two candidate predictions, denoted $\hat{x}_T^-$ and $\hat{x}_T^+$, one being an excellent predictor (which improves upon existing methods) and the other being rather poor. For instance, when applied to the nearest-neighbor predictor, the candidates are the two solutions to the equation:

$$(z - x_{i+1})^2 + (x_T - x_i)^2 + ... + (x_{T-d+2} - x_{i-d+2})^2 - |X_T - X_i|^2 e^{2\hat{\lambda}_i} = 0, \qquad (1)$$

where X_i is the phase-space nearest neighbor of the last observation, X_T. λ_i is estimated by $\hat{\lambda}_i$ using the method developed in Wolff (1992).[34]

Hence, accurate prediction boils down to being able to select the better of the two candidate predictors. Our goal here is to improve on previous work in Guégan & Leroux (2009a, 2009b) by developing a systematic selection method to accurately select the best of the two candidates, $\hat{x}_T^-$ and $\hat{x}_T^+$. To do so, we further exploit the information conveyed by the LLE. Indeed, the LLE being a measure of local chaoticity of a system (Abarbanel, 1992; Wolff, 1992), it may also yield important clues regarding the regularity of the trajectory.

In fact, even "globally chaotic" systems are typically made up of both "chaotic regions", where the LLE is positive, and more stable regions where it is negative (Bailey, 1997), as we illustrate in Figures 1, 2 and 3 for the Rössler[5], the Lorenz[6], and the Chua[7] systems, respectively[8]. In each figure we display, clockwise from the upper left corner: the 3-dimensional attractor in the (x, y, z)-space, the value of the LLE along the orbit (λ is displayed on the vertical axis), the value of the LLE along the trajectory, and the distribution of LLE values ranked from highest

---

[3] Other estimations of Lyapunov exponents exist. See, e.g., Gençay (1996), Delecroix et al (1997) and Bask & Gençay (1998).

[4] Details on this step of the method can be found in Guégan & Leroux (2009a, 2009b).

[5] We followed the z variable of the following Rössler system:

$$\begin{cases} \frac{dx}{dt} = -y - z \\ \frac{dy}{dt} = x + 0.1y \\ \frac{dz}{dt} = 0.1 + z(x - 14) \end{cases},$$

with initial values $x_0 = y_0 = z_0 = 0.0001$ and a step size of 0.01 (Guégan, 2003).

[6] We followed the x variable of the following Lorenz system:

$$\begin{cases} \frac{dx}{dt} = 16(y - x) \\ \frac{dy}{dt} = x(45.92 - z) - y \\ \frac{dz}{dt} = xy - 4z \end{cases},$$

with initial values $x_0 = -10$, $y_0 = -10$ and $z_0 = 30$, and a step size of 0.01 (Lorenz, 1963).

[7] We followed the z variable of the following Chua system:

$$\begin{cases} \frac{dx}{dt} = 9.35(y - h(x)) \\ \frac{dy}{dt} = x - y + z \\ \frac{dz}{dt} = -14.286y \end{cases},$$

with $h(x) = \frac{2}{7}x - \frac{3}{14}(|x + 1| - |x - 1|)$ initial values $x_0 = 0.3$, $y_0 = -0.3$ and $z_0 = 0.28695$, and a step size of 0.01. For an exhaustive gallery of double scroll attractors, see Bilotta et al (2007).

[8] For each attractor, we simulated 30,000 observations and deleted the first 5,000 ensure that we are working within the attractor.

to lowest. Notice that for each attractor, the value of the LLE takes on positive and negative values (i.e., above and below the $\lambda = 0$ plane depicted in the upper-right corner). Hence, we may expect very stable trajectories where the LLE is small, wheras regions where the LLE is large yield highly unstable behavior.

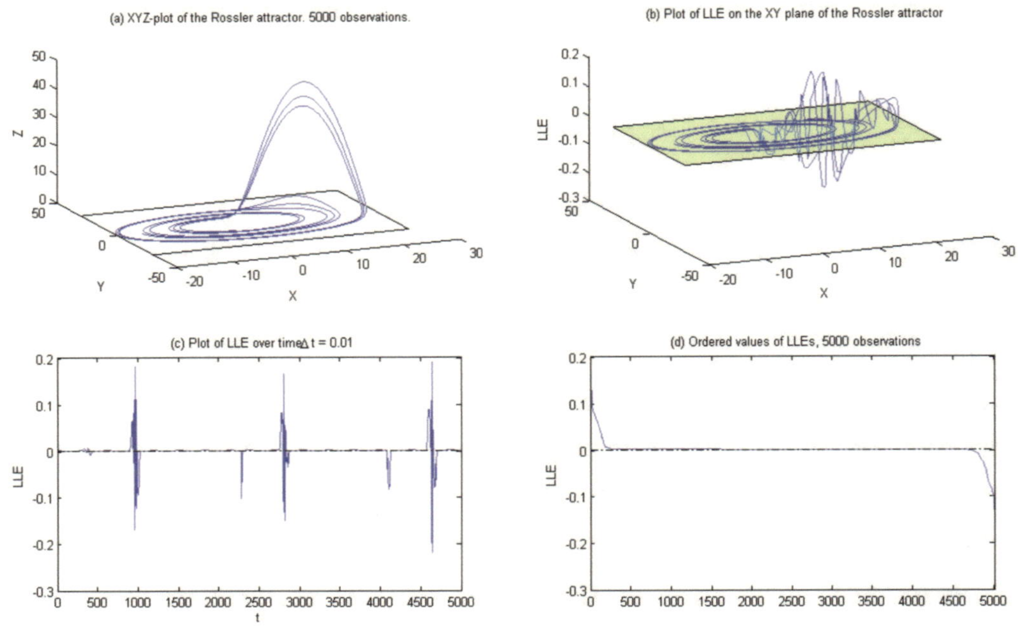

Fig. 1. Evolution of the LLE for the Rössler system

3. Solving the selection problem

Assuming that we observe $x_1, ..., x_T$, and following the insights of the previous section, we now investigate conditioning our selection process on the value of the LLE. Formally, our algorithm can be defined as follows:

$$\begin{cases} \text{If } \lambda_T \leq \bar{\lambda}, \text{select the "colinear" candidate} \\ \text{otherwise, select the "non colinear" candidate,} \end{cases} \tag{2}$$

where $\bar{\lambda}$ is an exogenously given threshold value. We abuse terminology slightly and denote by "colinear" the candidate which maximizes the following scalar product:

$$\hat{X}^c_{T+1} = \arg \max_{\hat{X}_{T+1} \in C} \frac{(\hat{X}_{T+1} - X_T) \cdot (X_{i+1} - X_T)}{||\hat{X}_{T+1} - X_T|| \times ||X_{i+1} - X_T||} \tag{3}$$

where $C = \{(\hat{x}^-_{T+1}, x_T, ..., x_{T-d+2}), (\hat{x}^+_{T+1}, x_T, ..., x_{T-d+2})\}$ and X_{i+1} is the successor of the nearest neighbor of X_T in phase space. Likewise, we denote by $\hat{X}^{nc}_{T+1}$, and call "non colinear", the candidate which minimizes the scalar product in Expression (3).

In words, the algorithm assumes that when the value of the LLE is low, the orbit is relatively smooth, suggesting that the trajectory to be predicted behaves similarly as the nearest

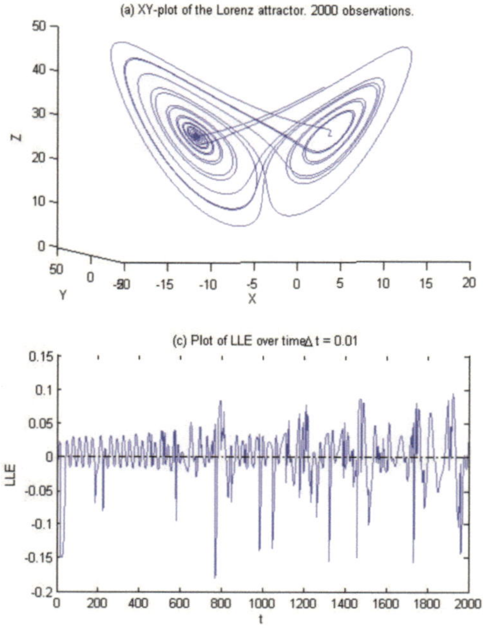

Fig. 2. Evolution of the LLE for the Lorenz system

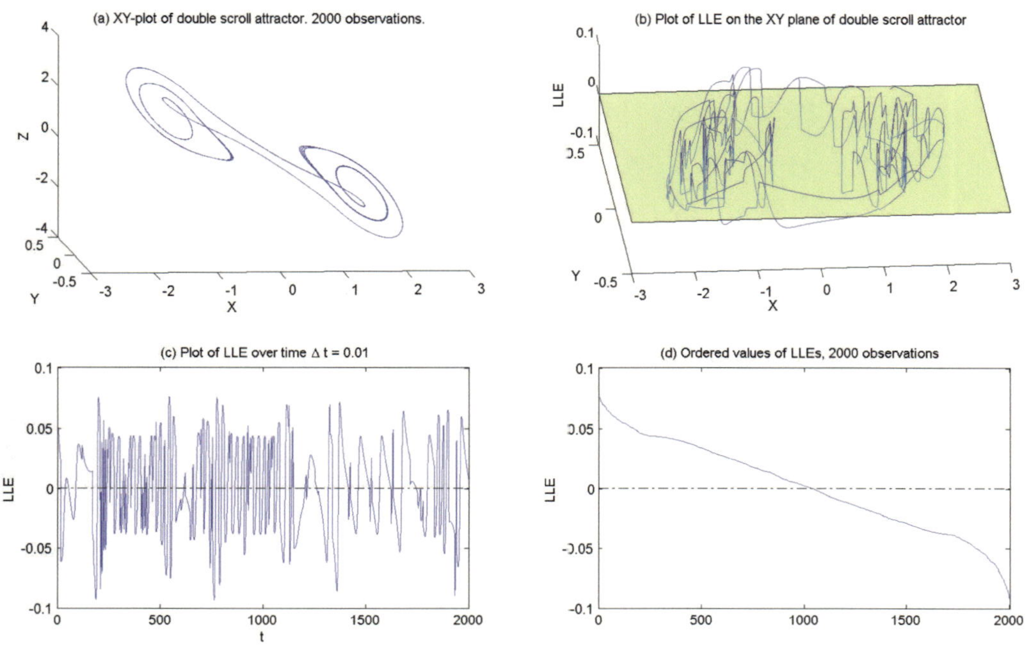

Fig. 3. Evolution of the LLE for the Chua system

neighbor's trajectory. Alternatively, when the LLE is "large", the trajectory is considered to behave erratically, so that the trajectory to be predicted is assumed to differ from that of its nearest neighbor.
Intuition suggests that one may need to estimate the optimal value of the threshold $\bar{\lambda}$ in terms of prediction accuracy for each chaotic system. Hence, we calculate the mean squared error (MSE) of the predictor using the above selection algorithm (2) in order to assess which threshold $\bar{\lambda}$ minimizes the MSE:

$$MSE^s(\bar{\lambda}) = \frac{1}{n} \sum_{t=T-n+1}^{T} \left(\hat{X}_t^s(\bar{\lambda}) - X_t\right)^2,$$

with $\hat{X}_t^s(\bar{\lambda}) = \hat{X}_t^c$ or $\hat{X}_t^{nc}$ according to selection algorithm (2), and where n is the number of predictions. We compute $MSE^s(\bar{\lambda})$ across all values of $\bar{\lambda}$ in the range of the system's LLE over the last 1000 observations of our sample ($n = 1000$) using the entire, true information set leading up to the predictee for each prediction. Figure 4 plots the values of MSE^s as a function of $\bar{\lambda}$ for the Rössler, Lorenz and Chua attractors. We find that $MSE^s(\bar{\lambda})$ is smallest when $\bar{\lambda}$ is the upper bound of the range. In other words, our method seems to not require estimating the optimal threshold, $\bar{\lambda}$, as one is better off always selecting the colinear candidate and *not* conditioning the selection process on the LLE, as intuition might have suggested.

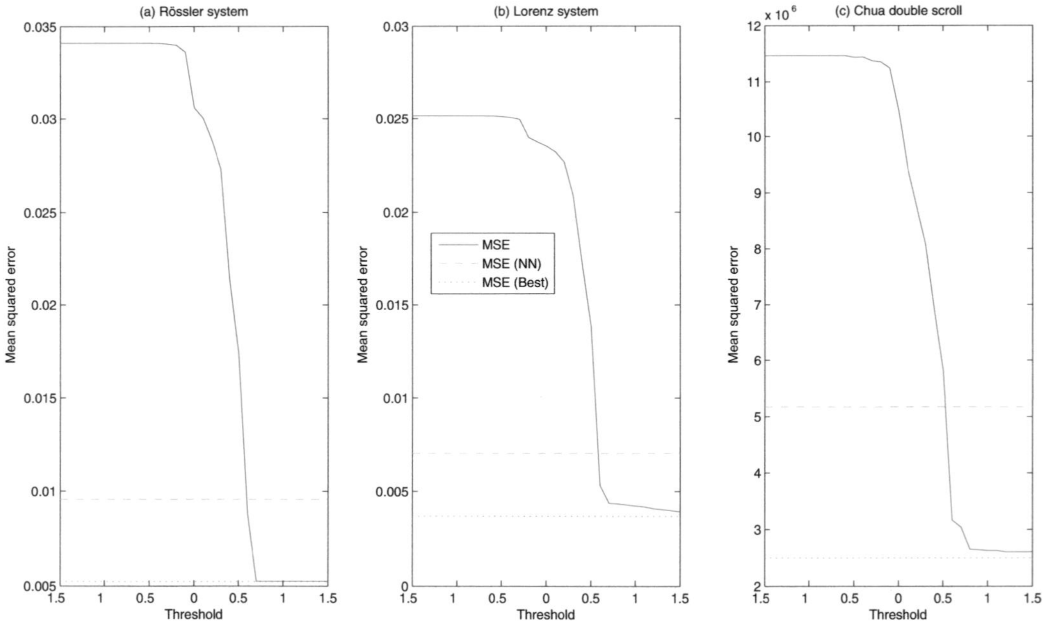

Fig. 4. MSE as a function of threshold $\bar{\lambda}$

In the remainder of the chapter, we shall focus on the performance of $\hat{X}^c$, the predictor which systematically selects the colinear candidate. For this predictor, the MSE writes as follows:

$$MSE^c = \frac{1}{n} \sum_{t=T-n+1}^{T} \left(\hat{X}_t^c - X_t\right)^2. \tag{4}$$

Table 1 displays the values of MSE^c along with the performances of the nearest-neighbor predictor:

$$MSE^{NN} = \frac{1}{n} \sum_{t=T-n+1}^{T} \left(\hat{X}_t^{NN} - X_t\right)^2 \tag{5}$$

and of the best of the two possible candidates

$$MSE^b = \frac{1}{n} \sum_{t=T-n+1}^{T} \min_{i=c,nc} \left(\hat{X}_t^i - X_t\right)^2 .^9 \tag{6}$$

Table 1 also shows the success rate, ρ, in selecting the better of the two candidate as well as information on the value of the LLE on the orbit (line 6) and information on the LLE on the observations where "wrong" candidate was selected (line 7).

Table 1: Prediction results. n =1,000 predictions.

		Rössler	Lorenz	Chua
MSE^c		0.0053	0.0039	2.6038e-6
MSE^{NN}		0.0156	0.0091	5.1729e-6
MSE^b		0.0052	0.0037	2.4947e-6
ρ		97.3%	94.30%	98.7%
$\hat{\lambda}_t$	mean	0.1302	0.1940	0.0593
	(min;max)	(-1.2453,0.9198)	(-1.4353;1.4580)	(-1.0593;1.1468)
$\hat{\lambda}_{t\|fail}$	mean	0.2582	0.4354	0.3253
	(min;max)	(-0.4824,09198)	(-0.5142;1.3639)	(-0.5648;0.5554)

Table 1. MSE^c, MSE^{NN} and MSE^b are as defined in (4), (5) and (6). ρ is the selection success rate of the colinear selector. $\hat{\lambda}_t$ is the value of the LLE on the 1,000 observations to be predicted. $\hat{\lambda}_{t|fail}$ is the value of the LLE on the observations where the colinear selector does not select the best candidate.

For all three systems, we find that MSE^c is substantially smaller than MSE^{NN}. Moreover, MSE^c is relatively close to MSE^b, suggesting that our procedure selects the best of the two candidates quite often. In fact, on all three attractors, we obtain success rate, ρ, close to 100%. Finally, on the few predictions where our predictor does select the "wrong" candidate, the value of the LLE is relatively high compared to the average LLE on the attractor (0.25 versus 0.13 for Rössler, 0.44 versus 0.19 for Lorenz, and 0.33 versus 0.06 for Chua). These findings are consistent with the intuition that prediction is more difficult in regions of the attractor which are more sensitive to initial conditions. While this finding seems to confirm that the value of the LLE plays a small role in the selection problem, recall that our results show that conditioning selection on the value of the LLE would not lead to improved predictions, as measured by $MSE^s(\bar{\lambda})$.

4. Forecasting

In this section, we detail the role of the value of the LLE on the size of errors and on the performance of the selection procedure as well as the performance of the predictor in the short and medium run.

4.1 Role of the LLE on error size

The following tables show the success rates of the selection procedure of $\hat{X}^c$ and the resulting MSE broken down in small value intervals for the LLE. Doing so allows one to assess how the performance of the procedure and of the predictor depends on the (local) chaoticity of the region considered. ρ represents the ratio of the number of times the best candidate was selected over the number of predictions in the interval considered. These predictions are then broken down into the number of good selection (n_{succ}) and the number of failures to select the best candidate (n_{fail}). Next, MSE^c shows the mean squared error of our predictor (using colinear selection) on each interval. $MSE^c|succ.$ and $MSE^c|fail$ show the value of MSE^c considering only the predictions where the best candidate was correctly and incorrectly selected, respectively. Finally, MSE^{NN} displays the mean squared error of the nearest neighbor predictor on the relevant interval.

Table 2: Rössler attractor, n =1000 predictions

$\hat{\lambda}_t$ range	ρ	n_{succ}	n_{fail}	MSE^c	$MSE^c\|succ$	$MSE^c\|fail$	MSE^{NN}
[-1.3,-1.1]	1	1	0	3.91e-11	3.91e-11	-	3.91e-11
[-1.1,-0.9]	-	-	-	-	-	-	-
[-0.9,-0.7]	1	5	0	1.32e-6	1.32e-6	-	1.34e-6
[-0.7,-0.5]	1	68	0	0.0073	0.0073	-	0.0073
[-0.5,-0.3]	0.98	106	2	0.0033	0.0033	2.096e-5	0.0034
[-0.3,-0.1]	0.97	105	3	0.0059	0.0060	0.0001	0.0072
[-0.1,0.1]	0.98	125	3	0.0089	0.0091	0.0000	0.0176
[0.1,0.3]	0.97	149	4	0.0019	0.0019	0.0009	0.0054
[0.3,0.5]	0.97	222	8	0.0059	0.0056	0.0132	0.0101
[0.5,0.7]	0.97	192	6	0.0051	0.0052	0.0009	0.0127
[0.7,0.9]	-	-	-	-	-	-	-
[0.9,1.1]	0	0	1	9.34e-10	-	9.34e-10	2.79e-11

Table 2. Each row relates to observations X_t for which the LLE belongs to $\hat{\lambda}_t$ range. ρ is the selection success ratio (1=100%). n_{succ} and n_{fail} are the number of predictions for which the colinear selector selects correctly and incorrectly, respectively. MSE^c and MSE^{NN} are as defined in (4) and (5). $MSE^c|succ$ and $MSE^c|fail$ correspond to MSE^c restricted to the previously defined n_{succ} and n_{fail} observations, respectively.

Notice that for all three attractors the size of errors is relatively stable over the range of LLEs when selection is successful. This indicates that our method accurately corrects for the dispersion of neighboring trajectories as measured by the value of the LLE. If this were not the case, one would expect the MSE to increase monotonically with the value of LLE. In fact, errors become large only for values of the LLE near the upper end of their range (above 0.9 for the Rössler attractor, above 1.1 for the Lorenz attractor, and above 0.5 for the Chua attractor). A possible reason for this sudden increase may be that our estimator for the value of the LLEs is not sufficiently robust in regions of high chaoticity. We expect that a more sophisticated estimation method for the LLE may solve this issue, which we address in a companion paper. Notice that for the Rössler attractor, for most values of the LLE, the size of errors when failing to select is on average less than when selecting accurately. For example, for $\hat{\lambda} \in [0.5, 0.7]$,

Table 3: Lorenz attractor, n =1000 predictions							
$\hat{\lambda}_t$ range	ρ	$n_{succ.}$	$n_{fail.}$	MSE^c	$MSE^c\|succ.$	$MSE^c\|fail.$	MSE^{NN}
[-1.5,-1.3]	1	1	0	0.0001	0.0001	-	0.0001
[-1.3,-1.1]	-	-	-	-	-	-	-
[-1.1,-0.9]	1	3	0	0.0016	0.0016	-	0.0016
[-0.9,-0.7]	1	3	0	0.0013	0.0013	-	0.0013
[-0.7,-0.5]	0.99	67	1	0.0033	0.0034	0.0003	0.0035
[-0.5,-0.3]	0.99	92	1	0.0049	0.0049	0.0000	0.0054
[-0.3,-0.1]	0.98	98	2	0.0056	0.0054	0.014	0.0098
[-0.1,0.1]	0.93	108	8	0.0038	0.0039	0.0026	0.0052
[0.1,0.3]	0.94	109	7	0.0041	0.0036	0.011	0.0077
[0.3,0.5]	0.96	195	8	0.0021	0.0020	0.0049	0.0088
[0.5,0.7]	0.91	223	22	0.0044	0.0038	0.0102	0.0079
[0.7,0.9]	0.90	18	2	0.0011	0.0008	0.0033	0.0012
[0.9,1.1]	0.81	13	3	0.0006	0.0003	0.0016	0.0016
[1.1,1.3]	0.82	9	2	0.0034	0.0031	0.0047	0.0027
[1.3,1.5]	0.80	4	1	0.042	0.052	0.0019	0.0015

Table 3. Each row relates to observations X_t for which the LLE belongs to $\hat{\lambda}_t$ range. ρ is the selection success ratio (1=100%). n_{succ} and n_{fail} are the number of predictions for which the colinear selector selects correctly and incorrectly, respectively. MSE^c and MSE^{NN} are as defined in (4) and (5). $MSE^c|succ$ and $MSE^c|fail$ correspond to MSE^c restricted to the previously defined n_{succ} and n_{fail} observations, respectively.

$MSE^c|_{succ} = 0.0052 > 0.0009 = MSE^c|_{fail}$.This apparently surprising observation is actually encouraging as it indicates that selection mistakes occur mostly when there is little need for correction. Such situations may arise because X_T's nearest neighbor is very close to X_T or, alternatively, when both candidates, $\hat{x}^-_{T+1}$ and $\hat{x}^+_{T-1}$ are both very close to x_{i+1} due to space orientation considerations. The same phenomenon can be observed for the Lorenz system up to $\hat{\lambda} = 0.1$ and for $\hat{\lambda} > 1.3$, but is less systematic for the Chua system.

Regarding the selection accuracy, as measured by ρ, we find that our algorithm selects almost perfectly for all three attractors, and in most ranges of $\hat{\lambda}$. As expected, ρ dips slightly for larger values of $\hat{\lambda}$ in the case of the Rössler and Lorenz attractors, which is in line with the common intuition according to which trajectories are more stable, or smoother, where the value of the LLE is small and more irregular for large values of the LLE. Surprisingly, the Chua attractor behaves somewhat differently. Interestingly, selection mistakes occur on all attractors for negative values of the LLE, where the system is supposedly locally "stable". Hence, our results suggest that the focal value of $\lambda = 0$, traditionally separating order from chaos, bears little meaning in terms of forecasting.

Table 4: Chua attractor, n =1000 predictions							
$\hat{\lambda}_t$ range	ρ	$n_{succ.}$	$n_{fail.}$	MSE^c $(\times 10^{-4})$	$MSE^c\|succ.$ $(\times 10^{-4})$	$MSE^c\|fail.$ $(\times 10^{-4})$	MSE^{NN} $(\times 10^{-4})$
[-1.3,-1.1]	1	1	0	0.3111	0.3111	-	.3111
[-1.1,-0.9]	1	1	0	0.1765	0.1765	-	0.1765
[-0.9,-0.7]	-	0	0	-	-	-	-
[-0.7,-0.5]	0.9873	78	1	0.0376	0.0381	0.0002	0.0391
[-0.5,-0.3]	0.98	98	2	0.0339	0.0332	0.0686	0.0362
[-0.3,-0.1]	1	116	0	0.0218	0.0218	-	0.0244
[-0.1,0.1]	0.9918	241	2	0.0074	0.0072	0.0285	0.0241
[0.1,0.3]	0.9917	120	1	0.0097	0.0097	0.0124	0.0228
[0.3,0.5]	0.9884	171	2	0.0199	0.0199	0.0183	0.0221
[0.5,0.7]	0.9740	150	4	0.0553	0.0508	0.2261	0.0239
[0.7,0.9]	0.8750	7	1	0.1333	0.0721	0.5619	0.0981
[0.9,1.1]	1	2	0	0.0884	0.0884	-	0.0025
[1.1,1.3]	1	2	0	0.2440	0.2440	-	0.0091

Table 4. Each row relates to observations X_t for which the LLE belongs to $\hat{\lambda}_t$ range. ρ is the selection success ratio (1=100%). n_{succ} and n_{fail} are the number of predictions for which the colinear selector selects correctly and incorrectly, respectively. MSE^c and MSE^{NN} are as defined in (4) and (5). $MSE^c|succ$ and $MSE^c|fail$ correspond to MSE^c restricted to the previously defined n_{succ} and n_{fail} observations, respectively.

4.2 Forecasting several steps ahead

We now explore the possibility of forecasting a chaotic time series several steps ahead using our correction method. In order to make predictions h-steps ahead, we proceed iteratively, including the successive one-step predictions.[10]

In addition to extending our predictions to several steps ahead, we jointly investigate the role of the number of neighbors to consider in the prediction and in the estimation of the LLE. We estimated the LLE using Wolff's (1992) algorithm with infinite bandwith and k neighbors, and applied our correction method to the average of the images of these neighbors ($k-$NNP).

4.2.1 Rössler attractor

The following table shows MSE^c and MSE^{NN} as a function of the number of neighbors and the prediction horizon in the top and bottom half of the table, respectively. For each column, and for each predictor, the numbers shown in bold are the smallest mean squared error for each horizon. Therefore, the corresponding number of neighbors, k, is optimal for that horizon.

As expected, predictions are more accurate in the shorter run. Moreover, increasing the number of neighbors, k, generally seems to decrease the accuracy of the prediction. Note

[10] For instance, $\hat{X}_{t+2}$ is obtained by constructing the (estimated) history $(X_1, ..., X_t, \hat{X}_{t+1})$. Next, $\hat{X}_{t+3}$ is obtained via history $(X_1, ..., X_t, \hat{X}_{t+1}, \hat{X}_{t+2})$, and so on. Hence,no further information is injected to the true information set $(X_1, ..., X_t)$.

Rössler attractor

	$h=1$	$h=2$	$h=6$	$h=7$	$h=10$
$k=1$	0.0053	**0.0117**	**0.1889**	**0.3107**	0.8575
$k=2$	**0.0045**	0.0144	0.2901	0.4890	1.6762
$k=3$	0.0058	0.0184	0.2114	0.3212	**0.8501**
$k=4$	0.0077	0.0240	0.3074	0.4301	1.3332
$k=5$	0.0091	0.0278	0.3650	0.5193	1.1830
$k=10$	0.0103	0.0412	0.6380	0.9228	2.2703
$k=20$	0.0283	0.1178	1.8714	2.7681	6.4980
MSE^{1-NN}	**0.0156**	**0.0315**	0.2392	0.3402	0.7928
MSE^{2-NN}	0.0194	0.0384	**0.2229**	**0.3017**	**0.6318**
MSE^{3-NN}	0.0228	0.0485	0.2784	0.3710	0.7410
MSE^{4-NN}	0.0242	0.0560	0.3513	0.4711	0.9528
MSE^{5-NN}	0.0295	0.0684	0.4224	0.5623	1.1133
MSE^{10-NN}	0.0500	0.1306	0.9188	1.2228	2.3539
MSE^{20-NN}	0.1247	0.3282	2.2649	2.9775	5.4714

Table 5. The top and bottom half of the table display MSE^c and MSE^{NN} as a function of the number of neighbors k and the prediction horizon, h, respectively.

that this is also true for the uncorrected nearest-neighbor predictor. Finally, our correction method improves upon the uncorrected nearest-neighbor predictor up until six steps ahead.

4.2.2 Lorenz attractor

Here also, predictions are more accurate in the shorter run. However, unlike for the Rössler attractor, the simulation results suggest that accuracy increases with k up to a point ($k = 4$). Beyond that, increasing the number of neighbors is detrimental to the accuracy of the method (except for $h = 20$, which is too large a horizon for our predictions to be trusted).
As is the case with the Rössler attractor, our method performs uniformly better than the corresponding uncorrected nearest-neighbor predictor for horizons of up to seven steps ahead.

4.2.3 Double scroll attractor

Again, we see that our prediction results improve upon those of the corresponding uncorrected k-nearest-neighbor predictor, but only in the very short run (up to $h = 2$). Also, as was the case with the other systems, the optimal number of neighbors is low: $k = 2$. Beyond that number, any information carried by neighbors farther away seems to only pollute the prediction results

5. Concluding comments

We further developed the methodology on using the information contained in the LLE to improve forecasts. Our contributions is threefold. First, the selection problem is not an issue, and does not require conditioning candidate selection on the value of the LLE. Next, our

Lorenz attractor

	$h=1$	$h=2$	$h=7$	$h=8$	$h=10$
$k=1$	0.0039	0.0176	0.6821	1.0306	1.9406
$k=2$	0.0024	0.0102	0.4151	0.6249	1.2429
$k=3$	0.0020	0.0081	0.3387	0.5103	0.9955
$k=4$	**0.0014**	**0.0057**	**0.2873**	**0.4347**	**0.8803**
$k=5$	0.0014	0.0061	0.3179	0.4852	0.9724
$k=10$	0.0016	0.0071	0.3374	05124	1.0329
$k=20$	0.0021	0.0101	0.4322	0.6474	1.2333
MSE^{1-NN}	0.0091	0.0246	0.3485	0.4877	0.8730
MSE^{2-NN}	0.0084	0.0226	0.2994	0.4152	0.7318
MSE^{3-NN}	**0.0081**	**0.0220**	**0.2951**	**0.4087**	0.7181
MSE^{4-NN}	0.0086	0.0231	0.2974	0.4096	0.7133
MSE^{5-NN}	0.0091	0.0243	0.2991	0.4104	**0.7123**
MSE^{10-NN}	0.0129	0.0349	0.3775	0.5001	0.8136
MSE^{20-NN}	0.0207	0.0562	0.5397	0.6893	1.0423

Table 6. The top and bottom half of the table display MSE^c and MSE^{NN} as a function of the number of neighbors k and the prediction horizon, h, respectively.

Chua double scroll

	$h=1$	$h=2$	$h=3$	$h=5$	$h=10$
$k=1$	2.6038e-6	1.1247e-5	3.2935e-5	1.3694e-4	0.0012
$k=2$	1.6569e-6	**5.5148e-6**	**1.5541e-5**	**6.1758e-5**	**5.5566e-4**
$k=3$	**1.5344e-6**	5.6257e-6	1.5912e-5	6.3038e-5	6.1618e-4
$k=4$	2.0762e-6	6.9228e-6	1.9519e-5	7.4392e-5	6.7625e-4
$k=5$	2.6426e-6	8.7472e-6	2.3965e-5	8.7017e-5	6.6244e-4
$k=10$	4.4688e-6	1.7896e-5	5.2198e-5	1.9949e-4	0.0014
$k=20$	6.4272e-6	2.7342e-5	9.3183e-5	4.4513e-4	0.0042
MSE^{1-NN}	5.1729e-6	8.7554e-6	1.6178e-5	5.2720e-5	4.8311e-4
MSE^{2-NN}	**4.3528e-6**	**7.9723e-6**	**1.5174e-5**	**4.9276e-5**	**4.3521e-4**
MSE^{3-NN}	5.9985e-6	1.1757e-5	2.2003e-5	6.4616e-5	4.7283e-4
MSE^{4-NN}	8.6114e-6	1.7168e-5	3.1539e-5	8.6965e-5	5.6469e-4
MSE^{5-NN}	1.1190e-5	2.3201e-5	4.2647e-5	1.1362e-4	6.7550e-4
MSE^{10-NN}	1.7453e-5	4.5731e-5	9.4048e-5	2.6532e-4	0.0014
MSE^{20-NN}	5.5861e-5	1.6005e-4	3.3975e-4	9.4208e-4	0.0042

Table 7. The top and bottom half of the table display MSE^c and MSE^{NN} as a function of the number of neighbors k and the prediction horizon, h, respectively.

results confirm that it is indeed possible to use information on the LLE to improve forecasts. We also highlight an interesting fact: the focal value of $\lambda = 0$, which traditionally separates order from chaos, does not play any role in the forecasting of chaotic systems. In other words, our methodology performs equally well on both stable and chaotic regions of the attractors studies. Finally, we examined the sensitivity of our methodology to varying the number k of neighbors as well as of the step-ahead horizon, h. While our goal was not to determine the optimal number of neighbors to consider for forecasting, it seems that each attractor admits a rather low optimal number of neighbors. We have worked with a fixed embedding dimension, d, throughout. Now that we have ascertained the validity of the approach, the next step is to confirm its performance on real physical or financial data.

6. References

[1] Abarbanel, H.D.I. (1992), Local and global Lyapunov exponents on a strange attractor. in Casdagli M and Eubank S Eds, Addison-Wesley, *Nonlinear Modeling and Forecasting, SFI Studies in the Science of Complexity*, Proc. Vol. XII: 229-247.

[2] B. Bailey, Local Lyapunov exponents: predictability depends on where you are. Nonlinear Dynamics and Economics, Kirman et al. Eds, 1997.

[3] Bask, M. & Gençay, R (1998). Testing chaotic dynamics via Lyapunov exponents, *Physica D*, 114: 1-2.

[4] Bilotta, E., Di Blasi, G., Stranges, F. & Pantano, P. (2007). A Gallery of Chua Atractors. Part VI. *International Journal of Bifurcation and Chaos*, 17: 1801-1910.

[5] Delecroix, M., Guégan, D. & Léorat, G. (1997) Determining Lyapunov exponents in deterministic dynamical systems, *Computational Statistics and Data Analysis*, 12: 93-107.

[6] Doerner, R., Hübinger, B. & Martienssen, W., Grossman, S. & Thomae, S. (1991). Predictability Portraits for Chaotic Motions, *Chaos, Solitons and Fractals*, 1: 553-571.

[7] Eckhardt, B. & Yao, D. (1993) Local Lyapunov exponents in chaotic systems, *Physica D*, 65: 100-108.

[8] Eckmann, J.P. & Ruelle, D (1985) Ergodic theory of chaos and strange attractors. *Review of Modern Physics*, 57: 615-656.

[9] Farmer, J.D. & Sidorowich, J.J. (1987) Predicting chaotic time series. *Physical Review Letters*, 59: 845 – 848.

[10] Gencay, R. (1996). A statistical framework for testing chaotic dynamics via Lyapunov exponents, *Physica D*, 89: 261-266.

[11] Guégan, D. (2003). *Les Chaos en Finance: Approche Statistique*, Economica Eds., Paris.

[12] Guégan, D. & Leroux, J. (2009b). Forecasting chaotic systems: The role of local Lyapunov exponents, *Chaos, Solitons and Fractals*, 41: 2401-2404.

[13] Guégan, D. & Leroux, J. (2009a). Local Lyapunov Exponents: A New Way to Predict Chaotic Systems, in World Scientific Eds., *Topics on Chaotic Systems: Selected papers from CHAOS 2008 International Conference*: 158-165.

[14] Guégan, D. & Mercier, L. (1998). Stochastic and chaotic dynamics in high-frequency financial data, in Prochazka Eds, *Signal Processing and Prediction*, 365-372.

[15] Lorenz, E.N. (1963). Deterministic non-periodic flow. *Journal of Atmospheric Science*, 20: 130-141.

[16] Murray, D. (1993). Forecasting a chaotic time series using an improved metric for embedding space, *Physica D*, 68: 318-325.

[17] Shintani, M. & Linton, O. (2004) Nonparametric neural network estimation of Lyapunov exponents and a direct test for chaos, *Journal of Econometrics*, 120: 1-33.
[18] Takens, F. (1996). Estimation of dimension and order of time series. *Progress in Nonlinear Differential Equations and their Applications*, 19: 405-422.
[19] Wolff, R.C.L. (1992). Local Lyapunov exponents: looking closely at chaos. *Journal of the Royal Statistical Society B*, 54: 353 – 371.
[20] Ziehmann, C., Smith, L.A. & Kurths, J. (2000) Localized Lyapunov exponents and the prediction of predictability. *Physics Letters A*, 271: 237-251.

3

Relationship between the Predictability Limit and Initial Error in Chaotic Systems

Jianping Li and Ruiqiang Ding
State Key Laboratory of Numerical Modeling for Atmospheric Sciences and Geophysical Fluid Dynamics, Institute of Atmospheric Physics, Chinese Academy of Sciences, Beijing 100029
China

1. Introduction

Since the pioneer work of Lorenz on predictability problems [1–2], many studies have examined the relationships between predictability and initial error in chaotic systems [3–7]; however, these previous studies focused on multi-scale complex systems such as the atmosphere and oceans [4–6]. Because large uncertainties exist regarding the dynamic equations and observational data related to such complex systems, there also exists uncertainty in any conclusions drawn regarding the relationship between the predictability of such systems and initial error. In addition, multi-scale complex systems such as the atmosphere are thought to have an intrinsic upper limit of predictability due to interactions among different scales [2, 4–6]. The predictability time of multi-scale complex systems, regardless of the errors in initial conditions, cannot exceed their intrinsic limit of predictability.

For relatively simple chaotic systems with a single characteristic timescale driven by a small number of variables (e.g., the logistic map [7] and the Lorenz63 model [1]), their predictability limits continuously depend on the initial errors: the smaller the initial error, the greater the predictability limit. If the initial perturbation is of size δ_0 and if the accepted error tolerance, Δ, remains small, then the largest Lyapunov exponent Λ_1 gives a rough estimate of the predictability time: $T_p \sim \frac{1}{\Lambda_1}\ln(\frac{\Delta}{\delta_0})$. However, reliance on the largest Lyapunov exponent commonly proves to be a considerable oversimplification [8]. This generally occurs because the largest Lyapunov exponent Λ_1, which we term the largest global Lyapunov exponent, is defined as the long-term average growth rate of a very small initial error. It is commonly the case that we are not primarily concerned with averages, and, even if we are, we may be interested in short-term behavior. Consequently, various local or finite-time Lyapunov exponents have been proposed, which measure the short-term growth rate of initial small perturbations [9–12]. However, the existing local or finite-time Lyapunov exponents, which are the same as the global Lyapunov exponent, are established based on the assumption that the initial perturbations are sufficiently small that their evolution can be approximately governed by the tangent linear model (TLM) of the nonlinear model, which essentially belongs to linear error dynamics. Clearly, as long as an uncertainty remains infinitesimal in the framework of linear error dynamics, it cannot pose a limit to predictability. To determine the limit of predictability, any proposed 'local Lyapunov exponent' must be defined with respect to the nonlinear behavior of nonlinear dynamical systems [13–14].

Recently, the nonlinear local Lyapunov exponent (NLLE) [15–17], which is a nonlinear generalization to the existing local Lyapunov exponents, was introduced to study the predictability of chaotic systems. NLLE measures the averaged growth rate of initial errors of nonlinear dynamical models without linearizing the governing equations. Using NLLE and its derivatives, the limit of dynamical predictability in large classes of chaotic systems can be efficiently and quantitatively determined. NLLE shows superior performance, compared with local or finite-time Lyapunov exponents based on linear error dynamics, in determining quantitatively the predictability limit of chaotic system. In the present study, we explore the relationship between the predictability limit and initial error in simple chaotic systems based on the NLLE approach, taking the logistic map and Lorenz63 model as examples.

2. Nonlinear local Lyapunov exponent (NLLE)

For an n-dimensional nonlinear dynamical system, its nonlinear perturbation equations are given by:

$$\frac{d}{dt}\boldsymbol{\delta}(t) = \mathbf{J}(\mathbf{x}(t))\boldsymbol{\delta}(t) + \mathbf{G}(\mathbf{x}(t),\boldsymbol{\delta}(t)), \tag{1}$$

where $\mathbf{x}(t) = (x_1(t), x_2(t), \cdots\cdots, x_n(t))^{\mathrm{T}}$ is the reference solution, T is the transpose, $\mathbf{J}(\mathbf{x}(t))\boldsymbol{\delta}(t)$ are the tangent linear terms, and $\mathbf{G}(\mathbf{x}(t),\boldsymbol{\delta}(t))$ are the high-order nonlinear terms of the perturbation $\boldsymbol{\delta}(t) = (\delta_1(t), \delta_2(t), \cdots\cdots, \delta_n(t))^{\mathrm{T}}$. Most previous studies have assumed that the initial perturbations are sufficiently small that their evolution could be approximately governed by linear equations [9–12]. However, linear error evolution is characterized by continuous exponential growth, which is not applicable to the description of a process that evolves from initially exponential growth to finally reaching saturation for sufficiently small errors (see Fig. 1). This linear approximation is also not applicable to situations in which the initial errors are not very small. Therefore, the nonlinear behaviors of error growth should be considered to determine the limit of predictability. Without linear approximation, the solutions of Eq. (1) can be obtained by numerical integration along the reference solution $\mathbf{x}(t)$ from $t = t_0$ to $t_0 + \tau$:

$$\boldsymbol{\delta}(t_0 + \tau) = \boldsymbol{\eta}(\mathbf{x}(t_0), \boldsymbol{\delta}(t_0), \tau)\boldsymbol{\delta}(t_0), \tag{2}$$

where $\boldsymbol{\eta}(\mathbf{x}(t_0), \boldsymbol{\delta}(t_0), \tau)$ is the nonlinear propagator. NLLE is then defined as

$$\lambda(\mathbf{x}(t_0), \boldsymbol{\delta}(t_0), \tau) = \frac{1}{\tau}\ln\frac{\|\boldsymbol{\delta}(t_0 + \tau)\|}{\|\boldsymbol{\delta}(t_0)\|}, \tag{3}$$

where $\lambda(\mathbf{x}(t_0), \boldsymbol{\delta}(t_0), \tau)$ depends in general on the initial state $\mathbf{x}(t_0)$ in phase space, the initial error $\boldsymbol{\delta}(t_0)$, and time τ. This differs from the existing local or finite-time Lyapunov exponents, which are defined based on linear error dynamics [9–12]. In the case of double limits of $\|\boldsymbol{\delta}(t_0)\| \to 0$ and $\tau \to \infty$, NLLE converges to the largest global Lyapunov exponent Λ_1. The ensemble mean NLLE over the global attractor of the dynamical system is given by

$$\bar{\lambda}(\boldsymbol{\delta}(t_0),\tau) = \int_\Omega \lambda(\mathbf{x}(t_0),\boldsymbol{\delta}(t_0),\tau)d\mathbf{x}$$

$$= \langle \lambda(\mathbf{x}(t_0),\boldsymbol{\delta}(t_0),\tau) \rangle_N, \ (N \to \infty) \tag{4}$$

where Ω represents the domain of the global attractor of the system, and $\langle\ \rangle_N$ denotes the ensemble average of samples of sufficiently large size N $(N \to \infty)$. The mean relative growth of initial error (RGIE) can be obtained by

$$\bar{E}(\boldsymbol{\delta}(t_0),\tau) = \exp(\bar{\lambda}(\boldsymbol{\delta}(t_0),\tau)\tau). \tag{5}$$

Using the theorem from Ding and Li [16], then we obtain

$$\bar{E}(\boldsymbol{\delta}(t_0),\tau) \xrightarrow{P} c \ (N \to \infty), \tag{6}$$

where $\xrightarrow{P}$ denotes the convergence in probability and c is a constant that depends on the converged probability distribution of error growth P. This is termed the saturation property of RGIE for chaotic systems. The constant c can be considered as the theoretical saturation level of $\bar{E}(\boldsymbol{\delta}(t_0),\tau)$. Once the error growth reaches the saturation level, almost all information on initial states is lost and the prediction becomes meaningless. Using the theoretical saturation level, the limit of dynamical predictability can be determined quantitatively [15–16]. In addition, for $\bar{\lambda}(\boldsymbol{\delta}(t_0),\tau) = \frac{1}{t}\ln\left[\bar{E}(\boldsymbol{\delta}(t_0),\tau)\right]$, based on the above analysis, we have

$$\bar{\lambda}(\boldsymbol{\delta}(t_0),\tau) \xrightarrow{P} \frac{1}{\tau} \times \ln c \ \text{ as } \tau \to \infty; \tag{7}$$

therefore, $\bar{\lambda}(\boldsymbol{\delta}(t_0),\tau)$ asymptotically decreases like $O(1/\tau)$ as $\tau \to \infty$. The magnitude of the initial error δ_0 is defined as the norm of the vector error $\boldsymbol{\delta}(t_0)$ in phase space at the initial time t_0; i.e., $\delta_0 = \|\boldsymbol{\delta}(t_0)\|$. The results show that the limit of dynamical predictability depends mainly on the magnitude of the initial error $\boldsymbol{\delta}(t_0)$ and rather than on its direction, because the error direction in the phase space becomes rapidly aligned toward the most unstable direction (Fig. 2).

3. Experimental predictability results

The first example is the logistic map [7],

$$y_{n+1} = a y_n (1 - y_n), \ 0 \le a \le 4, \tag{8}$$

Here, we choose the parameter value of $a = 4.0$, for which the logistic map is chaotic on the set (0,1) [18–19]. Figure 3 shows the dependence of the mean NLLE and the mean RGIE on the magnitude of the initial error. The mean NLLE is essentially constant in a plateau region that widens as decreasing initial error δ_0 (Fig. 3a). For a sufficiently long time, however, all the curves are asymptotic to zero. This finding reveals that for a very small initial error,

error growth is initially exponential, with a growth rate consistent with the largest global Lyapunov exponent, indicating that linear error dynamics are applicable during this phase. Subsequently, the error growth enters a nonlinear phase with a steadily decreasing growth rate, finally reaching a saturation value.

Figure 3b shows that the time at which the error growth reaches saturation also lengthens as δ_0 is reduced. Regardless of the magnitude of the initial error δ_0, all the errors ultimately reach saturation. To estimate the predictability time of a chaotic system, the predictability limit is defined as the time at which the error reaches 99% of its saturation level. The limit of dynamic predictability is found to decrease approximately linearly as increasing logarithm of initial error (Fig. 4). For a specific initial error, the limit of dynamic predictability is longer than the time for which the tangent linear approximation holds, which is defined as the time over which the mean NLLE remains constant. The difference between the predictability limit and the time over which the tangent linear approximation holds, remains largely constant as increasing logarithm of initial error, suggesting that the time over which the nonlinear phase of error growth lasts may be constant for initial errors of various magnitudes.

The second example is the Lorenz63 model [1],

$$\begin{cases} \dot{X} = -\sigma X + \sigma Y \\ \dot{Y} = rX - Y - XZ, \\ \dot{Z} = XY - bZ \end{cases} \tag{9}$$

where σ=10, r=28, and b=8/3, for which the well-known "butterfly" attractor exists. Figure 5 shows the mean NLLE and mean RGIE with initial errors of various magnitudes as a function of time τ. For all initial errors, the mean NLLE is initially unstable, then remains constant and finally decreases rapidly, approaching zero as increasing τ (Fig. 5a). For a very small initial error, it does not take long for error growth to become exponential, with a growth rate consistent with the largest global Lyapunov exponent, indicating that linear error dynamics are applicable during this phase. Subsequently, error growth enters a nonlinear phase with a steadily decreasing growth rate, finally reaching a saturation value (Fig. 5b). For initial errors of various magnitudes, the predictability limit of the Lorenz63 model is defined as the time at which the error reaches 99% of its saturation level, similar to the case for the logistic map.

Figure 6 shows the predictability limit and the time over which the tangent linear approximation holds as a function of the magnitude initial error. The predictability limit of the Lorenz63 model decreases approximately linearly as increasing logarithm of initial error, similar to the logistic map. For the Lorenz63 model, the difference between the predictability limit and the time over which the tangent linear approximation holds, remains largely constant as increasing logarithm of initial error.

4. Theoretical predictability analysis

As shown above, there exists a linear relationship between the predictability limit and the logarithm of initial error, for both the logistic map and Lorenz63 model. To understand the reason for this linear relationship, it is necessary to further investigate the relationship between the predictability limit and the logarithm of initial error using the theoretical

analysis, to determine if a general law exists between the predictability limit and the logarithm of initial error for chaotic systems.
For relatively simple chaotic systems such as the logistic map and Lorenz63 model, the predictability limit T_p is assumed to consist of the following two parts:

$$T_p = T_L + T_N , \tag{10}$$

where T_L is the time over which the tangent linear approximation holds, and T_N is the time over which the nonlinear phase of error growth occurs. When the mean error reaches a critical value δ_c, which is thought to be almost constant for a chaotic system under the condition of the given parameters, the tangent linear approximation is no longer valid and the error growth enters the nonlinear phase. Under the condition of the given parameters, the saturation value of error E^* is constant, which is not dependent on the initial error. Consequently, the time T_N taken for the error growth from δ_c to E^* can be considered as almost constant, not relying on the initial error. This assumption is confirmed by the experimental results shown in Figs. 3 and 5, which indicate that the interval between the predictability limit and the time over which the tangent linear approximation holds, remains almost constant as increasing logarithm of initial error. Then, T_N can be written as a constant:

$$T_N = C_1 . \tag{11}$$

For T_L, the time over which the tangent linear approximation holds, we get

$$\delta_c = \delta_0 exp(\Lambda_1 T_L) , \tag{12}$$

where δ_0 is the initial error and Λ_1 is the largest global Lyapunov exponent. From Eq. (12), we have

$$T_L = \frac{1}{\Lambda_1} \ln\left(\frac{\delta_c}{\delta_0}\right) . \tag{13}$$

From Eqs. (10), (11), and (13), we obtain

$$T_p = C_1 + \frac{1}{\Lambda_1}\left[\ln\delta_c - \ln\delta_0\right] . \tag{14}$$

Under the condition of the given parameters, Λ_1 of the chaotic system is fixed, as is $\frac{1}{\Lambda_1}\ln\delta_c$. Then, we have $\frac{1}{\Lambda_1}\ln\delta_c = C_2$ (where C_2 is a constant). Therefore, T_p can be written as

$$T_p = C - \frac{1}{\Lambda_1}\ln\delta_0 , \tag{15}$$

where $C = C_1 + C_2$. Eq. (15) can be changed to

$$T_p = C - \frac{1}{\Lambda_1}\frac{\log_{10}\delta_0}{\log_{10}e}. \quad (16)$$

If the largest global Lyapunov exponent Λ_1 and the constant C are known in advance, the predictability limit can be obtained for initial errors of any magnitude, according to Eq. (16). The constant C can be calculated from Eq. (16) if the predictability limit corresponding to a fixed initial error has been obtained in advance through the NLLE approach.

5. Experimental verification of theoretical results

Using the method proposed by Wolf et al. [20], the largest global Lyapunov exponent Λ_1 of the logistic map is 0.693 when $a = 4.0$. From Eq. (16), we have the formula that describes the relationship between the predictability limit and the initial error of the logistic map:

$$T_p = C - 3.321\log_{10}\delta_0. \quad (17)$$

For $\delta_0 = 10^{-6}$, the predictability limit of the logistic map is $T_p = 18$, as obtained using the NLLE approach. Then, we have $C = -1.92$ in Eq. (17). Therefore, the predictability limit for various initial errors can be obtained from Eq. (17). The predictability limits obtained in this way are in good agreement with those obtained using the NLLE approach (Fig. 7). This finding indicates that the assumptions presented in Section 3 are indeed reasonable. Therefore, it is appropriate to determine the predictability limit of the logistic map by extrapolating Eq. (17) to various initial errors.

The largest global Lyapunov exponent Λ_1 of the Lorenz63 model is obtained to be 0.906 when σ=10, r=28, b=8/3. From Eq. (16), we have the formula that describes the relationship between the predictability limit and the initial error of the Lorenz63 model:

$$T_p = C - 2.541\log_{10}\delta_0. \quad (18)$$

For $\delta_0 = 10^{-6}$, the predictability limit of the Lorenz63 model is $T_p = 22.19$, as obtained using the NLLE approach. Then, we have $C = 6.95$ in Eq. (17). Therefore, the predictability limits for various initial errors can be obtained by extrapolating the Eq. (17) to various initial errors. The resulting limits are in good agreement with those obtained using the NLLE approach (Fig. 8). The linear relationship between the predictability limit and the logarithm of initial error is further verified by the Lorenz63 model, and the relationship may be applicable to other simple chaotic systems.

6. Summary

Previous studies that examine the relationship between predictability and initial error in chaotic systems with a single characteristic timescale were based mainly on linear error dynamics, which were established based on the assumption that the initial perturbations are sufficiently small that their evolution could be approximately governed by the TLM of the nonlinear model. However, linear error dynamics involves large limitations, which is not applicable to determine the predictability limit of chaotic systems.

Taking the logistic map and Lorenz63 model as examples, we investigated the relationship between the predictability limit and initial error in chaotic systems, using the NLLE approach, which involves nonlinear error growth dynamics. There exists a linear relationship between the predictability limit and the logarithm of initial error. A theoretical analysis performed under the nonlinear error growth dynamics revealed that the growth of mean error enters a nonlinear phase after it reaches a certain critical magnitude, finally reaching saturation. For a given chaotic system, if the control parameters of the system are given, then the saturation value of error growth is fixed. The time taken for error growth from the nonlinear phase to saturation is also almost constant for various initial errors. The predictability limit is only dependent on the phase of linear error growth. Consequently, there exists a linear relationship between the predictability limit and the logarithm of initial error. The linear coefficient is related to the largest global Lyapunov exponent: the greater the latter, the more rapidly the predictability limit decreases as increasing logarithm of initial error. If the largest global Lyapunov exponent and the predictability limit corresponding to a fixed initial error are known in advance, the predictability limit can be extrapolated to various initial errors based on the linear relationship between the predictability limit and the logarithm of initial error.

It should be noted that the linear relationship between the predictability limit and the logarithm of initial error holds only in the case of relatively small initial errors. If the initial errors are large, the growth of the mean error would directly enter into the nonlinear phase, meaning that the linear relationship would fail to describe the relationship between the predictability limit and the logarithm of initial error. A more complex relationship may exist between the predictability limit and initial errors, which is an important subject left for future research.

7. Acknowledgment

This research was funded by an NSFC Project (40805022) and the 973 program (2010CB950400).

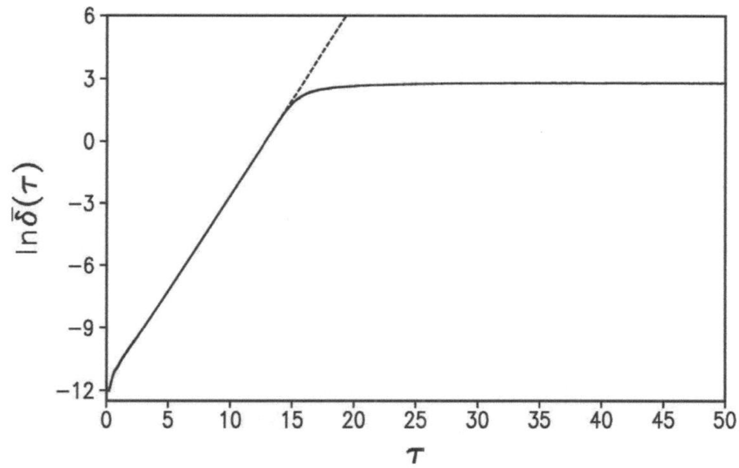

Fig. 1. Linear (dashed line) and nonlinear (solid line) average growth of errors in the Lorenz system as a function of time. The initial magnitude of errors is 10^{-5}.

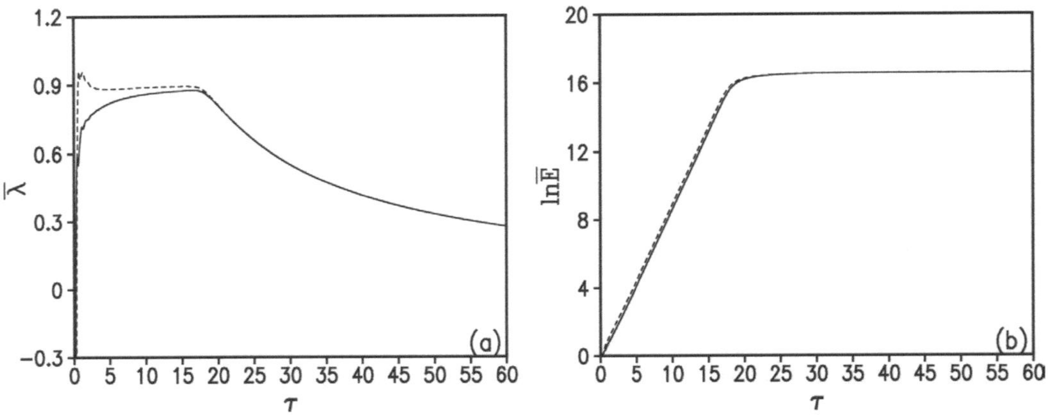

Fig. 2. Mean NLLE $\overline{\lambda}(\boldsymbol{\delta}(t_0),\tau)$ (a) and the logarithm of the corresponding mean RGIE $\overline{E}(\boldsymbol{\delta}(t_0),\tau)$ (b) in the Lorenz63 model as a function of time τ. In (a) and (b), the dashed and solid lines correspond to the initial errors $\boldsymbol{\delta}(t_0) = (10^{-6}, 0, 0)$ and $\boldsymbol{\delta}(t_0) = (0, 0, 10^{-6})$, respectively.

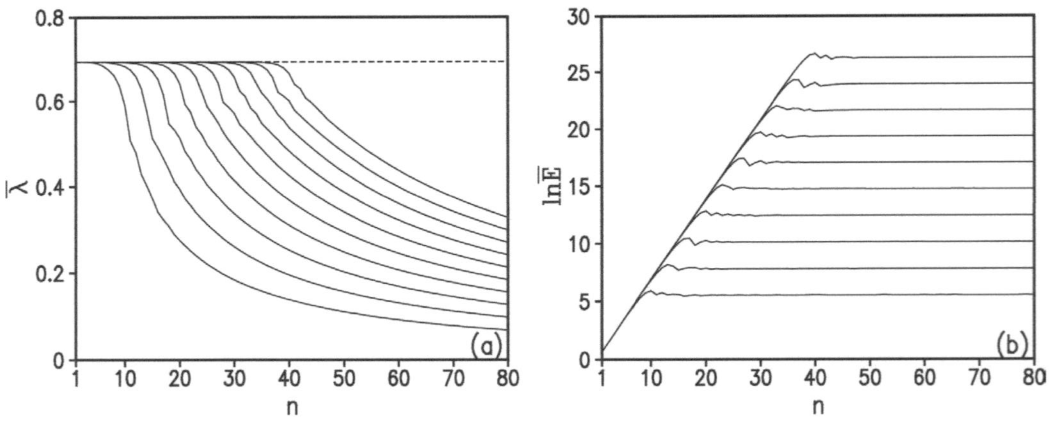

Fig. 3. Mean NLLE $\overline{\lambda}(\boldsymbol{\delta}(t_0),n)$ (a) and the logarithm of the corresponding mean RGIE $\overline{E}(\boldsymbol{\delta}(t_0),n)$ (b) in the logistic map as a function of time step n and δ_0 of various magnitudes. From above to below, the curves correspond to $\delta_0 = 10^{-12}$, 10^{-11}, 10^{-10}, 10^{-9}, 10^{-8}, 10^{-7}, 10^{-6}, 10^{-5}, 10^{-4}, and 10^{-3}, respectively. In (a), the dashed line indicates the largest global Lyapunov exponent.

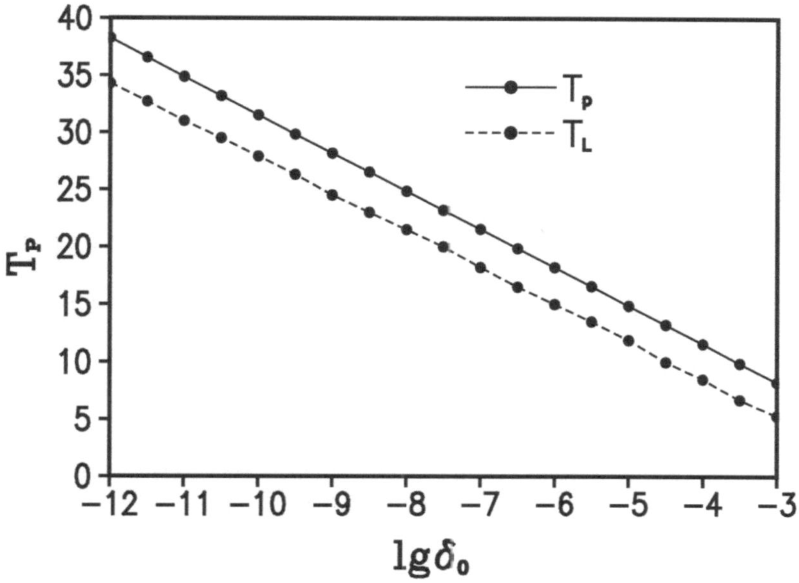

Fig. 4. Predictability limit T_P and the time T_L over which the tangent linear approximation holds in the logistic map as a function of δ_0 of various magnitudes.

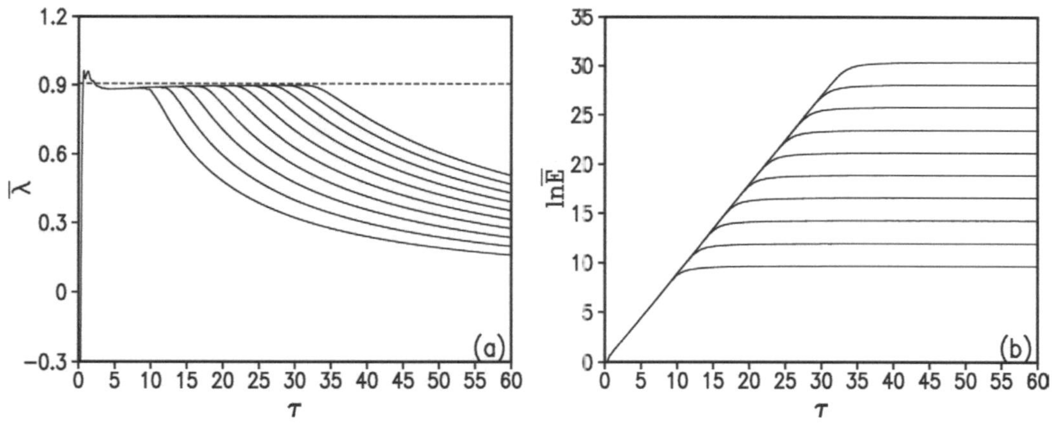

Fig. 5. Same as Fig. 3, but for the Lorenz63 model.

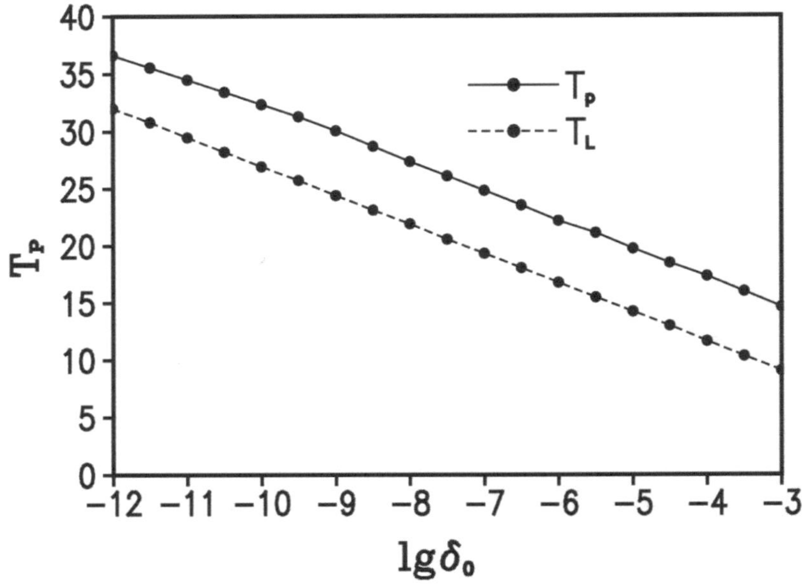

Fig. 6. Same as Fig. 4, but for the Lorenz63 model.

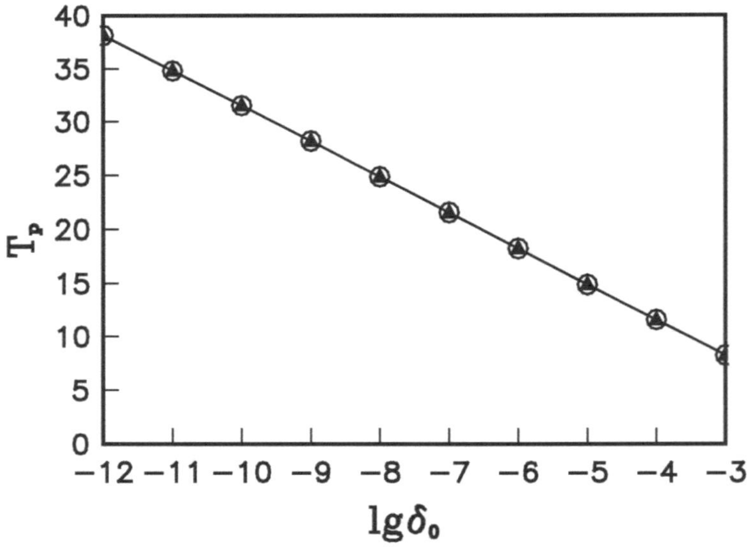

Fig. 7. Predictability limits obtained from Eq. (17) (open circles) and those obtained using the NLLE approach (closed triangles) in the logistic map as a function of δ_0 of various magnitudes.

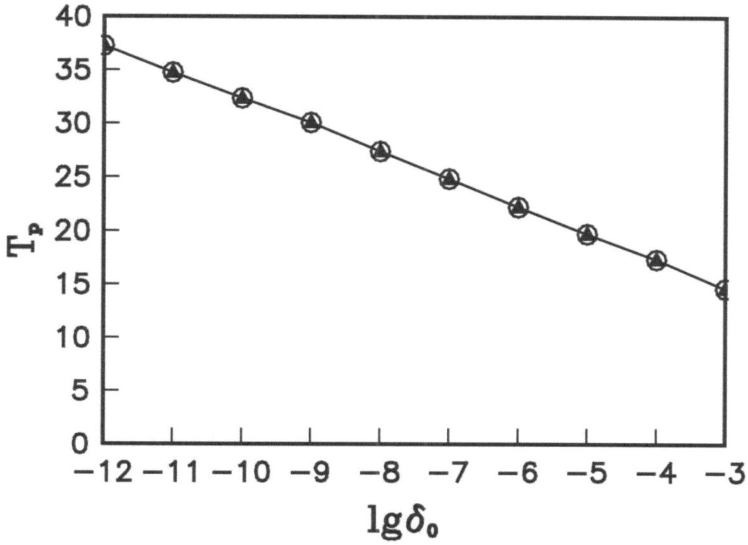

Fig. 8. Same as Fig. 7, but for the Lorenz63 model.

8. References

[1] E. N. Lorenz, J. Atmos. Sci. 20 (1963) 130.
[2] E. N. Lorenz, J. Atmos. Sci. 26 (1969) 636.
[3] J. P. Eckmann, D. Ruelle, Rev. Mod. Phys. 57 (1985) 617.
[4] Z. Toth, Mon. Wea. Rev. 119 (1991) 65.
[5] W. Y. Chen, Mon. Wea. Rev. 117 (1989) 1227.
[6] V. Krishnamurthy, J. Atmos. Sci. 50 (1993) 2215.
[7] R. M. May, Nature 261 (1976) 459.
[8] E. N., Lorenz, in Proceedings of a Seminar Held at ECMWF on Predictability (I), European Centre for Medium-Range Weather Forecasts, Reading, UK, 1996, p. 1.
[9] J. M. Nese, Physica D 35 (1989) 237.
[10] E. Kazantsev, Appl. Math. Comp. 104 (1999) 217.
[11] C. Ziemann, L. A. Smith, J. Kurths, Phys. Lett. A 4 (2000) 237.
[12] S. Yoden, M. Nomura, J . Atmos. Sci . 50 (1993) 1531.
[13] J. F. Lacarra, O. Talagrand, Tellus 40A (1988) 81.
[14] M. Mu, W. S. Duan, B. Wang, Nonlinear Process. Geophys. 10 (2003) 493.
[15] J. P. Li, R. Q. Ding, B. H. Chen, in Review and prospect on the predictability study of the atmosphere, *Review and Prospects of the Developments of Atmosphere Sciences in Early 21st Century*, China Meteorology Press, 96.
[16] R. Q. Ding, J. P. Li, *Phys. Lett. A* 364 (2007) 396.
[17] R. Q. Ding, J. P. Li, K. J. Ha, *Chin. Phys. Lett.* 25 (2008) 1919.
[18] C. Rose, M. D. Smith, Mathematical Statistics with Mathematica, Springer-Verlag, New York, 2002.

[19] J. Guckenheimer, P. J. Holmes, Nonlinear Oscillations, Dynamical Systems, and Bifurcations of Vector Fields, Springer-Verlag, New York, 1983.
[20] A. Wolf, J. B. Swift, H. L. Swinney, J. A. Vastano, Physica D 16 (1985) 285.

4

Microscopic Theory of Transport Phenomenon in Hamiltonian Chaotic Systems

Shiwei Yan
College of Nuclear Science and Technology, Beijing Normal University
China

1. Introduction

It has been one of the important fields of contemporary science to explore the microscopic origin of the damping phenomenon of collective motion in the finite many-body system. The evolution of the early universe, that of the chemical reaction, many active processes in biological system, the fission and fusion processes in nuclear system, the quantum correspondent of the classically chaotic system and the measurement theory are typical examples among others(1–14). Although these processes have been successfully described by the phenomenological transport equation, there still remain some basic problems, such as, how to derive the *macro*-level transport equation describing the macroscopic irreversible motion from the *micro*-level reversible dynamics from the fundamental level dynamics; how the statistical state is realized in the irrelevant subsystem and why the irreversible macro-level process is generated as a result of the reversible micro-level dynamics.
The study on this subject has been one of the most fundamental and challenging fields in the various fields of contemporary science. Intensive studies have been carried out (15–29), however, an acceptance microscopic understanding is still far from realization and there still remain a lot of studies(30–33).

1.1 From reversible to irreversible: Foundation of statistical physics

Before discussing the microscopic origin of irreversibility phenomenon, one should be aware of an informal indication of the problem in explaining the meaning of the foundation of statistical physics, which can be seen in the presence of two types of processes: (1) time-irreversible macroscopic (*relevant or collective*) process which obey the thermodynamics, or kinetic, laws; and (2) time-reversible microscopic (*irrelevant or intrinsic*) process which obey, say, the Newton and Maxwell equations of motion. The great difference between both descriptions of the processes in nature, is not clearly understood and an acceptance explanation on the origin of irreversibility is still lack(34). The formal definition of the problem is to derive a macroscopic equation which describes an irreversible evolution which begins with a reversible Hamiltonian equation.
Before the recognition of the importance of chaos, the attempts to unite, in a formal way, the statistical and dynamical description of a system, usually starts with dividing the total system into the relevant and irrelevant degrees of freedom by hand and assuming the irrelevant system placed in a state of micro-canonical equilibrium (thermodynamical) state

(Ref. Boltzmann's pioneer proposal(35) and the textbooks as (36)). This is the Boltzmann principle

$$S = k \ln \mathcal{A}(E). \tag{1}$$

where $\mathcal{A}(E)$ is the area of the phase space explored by the system in a micro-canonical state, k the Boltzmann constant and S the entropy. However, such the derivations are essentially based on the assumption of an infinitely large number of degrees of freedom and the existence of two different time scales $\tau_r \gg \tau_i$, where τ_r is the time scale of relevant degrees of freedom and τ_i is that of irrelevant ones. Under such assumption, the irreversibility or the equilibrium condition is supplemented for the dynamical equations, and the resultant distribution has the form

$$P(\epsilon) \sim e^{-\beta\epsilon} \quad \beta \equiv 1/kT \tag{2}$$

where ϵ is the energy of the irrelevant degrees of freedom and T the temperature of the system. Distribution (2) is called the equilibrium Boltzmann distribution which corresponds to the thermodynamical state and thus only can be adopted to describe the *equilibrium process rather than nonequilibrium states*. It also should be mentioned that Poincaré recurrence theorem says that for a finite and area-preserving motion, any trajectory should return to an arbitrarily taken domain Σ in a finite time and should do so repeatedly for an infinite number of time. However, Boltzmann had rightly argue that for a large number of particles, this recurrence time would be astronomically long. This assumption only can be justified for a system with infinite number of degrees of freedom. When one want to study the origin of irreversibility of a finite system where dynamical chaos occurs, this assumption of infinite occurrence time will cause some serious problems.

Many attempts have been successfully achieved in different ways and with some supplementary conditions on microscopic Hamiltonian equations, such as the random phase approximation (mixing)(37; 38), Gaussian orthogonal ensemble (GOE), or other equivalent conditions played the role of statistical element(15–20; 25–29; 39). The ergodic and irreversible property is assumed for the irrelevant system with infinite number of degree of freedom. Temperature, so as thermodynamics, is introduced by hand through the supplementary conditions. From dynamical point of view, such the derivation is unsatisfactory since the strong condition like randomness of some variables or statistical ansatz should be introduced by hand. Following the recognition of the importance of chaos, it has been supposed that *there is an intimate relation between the realization of irreversibility and the order-to-chaos transition within the microscopic Hamilton dynamics*. When one derives the macroscopic irreversibility from the fundamental Hamiltonian equations, the stochastic processes can be obtained for some specific parameters and initial conditions. However even in this case, such the supplementary assumptions still remain to be justified. The main problems are: whether or not one may substantiate statistical state in the way dynamical chaos is structured in real Hamiltonian system, whether or not there are some difficulties of using the properties of dynamical chaos as a source of randomness, whether one can derive a random process from the dynamical chaotic motion and whether or in what conditions, the derived stochastic process may correspond to the above-mentioned random assumptions. It is well known that Poincaré recurrence time is finite for finite Hamiltonian systems and its phase space has fractal (or multi-fractal) structure, where the ergodicity of motion is not generally satisfied. Therefore, specially in the finite system, it is not a trivial discussion whether or not the irrelevant subsystem can be effectively replaced by a statistical object as a heat bath, even when it shows chaotic behavior and its Lyapunov exponent has a positive value everywhere in the phase space. It is also an interesting question to explore the relation between the dynamical definition of the statistical state, if it exists, and the static definition of it.

1.2 From infinite to finite system

It should say that there is substantial difficulty, or it is almost impossible in some extent, for us to derive the macroscopic irreversibility from the fundamental Hamiltonian equations for an infinite system because which has an infinite (or extremely large) number of degrees of freedom. This fact is generally accepted as the reason for the introduction of the statistical assumptions. On another hand, when one derive macroscopic equations by averaging over microscopic random variables resulted in a reduced description of an *in□nite* system, the detailed structure of micro phase space will lose its importance. In this sense, for an *in□nite* system, such the statistical approach seems to be reasonable and will not cause any serious problems.

However, in such systems as atoms, nuclei and biomolecules whose environment is not infinite, where assumption of a large number of degrees of freedom is not justified, and in a case when one intends to derive the macroscopic irreversibility and phenomenological transport equation from the fundamental level dynamics, it is not obvious whether or not one may introduce the statistical assumptions for the irrelevant degrees of freedom. The decisive problem in the finite system is how to justify an introduction of some statistical state or some statistical concept like the temperature or the heat bath, which is one of the basic ingredient to derive an irreversible process to the Hamilton system.

With regards to the damping phenomena observed in the giant resonance on top of the highly excited states in the nuclear system, its microscopic description has been mainly based on the temperature dependent mean-field theory(40–45). However, an introduction of the temperature in the finite-isolated nuclei is by no means obvious, when one explicitly introduce many single-particle excitation modes on top of the temperature-dependent shell model. Could one introduce a chaotic (complex) excitation mode on top of the chaotic (heat bath characterized by the temperature) system? When one considers the $2p$-$2h$ (two-particle two-hole) state as a door way state to be coupled with the $1p$-$1h$ collective excitation mode, a naive classical model Hamilton would be something like a β Fermi-Pasta-Ulam (FPU) system(46–49) where no heat bath is assumed, rather than the temperature-dependent shell model where the Matsubara Green function is used.

The recent development in the classical theory of nonlinear Hamiltonian system (22; 34; 50–53) has shown that there appears an exceedingly rich structure in the phase space, which is usually considered to prevent a fully developed chaos. The existence of fractal structure is a remarkable property of Hamilton chaos and a typical feature of the phase space in real system. Due to the fractal structure of the phase space, the motion of Hamilton system of general type is not ergodic, specially for a finite Hamiltonian system. In this case, the questions then arise: what kind random process corresponds to the dynamical chaotic motion? whether or not the system dynamically reaches some statistical object? The microscopic derivation of the non-equilibrium statistical physics in relation with the exceedingly rich structure of the phase space as well as with the order-to-chaos transition might be explored within the microscopic Hamilton dynamics. This subject will be further discussed in Sec. 4.1.2.

Another important issue related to this study is how to divide the total system into the relevant and irrelevant degrees of freedom. However, in many approaches(24; 26; 27), one usually starts with dividing the total system into the relevant and irrelevant degrees of freedom

by hand. In the system where a total number of degrees of freedom can be approximately treated as an infinite, there does not arise any serious problem how to introduce the relevant degrees of freedom. In the finite system as nuclei where a number of the degrees of freedom is not large enough, and a time scale of the relevant motion and that of the irrelevant one is typically less than one order of magnitude difference, there arises an important problem how to distinguish the relevant ones from the rest in a way consistent with the underlying microscopic dynamics for aiming to properly characterize the collective motion. Here it worth to mention another important issue is related with an applicability of the *linear response theory* (LRT)(54–59), because a validity of the linear approximation for the macro-level dynamics does not necessarily justify that for the micro-level dynamics. Furthermore, there arises a basic question whether or not one may divide the total system into the relevant and irrelevant subsystems by leaving the *linear* coupling between them(30; 50; 60–62). At the best of our knowledge, it seems that there is no compelling physical reason to choose the linear coupling interaction between the relevant and irrelevant subsystems.
Summarily speaking, in exploring the microscopic dynamics in □*nite Hamiltonian system*, says, answering the basic questions as listed in the beginning of this section, there are two main subjects. *One is how to divide the total system into the relevant and irrelevant ones and another is how to derive the macroscopic statistical properties from microscopic dynamics.*

1.3 The nonlinear theory of the classical Hamiltonian system

From above discussion, one can conclude that the theory of chaotic dynamics should play a decisive role in understanding the origin of microscopic irreversibility within the microscopic Hamilton dynamics. It is imperative to remember the recent development in the classical theory of nonlinear Hamilton system(34; 51–53).
The *chaos* phenomenon is often used to describe the motions of the system's trajectories which are sensitive to the slightest changes of the initial condition. The motion known as chaotic occupies a certain area (called stochastic sea) in the phase space. In idea chaos, the stochastic sea is occupied in uniform manner. This is, however, not the case in real systems. The phase space has exceedingly rich structure where the chaotic and regular motions co-exist and there are many *islands* which a chaotic trajectory can not penetrate (as stated in *KAM Theorem*). Many important properties of chaotic dynamics, such as the order-to-chaos transition dynamics, are determined by the properties of the motion near the boundary of islands.
Thanks to H. Poincaré and his successors, we know how important it is to understand why there appears an exceedingly rich structure in the phase space and how the order-to-chaos transition occurs, rather than to understand individual trajectory under a specific initial condition. A set of closed orbits having the same property (characterized by a set of local constants of motion) forms a torus structure around a certain stable fixed point in the phase space, and is separated from the other types of closed orbits (characterized by another set of local constants of motion) through separatrices. Depending on the strength of the nonlinear interaction or on the energy of the system, there appear many kinds of new periodic orbits characterized by respective *local* constants of motion along the known periodic orbits, which are called *bifurcation* phenomena.
When different separatrices start to overlap in a small region of the phase space, there appears a local chaotic sea. In this overlap region where two kinds of periodic orbits characterized by different sets of constants of motion start to coexist, it might become difficult to realize a well-developed closed orbit characterized by a single set of local constants of motion any

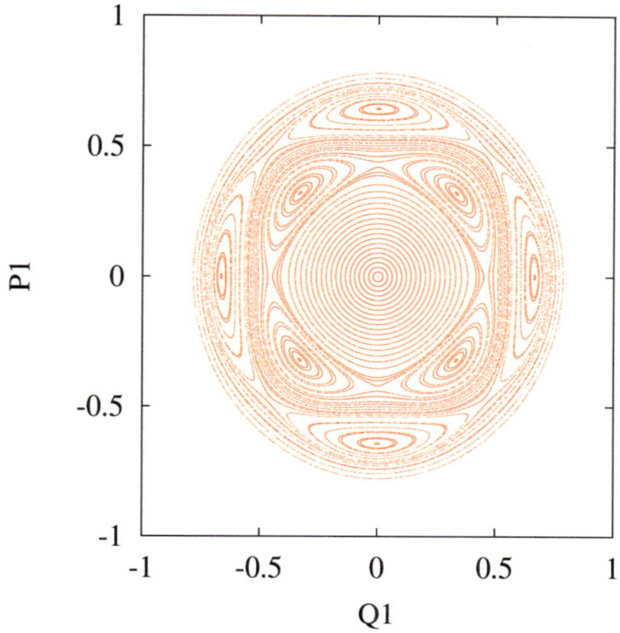

Fig. 1. Poincaré section map of SU(3) Hamiltonian on (q_1, p_1) plane for a case with $E = 40$ and $V_i = -0.01$

more. This overlap criterion on an appearance of the chaotic sea has been considered to be a microscopic origin of the order-to-chaos transition dynamics.

A classical example of the order-to-chaos transition for the SU(3) classical Hamiltonian system (66) is shown in Figs. 1 to 4 for the cases with V_i =-0.01, -0.03, -0.045 and -0.07, respectively. In the cases with V_i =-0.01 and -0.03, i.e., the smaller interaction strength or weaker nonlinearity, the whole phase space is covered by the regular motions, forming many islands structure. When the nonlinearity of interaction goes to stronger, there appears chaotic sea in a region where the crossing point of the separatrics (Fig. 3), i.e., the unstable fixed point is expected in Fig. 2. Moreover, there appear many secondary islands around the primary island structure, which has already existed in Fig. 2. A chaotic trajectory can not penetrate the island and a regular trajectory from an island is not be able to escape from it. Around some secondary island, one may find some tertiary island structure, and so forth, as shown in Fig. 5. This repeated complex structure is called *fractal* phenomena. The fractal structure of phase space is a remarkable property of Hamiltonian chaos and a typical feature of the phase space in real systems. For a classical Hamiltonian system, the distribution of the Poincaré recurrence is time- and space-fractal, which plays a crucial role in an understanding of the general properties of chaotic dynamics and the foundation of statistical physics.

The general theory of the nonlinear dynamics has been developed for aiming to understand these complex structure by studying why there appear many stable and unstable fixed points, and how to get an information on their constants of motion. And also the theory of nonlinear chaotic dynamics plays an important role in understanding the foundation of statistical physics.

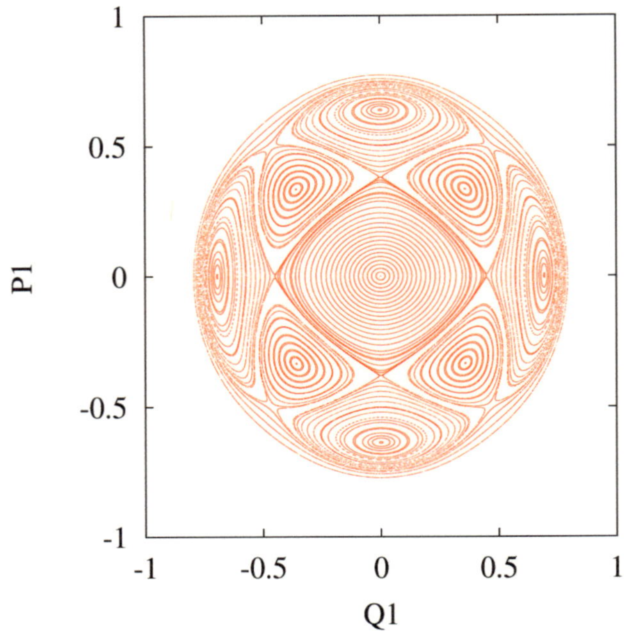

Fig. 2. Poincaré section map of SU(3) Hamiltonian on (q_1, p_1) plane for a case with $E = 40$ and $V_i = -0.03$

1.4 The self-consistent collective coordinate (SCC) method & the optimum coordinate system

As discussed in Sect. 1.2, for finite system, an important problem is to explore how to divide the total system into the relevant and irrelevant degrees of freedom in a way consistent with the underlying microscopic dynamics for aiming to properly characterize the collective motion. In a case of the Hamiltonian system, a division may be performed by applying the self-consistent collective coordinate (SCC) method(60). In the following, for the sake of self-containedness, the SCC method is briefly reformulated within the classical Hamiltonian system. The detailed description can be found in Ref. (60) and a review article (50).

The SCC method was proposed within the usual symplectic manifold, which intends to define the *maximally-decoupled coordinate system* where the minimum number of coordinates is required in describing the trajectory under discussion. In such a finite system as the nucleus, it is not obvious how to introduce the relevant (collective or distinguished) coordinates which are used in describing macroscopic properties of the system. This problem is also very important to explore why and how the statistical aspect could appear in the finite nuclear system, and whether or not the irrelevant system could be expressed by some statistical object, because there is no obvious reason to divide the nuclear system into two, unlike a case with the Brownian particle plus molecular system.

The basic idea of the SCC method rests on the following point: The nonlinear canonical transformation between the original coordinate system and a new coordinate one is defined in such a way that the anharmonic effects causing the microscopic structure change of the relevant coordinates are incorporated into the latter coordinate system as much as possible, and the coupling between the relevant and irrelevant subsystems is optimally minimized.

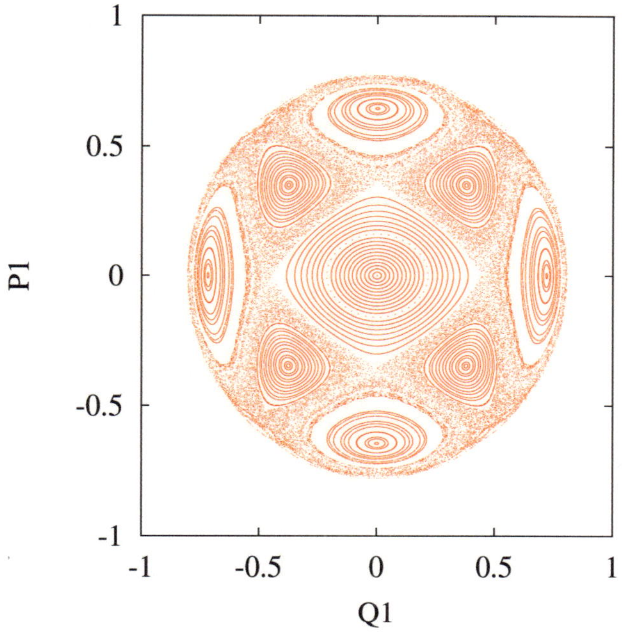

Fig. 3. Poincaré section map of SU(3) Hamiltonian on (q_1, p_1) plane for a case with $E = 40$ and $V_i = -0.045$

Trajectories in a 2K dimensional symplectic manifold expressed by

$$M^{2K}: \quad \left\{C_j^*, C_j; \quad j = 1, \cdots, K\right\} \tag{3}$$

are organized by the canonical equations of motion given as

$$i\dot{C}_j = \frac{\partial H}{\partial C_j^*}, \quad i\dot{C}_j^* = -\frac{\partial H}{\partial C_j}, \quad j = 1, \cdots, K, \tag{4}$$

where H denotes the Hamiltonian of the system. Let us consider one of the trajectories which are obtained by solving Eq. (4) under a set of specific initial conditions. In describing a given trajectory, it does not matter what coordinate system one may use provided one employs the whole degrees of freedom without any truncation. An arbitrary representation used in describing the canonical equations of motion in Eq. (4) will be called the initial representation (IR). Out of many coordinate systems which are equivalent with each other and are related through the canonical transformations with one another, however, one may select a *maximally-decoupled coordinate system* where the minimum number of coordinates is required in describing a given trajectory. What one has to do is to extract a small dimensional submanifold denoted as $M^{2L}(L < K)$ on which the given trajectory is confined. The representation characterizing the maximally-decoupled coordinate system will be called the dynamical representation (DR). Let us introduce a set of canonical variables in the DR. A set of coordinates $\{\eta_a^*, \eta_a; a = 1, \cdots, L\}$ are called the *relevant* degrees of freedom and are used in describing the given trajectory, whereas $\{\xi_\alpha^*, \xi_\alpha; \alpha = L+1, \cdots, K\}$ are called the *irrelevant*

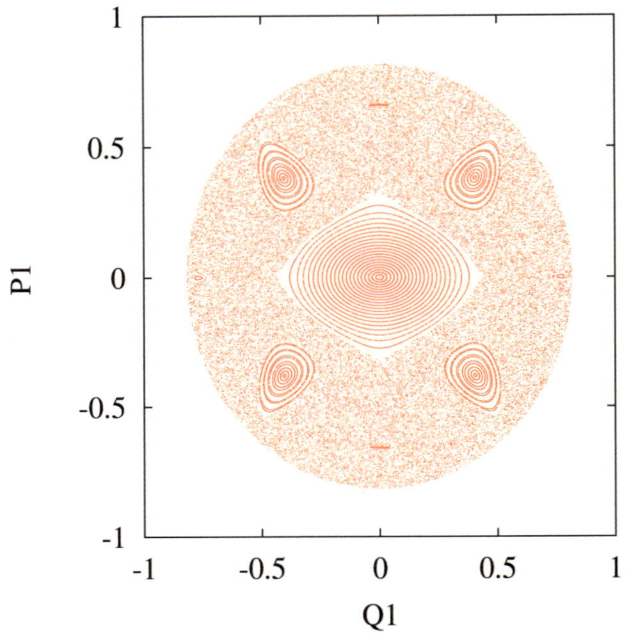

Fig. 4. Poincaré section map of SU(3) Hamiltonian on (q_1, p_1) plane for a case with $E = 40$ and $V_i = -0.07$

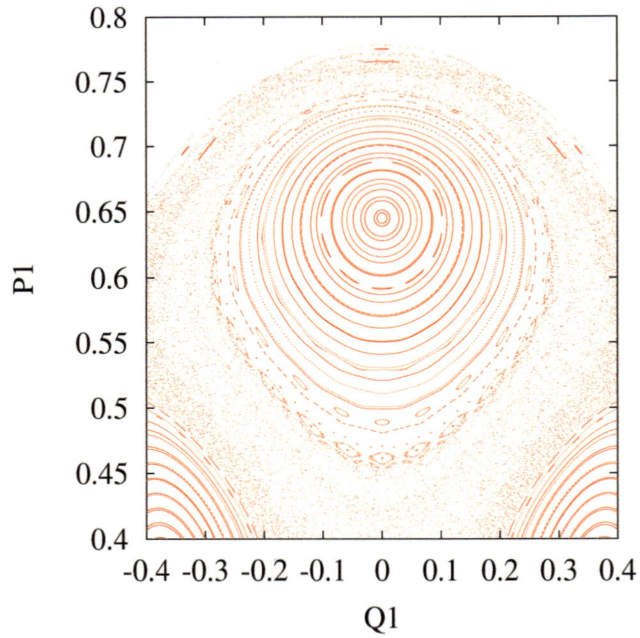

Fig. 5. Magnification of the top island of Fig. 3.

degrees of freedom, and this new coordinate system provides us with another chart expressed as I^{2K}.

In order to find the DR, one has to know the canonical transformation between IR and DR,

$$M^{2K}: \quad \left\{C_j^*, C_j\right\} \Leftrightarrow I^{2K}: \quad \{\eta_a^*, \eta_a; \xi_\alpha^*, \xi_\alpha\}. \tag{5}$$

Ensuring Eq. (5) to be a canonical transformation, there should hold the following *canonical variable condition* given by

$$\sum_j \left\{ C_j \frac{\partial C_j^*}{\partial \eta_a^*} - C_j^* \frac{\partial C_j}{\partial \eta_a^*} \right\} = \eta_a + i \frac{\partial S}{\partial \eta_a^*}, \tag{6a}$$

$$\sum_j \left\{ C_j \frac{\partial C_j^*}{\partial \xi_\alpha^*} - C_j^* \frac{\partial C_j}{\partial \xi_\alpha^*} \right\} = \xi_\alpha + i \frac{\partial S}{\partial \xi_\alpha^*}, \tag{6b}$$

where S is a generating function of the canonical transformation, and is an arbitrary real function of η_a, η_a^*, ξ_α and ξ_α^* satisfying $S^* = S$. From Eq. (6), one may obtain the following relations

$$\sum_j \left\{ \frac{\partial C_j}{\partial \eta_b} \frac{\partial C_j^*}{\partial \eta_a^*} - \frac{\partial C_j}{\partial \eta_a^*} \frac{\partial C_j^*}{\partial \eta_b} \right\} = \delta_{a,b}, \tag{7a}$$

$$\sum_j \left\{ \frac{\partial C_j}{\partial \xi_\beta} \frac{\partial C_j^*}{\partial \xi_\alpha^*} - \frac{\partial C_j}{\partial \xi_\alpha^*} \frac{\partial C_j^*}{\partial \xi_\beta} \right\} = \delta_{\alpha,\beta}, \tag{7b}$$

$$\sum_j \left\{ \frac{\partial C_j}{\partial \xi_\alpha} \frac{\partial C_j^*}{\partial \eta_a^*} - \frac{\partial C_j}{\partial \eta_a^*} \frac{\partial C_j^*}{\partial \xi_\alpha} \right\} = 0, \quad \text{etc.} \tag{7c}$$

Since the transformation in Eq. (5) is canonical, the new variables in the DR also satisfy the canonical equations of motion given as

$$i\dot{\eta}_a = \frac{\partial H}{\partial \eta_a^*}, \quad i\dot{\eta}_a^* = -\frac{\partial H}{\partial \eta_a}, \quad i\dot{\xi}_\alpha = \frac{\partial H}{\partial \xi_\alpha^*}, \quad i\dot{\xi}_\alpha^* = -\frac{\partial H}{\partial \xi_\alpha}. \tag{8}$$

Since the trajectory under consideration is supposed to be described by the relevant degrees of freedom alone, and since the irrelevant degrees of freedom are assumed to describe a small-amplitude motion around it, one may introduce a Taylor expansion of C_j^* and C_j with respect to ξ_α^* and ξ_α on the surface of the submanifold M^{2L} as

$$C_j = \left[C_j\right] + \sum_\alpha \left\{ \xi_\alpha \left[\frac{\partial C_j}{\partial \xi_\alpha}\right] + \xi_\alpha^* \left[\frac{\partial C_j}{\partial \xi_\alpha^*}\right] \right\} + \cdots, \tag{9}$$

where the symbol $[g]$ for an arbitrary function $g(\eta_a^*, \eta_a; \xi_\alpha^*, \xi_\alpha)$ denotes a function on the surface M^{2L}, and is a function of the relevant variables alone,

$$[g] \equiv g(\eta_a^*, \eta_a; \xi_\alpha^* = 0, \xi_\alpha = 0). \tag{10}$$

Here, it should be noticed that a set of functions $[C_j]$ and $[C_j^*]$ provides us with a knowledge on how the submanifold M^{2L} is embedded in M^{2K}. In other words, a diffeomorphic mapping

$$I^{2L} \rightarrow M^{2L} \quad \text{embedded in} \quad M^{2K}: \quad \{\eta_a^*, \eta_a\} \rightarrow \left\{[C_j], [C_j^*]\right\}. \tag{11}$$

is determined by the set of $[C_j]$ and $[C_j^*]$ which are functions of the relevant variables η_a^* and η_a alone.

In the same way, one may have an expansion form as

$$\frac{\partial H}{\partial C_j^*} = \left[\frac{\partial H}{\partial C_j^*}\right] + \sum_\alpha \left\{ \xi_\alpha \left[\frac{\partial^2 H}{\partial \xi_\alpha \partial C_j^*}\right] + \xi_\alpha^* \left[\frac{\partial^2 H}{\partial \xi_\alpha^* \partial C_j^*}\right] \right\} + \cdots, \quad \text{and} \quad c.c., \tag{12}$$

which appears on the r.h.s. in Eq. (4).

Here, one has to notice that there hold the following relations,

$$\frac{\partial H}{\partial \eta_a} = \sum_j \left\{ \frac{\partial C_j}{\partial \eta_a}\frac{\partial H}{\partial C_j} + \frac{\partial C_j^*}{\partial \eta_a}\frac{\partial H}{\partial C_j^*} \right\}, \tag{13a}$$

$$\frac{\partial H}{\partial \xi_\alpha} = \sum_j \left\{ \frac{\partial C_j}{\partial \xi_\alpha}\frac{\partial H}{\partial C_j} + \frac{\partial C_j^*}{\partial \xi_\alpha}\frac{\partial H}{\partial C_j^*} \right\}. \tag{13b}$$

Using Eqs. (9) and (12), one may apply the Taylor expansion to the quantities appearing on the lhs in Eq. (13). Its lowest order equation is given as

$$\left[\frac{\partial H}{\partial \eta_a}\right] = \sum_j \left\{ \left[\frac{\partial C_j}{\partial \eta_a}\right]\left[\frac{\partial H}{\partial C_j}\right] + \left[\frac{\partial C_j^*}{\partial \eta_a}\right]\left[\frac{\partial H}{\partial C_j^*}\right] \right\}, \tag{14a}$$

$$\left[\frac{\partial H}{\partial \xi_\alpha}\right] = \sum_j \left\{ \left[\frac{\partial C_j}{\partial \xi_\alpha}\right]\left[\frac{\partial H}{\partial C_j}\right] + \left[\frac{\partial C_j^*}{\partial \xi_\alpha}\right]\left[\frac{\partial H}{\partial C_j^*}\right] \right\}. \tag{14b}$$

The basic idea of the SCC method formulated within the TDHF theory rests on the *invariance principle of the Schrödinger equation*(63). In the present case of the classical system, it is expressed as the *invariance principle of the canonical equations of motion*, which is given by

$$i\frac{d}{dt}\left[C_j\right] = \left[\frac{\partial H}{\partial C_j^*}\right], \quad i\frac{d}{dt}\left[C_j^*\right] = -\left[\frac{\partial H}{\partial C_j}\right], \quad j = 1, \cdots, K. \tag{15}$$

Since the time-dependence of $[C_j]$ and $[C_j^*]$ is supposed to be described by that of η_a and η_a^*, Eq. (15) is expressed as

$$\left[\frac{\partial H}{\partial C_j^*}\right] = i\sum_a \left\{ \dot{\eta}_a \frac{\partial \left[C_j\right]}{\partial \eta_a} + \dot{\eta}_a^* \frac{\partial \left[C_j\right]}{\partial \eta_a^*} \right\}, \quad \text{and} \quad c.c., \quad j = 1, \cdots, K. \tag{16}$$

Substituting Eq. (16) into the r.h.s. of Eq. (14), one gets

$$\left[\frac{\partial H}{\partial \eta_a^*}\right] = i\sum_b \dot{\eta}_b \sum_j \left\{ \frac{\partial \left[C_j\right]}{\partial \eta_b}\frac{\partial \left[C_j^*\right]}{\partial \eta_a^*} - \frac{\partial \left[C_j\right]}{\partial \eta_a^*}\frac{\partial \left[C_j^*\right]}{\partial \eta_b} \right\}$$
$$+ i\sum_b \dot{\eta}_b^* \sum_j \left\{ \frac{\partial \left[C_j\right]}{\partial \eta_b^*}\frac{\partial \left[C_j^*\right]}{\partial \eta_a^*} - \frac{\partial \left[C_j\right]}{\partial \eta_a^*}\frac{\partial \left[C_j^*\right]}{\partial \eta_b^*} \right\}, \quad \text{and} \quad c.c.. \tag{17}$$

When there holds the lowest order relation derived from Eq. (6), i.e.,

$$\text{Condition I} \quad \sum_j \left\{ \left[C_j\right]\frac{\partial \left[C_j^*\right]}{\partial \eta_a^*} - \left[C_j^*\right]\frac{\partial \left[C_j\right]}{\partial \eta_a^*} \right\} = \eta_a, \tag{18}$$

called the *Canonical Variable Condition*, Eq. (17) reduces into

$$i\dot{\eta}_a = \left[\frac{\partial H}{\partial \eta_a^*}\right], \quad i\dot{\eta}_a^* = -\left[\frac{\partial H}{\partial \eta_a}\right], \tag{19}$$

which just corresponds to the lowest order equation of Eq. (8), and is called the *Equation of Collective Motion*.

$$\text{Condition II} \quad 0 = \left[\frac{\partial H}{\partial C_j^*}\right] - \sum_a \left\{ \frac{\partial [H]}{\partial \eta_a^*}\frac{\partial \left[C_j\right]}{\partial \eta_a} - \frac{\partial [H]}{\partial \eta_a}\frac{\partial \left[C_j\right]}{\partial \eta_a^*} \right\}, \quad \text{and} \quad c.c., \tag{20}$$

which is called the *Maximally-Decoupling Condition*.
Conditions I and II constitute a set of basic equations of the SCC method in the classical Hamilton system. From the *Maximally-Decoupling Condition*, one can get the following relation,

$$\left[\frac{\partial H}{\partial \xi_\alpha}\right] = 0. \tag{21}$$

Equation (21) simply states that the new coordinate system $\{\eta_a, \eta_a^*, \xi_\alpha, \xi_\alpha^*\}$ determined by the SCC method has no first order couplings between the relevant and irrelevant degrees of freedom. With the aid of the SCC method, one may introduce the *maximally-decoupled coordinate system*, where the linear coupling between the relevant and irrelevant degrees of freedom is eliminated. This result is very important to treat the collective dissipative motion coupled with the irrelevant system. In a case of the infinite system, one may usually apply the linear response theory where the relevant system is assumed to be coupled with the irrelevant one through the *linear* coupling, and the latter is usually expressed by a thermal reservoir. As we have discussed in this section, however, one may introduce a concept of "relevant" degrees of freedom in the finite system after requiring an elimination of the linear coupling with leaving only the nonlinear couplings.

1.5 The scope of the present work

In order to explore the microscopic dynamics responsible for the macroscopic transport phenomena, a theory of coupled-master equation has been formulated as a general framework for deriving the transport equation, and for clarifying its underlying assumptions(23). In order to *self-consistently* and *optimally* divide the finite system into a pair of weakly coupled systems, the theory employs the SCC method(60) as mentioned in Sec. 1.4. The self-consistent and optimal separation in the degrees of freedom enables us to study the dissipation mechanisms of large-amplitude relevant motion and nonlinear dynamics between the relevant and irrelevant modes of motion. An important point of using the SCC method(60) for dynamically dividing the total system into two subsystems is a form of the resultant coupling between them, where a *linear* coupling is eliminated by the maximal decoupling condition imposed by the method.

In this chapter, with the microscopic Hamiltonian, we will discuss how to derive the transport equation from the general theory of coupled-master equation and how to realize the dissipation phenomena in the finite system on the basis of the microscopic dynamics, what kinds of necessary conditions there are in realizing the dissipative process, what kinds of dynamical relations there are between the micro-level and phenomenological-level descriptions, without introducing the any statistical anastz.

It will be clarified(30) that the macroscopic transport equation is obtained from the fully microscopic master equation under the following microscopic conditions: (I) The effects coming from the irrelevant subsystem on the relevant one are taken into account and mainly expressed by an average effect over the irrelevant distribution function. Namely, the fluctuation effects are considered to be sufficiently small and are able to be treated as a perturbation around the path generated by the average Hamiltonian. (II) The irrelevant distribution function has already reached its time-independent stationary state before the main microscopic dynamics responsible for the damping of the relevant motion dominates. As discussed in Sec. 3.1.2, this situation was turned out to be well realized even in the two degrees of freedom system. (III) The time scale of the motion for the irrelevant subsystem is much shorter than that for the relevant one.

The numerical simulations are carried out for a microscopic system composed of the relevant one-degree of freedom system coupled to the irrelevant two-degree of freedom system (described by a classical SU(3) Hamiltonian) through a weak coupling interaction. The novelties of our approach are: (I) the total system is dynamically and optimally divided into the relevant and irrelevant degrees of freedom in a way consistent with the underlying microscopic dynamics for aiming to properly characterize the collective motion; (II) the macroscopic irreversibility is dynamically realized for a finite system rather than introducing any statistical anastz as for infinite system with extremely large number of degrees of freedom. The transport phenomenon will been established numerically(30). It will be also clarified that for the case with a small number degrees of freedom (say, two), the microscopic dephasing mechanism, which is caused by the chaoticity of irrelevant system, is responsible for the energy transfer from the collective system to the environment. Although our numerical simulation by employing the Langevin equation was able to reproduce the macro-level transport phenomenon, it was also clarified that there are substantial differences in the micro-level mechanism between the fully microscopic description and the Langevin description, and in order to reproduce the same results the parameters used in the Langevin equation do not satisfy the fluctuation-dissipation theorem.

Therefore various questions related to the transport phenomenon realized in the finite system on how to understand the differences between the above-mentioned two descriptions, what kinds of other microscopic mechanisms are there besides the *dephasing*, and when the fluctuation-dissipation theorem comes true etc. are still remained. In the conventional approaches like the Fokker-Planck or Langevin type equations, the irrelevant subsystem is always assumed to have a large (even *infinite*) number of degrees of freedom and is placed in a canonically equilibrated state. It is then quite natural to ask whether these problems are caused by a limited number (only two) of degrees of freedom in the irrelevant subsystem considered in our previous work. In order to fill the gap between two and infinite degrees of freedom for the irrelevant subsystem, it is extremely important to study how the microscopic dynamics depends on the number of the degrees of freedom in the irrelevant subsystem.

In this chapter, we will further use a β-Fermi-Pasta-Ulam (β-FPU) system representing the irrelevant system, which allows us to change the number of degrees of freedom very conveniently and meanwhile retain the chaoticity of the dynamics of β-FPU system with the same specific dynamical condition. It will be shown that although the dephasing mechanism is the main mechanism for a case with a small number of degrees of freedom (say, two), the diffusion mechanism will start to play a role as the number of degrees of freedom becomes large (say, eight or more), and, in general, the energy transport process occurs by passing through three distinct stages, such as the dephasing, the statistical relaxation, and the equilibrium regimes. By examining a time evolution of a non-extensive entropy(84), an existence of three regimes will be clearly exhibited.

Exploiting an analytical relation, it will be shown that the energy transport process is described by the *generalized* Fokker-Planck and Langevin type equation, and a phenomenological fluctuation-dissipation relation is satisfied in a case with relatively large degrees of freedom system. It will be clarified that the irrelevant subsystem with finite number of degrees of freedom can be treated as a heat bath with a finite correlation time, and the statistical relaxation turns out to be an anomalous diffusion, and both the microscopic approach and the conventional phenomenological approach may reach the same level description for the transport phenomena only when the number of irrelevant degrees of freedom becomes very large.

It should be mentioned that a necessity of using a non-extensive entropy for characterizing the damping phenomenon in the finite system is very interesting in connecting the microscopic dynamics and the statistical mechanics, because the non-extensive entropy(83; 84) might characterize the non-statistical evolution process more properly than the physical Boltzmann-Gibbs entropy. This might suggest us that the damping mechanism in the finite system is a non-statistical process, where the usual fluctuation-dissipation theorem is not applicable.

We will be able to reach all these goals only within a microscopic classical dynamics of a finite system. The outline of this chapter is as follows. In Sec. 1, we have briefly introduced some background knowledge and motivations of this study. This section is written in a very compact way because I want to pay my most attention on introducing our new progresses what the readers really want to know. The detailed information can be easily found in references. In Sec. 2, we briefly recapitulate the theory of coupled-master equation(23) for the sake of self-containedness. Starting from the most general coupled-master equation, we try to derive the Fokker-Planck and Langevin type equation, by clarifying necessary underlying conditions. Aiming to realize such a physical situation where these conditions are satisfied, in Sec. 3.1, various numerical simulations will be performed for a system where a relevant (collective) harmonic oscillator is coupled with the irrelevant (intrinsic) SU(3) model. After numerically realizing a macro-level transport phenomena, we will try to reproduce it by using a phenomenological Langevin equation, whose potential is derived microscopically. In Sec. 3.2, special emphasis will be put on the effects depending on the number of irrelevant degrees of freedom with a microscopic Hamiltonian where irrelevant system is described by a β-Fermi-Pasta-Ulam (β-FPU) system. We will discuss the behavior of the energy transfer process, energy equipartition problem and their dependence on the number of degrees of freedom. The time evolution of entropy by using the nonextensive thermo-dynamics and microscopic dynamics of non-equilibrium transport process will be examined in Sec. 4. In Sec. 5, we will further explore our results in an analytical way with deriving a *generalized* Fokker-Planck equation and a *phenomenological* Fluctuation-Dissipation relation, and will discuss the underlying physics. By using the β-FPU model Hamiltonian, we will further explore how different transport phenomena will appear when the two systems are coupled with linear or nonlinear interactions in Sec. 6. The last section is devoted for summary and discussions.

2. Theory of coupled-master equations and transport equation of collective motion

As repeatedly mentioned in Sec. 1, when one intends to understand a dynamics of evolution of a finite Hamiltonian system which connects the macro-level dynamics with the micro-level dynamics, one has to start with how to divide the total system into the weakly coupled relevant (collective or macro η, η^*) and irrelevant (intrinsic or micro ξ, ξ^*) systems. As an example, the nucleus provides us with a very nice benchmark field because it shows a coexistence of "macroscopic" and "microscopic" effects in association with various "phase transitions", and a mutual relation between "classical" and "quantum" effects related with the macro-level and micro-level variables, respectively. At certain energy region, the nucleus exhibits some statistical aspects which are associated with dissipation phenomena well described by the phenomenological transport equation.

2.1 Nuclear coupled master equation

Exploring the microscopic theory of nuclear large-amplitude collective dissipative motion, whose characteristic energy per nucleon is much smaller than the Fermi energy, one may start with the time-dependent Hartree-Fock (TDHF) theory. Since the basic equation of the TDHF theory is known to be formally equivalent to the classical canonical equations of motion (64), the use of the TDHF theory enables us to investigate the basic ingredients of the nonlinear nuclear dynamics in terms of the TDHF trajectories. The TDHF equation is expressed as :

$$\delta\langle\Phi(t)|(i\frac{\partial}{\partial t} - \hat{H})|\Phi(t)\rangle = 0, \tag{22}$$

where $|\Phi(t)\rangle$ is the general time-dependent single Slater determinant given by

$$|\Phi(t)\rangle = \exp\{i\hat{F}\}\,|\Phi_0 > e^{iE_0 t}, \quad i\hat{F} = \sum_{\mu i}\{f_{\mu i}(t)\hat{a}^\dagger_\mu \hat{b}^\dagger_i - f^*_{\mu i}(t)\hat{b}_i\hat{a}_\mu\}, \tag{23}$$

where $|\Phi_0\rangle$ denotes a HF stationary state, and $\hat{a}^\dagger_\mu(\mu = 1, 2, ..., m)$ and $\hat{b}^\dagger_i(i = 1, 2, ..., n)$ mean the particle- and hole-creation operators with respect to $|\Phi_0\rangle$. The HF Hamiltonian H and the HF energy E_0 are defined as

$$H = \langle\Phi(t)|\hat{H}|\Phi(t)\rangle - E_0, \quad E_0 = \langle\Phi_0|\hat{H}|\Phi_0\rangle. \tag{24}$$

With the aid of the self-consistent collective coordinate (SCC) method (60), the whole system can be optimally divided into the relevant (collective) and irrelevant (intrinsic) degrees of freedom by introducing an optimal canonical coordinate system called the dynamical canonical coordinate (DCC) system for a given trajectory. That is, the total closed system $\eta \oplus \xi$ is dynamically divided into two subsystems η and ξ, whose optimal coordinate systems are expressed as $\eta_a, \eta_a^* : a = 1, \cdots$ and $\xi_\alpha, \xi_\alpha^* : \alpha = 1, \cdots$, respectively. The resulting Hamiltonian in the DCC system is expressed as:

$$H = H_\eta + H_\xi + H_{coupl}, \tag{25}$$

where H_η depends on the relevant, H_ξ on the irrelevant, and H_{coupl} on both the relevant and irrelevant variables. The TDHF equation (22) can then be formally expressed as a set of canonical equations of motion in the classical mechanics in the TDHF phase space (symplectic manifold), as

$$i\dot{\eta}_a = \frac{\partial H}{\partial \eta_a^*}, \qquad i\dot{\eta}_a^* = -\frac{\partial H}{\partial \eta_a}, \qquad i\dot{\xi}_\alpha = \frac{\partial H}{\partial \xi_\alpha^*}, \qquad i\dot{\xi}_\alpha^* = -\frac{\partial H}{\partial \xi_\alpha} \tag{26}$$

Here, it is worthwhile mentioning that the SCC method defines the DCC system so as to eliminate the *linear* coupling between the relevant and irrelevant subsystems, i.e., the maximal decoupling condition(23) given by Eq. (20),

$$\left.\frac{\partial H_{coupl}}{\partial \eta}\right|_{\xi=\xi^*=0} = 0, \tag{27}$$

is satisfied. This separation in the degrees of freedom will turn out to be very important for exploring the energy dissipation process and nonlinear dynamics between the collective and intrinsic modes of motion.

The transport, dissipative and damping phenomena appearing in the nuclear system may involve a dynamics described by the wave packet rather than that by the eigenstate. Within the mean-field approximation, these phenomena may be expressed by the collective behavior of the ensemble of TDHF trajectories, rather than the single trajectory. A difference between the dynamics described by the single trajectory and by the bundle of trajectories might be related to the controversy on the effects of one-body and two-body dissipations(28; 40; 41; 65; 66), because a single trajectory of the Hamilton system will never produce any energy dissipation. Since an effect of the collision term is regarded to generate many-Slater determinants out of the single-Slater determinant, an introduction of the bundle of trajectories is considered to create a very similar situation which is produced by the two-body collision term.

In the classical theory of dynamical system, the order-to-chaos transition is usually regarded as the microscopic origin of an appearance of the statistical state in the finite system. Since one may express the heat bath by means of the infinite number of *integrable* systems like the harmonic oscillators whose frequencies have the Debye distribution, it may not be a relevant question whether the chaos plays a decisive role for the dissipation mechanism and for the microscopic generation of the statistical state in a case of the infinite system. In the finite system where the large number limit is not secured, the order-to-chaos is expected to play a decisive role in generating some statistical behavior.

To deal with the ensemble of TDHF trajectories, we start with the Liouville equation for the distribution function:

$$\dot{\rho}(t) = -i\mathcal{L}\rho(t), \qquad \mathcal{L}* \equiv i\{H, *\}_{PB}, \tag{28}$$

$$\rho(t) = \rho(\eta(t), \eta(t)^*, \xi(t), \xi(t)^*),$$

which is equivalent to TDHF equation (22). Here the symbol $\{\}_{PB}$ denotes the Poisson bracket. Since we are interested in the time evolution of the bundle of TDHF trajectories, whose bulk properties ought to be expressed by the relevant variables alone, we introduce the reduced distribution functions as

$$\rho_\eta(t) = Tr_\xi \rho(t), \quad \rho_\xi(t) = Tr_\eta \rho(t). \tag{29}$$

Here, the total distribution function $\rho(t)$ is normalized so as to satisfy the relation

$$Tr\rho(t) = 1, \tag{30}$$

where

$$Tr \equiv Tr_\eta Tr_\xi, \tag{31}$$

$$Tr_\eta \equiv \prod_a \int\int d\eta_a d\eta_a^*, \quad Tr_\xi \equiv \prod_\alpha \int\int d\xi_\alpha d\xi_\alpha^*. \tag{32}$$

With the aid of the reduced distribution functions $\rho_\eta(t)$ and $\rho_\xi(t)$, one may decompose the Hamiltonian in Eq. (25) into the form

$$H = H_\eta + H_\xi + H_{coupl} \tag{33a}$$

$$= H_\eta + H_\eta(t) + H_\xi + H_\xi(t) + H_\Delta(t) - E_0(t), \tag{33b}$$

$$H_\eta(t) \equiv Tr_\xi H_{coupl} \rho_\xi(t), \tag{33c}$$

$$H_\xi(t) \equiv Tr_\eta H_{coupl} \rho_\eta(t), \tag{33d}$$

$$H_{aver}(t) \equiv H_\eta(t) + H_\xi(t), \tag{33e}$$

$$E_0(t) \equiv Tr H_{coupl} \rho(t), \tag{33f}$$

$$H_\Delta(t) \equiv H_{coupl} - H_{aver}(t) + E_0(t). \tag{33g}$$

The corresponding Liouvillians are defined as

$$\mathcal{L}_\eta* \equiv i\{H_\eta, *\}_{PB} \tag{34a}$$

$$\mathcal{L}_\eta(t)* \equiv i\{H_\eta(t), *\}_{PB} \tag{34b}$$

$$\mathcal{L}_\xi* \equiv i\{H_\xi, *\}_{PB} \tag{34c}$$

$$\mathcal{L}_\xi(t)* \equiv i\{H_\xi(t), *\}_{PB} \tag{34d}$$

$$\mathcal{L}_{coupl}* \equiv i\{H_{coupl}, *\}_{PB} \tag{34e}$$

$$\mathcal{L}_\Delta(t)* \equiv i\{H_\Delta(t), *\}_{PB} \tag{34f}$$

Through above optimal division of the total system into the relevant and irrelevant degrees of freedom, one can treat the two subsystems in a very parallel way. Since one intends to explore how the statistical nature appears as a result of the microscopic dynamics, one should not introduce any statistical ansatz for the irrelevant distribution function ρ_ξ by hand, but should properly take account of its time evolution. By exploiting the time-dependent projection operator method (67), one may decompose the distribution function into a separable part and a correlated one as

$$\begin{aligned}\rho(t) &= \rho_s(t) + \rho_c(t),\\ \rho_s(t) &\equiv P(t)\rho(t) = \rho_\eta(t)\rho_\xi(t),\\ \rho_c(t) &\equiv (1 - P(t))\rho(t),\end{aligned} \tag{35}$$

where $P(t)$ is the time-dependent projection operator defined by

$$P(t) \equiv \rho_\eta(t)Tr_\eta + \rho_\xi(t)Tr_\xi - \rho_\eta(t)\rho_\xi(t)Tr_\eta Tr_\xi. \tag{36}$$

From the Liouville equation (28), one gets

$$\dot{\rho}_s(t) = -iP(t)\mathcal{L}\rho_s(t) - iP(t)\mathcal{L}\rho_c(t), \tag{37a}$$

$$\dot{\rho}_c(t) = -i(1 - P(t))\mathcal{L}\rho_s(t) - i(1 - P(t))\mathcal{L}\rho_c(t). \tag{37b}$$

By introducing the propagator

$$g(t,t') \equiv \mathrm{Texp}\left\{-i\int_{t'}^{t}\left[1 - P(\tau)\right]\mathcal{L}d\tau\right\}, \tag{38}$$

where T denotes the time ordering operator, one obtains the master equation for $\rho_s(t)$ as

$$\begin{aligned}\dot{\rho}_s(t) &= -iP(t)\mathcal{L}\rho_s(t) - iP(t)\mathcal{L}g(t,t_I)\rho_c(t_I)\\ &\quad - \int_{t_I}^{t} dt' P(t)\mathcal{L}g(t,t')\{1 - P(t')\}\mathcal{L}\rho_s(t'),\end{aligned} \tag{39}$$

where t_I stands for an initial time. In the conventional case, one usually takes an initial condition

$$\rho_c(t_I) = 0, \quad \text{i.e.,} \quad \rho(t_I) = \rho_\eta(t_I)\cdot\rho_\xi(t_I). \tag{40}$$

That is, there are no correlation at the initial time. According to this assumption, one may eliminate the second term on the rhs of Eq. (39). In our present general case, however, we have to retain this term, which allows us to evaluate the memory effects by starting from various time t_I.

With the aid of some properties of the projection operator $P(t)$ defined in Eq. (36) and the relations

$$Tr_\eta\mathcal{L}_\eta = 0, \quad Tr_\xi\mathcal{L}_\xi = 0, \quad Tr_\eta\mathcal{L}_\eta(t) = 0, \quad Tr_\xi\mathcal{L}_\xi(t) = 0,$$

$$\mathcal{L}_\eta * \equiv i\left\{H_\eta, *\right\}_{PB}, \quad \mathcal{L}_\eta(t) * \equiv i\left\{H_\eta(t), *\right\}_{PB}, \tag{41}$$

$$\mathcal{L}_\xi * \equiv i\left\{H_\xi, *\right\}_{PB}, \quad \mathcal{L}_\xi(t) * \equiv i\left\{H_\xi(t), *\right\}_{PB},$$

as is easily proved, the Liouvillian $\mathcal{L}$ appearing inside the time integration in Eq. (39) is replaced by $\mathcal{L}_{coupl}$ defined by $\mathcal{L}_{coupl}* = \{H_{coupl}, *\}_{PB}$ and Eq. (39) is reduced to

$$\begin{aligned}\dot{\rho}_s(t) &= -iP(t)\mathcal{L}\rho_s(t) - iP(t)\mathcal{L}g(t,t_I)\rho_c(t_I) \\ &\quad - \int_{t_I}^{t} dt' P(t)\mathcal{L}_\Delta(t)g(t,t')\{1-P(t')\}\mathcal{L}_\Delta(t')\rho_s(t'),\end{aligned} \tag{42}$$

Expressing $\rho_s(t)$ and $P(t)$ in terms of $\rho_\eta(t)$ and $\rho_\xi(t)$, and operating Tr_η and Tr_ξ on Eq. (39), one obtains a coupled master equation

$$\begin{aligned}\dot{\rho}_\eta(t) &= -i[\mathcal{L}_\eta + \mathcal{L}_\eta(t)]\rho_\eta(t) - iTr_\xi[\mathcal{L}_\eta + \mathcal{L}_{coupl}]g(t,t_I)\rho_c(t_I) \\ &\quad - \int_{t_I}^{t} d\tau Tr_\xi \mathcal{L}_\Delta(t)g(t,\tau)\mathcal{L}_\Delta(\tau)\rho_\eta(\tau)\rho_\xi(\tau),\end{aligned} \tag{43a}$$

$$\begin{aligned}\dot{\rho}_\xi(t) &= -i[\mathcal{L}_\xi + \mathcal{L}_\xi(t)]\rho_\xi(t) - iTr_\eta[\mathcal{L}_\xi + \mathcal{L}_{coupl}]g(t,t_I)\rho_c(t_I) \\ &\quad - \int_{t_I}^{t} d\tau Tr_\eta \mathcal{L}_\Delta(t)g(t,\tau)\mathcal{L}_\Delta(\tau)\rho_\eta(\tau)\rho_\xi(\tau),\end{aligned} \tag{43b}$$

where $\mathcal{L}_\Delta(t)* \equiv \{H_\Delta(t), *\}_{PB}$. The first (instantaneous) term describes the reversible motion of the relevant and irrelevant systems while the second and third terms bring on irreversibility. The coupled master equation (43) is still equivalent to the original Liouville equation (28) and can describe a variety of dynamics of the bundle of trajectories. In comparison with the usual time-independent projection operator method of Nakajima-Zwanzig (68) (69) where the irrelevant distribution function ρ_ξ is assumed to be a stationary heat bath, the present coupled-master equation (43) is rich enough to study the microscopic origin of the large-amplitude dissipative motion.

2.2 Dynamical response and correlation functions

As was discussed in Sec. 3.1.2 and Ref.(22), a bundle of trajectories even in the two degrees of freedom system may reach a statistical object. In this case, it is reasonable to assume that the effects on the relevant system coming from the irrelevant one are mainly expressed by an averaged effect over the irrelevant distribution function (*Assumption*). Namely, the effects due to the fluctuation part $H_\Delta(t)$ are assumed to be much smaller than those coming from $H_{aver}(t)$. Under this assumption, one may introduce the *mean-field* propagator

$$g_{mf}(t,t') = Texp\left\{-i\int_{t'}^{t}[1-P(\tau)]\mathcal{L}^{mf}(\tau)d\tau\right\}, \tag{44a}$$

$$\mathcal{L}^{mf}(t) = \mathcal{L}_\eta^{mf}(t) + \mathcal{L}_\xi^{mf}(t), \tag{44b}$$

$$\mathcal{L}_{\eta}^{mf}(t) \equiv \mathcal{L}_{\eta} + \mathcal{L}_{\eta}(t), \tag{44c}$$

$$\mathcal{L}_{\xi}^{mf}(t) \equiv \mathcal{L}_{\xi} + \mathcal{L}_{\xi}(t), \tag{44d}$$

which describes the major time evolution of the system, while the fluctuation part is regarded as a perturbation. By further introducing the following propagators given by

$$G_{mf}(t,t') \equiv \mathrm{Texp}\left\{ -i \int_{t'}^{t} \mathcal{L}^{mf}(\tau) d\tau \right\} = G_{\eta}(t,t') G_{\xi}(t,t'), \tag{44a}$$

$$G_{\eta}(t,t') \equiv \mathrm{Texp}\left\{ -i \int_{t'}^{t} \mathcal{L}_{\eta}^{mf}(\tau) d\tau \right\}, \tag{44b}$$

$$G_{\xi}(t,t') \equiv Texp\left\{ -i \int_{t'}^{t} \mathcal{L}_{\xi}^{mf}(\tau) d\tau \right\}, \tag{44c}$$

one may prove that there holds a relation

$$g_{mf}(t,\tau)\mathcal{L}_{\Delta}(\tau)\rho_{\eta}(\tau)\rho_{\xi}(\tau) = G_{mf}(t,\tau)\mathcal{L}_{\Delta}(\tau)\rho_{\eta}(\tau)\rho_{\xi}(\tau). \tag{45}$$

The coupling interaction is generally expressed as

$$H_{coupl}(\eta,\xi) = \sum_{l} A^{l}(\eta) B^{l}(\xi). \tag{46}$$

For simplicity, we hereafter discard the summation l in the coupling. By introducing the generalized two-time correlation and response functions, which have been called *dynamical* correlation and response functions in Ref. (21), through

$$\phi(t,\tau) \equiv Tr_{\xi} G_{\xi}(\tau,t) B \cdot (B - < B >_{t}) \rho_{\xi}(\tau), \tag{47}$$

$$\chi(t,\tau) \equiv Tr_{\xi} \left\{ G_{\xi}(\tau,t) B, B \right\}_{PB} \rho_{\xi}(\tau), \tag{48}$$

with $< B >_{t} \equiv Tr_{\xi} B \rho_{\xi}(t)$, the master equation in Eq.(43) for the relevant degree of freedom is expressed as

$$\begin{aligned} \dot{\rho}_{\eta}(t) &= -i[\mathcal{L}_{\eta} + \mathcal{L}_{\eta}(t)]\rho_{\eta}(t) - iTr_{\xi}[\mathcal{L}_{\eta} + \mathcal{L}_{coupl}] g(t,t_I) \rho_c(t_I) \\ &+ \int_{0}^{t-t_I} d\tau \chi(t,t-\tau) \left\{ A, G_{\eta}(t,t-\tau)(A - < A >_{t-\tau}) \rho_{\eta}(t-\tau) \right\}_{PB} \\ &+ \int_{0}^{t-t_I} d\tau \phi(t,t-\tau) \left\{ A, G_{\eta}(t,t-\tau) \left\{ A, \rho_{\eta}(t-\tau) \right\}_{PB} \right\}_{PB}, \end{aligned} \tag{49}$$

with $< A >_{t} \equiv Tr_{\eta} A \rho_{\eta}(t)$. Here, it should be noted that the whole system is developed exactly up to t_I. In order to make Eq.(49) applicable, t_I should be taken to be very close to a time when the irrelevant system approaches very near to its stationary state (, i.e., the irrelevant system is very near to the statistical state where one may safely make the assumption to be stated in next subsection). In order to analyze what happens in the microscopic system which is situated far from its stationary states, one has to study $\chi(t_I, t_I - \tau)$ and $\phi(t_I, t_I - \tau)$ by changing t_I. Since both $\chi(t_I, t_I - \tau)$ and $\phi(t_I, t_I - \tau)$ are strongly dependent on t_I, it is not easy to explore the dynamical evolution of the system far from the stationary state. So as to make Eq.(49) applicable, we will exploit the further assumptions.

2.3 Macroscopic transport equation

In this subsection, we discuss how the macroscopic transport equation is obtained from the fully microscopic master equation (49) by clearly itemizing necessary microscopic conditions.

Condition I Suppose the relevant distribution function $\rho_\eta(t-\tau)$ inside the time integration in Eq. (49) evolves through the mean-field Hamiltonian $H_\eta + H_\eta(t)$[1]. Namely, $\rho_\eta(t-\tau)$ inside the integration is assumed to be expressed as $\rho_\eta(t) = G_\eta(t, t-\tau)\rho_\eta(t-\tau)$, so that Eq.(49) is reduced to

$$\begin{aligned}\dot{\rho}_\eta(t) &= -i[\mathcal{L}_\eta + \mathcal{L}_\eta(t)]\rho_\eta(t) - iTr_\xi[\mathcal{L}_\eta + \mathcal{L}_{coupl}]g(t, t_I)\rho_c(t_I) \\ &+ \int_0^{t-t_I} d\tau \chi(t, t-\tau)\left\{A, G_\eta(t, t-\tau)(A - < A >_{t-\tau}) \cdot \rho_\eta(t)\right\}_{PB} \\ &+ \int_0^{t-t_I} d\tau \phi(t, t-\tau)\left\{A, \left\{G_\eta(t, t-\tau)A, \rho_\eta(t)\right\}_{PB}\right\}_{PB}. \end{aligned} \quad (50)$$

This condition is equivalent to *Assumption* discussed in the previous subsection, because the fluctuation effects are sufficiently small and are able to be treated as a perturbation around the path generated by the mean-field Hamiltonian $H_\eta + H_\eta(t)$, and are sufficient to be retained in Eq. (50) up to the second order.

Condition II Suppose the irrelevant distribution function $\rho_\xi(t)$ has already reached its time-independent stationary state $\rho_\xi(t_0)$. According to our previous paper(22), this situation is able to be well realized even in the 2-degrees of freedom system. Under this assumption, the relevant mean-field Liouvillian $\mathcal{L}_\eta + \mathcal{L}_\eta(t)$ becomes a time independent object. Under this assumption, a time ordered integration in $G_\eta(t, t')$ defined in Eq. (44) is performed and one may introduce

$$G_\eta(t, t-\tau) \approx G_\eta(\tau) \equiv \exp\left\{-i\mathcal{L}_\eta^{mf}\tau\right\}, \qquad \mathcal{L}_\eta^{mf} \equiv \mathcal{L}_\eta + \mathcal{L}_\eta(t_0), \quad (51)$$

where t_0 denotes a time when the irrelevant system has reached its stationary state.

Condition III Suppose the irrelevant time scale is much shorter than the relevant time scale. Under this assumption, the response $\chi(t, t-\tau)$ and correlation functions $\phi(t, t-\tau)$ are regarded to be independent of the time t, because t in Eq.(50) is regarded to describe a very slow time evolution of the relevant motion. By introducing an approximate one-time response and correlation functions

$$\chi(\tau) \approx \chi(t, t-\tau), \quad \phi(\tau) \approx \phi(t, t-\tau), \quad (52)$$

[1] The same assumption has been introduced in a case of the linear coupling(27).

one may get

$$\dot{\rho}_\eta(t) = -i[\mathcal{L}_\eta + \mathcal{L}_\eta(t)]\rho_\eta(t) - iTr_\xi[\mathcal{L}_\eta + \mathcal{L}_{coupl}]g(t,t_I)\rho_c(t_I)$$
$$+\int_0^\infty d\tau\chi(\tau)\left\{A, \exp\left\{-i\mathcal{L}_\eta^{mf}\tau\right\}(A- < A >_{t-\tau})\cdot\rho_\eta(t)\right\}_{PB}$$
$$+\int_0^\infty d\tau\phi(\tau)\left\{A, \left\{\exp(-i\mathcal{L}_\eta^{mf}\tau)A, \rho_\eta(t)\right\}_{PB}\right\}_{PB}. \quad (53)$$

This condition is different from the diabatic condition(17; 19), where the ratio between the characteristic times of the irrelevant degrees of freedom and of the relevant one is considered arbitrary small. However this condition is only partly satisfied for the most realistic cases. The dissipation is necessarily connected to some degree of chaoticity of the overall dynamics of the system(28).

Here it should be noted that such one-time response and correlation functions are still different from the usual ones introduced in the LRT where the concepts of linear coupling and of heat bath are adopted. Under the same assumption, the upper limit of the integration $t - t_I$ in Eq. (53) can be extended to the infinity, because the $\chi(\tau)$ and $\phi(\tau)$ are assumed to be very fast damping functions when it is measured in the relevant time scale.
Here, one may introduce the susceptibility $\zeta(t)$

$$\zeta(t) = \int_0^t d\tau\chi(\tau), \quad \zeta(0) = 0. \quad (54)$$

Defining $\zeta \equiv \zeta(\infty)$, one may further introduce another dynamical function $c(t)$:

$$\zeta(t) = [1 - c(t)]\zeta, \quad \text{with} \quad c(0) = 1, \qquad c(\infty) = 0, \quad (55)$$

which satisfies the following relation

$$\chi(t) = \frac{\partial\zeta(t)}{\partial t} = -\zeta\frac{\partial c(t)}{\partial t}. \quad (56)$$

Inserting Eq. (56) into Eq. (53) and integrating by part, one gets

$$\dot{\rho}_\eta(t) = -i[\mathcal{L}_\eta + \mathcal{L}_\eta(t)]\rho_\eta(t) - iTr_\xi[\mathcal{L}_\eta + \mathcal{L}_{coupl}]g(t,t_I)\rho_c(t_I)$$
$$+\zeta\left\{A, (A- < A >_t)\cdot\rho_\eta(t)\right\}_{PB}$$
$$+\zeta\int_0^\infty d\tau c(\tau)\left\{A, \frac{d}{d\tau}(\exp(-i\mathcal{L}_\eta^{mf}\tau)(A- < A >_t))\cdot\rho_\eta(t)\right\}_{PB}$$
$$+\int_0^\infty d\tau\phi(\tau)\left\{A, \left\{\exp(-i\mathcal{L}_\eta^{mf}\tau)A, \rho_\eta(t)\right\}_{PB}\right\}_{PB}. \quad (57)$$

This equation is a Fokker-Planck type equation. The first term on the right-hand side of Eq. (57) represents the contribution from the mean-field part, and the second term a contribution

from the correlated part of the distribution function at time t_I. The last three terms represent contribution from the dynamical fluctuation effects H_Δ. The friction as well as fluctuation terms are supposed to emerge as a result of those three terms. We will discuss the role of each term with our numerical simulation in the next section.
At the end of this subsection, let us discuss how to obtain the Langevin equation from our fully microscopic coupled master equation, because it has been regarded as a final goal of the microscopic or dynamical approaches to justify the phenomenological approaches. For a sake of simplicity, let us discuss a case where the interaction between relevant and irrelevant degrees of freedom has the following linear form,

$$H_{coupl} = \lambda Q \sum_i q_i, \quad \text{i.e.} \quad A = \sqrt{\lambda} Q, \quad B = \sqrt{\lambda} \sum_i q_i, \tag{58a}$$

$$Q = \frac{1}{\sqrt{2}}(\eta + \eta^*), \quad P = \frac{i}{\sqrt{2}}(\eta^* - \eta), \tag{58b}$$

$$q_i = \frac{1}{\sqrt{2}}(\xi_i + \xi_i^*), \quad p_i = \frac{i}{\sqrt{2}}(\xi_i^* - \xi_i). \tag{58c}$$

Here, we assume that the relevant system consists of one degree of freedom described by P, Q. Even though we apply the linear coupling form, the generalization for the case with more general nonlinear coupling is straightforward. In order to evaluate Eq. (57), one has to calculate

$$Q(\tau) = \exp(-i\mathcal{L}_\eta^{mf}\tau)Q, \tag{59}$$

where $Q(\tau)$ is a phase space image of Q through the backward evolution. Thus the Poisson bracket $\{Q(\tau), \rho_\eta(t)\}_{PB}$ in Eq. (57) is expressed as

$$\{Q(\tau), \rho_\eta(t)\}_{PB} = \frac{\partial Q(\tau)}{\partial Q}\frac{\partial \rho_\eta(t)}{\partial P} - \frac{\partial Q(\tau)}{\partial P}\frac{\partial \rho_\eta(t)}{\partial Q}. \tag{60}$$

By introducing the following quantities,

$$\alpha_1(P,Q) \equiv \lambda \int_0^\infty d\tau \phi(\tau) \frac{\partial Q(\tau)}{\partial Q}, \tag{61a}$$

$$\alpha_2(P,Q) \equiv -\lambda \int_0^\infty d\tau \phi(\tau) \frac{\partial Q(\tau)}{\partial P}, \tag{61b}$$

$$\beta(P,Q) \equiv \lambda\zeta \int_0^\infty d\tau c(\tau) \frac{\partial Q(\tau)}{\partial \tau}, \tag{61c}$$

Eq. (57) is reduced to

$$\begin{aligned}\dot{\rho}_\eta(t) = &-iTr_\xi[\mathcal{L}_\eta + \mathcal{L}_{coupl}]g(t,t_I)\rho_c(t_I) \\ &+\left\{-i(\mathcal{L}_\eta + \mathcal{L}_\eta(t)) + \lambda\zeta(Q - \langle Q\rangle_t)\frac{\partial}{\partial P}\right. \\ &\left.+\frac{\partial}{\partial P}\beta(P,Q) + \frac{\partial}{\partial P}\alpha_1(P,Q)\frac{\partial}{\partial P} + \frac{\partial}{\partial P}\alpha_2(P,Q)\frac{\partial}{\partial Q}\right\}\rho_\eta(t)\end{aligned} \tag{62}$$

As discussed in Ref. (26), Eq. (62) results in the Langevin equation with a form

$$\ddot{Q} = -\frac{1}{m}\frac{\partial U(Q)}{\partial x} - \gamma\dot{Q} + f(t), \tag{63}$$

by introducing a concept of mechanical temperature.
The above derivation of the Langevin equation is still too formal to be applicable for the general cases. However it might be naturally expected that the Conditions I, II and III are met in the actual dynamical processes.

3. Dynamic realization of transport phenomenon in finite system

In order to study the dissipation process microscopically, it is inevitable to treat a system with more than two degrees of freedom, which is able to be divided into two weakly coupled subsystems: one is composed of at least two degrees of freedom and is regarded as an irrelevant system, whereas the rest is considered as a relevant system. The system with two degrees of freedom is too simple to assign the relevant degree of freedom nor to discuss its dissipation, because the chaotic or statistical state can be realized by a system with at least two degrees of freedom.

3.1 The case of the system with three degrees of freedom

3.1.1 Description of the microscopic system

The system considered in our numerical calculation is composed of a collective degree of freedom coupled to intrinsic degrees of freedom through weak interaction, which simulates a nuclear system. The collective system describing, e.g., the giant resonance is represented by the harmonic oscillator given by

$$H_\eta(q,p) = \frac{p^2}{2M} + \frac{1}{2}M\omega^2 q^2. \tag{64}$$

and the intrinsic system mimicking the hot nucleus is described by the modified SU(3) model Hamiltonian (70) given by

$$\hat{H} = \sum_{i=0}^{2}\epsilon_i\hat{K}_{ii} + \frac{1}{2}\sum_{i=1}^{2}V_i\left\{\hat{K}_{i0}\hat{K}_{i0} + h.c.\right\}; \quad \hat{K}_{ij} = \sum_{m=1}^{N}C^\dagger_{im}C_{jm} \tag{65}$$

where $C^\dagger_{im}$ and C_{im} represent the fermion creation and annihilation operators. There are three N-fold degenerate levels with $\epsilon_0 < \epsilon_1 < \epsilon_2$. In the case with an even N particle system, the TDHF theory gives a classical Hamiltonian with two degrees of freedom as

$$\begin{aligned} H_\xi(q_1,p_1,q_2,p_2) = \; & \frac{1}{2}(\epsilon_1-\epsilon_0)(q_1^2+p_1^2) + \frac{1}{2}V_1(N-1)(q_1^2-p_1^2) \\ & +\frac{1}{2}(\epsilon_2-\epsilon_0)(q_2^2+p_2^2) - \frac{1}{2}V_2(N-1)(q_2^2-p_2^2) \\ & -\frac{N-1}{4N}V_1(q_1^4-p_1^4) - \frac{N-1}{4N}V_2(q_2^4-p_2^4) \\ & +\frac{N-1}{4N}\left[-V_1(q_1^2-p_1^2)(q_2^2+p_2^2) - V_2(q_1^2+p_1^2)(q_2^2-p_2^2)\right]. \end{aligned} \tag{66}$$

In our numerical calculation, the used parameters are M=18.75, ω^2=0.0064, ϵ_0=0, ϵ_1=1, ϵ_2=2, N=30 and V_i=-0.07. In this case, the collective time scale τ_{col} characterized by the harmonic oscillator in Eq. (64) and the intrinsic time scale τ_{in} characterized by the harmonic part of the intrinsic Hamiltonian in Eq.(66) satisfies a relation $\tau_{col} \sim 10\tau_{in}$.
For the coupling interaction, we use the following nonlinear interaction given by

$$H_{coupl} = \lambda(q - q_0)^2 \sum_{i=1}^{2} \left\{ q_i^2 + p_i^2 \right\}. \tag{67}$$

A physical meaning of introducing a quantity q_0 in Eq. (67) will be discussed at the end of this subsection as well as the next subsection.
In performing the numerical simulation, the time evolution of the distribution function $\rho(t)$ is evaluated by using the pseudo-particle method as:

$$\rho(t) = \frac{1}{N_p} \sum_{n=1}^{N_p} \prod_{i=1}^{2} \delta(q_i - q_{i,n}(t))\delta(p_i - p_{i,n}(t)) \cdot \delta(q - q_n(t))\delta(p - p_n(t)), \tag{68}$$

where N_p means the total number of pseudo-particles. The distribution function in Eq. (68) defines an ensemble of the system, each member of which is composed of a collective degree of freedom coupled to a single intrinsic trajectory. The collective coordinates $q_n(t)$ and $p_n(t)$, and the intrinsic coordinates $q_{i,n}(t)$ and $p_{i,n}(t)$ determine a phase space point of the n-th pseudo-particle at time t, whose time dependence is described by the canonical equations of motion given by

$$\dot{q} = \frac{\partial H}{\partial p}, \quad \dot{p} = -\frac{\partial H}{\partial q}, \tag{69a}$$

$$\dot{q}_i = \frac{\partial H}{\partial p_i}, \quad \dot{p}_i = -\frac{\partial H}{\partial q_i}, \quad \{i = 1, 2\} \tag{69b}$$

$$H \equiv H_\eta(q, p) + H_\xi(q_1, p_1, q_2, p_2) + H_{coupl} \tag{69c}$$

We use the fourth order simplectic Runge-Kutta method(75; 76) for integrating the canonical equations of motion and N_p is chosen to be 10,000. The initial condition for the intrinsic distribution function is given by a uniform distribution in a tiny region of the stochastic sea as stated in Ref. (22). That for the collective distribution function is given by the δ function centered at $q(0) = 0$ and $p(0)$, $p(0)$ being defined by a given collective energy E_η together with $q(0) = 0$. The distribution function in Eq. (68) defines an ensemble of the system, each member of which is composed of a collective degree of freedom coupled to a single intrinsic trajectory.
In our numerical simulation, the coupling interaction is not activated at an initial stage. In the beginning, the coupling between the collective and intrinsic systems is switch off, and they evolve independently. Namely, the collective system evolves regularly, whereas, as discussed in the subsection 3.1.2, the intrinsic system tends to reach its time-independent stationary state (chaotic object). After the statistical state has been realized in the intrinsic system, the coupling interaction is activated. A quantity q_0 in Eq.(67) denotes a value of the collective trajectory q at the switch on time. A purpose of introducing q_0 is to insert the coupling *adiabatically*, and to conserve the total energy before and after the switch on time. (Hereafter, τ_{sw} denotes the

moment when the interaction is switch on, and in our numerical calculation τ_{sw} is set to be $\tau_{sw} = 12\tau_{col}$).

Here it is worthwhile to discuss why we let the two systems evolve independently at the initial stage. As is well known, the ergodic and irreversible property of the intrinsic system is assumed in the conventional approach, and the intrinsic system for the *in□nite* system is usually represented by the time independent canonical ensemble. In the *□nite* system, however, one has to explore whether or not the intrinsic system tends to reach such a state that is effectively replaced by a statistical object, how it evolves after the coupling interaction is switch on, and what its final state looks like.

As is discussed at the end of the subsection 2.2, it is not easy to apply Eq. (49) for analyzing what happens in the dynamical microscopic system which is in the general situation. Our present primarily aim is to microscopically generate such a transport phenomenon that might be understood in terms of the Langevin equation. Namely, we have to construct such a microscopic situation that seems to satisfy the Condition I, II and III discussed in subsection 2.3. In this context, we firstly let the intrinsic system reach a chaotic situation in a dynamical way, till the ergodic and irreversible property are well realized *dynamically*. In the next subsection, it will be shown that above microscopic situation is indeed realized *dynamically* for the intrinsic system (66).

3.1.2 Dynamic realization of statistical state in finite system

It is not a trivial discussion how to dynamically characterize the statistical state in the finite system. Even though the Hamilton system shows chaotic situation and the Lyapunov exponent has a positive value everywhere in the phase space, there still remain a lot of questions, such as, whether or not one may substantiate statistical state in the way dynamical chaos is structured in real Hamiltonian system, how the real macroscopic motion looks like in such system, whether or not there are some difficulties of using the properties of dynamical chaos as a source of randomness, whether or not there is difference between real Hamiltonian chaos and a conventional understanding of the laws of statistical physics and whether or not the system dynamically reaches some statistical object. It is certainly interesting question especially for the nuclear physics to explore the relation between the dynamical definition of the statistical state and the static definition of it. The former definition will be discussed in the following, whereas the latter definition is usually given by employing a concept of "temperature" like

$$\rho = e^{-\beta H}, \quad \beta = \frac{1}{kT}. \tag{70}$$

Even in the nuclear system, there are many phenomena well explained by using the concept of temperature. To make the discussion simple, we treat the Hamilton system given in Eq. (66). In Fig. 4, the Poincaré section for the case with $N = 30$, $\epsilon_0 = 0$, $\epsilon_1 = 1$, $\epsilon_2 = 2$, $V_1 = V_2 = -0.07$ and $E = 40$ is illustrated. From this figure, one may see that the phase space is dominated by a chaotic sea, with some remnants of KAM torus(71). The toughness of the torus structure is a quite general property in the Hamilton system. Since the KAM torus means an existence of a very sticky motion which travels around the torus for a quite long time, one might expect a very long correlation time which would prevent us from introducing some statistical objects.

As is well known, the nearest-neighbor level-spacing statistics of the quantum system is well described by the GOE, when the phase space of its classical correspondent is covered by a chaotic sea(39). Here it should be remembered that the GOE is derived under the assumption that the matrix elements of Hamiltonian should be *representation independent*(72). This assumption would be considered to be a *statistical* ansatz introduced for the quantum system. Let us consider the classical analogue of the quantum concept of representation independence. We repeatedly point out an importance of the choice of coordinate system, because it has shown to be very useful in exploring how simply the trajectory under discussion is described, how to obtain its approximate constants of motion, how optimally the total system is divided into the relevant and irrelevant subsystems for a given trajectory and how analytically one may understand an exceedingly rich structure of the phase space. In a case of the chaotic situation where no constants of motion exist except for the total energy, however, there should be no dynamical reason to select some specific coordinate system. In other words, the classical statistical state is expected to be characterized by the *coordinate system independence.*

The coordinate system $\{q_1, p_1, q_2, p_2\}$ used in describing the Hamilton system in Eq. (66) just corresponds to the maximal-decoupled coordinate system, because it satisfies the maximum-decoupling condition (27). The coordinate system $\{q_1, p_1, q_2, p_2\}$ is identified to be the optimum coordinate system, when an amplitude of the trajectory is sufficiently small and the harmonic term in Eq. (66) is dominated. When the amplitude becomes large, there appears such a situation for the bundle of trajectories, where the following relations are fulfilled,

$$< q_i >_t < \sqrt{\langle q_i^2 - < q_i >_t^2 \rangle_t}, \tag{71a}$$

$$< p_i >_t < \sqrt{\langle p_i^2 - < p_i >_t^2 \rangle_t}, \quad \{i = 1, 2\} \tag{71b}$$

with

$$< A >_t \equiv \int\int\int\int dq_1 dp_1 dq_2 dp_2 A \rho(t). \tag{72}$$

In this case, the coordinate system $\{q_1, p_1, q_2, p_2\}$ looses its particular advantage in describing the bundle of trajectories under discussion. When there realizes a stationary state satisfying

$$\frac{d}{dt} < q_i >_t = 0, \quad \frac{d}{dt}\left\langle q_i^2 - < q_i >_t^2 \right\rangle_t = 0, \quad \text{etc}, \tag{73}$$

Equation (71) is considered to be a *dynamical* condition to characterize the system to be in the *statistical object*, because the system does not show any regularity associated with a certain specific coordinate system. In other words, the system has dynamically reached such a state that is *coordinate system independent*.

In Fig. 6, the time dependence of the variance $< p_1^2 - < p_1 >^2 >$ of the momentum for the first degree of freedom is shown for the cases with $E = 40$ and $V = -0.01, -0.04$ and -0.07. A unit of time is given by $\tau_1 = \omega_1 / 2\pi$, where ω_1 is an eigen frequency of low-lying normal mode obtained by applying the RPA to Eq. (65). In the case with $V = -0.01$ where the whole phase space is covered by the regular motions illustrated in Fig. 1, the variance is oscillating and its amplitude is increasing. In the case with a much stronger interaction $V = -0.04$, the variance increases exponentially and then oscillates around some saturated value. Since the amplitude of oscillation is not small, a stationary state is not expected to be realized for a very long time. Note that the Poincaré section map for the case with $V = -0.04$ is still dominated by many kinds of island structure like the case with $V = -0.01$. Even though an initial distribution is chosen around the unstable fixed point where many trajectories with different characters come across with each other, domination of the KAM torus in the Poincaré section prevents the system from reaching some statistical object.

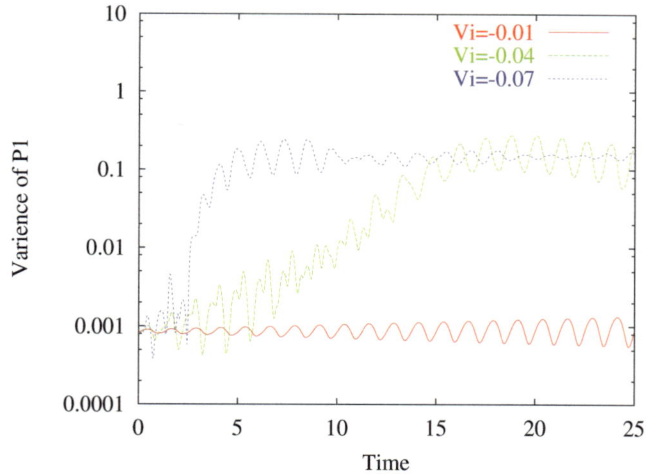

Fig. 6. Variance $< p_1^2 - < p_1 >^2 >$ for the cases with $V = -0.01, -0.04$ and -0.07.

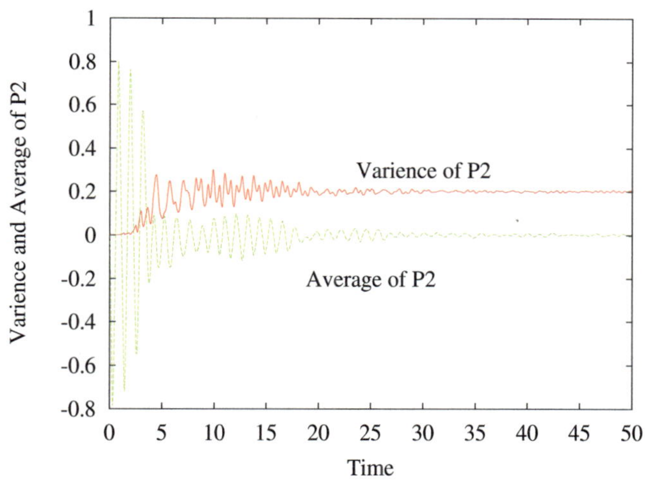

Fig. 7. Averaged value $< p_2 >$ and variance $< p_2^2 - < p_2 >^2 >$ for the case with $V = -0.07$.

In the case of $V = -0.07$, where the overwhelming region of the Poincaré section map is covered by the chaotic sea as is depicted in Fig. 4, a quite different situation is realized. As is observed in Fig. 6, the time dependence of the variance of p_1 almost dies out around $\tau \approx 25\tau_1$. In Fig. 7, the averaged value $< p_2 >$ and its variance $< p_2^2 - < p_2 >^2 >$ for the second degree of freedom are shown for the case with $V = -0.07$. Since $< p_2 >$ has reached null value around $\tau \approx 30\tau_1$ and the variance become almost constant around $\tau \approx 25\tau_1$ like $< p_1^2 - < p_1 >^2 >$, the system is considered to be in a stationary statistical state where the relation in Eqs. (71) and (73) are well realized at around $\tau \approx 30\tau_1$. In this case, the choice of a particular coordinate system does not have any profit for the present the system with $V = -0.07$, like the quantum system described by GOE.

Another information on the dynamic realization of the statistical state might be obtained from the two-time dynamic response $\chi_{lm}(t,\tau)$, $X_{lm}(t,\tau)$ and correlation functions $\phi_{lm}(t,\tau)$, $\Phi_{lm}(t,\tau)$ defined in Eqs. (47) and (48). Suppose the system described by a bundle of trajectories has been developed exactly till t_I following the original Liouville equation (28) or equivalently by the coupled-master equation (43). The approximate coupled master equations in Eqs. (49), which depend on the two-time dynamic response and correlation functions, are derived from Eq. (43) under the assumption that the effects coming from the fluctuation $H_\Delta(t)$ are sufficiently small so as to be evaluated by the second order perturbation theory. Consequently, Eqs. (49) is considered to be applicable either in a case with very small fluctuation effects or in a case with a very short time interval $\tau = t - t_I$ just after t_I. When one evaluates the t_I dependence of the dynamic response and correlation functions

$$\chi_{lm}(t_I+\tau,t_I), \quad \phi_{lm}(t_I+\tau,t_I), \quad X_{lm}(t_I+\tau,t_I), \quad \Phi_{lm}(t_I+\tau,t_I), \tag{74}$$

one may study how their τ-dependence change as a function of t_I. Since the dynamic response and correlation functions depend on the time derivative of $< q_i^2 - < q_i >_t^2 >$, their t_I-independence gives a more severe stationary condition than the condition (73).

When $\rho(t)$ reaches some stationary state after a long time-evolution through the original Liouville equation, the dynamic response and correlation functions show no t_I-dependence so as to be approximated by the usual one-time response and correlation functions appeared in the LRT. According to the recent work(22), it turned out that a dynamic realization of statistical state is established around $t_I \approx 50\tau_1$ for the system described by the Hamiltonian in Eq. (66) with $V = -0.07$.

3.1.3 Energy interchange between the collective and intrinsic systems

Our attention is mainly focused on examining the energy interchange between these two systems, and what final states these two systems can reach and their interaction-dependence. For studying the energy interchange, we make numerical calculation for the following cases: The collective energy is much larger, comparable and much smaller than the intrinsic energy. Namely, the collective energy is chosen to be $E_\eta = 20$, 40 and 60, whereas the intrinsic energy is fixed at $E_\xi = 40$. Here $E_\xi = 40$ is chosen, because the phase space of the intrinsic system is almost covered by the chaotic sea at this energy. In order to examine the interaction dependence of the final state, the interaction strength parameter λ is chosen to be 0.005 (relatively weak), 0.01 and 0.02 (relatively strong).

Figures 8 (a)-(d) show the time-dependent averaged values of the partial Hamiltonian $\langle H_\eta \rangle$, $\langle H_\xi \rangle$ and $\langle H_{coupl} \rangle$ and the total Hamiltonian $\langle H \rangle$ defined through

$$\langle X \rangle = \int X\rho(t)dqdp\prod_{i=1}^{2} dq_i dp_i, \tag{75}$$

for the case with $E_\eta = 40$. One may see that the main change occurs in the collective energy as well as the interaction energy, but not in the intrinsic energy.

When one precisely looks for the independent trajectories of the bundle, the collective, intrinsic and interaction energies of each trajectory are changing in time in accordance with the usual Hamilton system. Since the intrinsic system has already reached some stochastic

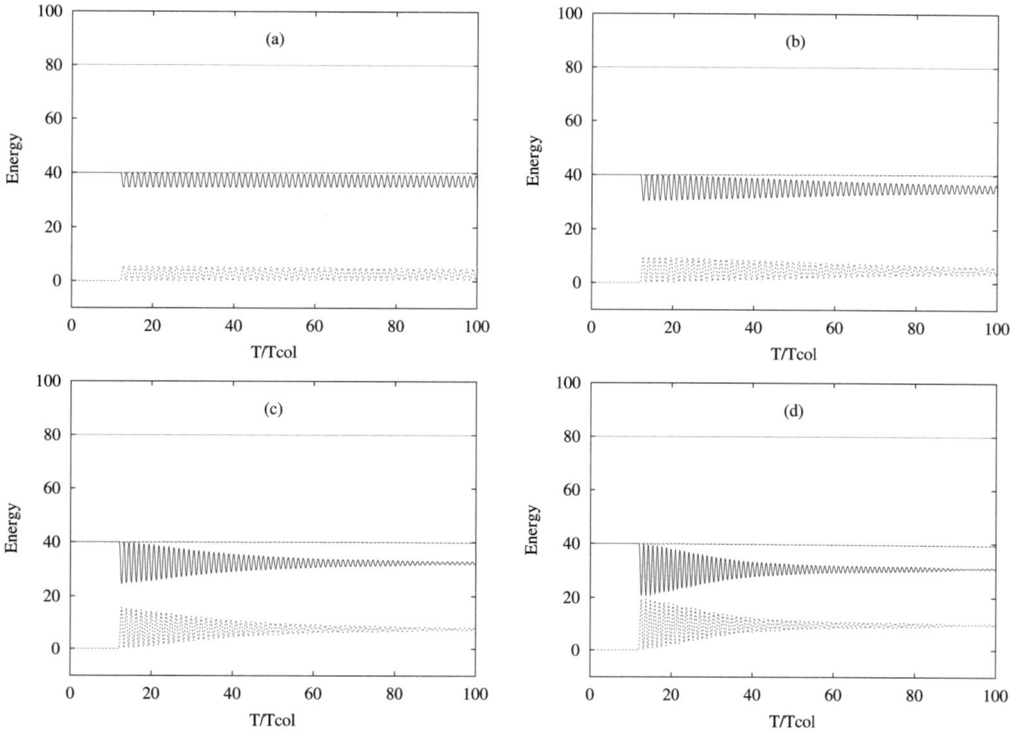

Fig. 8. Time-dependence of the averaged partial Hamiltonian $\langle H_\eta \rangle$, $\langle H_\xi \rangle$, $\langle H_{coupl} \rangle$ and $\langle H \rangle$ for E_η=40, E_ξ=40 and (a) λ=0.005; (b) λ=0.01; (c) λ=0.02 and (d) λ=0.03. Solid line refers to $\langle H_\eta \rangle$; long dashed line refers to $\langle H_\xi \rangle$; short dashed line refers to $\langle H_{coupl} \rangle$ and dotted line refers to $\langle H \rangle$. τ_{col} denotes a characteristic periodic time of collective oscillator.

state when the interaction is switch on, a time-dependence of the intrinsic energy for each trajectory is canceled out when one takes an average over many trajectories of the bundle. For a case with small interaction strength ($\lambda = 0.005$), the collective energy oscillates for a long time and seems not to reach any saturated value. In a case with a relatively large interaction strength ($\lambda \sim$0.02), it will reach some time-independent value.

Figures 9 (a) and (b) represent the numerical results for the cases with $E_\eta = 20$ and 60, showing almost the same result as for the case with $E_\eta = 40$.

From the above numerical simulation, one may see that the energy is dissipated from the collective to an 'environment', when the intrinsic system and the coupling interaction are regarded as an 'environment'. Before understanding the above energy transfer in terms of the phenomenological Langevin equation, it is important to microscopically explore what happens in the intrinsic system when the collective system is attached to the intrinsic system through the coupling interaction.

In Fig. 10, a time dependence of the variance of the intrinsic momentum $< p_1^2 >$ is shown. The other intrinsic variances $< q_1^2 >$, $< q_2^2 >$ and $< p_2^2 >$ show almost the same time dependence as in Fig. 10. As discussed in our previous paper(22), an appearance of some chaotic state is expected when the variance has reached its stationary value. Since the variance of the intrinsic

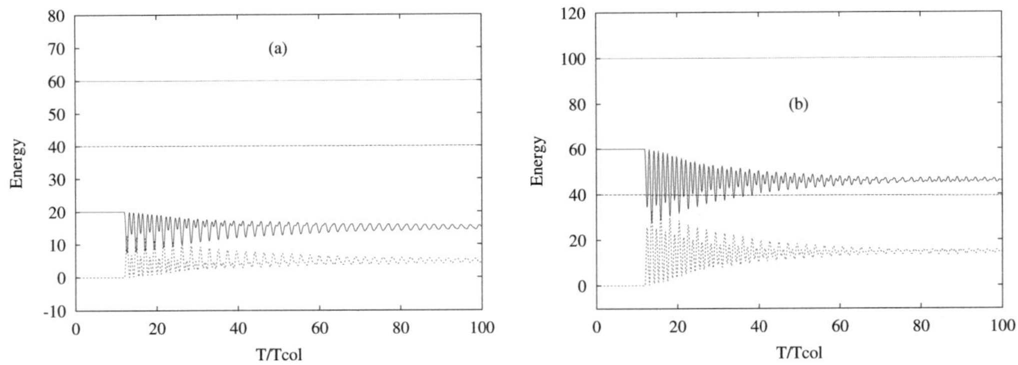

Fig. 9. Time-dependence of the averaged partial Hamiltonian for (a) E_η=20, E_ξ=40, λ=0.02; (b) E_η=60, E_ξ=40, λ=0.02. Reference of lines is the same as in Fig. 8.

system reaches some stationary value before τ_{sw} and since the intrinsic system is regarded to be in the chaotic state, the coupling interaction is activated at τ_{sw} in our simulation. After $\tau_{sw} = 12\tau_{col}$, its value remains almost the same for the small interaction strength case, and reaches quickly a little bit larger stationary value for the large coupling strength case ($\lambda = 0.02$). This small increase corresponds to a slight enlargement of the chaotic sea in the intrinsic phase space. Practically, the values of variances are regarded to be constant before and after τ_{sw}.

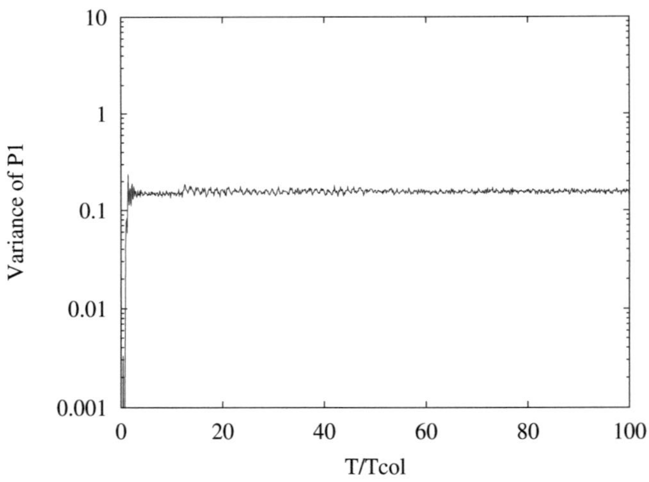

Fig. 10. Time-dependence of variance of p_1 for E_η=40, E_ξ=40 and λ=0.02. Coupling is switch on at $\tau_{sw} = 12\tau_{col}$.

From our numerical simulation, one may deduce such a conclusion that the intrinsic system even with only two degrees of freedom can be treated as a time independent statistical object before and after the coupling interaction is activated. This conclusion provide us with the dynamical foundation for understanding the statistical ansatz adopted in the conventional transport theory, where the irrelevant system is always regarded as a time-independent statistical object.

Since the variance has reached its stationary value shortly after τ_{sw}, it is reasonable to introduce the following time independent quantity:

$$< p_i^2 + q_i^2 >= \int \prod_{i=1}^{2} dp_i dq_i \{p_i^2 + q_i^2\}\rho(t) \tag{76}$$

In accordance with the mean-field Liouvillian in Eq. (44), one may introduce the *time-independent* collective mean-field Hamiltonian as

$$H_\eta + H_\eta(t)\Bigg|_{t>\tau_{sw}} = \frac{p^2}{2M} + \frac{1}{2}M\omega_0^2 q^2 + \lambda(q - q_0)^2 \sum_{i=1}^{2} < p_i^2 + q_i^2 > . \tag{77}$$

Except for the effects coming from the fluctuation part $H_\Delta(t)$, the collective trajectory is supposed to be described by the mean field Hamiltonian in Eq. (77) after the coupling interaction is switch on. The solution of Eq. (77) is expressed as

$$q = A\cos\omega(t - \tau_{sw}), \quad p = -M\omega A\sin\omega(t - \tau_{sw}), \tag{78}$$

where

$$\omega^2 = \omega_0^2 + \omega_1^2, \quad \omega_1^2 \equiv \frac{2\lambda}{M} < p_i^2 + q_i^2 >, \quad A = q_0 \left(\frac{\omega_0}{\omega}\right)^2, \tag{79}$$

the amplitude A being fixed by using the initial condition $q(\tau_{sw}) = q_0$. In accordance with this initial condition, there holds the following energy conservation before and after τ_{sw} as

$$H_\eta\Bigg|_{t=\tau_{sw}-0} = H_\eta + H_\eta(t)\Bigg|_{t=\tau_{sw}+0} = \frac{M}{2}q_0^2\omega_0^2. \tag{80}$$

In order to understand a oscillating property of the collective energy observed in Figs. 1 and 2, let us substitute the solution in Eq. (78) into the collective Hamiltonian H_η. Then one gets

$$H_\eta = \frac{M}{2}q_0^2\omega_0^2 \left\{1 - 4\frac{\omega_1^2\omega_0^2}{\omega^4}\sin^4\frac{\omega}{2}(t - \tau_{sw})\right\}. \tag{81}$$

In Fig. 11, the numerical result of Eq. (81) is shown together with the exact simulated result. As is clearly recognized from Fig. 11 and Eq. (81), the mean field description can well reproduce the oscillating property (the amplitude, the central energy of the oscillation as well as the frequency) of the collective energy $< H_\eta >$, whereas it can not reproduce a reduction mechanism of the amplitude. That is the mean field Hamiltonian can not describe the dissipation process. More precisely, one may see that the mean-field approximation provides us with a decisive information on the following two points: (a) the amplitude A of the collective energy is mainly determined by the coupling interaction strength λ as well as the averaged properties of the intrinsic system $\langle \sum_{i=1}^{2} p_i^2 + q_i^2 \rangle$; (b) the frequency ω is related with the characteristic frequency of the collective oscillator ω_0, the coupling interaction strength λ and the averaged properties of intrinsic system $\langle \sum_{i=1}^{2} p_i^2 + q_i^2 \rangle$. From the above discussion

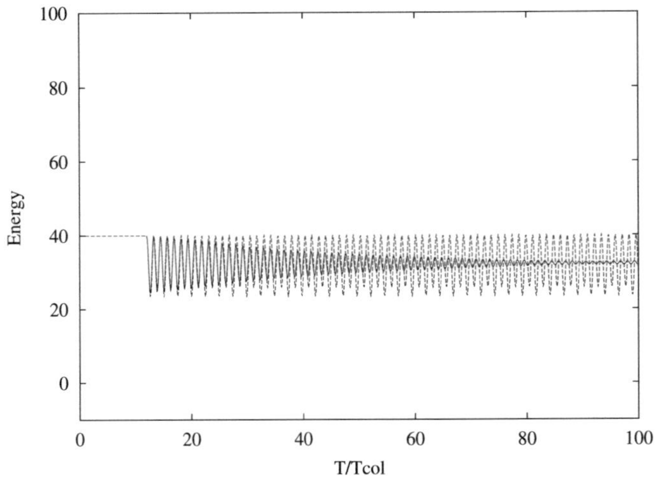

Fig. 11. Time-dependence of average collective energy (dashed line) H_η in Eq. (81), in which the mean-field energy of the coupling interaction is considered as shown in Eq. (77), together with the exact simulated result (solid line). Parameters used in the mean-field potential is the same as Fig. 8(c).

and from Figs.1 and 2, the dissipation process should be attributed to the fluctuation effects coming from H_Δ.

3.1.4 Analysis with a phenomenological transport equation

Before discussing the microscopic dynamics responsible for the damping and diffusion process, let us apply the phenomenological transport equation to our present simulated process. Let us suppose that the collective motion will be subject to both a friction force and a random force, and can be described by the Langevin equation. A simple Langevin equation is given by

$$M\ddot{q} + \frac{\partial U^{mf}(q)}{\partial q} + \gamma\dot{q} = f(t), \tag{82}$$

where $U^{mf}(q)$ represents the potential part of $H_\eta + H_\eta(t)$ in Eq. (77) and γ the friction strength parameter. A function $f(t)$ represents the random force and, in our calculation, it is taken to be the Gaussian white noise characterized by the following moments:

$$\langle f(t)\rangle = 0, \quad \langle f(t)f(s)\rangle = kT\delta(t-s). \tag{83}$$

The numerical result for Eq. (82) is shown in Fig. 12 with the parameters γ=0.0033 and kT=1.45. The used parameters appearing in $U^{mf}(q)$ is the same as in Fig. 8 (c).

As is understood from Fig. 12, the Langevin equation do reproduce the energy transfer from the collective system to the environment quite well. This means that our dynamical simulation shown in Fig. 8 is satisfactory linked with the conventional transport equation, and our schematic model Hamiltonian introduced by Eqs. (64), (66) and (67) is successfully considered as a dynamical *analogue* of the Brownian particle coupled with the classical statistical system. Based on the above analogy and on Eqs. (57) and (82), one may learn the collective degree of freedom is subject to both an average force coming from the mean field Hamiltonian in

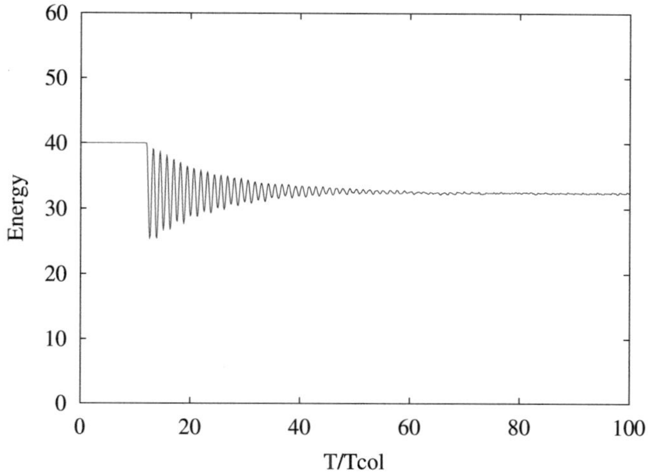

Fig. 12. Time-dependence of average collective energy simulated with Langevin equation (82) with γ=0.0033 and kT=1.45. Parameters used in the mean-field potential is the same as Fig. 8(c).

Eq. (77) and the fluctuation term H_Δ. Namely, the fluctuation H_Δ described by the last three terms on the right hand side of Eq. (57) is responsible for not only the damping of the oscillation amplitude but also for the dissipative energy flow from the collective system to the environment.

At the end of this subsection, it should be noticed that our choice of γ and kT does not satisfy the fluctuation-dissipation theorem. This means that our simulated dissipative phenomenon is not the same as the usual damping phenomena described within the LRT. Since our simulated dissipation phenomenon is induced not by the linear coupling but by the nonlinear coupling, there still remain interesting questions for comprehensively understanding the macroscopic transport phenomena.

3.1.5 Microscopic origin of damping and diffusion mechanism

In the Langevin equation, there are two important forces, the friction force and the random force. The former describes the average effect on the collective degree of freedom causing an irreversible dissipation, while the latter the diffusion of it. According to the parameter values adopted in our Langevin simulation in Fig. 12, it is naturally expected that the dissipative-diffusion mechanism plays a crucial role in reducing the oscillation amplitude of collective energy, and in realizing the steadily energy flow from the collective system to the environment.

In order to explore this point, a time development of the collective distribution function $\rho_\eta(t)$ is shown in Figs. 13 and 14 for two cases with λ=0.005 (small coupling strength) and 0.02 (large coupling strength), respectively. In Figs. 13(a) and 14(a), it is illustrated how a shape of the distribution function $\rho_\eta(t)$ in the collective phase space disperses depending on time. In these figures, an effect of the friction force ought to be observed when a location of the distribution function changes from the outside (higher energy) region to the inside (lower energy) region of the phase space. On the other hand, a dissipative diffusion mechanism is

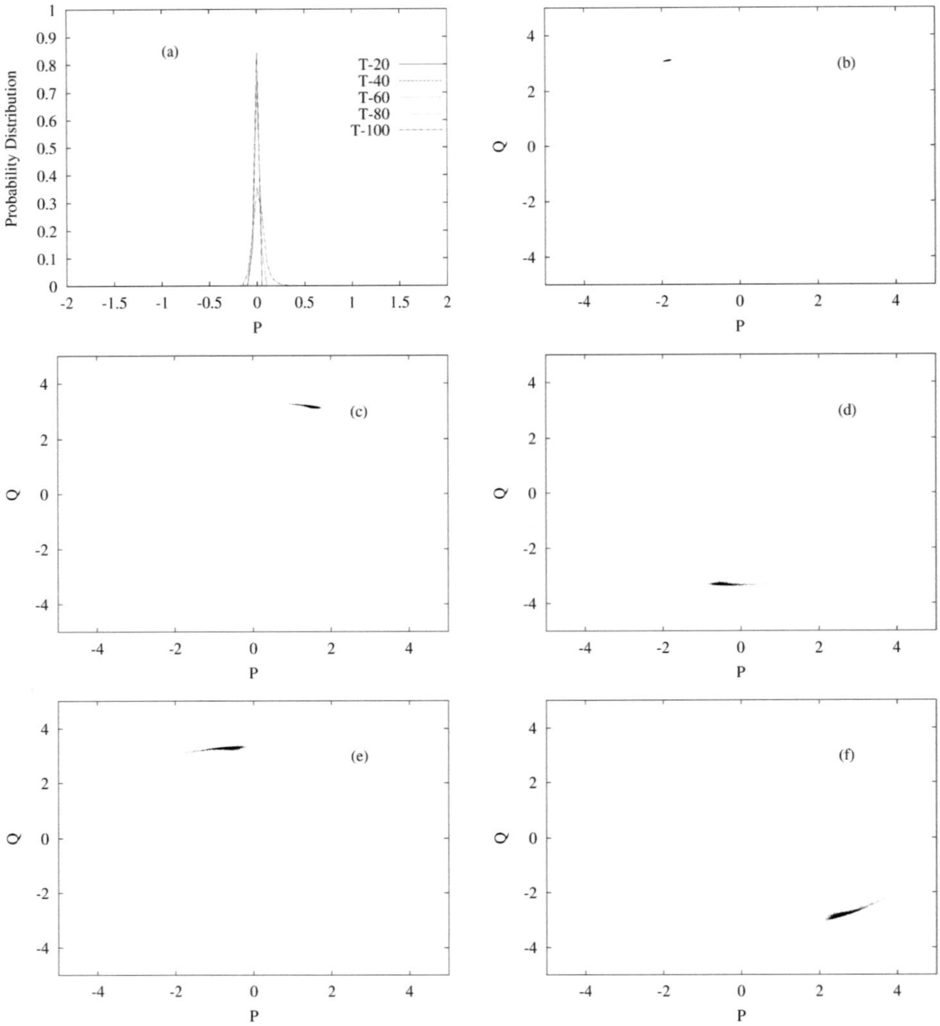

Fig. 13. (a) Probability distribution function of collective trajectories which is defined as $PD_\eta(p') = \int \rho_\eta(t) \Big|_{p=p_m+p'} dq$ and p_m satisfies $\frac{\partial \rho_\eta(t)}{\partial p}\Big|_{p=p_m} = 0$; (b-f) the collective distribution function in (p,q) space at T=20τ_{col}; T=40τ_{col}; T=60τ_{col}; T=80τ_{col}; and T=100τ_{col} for E_η=40, λ=0.005. The parameters are the same as in Fig. 8(c).

studied from Figs. 13(a) and 14(a) by observing how strongly a distribution function initially (at $t = \tau_{sw}$) centered at one point in the collective phase space disperses depending on time. One may see that for the case with λ=0.005, $\rho_\eta(t)$ is slightly enlarged from the initial δ-distribution, but is still concentrated in a rather small region even at $t = 100\tau_{col}$. On the other hand, for the case with λ=0.02, one may see that $\rho_\eta(t)$ quickly disperses after the coupling interaction is switch on and tends to cover a whole ring shape in the phase space at $t = 100\tau_{col}$.

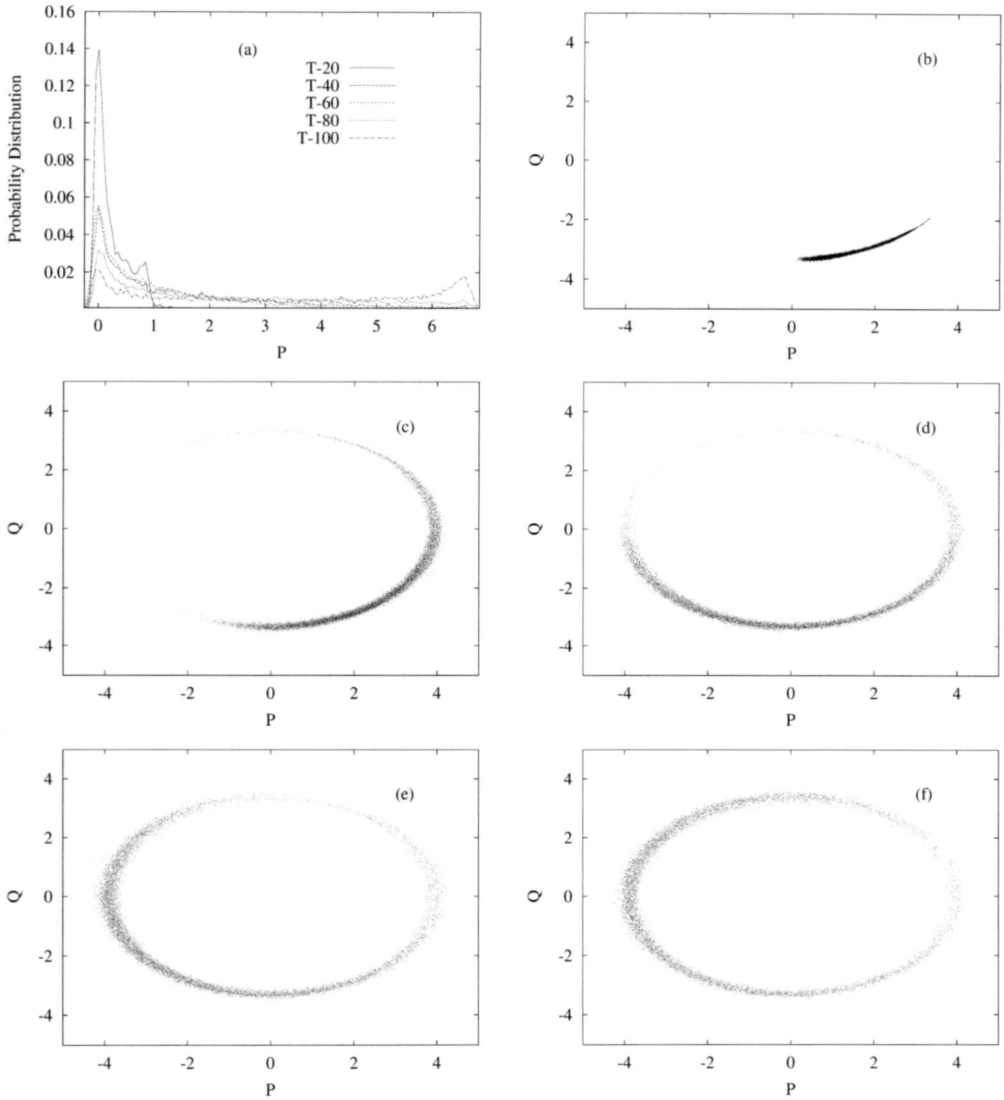

Fig. 14. (a) Probability distribution function of collective trajectories which is defined as $PD_{\eta}(p') = \int \rho_{\eta}(t)\Big|_{p=p_m+p'} dq$ and p_m satisfies $\frac{\partial \rho_{\eta}(t)}{\partial p}\Big|_{p=p_m} = 0$; (b-f) the collective distribution function in (p,q) space at T=$20\tau_{col}$; T=$40\tau_{col}$; T=$60\tau_{col}$; T=$80\tau_{col}$; and T=$100\tau_{col}$ for E_{η}=40, λ=0.02. The parameters are the same as in Fig. 8(c).

Let us discuss a relation between the reduction mechanism in the amplitude of collective energy and the dispersing property of $\rho_{\eta}(t)$. Suppose $\rho_{\eta}(t)$ does not show any strong disperse property by almost keeping its original δ-function shape, in this case, the effects coming from $H_{\Delta}(t)$ is considered to be small. The collective part of each trajectory has a time dependence expressed in Eq. (78) and its collective energy H_{η} has a time dependence given by Eq. (81).

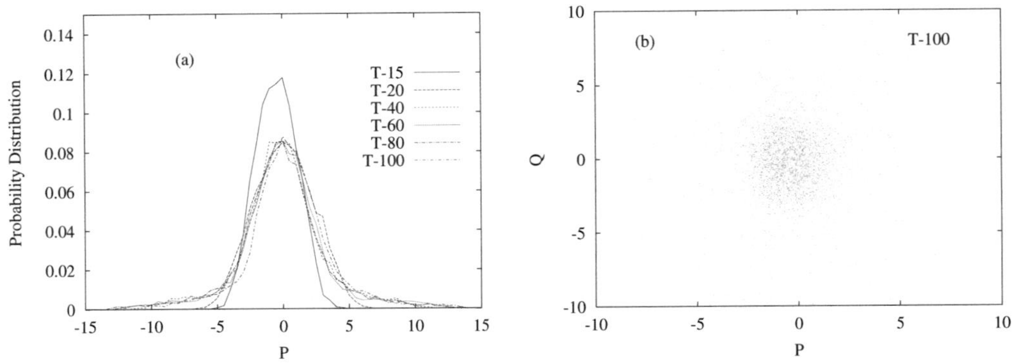

Fig. 15. (a) The probability distribution function of collective trajectories as defined in the caption of Fig. 13(a); (b) collective distribution function in (p,q) space at t=100τ_{col} simulated with Langevin equation (82) with γ=0.0033 and kT=1.45. The parameters used in mean-field potential is the same as Fig. 8(c)

Since there is a well developed *coherence* among the trajectories in $\rho_\eta(t)$ when $\lambda = 0.005$, the averaged collective energy $< H_\eta >$ over the bundle of trajectories still has a time dependence given by Eq. (81). Consequently, one may not expect a reduction of the oscillation amplitude in the collective energy as is shown in Fig. 8(a).

When the distribution function tends to expand over the whole ring shape, the collective part of each trajectory is not expected to have the same time dependence as in Eq. (78). This is due to the effects coming from the stochastic force $H_\Delta(t)$, and some trajectories have a chance to have an advanced phase whereas other trajectories have a retarded phase in comparison with the phase in Eq. (78). According to the *decoherent* effects coming from $H_\Delta(t)$, the time dependence of the collective energy for the each trajectory in Eq. (78) cancels out due to the randomness of the phases when one takes an average over the bundle of trajectories. This dephasing mechanism is induced by $H_\Delta(t)$, and is considered to be the microscopic origin of the damping, i.e. the energy transfer from the collective system to the environment.

In order to compare the above mechanism with what happens in the phenomenological transport equation, the solution of the Langevin equation represented in the collective phase space is shown in Fig. 15 for the cases with γ=0.0033 and kT=1.45. From this figure, one may understand that the damping (a change of the distribution from the outside to the inside of the phase space) as well as the diffusion (an expansion of the distribution) are taking place so as to reproduce the numerical result in Fig. 12. Even though the Langevin equation gives almost the same result as in Fig.8 in the macroscopic-level, as is recognized by comparing Figs. 13 and 14 with Fig. 15, there are substantial differences in the microscopic-level dynamics. Namely, the distribution function $\rho_\eta(t)$ of our simulation evolves into the whole ring shape with staying almost the same initial energy region of the phase space, while the solution of the Langevin equation evolves to a round shape with covering the whole energetically allowed region. In the case of the Langevin simulation, the dissipation and dephasing mechanisms are seemed to contribute to reproduce the result in Fig. 12, while the dephasing mechanism is essential for the damping of the collective energy in our microscopic simulation.

Here, it is worthwhile mentioning that the *decoherence* or *dephasing* process due to the interaction with the environment has also been discussed in the quantum system(13; 73).

3.2 The Case of the system with multi-degree of freedom

As shown in last section, it has been clarified that the main damping mechanism(30) of the collective motion *nonlinearly* coupled with the intrinsic system composed by two degrees of freedom is *dephasing* caused by the chaoticity of intrinsic system. Here, it should be noted that the dephasing process only appears under the nonlinear coupling interaction, specially for the small number of degrees of freedom, as in a case of the quantum dynamical system(13). It was also found that the collective distribution function organized by the Liouville equation and that by the phenomenological Langevin equation show quite different structure in the collective phase space, even though they give almost the same macro-level description for the averaged property of the collective motion.

Now we are facing the questions as how to understand such the difference between two descriptions, and in what condition we can expect the same microscopic situation as the Langevin equation described and when the fluctuation-dissipation theorem comes true. In fact, underlying the conventional approach to the Fokker-Planck- or Langevin-type equation, the intrinsic subsystem is considered with large (or say, *in□nite*) number of degrees of freedom placed in an initial state of canonical equilibrium. So, for understanding the fundamental background of phenomenological transport equation and the basis of dissipation-dissipation relation, there still remain interesting questions for comprehensively understanding the effect, which changes depending on the number of degrees of freedom of intrinsic system.

For this purpose, we will use a Fermi-Pasta-Ulam (FPU) system for describing the intrinsic system, which allows us more conveniently to change the number of degrees of freedom of intrinsic system. It will be shown that dephasing mechanism is the main mechanism for small number degrees of freedom (say, two) case. When the number of degrees of freedom becomes relative large (say, eight or more), the diffusion mechanism will start to play the role and the energy transport process can be divided into three regimes, such as a dephasing regime, a statistical relaxation regime, and an equilibrium regime. By examining the time evolution of entropy with using the nonextensive thermodynamics in Sec. 4, we will find that an existence of three regimes is clearly shown.

Under the help of analytical analysis carried in Sec. 5, we will also show that for the case with relative large number of degrees of freedom, the energy transport process can be described by the generalized Fokker-Planck- and Langevin-type equation, and a phenomenological Fluctuation-Dissipation relation is satisfied. For the finite system, the intrinsic system plays the role as a finite heat bath with finite correlation time and the statistical relaxation is anomalous diffusion. Only for the intrinsic system with very large number of degrees of freedom, the dynamical description and conventional transport approach may provide almost the same macro- and micro-level mechanisms.

3.2.1 β-fermi-pasta-Ulam (FPU) system

The collective subsystem, for simplicity and without any lose of generality, is represented by a harmonic oscillator as the case of the system with three degrees of freedom as Eq. (64). The intrinsic subsystem, mimicking the environment, is described by a β Fermi-Pasta-Ulam (FPU) system (sometime called β-FPU system, as with quadrtic interaction), which was posed in the famous paper (49) and reviewed in (74):

$$H_{\xi} = \sum_{i=1}^{N_d} \frac{p_i^2}{2} + \sum_{i=2}^{N_d} W(q_i - q_{i-1}) + W(q_{N_d}), \tag{84}$$
$$W(q) = \frac{q^4}{4} + \frac{q^2}{2}$$

where

$$q = \frac{1}{\sqrt{2}}(\eta + \eta^*), \quad p = \frac{i}{\sqrt{2}}(\eta^* - \eta), \tag{85a}$$

$$q_i = \frac{1}{\sqrt{2}}(\xi_i + \xi_i^*), \quad p_i = \frac{i}{\sqrt{2}}(\xi_i^* - \xi_i), \quad \{i = 1, \cdots, N_d\} \tag{85b}$$

N_d represents the number of degrees of freedom (i.e., the number of nonlinear oscillators). According to the related literatures(26; 48; 74), the dynamics of β-FPU becomes strongly chaotic and relaxation is fast, when the energy per DOF ϵ is chosen to be larger than a certain value (called as the critical value(48), say $\epsilon_c \approx 0.1$). In the this thesis, ϵ is chosen as 10 to guarantee that our irrelevant subsystem can reach fully chaotic situation. Indeed, in this case, the calculated largest Lyapunov exponent $\sigma(N_d)$ turns out to be positive, for instance $\sigma(N_d)$ =0.15, 0.11, and 0.11 for N_d =2, 4, and 8, respectively. Thus, a "fully developed chaos" is expected for the β-FPU system, and an appearance of statistical behavior in its chain of oscillators and an energy equipartition among the modes are expected to be realized.
For the coupling interaction, we use the following nonlinear interaction given by

$$H_{coupl} = \lambda \left\{ q^2 - q_0^2 \right\} \left\{ q_1^2 - q_{1,0}^2 \right\}. \tag{86}$$

A physical meaning of introducing the quantities q_0 and $q_{1,0}$ in Eq. (86) is discussed in Sec. 3.1.1 and our previous paper(30). Such the choice of the coupling interaction form means that q_1 is considered as a doorway variable, through which the intrinsic subsystem exerts its influence on the collective subsystem(26). It should be pointed out that the form of coupling interaction in Eq. (86) is a little bit different from the one used in our previous paper(30) since here we want to treat the collective and doorway variables in a more parallel way. The numerical comparison between this two forms shows there is no substantial differences between these two forms on the final results.
As discussed in Sec. 3.1.1, the time evolution of the distribution function $\rho(t)$ is evaluated by using the pseudo-particle method as:

$$\rho(t) = \frac{1}{N_p} \sum_{n=1}^{N_p} \prod_{i=1}^{N_d} \delta(q_i - q_{i,n}(t))\delta(p_i - p_{i,n}(t))$$
$$\cdot\delta(q - q_n(t))\delta(p - p_n(t)), \tag{87}$$

where N_p means the total number of pseudo-particles. The distribution function in Eq. (87) defines an ensemble of the system, each member of which is composed of a collective degree of freedom coupled to a single intrinsic trajectory. The collective coordinates $q_n(t)$ and $p_n(t)$, and the intrinsic coordinates $q_{i,n}(t)$ and $p_{i,n}(t)\{i = 1, \cdots, N_d\}$ determine a phase space point of the n-th pseudo-particle at time t, whose time dependence is described by the canonical equations of motion given by

$$\dot{q}_i = \frac{\partial H}{\partial p_i}, \quad \dot{p}_i = -\frac{\partial H}{\partial q_i}, \quad \{i = 1, \cdots, N_d\}$$
$$\dot{q} = \frac{\partial H}{\partial p}, \quad \dot{p} = -\frac{\partial H}{\partial q} \tag{88}$$

We use the fourth order simplectic Runge-Kutta algorithm(75; 76) for integrating the canonical equations of motion and N_p is chosen to be 10,000. In our study, the coupling strength parameter is chosen as $\lambda \sim 0.002$.

3.2.2 Energy dissipation and equipartition

We have discussed a microscopic dynamical system with three degrees of freedom in Sec. 3.1.3, 3.1.4 and 3.1.5, and shown that the dephasing mechanism induced by fluctuation mechanism turned out to be responsible for the energy transfer from collective subsystem to environment(30). In that case, as we shown, the fluctuation-dissipation relation does not hold and there is substantial difference in the microscopic behaviors between the microscopic dynamical simulation based on the Liouville equation and the phenomenological transport equation even if these two descriptions provide almost same macroscopic behaviors. Namely, the collective distribution function organized by the Liouville equation evolves into the whole ring shape with staying almost the same initial energy region of the phase space, while the solution of the Langevin equation evolves to a round shape, whose collective energy is ranging from the initial value to zero.

For answering the questions as how to understand the above stated differences, and in what condition where the microscopic descriptions by the Langevin equation and by the Liouville equation give the same results and in what physical situation where the fluctuation-dissipation theorem comes true, a naturally extension of our work(30) is to considered the effects of the number of degrees of freedom in intrinsic subsystem because no matter how our simulated dissipation phenomenon is obtained by a simplest system which is composed of only three degrees of freedom, as described in Sec. 3.1.

In our numerical calculation, the used parameters are M=1, ω^2=0.2. In this case, the collective time scale τ_{col} characterized by the harmonic oscillator in Eq. (64) and the intrinsic time scale τ_{in} characterized by the harmonic part of the intrinsic Hamiltonian in Eq.(84) satisfies a relation $\tau_{col} \gg \tau_{in}$. The switch-on time τ_{sw} is set to be $\tau_{sw} = 100\tau_{col}$

Figures 16 (a-d) show the time-dependent averaged values of the partial Hamiltonian $\langle H_\eta \rangle$, $\langle H_\xi \rangle$ and $\langle H_{coupl} \rangle$ and the total Hamiltonian $\langle H \rangle$ for the case with $E_\eta = 30$, λ=0.002, N_d=2, 4, 8 and 16, respectively. The definition of ensemble average is the same as Eq. (75).

In order to show how the dissipation of the collective energy changes depending on the number of degrees of freedom in intrinsic subsystem, the time-dependent averaged values of the partial Hamiltonian $\langle H_\eta \rangle$ are also shown in Fig. 17 for the cases with N_d=2, 4, 8 and 16, respectively.

It can be clearly seen that a very similar result has been obtained for the case with N_d=2 as described in our previous paper(30), that is, the main change occurs in the collective energy as well as the interaction energy, and the main process responsible for this change is coming from the dephasing mechanism. One may also learn from our previous paper(30) that the dissipative-diffusion mechanism plays a crucial role in reducing the oscillation amplitude of

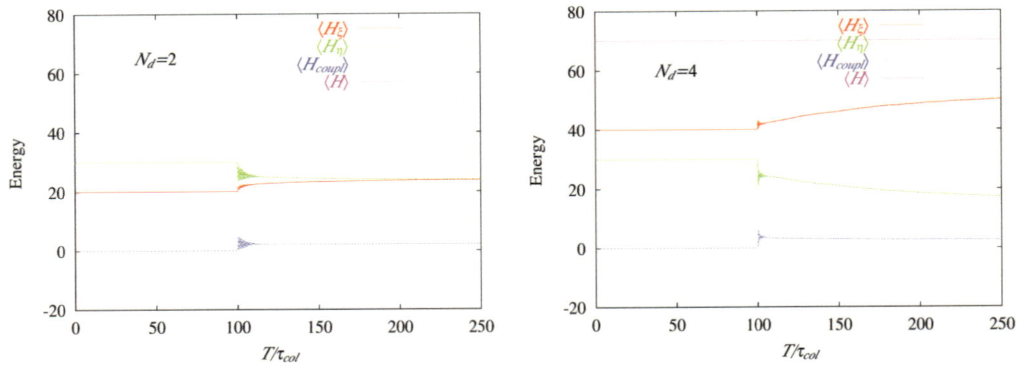

Fig. 16. Time-dependence of the average partial Hamiltonian $\langle H_\eta \rangle$, $\langle H_\xi \rangle$, $\langle H_{coupl} \rangle$ and the total Hamiltonian $\langle H \rangle$ for E_η=30, λ=0.002. (a) N_d=2, (b) N_d=4, (c) N_d=8 and (d) N_d=16.

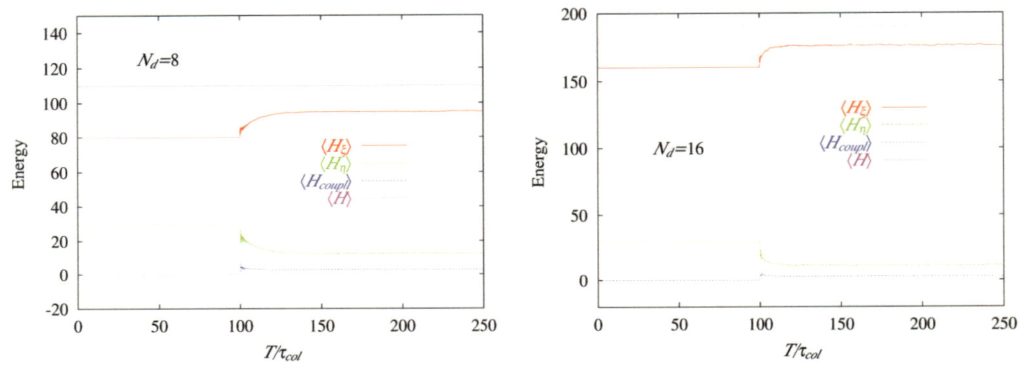

Fig. 16. *continued.*

N_d	2	4	8	16
$\langle H_\xi \rangle$	11.92	12.54	11.851	10.996
$\langle H_\eta \rangle$	24.03	17.15	12.499	11.32

Table 1. An asymptotic average energy for every degree of freedom in the intrinsic system and that for the collective system

collective energy, and in realizing the steadily energy flow from the collective system to the environment.

However, with the increasing of the number of degrees of freedom of intrinsic subsystem, the collective energy, after finishing the dephasing process, gradually decreases and finally reaches to a saturated value. This saturated asymptotic may be understood as a realization of the dynamics balance between an input of energy into the collective subsystem from the fluctuation of nonlinear coupling interaction between the two subsystems and an output of energy due to its dissipation into the environment. It is no doubt that *there appears another mechanism for the N_d larger than 2.*

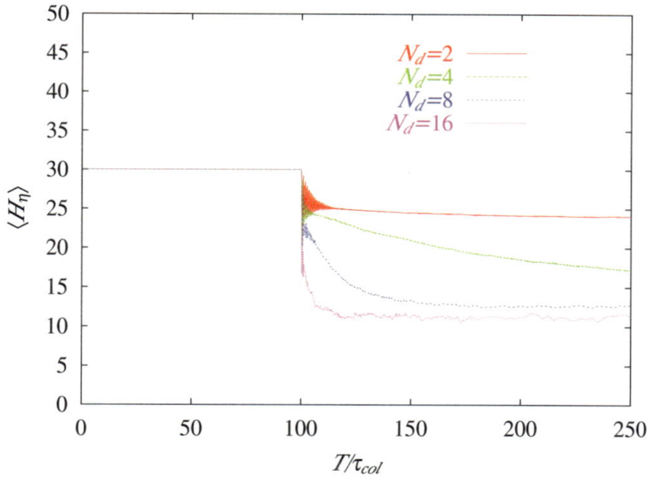

Fig. 17. Time-dependent average value of collective energy $\langle H_{col} \rangle$ for the cases with N_d=2, 4, 8 and 16. Parameters are the same as Fig. 16.

Here we also should noticed the asymptotic average energies for every degrees of freedom in the intrinsic subsystem and that of collective subsystem as shown in Table 1. Considering a boundary effect of the finite system. i.e., the two ends oscillator in β-FPU Hamiltonian, one may see that the equipartition of the energy among every degree of freedom is expected in the final stage for the case with relatively large number of degrees of freedom, as $N_d \geq 8$.

3.2.3 Three regimes of collective dissipation dynamics

One can understand from Figs. 16 and 17 that the energy transfer process of collective subsystem can be divided into three regimes: (1) *Dephasing regime*. In this regime, the fluctuation interaction reduces the coherence of collective trajectories and damps the average amplitude of collective motion. This regime is the main process in the case when system with small number of degrees of freedom (say, two). When the number of degrees of freedom increases, the time scale of this regime will decrease; (2) *Non-equilibrium relaxation regime*, which will also be called as thermodynamical regime in the next section. In this regime, the energy of collective motion irreversibly transfers to the "environment"; (3) *Saturation regime*. This is an asymptotic regime where the total system reaches to another equilibrium situation and the total energy is equally distributed over every degree of freedom realized in the cases with $N_d \geq 8$. We will mention above three regimes again in our further discussion.

From the conventional viewpoint of transport theory, we can see that such the gradually decreasing behaviour of collective energy is due to an irreversible dissipative perturbation, which comes from the interaction with intrinsic subsystem and damps the collective motion. The asymptotic and saturated behaviour reveals that a fluctuation-dissipation relation may be expected for the cases with $N_d \geq 8$. Remembering our previous simulation(30) by using Langevin equation for the case with N_d=2, we can see, in that case, the role of fluctuation interaction mainly contribute to provide the diffusion effect which reduce the coherence of collective trajectories. The irreversible dissipative perturbation (friction force) is relatively small. However, an appearance of the second regime may indicate that the contribution of the dissipative (damping) mechanism will become large with the increasing of N_d. We will show

in the next section that it is the dissipative (damping) mechanism that makes the collective distribution function of the cases with $N_d \geq 8$ evolves to cover the whole energetically allowed region as the solution of the Langevin equation. In this sense, one may expect that the above mentioned numerical simulation provide us with very richer information about the dissipative behaviour of collective subsystem, which changes depending on the number of degrees of freedom in intrinsic subsystem.
According to a general understanding, the non-equilibrium relaxation regime (or called as thermodynamical regime) may also be understood by the Linear Response Theory (24; 26; 27) provided that the number of degrees of freedom is sufficient large. However, as in the study of quantum dynamical system, the dephasing process only can be understood under the scheme with non-linear coupling interaction, specially for the small number of degrees of freedom. From our results, as shown in Fig. 17, it is clarified that the time scale of dephasing process changes to small with the increasing of the number of degrees of freedom. For the case with two degrees of freedom, the dephasing process lasts for a very long time and dominates the time evolution process of the system. When the number of degrees of freedom increases upto sixteen, the time scale is very small and nonequilibrium relaxation process becomes the main process for energy dissipation. So, in our understanding, for the case with small number of degrees of freedom (N_d <8) where the applicability of Linear Response Theory is still a question of debate(61; 77), the dephasing mechanism plays important role for realizing the transport behaviors. When the number of degrees of freedom becomes large (more than sixteen), the thermodynamical mechanism will become a dominant mechanism and there will be no much difference between the Nonlinear and Linear Response Theory.

4. Entropy evolution of nonequilibrium transport process in finite system

It is not a trivial discussion how to understand the three regimes as mentioned in above section in a more dynamical way. As mentioned in Sec. II, the transport, dissipative and damping phenomena could be expressed by the collective behavior of the ensemble of trajectories. In the classical theory of dynamical system, the order-to-chaos transition is usually regarded as the microscopic origin of an appearance of the statistical state in the finite system. Since one may express the heat bath by means of the infinite number of *integrable* systems like the harmonic oscillators whose frequencies have the Debye distribution, it may not be a relevant question whether the chaos plays a decisive role for the dissipation mechanism and for the microscopic generation of the statistical state in a case of the infinite system. In the finite system where the large number limit is not secured, the order-to-chaos transition is expected to play a decisive role in generating some statistical behavior. There should be the relation between the generating the chaotic motion of a single trajectory and the realizing a statistical state for a bundle of trajectories.

4.1 Nonequilibrium relaxation process & entropy production

4.1.1 Physical Boltzmann-Gibbs (BG) entropy

This phenomenon is still represented in the study for clarifying the dynamical relation between the Kolmogorov-Sinai (KS) entropy and the physical entropy for a chaotic conservative dynamical system in classical sense(78), or the status of quantum-classical correspondence for quantum dynamical system(13). The KS entropy is a single number κ, which is related to the average rate of exponential divergence of nearby trajectories, that is, the summation of all the positive Lyapunov exponents of the chaotic dynamical system considered. As for the physical Boltzmann-Gibbs (BG) entropy S(t), the entropy of the second law of thermodynamics, is defined by the distribution function $\rho(t)$ (68) of a bundle of trajectories as:

$$S(t) = -\int \rho(t) \ln \rho(t) d\mathbf{q} d\mathbf{p} \prod_{i=1}^{N_d} dq_i dp_i, \tag{89}$$

which depends not only on the particular dynamical system, but also on the choice of an initial probability distribution for the state of that system, which is described by *a bundle of trajectories*. Therefore the connection between KS entropy and physical (BG) entropy can be considered to given an equivalent relation to that between the chaoticity of a single trajectory and the statistical state for a bundle of trajectories. However, this relation may be not so simple because the KS entropy is the entropy of a single trajectory and in principle, might not coincide with the Gibbs entropy expressed in terms of probability density of a bundle of trajectories.

It has been concluded(78) that the time evolution of S(t) goes through three time regimes: (1) An early regimes where the S(t) is heavily dependent on the details of the dynamical system and of the initial distribution. This regime sometimes is called as the decoherence regime for a Quantum system or dephasing regime for classical system. In this regime, there is no generic relation between S(t) and κ; (2) An intermediate time regime of linear increase with slope κ, i.e., $|\frac{dS(t)}{dt}| \sim \kappa$, which is called the Kolmogorov-Sinai regime or thermodynamical regime. In this regime, a transition from dynamics to thermodynamics is expected to occur; (3) A saturation regime which characterizes equilibrium, for which the distribution is uniform in the available part of phase space. In accordance with the view of Krylov(79), a coarse graining process is required here by the division of space.

4.1.2 Generalized nonextensive entropy & anomalous diffusion

It should be mentioned that the physical (BG) entropy S(t)(89) is unable to deal with a variety of interesting physical problems such as the thermodynamics of self gravitating systems, some anomal diffusion phenomena, Lévy flights and distributions, among others(80–83). In order to deal with these difficulties, a generalized, nonextensive entropy form is introduced(84):

$$S_\alpha(t) = \frac{1 - \int [\rho(t)]^\alpha d\mathbf{q} d\mathbf{p} \prod_{i=1}^{N_d} dq_i dp_i}{\alpha - 1}, \tag{90}$$

where α is called the entropic index, which characterizes the entropy functional $S_\alpha(t)$. When $\alpha = 1$, $S_\alpha(t)$ reduces to the conventional physical (BG) entropy S(t)(89).

How to understand the departure of α from $\alpha = 1$ has been discussed in Refs.(80; 82). From a macroscopic point of view, the diversion of α from $\alpha = 1$ measures how that the dynamics of the system do not fulfil the condition of short-range interaction and correlation that according to the traditional wisdom are necessary to establish thermodynamical properties(80). On the other hand, such diversion can be attributed to the *mixing* (and not only ergodicity) situation in phase space, that is, if the mixing is exponential (strong mixing), the $\alpha = 1$ and physical (BG) entropy S(t) is the adequate hypothesis, whereas the *mixing* is weak and then nonextensive entropy form should be used(82). We will show in the following that $\alpha \neq 1$ implies the non-uniform distribution in the collective phase space.

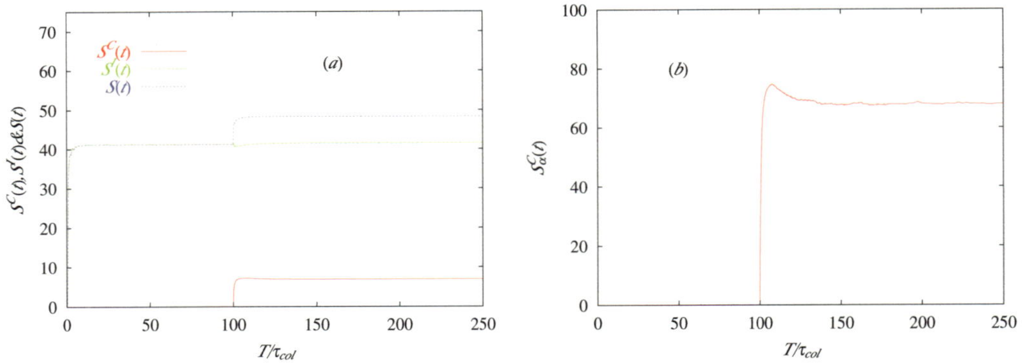

Fig. 18. (a) Physical Boltzmann-Gibbs entropy S(t). Nonextensive entropy $S_\alpha(t)$ for collective (b), intrinsic (c) and total phase space (d), for the case with N_d=8. Entropic index α=0.7. Parameters are the same as Fig. 16.

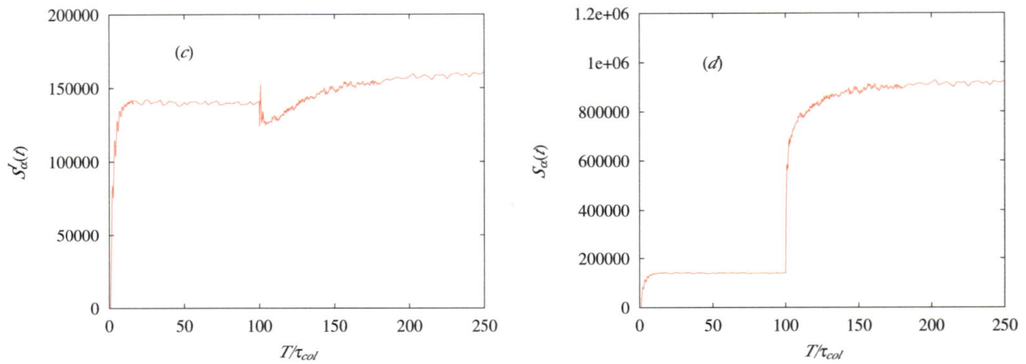

Fig. 18. *continued.*

It should be very interesting that our simulated energy transfer processes show also three regimes as mentioned in Sec. 3.2.3. Consequently, it is an interesting question whether there is some relation between our numerical simulation and the time evolution of S(t) or $S_\alpha(t)$. To understand the underlying connection between these two results, we calculated the entropy evolution process for our system by employing a generalized, nonextensive entropy:

$$S_\alpha^C(t) = \frac{1 - \int [\rho_\eta(t)]^\alpha dq dp}{\alpha - 1}, \tag{91a}$$

$$S_\alpha^I(t) = \frac{1 - \int [\rho_\xi(t)]^\alpha \prod_{i=1}^{N_d} dq_i dp_i}{\alpha - 1} \tag{91b}$$

where $\rho_\eta(t)$ and $\rho_\xi(t)$ are the reduced distribution functions (29) of collective and intrinsic subsystems, respectively. For comparison in the following, we also define the physical (BG) entropy for collective and intrinsic subsystems as:

$$S^C(t) = -\int \rho_\eta(t) \ln \rho_\eta(t) dq dp, \tag{92a}$$

$$S^I(t) = -\int \rho_\xi(t) \ln \rho_\xi(t) \prod_{i=1}^{N_d} dq_i dp_i \tag{92b}$$

Figure 18 shows the comparison between the physical (BG) entropy S(t) in Fig. 18(a) and nonextensive entropy $S_\alpha(t)$ Fig. 18(b-d) for collective, intrinsic subsystems and total system for the case with $N_d = 8$. From this figure, it is understood that there is no entropy produced for collective subsystem before the coupling interaction is activated. However the entropy evaluation process for intrinsic subsystem shows very obviously three regimes both in physical (BG) entropy and in nonextensive entropy. This means that the intrinsic subsystem (β-FPU system) can normally diffuse far from equilibrium state to equilibrium state, where the trajectories are uniformly distributed in the phase space. This conclusion is consistent with Ref. (26). After the coupling interaction is switched on, one can see much different situation when one use the physical (BG) entropy or nonextensive entropy in evaluating the entropy production. For intrinsic subsystem, because its time scale is much smaller than collective one, it should be always in time-independent stationary state even after switch-on time t_{sw}(30). This point can be clearly seen from the present simulation in Fig. 18, where there is no change for $S^I(t)$ around t_{sw}. However, the distribution of trajectories in phase space ought to be changed after t_{sw}(85) which can not be observed by BG entropy. Such the change of the distribution of trajectories in phase space is observed by means of $S^I_\alpha(t)$ as shown in Fig. 18 (c). We will mention this point furthermore in the following context.
With regard to collective subsystem, our calculated results for $S^C(t)$ and for $S^C_\alpha(t)$ have been shown in Fig. 18(a) and (b) . From Fig. 18(a), one may observe that $S^C(t)$ increase exponentially to a maximum value just after t_{sw}. It is not trivial to answer whether or not this maximum value indicates the stationary state for collective degree of freedom because as mentioned in the last section, the energy interchange between collective and intrinsic subsystems is still continuous in this moment. We can understand this point if we examine the nonextensive entropy $S^C_\alpha(t)$ in Fig. 18(b). Fig. 18(b) shows that $S^C_\alpha(t)$ exponentially increases to a maximal value as $S^C(t)$, but then almost linearly decrease and finally tends to a saturated time-independent value. The calculated results of second moment of $\langle q^2 \rangle$ has shown that such the linearly decreasing process is a superdiffusion process. Those calculated results tells that, for $N_d = 8$, the time evolution of $S^C_\alpha(t)$ shows clearly three regimes after t_{sw}, says, exponentially increasing regime, linearly decreasing regime and saturated regime.
For understanding the N_d-dependence of three regimes of transport process, furthermore, we show the comparison of $S^C_\alpha(t)$ for N_d=2, 4, 8 and 16, respectively in Fig. 19 . One may see that the line for the case with N_d=2 only shows the exponentially increasing behaviour. It has been pointed out(30) that, the dephasing mechanism is mainly contributed to the transport process in the case with $N_d = 2$. With this point of view, it is easy to understand that the *exponentially increasing part corresponds to the dephasing regime.* As our understanding, the time scale of dephasing regime mainly depends on the strength of coupling interaction and the chaoticity of intrinsic subsystem, as well as the number of degrees of freedom. In our result, the time scales of dephasing regime for different N_d are different with the selection interaction strength λ and the largest Lyapunov exponents $\sigma(N_d)$ for intrinsic subsystem.

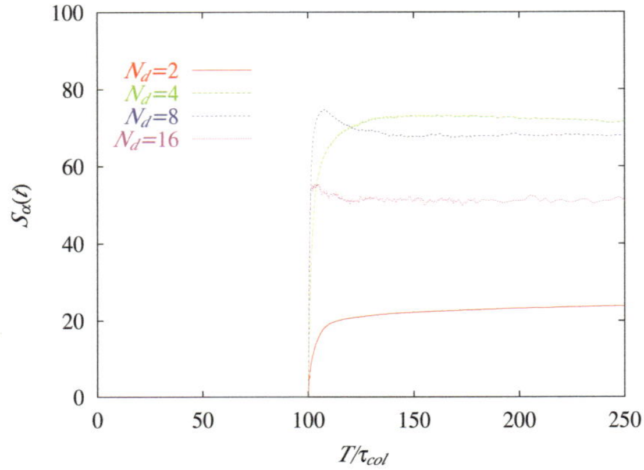

Fig. 19. Comparison of $S_\alpha^C(t)$ for N_d=2, 4, 8 and 16. Parameters are the same as Fig. 18.

With the N_d increasing upto 8, a linearly decreasing process for $S_\alpha^C(t)$ appears after an exponentially increasing stage. As we understand in last subsection, this should be correspondent to the nonequilibrium relaxation process in which the energy of collective motion irreversibly transfers to the "environment".

It is interesting to mention that there also appears three stages in the entropy production for far-from-equilibrium processes, which is also characterized by using the nonextensive entropy(78). Here it should be noted the point that why the second regime is linearly decreasing, not linearly increasing as V. Latora and M. Baranger's findings(78). The systems considered by V. Latora and M. Baranger(78) and others (13; 80; 81) are conservative chaotic systems. As we know, for conservative chaotic systems, the entropy will uniquely increase if it is put in a state far from equilibrium state. Our calculated results is consistent with this phenomenon for the total system, which is a conservative system, as shown in Fig. 3 (d), and for intrinsic subsystem, which also can be treated as a conservative system before t_{sw}, as shown in Fig. 3 (c). Especially, the collective subsystem is a dissipative system after t_{sw}. In the second regime of energy dissipation as described in the last section, the energy of collective motion irreversibly dissipate to intrinsic motion, which should cause the shrink of the distribution of collective trajectories in phase space.

A necessity of using a non-extensive entropy in connecting the microscopic dynamics and the statistical mechanics, and in characterizing the damping phenomenon in the finite system, might suggest us that the damping mechanism in the finite system is an anomalous process, where the usual fluctuation-dissipation theorem is not applicable.

Here it is worthwhile to clarify a relation between an anomalous diffusion and the above mentioned nonextensive entropy expressed by the time evolution of the subsystems with $\alpha < 1$, because the non-equilibrium relaxation regime is characterized not by the physical BG entropy but by the nonextensive entropy with $\alpha < 1$. Generally, the diffusion process is characterized by the average square displacement or its variance as

$$\sigma^2(t) \sim t^\mu, \tag{93}$$

with $\mu = 1$ for normal diffusion. All processes with $\mu \neq 1$ are termed anomalous diffusion, namely, subdiffusion for $0 < \mu < 1$ and superdiffusion for $1 < \mu < 2$.

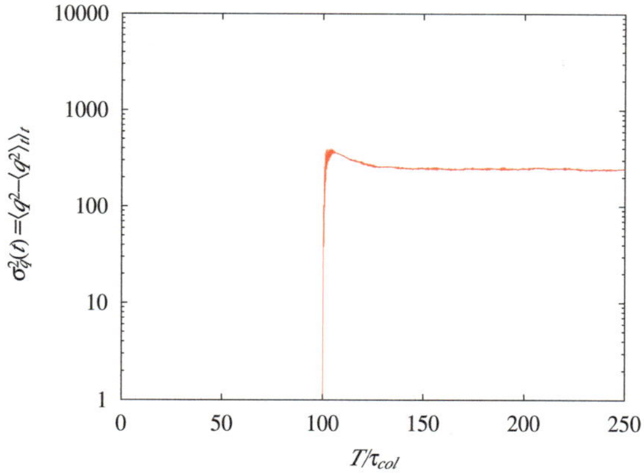

Fig. 20. Time-dependent variance $\sigma_q^2(t)$ for the case with N_d=8. Parameters are the same as Fig. 16

We calculate a time-dependent variance of collective coordinate $\sigma_q^2(t) = \langle q^2 - \langle q^2 \rangle_t \rangle_t$ for the case with N_d=8 as depicted in Fig. 20, which also clearly shows the three stages as discussed above. Here one should mentioned that $\sigma_q^2(t)$ decreasing from a maximal value to a saturation one in the non-equilibrium relaxation regime, rather than increases from a minimal value to a saturation one as in the conventional approach. In the conventional approach, there does not appear dephasing regime. The collective distribution function $\rho_\eta(t)$ spread out from a localized region (say, as δ-distribution) till saturation with an equilibrium Boltzmann distribution. In this case, $\sigma_q^2(t)$ increases from a minimal value (say, zero) to a saturation one corresponding to the Boltzmann distribution. However, in present case for finite system, $\sigma_q^2(t)$ exponentially increases from 0 up to a maximal value in dephasing regime as the behavior of entropy $S_\alpha^C(t)$ in Fig. 18(b) because in this regime, the collective distribution function $\rho_\eta(t)$ quickly disperses after the coupling interaction is switched on and tends to cover a ring shape in the phase space. In the second regime of energy dissipation, the collective energy irreversibly dissipates into the intrinsic system with making the distribution of collective trajectories in phase space shrunk until saturation with an equilibrium Boltzmann distribution. It is due to the finite effect that $\sigma_q^2(t)$ becomes much bigger than its saturation value in the dephasing regime. Therefore, in the second regime, $\sigma_q^2(t)$ will decreases from this maximal value to a saturation one with shrinking of distribution function of collective trajectories in phase space.

As discussed in Sec. 3.2.3, dephasing regime is the main process for a system with small number of intrinsic degrees of freedom (say, two). A lasting time of this regime decreases with increasing of the number of intrinsic degrees of freedom. When the number of intrinsic degrees of freedom becomes infinite, there might be no dephasing regime. In this case, $\sigma_q^2(t)$ will show the same behavior as in the conventional approach.

The result of $\sigma_q^2(t)$ in non-equilibrium relaxation regime can be characterized with the expression

$$\sigma_q^2(t) = \sigma_q^2(t_0) - D(t - t_0)^{\mu_q}, \tag{94}$$

where $t_0 = 110\tau_{col}$ is a moment when the dephasing regime has finished, $\sigma_q^2(t_0) = 335.0$ the value of $\sigma_q^2(t)$ at time t_0. We fit the diffusion coefficient D and diffusion exponent μ_q in Eq.

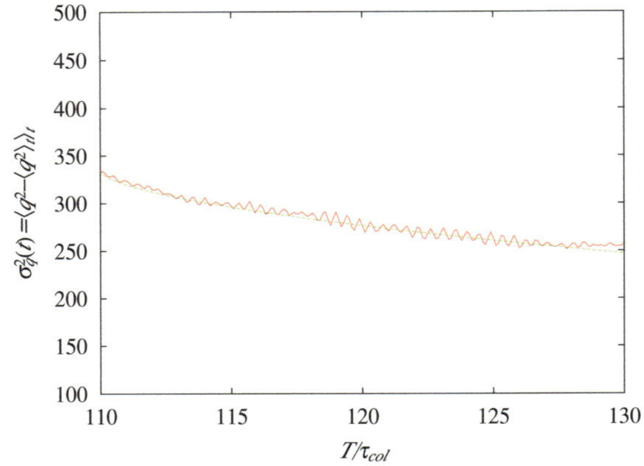

Fig. 21. Time-dependent variance $\sigma_q^2(t)$ for the case with N_d=8. Solid line refers to the result of dynamical simulation as shown in Fig. 20; long dashed line refers to the fitting results of Eq. (94) with parameters $D = 15.5, \mu_q = 0.58$.

(94) for the non-equilibrium relaxation regime as plotted in Fig 21. The resultant values are D=15.5 and $\mu_q = 0.58$, which suggest us that the non-equilibrium relaxation process of a finite system correspond to an *anomalous* diffusion process.

4.2 Microscopic dynamics of nonequilibrium process & Boltzmann distribution

In order to explore this understanding more deeply, a time development of the collective distribution function $\rho_\eta(t)$ in collective (p,q) space and probability distribution function of collective trajectories which is defined as

$$\mathrm{P}_\eta(\epsilon) = \int \rho_\eta(t) \Big|_{H_\eta(q,p)=\epsilon} dqdp \tag{95}$$

are shown in Figs. 22 and 23 at different time for $N_d = 8$. In these figures, it is illustrated how a shape of the distribution function $\rho_\eta(t)$ in the collective phase space disperses depending on time. An effect of the damping mechanism ought to be observed when a peak location of the distribution function changes from the outside (higher collective energy) region to the inside (lower collective energy) region of the phase space. On the other hand, a dissipative diffusion mechanism is studied by observing how strongly a distribution function initially (at $t = \tau_{sw}$) centered at one point in the collective phase space disperses depending on time.

One may see that from T=t_{sw} to $110\tau_{col}$, $\rho_\eta(t)$ quickly disperses after the coupling interaction is switched on and tends to cover a ring shape in the phase space. When the distribution function tends to expand over the whole ring shape, the relevant part of each trajectory is not expected to have the same time dependence. Some trajectories have a chance to have an advanced phase, whereas other trajectories have a retarded phase in comparison with the averaged motion under mean-field approximation. This dephasing mechanism is considered to be the microscopic origin of the entropy production in the exponential regime.

The more interesting things appear from T=$110\tau_{col}$ through T=$140\tau_{col}$. One may see that the distribution function gradually expand to center region from T=$110\tau_{col}$. The region of maximal probability distribution gradually moves to center, meanwhile the density of

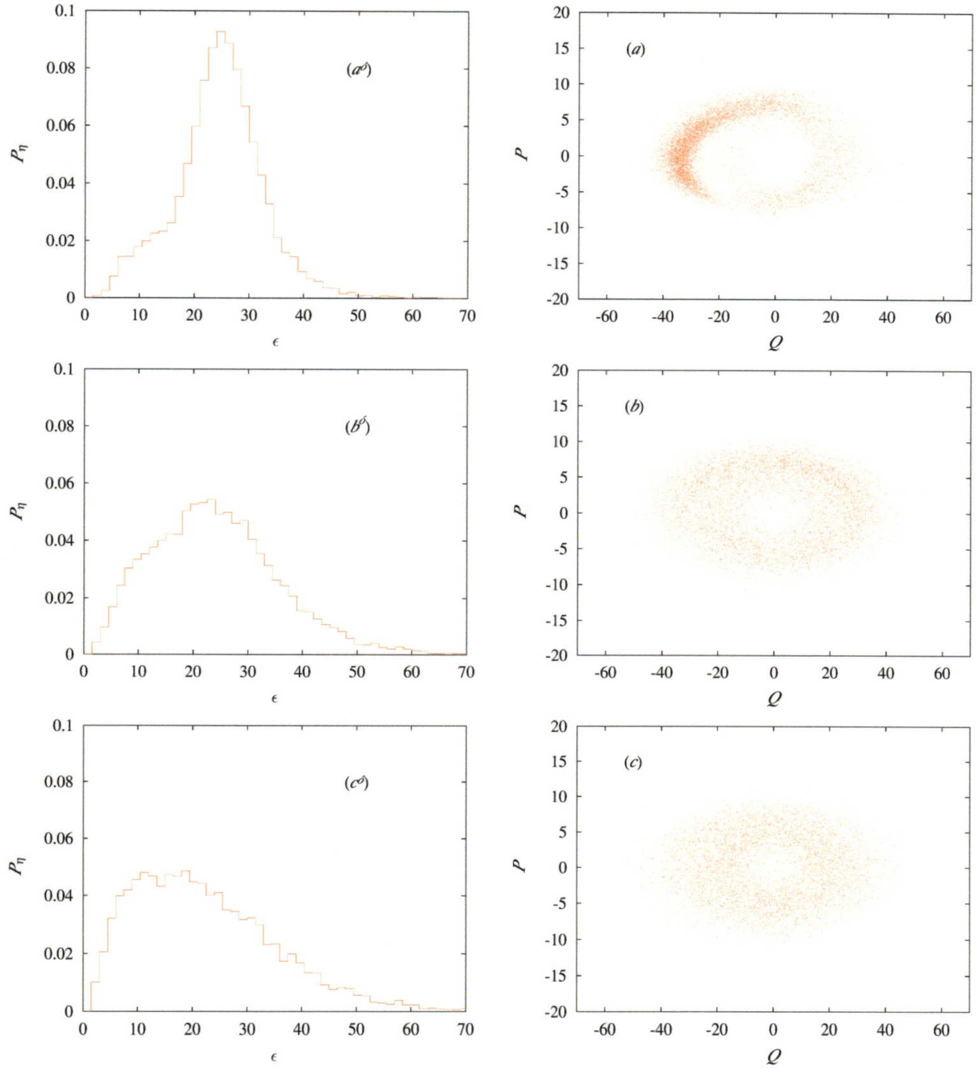

Fig. 22. (a-c) Collective distribution function in (p,q) phase space; ($a^{\dagger}$-$c^{\dagger}$) Probability distribution function $P_{\eta}(\epsilon)$ of collective trajectories at T=102.5τ_{col}, 110τ_{col} and 120τ_{col} for E_{η}=30 and λ=0.002.

distribution in the out ring (as at T=110τ_{col}) goes to low. And finally at T=160τ_{col}, one can see the distribution tend to the equilibrium Boltzmann distribution as:

$$P_{\eta}(\epsilon) \sim e^{-\beta\epsilon} \tag{96}$$

After T=160τ_{col} to 240τ_{col}, the distribution function does not practically changed anymore, which is correspondent to the saturated regime. Comparison the distribution in Fig. 23 (f) with the one obtained by the phenomenological transport equation (as Langevin equation) in Fig. 15(b) and in our previous paper(30), one can see that such the distribution is consistent

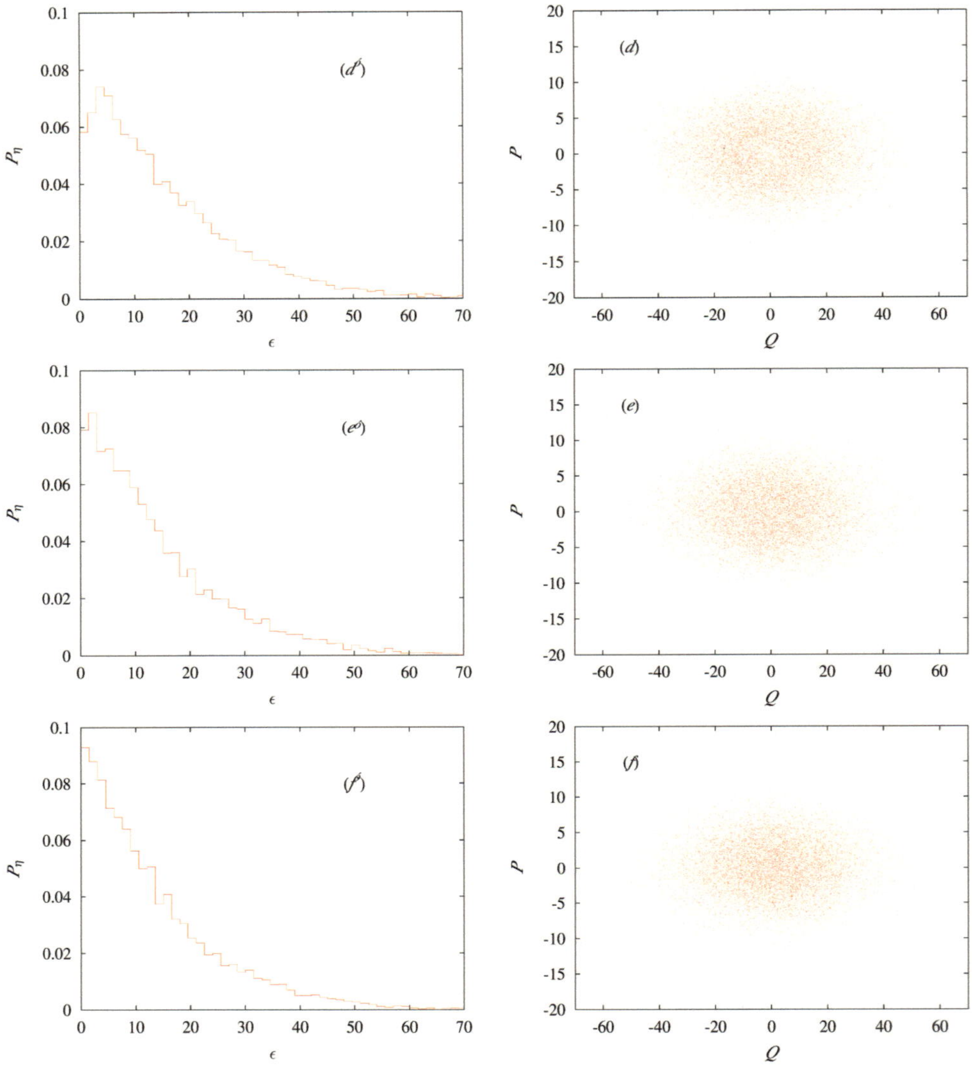

Fig. 23. (d-f) Collective distribution function in (p,q) phase space; (d†-f†) Probability distribution function $P_\eta(\epsilon)$ of collective trajectories at T=140τ_{col}, 160τ_{col}, and 240τ_{col} for E_η=30 and λ=0.002.

with the results simulated by Langevin equation. So one can see that *a transition from dynamics to thermodynamics occurs indeed and the collective subsystem finally reaches to equilibrium state.*
At the end of this section, one may conclude that: (i) When the physical BG entropy is used to evaluate the entropy production for the system considered in this work, the three characteristic regimes can not be detected in the collective system. When the non-extensive entropy is used with $\alpha < 1.0$, the three dynamical stages, i.e., the dephasing regime, non-equilibrium relaxation regime and equilibrium regime, appear for a relatively large number of intrinsic degrees of freedom as $N_d \geq 8$. The second regime may disappear for a small number of degrees of freedom case like $N_d = 2$. (ii) Since the collective system is a

dissipative system whose distribution function varies non-uniformly in the non-equilibrium relaxation regime, one has to use the entropy index x different from 1 . (iii) As is shown by the $\sigma_q^2(t)$ and by $\alpha < 1$, the non-equilibrium relaxation process of a finite system considered in this thesis corresponds to the anomalous diffusion process. (iv) The final regime is consistent with the simulation obtained by the phenomenological transport equation. Namely, the statistical state is actually realized dynamically in a finite system which is composed by the collective and intrinsic systems coupled with the nonlinear interaction.

5. A generalized fluctuation-dissipation relation of collective motion

5.1 Derivation of a generalized Fokker-Planck equation

Now we are at the position to analytically understand why and how the second regime, i.e., thermodynamical regime, appears when the number of degrees of freedom of intrinsic subsystem increases from $N_d = 2$ to larger one, as $N_d = 8$. In principle, we can start from the coupled master equation (43), which includes the full information about the time evolution of the two subsystems. However, the coupled master equation (43) is still equivalent to the original Liouville equation (28) and is, in fact, not yet tractable specially for a system far from the stationary states(30).

As was discussed in above sections, when we mainly focus our discussion on the second regime, the intrinsic degrees of freedom can be considered to be in fully developed chaotic situation. In this case, it is reasonable to assume that the effects on the collective system coming from the intrinsic one are mainly expressed by an averaged effect over the intrinsic distribution function (*Assumption*). Namely, the effects due to the fluctuation part $H_\Delta(t)$ are assumed to be much smaller than those coming from $H_\eta + H_\eta(t)$ and are able to be treated as a stochastic perturbation around the path generated by the mean-field Hamiltonian $H_\eta + H_\eta(t)$[2]. In Sec. 3.1.4, a phenomenological transport equation (82) was used in reproducing our simulated results phenomenologically.

$$M\ddot{q} + \frac{\partial U^{mf}(q)}{\partial q} + \gamma\dot{q} = f(t), \quad q = \frac{\eta + \eta^*}{\sqrt{2}}, \tag{97}$$

was used in reproducing our simulated results phenomenologically. Here $U^{mf}(q)$ denotes the potential part of $H_\eta + H_\eta(t)$, γ the friction parameter and $f(t)$ the Gaussian white noise with an appropriate temperature. Since our present main concern is to make clear a relation between the macro-level dynamics organized by the phenomenological equation like Eq. (97) (or like Fokker-Planck equation (118) or the macro-level equation (123) discussed in the following) and the micro-level dynamics by the coupled master equation (43) one step further, we start with the Hamiltonian of collective degree of freedom, which organizes the collective distribution function $\rho_\eta(t)$, formally written as:

$$H_\eta^T = H_\eta + H_\eta(t) + \lambda H_{\Delta,\eta}(t) \tag{98}$$

where H_η and $H_\eta(t)$ are defined in Eq. (64) and Eq. (33), respectively. The main differences between Eq. (97) and Eq. (98) are i) γ and $f(t)$ in Eq. (97) are given by hand, ii) $\rho_\xi(t)$ specifying the fluctuation effects $H_{\Delta,\eta}(t)$ in Eq.(98) is determined microscopically by Eq. (43). What we are going to discuss in the following, with the aid of Eq. (98), is to understand a change of

[2] Hereafter, 'mean-field' is used to express an average effect over the intrinsic distribution function $\rho_\xi(t)$.

phenomenological parameters in Eqs. (97), (118) or (123) in terms of the fluctuation associated with the microscopic dynamics $\rho_\xi(t)$ determined by Eq. (43).
In terms of Eqs. (85) and (86), the coupling interaction can generally expressed as

$$H_{coupl}(\eta,\xi) = \lambda \sum_l A^l(\eta) B^l(\xi). \tag{99}$$

For simplicity, we hereafter discard the summation l in the coupling. The fluctuation Hamiltonian $H_{\Delta,\eta}(t)$ in Eq. (98) then reads

$$H_{\Delta,\eta}(t) = \phi'(t) A(\eta) \qquad \phi'(t) = B(\xi) - \langle B(\xi) \rangle^3. \tag{100}$$

With the aid of the partial Hamiltonian (98), the distribution function of collective subsystem $\rho_\eta(t)$ determined by Eq. (43) then may be explored by using the Liouville equation given by:

$$\begin{aligned} \dot{\rho}_\eta(t) &= -i\mathcal{L}_\eta^T \rho_\eta(t) \\ &= -i\Big(\mathcal{L}_\eta + \mathcal{L}_\eta(t) + \lambda \mathcal{L}_{\Delta,\eta}(t)\Big)\rho_\eta(t) \end{aligned} \tag{101}$$

where $\mathcal{L}_\eta^T$ and $\mathcal{L}_{\Delta,\eta}(t)$ are defined as in Eq. (34).

$$\mathcal{L}_\eta^T * \equiv i\{H_\eta^T, *\}_{PB}, \tag{102a}$$

$$\mathcal{L}_{\Delta,\eta}(t) * \equiv i\{H_{\Delta,\eta}(t), *\}_{PB} \tag{102b}$$

Here $\{,\}_{PB}$ denotes a Poisson bracket with respect to the collective variables.
Since, in this section, we are interested in understanding the microscopic dynamics which is responsible for the appearance of the second regime, we can start our discussion from a situation where the dephasing processes have finished, which means that the collective subsystem has reached the situation where the distribution function has the space-reversal symmetry as shown in Figs. 22 and 22 for $t > 100\tau_{col}$. Considering that the time scale of dephasing process is much smaller than that of thermodynamical process, the correlation between dephasing and thermodynamical process might be omissible. In this case, the Liouvillian equation (101) can be considered to describe the evolution of distribution function $\rho_\eta(t)$ only caused by dissipative mechanism.
Although $H_{\Delta,\eta}(t)$ contains the intrinsic variables, in the present formulation, the fluctuation $H_{\Delta,\eta}(t)$ should be considered to be a time dependent stochastic force expressed as $\phi'(t)$ in Eq. (100), and a stochastic average is obtained by taking the integration over the intrinsic variables with a weight function $\rho_\xi(t)$. Here it should be noticed that the Liouville equation (101) is an approximation to Eq. (43). Since our present aim is to explore how the effects on the collective system coming from the intrinsic fluctuation $\phi'(t)$ change depending on the number of intrinsic degrees of freedom as simple as possible, we start with Eq. (101) rather than Eq. (43). Namely, the collective fluctuation effects originated from $A(\eta) - Tr_\eta A(\eta)\rho_\eta$ on the intrinsic system ought to be disregarded, because we are now studying the average dynamics of collective motion.

[3] Except specific definition, thereafter, the average is obtained by taking the integration over the intrinsic variables with a weight function $\rho_\xi(t)$ at time t, say $< * >= Tr_\xi * \rho_\xi(t)$.

It should be emphasized that we formally express the partial Hamiltonian and Liouville equation of collective degree of freedom as Eqs. (98) and (101). However, in order to closely relate our analysis carried out in this section with our numerical simulation as shown in last two section, the Liouville equation (101) will not be used to determine $\rho_\eta(t)$, but be used only to understand what happens in the collective distribution function $\rho_\eta(t)$, which is numerically obtained by integrating the canonical equations of motion (69) with the Hamiltonian in Eq. (25).

Let us start our discussion just after the dephasing process has finished. Eq. (101) may now be a linear stochastic equation with fluctuation term $\mathcal{L}_{\Delta,\eta}(t)$. When the fluctuation part is regarded as a perturbation, one may introduce the *mean-field* propagator

$$G_\eta(t,t') = Texp\left\{-i\int_{t'}^{t}\left[\mathcal{L}_\eta + \mathcal{L}_\eta(\tau)\right]d\tau\right\} \tag{103}$$

which describes an average time-evolution of the collective system.

Under the help of the *mean-field* propagator $G_\eta(t,t')$ and taking the stochastic average over $\rho_\xi(t)$, one may obtain the master equation for $\rho_\eta(t)$ from Eq. (101), as

$$\begin{aligned}\dot{\rho_\eta}(t) = &-i\left\{\mathcal{L}_\eta + \mathcal{L}_\eta(t)\right\}\rho_\eta(t)\\ &-\lambda^2\int_0^\infty d\tau\langle\langle\mathcal{L}_{\Delta,\eta}(t)G_\eta(t,t-\tau)\mathcal{L}_{\Delta,\eta}(t-\tau)\rangle\rangle G_\eta(t-\tau,t)\rho_\eta(t)\end{aligned} \tag{104}$$

where a symbol $\ll\cdots\gg$ denotes a cumulant defined as:

$$\ll \mathcal{AB} \gg \equiv < \mathcal{AB} > - < \mathcal{A} >< \mathcal{B} > \tag{105}$$

which relates to the average $< * >_t = Tr_\xi * \rho_\xi(t)$. A derivation of Eq. (104) is given in Appendix 10.

In getting Eq. (104) from Eq. (142), we have supposed[4] that the collective distribution function $\rho_\eta(t)$ evolves through the mean-field Hamiltonian $H_\eta + H_\eta(t)$ from $t-\tau$ to t. This is because the fluctuation effects are so small as to be treated as a perturbation around the path generated by the mean-field Hamiltonian $H_\eta + H_\eta(t)$, and are sufficient to be retained in Eq. (104) up to the second order in λ. Under the assumption of a weak coupling interaction and of a finite correlation time τ_c

$$\langle\langle\phi'(t)\phi'(t')\rangle\rangle = 0 \qquad \text{for} \quad |t-t'| > \tau_c$$

an upper limit in the time integration in Eq. (104) may be extended to ∞.

Eq. (104) is valid upto the second-order cumulant expansion. Here

$$\langle\langle\phi'(t)\phi'(t')\rangle\rangle = \langle\phi'(t)\phi'(t')\rangle - \langle\phi'(t)\rangle\langle\phi'(t')\rangle$$

The *mean-field* propagator operator $G_\eta(t,t-\tau)$ provides the solution of unperturbed equation. That is, there holds a relation

$$f(\eta,t) = G_\eta(t,t-\tau)f(\eta,t-\tau), \tag{106}$$

[4] as **Condition I** in Sect. 2.3.

provided $f(\eta,t)$ satisfies a relation

$$\frac{\partial f(\eta,t)}{\partial t} = -i\Big(\mathcal{L}_\eta + \mathcal{L}_\eta(t)\Big) f(\eta,t) \tag{107}$$

Since the Liouville equation (107) is equivalent to the canonical equation of motion given by

$$i\dot{\eta}_a = \frac{\partial\Big(H_\eta + H_\eta(t)\Big)}{\partial \eta_a^*}, \tag{108a}$$

$$i\dot{\eta}_a^* = -\frac{\partial\Big(H_\eta + H_\eta(t)\Big)}{\partial \eta_a} \tag{108b}$$

there holds a relation

$$f(\eta,t) = f(\eta^{t-\tau}, t-\tau)\left|\frac{d\eta^{t-\tau}}{d\eta}\right| = G_\eta(t,t-\tau) f(\eta,t-\tau) \tag{109}$$

$\left|d\eta^{t-\tau}/d\eta\right|$ being a Jacobian determinant.
Using the above relation, Eq. (104) can be simplified as

$$\begin{aligned} \dot{\rho_\eta}(t) = & -i\left\{\mathcal{L}_\eta + \mathcal{L}_\eta(t)\right\}\rho_\eta(t) \\ & -\lambda^2 \int_0^\infty d\tau \left|\frac{d\eta^{t-\tau}}{d\eta}\right| \langle\langle \mathcal{L}_{\Delta,\eta}(t)\mathcal{L}_{\Delta,\eta}^{-\tau}(t-\tau)\rangle\rangle \left|\frac{d\eta}{d\eta^{t-\tau}}\right| \rho_\eta(t) \end{aligned} \tag{110}$$

where

$$\mathcal{L}_{\Delta,\eta}(t)* \equiv i\phi'(t)\left\{A(\eta), *\right\}, \tag{111}$$

$$\mathcal{L}_{\Delta,\eta}^{-\tau}(t-\tau)* \equiv i\phi'(t-\tau)\left\{A(\eta^{t-\tau}), *\right\}. \tag{112}$$

With Hamiltonians H_η and $H_\eta(t)$ as defined in Eq. (64) and (33), one may easily get an analytical form of mapping $\eta \to \eta^\tau$ by solving the unperturbed equation (108)

$$q(\tau) = q\cos\omega'\tau + \frac{p}{M\omega'}\sin\omega'\tau \tag{113a}$$

$$p(\tau) = -qM\omega'\sin\omega'\tau + p\cos\omega'\tau \tag{113b}$$

where we have used the relation (85) and the relation defined by

$$\omega'^2 = \omega^2 + \frac{2\lambda\langle\left\{q_1^2 - q_{1,0}^2\right\}\rangle}{M}$$

The Jacobian determinant of this mapping reads

$$\left|\frac{d\eta^{-\tau}}{d\eta}\right| = \left|\frac{d\eta}{d\eta^{-\tau}}\right| = 1 \tag{114}$$

because ω' does not practically depend on time. In terms of the coupling interaction (86), the fluctuation Hamiltonian $H_{\Delta,\eta}(t)$ in Eq. (100) can be explicitly written as

$$H_{\Delta}^{\eta}(t) = \phi'(t)\left\{q^2 - q_0^2\right\}, \tag{115a}$$

$$\phi'(t) = \left\{q_1^2 - q_{1,0}^2\right\} - \langle\left\{q_1^2 - q_{1,0}^2\right\}\rangle. \tag{115b}$$

With the help of Eq. (115), the culmulant in Eq. (110) can therefore be expressed

$$\langle\langle \mathcal{L}_{\Delta,\eta}(t)\mathcal{L}_{\Delta,\eta}^{-\tau}(t-\tau)\rangle\rangle = -\langle\langle \phi(t)\phi(t-\tau)\rangle\rangle q\frac{\partial}{\partial p}q(t-\tau)\frac{\partial}{\partial p(t-\tau)} \tag{116}$$

where $\phi(t) = 2\phi'(t)$. Considering $(\eta^{-\tau})^{\tau} = \eta$ and using Eqs. (113), one gets

$$\begin{aligned} q(t-\tau)\frac{\partial}{\partial p(t-\tau)} &= \left(q\frac{\sin\omega'\tau\cos\omega'\tau}{M\omega'} - p\frac{\sin^2\omega'\tau}{M^2\omega'^2}\right)\frac{\partial}{\partial q} \\ &+ \left(q\cos^2\omega'\tau - p\frac{\sin\omega'\tau\cos\omega'\tau}{M\omega'}\right)\frac{\partial}{\partial p} \end{aligned} \tag{117}$$

Finally, Eq. (110) can be explicitly written as:

$$\frac{\partial\rho_\eta(t)}{\partial t} = \left\{\mathcal{L}_{eff} + \lambda^2\left(\beta_1 q\frac{\partial}{\partial p}\left(q\frac{\partial}{\partial q} - p\frac{\partial}{\partial p}\right) + \beta_2 q^2\frac{\partial}{\partial p^2} - \beta_3 q\frac{\partial}{\partial p}p\frac{\partial}{\partial q}\right)\right\}\rho_\eta(t) \tag{118}$$

where

$$\mathcal{L}_{eff} = -\frac{p}{M}\frac{\partial}{\partial q} + M\omega'^2 q\frac{\partial}{\partial p}$$

is an effective unperturbed (mean-field) Liouvillian of the collective system. The parameters β_1, β_2 and β_3 are expressed as the Fourier transformations of the correlation functions of intrinsic system:

$$\beta_1 = \frac{1}{M\omega'}\int_0^\infty d\tau\langle\langle\phi(t)\phi(t-\tau)\rangle\rangle\cos\omega'\tau\sin\omega'\tau \tag{119a}$$

$$\beta_2 = \int_0^\infty d\tau\langle\langle\phi(t)\phi(t-\tau)\rangle\rangle\cos^2\omega'\tau \tag{119b}$$

$$\beta_3 = \frac{1}{M^2\omega'^2}\int_0^\infty d\tau\langle\langle\phi(t)\phi(t-\tau)\rangle\rangle\sin^2\omega'\tau \tag{119c}$$

Eq. (118) is the two-dimensional Fokker-Planck equation. The first term on the right-hand side of Eq. (118) represents the contribution from the mean-field part $H_\eta + H_\eta(t)$, and the last three terms represent contributions from the dynamical fluctuation effects $H_{\Delta,\eta}$. The parameters β_1, β_2 and β_3 establish the connection between the macro-level dynamical evolution of collective system and the micro-level fluctuation of intrinsic one.

5.2 Fluctuation-dissipation relation & correlation functions

With the same definition of ensemble average[5] as Eq. (75), one can find the identity

$$\frac{d\langle X\rangle}{dt} = \int X \frac{d\rho_\eta(t)}{dt} dq dp \tag{120}$$

which is valid for any collective variable which does not explicitly depend on time. When one inserts the equation (118) into (120), and evaluates the individual term by observing the standard rule:

$$\int A\{B,C\}_{PB} dqdp = \int \{A,B\}_{PB} C dqdp \tag{121}$$

one can obtain the equation of first moment:

$$\begin{aligned} \frac{d\langle q\rangle}{dt} &= \frac{\langle p\rangle}{M} \\ \frac{d\langle p\rangle}{dt} &= -\frac{\lambda\beta_3}{M}\langle p\rangle - \left[M\omega'^2 - \lambda^2\frac{\beta_1}{M}\right]\langle q\rangle \end{aligned} \tag{122}$$

or in a compact way as

$$M\langle\ddot{q}\rangle + \Gamma\langle\dot{q}\rangle + \left[M\omega'^2 - \lambda^2\frac{\beta_1}{M}\right]\langle q\rangle = 0 \tag{123}$$

$$\Gamma = \frac{\lambda\beta_3}{M} = \frac{\lambda}{M^3\omega'^2}\int_0^\infty d\tau\langle\langle\phi(t)\phi(t-\tau)\rangle\rangle \sin^2\omega'\tau \tag{124}$$

Here the parameter Γ (or β_3) represents the damping effects on collective dynamical motion coming from the fluctuation interaction, which originates from the chaoticity of intrinsic subsystem. Eq. (124) can be regarded as a *phenomenological Fluctuation-Dissipation relation* and the damping phenomenon (described by β_3 or Γ) implies that the energy is irreversibly dissipated from collective subsystem and absorbed by intrinsic one.

Applying the similar procedures for obtaining Eq. (123), one may derive an equation of motion for the second moments

$$\frac{d}{dt}\begin{bmatrix}\langle qq\rangle \\ \langle pp\rangle \\ \langle qp\rangle\end{bmatrix} = \begin{bmatrix} 0 & 0 & \frac{2}{M} \\ 4\lambda^2M^2\omega'^2\beta_3 + 2\lambda^2\beta_2 & -4\lambda^2\beta_3 & -2M\omega'^2 - 2\lambda\beta_0 \\ -M^2\omega'^2 - \lambda\beta_0 + 2\lambda^2\beta_1 & \frac{1}{M} & -4\lambda^2\beta_3 \end{bmatrix}\begin{bmatrix}\langle qq\rangle \\ \langle pp\rangle \\ \langle qp\rangle\end{bmatrix} \tag{125}$$

A real eigenvalue of the matrix in above equation indicates an instability of collective trajectory which is caused by the chaoticity of intrinsic trajectory through fluctuation Hamiltonian $H_{\Delta,\eta}$(48).

Equations (118), (123) and (125) have set up an phenomenological relation among the micro-level properties of the intrinsic subsystem and the macro-level time evolution of collective subsystem through microscopic correlation functions.

Employing the numerical simulation results for Eq. (69), we calculate the correlation function $\langle\langle\phi(t)\phi(t-\tau)\rangle\rangle$ at $t = 120\tau_{col}$ for the case with $N_d = 2, 4$ and 8 as shown in Fig. 24. Generally

---

[5] Ensemble average means integration over the collective variables with a weight function $\rho_\eta(t)$ at time t, say $< * >= Tr_\eta * \rho_\eta(t)$.

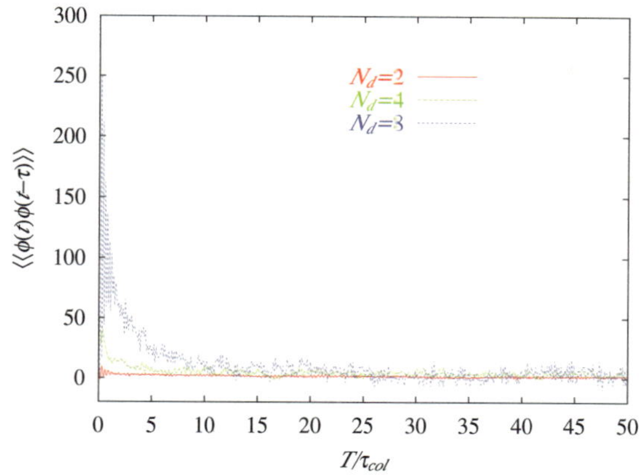

Fig. 24. Correlation function at $t = 120\tau_{col}$ for the case with $N_d = 2, 4$ and 8. Parameters are the same as Fig. 16.

speaking, the correlation function $\langle\langle\phi(t)\phi(t-\tau)\rangle\rangle$, as well as the parameters β_1, β_2 and β_3 may have a strong time dependence, when the intrinsic system undergoes a drastic change like in the dephasing regime. Since, in the present context, we want to understand why the second regime, i.e., thermodynamical regime, appears when the number of degrees of freedom of intrinsic subsystem increases from $N_d = 2$ to larger one, as $N_d = 8$, it is reasonable for us to select a moment, just after the dephasing process has finished. From Figs. 16 $\sim$ 23, it can be seen that $t = 120\tau_{col}$ is just corresponds to such the moment. This is the reason why we calculate the correlation function at $t = 120\tau_{col}$.
From Fig. 24, one can see that the correlation function for the case with $N_d = 2$ is very weak and oscillates around $\langle\langle\phi(t)\phi(t-\tau)\rangle\rangle_t = 0$. In this case, the main influence of the intrinsic subsystem on collective one acts as a source of dephasing, and has finished before $t = 120\tau_{col}$. As N_d increases, the magnitude of the correlation function becomes large and behaves like a "colored noise" with finite correlation time τ_c:

$$\langle\langle\phi(t)\phi(t-\tau)\rangle\rangle \sim e^{-\frac{\tau}{\tau_c}}$$

From this calculation, the correlation function seems to reach a δ function which represents a "white noise" when N_d increases to infinite. This results verify our understanding as shown in Sec. 3.2 and 4:

- The *dephasing regime* is the main mechanism for the small number of freedom (say, two) case.
- Both the dynamical description and conventional transport approach can provide us with almost same macro- and micro-level mechanisms only for the system with very large number of degrees of freedom, however, for the finite system, the statistical relaxation is *an anomalous diffusion* and the fluctuation effects have *□nite correlation time.*

In fact, the approximation of "white noise" is never exactly realized for the realistic physical system, specially for the finite system. What must be done is to consider the noise and the physical system within which, or upon which, it is operating together. Specifically, the finite-time correlation of noise must be taken into account.

N_d	2	4	8	16
β_3	0.201	0.530	0.820	1.773

Table 2. Calculated values of parameter β_3 at $t = 120\tau_{col}$ for the case with N_d=2, 4, 8 and 16, respectively.

Using above results of correlation function, we calculate the parameter β_3 as shown in Table 2. As is obviously seen, the damping effects on collective dynamical motion will increases when the number of degree of freedom increases. For the case with small number of degree of freedom, the damping effects are too small to make the second regime realized. This understanding is consistent with our conclusion stated in Sec. 3.1.4-3.1.5 and in our previous paper(30), where we pointed out that the dephasing mechanism is essential for the damping of the collective energy in the case with two degrees of freedom. However for the case with larger number of degree of freedom as $N_d = 8$ or more, the damping effects become appreciable and make the collective system thermodynamically relaxed to an equilibrium state. This result provides us with a microscopically understanding on how and why the second and third regimes are realized for the collective system coupled to the intrinsic system with an appropriately large number of degrees of freedom.
At the end of this section, we want to discuss on the fluctuation-dissipation relation of collective motion (124). As mentioned in Sec. 3.2.2, the energy equipartition among every degrees of freedom can be expected in the final regime for the case with relatively larger number of degrees of freedom, as N_d=8. This situation just corresponds to a case where the conventional transport equation is applied and the fluctuation-dissipation relation of the collective motion is expected.
Since the collective energy is given by

$$\langle E\rangle = \frac{\langle p^2\rangle}{2M} + \frac{1}{2}m\omega^3\langle q^2\rangle, \tag{126}$$

which is derived from Eq. (64), one may evaluate a rate of collective energy change as

$$\frac{d\langle E\rangle}{dt} = \left[\frac{4\lambda^2M^2\omega'^2\beta_3 + 2\lambda^2\beta_2}{2M}\langle qq\rangle - \frac{4\lambda^2\beta_3}{2M}\langle pp\rangle\right] \tag{127}$$

by using Eq. (125). Since the energy interchange between the two subsystems is supposed to have finished on the average in the third regime,, that is, from Eq. (127), the relation

$$\left[(2M^2\omega'^2\beta_3 + \beta_2)\langle qq\rangle - 2\beta_3\langle pp\rangle\right] = 0 \tag{128}$$

should be satisfied. Figure 25 shows the results of the right-hand-side of equation (127). It is clearly seen that a relation (128) is actually satisfied on the third regime.
To summarize this section, one may get the following conclusions. The damping mechanism caused by fluctuation interaction is the main reason of the appearance of the thermodynamical process. When the number of intrinsic degrees of freedom is relatively large (as N_d=8), the damping mechanism makes the realization of the thermodynamical process and the saturated

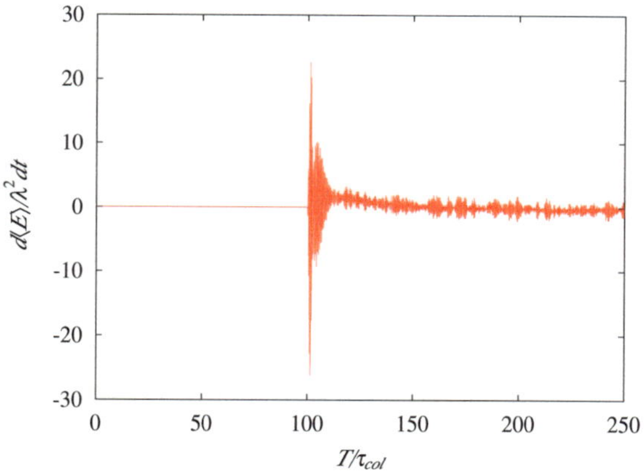

Fig. 25. Rate of collective energy change in Eq. (127). Correlation function $\langle\langle\phi(t)\phi(t-\tau)\rangle\rangle$ is calculated at $t = 240\tau_{col}$ for $N_d = 8$. Parameters are the same as Fig. 16

situation. In this case, the traditional Fokker-Planck equation is safely used in describing the thermodynamical process, and a Fluctuation-Dissipation relation is well realized.

It should be pointed out that, in this section, we have used the microscopic master equation (104) rather than the coupled master equation (43), in order to analytically study the microscopic dynamics responsible for the macro-level dissipative motion as plainly as possible. Although the similarity between Eq. (104) and Eq. (43) is obvious, the former does not includes the effects coming from the response functions which are also known to play an important role in understanding an interrelation between the micro-level and macro-level dynamics. Since the effects of the response function was explored in our previous paper(21), and since the former is convenient to show the physical role of the correlation function clearly, in this section, we have started our analytical discussion from Eq. (104). Apparently, it is our next subject to study the role of the dynamical correlation and dynamical response functions more deeply and more comprehensive way.

6. Linear and nonlinear coupling

According to the SCC method, which has been developed to optimally divide the total space into the relevant and irrelevant subspaces, there should not remain any linear coupling interaction between two spaces. In other words, one may optimally divide the total system into the two *decoupled* subsystems by using such a dynamical condition that the linear coupling between them should be eliminated. Since a ratio between the time scale of the well developed collective motion and that of the single-particle motion is typically less than one order of magnitude in such a finite system as nucleus, it is a very important task to carefully study how the relevant degrees of freedom are distinguished from the rest degrees of freedom. On the basis of the SCC method, one may state that the separation of the total system into two subsystems coupled with a linear interaction has no physical meaning in a finite system, because a choice of the coordinate system, i.e., a separation between the relevant and irrelevant coordinates remains arbitrary when there remains a linear coupling between them. This statement is easily recognized when one remembers that the harmonic oscillators coupled with the linear interaction reduce to the uncoupled harmonic oscillators by a proper choice of the coordinate system. Here, we do not intend to extend the above statement for

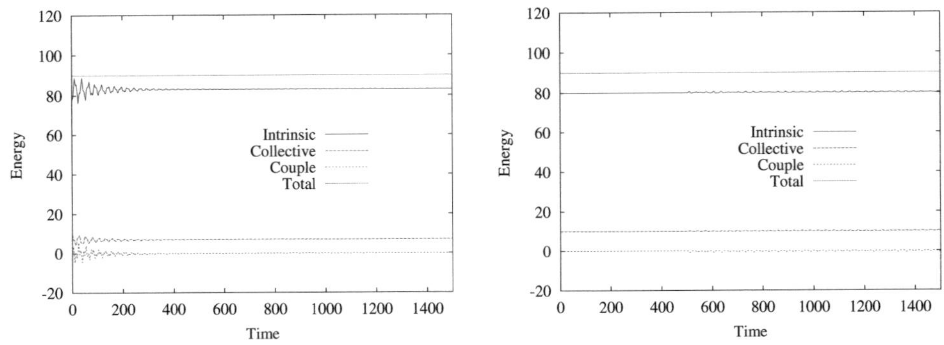

Fig. 26. The distribution of the partial Hamiltonian $\langle H_\eta \rangle$, $\langle H_\xi \rangle$, $\langle H_{coupl} \rangle$ and $\langle H \rangle$ for $N_d = 8$ and $\Delta = 0.02$

the infinite system, because there is many order of magnitude difference between a time scale of the macroscopic motion and that of the microscopic one, and there are huge number of degrees of freedom in the infinite irrelevant system.

In order to explore the different effects between the linear and nonlinear coupling interactions on the dissipative process, we have made a numerical simulation for the β Fermi-Pasta-Ulam (β-FPU) model described in Sec. 3.2.1. The collective H_η, intrinsic H_ξ are the same as in Sec. 3.2.1, but a coupling H_{coupl} Hamiltonians is given as

$$H_{coupl} = \Delta q \cdot q_1. \tag{129}$$

The numerical results are illustrated in Fig. 26. In Fig. 26(a), the coupling is switch on from the beginning, whereas in Fig. 26(b) it is switch on at $\tau_{sw} = 500\tau_{in}$ when a chaotic situation has been well realized in the intrinsic system. In Fig. 26(a), one may observe small energy transfer from the collective to the intrinsic system when the system reach its stationary state at $t \approx 400\tau_{in}$. Namely $< H_\xi >$ becomes a little bit greater than 80 and $< H_\eta >$ less than 10. Before reaching their stationary states, especially at the early stage at $t \leq 100\tau_{in}$, there are violent energy exchange between the collective and intrinsic systems. Since it is not allowed to apply some statistical treatment for the intrinsic system in this early stage when no stationary state is realized for it, there might be no reason to apply the Langevin type equation for a case in Fig. 26(a). In other words, the above energy transfer may not be understood in terms of the macroscopic terms. When one switches on the coupling after the chaotic state has been realized in the intrinsic system, there is almost no energy dissipation in the collective motion as is seen from Fig. 26(b).

An essential difference between the linear and nonlinear coupling cases may be understood as follows: As is seen from Eq. (77), the coupling H_{coupl} produces the mean field potential $H_\eta(t)$ in the case of the nonlinear coupling, because the second moment $< \sum_{i=1}^{2}\{q_i^2 + p_i^2\} >$ has some value when the intrinsic system reaches some stationary state. It is recognized from Eq. (81) that this average effect plays a decisive role to define an amount of transferred energy from the collective system to the environment, like the friction force. On the other hand, H_{coupl} does not produce any averaged effects on the collective motion in the case with the linear coupling, because there holds a relation $< q_i >= 0$ when the statistical state is realized in the intrinsic system. With regards to the β-FPU model, one may conclude that the

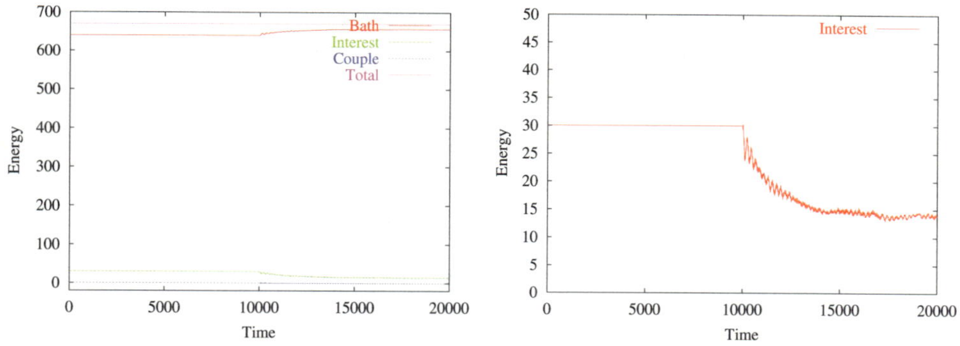

Fig. 27. The distribution of the partial Hamiltonian $\langle H_\eta \rangle$, $\langle H_\xi \rangle$, $\langle H_{coupl} \rangle$ and $\langle H \rangle$ for $\Delta = 0.02$, N_d is 64 which almost can be treated as the case with infinite number of degrees of freedom.

energy dissipation phenomena may not be expected for a finite system, although the other main numerical results described in Ref. (26) have been reproduced.

However, as mentioned in Sec. 3.2.3, the nonequilibrium relaxation regimen (or called as thermodynamical regimen) may also be understood by the Linear Response Theory (24; 26; 27) provided that the number of degrees of freedom is sufficient large. Our numerical results, as shown in Fig. 27, confirm this conclusion. The number of degrees of freedom N_d is chosen as 64, which almost can be considered as infinite. There still remain some unsolved questions for the case with a linear coupling interaction, such as: what is the microscopic reason for energy dissipation in the case with very large number of degrees of freedom (as $N_d > 64$); what is the difference in microscopic dynamics between the cases with very large and small number of degrees of freedom, and furthermore, why a linear coupling interaction can remain between relevant and irrelevant degrees of freedom for producing the Ohmic dissipation for relevant motion, why the linear response theory can be applied for the micro-variables which have a very short time scale in comparison with that for the macro-variables. Such the problem will be investigated in our further works.

7. Summary

We have systematically discussed the characteristic features of non-equilibrium processes for a microscopic Hamilton system with finite degrees of freedom without introducing any statistical ansatz.

The total system is self-consistently and optimally divided into the relevant and irrelevant degrees of freedom in a way consistent with the underlying microscopic dynamics for aiming to properly characterize the collective motion, where the linear coupling between the relevant and irrelevant degrees of freedom is eliminated by the maximally-decoupled coordinate system. This division in the degrees of freedom turns out to be very important for exploring the energy dissipation process and nonlinear dynamics between the collective and intrinsic modes of motion.

A macroscopic transport equation has been derived from the fully microscopic master equation for a microscopic system composed of the one collective degree of freedom system coupled to an intrinsic system with finite degrees of freedom through a weak interaction, by clarifying necessary underlying conditions.

It has been found that the macro-level statistical aspects are strongly related to an appearance of micro-level chaotic motion, and the dissipation of collective motion is realized through dephasing, statistical relaxation and equilibrium regimes. Dominant stage changes depending on the number of intrinsic degrees of freedom. It has been clearly clarified that both the dynamical description and conventional transport approach can provide us with almost same macro- and micro-level mechanisms only for the system with very large number of degrees of freedom, however for the finite system, the statistical relaxation is anomalous diffusion and the fluctuation effects have finite correlation time.

It is interesting to notice that the nonequilibrium relaxation regime is characterized not by the usual BG entropy, but by the nonextensive entropy with $\alpha < 1$, which has been used to extend the thermodynamics to a system with a fractal structure.

Under the help of analytical analysis, we have shown that the energy transport process can be safely described by a Fokker-Planck- and Langevin-type equation, when the number of intrinsic degrees of freedom is relatively large. In this case, the intrinsic subsystem exhibits a very interesting role as a finite *heat bath* and the fluctuation has the finite correlation time (as colored noise). Only when the number of degrees of freedom for the intrinsic system is infinite, the intrinsic subsystem can be treated as a statistical heat bath with white noise.

This study provides a general framework for studying the dissipative collective motion of such the systems as atomic, nuclei and biomolecule whose environment is not infinite.

8. Acknowledgements

The ideas developed in this chapter have matured through collaboration with my colleagues: Professors F. Sakata and Y. Zhuo. This work was partially supported by the National Natural Science Foundation of China under Grant Nos. 10475008 and 10975019, the Scientific Research Foundation for the Returned Overseas Chinese Scholars, Ministry of Personnel of China (Grant No.: MOP2006138) and the Japan-China cooperative research program organized by the Japan Society for the Promotion of Science.

9. References

[1] M. J. Klein, Science 169, (1970)361
[2] C. O. Escobar, L. F. dos Santos and P.C. Marques, *Phys. Rev.* A50 (1994) 1913.
[3] M. Gell-Mann and J. B. Hartle, Phys. Rev. D47,3345(1993).
[4] H. A. Kramers, Physica VII 4(1940)284.
[5] H. Rishen, *The Fooker-Planck Equation*, (Springer, Berlin, 1984).
[6] P. Hänggi, P. Talkner and M. Borkovec, Rev. Mod. Phys. Vol.62, 251(1990).
[7] P. Jung, J. G. Kissner, and P. Hänggi, Phys. Rev. Lett. 76, 3436(1996).
[8] I. Derányi, and R. D. Astumian, Phys. Rev. Lett. 82, 2623(1999).
[9] M. E. Fisher, and A. B. Kolomeisky, Physica A274, 241(1999).
[10] Y. Abe, S. Ayik, P.-G. Reinhard And E. Suraud, Phys. Rep. 275, 49(1996).
[11] H. A. Weidenmüller, Prog. Nucl. Part. Phys. 3, 49(1980).
[12] D. Hilscher, and H. Rossner,Ann. Phys. 17, 471(1992).
[13] S. Habib, K. Shizume and W. H. Zurek, Phys. Rev. Lett. 80, 4361(1998).
[14] Arjendu K. Pattanayak, Phys. Rev. Lett. 83, 4526(1999).
[15] J. Blocki et al., Ann. Phys. (N. Y.) 113, 330(1978).
[16] E. Ott, Phys. Rev. Lett. 42, 1628(1979).

[17] M. Wilkinson, J. Phys. A23, 3603(1990);
M. Wilkinson and E. J. Austin, J. Phys. A28, 2277(1995)
[18] M. V. Berry and J. M. Robbins, Proc. R. Soc. London A442, 659(1993);
J. M. Robbins and M. V. Berry, J. Phys. A25, L961(1992).
[19] C. Jarzynski, Phys. Rev. A46, 7498(1992);
Phys. Rev.Lett. 74, 2937(1995); 71, 839(1993).
[20] S. E. Koonin, R. L. Hatch, and J. Randrup, Nucl. Phys. A283, 87(1977);
S. E. Koonin and J. Randrup, Nucl. Phys. A289, 475(1977).
[21] X. Wu,F. Sakata, Y. Zhuo and Z. Li, Phys. Rev. C48, 1183(1993)
[22] X. Wu,F. Sakata, Y. Zhuo, Z. Li and N. D. Dang, Phys. Rev. C53, 1233(1996).
[23] F. Sakata, M. Matsuo, T. Marumori and Y. Zhuo. Ann. Phys. (N.Y.) 194, 30(1989).
[24] G. Do Dang, A. Klein and P. -G Reinhard, Phys. Rev. C59, 2065(1996).
[25] D. Cohen, Phys. Rev. Lett. 78, 2878(1997); Phys. Rev. Lett. 82, 4951(1999).
[26] M. Bianucci, R. Mannella, B. J. West and P. Grigilini, Phys. Rev. E51, 3002(1995), and references therein.
[27] H. Hofmann, Phys. Rep. 284, 137(1997).
[28] M. Baldo, G. F. Burgio, A. Rapisarda and P. Schuck, Phys. Rev. C58, 2821(1998).
[29] H. C. Fogedby, Phys. Rev. E58, 1690(1998).
[30] S. Yan, F. Sakata, Y. Zhuo, and X. Wu, Phys. Rev. E63, 021116(2001).
[31] S. Yan, F. Sakata, and Y. Zhuo, Phys. Rev. E65, 031111(2002).
[32] F. Sakata, Y. Hashimoto, S. Yan, L. Guo, H. Imagawa, A. Seki, and S. Fujiwara, AIP Conf. Proc., Vol. 597, 249-257(2001)
[33] S. Yan, F. Sakata, and Y. Zhuo, Phys. Lett. A319, 60(2003).
[34] G. M. Zaslavsky, *Physics of Chaos in Hamiltonian Systems: on the Foundations of Statistical Physics*, (Imperial College Press, London, 1998).
[35] L. Boltzmann, Wiss. Ber. 58, 517(1968); 66, 275(1972)
[36] K. Huang, *Statistical Mechanics*, (Wiley,Singapore, 1987).
[37] K. Lindenberg and V. Seshadri, Physica A109,483(1981).
[38] B. Carmeli and A. Nitzan, Chem. Phys. Lett. 102,517(1983)
[39] O. Bohigas and M. G. Giannoni, *Lecture notes in Phys.* 209 (Springer, Heidelberg, 1984) 1, and references therein.
[40] S. Ayik and J. Randrup, Phys. Rev. C50, 2947(1994).
[41] S. Ayik, O. Yilmaz, A. Gokalp and P. Shuck, Phys. Rev. C58,1594(1998).
[42] G. F. Bertsch, P. F. Bortignon and R. A. Broglia, Rev. Mod. Phys., 55, 287(1983).
[43] J. da Providência, M. Yamamura and A. Kuriyama, Phys. Rev. C50, 1720(1994).
[44] A. Kuriyama, J. da Providência and M. Yamamura, Prog. Theor. Phys. 84, 1115(1990).
[45] A. Kuriyama, M. Yamamura, J. da Providência and C. da Providência, Phys. Rev. C45,2196(1992).
[46] M. Pettini and M. Landolfi, Phys. Rev. A41, 768(1990).
[47] M. Pettini and M. Cerruti-Sola, Phys. Rev. A44, 975(1991).
[48] L. Casetti and M. Pettini, Phys. Rev. E48, 4320(1993).
[49] E. Fermi, J. Pasta, and S. Ulam, in *Collected Papers of Enrico Fermi* (Accademia Nazionale dei Lincei and University of Chicago, Roma,1965), Vol. II, P.978.
[50] F. Sakata, T. Marumori, Y. Hashimoto and S. Yan, Suppl. Prog. Theor. Phys. 141, 1-111(2001)
[51] J. R. Carry, Phys. Rep., 79, 129(1981).
[52] B. V. Chirikov, Phys. Rep., 52, 263(1979).

[53] A. J. Lichtenberg and M. A. Lieberman, *Regular and Stochastic Motion, Applied Mathematical Science* 38 (Springer, New York, 1983).
[54] R. Kubo, Prog. Theor. Phys., 12,570(1957).
[55] R. Kubo, M. Toda, and N. Hashitsume, *Statistical Physics II: Nonequilibrium Statistical Mechanics*, Springer-Verlag, Now York 1985.
[56] R. Zwanzig, Ann. Rev. Phys. Chem. 16,67(1965).
[57] M. S. Green, J. Chem. Phys. 20,1281(1952).
[58] M. S. Green, J. Chem. Phys. 22,398(1954).
[59] R. Zwanzig, Ann. Rev. Phys. Chem. 16,67(1965).
[60] T. Marumori, T. Maskawa, F. Sakata, and A. Kuriyama, Prog. Theor. Phys. 64, 1294(1980).
[61] M. Bianucci, R. Mannella and P. Grigolini, Phys. Rev. Lett. 77, 1258(1996).
[62] E. Lutz and H. A. Weidenmüller, Physica A267, 354(1999).
[63] T. Marumori, Prog. Theor. Phys. 57, 112(1977).
[64] J. W. Negele, Rev. Mod Phys. 54, 913(1982).
[65] F. V. De Blasio, W. Cassing, M. Tohyama, P. F. Bortignon and R.A. Broglia, Phys. Rev. Lett. 68,1663(1992).
[66] A. Smerzi, A. Bonasera and M. Di Toro, Phys. Rev. C44,1713(1991).
[67] C. R. Willis and R. H. Picard, Phys. Rev. A9, 1343(1974).
[68] S. Nakajima, Prog. Theor. Phys.,20,948(1958)
[69] R. W. Zwanzig, J. Chem. Phys., 33,1338(1960).
[70] S. Y. Li, A. Klein, and R. M. Dreizler, J. Math. Phys. 11, 975(1970).
[71] A. N. Komologorov, Dokl. Akad. Nauk SSSR, 98, 527(1954).
[72] A. Bohr and B. R. Mottelson, *Nuclear Structure* I Benjamin, New York, 1969.
[73] W. H. Zurek and J. P. Paz, Phys. Rev. Lett. 72, 2508(1994);
W. H. Zurek, Phys. Rev. D24, 1516(1981);
E. Joos and H. D. Zeh, Z. Phys. B59, 229(1985).
[74] J. Ford, Phys. Rep. 5, 271(1992).
[75] H. Yoshida, Phys. Lett. A150, 262(1990).
[76] M. Sofroniou and W. Oevel, SIAM Journal of Numerical Analysis 34 (1997), pp. 2063-2086.
[77] N. G. van Kampen, Phys. Nor. 5, 279(1971)
[78] V. Latora and M. Baranger, Phys. Rev. Lett. 82, 520(1999).
[79] N. S. Krylov, *Works on the Foundations of Statistical Physics*, Princeton Series in Physics(Princeton University Press, Princeton, NJ, 1979).
[80] P. Grigolini, M. G. Pala, L. Palatella and R. Roncaglia, Phys. Rev. E 62, 3429(2000).
[81] U. M. S. Costa, M. L. Lyra, A. R. Plastino and C. Tsallis, Phys. Rev. E 56, 245(1997).
[82] V. Latora, M. Baranger, A. Rapisarda and C. Tsallis, Phys. Lett. A273, 97(2000).
[83] C. Tsallis, Fractals 3, 541(1995).
[84] C. Tsallis, J. Stat. Phys. 52, 479(1988);
E. M. E. Curado and C. Tsallis, J. Phys. A24, L69(1991); 24, 3187E(1991); 25, 1019E(1992);
C. Tsallis,Phys. Lett. A206, 389(1995).
[85] S. Yan, F. Sakata, Y. Zhuo and X. Wu, RIKEN Review, No.23, 153(1999).
[86] F. Sakata, T. Marumori, Y. Hashimoto and T. Une, Prog. Theor. Phys. 70, 424(1983).

10. Appendix

Derivation of Eq. (104)

In this appendix, a derivation of the master equation (104) is discussed. From the definition in Eq. (103), one can get that the mean-field propagator $G_\eta(t,t')$ satisfies the relation

$$\frac{dG_\eta(t,t')}{dt} = -i\lambda(\mathcal{L}_\eta + \mathcal{L}_\eta(t))G_\eta(t,t') \tag{130}$$

and has the properties

$$G_\eta(t,t_1)G_\eta(t_1,t') = G_\eta(t,t') \tag{131a}$$

$$G_\eta^{-1}(t,t') = G_\eta(t',t) \tag{131b}$$

where $G_\eta^{-1}(t,t')$ is the inverse propagator of $G_\eta(t,t')$
With the aid of the mean-field propagator, the solution of Eq. (101) can be formally expressed as:

$$\rho_\eta(t) = G_\eta(t,0)\rho'_\eta(t) \tag{132}$$

which satisfies the equation

$$\dot{\rho}_\eta(t) = \dot{G}_\eta(t,0)\rho'_\eta(t) + G_\eta(t,0)\dot{\rho}'_\eta(t) \tag{133}$$

With Eq. (130), one gets

$$\dot{\rho}_\eta(t) = -i\lambda(\mathcal{L}_\eta + \mathcal{L}_\eta(t))G_\eta(t,0)\rho'_\eta(t) + G_\eta(t,0)\dot{\rho}'_\eta(t) \tag{134}$$

Inserting Eq. (132) into the r.h.s. of Eq. (101) and comparing with Eq. (134), one can easily get

$$\dot{\rho}'_\eta(t) = -i\lambda\mathcal{L}'_{\Delta,\eta}(t)\rho'_\eta(t), \tag{135}$$

where

$$\mathcal{L}'_{\Delta,\eta}(t) = G_\eta^{-1}(t,0)\mathcal{L}_{\Delta,\eta}(t)G_\eta(t,0) \tag{136}$$

Eq. (135) is a linear stochastic differential equation. Applying cumulant expansion method(77), one has

$$\begin{aligned}\dot{\rho}'_\eta(t) = &-i\lambda\langle\langle\mathcal{L}'_{\Delta,\eta}(t)\rangle\rangle\rho'_\eta(t)\\ &-\lambda^2\int_0^t d\tau\langle\langle\mathcal{L}'_{\Delta,\eta}(t)\mathcal{L}'_{\Delta,\eta}(\tau)\rangle\rangle\rho'_\eta(t)\end{aligned} \tag{137}$$

where a symbol $\ll \cdots \gg$ denotes a cumulant defined as:

$$\ll \mathcal{AB} \gg \equiv < \mathcal{AB} > - < \mathcal{A} >< \mathcal{B} > \tag{138}$$

which is related to the average over the intrinsic degrees of freedom

$$< \cdots > \equiv Tr\{\cdots\}$$

Eq. (137) is valid upto the second order in λ. According to a definition of the fluctuation Hamiltonian $H_{\Delta,\eta}(t)$ in (100), the first-order term in (137) is zero since there holds a relation

$$\langle\langle \mathcal{L}'_{\Delta,\eta}(t)\rangle\rangle \sim \langle\langle \phi'(t)\rangle\rangle = \langle \phi'(t)\rangle = 0 \tag{139}$$

one thus obtains

$$\dot{\rho}'_\eta(t) = -\lambda^2 \int_0^t d\tau \langle\langle \mathcal{L}'_{\Delta,\eta}(t)\mathcal{L}'_{\Delta,\eta}(\tau)\rangle\rangle \rho'_\eta(t) \tag{140}$$

Inserting (140) into (134), one has

$$\begin{aligned}\dot{\rho}'_\eta(t) &= -i\lambda\big(\mathcal{L}_\eta + \mathcal{L}_\eta(t)\big)G_\eta(t,0)\rho'_\eta(t) \\ &\quad -\lambda^2 \int_0^t d\tau G_\eta(t,0)\langle\langle \mathcal{L}'_{\Delta,\eta}(t)\mathcal{L}'_{\Delta,\eta}(\tau)\rangle\rangle \rho'_\eta(t)\end{aligned} \tag{141}$$

With the relation (131), (132) and (136), Eq. (141) can be read as

$$\begin{aligned}\dot{\rho}'_\eta(t) &= -i\lambda\big(\mathcal{L}_\eta + \mathcal{L}_\eta(t)\big)\rho_\eta(t) \\ &\quad -\lambda^2 \int_0^t d\tau \langle\langle \mathcal{L}_{\Delta,\eta}(t)G_\eta(t,\tau)\mathcal{L}_{\Delta,\eta}(\tau)\rangle\rangle G_\eta(\tau,t)\rho_\eta(t)\end{aligned} \tag{142}$$

Making the variable transformation $\tau \longrightarrow t-\tau$, one can have

$$\begin{aligned}\dot{\rho}'_\eta(t) &= -i\lambda\big(\mathcal{L}_\eta + \mathcal{L}_\eta(t)\big)\rho_\eta(t) \\ &\quad -\lambda^2 \int_0^t d\tau \langle\langle \mathcal{L}_{\Delta,\eta}(t)G_\eta(t,t-\tau)\mathcal{L}_{\Delta,\eta}(t-\tau)\rangle\rangle G_\eta(t-\tau,t)\rho_\eta(t)\end{aligned} \tag{143}$$

This is just Eq. (104).

Part 2

Chaos Control

5

Chaos Analysis and Control in AFM and MEMS Resonators

Amir Hossein Davaie-Markazi and Hossein Sohanian-Haghighi
School of Mechanical Engineering, Iran University of Science and Technology, Tehran, Iran

1. Introduction

For years, chaotic phenomena have been mainly studied from a theoretical point of view. In the last two decades, considerable developments have occurred in the control, prediction and observation of chaotic behaviour in a wide variety of dynamical systems, and a large number of applications have been discovered and reported (Moon & Holmes, 1999; Endo & Chua, 1991; Kennedy, 1993). Chaotic behaviour can only be observed in particular nonlinear dynamical systems. In recent years, nonlinearity is known as a key characteristic of micro resonant systems. Such devices are used widely in variety of applications, including sensing, signal processing, filtering and timing. In many of these applications some purely electrical components can be replaced by micro mechanical resonators. The benefits of using micro mechanical resonators include smaller size, lower damping, and improved the performance. Two examples of micro mechanical resonators that their complex behaviour is described briefly in this chapter are atomic force microscopy (AFM) and micro electromechanical resonators. AFM has been widely used for surface inspection with nanometer resolution in engineering applications and fundamental research since the time of its invention in 1986 (Hansma et al., 1988). The mechanism of AFM basically depends on the interaction of a micro cantilever with surface forces. The tip of the micro cantilever interacts with the surface through a surface–tip interaction potential. One of the performance modes of an AFM is the so called "tapping mode". In this mode, the micro-cantilever is driven to oscillate near its resonance frequency, by a small piezoelectric element mounted in the cantilever. In this chapter it will be shown that micro-cantilever in tapping mode may exhibit chaotic behaviour under certain conditions. Such a chaotic behaviour has been studied by many researchers (Burnham et al. 1995; Basso et al., 1998; Ashhab et al., 1999; Jamitzky et al., 2006; Yagasaki, 2007).

In section 3, the chaotic behaviour of micro electromechanical resonators is studied. Micro electromechanical resonant systems have been rapidly growing over recent years because of their high accuracy, sensibility and resolution (Bao, 1996). The resonators sensing application concentrate on detecting a resonance frequency shift due to an external perturbation such as accreted mass (Cimall et al., 2007). The other important technological applications of mechanical resonators include radiofrequency filter design (Lin et al., 2002) and scanned probe microscopy (Garcia et al., 1999). Many researchers have tried to analyze nonlinear behaviour in micro electeromechanical systems (MEMS) (Mestrom et al., 2007;

Younis & Nayfeh, 2003; Braghin et al., 2007). We will examine the mathematical model of a micro beam resonator, excited between two parallel electrodes. Chaotic behaviour of this model is studied. A robust adaptive fuzzy method is introduced and used to control the chaotic motion of micro electromechanical resonators.

2. Atomic force microscopy

The mechanism of an AFM basically depends on the interaction of a micro cantilever with surface forces. The tip of the micro cantilever interacts with the surface through a surface-tip interaction potential. One of the performance modes of an AFM is the so called "tapping mode". In this mode, the micro-cantilever is driven to oscillate near its resonance frequency, by a small piezoelectric element mounted in the cantilever. When the tip comes close to an under scan surface, particular interaction forces, such as Van der Waals, dipole-dipole and electrostatic forces, will act on the cantilever tip. Such interactions will cause a decrease in the amplitude of the tip oscillation. A piezoelectric servo mechanism, acting on the base structure of the cantilever, controls the height of the cantilever above the sample so that the amplitude of oscillation will remain close to a prescribed value. A tapping AFM image is therefore produced by recording the control effort applied by the base piezoelectric servo as the surface is scanned by the tip.

From theoretical investigations it is known that the nonlinear interaction with the sample can lead to chaotic dynamics although the system behaves regularly for a large set of parameters. In this section, the model of micro cantilever sample interaction is described and dynamical behaviour of forced system is investigated. The cantilever tip sample interaction is modelled by a sphere of radius R and equivalent mass m which is connected to a spring of stiffness k. A schematic of the model is shown in Fig.1. The interaction of an intermolecular pair is given by the Lennard Jones potential which can be modelled as (Ashhab et al., 1999)

$$V(x,Z) = -\frac{A_2 R}{6(Z+x)} + \frac{A_1 R}{1260(Z+x)^7} \tag{1}$$

where A_1 and A_2 are the Hamaker constants for the attractive and repulsive potentials. To facilitate the study of the qualitative behaviour of the system, the following parameters are defined:

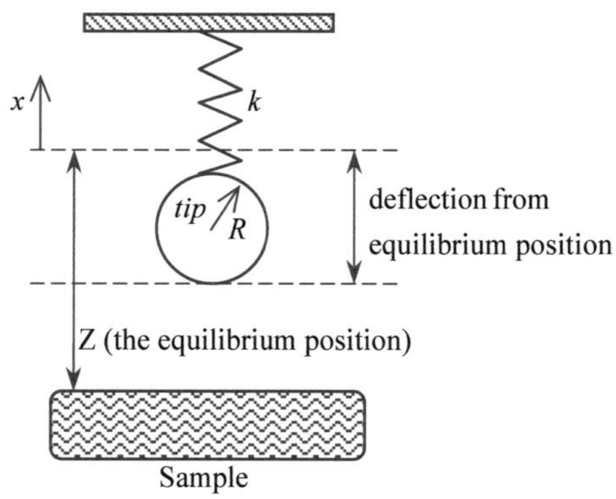

Fig. 1. The tip sample model.

$$D = \frac{A_2 R}{6k}, Z_s = \frac{3}{2}(2D)^{\frac{1}{3}}, \alpha_0 = \frac{Z}{Z_s}, d_0 = \frac{4}{27}, \Sigma = \left(\frac{A_1}{A_2}\right)^{\frac{1}{6}} \frac{1}{Z_s}, \zeta_1 = \frac{x}{Z_s}, \zeta_2 = \dot{\zeta}_1, \omega = \sqrt{\frac{k}{m}}, \tau = \omega t \quad (2)$$

where t denotes time and the dot represents derivative with respect τ.
Using these parameters, the cantilever equation of motion with air damping effect, is described in state space as below

$$\begin{aligned} \dot{\zeta}_1 &= \zeta_2 \\ \dot{\zeta}_2 &= -\zeta_1 - \delta\zeta_2 - \frac{d_0}{(\alpha_0 + \zeta_1)^2} + \frac{\Sigma^6 d_0}{30(\alpha_0 + \zeta_1)^8} + \Gamma\cos\Omega\tau \end{aligned} \quad (3)$$

where δ is the damping factor and Γ and Ω are the amplitude and frequency of driving force respectively. Fig.2 shows a qualitative phase portrait of unforced system. There are two homoclinic trajectories each one connected to itself at the saddle point.

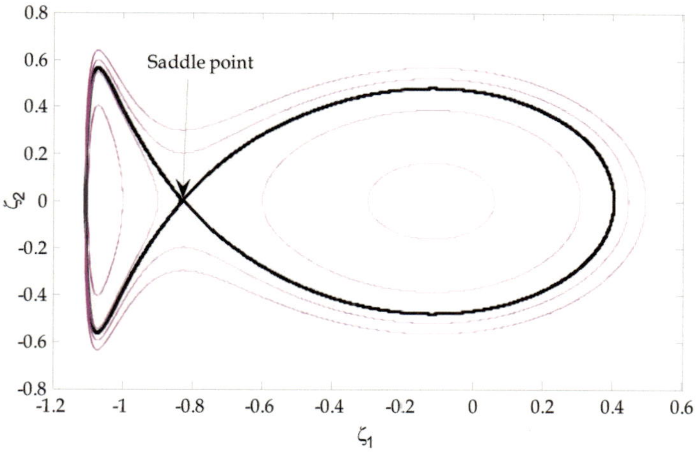

Fig. 2. Phase diagram for unforced AFM model.

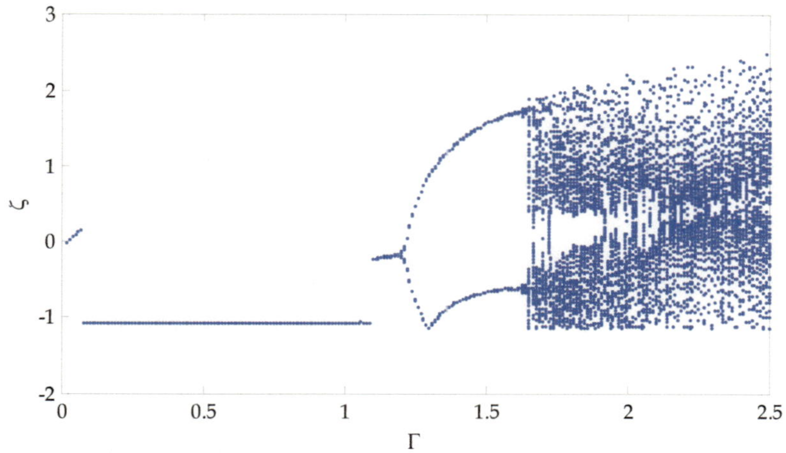

Fig. 3. The bifurcation diagram obtained by varying Γ from 0 to 2.5.

For numerical simulation, we consider (3), where the parameters have been set as follows: $\Sigma = 0.3$, $\alpha = 1.25$, $\delta = 0.05$, $\Omega = 1$ .For these values, the bifurcation diagram of AFM model is shown in Fig. 3, where the parameter Γ is plotted versus the cantilever tip positions in the corresponding Poincare map. The obtained diagram reveals that, starting at $\Gamma = 1.2$, the period orbit undergoes a sequence of period doubling bifurcation. For the range $\Gamma \in (1.7, 2.5)$, the system shows complex behaviours. Fig. 4 shows various types of system responses for $\Gamma = 1$, $\Gamma = 1.5$ and $\Gamma = 2$.

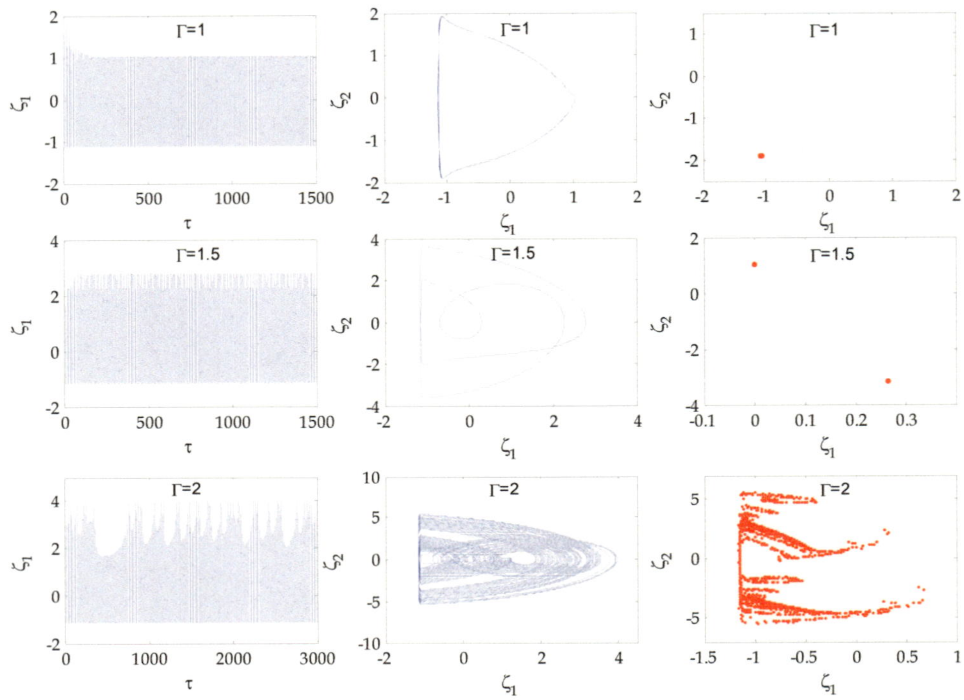

Fig. 4. Time histories, corresponding phase diagrams and Poincare maps obtained by simulating (3).

3. Micro electromechanical resonators

In many cases it is highly desirable to reduce the size of MEMS mechanical elements (Roukes, 2001). This allows increasing the frequencies of mechanical resonances and improving their sensitivity as sensors. Although miniaturized MEMS resonant systems have many attractions, they also provide several important challenges. A main practical issue is to achieve higher output energy, in particular, in devices such as resonators and micro-sensors. A common solution to the problem is the well-known electrostatic comb-drive (Xie & Fedder, 2002). However, this solution adds new constraints to the design of the mechanical structure due to the many complex and undesirable dynamical behaviours associated with it. Another way to face this challenge is to use a strong exciting force (Logeeswaran et al., 2002; Harley, 1998). The major drawback of this approach is the nonlinear effect of the electrostatic force. When a beam is oscillating between parallel electrodes, the change in the capacitance is not a perfectly linear function. The forces attempting to restore the beam to its neutral position vary as the beam bends; the more the beam is deflected, the more nonlinearity can be observed. In fact nonlinearities in MEMS resonators generally arise from two distinct sources: relatively large structural deformations and displacement-dependent excitations. Further increasing in the magnitude of the excitation force will result in nonlinear vibrations, which will affect the dynamic behavior of the resonator, and may lead to chaotic behaviors (Wang et al., 1998). The chaotic motion of MEMS resonant systems in the vicinity of specific resonant separatrix is investigated based on the corresponding resonant condition (Luo & Wang., 2002). The chaotic behavior of a micro-electromechanical oscillator was modelled by a version of the Mathieu equation and investigated both numerically and experimentally in (Barry et al., 2007). Chaotic motion was also reported for a micro electro mechanical cantilever beam under both open and close loop control (Liu et al., 2004).

In this section, the chaotic dynamics of a micro mechanical resonator with electrostatic forces on both upper and lower sides of the cantilever is investigated. Numerical studies including phase portrait, Poincare map and bifurcation diagrams reveal the effects of the excitation amplitude, bias voltage and excitation frequency on the system transition to chaos. Moreover a robust adaptive fuzzy control algorithm is introduced and applied for controlling the chaotic motion. Additional numerical simulations show the effectiveness of the proposed control approach.

3.1 Mathematical model

An electrostatically actuated microbeam is shown in Fig.5. The external driving force on the resonator is applied via an electrical driving voltage that causes electrostatic excitation with a dc-bias voltage between electrodes and the resonator: $V_i = V_b + V_{AC} Sin\Omega t$, where, V_b is the bias voltage, and V_{AC} and Ω are the AC amplitude and frequency, respectively. The net actuation force, F_{act}, can then be expressed as (Mestrom et al., 2007)

$$F_{act} = \frac{1}{2}\frac{C_0 d}{(d-z)^2}(V_b + V_{AC} Sin\Omega t)^2 - \frac{1}{2}\frac{C_0 d}{(d+z)^2}(V_b^2) \quad (4)$$

where C_0 is the capacitance of the parallel-plate actuator at rest, d is the initial gap width and z is the vertical displacement of the beam. The governing equation of motion for the dynamics of the MEMS resonator can be expressed as

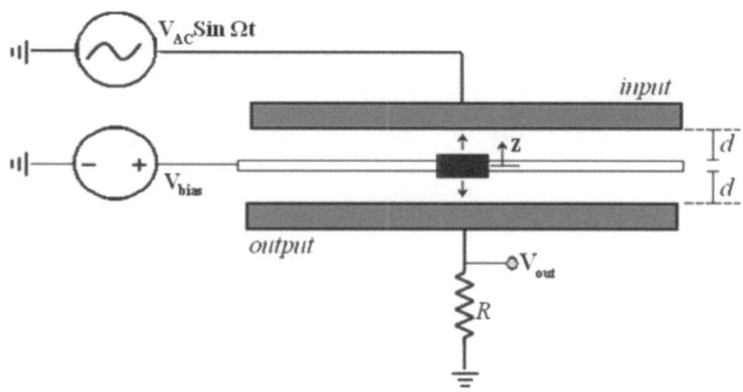

Fig. 5. A schematic picture of the electrostatically actuated micromechanical resonator.

$$m_{eff}z'' + bz' + k_1 z + k_3 z^3 = F_{act} \tag{5}$$

where, z' and z'' represent the first and second time derivative of z, and m_{eff}, b, k_1 and k_3 are effective lumped mass, damping coefficient, linear mechanical stiffness and cubic mechanical stiffness of the system respectively.
It is convenient to introduce the following dimensionless variables:

$$\tau = \omega_0 t,\ \omega = \frac{\Omega}{\omega_0}, x = \frac{z}{d}, \mu = \frac{b}{m_{eff}\omega_0}, \alpha = \frac{k_1}{m_{eff}\omega_0^2}, \beta = \frac{k_3 d^2}{m_{eff}\omega_0^2}, \gamma = \frac{C_0 V_b^2}{2m_{eff}\omega_0^2 d^2},\ A = 2\gamma\frac{V_{AC}}{V_b} \tag{6}$$

where ω_0 is the purely elastic natural frequency defined as

$$\omega_0 = \sqrt{\frac{k_1}{m_{eff}}} \tag{7}$$

Assuming the amplitude of the AC driving voltage to be much smaller than the bias voltage, with the dimensionless quantities defined in (6) the nondimensional equation of motion is obtained:

$$\ddot{x} + \mu\dot{x} + \alpha x + \beta x^3 = \gamma\left(\frac{1}{(1-x)^2} - \frac{1}{(1+x)^2}\right) + \frac{A}{(1-x)^2} Sin\omega\tau \tag{8}$$

Here, the new derivative operator, $(\dot{\ })$, denotes the derivative with respect to τ. It is worth mentioning that, if the potential is set to be zero at $x = 0$, the corresponding potential can be described as

$$V(x) = \frac{\alpha x^2}{2} + \frac{\beta x^4}{4} - \gamma\left(\frac{1}{1-x} + \frac{1}{1+x}\right) + 2\gamma \tag{9}$$

Fig. 6 shows that the change in the number of equilibrium points, when the applied voltage is changed. For the case where the bias voltage does not exist, only one stable state exists,

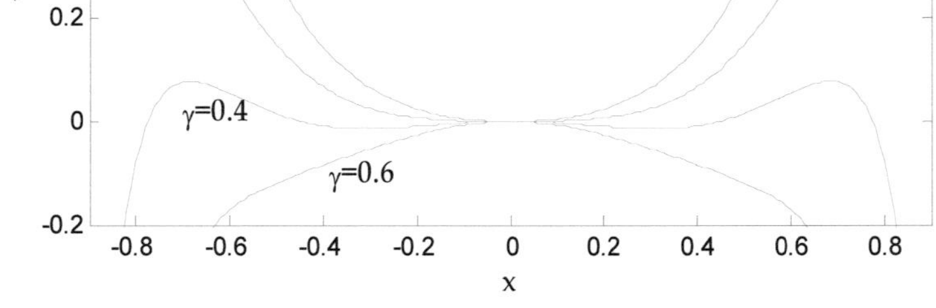

Fig. 6. The potential function for four values of γ ($\gamma = 0, 0.2, 0.4, 0.6$), $\alpha = 1$ and $\beta = 10$.

and the equilibrium point is a stable center point at x=0. When the bias voltage is not zero, however, at a critical position, the resonator becomes unstable and is deflected against one of the stationary transducer electrodes (pull-in phenomena). If the bias is small, the structure stays in the deflected position, smaller than the critical one. For this case, three associated equilibrium points are one stable center point and two unstable saddle points. As the bias voltage increases, the equilibrium point at x=0 becomes unstable and the potential function V(x) will have a local peak at this point. The original equilibrium point at the center position becomes a saddle point and two new center points emerge at either side of the origin. For a large enough bias voltage, there is only one unstable equilibrium point at x=0 and the resonator becomes completely unstable.

3.2 Transition to chaos

To verify the analytical findings, a series of numerical simulations of the exact nonlinear differential equation (5) is performed with the following dimensionless parameters:

$m = 5\times10^{-12}kg,\ b = 5\times10^{-8}\,kg/s,\ k_1 = 5\mu N/\mu m,\ k_3 = 15\mu N/\mu m^3,\ d = 2\mu m,\ C_0 = 1.5\times10^{-14}F,$

$V_b = 30V, \omega = 0.5.$

The unforced system has a saddle point at $x = 0$ as can be seen from Fig. 7. Existence of this point makes homoclinic bifurcations to take place possible. This means that the system has the necessary condition for chaotic behaviour.

The phase portrait and time histories are plotted for different values of the AC voltage. To study the effect of the AC voltage on the beam dynamics, the bias voltage is kept fix and the AC voltage is varied. Starting from the vicinity of the critical amplitude for $V_{AC} = 0.06V$, the system response contains transient chaos and periodic motion around one of the center points (Fig. 8a). Fig. 8b reveals that following the transient chaos, the beam oscillates in the vicinity of the other center point for $V_{AC} = 0.17V$. The more increase in the AC voltage causes a longer transient chaotic motion. The chaotic transient oscillation is large in amplitude and jumping between potential wells. After a while in such a regime of motion, a steady state regular vibration with much smaller amplitude, and located in a single potential well, is observed. As can be seen from Fig. 8c, after the transient chaotic response, a periodic motion may be observed, evolving out of the homoclinic orbit and, with much larger

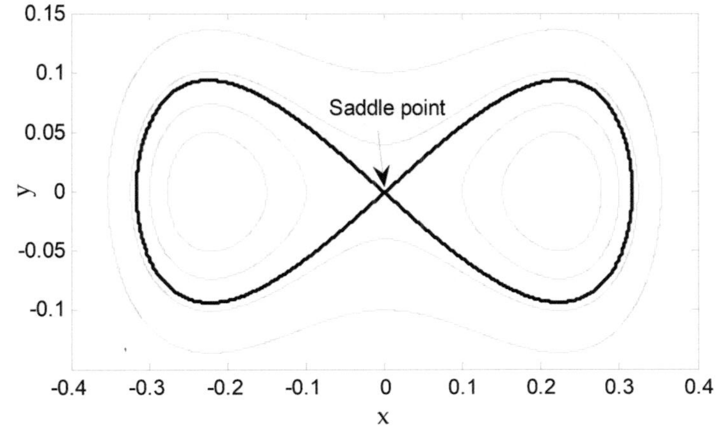

Fig. 7. Phase portraits of unforced system.

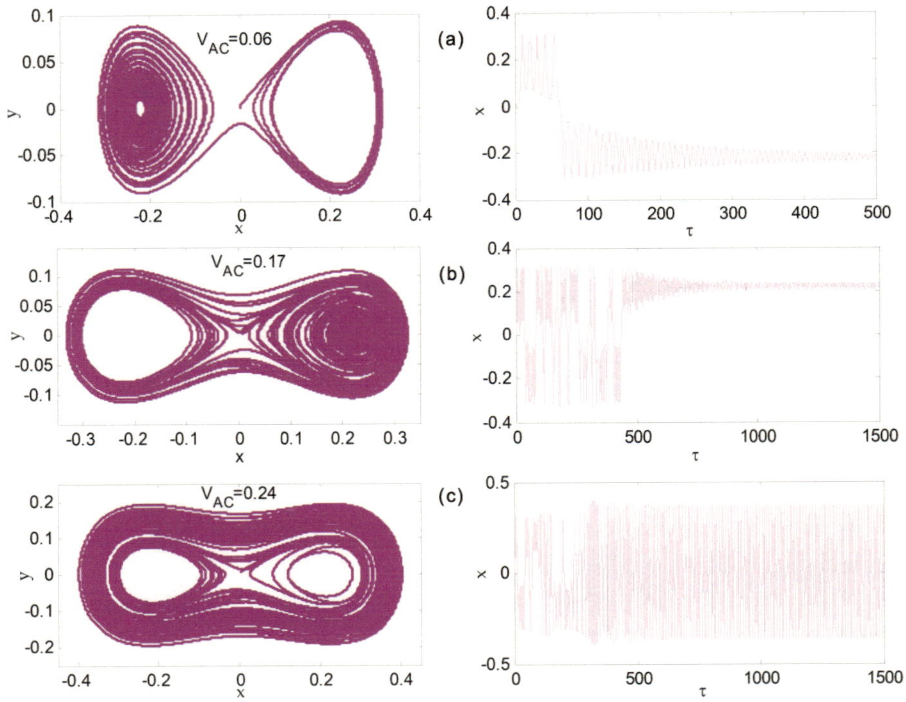

Fig. 8. Phase diagrams and time histories obtained by simulating (5). Corresponding AC voltages are indicated in phase diagrams.

amplitude. ($V_{AC} = 0.24V$) . With a large enough stimulation time, the system is brought back to chaotic steady state. Fig.9 shows the phase trajectory and the Poincare map of the chaotic motion, with $V_{AC} = 1.8V$. The system behavior is different from that of the Duffing attractor because of the electrostatic terms in the MEMS equations. Because of the two unstable points near the fixed electrodes, there is an upper limit for the applied AC voltage.

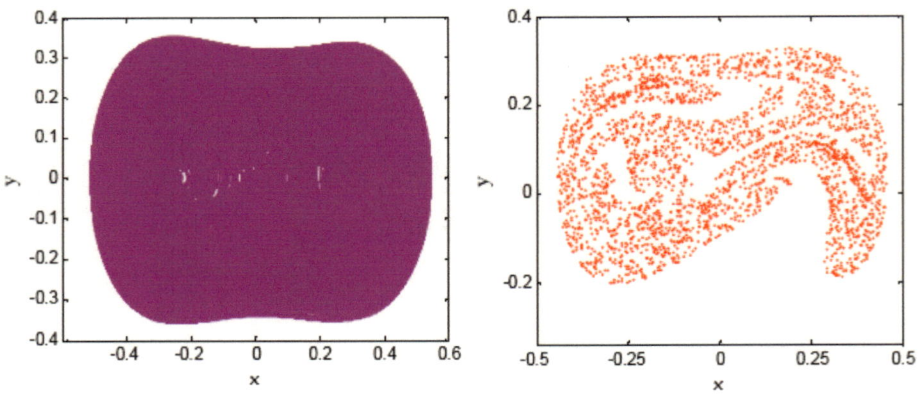

Fig. 9. The phase trajectory and the Poincare map when $V_{AC} = 1.8V$.

Any more increase in the AC voltage, leads to a dynamic pull-in phenomena, which could to instability at a voltage lower than the static pull-in voltage. In interpreting the results in

Fig. 10, note that $V_{AC} = 2.8V$ corresponds to collapse of the microbeam into the fixed electrode.

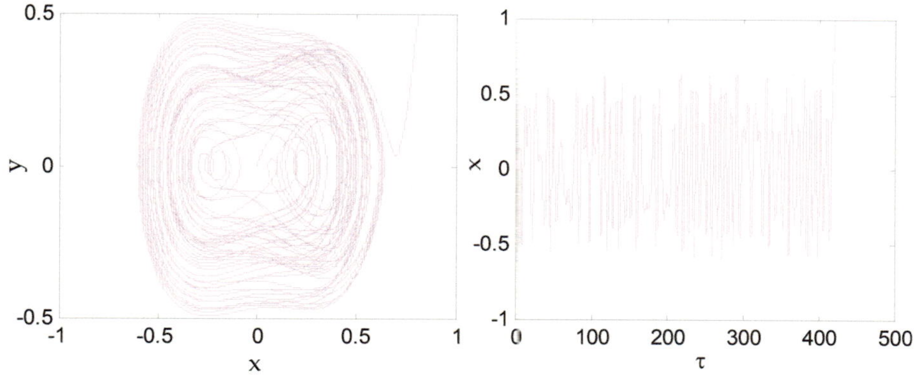

Fig. 10. The phase trajectory and time history for x(τ) obtained with $V_{AC} = 2.8V$.

3.3 Bifurcation diagrams

Fig.11 shows the bifurcation diagram. In this case, the qualitative behavior of the system is shown against a varying AC voltage from 0 to 2.8. In the bifurcation diagram, the final system states of the previously iterated value of the AC voltage is chosen as the initial condition for the next system iteration with the new value of the AC voltage. Chaotic behavior of system starts when $V_{AC} = 1.4V$ and continues until $V_{AC} = 2.8V$. For AC voltages larger than 2.8V, the dynamic pull-in may occur, where, the electric force increases and becomes much higher than the spring restoring force and the resonator sticks to one of the stationary electrodes (Nayfeh &Younis, 2007). The initial conditions are assumed as $(x_{in}, v_{in}) = (0,0)$ for all simulation studies.

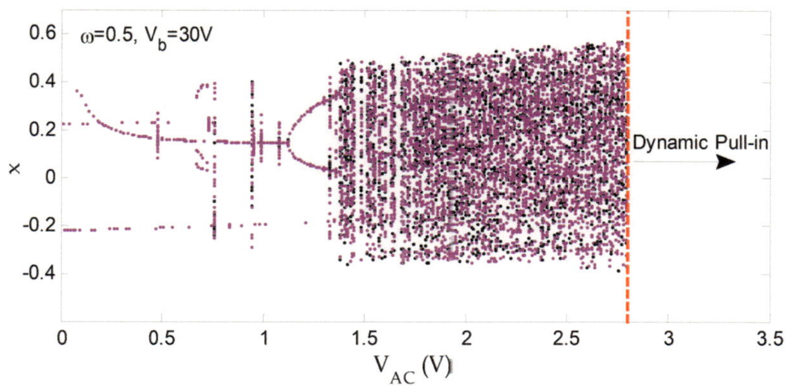

Fig. 11. The bifurcation diagram obtained by varying AC voltage from 0 to 2.8V.

The characteristic dynamical behaviors are investigated by varying the bias voltage. Fig.12 shows the bifurcation diagram of the micro beam displacement via the applied bias voltage. The figure indicates that, with an increase in the applied bias voltage, a period-doubling bifurcation occurs, i.e., a period-1 motion becomes a period-2 motion. If the applied bias voltage is increased, a chaotic behavoir may occur. The figure demonstrates that the chaotic region becomes wider as the applied bias voltage is increased.

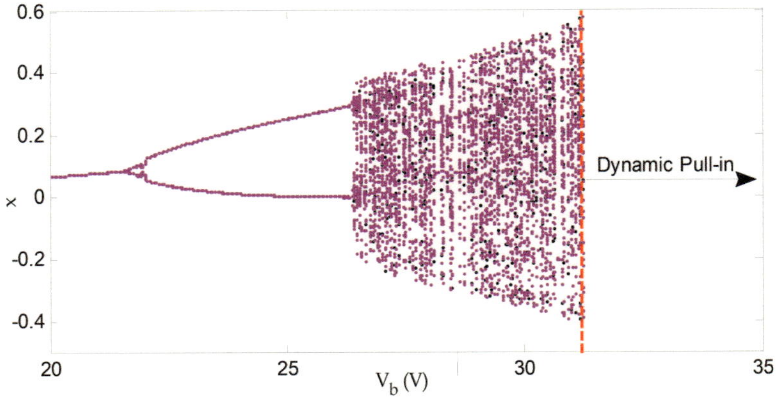

Fig. 12. The bifurcation diagram obtained by varying the bias voltage from 20 to 32V.

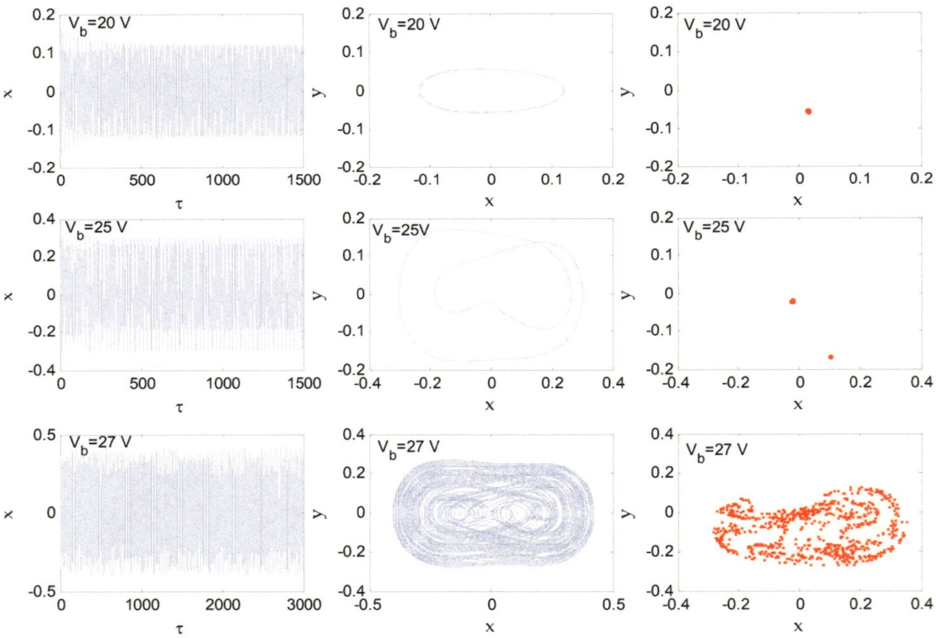

Fig. 13. Time histories and corresponding phase diagrams and Poincare maps obtained by simulating (5) with $\omega = 0.5$ and $V_{AC} = 1.8V$.

It can be seen from Fig. 13, that the system responses contain periodic and chaotic motions. When $V_b = 20V$, the vibration amplitude of the cantilever is small, the period-1 motion with only one isolated point in Poincare map and one circle in phase portrait can be observed. With an increase in the amplitude of the applied bias voltage, the motion becomes synchronous with period-two, as illustrated in Fig. 13 for $V_b = 25V$. Moreover, at $V_b = 27V$, the micro beam displacement response becomes chaotic and no regular pattern can be observed in the corresponding Poincare map and the phase portrait.

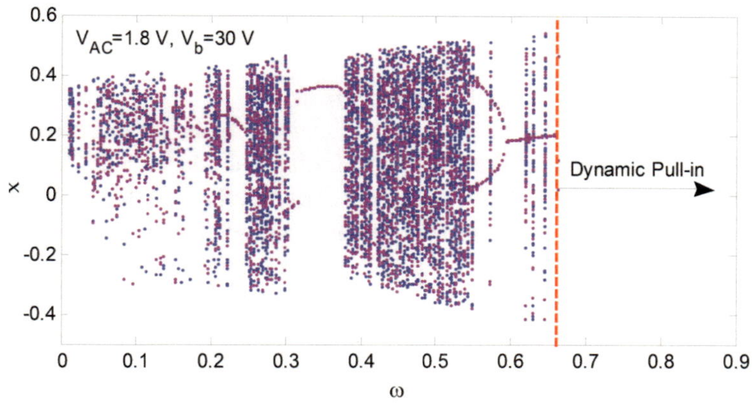

Fig. 14. The bifurcation diagram obtained by varying ω from 0 to 0.67.

Fig. 14 shows that the system responses exhibit an alternation of periodic and chaotic motions. The system response comes into a steady-state synchronous motion with period-1, and returns to the chaotic motion alternatively, as the excitation frequency is increased. Period-doubling motions are also observed for a small range of excitation frequencies.

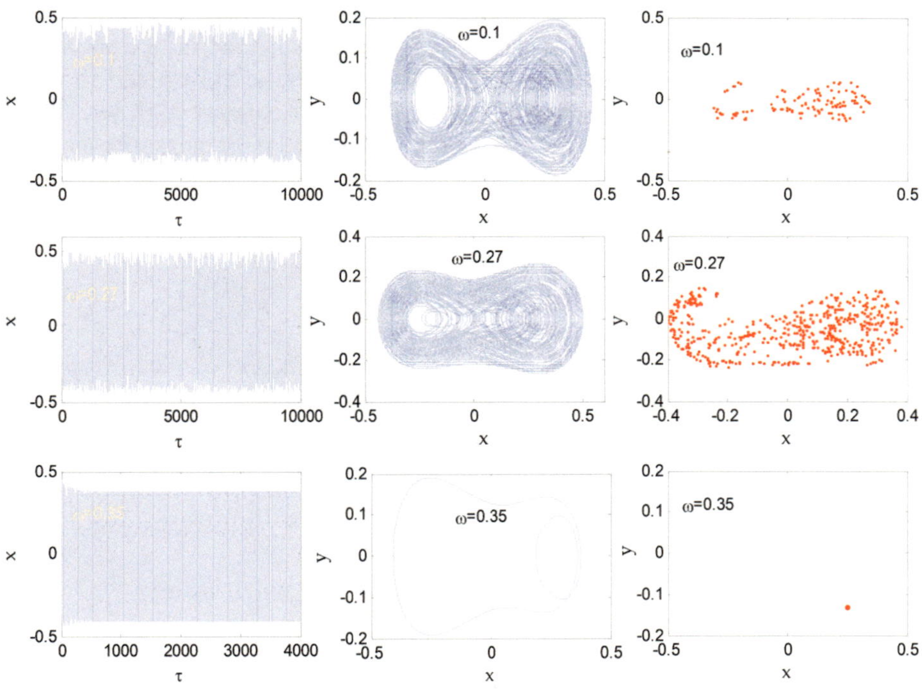

Fig. 15. Time histories, corresponding phase diagrams and Poincare maps obtained by simulating (5) with $V_b = 30V$ and $V_{AC} = 1.8V$.

Fig. 15 depicts the time history, phase plane portraits and the Poincare maps based on the responses of the electrostatically actuated system over a range of frequencies. Various chaotic behavior is observed for $\omega = 0.2$ and $\omega = 0.27$. It can be seen that, for $\omega = 0.35$, the motion of the system is synchronized with period-one.

3.4 Control of chaotic motion in MEMS resonator

Various fuzzy control methods for control of chaotic systems are proposed in the literature e.g., (Calvo, 1998; Poursamad & Markazi, 2009-a; Haghighi & Markazi, 2010). In this section, a robust adaptive fuzzy control algorithm is used to stabilize a MEMS beam in a high-amplitude oscillation state. A key issue that arises in chaos control, particularly in MEMS resonators, is that the system parameters are not known precisely, and are perturbed during operation (Wang et al., 1998). Unlike most conventional control systems whose equilibriums are assumed known and fixed regardless of values of the system parameters, the equilibriums of chaotic systems are a function of their system constant parameters. This suggests that, when the system parameters are not precisely known, and hence, the equilibriums are then unknown, the conventional control methodologies may not be applied directly. In addition, the presence of external disturbance and measurement noise, may adversely affect the system performance. Therefore, development of alternative control strategies for efficient control and robust tracking of chaotic systems, under the presence of uncertainties is highly desirable.

The controller proposed in this section comprises a fuzzy system and a robust controller. The fuzzy system, whose parameters are adaptively tuned, is designed based on the sliding-mode control (SMC) strategy to mimic the ideal controller, i.e., when the model of the plant is exactly known. The robust controller is then designed to compensate for deviations of the fuzzy controller, compared to the ideal one. The uncertainty bound needed in the robust controller is also adaptively tuned online to avoid using unnecessary high switching gain, due to the, most often, conservative bounds. A comprehensive presentation of the proposed control method and proof of the asymptotic stability can be found in (Poursamad & Markazi, 2009-a ; Poursamad & Markazi, 2009-b).

In order to write (5) in a more convenient form, it is rewritten as

$$\ddot{x} = f(\dot{x}, x, t) + u\,, \tag{10}$$

where u is the appended control input and f is a smooth function obtained from (5). Now let define a sliding surface, $S(t)$, using $s(\dot{\tilde{x}}, \tilde{x}) = 0$ with $s(\dot{\tilde{x}}, \tilde{x}) = \dot{\tilde{x}} + \lambda \tilde{x}$, where $\tilde{x} = x_d - x$ is the tracking error, $\dot{\tilde{x}}$ is the time derivative of $\tilde{x}$, x_d is the desired trajectory and λ is a to be selected strictly positive constant. Now, an ideal (central) control signal is obtained as

$$u^* = -f + \ddot{x}_d + \lambda \dot{\tilde{x}} \tag{11}$$

and the control law is defined as

$$u = u^* + u_{rb}\,, \tag{12}$$

where, the robust control signal, u_{rb}, is designed to overcome the deviations from the sliding surface, by employing a switching strategy:

$$u_{rb} = \delta \,\text{sgn}(s) \tag{13}$$

Here, δ is the bound of uncertainties. It is noted that, in the design of a conventional SMC, the uncertainty bound δ, must be known or estimated at the outset of the control design, a matter which is not easily achievable in practice. Such uncertainties may include unknown plant dynamics, parameter variations, and external load disturbances. In particular, the dynamics of micro/nano electromechanical systems are not known exactly, so the ideal controller proposed in (11) may not actually work in practice. As an alternative, the ideal controller can be approximated by a fuzzy inference system

$$u^* = \hat{B}^T W(s) + \psi \tag{14}$$

Here, $\hat{B}$ is the estimated value for the optimal weighting vector, and $W = \begin{bmatrix} w_1 & \cdots & w_n \end{bmatrix}^T$ is a vector with components $w_r(s) = \mu_r \big/ \sum_{r=1}^{n} \mu_r$ and, where, μ_r is the firing strength of the rth rule of the fuzzy algorithm. The bias term ψ represents unmodeled dynamics and external disturbances and is assumed to be bounded as $|\psi| \le \psi$. The weighting vector can be updated by the adaptation rule $\dot{\hat{B}} = \alpha_1 s(t) W$, and the bound of uncertainties is estimated by the adaptation rule $\dot{\psi} = \alpha_2 |s(t)|$, where α_1 and α_2 are strictly positive constants, adaptation rates.

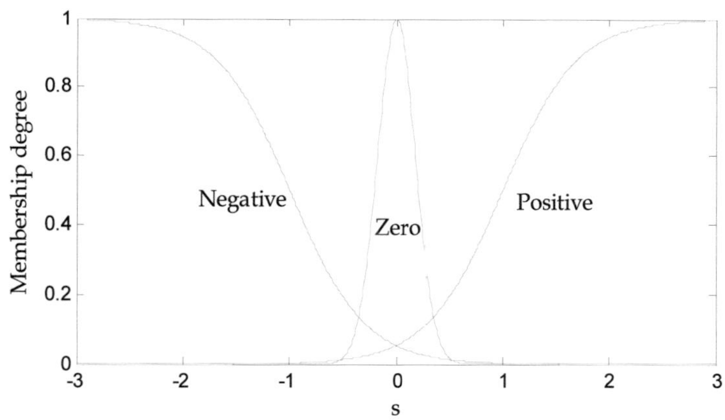

Fig. 16. Membership functions of s for robust adaptive fuzzy control.

The objective is to control the position variable x so as to track the desired trajectory $x_d = 0.6\sin 0.5\tau$. The resonator properties are the same as introduced in Section 3.2 and $V_{AC} = 1.8V$. The input membership functions are selected as shown in Fig. 16 and the sliding surface is defined as $s = \dot{\tilde{x}} + \tilde{x}$. The parameters of these membership functions are chosen such that the parameter s remains close to zero. The initial weighting vector is arbitrarily selected as $\hat{B} = \begin{bmatrix} 1 & 0 & 1 \end{bmatrix}^T$, the initial value of the uncertainty bound is chosen as $\psi = 0.01$ and the learning rates are set to $\alpha_1 = 1$ and $\alpha_2 = 2 \times 10^{-4}$. The controller is activated at $\tau = 200$, for which the resulting output is depicted in Fig. 17, showing the effectiveness of the proposed control strategy.

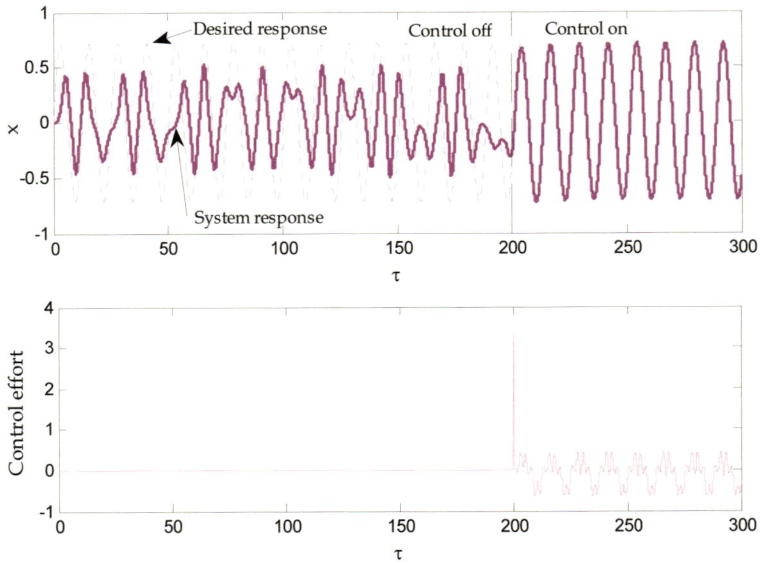

Fig. 17. Simulation results for MEMS resonator with proposed control strategy.

4. Conclusions

This chapter deals with the chaotic motion of micromechanical resonators. The source of nonlinearities in AFM is the Lennard Jones force while nonlinearities in MEMS resonator system include mechanical nonlinearity due to large deformation and nonlinear electrostatic forces. It is shown that each of these systems has one unstable fix point that connects the corresponding homoclinic trajectory to itself. Certain set of parameters may cause homoclinic bifurcation in these systems. Such a bifurcation corresponds to double periodic behavior of the system. It is seen that increase in the amplitude of driving force could lead to a chaotic motion. Finally, an adaptive fuzzy-sliding mode strategy was proposed for control of the chaotic motion. It was shown through simulations study that such a control strategy could successfully eliminate the chaotic motion and force the system response towards a stable orbit.

5. References

Ashhab, M. ; Salapaka, M.V.; Dahleh, M. & Mezic, I. (1999). Dynamical analysis and control of micro-cantilevers, *Automatica,* Vol. 35 , pp. 1663–1670.

Barry, E.; DeMartini, B. E.; Butterfield, E. ; Moehlis, J. & Turner, K. (2007). Chaos for a Microelectromechanical Oscillator Governed by the Nonlinear Mathieu Equation, *Journal of Microelectromechanical Systems*, Vol. 16, pp. 1314–1323.

Basso, M.; Giarrk, L.; Dahleh, M. & Mezic, I. (1998). Numerical analysis of complex dynamics in atomic force microscopes, *Proc. IEEE Int. Conf. Control Appl.*

Burnham, N.A. ; Kulik, A.J. ; Gremaud, G. & Briggs, G.A.D. (1995). Nanosubharmonics: The dynamics of small nonlinear contacts, *Phys. Rev. Lett.*, Vol. 74, pp. 5092–5059.

Calvo, O. (1998), Fuzzy control of chaos, *International Journal of Bifurcation and Chaos*, Vol. 8, No. 8, pp 1743–1747.

Chacon, R. (1999). General results on chaos suppression for biharmonically driven dissipative systems. *Phys Lett A*; 257, pp. 293–300.

Endo, T. & Chua, L. O. (1991). Synchronization of chaos in phase-locked loops, *IEEE Trans. Circuits Syst.*, Vol. 38, pp. 1580-1588.

Garcia, R.; Tamayo, J. & San Paulo, A. (1999). Phase contrast and surface energy hysteresis in tapping mode scanning force microscopy, *Surface Interface Anal* 27, pp.312–316.

Haghighi, H.S. & Markazi, A.H.D. (2010), Chaos prediction and control in MEMS resonators, *Commun Nonlinear Sci Numer Simulat*, Vol. 15, pp. 3091–3099.

Hansma, P.K. ; Elings, V.B. ; Marti, O. & Bracker, C.E. (1988). Scanning tunneling microscopy and atomic force microscopy: Application to biology and technology, *Science*, Vol. 242 , pp. 209-242.

Harley, J.A. ; Chow, E.M. & Kenny, T.W. (1998). Design of resonant beam transducers: An axial force probe for atomic force microscopy, *In Micro-Electro-Mechanical Systems: ASME Intl. ME Congress and Exposition*, pp 274-252, Anaheim, Ca.

Jamitzky, F.; Stark, M.; Bunk, W. ; Heckl, W.M. & Stark, R.W. (2006). Chaos in dynamic atomic force microscopy, *Nanotechnology*, Vol. 17 pp. 213–220.

Kennedy, M. P. (1993). Three steps to chaos, Part I: Evolution, Part II: A Chua's circuit primer, *IEEE Trans. Circuits Syst.* I, Vol. 40, No.10, pp.640-656.

Lin, L.; Howe, R. & Pissano, A.P. (1998). Microelectromechanical filters for signal processing, *J. Microelectromech. Syst.* Vol. 7, No.3, pp. 286–294.

Liu, S; Davidson, A; & Lin, Q. (2004). Simulation studies on nonlinear dynamics and chaos in a MEMS cantilever control system, *Journal of Micromechanics and Microengineering*,Vol. 14, pp. 1064–1073.

Logeeswaran, V.J.; Tay, F.E.H.; Chan, M.L.; Chau, F.S. & Liang, Y.C. (2002). *Proceedings of the DTIP 2002 on A 2f Method for the Measurement of Resonant Frequency and Q-factor of Micromechanical Transducers*, ,pp. 584–590, Cannes, May 2002.

Luo, A. & Wang Fei-Yue. (2002). Chaotic motion in a micro-electro-mechanical system with non-linearity from capacitors, *Commun Nonlinear Sci Numer Simul*, Vol. 7, pp. 31–49.

Melnikov, VK. (1963). On the stability of the center for time periodic perturbations. *Trans Moscow Math Soc*,12, pp. 1–57.

Mestrom, R.M.C. ; Fey, R.H.B.; van Beek, J.T.M.; Phan, K.L. & Nijmeijer, H. (2007). Modeling the dynamics of a MEMS resonator: Simulations and experiments, *Sens. Actuators A*, Vol. 142 ,pp. 306-315.

Moon, F. C. & Holmes, P. A magnetoelastic strange attractor, *J. Sound Vib.*, Vol. 65, No. 2, pp. 285–296.

Nayfeh, A.H.; Younis, M.I.; Abdel-Rahman, E. (2007). Dynamic pull-in phenomenon in MEMS resonators, *Nonlinear Dynamics*,Vol. 48,pp. 153-63.

Poursamad, A. & Davaie-Markazi, A.H. (2009-a). Robust adaptive fuzzy control of unknown chaotic systems, *Applied Soft Computing*, Vol. 9, pp. 970–976.

Poursamad, A. & Markazi, A.H.D. (2009-b) Adaptive fuzzy sliding-mode control for multi-input multi-output chaotic systems, *Chaos, Solitons Fractals*, Vol. 42, pp. 3100–3109.

Roukes, M. (2001). Nanoelectromechanical systems face the future, *Phys.World*, Vol. 14 , pp. 25.

Wang, Y.C.; Adams, S.G.; Thorp, J.S.; MacDonald, N.C.; Hartwell, P. & Bertsch, F. (1998). Chaos in MEMS, parameter estimation and its potential application, *IEEE Trans. Circuits Syst. I*, Vol. 45, pp. 1013–1020.

Xie, H. & Fedder, G. (2002). Vertical comb-finger capacitive actuation and sensing for coms-MEMS, *Sens. Actuators A*, Vol. 95 , pp. 212–221.

Yagasaki, K. (2007), Bifurcations and chaos in vibrating microcantilevers of tapping mode atomic force microscopy, *Journal of Non-Linear Mechanics*, Vol. 42, pp. 658 - 672.

Younis, M. I. & Nayfeh, A. H. (2003). A Study of the Nonlinear Response of a Resonant Microbeam to an Electric Actuation, *Nonlinear Dynamics*, Vol. 31, No. 1 pp. 91–117.

6

Control and Identification of Chaotic Systems by Altering the Oscillation Energy

Valery Tereshko
University of the West of Scotland
United Kingdom

1. Introduction

Last years, researchers paid a major attention to the controlling chaos schemes that use information obtained from the experimental time series of system's accessible variables. When the trajectory is in a neighbourhood of desired UPO, the Ott-Grebogi-Yorke (OGY) controlling chaos scheme can be applied (Ott et al., 1990). Exploiting the linearity of return map near corresponding unstable fixed point, it stabilizes UPOs with one unstable direction by directing the trajectory to the orbit stable manifold. The technique requires performing several calculations to generate a control signal. This approach may fail (i) if the dynamics is so fast that the controller cannot follow it, and (ii) if the dynamics is highly unstable, i.e. the trajectory diverges from a target so far that small perturbations cannot be effective. For highly dissipative systems that are well characterized by a one-dimensional return map, occasional proportional feedback (Hunt, 1991; Peng et al., 1991) and occasional feedback (Myneni et al., 1999) techniques was developed. The occasional proportional feedback utilizes an amplitude of parametric perturbation that is proportional to the deviation of system's current state from its desired state (Hunt, 1991; Peng et al., 1991). Similar technique but with application to a system accessible variable instead of a parameter is called proportional perturbation feedback (Garfinkel et al., 1992). Alternatively, occasional feedback utilizes a control pulse duration that is equal to the transit time of trajectory through a specified window placed on either side of saddle fixed point (Myneni et al., 1999). Owing to simplicity, these methods do not require any processor and can be implemented at high speeds.

For highly unstable orbits, quasicontinuous extensions of original OGY technique can be applied when more than one control points per period are taken (Hübinger et al., 1994; Reyl et al., 1993). Another option is to use a continuous-time control (Gauthier et al., 1994; Just et al., 1999b; Pyragas, 1992; 1995; Socolar et al., 1994). However, obtaining complete information about desired trajectory can be difficult (or even impossible, say, at high frequencies or spatial complexity). Therefore, the continuous-time delayed feedback using information only about a period of desired UPO became most popular. Here, the control signal is proportional to the difference between a system current state and its state at some earlier time, the delay being set to a period of desired UPO (Gauthier et al., 1994; Pyragas, 1992). This approach is found effective to control low-period UPOs at high frequencies (Gauthier et al., 1994), but it may fail for high-period UPOs or for highly unstable orbits (Just et al., 1999b). An extension of method that incorporates information from many previous states of the system is suitable for controlling UPOs in fast dynamical systems, with large value of Lyapunov exponents, and of high periods (Socolar et al., 1994). The attractiveness of delayed feedback scheme consists in the self-organizing ability of a system to autosynchronize its own behaviour. However, unlike the OGY-based schemes where the trajectory is targeted to a predefined UPO, the delayed feedback control does not discriminate between different periodic orbits of the same period, and does not necessarily lead to the stabilization of orbits embedded in a chaotic attractor (Hikihara et al., 1997; Simmendinger et al., 1998). The success of this control is significantly restricted by a control loop latency (Just et al., 1999a).

In the nonfeedback, or open-loop, schemes, the control signal does not depend on a system state. One of approaches is a nonlinear entrainment method (Hübler & Lüscher, 1989; Jackson & Hübler, 1990). It requires knowledge of the system equations to construct control forces that can have large amplitude and complicated shape. The basins of entrainment, in turn, can have very complicated structure. Typically, this method can require as many control forces, as there are dimensions of the system.

In contrast, there are many examples of converting chaos to a periodic motion by exposing a system to only one, weak periodic force or weak parameter modulation (Alexeev & Loskutov, 1987; Braiman & Goldhirsch, 1991; Cao, 2005; Chacón, 1996; Chacón & Díaz Bejarano, 1993; Chizhevsky & Corbalán, 1996; Chizhevsky et al., 1997; Dangoisse et al., 1997; Fronzoni et al., 1991; Kivshar et al., 1994; Lima & Pettini, 1990; Liu & Leite, 1994; Meucci et al., 1994; Qu et al., 1995; Ramesh & Narayanan, 1999; Rödelsperger et al., 1995; Tereshko & Shchekinova, 1998). Typically, this approach utilizes only a period and an amplitude of perturbation (Alexeev & Loskutov, 1987; Braiman & Goldhirsch, 1991; Kivshar et al., 1994; Lima & Pettini, 1990; Liu & Leite, 1994; Ramesh & Narayanan, 1999). If the amplitude is kept small enough, one can expect a controlled periodic orbit or an equilibrium to trace closely the corresponding unperturbed one (provided that no crises are induced). The periodic perturbation methods can be easily realized in practice. However, the independence of the perturbation from a system state leads to some limitations of above approach: the control by periodic perturbations relying only on their period and amplitude is not, in general, a goal-oriented technique (Shinbrot et al., 1993). On the other hand, the importance of a phase (Cao, 2005; Chacón, 1996; Chizhevsky & Corbalán, 1996; Chizhevsky et al., 1997; Dangoisse et al., 1997; Fronzoni et al., 1991; Meucci et al., 1994; Qu et al., 1995; Tereshko & Shchekinova, 1998) and even a shape (Azevedo & Rezende, 1991; Chacón, 1996; Chacón & Díaz Bejarano, 1993; Rödelsperger et al., 1995) of perturbation became evident. The utilization of extra parameters allows tuning the perturbation to a desired target shape more selectively. The above findings were generalized in a concept of geometrical resonance that reveals the underlying mechanism of nonfeedback resonant control for a general class of chaotic oscillators (Chacón, 1996). The phase of perturbation is crucial for the success of nonfeedback resonant control. First of all, it determines the direction and, hence, the targets where a trajectory is driven to. Secondly, keeping the perturbation precisely in phase with the controlled signal ensures smallest control amplitudes, whereas dephasing can destroy the control. By changing only the perturbation phase, one can switch the trajectory from one controlled state to another (Tereshko & Shchekinova, 1998).

In real-life systems, the existing uncontrolled drifts can spoil resonant conditions. Small deviation of the perturbation frequency from the resonance is equivalent to slowly varying modulation of the phase. This results in a temporal evolution consisting of regular alternations between a stabilized orbit and the chaotic behaviours (Chizhevsky & Corbalán, 1996; Meucci et al., 1994; Qu et al., 1995). The real-life nonfeedback control may, thus, demand an occasional adjustment of the perturbation frequency. To overcome the above problem, a feedback control where the perturbation depends on the controlled signal can be used.

Have analyzed the existing approaches, we developed a following control method. To any type of system behaviour, we put in correspondence a value of averaged oscillation energy that is an averaged (over the time) compound of the system kinetic and potential energy. The objective is to alter this energy so as to correspond to a desired behaviour. This is a general approach that does not depend on particular oscillator equations. Simple feedback depending solely on an output signal is utilized for this purpose. We start with identifying the type of control perturbations appropriate for the above control. One simply increases the feedback strength, and, thus, depending on the perturbation phase, increases or decreases the oscillation energy. The above strategy does not require any computation of the control signal and, hence, is applicable for control as well as identification of unknown systems. The above approach was applied to control isolated oscillators, as well as coupled ones (Tereshko, 2009; Tereshko et al., 2004a;b). Here, we summarize the obtained results and present our new findings in controlling spatially-extended systems.

2. General approach

Let us consider controlling a general type nonlinear oscillator

$$\ddot{x} + \chi(x,\dot{x}) + \xi(x) = F(t) + g(x,\dot{x}) \tag{1}$$

where $\chi(x,\dot{x})$, $\xi(x)$ and $g(x,\dot{x})$ are dissipative or energy-generating component, restoring force, and control force, respectively. These functions are nonlinear in general case. Also, $\chi(x,\dot{x})$ and $g(x)$ are assumed not to contain an additive function of x. $F(t)$ is an external time-dependent driving force.

At $F(t) = 0$ and $g(x,\dot{x}) = 0$, Eq. (1) possesses the equilibriums defined by equation $\xi(x) = 0$. In oscillators with nonlinear damping (say, van der Pol and Reyleigh oscillators), an equilibrium becomes unstable at some parameter values, and stable self-sustained oscillations are excited. In other types of oscillators, say Duffing oscillator, a limit cycle arises under the action of periodic driving force. We assume that at some driving amplitudes, a limit cycle becomes saddle, and new attractor, say period-2 cycle, arises. In many well-known examples, this scenario leads, through the sequence of bifurcations, to the birth of chaotic attractor.

One can define an energy of oscillations as the sum of "potential" and "kinetic" energy:

$$E(t) = \int \xi(x)\,\mathrm{d}x + \frac{1}{2}\dot{x}^2 . \tag{2}$$

An averaged (over period T) energy yields

$$\langle E \rangle = \frac{1}{T}\int_0^T \Big(\int \xi(x)\,\mathrm{d}x + \frac{1}{2}\dot{x}^2 \Big)\,\mathrm{d}t . \tag{3}$$

For periodic dynamics T is an oscillation period, whereas for chaotic one $T \to \infty$. Each attractor of an oscillator is assigned to a value of averaged energy (3). If an oscillation amplitude is sufficiently small, the limit cycle oscillations can be approximated as $x \simeq \rho \sin \omega t$, which gives $\langle E \rangle = \frac{1}{2}\rho^2$.

Typically, transitions to a chaotic attractor correspond to the increase of energy (3). Let us clarify this statement on the example of a period-doubling process. Suppose that changing some of the system parameters results in an oscillation period doubling and, eventually, in a chaos. Starting at period-1 cycle, its amplitude grows with increasing the above parameter, and, hence, energy (3) does. Every period-doubling bifurcation contributes subharmonic (as well as its odd harmonic) to the fundamental frequency, which again increases energy (3). Thus, the higher the orbit period is, the higher the averaged energy corresponding to this orbit. A stationary point, around which a limit cycle develops, can be viewed as a zero-amplitude cycle possessing, thus, zero energy.

A following control strategy can be proposed. Starting at a lower energy attractor, one stabilizes higher energy repellors by sequential increasing the averaged oscillation energy. On the contrary, decreasing this energy leads to the stabilization of lower energy repellors.

A change of energy (2) yields

$$\dot{E}(t) = \xi(x)\dot{x} + \dot{x}\ddot{x} = \big(-\chi(x,\dot{x}) + F(t) + g(x,\dot{x})\big)\dot{x}\,. \tag{4}$$

The last term of (4) represents an energy change caused solely by the control. We require that

$$g(x,\dot{x})\,\dot{x} > 0\ (< 0) \tag{5}$$

for $\forall(x,\dot{x})$. A minimal feedback satisfying (5) is achieved at $g = g(\dot{x})$. Indeed, simple linear (relative to the velocity) control $g(\dot{x}) \sim \dot{x}$ as well as nonlinear controls of higher power, say $g(\dot{x}) \sim \dot{x}^3$ suffice. In general

$$g(\dot{x}) = k\,h(\dot{x}) \tag{6}$$

where $h(\dot{x})$ is assumed to be odd, i.e. $h(\dot{x}) = -h(-\dot{x})$. One can, thus, define

$$h(\dot{x}) \begin{cases} > 0, & \text{if } \dot{x} > 0 \\ = 0, & \text{if } \dot{x} = 0 \\ < 0, & \text{if } \dot{x} < 0\,. \end{cases} \tag{7}$$

To guarantee a control perturbation tininess even at high values of $\dot{x}$, $h(\dot{x})$ is taken to be bounded. Throughout, we consider $g(\dot{x}) = k\tanh(\beta\dot{x})$ with $0 < \beta \leqslant \infty$ determining the function slope.

Perturbation (6-7) is specially tuned to control equilibriums: their positions are not changed by the control as the latter vanishes at $\dot{x} = 0$. $\dot{E} = 0$ at equilibriums respectively. The above control does not vanish at dynamic attractors. Our aim, however, is not controlling the UPOs of unperturbed system existing at given parameter values, but rather the shift of a system into a region of desired behaviours. Energy (3) is changed so as to match energy of a desired state. For small oscillations, one can find amplitude ρ by substituting $x = \rho\sin\omega t$ into an averaged (over period T) energy change and solving equation

$$\langle\dot{E}\rangle = \frac{1}{T}\int_0^T \dot{E}(t)\,\mathrm{d}t = \frac{1}{T}\int_0^T \big(-\chi(x,\dot{x}) + F(t) + g(x,\dot{x})\big)\dot{x}\,\mathrm{d}t = 0\,. \tag{8}$$

Equation (8) describes the balance of dissipation and energy supply brought by damping, driving, and control forces. For general orbit defined by the infinite series of periodic modes, a fundamental mode as well as its harmonics should, in principle, be counted.

In this paper, we alter the feedback strength to adjust the oscillation energy to different levels. The above strategy does not require any computation of control signal and, hence, is applicable for control as well as identification of unknown systems.

Another strategy is based on a goal-oriented control of desired target. It can be applied in cases when the system equations are known or a desired target can be identified (say, extracted from the system time series). The amplitude of system's natural response is derived from equation

$$\frac{1}{T}\int_0^T\big(-\chi(x,\dot{x})+F(t)\big)\dot{x}\,dt=0\,. \tag{9}$$

Equation (9) describes the balance of dissipation and supply of system's intrinsic energy. For free self-sustained oscillations, this balance is supported entirely by nonlinear damping. To eliminate the natural response distortion imposed by the control, the following condition must be satisfied:

$$\frac{1}{T}\int_0^T\big(g(x,\dot{x})\big)\dot{x}\,dt=0\,. \tag{10}$$

For small oscillations, substitution of $g(x,\dot{x})=k\tanh(\beta\dot{x})\approx k(\beta\dot{x}-\frac{1}{3}\beta^3\dot{x}^3)$ into (10) yields

$$\beta=\frac{2}{\rho\omega}\,. \tag{11}$$

Thus, the distortion can be minimized solely by tuning a perturbation shape. If $\rho\ll 1$, β should be sufficiently large so as to preserve the underlying natural response.
Control (6-7) does not depend on the type of functions $\chi(x,\dot{x})$, $\xi(x)$, and $F(t)$, and, hence, can be applied to linear and nonlinear oscillators, to regular and chaotic dynamics.
The approach can be easily generalized to a case of coupled oscillator networks (Tereshko et al., 2004b).

3. Controlling 2-D oscillators

3.1 Van der Pol oscillator

Consider the van der Pol oscillator with $\chi(x,\dot{x})=(x^2-\mu)\dot{x}$ and $\xi(x)=x$ controlled by feedback $g(\dot{x})=k\tanh(\beta\dot{x})$. Linearizing the dynamic equation (1) in the vicinity of $x=0$, one obtains the eigenvalues: $\lambda_1=\big(\mu+k\beta-\sqrt{(\mu+k\beta)^2-4}\big)/2$ and $\lambda_2=\big(\mu+k\beta+\sqrt{(\mu+k\beta)^2-4}\big)/2$. At $\mu>0$ and $k<0$, the perturbation with $k<-(1/\beta)\mu$ or $\beta>(1/|k|)\mu$ stabilizes the unstable equilibrium. Thus, two control strategies can be applied: (i) altering the perturbation magnitude; (ii) reshaping the perturbation. When $\beta\to\infty$, $\tanh(\beta\dot{x})\to\text{sign}(\dot{x})$. The energy change caused by the control yields $g(\dot{x})\dot{x}=k\,\text{sign}(\dot{x})\,\dot{x}=k\,|\dot{x}|$. This strategy corresponds to maximizing the rejection (injection) of the oscillation energy and is, in fact, the first approximation of optimal control for a van der Pol oscillator with small dissipation (Kolosov, 1999).

3.2 Forced two-well Duffing oscillator

To analyze controlling chaotic oscillators, consider the forced two-well Duffing oscillator with negative linear and positive cubic restoring terms:

$$\ddot{x}+e\dot{x}-x+x^3=b\cos\omega t+k\tanh(\beta\dot{x})\,. \tag{12}$$

In unperturbed system, at $e=0.3$, $\omega=1.2$, and $b<0.3$, the "particle" become trapped into other left or right potential well oscillating around $x=-1$ and $x=1$ respectively (or tending to these stationary states when $b=0$). At $b\gtrsim 0.3$, the particle is able to escape the wells, its irregular wandering between two potential wells corresponding to chaotic oscillations. Taking

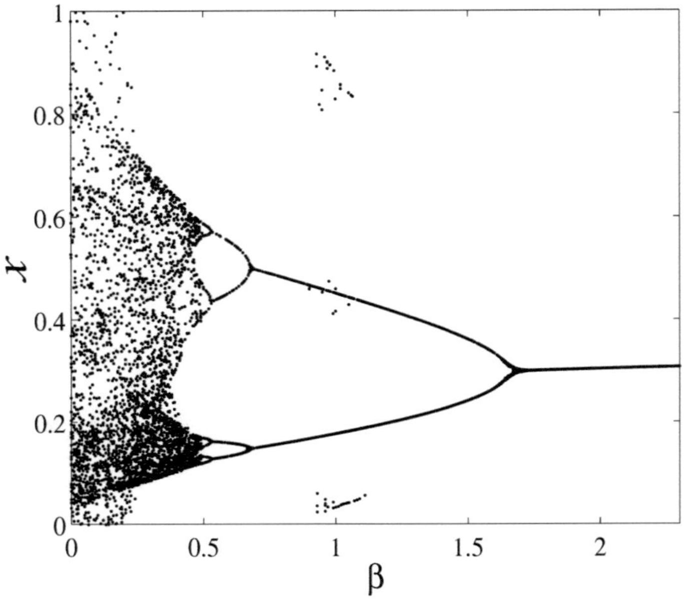

Fig. 1. Bifurcation diagram of oscillator (12) at $e = 0.3$, $\omega = 1.2$, $b = 0.31$, and $k = -0.06$.

the linear approximation $\tanh(\beta\dot{x}) \approx \beta\dot{x}$, obtain $\dot{E} = \big((-e + k\beta)\dot{x} + b\cos\omega t)\big)\dot{x}$. At small β's, the control action is, thus, equivalent to linear adjustment of the oscillator damping. With increasing β, the influence of the perturbation nonlinearity respectively increases.

Let us fix the amplitude k and change only the perturbation slope β. This induces the double action: (i) reshaping the perturbation, and (ii) changing its effective amplitude k_{ef}. Increasing the slope leads to the increase of k_{ef} (it changes from 0 to k when β changes from 0 to ∞). As a result, when $k < 0$ the sequential stabilization of orbits of the period-doubling cascade occurs in the reverse order (Fig. 1). These orbits are stabilized at relatively small β and k. Around $\beta = 1$, the coexisting orbits multiple of period 3 appear. They can be eliminated by the slow modulation of either k or h. The similar effect of reverse period-doubling is reached at increasing e. However, suppressing the oscillations (to a state where the trajectory remains in the vicinity of either 1 or -1) occurs only at extremely high e. Hereupon, the system dynamics becomes overdamped, which requires extremely long transitional times. In contrast, the perturbations with large β effectively suppress the oscillations when k remains relatively small (Fig. 2). Note, the requirement for large β follows from condition (11): when $\rho \to 0$, $\beta \to \infty$. Unlike stabilization of stationary points in unforced oscillators, the system trajectory slightly deviates around the controlled point (with the amplitude less than 10^{-3} in Fig. 2), and the control, hence, does not vanish there. This happens because stationary points in forced oscillators are not the invariants of dynamics and become these only at zero forcing. Figure 3 demonstrates the entrainment between the feedback force at very small and large β's, when stabilizing the period-1 orbit and the stationary point respectively, and the driving force waveforms. The larger β the better the perturbation force waveform fits (in anti-phase) the driving force to suppress the latter. Tuning the phase and the shape of perturbation to their driving force counterparts is equivalent to combining the driving and the perturbation forces into the one effective force $F_{ef} = (b + k)\cos\omega t$.

Changing the perturbation phase on the opposite one leads to the increase of the averaged oscillation energy allowing the UPOs corresponding to the higher values of energy (2) be

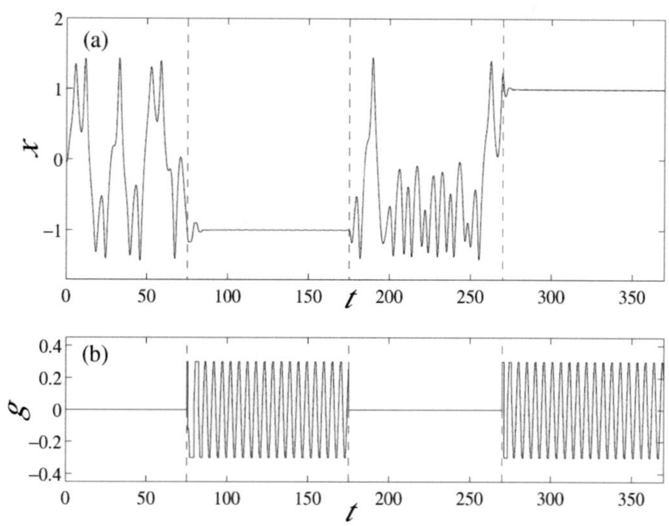

Fig. 2. Dynamics of (a) the state variable and (b) the control perturbation of oscillator (12) at $e = 0.3$, $\omega = 1.2$, $b = 0.31$, $k = -0.3$, and $\beta = 5000$.

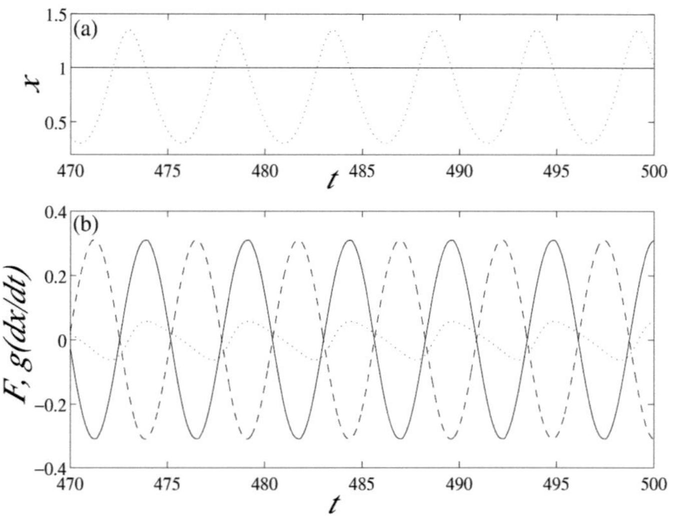

Fig. 3. Dynamics of (a) the state variable at $\beta = 5000$ and $k = -0.31$ (solid line); $\beta = 0.01$ and $k = -9$ (dotted line), and (b) the control perturbation at $\beta = 5000$ and $k = -0.31$ (solid line); $\beta = 0.01$ and $k = -9$ (dotted line), and the driving force (dashed line) of oscillator (12). For all graphs, $e = 0.3$, $\omega = 1.2$, and $b = 0.31$.

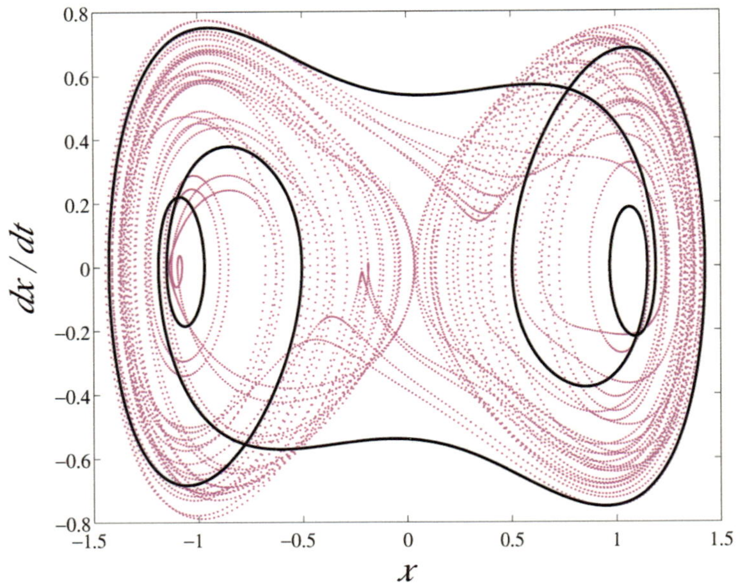

Fig. 4. Phase space of oscillator (12) at $e = 0.3$, $\omega = 1.2$, $b = 0.31$, $\beta = 2$, and $k = 0$ (grey dotted line); $k = 0.06$ (bold solid line).

stabilized. Figure 4 demonstrates the stabilization of period-5 orbit. The similar strategy can destabilize the initially stable system by shifting it to the chaotic regions.

3.3 Forced van der Pol oscillator

Controlling chaotic oscillators with nonlinear damping shows the clearly different scenarios of the control. Let us analyze the forced van der Pol oscillator:

$$\ddot{x} + e(x^2 - \mu)\dot{x} + x = b\cos\omega t + k\tanh(\beta\dot{x})\,. \tag{13}$$

In the unperturbed system, no regularity is observed at $e = 5$, $\mu = 1$, $b = 5$ and $\omega = 2.463$ (Fig. 5(a)). At small enough β, obtain $\dot{E} = \Big(-e\big(x^2 - (\mu + e^{-1}k\beta)\big)\dot{x} + b\cos(\omega t)\Big)\dot{x}$. Unlike the previous case, even a weak control perturbation changes nonlinearly the oscillator damping. One can expect the markedly different manifestations of the control at small and large β, respectively. Indeed, the control with $k < 0$ decreases the negative damping term, which leads to stabilization of the period-3 and the period-1 orbits (Fig. 5(b)). These orbits are different from the orbits stabilized by decreasing the driving force amplitude. We compared the stabilized orbits and their unperturbed counterparts. To stabilize the period-1 orbit, the control perturbation induces the shift of μ to $\mu' = \mu - e^{-1}k\beta$ (see Fig. 5(b)). As predicted by the theory, the stabilized orbit and the unperturbed orbit that corresponds to this shift coincide. For orbits with more complicated shapes, the stabilized orbits trace closely their unperturbed counterparts.

With the increase of β, the control perturbation begins to affect the driving force term. Figure 5(c) demonstrates the stabilization of period-5 orbit corresponding to the lower amplitudes of driving force.

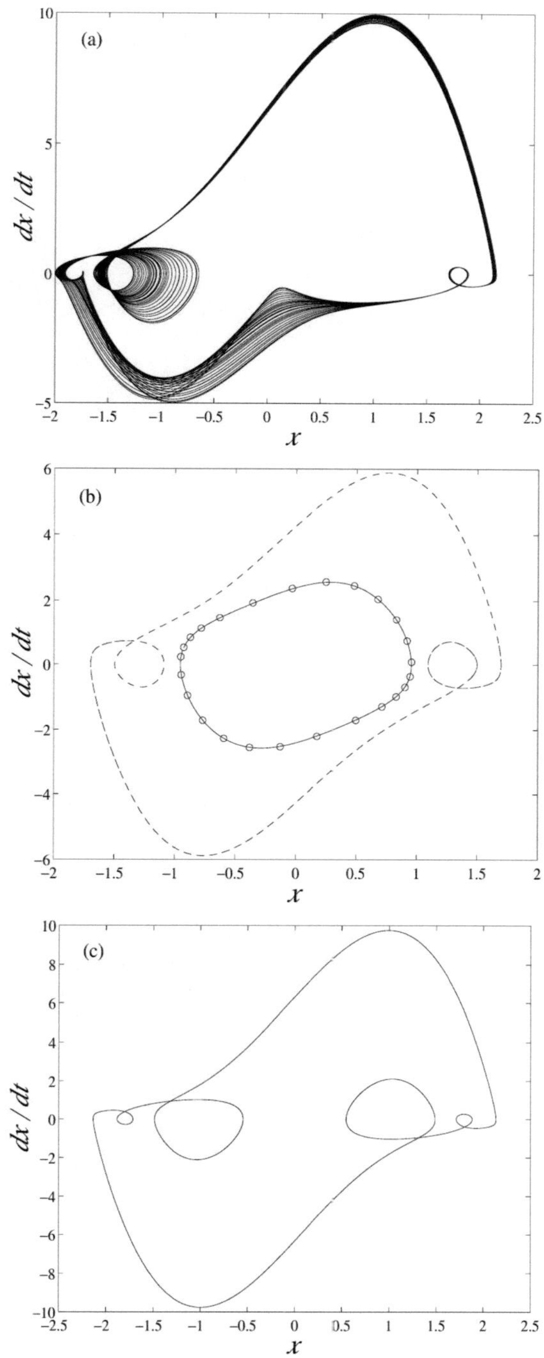

Fig. 5. Phase space of oscillator (13) at $e = 5$, $\mu = 1$, $\omega = 2.463$, $b = 5$, and (a) $k = 0$; (b) $\beta = 0.1$, and $k = -20$ (dashed line); $k = -40$ (solid line); circles indicate the period-1 cycle of the unperturbed system at $e = 5$, $\mu = 0.2$, $\omega = 2.463$, and $b = 5$; (c) $\beta = 3$, and $k = -0.13$.

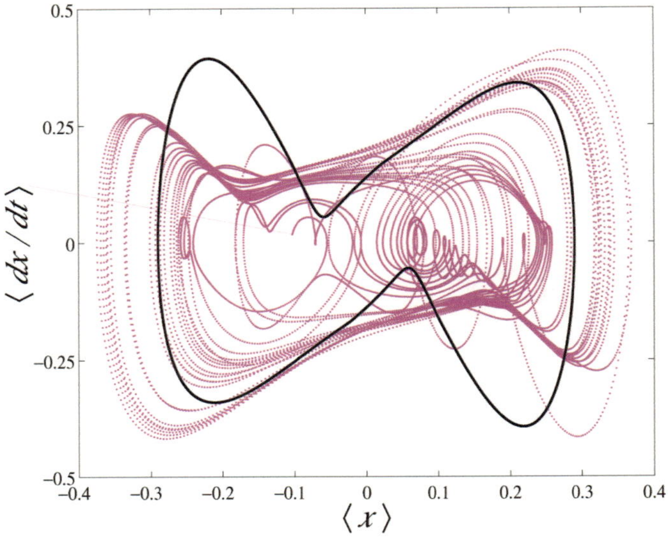

Fig. 6. Phase space of oscillator network (14) for the averaged trajectory ($\langle x \rangle = \frac{1}{n}\sum_{i=1}^{n} x$ and $\langle \dot{x} \rangle = \frac{1}{n}\sum_{i=1}^{n} \dot{x}$) at $e = 0.18$, $\nu = 8$, $\omega = 1.02$, $b = 0.35$, $\frac{1}{n}(\alpha_1, \alpha_2, .., \alpha_n)$ = (1.7861, -2.1131, 0.2561, 2.2297, -1.3585, -0.6648, 1.1977, 0.2451, -2.2229, 0.4282), $n = 10$ and $k = 0$ (grey dotted line); $k = -0.18$ (solid line). $j = \arg\{\min(|\alpha_1|, |\alpha_2|, .., |\alpha_n|)\} = 8$, which implies the perturbation to be applied to 8th oscillator.

3.4 Coupled oscillators

Consider controlling the network of n oscillators coupled via the mean field. As the network element, take the forced van der Pol-Duffing oscillator, an oscillator with the van der Pol nonlinear damping and the modified Duffing restoring force containing only the cubic term. This oscillator describes the dynamics of nonlinear circuit (Ueda, 1992). Let us assume that the oscillators are identical but their coupling strengths are randomly varied, and only single element of the network is subjected to the control. The oscillator with the weakest coupling strength is least affected by the mean field, and, hence, is most preserving own intrinsic dynamics. We apply the control to this oscillator. The oscillator network equations, thus, read

$$\ddot{x}_j + e(\nu x_j^2 - 1)\dot{x}_j + x_j^3 + \alpha_j \frac{1}{n}\sum_{i=1}^{n} x_i = b\cos\omega t + k\tanh(\beta \dot{x})$$

$$\ddot{x}_l + e(\nu x_l^2 - 1)\dot{x}_l + x_l^3 + \alpha_l \frac{1}{n}\sum_{i=1}^{n} x_i = b\cos\omega t \tag{14}$$

where $j = \arg\{\min(|\alpha_1|, |\alpha_2|, .., |\alpha_n|)\}, l = 1, 2, .., n,\ l \neq j$.

For single oscillator, the dynamics is chaotic at $e = 0.2$, $\nu = 8$, $\omega = 1.02$, and $b = 0.35$ (Ueda, 1992). Coupling 10 chaotic oscillators by the connections with strengths varied randomly according to the Gaussian distribution (with the mean equal to 0, and the variance and the standard deviation equal to 1) produces various dynamics. Figure 6 demonstrates the averaged trajectory of the network that reveals all futures of chaotic behaviour. The perturbation decreasing the averaged oscillation energy, being applied to the most weakly connected oscillator, stabilizes the network dynamics. Controlling, in opposite, the most

strongly connected oscillator leads to the similar results requiring, however, much larger control amplitudes.
We performed the simulations of higher dimensional networks. For 50 oscillator network with random normally distributed coupling strengths, the control perturbation applied to the most weakly coupled oscillator is found to stabilize the dynamics.

4. Controlling 3-D oscillators

4.1 Colpitts oscillator

The chaotic attractors have been observed in several electronic circuits. One of such circuit is the Colpitts oscillator (Baziliauskas, 2001; De Feo, 2000; Kennedy, 1994). It consists of a bipolar junction transistor (the circuit active nonlinear element) and a resonant L-C circuit. The oscillator is widely used in electronic devices and communication systems.
The Colpitts oscillator dynamics can be described by the following dynamical system (Baziliauskas, 2001):

$$\begin{aligned} \dot{x} &= y - f(x) \\ \dot{y} &= c - x - by - z \\ \varepsilon\dot{z} &= y - d \end{aligned} \tag{15}$$

where function

$$f(x) = \begin{cases} -a(z+1), & z < -1, \\ 0, & z \geqslant -1, \end{cases}$$

dimensionless variables x and z correspond to circuit's capacitor voltages, and variable y corresponds to circuit's inductor current. a, b, c, d are the dimensionless parameters. This model is equivalent to the so-called ideal model of the circuit (De Feo, 2000). It maintains, however, all essential features exhibited by the real Colpitts oscillator. For $z < -1$, the transistor works in its forward-active region, while for $z \geqslant -1$, it is cut-off.
Substituting $y = \varepsilon\dot{z} + d$ to the second equation of (16), obtain

$$\begin{aligned} \varepsilon\ddot{z} + \varepsilon b\dot{z} + z &= c - bd - x \\ \dot{x} &= -f(x) + \varepsilon\dot{z} + d\,. \end{aligned} \tag{16}$$

To apply the above approach, one need to add feedback $g(\dot{x})$ to the first equation of system (16). For the above oscillator, the change of energy (2) caused by this control yields $\dot{z}g(\dot{z})$. If $g(\dot{z})$ takes form (6-7), the latter term always provides the increase (decrease) of the oscillation energy for positive (negative) perturbation magnitudes. We, thus, consider $g(\dot{z}) = k\ \tanh(\beta\dot{z})$. Taking $\dot{z} = \frac{1}{\varepsilon}(y - d)$, obtain the control feedback to apply to the second equation of system (16):

$$g(y) = k\ \tanh\left(\frac{1}{\varepsilon}\beta(y-d)\right)\,. \tag{17}$$

Perturbation (17) is specially tuned to control the equilibrium of system (16). Figure 7 demonstrates the latter. k is chosen to be negative, which results in decreasing the averaged oscillation energy.
Note, the stationary point exists only in the forward-active region. Unlike, the periodic orbit trajectories spend most of their times in the cut-off region. The circuit oscillations are balanced, thus, not around the above stationary point but rather around the total collector voltage equilibrium. The latter is proportional to $x + z$. Let us consider $\varepsilon = 1$ and define $w = x + z$. In

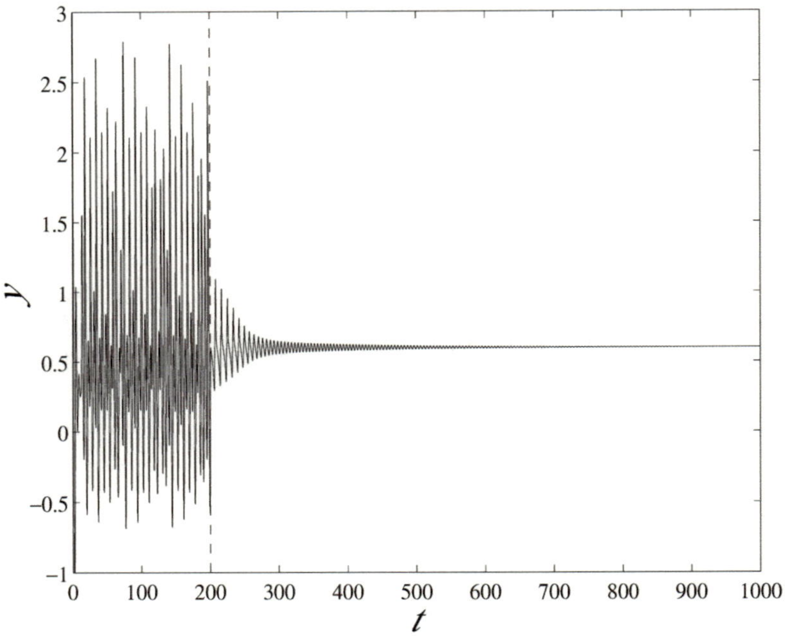

Fig. 7. Dynamics of the state variable of oscillator (16) at $\varepsilon = 1$, $a = 30$, $b = 0.8$, $c = 20$, $d = 0.6$, $\beta = 10$, and $k = 0$ ($t < 200$); $k = -1.6$ ($t \geqslant 200$). Dashed line indicates the time of starting the control.

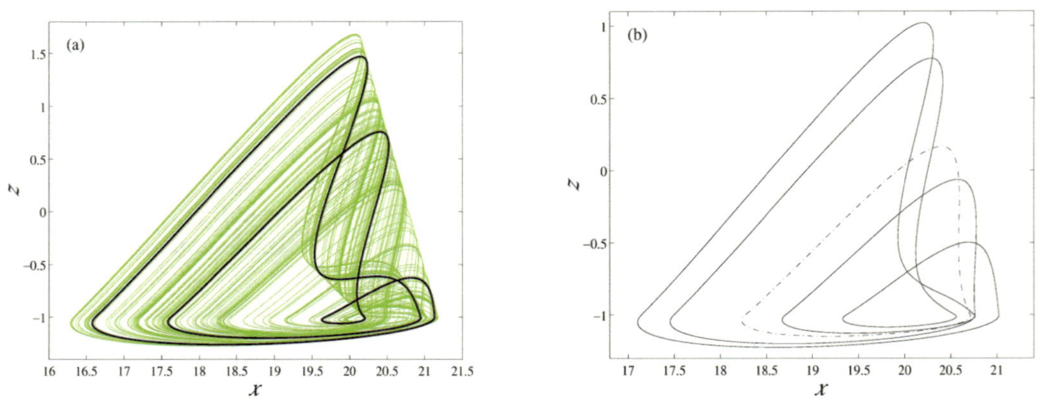

Fig. 8. Phase space of oscillator (16) at $\varepsilon = 1$, $a = 30$, $b = 0.8$, $c = 20$, $d = 0.6$, $\beta = 10$, and (a): $k = 0$ (grey line); $k = -0.009$ (bold black line); (b): $k = -0.012$ (solid line); $k = -0.24$ (dot-dashed line)

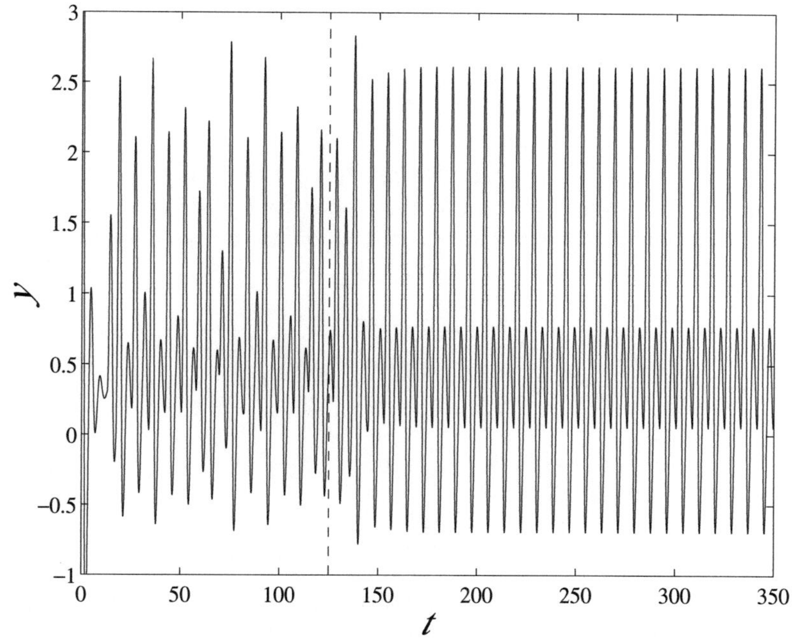

Fig. 9. Dynamics of the state variable of oscillator (16) at $\varepsilon = 1$, $a = 30$, $b = 0.8$, $c = 20$, $d = 0.6$, $\beta = 10$, and $k = 0$ ($t < 125$); $k = 0.08$ ($t \geqslant 125$). Dashed line indicates the time of starting the control.

the cut-off region, the summation of first and third equations of system (16) yields $\dot{w} = 2y - d$. Substitution of $y = \frac{1}{2}(\dot{w} + d)$ to the second equation of system (16) results in the following dynamics of the total collector voltage:

$$\ddot{w} + b\dot{w} + 2w = 2c - bd\,. \tag{18}$$

Perturbation $g(\dot{w})$ satisfying conditions (6-7) being applied to oscillator (18) results in the following:

$$g(y) = k\ \tanh\left(\beta(y - \frac{d}{2})\right) \tag{19}$$

To control circuit's periodic orbits, the second equation of system (16) should be exposed to the latter feedback.

Figures 8 and 9 demonstrate controlling the oscillator periodic orbits. At $k = 0$, the system exhibits chaotic oscillations (Fig. 8(a), grey line). Let us apply the feedback that decreases the oscillation energy. Strengthening its force, one sequentially stabilizes the orbits corresponding to the windows of chaotic attractor and then the period-doubling orbits of main cascade in their reverse order. At $k \simeq -0.009$, one obtains the period-3 orbit corresponding to the largest window of chaotic attractor (Fig. 8(a), bold black line). The period-8, -4, -2, and -1 orbits are stabilized at $k \simeq -0.11, -0.12, -0.14, -0.22$ respectively. Figure 8(b) demonstrates the stabilized period-4 (solid line) and the period-1 (dot-dashed line) orbit respectively.

Increasing the oscillation energy leads to the stabilization of orbits corresponding to these energy levels. As example, Fig. 9 demonstrates the stabilization of so-called 2-pulse orbit.

We also considered a chain (ring) of 10 Colpitts oscillators with the diffusion-type couplings (with coupled emitters and collectors of the circuit transistor (Baziliauskas, 2001)). Different UPOs were stabilized with control perturbations applied to only single oscillators.

4.2 Chua's oscillator

Let us consider controlling a system that produces two major mechanisms of chaotic behaviour in continuous systems — the Rössler and the Lorenz types. This system is the Chua's circuit, an autonomous electronic circuit modelled by equations (Chua et al., 1986; Wu, 1987):

$$\begin{aligned} \dot{x} &= a(y - f(x)) \\ \dot{y} &= x - y + z + g(y) \\ \dot{z} &= -by \end{aligned} \tag{20}$$

where function $f(x) = m_1 x + \frac{1}{2}(m_0 - m_1)(|x+1| - |x-1|)$, a is the bifurcation parameter, and $g(y)$ is the control perturbation.

We take $b = 15$, $m_0 = -\frac{1}{7}$, and $m_1 = \frac{2}{7}$. With increasing a in the unperturbed system, the steady states, ($x^{(s)} = p, y^{(s)} = 0, z^{(s)} = -p$) and its symmetric image ($x^{(s)} = -p, y^{(s)} = 0, z^{(s)} = p$), where $p = \frac{(m_1 - m_0)}{m_1}$, become unstable, and a limit cycle arises through the Andronov-Hopf bifurcation. Further increasing the bifurcation parameter leads firstly to the Rössler-type chaos through the period-doubling cascade, and then to merging two Rössler bands and to forming the double scroll attractor (Chua et al., 1986). The oscillation amplitude grows as α increases.

Substituting $y = -\frac{\dot{z}}{b}$ to the second equation of (20) and assuming $g(y)$ to be the odd function, obtain

$$\begin{aligned} \ddot{z} + \dot{z} + bz &= -bx + bg(\frac{\dot{z}}{b}) \\ \dot{x} &= a(-\frac{\dot{z}}{b} - f(x)) \,. \end{aligned} \tag{21}$$

For oscillator (21), the change of energy caused by the control yields $b\dot{z}g(\frac{\dot{z}}{b})$. If $g(\frac{\dot{z}}{b})$ takes form (6-7), the latter term always provides the increase (decrease) of the oscillation energy for the positive (negative) perturbation magnitudes. We, thus, consider $g(\frac{\dot{z}}{b}) = k \tanh(\beta \frac{\dot{z}}{b})$. Taking into account that $\dot{z} = -by$ and considering the limit $\beta \to \infty$, obtain the following control term:

$$g(y) = k\,\mathrm{sign}(y)\,. \tag{22}$$

At negative k, perturbation (22) reduces the oscillation energy. The increase of perturbation amplitude recovers all lower energy repellors of system (20). Figure (10) demonstrates the bifurcation diagram of system (20) at $a = 9$. Here, we considered only the trajectories corresponding to the right hand wing of the attractor. The unperturbed system exhibits the chaotic behaviour that corresponds to the screw-type chaos of the Rössler band attractor. At $0.0083 \lesssim k \lesssim 0.0097$, the orbits of period $3 \cdot 2^i, i = 0, 1, 2...$ (in the reverse order beginning with the highest period) are stabilized. These orbits correspond to the largest window of the Rössler band. As known, this window separates the two different types of Rössler chaos in Chua's circuit, the screw-type chaos and the spiral chaos. At the higher amplitudes of control perturbation, the behaviour becomes converted to the spiral chaos featuring, thus, the control of chaotic repellor. The further increase of control amplitude leads firstly to the sequential stabilization of $2^i, i = 0, 1, 2...$ orbits (these UPOs are controlled at $0.0193 \lesssim k \lesssim 0.0392$, again, in the reverse order beginning with the highest period orbit) and finally to the stabilization of the steady state corresponding to the controlled band (Fig. 11). In the latter case, the perturbation evolves to the high-frequency periodic oscillations controlling the stationary state. One can draw a clear parallel between this case and the stabilization of unstable equilibrium in a rapidly oscillating field, which is the classical example of physics (Landau & Lifshitz, 1976).

The last example demonstrates the self-tuning nature of given control. Indeed, to stabilize the periodic orbits, the perturbation evolves to the required resonant one. Unlike, when controls the chaotic repellors, the perturbation switches chaotically between $-k$ and k.

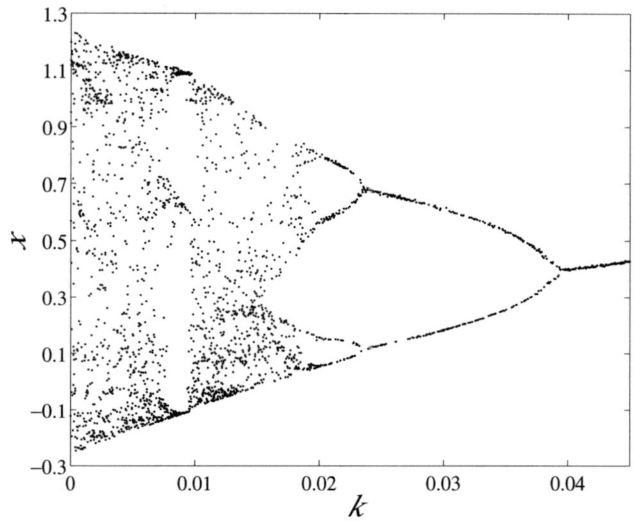

Fig. 10. Bifurcation diagram of perturbed Chua's circuit (20) at $b = 15$, $m_0 = -1/7$, and $m_1 = 2/7, a = 9$.

In the nonchaotic regimes, one can apply the similar strategy. Consider, for example, $a = 8$, which corresponds to the period-1 oscillations. Taking positive k and increasing it, the system will be driven to the higher energy states. As a result, all these states can be controlled, namely: the period-doubled orbits, the repelling Rössler band and double scroll, and the UPOs of latter repellors.

Consider now the double scroll attractor ($a = 10$, Fig. 12(a)). At negative k, strengthening the perturbation decreases the oscillation energy, allowing to control the lower energy repellors. Figure 12(b) illustrates the control of UPO corresponding to a window of the double scroll. At the higher amplitude of control perturbation, one observes the reverse bifurcation of the double scroll birth when the trajectories from two loci diverge and form two separate odd-symmetric Rössler bands. Depending on the locus where the control is turned on, one or another band can be controlled. Figure 12(c) illustrates controlling the right-hand Rössler band. Increasing the control amplitude, one stabilizes sequentially the period-doubling orbits in their reverse order. Fig. 12(d) shows controlling the period-4 orbit. The further increase of control amplitude leads to the stabilization of steady states. However, the unstable steady states can be controlled by a weaker perturbation, if the control is turned on in the vicinity of

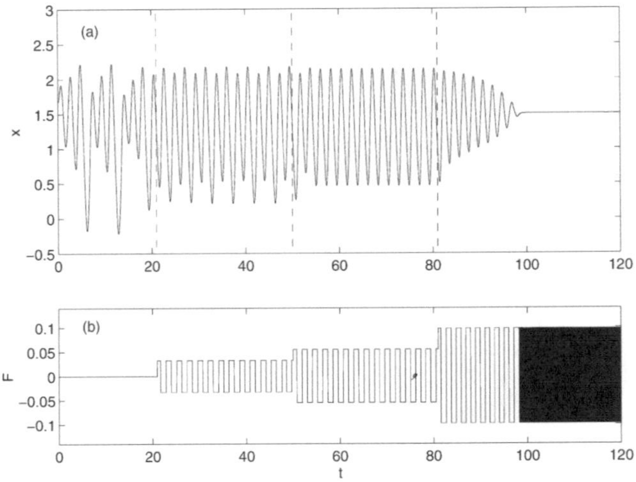

Fig. 11. Dynamics of (a) perturbed Chua's circuit (20) and (b) its control perturbation at $b = 15$, $m_0 = -1/7$, $m_1 = 2/7$, $a = 9$, and $k = 0$ $(0 \leq t < 21)$; $k = -0.033$ $(21 \leq t < 50)$; $k = -0.055$ $(50 \leq t < 81)$; $k = -0.098$ $(t > 81)$.

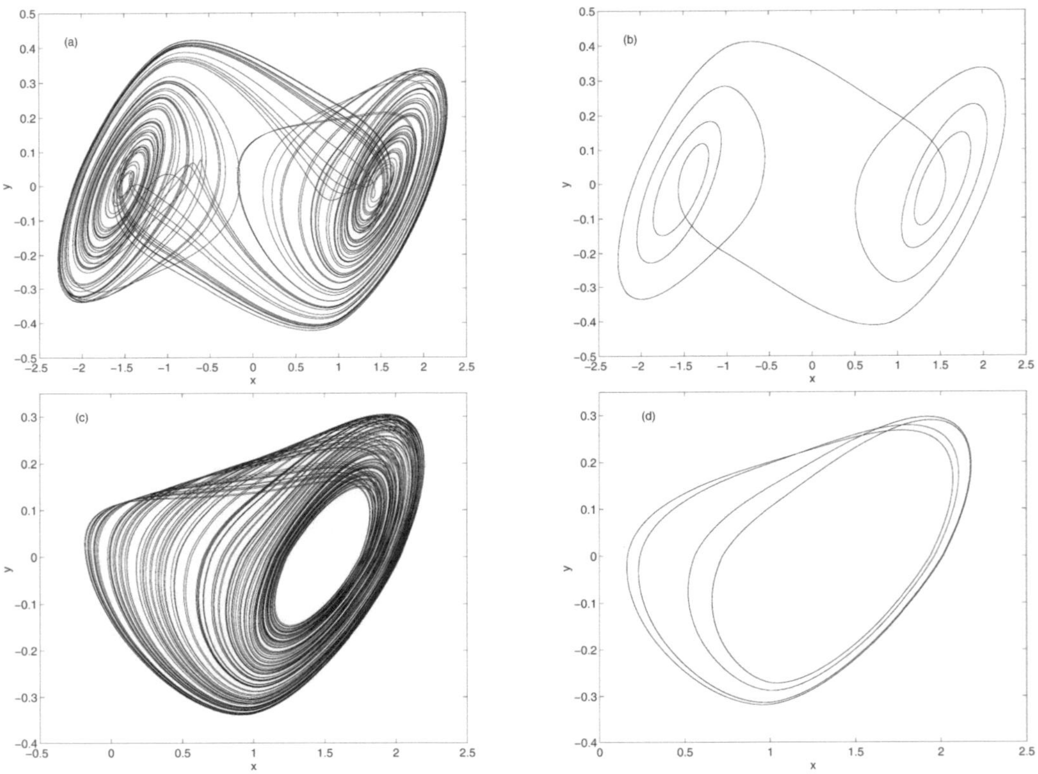

Fig. 12. State space of perturbed Chua's circuit (20) at $b = 15$, $m_0 = -1/7$, $m_1 = 2/7$, $a = 10$, and (a) $k = 0$; (b) $k = -0.0085$; (c) $k = -0.068$; (d) $k = -0.085$.

these states. To control the UPOs corresponding to the lower energy levels, the perturbation decreasing the oscillation energy, i.e. one with the positive k, should be applied.

5. Controlling reaction-diffusion media

The above strategy can be generalized to control the pattern dynamics in the spatially-extended systems. Consider a general reaction-diffusion system:

$$\frac{\partial u}{\partial t} = \xi(u) + \frac{\partial^2 u}{\partial r^2} \,. \tag{23}$$

This equation possesses a special solution of the form $u = u(r - ct)$, where c is the wave speed, called a travelling wave (23). Taking new variable $\varrho = r - ct$, obtain

$$\ddot{u} + c\dot{u} + \xi(u) = 0 \tag{24}$$

where all derivatives are taken over ϱ. Perturbation (6-7) is able to effectively increase or decrease the oscillation energy of travelling wave enhancing or suppressing the latter respectively.

Let us consider an excitable medium. It is characterized by the existence of the only equilibrium, the resting state, yet being perturbed the system trajectory is able to spend a substantial time outside of the equilibrium, in the firing state. Let us augment equation (23) with new "recovery" variable v that allows the system dynamics to return to its resting state:

$$\dot{v} = \psi(u, v) \tag{25}$$

Assuming the existence of travelling wave solution, throughout we consider the following system:

$$\begin{aligned} \ddot{u} + c\dot{u} + \zeta\big(\xi(u) + \varphi(u,v)\big) &= 0 \\ \dot{v} + \frac{1}{c}\psi(u,v) &= 0 \,. \end{aligned} \tag{26}$$

Typically, $\varphi(u,v)$ and $\psi(u,v)$ are the linear combinations of u and v, and $\xi(u,v)$ is a nonlinear function. The most known examples of nonlinear kinetics in the excitable media are represented by functions $\xi(u) = u - \frac{1}{3}u^3$ and $\xi(u) = \Theta(u - \delta)$ where Θ is the Heaviside step function. The latter is equal to 1 when v exceeds the threshold value δ, and 0 otherwise. These choices belong to the classical FitzHugh-Nagumo (FitzHugh, 1961) and Rinzel-Keller (Rinzel & Keller, 1973) models respectively.

To control the travelling waves, we apply the control perturbation to the right-hand side of the first equation of system (26):

$$\ddot{u} + c\dot{u} + \zeta\big(\xi(u) + \varphi(u,v)\big) = k\tanh(\beta\dot{u}) \,. \tag{27}$$

The latter is, in fact, the introduction of some form of nonlinear damping into the system. For small β, the linear approximation yields $\tanh(\beta\dot{u}) \approx \beta\,\dot{u}$, and the control reduces to the adjustment of the travelling wave speed:

$$\ddot{u} + (c - k\beta)\dot{u} + \zeta\big(\xi(u) + \varphi(u,v)\big) = 0 \,. \tag{28}$$

The distributed version of the above control can be directly applied to system (23), viewing it as a spatially distributed overdamped oscillator. Note, ϱ is the function of both t and r giving the opportunity for the two types of control. The first type reads:

$$\frac{\partial u}{\partial t} = \xi(u) + \frac{\partial^2 u}{\partial r^2} + k(r,t)\tanh\left(\beta\frac{\partial u}{\partial t}\right). \tag{29}$$

Generally, k is the function of r and t. Throughout, however, we demonstrate the efficiency of the spatially localized perturbations with the constant in time amplitudes. In the limit of small β and constant k, the control reduces to the simple timescale and diffusion coefficient adjustments:

$$\frac{\partial u}{\partial t} = \frac{1}{(1-k\beta)}\left(\xi(u) + \frac{\partial^2 u}{\partial r^2}\right). \tag{30}$$

Unlike the adjustment of the travelling wave speed in (28), the above one affects the whole right-hand side of the equation and, hence, must be bounded to $k\beta < 1$ (unless one intends to drastically modify the system).
The second type of control reads:

$$\frac{\partial u}{\partial t} = \xi(u) + \frac{\partial^2 u}{\partial r^2} + k(r,t)\tanh\left(\beta\frac{\partial u}{\partial r}\right). \tag{31}$$

Here, the last term is nothing but the nonlinear flow, which, in the limit of small β, tends to its linearized version.
When suppressing the travelling waves in excitable media, after some period of exposition, the control can be switched off. Indeed, the rest state is the stable equilibrium here, and the perturbation should only be imposed while the trajectory is out of its basin of attraction.
Below, consider the above control on the examples of two models of excitable reaction-diffusion media.

5.1 Distributed FitzHugh Nagumo model

This system is the approximation of Hodgkin-Huxley model (Hodgkin & Huxley, 1952) of the propagation of voltage pulses along a nerve fibre. The dynamics is described by the system of coupled equations (Scott, 1975):

$$\begin{aligned}\frac{\partial u}{\partial t} &= u - \frac{1}{3}u^3 - v + \iota + \frac{\partial^2 u}{\partial r^2}\\ \frac{\partial v}{\partial t} &= \alpha(u - av + b)\end{aligned} \tag{32}$$

where u represents the local electric potential across the cell membrane and v represents the conductivity of the voltage-sensitive ionic channels. Parameters ϱ, a and b represent the membrane's current, radius and resistivity respectively, and parameter α constitutes the temperature factor.

5.1.1 Excitable regime

When looking for a travelling wave solution, the problem reduces to solving the ODEs equations:

$$\begin{aligned}&\ddot{u} + c\dot{u} + u - \frac{1}{3}u^3 - v + \iota = 0\\ &\dot{v} = -\frac{\alpha}{c}(u - av + b).\end{aligned} \tag{33}$$

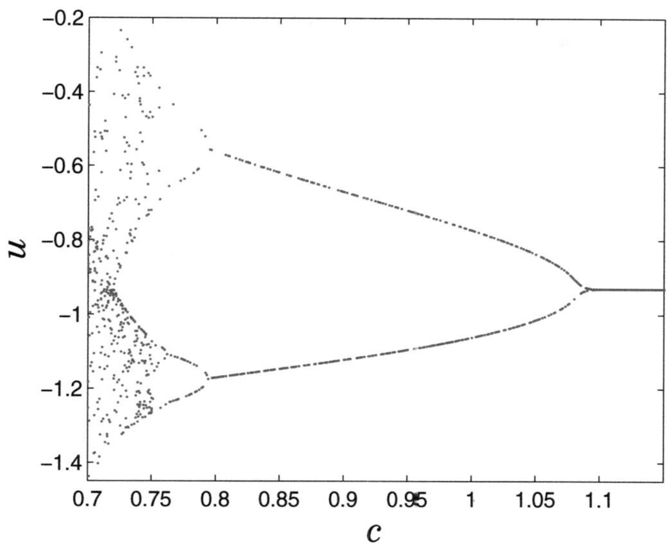

Fig. 13. Bifurcation diagram of system (33) at $a = 0.5$, $b = 0.6$, $\alpha = 0.1$, and $\iota = 0$.

The forced-free system, i.e. one with $\iota = 0$, demonstrates the transition to chaos with the decrease of c (Fig. 13). Obviously, the linear damping control (28) will stabilize the dynamics. More efficient, however, to utilize the nonlinearity of sigmoid-type control perturbation as in (27). Fig. 14 illustrates the control of various period orbits by the tanh-perturbation.
The similar strategy is applied to the periodically driven system. When the membrane is subjected to the periodic current, i.e. $\iota = \rho\cos(\omega t)$, system (33) demonstrates the chaotic behaviour as well as its driven-free analogue (Rajesekar & Lakshmanan, 1994). Fig. 15 illustrates the control of above system.

5.1.2 Oscillatory regime

Fig. 16 illustrates controlling the system in the oscillatory mode applying the linearized version of control (31). Depending on the sign of control perturbation, one can either increase the oscillation frequency or suppress the oscillations.

5.2 Kahlert-Rössler model

The Kahlert-Rössler model is a variant of the Rinzel-Keller system (Rinzel & Keller, 1973) of the nerve conduction (Kahlert & Rössler, 1984):

$$\begin{aligned} \frac{\partial u}{\partial t} &= \mu(-u + \Theta(u-\delta) + v - \gamma) + \frac{\partial^2 u}{\partial r^2} \\ \frac{\partial v}{\partial t} &= -\epsilon u + v \end{aligned} \tag{34}$$

where $\Theta(\vartheta) = 1$ if $\vartheta > 0$ and 0 otherwise; δ is the threshold parameter.

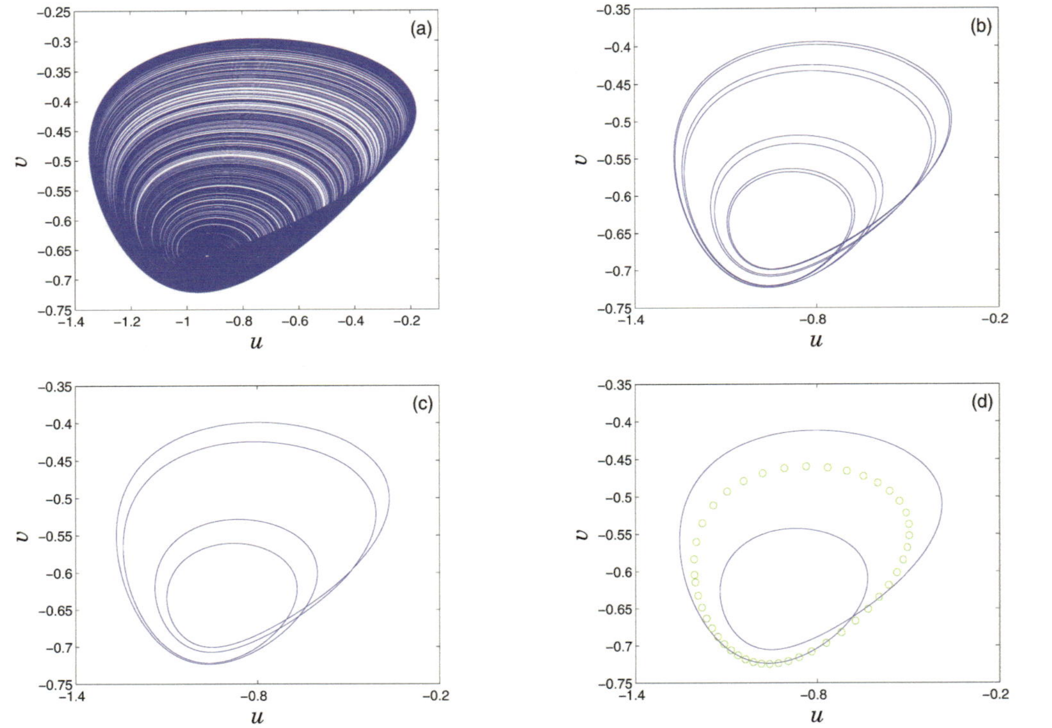

Fig. 14. State space of controlled system (33) at $a = 0.5$, $b = 0.b$, $\alpha = 0.1$, $c = 0.72$, $\iota = 0$, $\beta = 10$ and (a) $k = 0$; (b) $k = -0.0118$; (c) $k = -0.013$; (d) $k = -0.015$ (solid line) $k = -0.03$ (open circles).

5.2.1 Excitable regime

Looking for the travelling wave solution, obtain the following system of ODEs:

$$\ddot{u} + c\dot{u} + \mu\big(-u + \Theta(u - \delta) + v - \gamma\big) = 0$$
$$\dot{v} = \frac{1}{c}(\epsilon u - v) \qquad (35)$$

where all derivatives are taken over the wave variable $\varrho = r - ct$.
System (35) demonstrates the "screw-type" chaos at some parameter values (Kahlert & Rössler, 1984). Applying the tanh-perturbation, the chaos is tamed to the periodic oscillations (Fig. 17).

5.2.2 Oscillatory regime

The adjustment of system's timescale and diffusion rate can stabilize the dynamics. Fig. 18(a) illustrates the emergence of low-frequency stabilizing modulation. Changing $k\beta$ leads to different patterns. Fig. 18(b) illustrates the temporal dynamics at the system middle point, i.e at $r = l/2$ where l is the system size.

6. Discussion and conclusions

The two control strategies are found to be effective: (i) altering a perturbation magnitude; (ii) reshaping a perturbation. In the majority of considered cases, the control represents

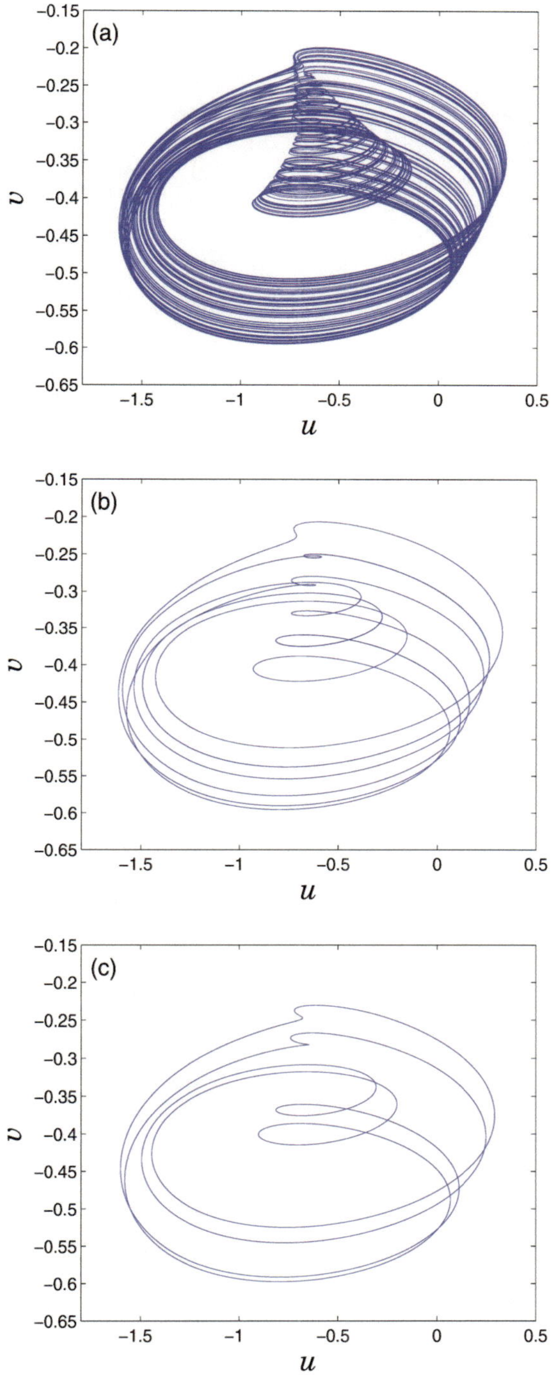

Fig. 15. State space of controlled system (33) at $a = 0.5$, $b = 0.5$, $\alpha = 0.1$, $c = 0.9$, $\rho = 0.55$, $\omega = 1$, $\beta = 100$ and (a) $k = 0$; (b) $k = -0.001$; (c) $k = -0.005$.

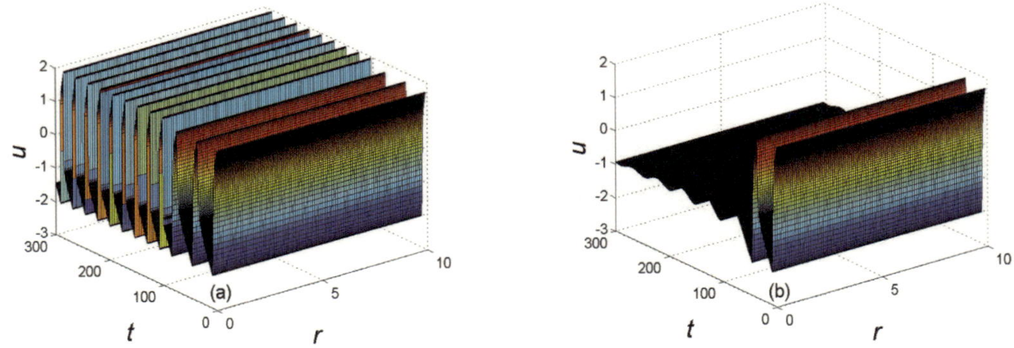

Fig. 16. Dynamics of controlled system (32) at $a = 0.5$, $b = 0.6$, $\alpha = 0.1$, $\delta = 0$ and (a) $k\beta = 0.99$; (b) $k\beta = -3.9$.

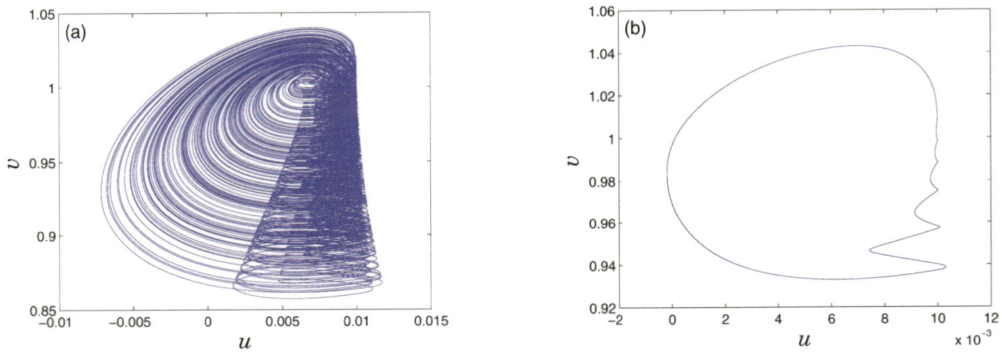

Fig. 17. State space of controlled system (35) at $\mu = 10$, $\gamma = 1$, $\delta = 0.01$, $\epsilon = 150$, $c = 3.5$, $\beta = 100$ and (a) $k = 0$; (b) $k = -0.21$.

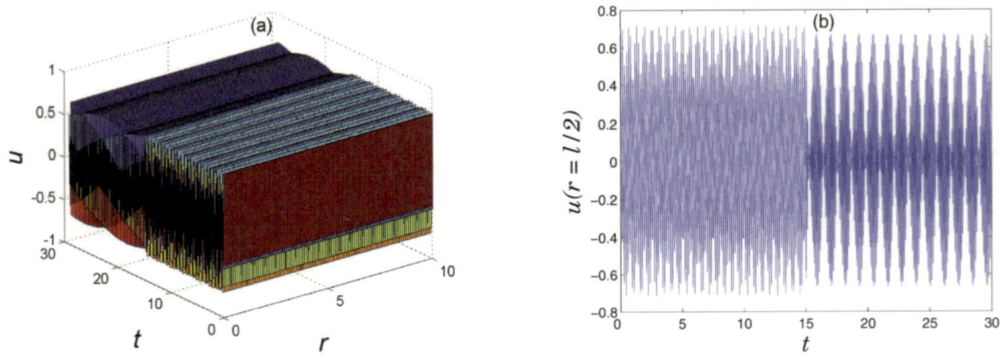

Fig. 18. Dynamics of controlled system (34) at $\mu = 10$, $\gamma = 1$, $\delta = 0.01$, $\epsilon = 150$ and (a) $k\beta = 0.5$; (b) $k\beta = 0.6$.

an addition of extra nonlinear damping to a system. Depending on the level of perturbation nonlinearity, two different scenarios take place. Recall that simple changing the tanh-perturbation slope transforms the feedback from near-linear to extremely nonlinear one. The above controls manifests themselves in (i) changing an oscillator natural damping; (ii) suppressing (enhancing) an external driving force, respectively. The perturbation shape, once again, reveals its significance determining the control mechanisms.

The occurrence of second scenario depends on the oscillator features. In our approach, a control perturbation is naturally locked to an oscillator velocity. If there is any phase shift between the velocity, and, hence, the control perturbation and the driving force, than a delayed version of control, i.e. $g(\dot{x}(t-\tau))$ with a time lag τ between the control perturbation and the driving force, will be most effective. Note, a phase of chaotic oscillator is determined using the approach developed in (Pikovsky et al., 1997; Rosenblum et al., 1996). When the phase difference between chaotic oscillations and a driving force exhibits large deviations, the coherence between the control action and the driving force can be destroyed. In this case independently on β, the control affects only an oscillator damping. This scenario is observed, for example, in the "broken egg" attractor (Ueda, 1992).

Though derived differently, in approximation $\dot{x} \approx \tau^{-1}(x(t) - x(t-\tau))$, the proposed control can be viewed as a continuous-delay control with saturation (or simply a continuous-delay control when $h(\dot{x}) = \dot{x}$) (Gauthier et al., 1994; Pyragas, 1992) adapted to the stabilization of fixed points. To control a fixed point, return time τ must tend to 0.

Recently our method was applied to mechanical systems where the forcing source has a limited available energy supply (de Souza et al, 2007). These oscillators, called non-ideal ones, are described by a combination of passive and active parts (the oscillator and the motor). The authors demonstrated the efficiency of approach applying the control altering the oscillation energy to the driving motor part.

Some of the existing methods of control can be reconsidered in the light of proposed approach. Look at so-called active control applied for suppressing oscillations driven by the dry friction forces (Heckl & Abrahams, 1996). These oscillations are produced by a mass-spring system sliding on a moving belt. The active control represents a feedback loop which senses the mass velocity, passes it to a filter, then to a phase shifter, to a variable-gain amplifier, and finally to shaker attached to the mass. The control force is $g(\dot{x}, \phi) = \alpha e^{i\phi}\dot{x}$ where α is a measure for amplification and ϕ is a phase shift. In terms of a time lag τ, $g(\dot{x}, \tau) = \alpha\dot{x}(t-\tau)$. Immediately, one find that at $\phi = 0$ ($\tau = 0$), or $\phi = \frac{\pi}{2}$ ($\tau = \frac{\pi}{2}$), the active control is nothing but the proposed energy alteration control. No surprise that, keeping positive α, the authors found their control to be optimal at $\phi = \frac{\pi}{2}$ ($\tau = \frac{\pi}{2}$). In this case, the averaged energy change brought about by the control decreases as $\langle\dot{x}(t)\dot{x}(t-\tau)\rangle = -\langle\dot{x}^2(t)\rangle$, which leads to recovering of lower energy repellors, and, generally, to the stabilization of dynamics.

The nonfeedback control methods can be reviewed in terms of energy alteration too. The resonance between a controlled signal and a control perturbation is usually the general condition for the efficient shift of the trajectory to a desired target, or, in other words, to altering the system energy. The phase of perturbation is used both to fine-tune the control or and to switch the drive direction on the opposite one, i.e. to switch between the directions of energy increase and decrease (Tereshko & Shchekinova, 1998).

An important issue is the application of control in practice. The authors in (Heckl & Abrahams, 1996) discussed the applications of their technique to real-life friction-driven oscillations, in particular, to a squeal noise. This disturbing type of noise occurs when there is a lateral progression of a wheel relative to a rail. The excited bending vibrations of the wheel

are radiated in the surrounding air and heard as intensive high pitched squeal. The authors present an experimental set where their control technique was tested.
A development of methods of controlling spatially-extended systems has great practical importance too. The considered excitable dynamics of active reaction-diffusion systems, for example, lies at the core of neuron functioning. Controlling the neural activity patterns can potentially treat mental, movement and sleep disorders, pain, and other illnesses associated with a neural system.
To summarize, we developed the control based on an alteration of oscillation energy. Since the approach utilizes a feedback that depends solely on the output signal, it is especially useful when the system parameters are inaccessible or hardly adjustable. The particular type of perturbation is rather relative — most important, it should comply with condition (5), which guarantees the monotonic change of a system oscillation energy. Then, the repellors are stabilized when the energy passes levels corresponding to their stable counterparts.

7. Acknowledgments

The author grateful to the University of the West of Scotland for sabbatical grant and to the Carnegie Trust for the Universities of Scotland for the grant that supported a part of presented research.

8. References

Alexeev, V.V. & Loskutov, A.Yu. (1987). Control of a system with a strange attractor through periodic parametric action. *Sov. Phys.-Dokl.* 32, 270–271.

Azevedo, A. & Rezende, S.M. (1991). Controlling chaos in spin-wave instabilities. *Phys. Rev. Lett.* 66, 1342–1345.

Baziliauskas, A.; Tamaševičius, A.; Bumeliene, S.; & Lindberg, E. (2001). Synchronization of chaotic Colpitts oscillators. *Scienti□c Proceedings of Riga Technical University, Ser. 7. Telecommunications and Electronics*, vol. 1, p. 55–58.

Braiman, Y. & Goldhirsch, I. (1991). Taming chaotic dynamics with weak periodic perturbations. *Phys. Rev. Lett.* 66, 2545–2548.

Cao, H. (2005). Primary resonant optimal control for homoclinic bifurcations in single-degree-of-freedom nonlinear oscillators. *Chaos, Solitons and Fractals* 24, 1387–1398.

Chacón, R. (1996). Geometrical resonance as a chaos eliminating mechanism. *Phys. Rev. Lett.* 77, 482–485.

Chacón, R. & Díaz Bejarano, J. (1993). Routes to suppressing chaos by weak periodic perturbations. *Phys. Rev. Lett.* 71, 3103–3106.

Chizhevsky, V.N. & Corbalán, R. (1996). Experimental observation of perturbation-induced intermittency in the dynamics of a loss-modulated CO2 laser. *Phys. Rev. E* 54, 4576–4579.

Chizhevsky, V.N.; Corbalán, R. & Pisarchik, A.N. (1997). Attractor splitting induced by resonant perturbations. *Phys. Rev. E* 56, 1580–1584.

Chua, L.O.; Komuro, M. & Matsumoto, T. (1986). The double scroll family. *IEEE Trans. Circuits Syst.* CAS-33, 1072–1118.

Dangoisse, D.; Celet, J.-C. & Glorieux, P. (1997). Global investigation of the influence of the phase of subharmonic excitation of a driven system. *Phys. Rev. E* 56, 1396–1406.

De Feo, O.; Maggio, G.M. & Kennedy, M.P. (2000). The Colpitts oscillator: Families of periodic solutions and their bifurcations. *Int. J. Bifurcation and Chaos* 10, 935–958.

de Souza, S.L.T.; Caldas, I.L.; Viana, R.L.; Balthazar, J.M. & Brasil, R.M.L.R.F. (2007). A simple feedback control for a chaotic oscillator with limited power supply. *J. Sound and Vibration* 299, 664–671.

Ding, W.X.; She, H.Q.; Huang, W. & Yu, C.X. (1994). Controlling chaos in a discharge plasma. *Phys. Rev. Lett.* 72, 96–99.

FitzHugh, R. (1961). Impulses and physiological states in models of nerve membrane. *Biophys. J.* 1, 445–466.

Fronzoni, L.; Giocondo, M. & Pettini, M. (1991). Experimental evidence of suppression of chaos by resonant parametric perturbations. *Phys. Rev. A* 43, 6483–6487.

Garfinkel, A.; Spano, M.L.; Ditto, W.L. & Weiss, J. (1992). Controlling cardiac chaos. *Science* 257, 1230–1235.

Gauthier, D.J.; Sukow, D.W.; Concannon, H.M. & Socolar, J.E.S. (1994). Stabilizing unstable periodic orbits in a fast diode resonator using continuous time-delay auto-synchronization. *Phys. Rev. E* 50, 2343–2346.

Heckl, M.A. & Abrahams, I.D. (1996). Active control of friction-driven oscillations. *J. Sound and Vibrations* 193, 417–426.

Hikihara, T.; Touno, M.; & Kawagoshi, T. (1997). Experimental stabilization of unstable periodic orbit in magneto-elastic chaos by delayed feedback control. *Int. J. Bifurcation and Chaos* 7, 2837–2846.

Hodgkin, A. L. & Huxley, A. F. (1952). A quantitative description of membrane current and its application to conduction and excitation in nerve. *J. Physiol.* 117, 500–544.

Hunt, E.R. (1991). Stabilizing high-period orbits in a chaotic system: The diode resonator. *Phys. Rev. Lett.* 67, 1953–1955.

Hübinger, B.; Doerner, R; Martienssen, W.; Herdering, M.; Pitka, R. & Dressler, U. (1994). Controlling chaos experimentally in systems exhibiting large effective Lyapunov exponents. *Phys. Rev. E* 50, 932–948.

Hübler, A. & Lüscher, E. (1989). Resonant stimulation and control of nonlinear oscillators. *Naturwissenschaften* 76, 67–69.

Jackson, E.A. & Hübler, A. (1990). Periodic entrainment of chaotic logistic map dynamics. *Physica D* 44, 407–420.

Just, W.; Reckwerth, D.; Reibold, E. & Benner, H. (1999a). Influence of control loop latency on time-delayed feedback control. *Phys. Rev. E* 59, 2826–2829.

Just, W.; Reibold, D.E.; Benner, H.; Kacperski, K.; Fronczak, P. & Hołyst, J. (1999b). Limits of time-delayed feedback control. *Phys. Lett. A* 254, 158–164.

Kahlert, C. & Rössler, O. E. (1984). Chaos as a limit in a boundary value problem. *Z. Naturforsch.* 39a, 1200–1203.

Kennedy, M.P. (1994). Chaos in the Colpitts oscillator. *IEEE Trans. Circuits Syst.* 41, 771–774.

Kivshar, Y.S.; Rödelsperger, F. & Benner, H. (1994). Suppression of chaos by nonresonant parametric perturbations. *Phys. Rev. E* 49, 319–324.

Kolosov, G.E. (1999). *Optimal Design of Control Systems: Stochastic and Deterministic Problems*, Marcel Dekker, Inc., New York.

Landau, L.D. & Lifshitz, E.M. (1976). *Mechanics (Course of Theoretical Physics, Vol. 1)*, Pergamon Press, Oxford, third edition.

Lima, R. & Pettini, M. (1990). Suppression of chaos by resonant parametric perturbations. *Phys. Rev. A* 41, 726–733.

Liu, Y. & Leite, J.R. (1994). Control of Lorenz chaos. *Phys. Lett. A* 185, 35–37.
Meucci, R. Gadomski, W.; Ciofini, M. & Arecchi, F.T. (1994). Experimental control of chaos by means of weak parametric perturbations. *Phys. Rev. E* 49, R2528–R2531.
Myneni, K; Barr, Th. A.; Corron, N.J. & Pethel, S.D. (1999). New method for the control of fast chaotic oscillations. *Phys. Rev. Lett.* 83, 2175–2178.
Ott, E.; Grebogi, C. & Yorke, J.A. (1990). Controlling chaos. *Phys. Rev. Lett* 64, 1196-1199.
Peng, B., Petrov, V. & Showalter, K. (1991). Controlling Chemical Chaos. *J. Phys. Chem.* 95, 4957–4959.
Pikovsky, A.S.; Rosenblum, M.G.; Osipov, G.V. & Kurths, J. (1997). Phase synchronization of chaotic oscillators by external driving. *Physica D* 104, 219–238.
Pyragas, K. (1992). Continuous control of chaos by self-controlling feedback. *Phys. Lett. A* 170, 421–428.
Pyragas, K. (1995). Control of chaos via extended delay feedback. *Phys. Lett. A* 206, 323–330.
Qu, Z.; Hu, G.; Yang, G. & Qin, G. (1995). Phase effect in taming nonautonomous chaos by weak harmonic perturbations. *Phys. Rev. Lett.* 74, 1736–1739.
Rajesekar, S. & Lakshmanan, M. (1994). Bifurcation, chaos and suppression of chaos in FitzHughŰNagumo nerve conduction modelation. *J. Theor. Biol.* 166, 275–288.
Ramesh, M. & Narayanan, S. (1999). Chaos control by nonfeed- back methods in the presence of noise. *Chaos, Solitons and Fractals* 10, 1473–1489.
Reyl, C.; Flepp, L.; Badii, R. & Brun, E. (1993). Control of NMR-laser chaos in high-dimensional embedding space. *Phys. Rev. E* 47, 267–272.
Rinzel, J. & Keller, J.B. (1973). Traveling wave solutions of a nerve conduction equation. *Biophys. J.* 13, 1313-1337.
Rosenblum, M.G.; Pikovsky, A.S. & Kurths, J. (1996). Phase synchronization of chaotic oscillators. *Phys. Rev. Lett.* 76, 1804–1807.
Rödelsperger, F., Kivshar, Y.S. & Benner, H. (1995). Reshaping-induced chaos suppression. *Phys. Rev. E* 51, 869-872.
Scott, A. F. (1975). The electrophysics of a nerve fiber. *Rev. Mod. Phys.* 47, 487–533.
Shinbrot, T.; Ott, E.; Grebogi, C. & Yorke, J.A. (1993). Using small perturbations to control chaos. *Nature* 363, 411–417.
Simmendinger, C.; Hess, O. & Wunderlin, A. (1998). Analytical treatment of delayed feedback control. *Phys. Lett. A* 245, 253–258.
Socolar, J.E.S.; Sukow, D.W.; & Gauthier, D.J. (1994). Stabilizing unstable periodic orbits in fast dynamical systems. *Phys. Rev. E* 50, 3245–3248.
Tereshko, V. (2009). Control and identification of chaotic systems by altering their energy. *Chaos, Solitons and Fractals* 40, 2430Ű-2446.
Tereshko, V.; Chacón, R. & Carballar, J. (2004a). Controlling the chaotic Colpitts oscillator by altering its oscillation energy. *Proc. 12th Intern. IEEE Workshop on Nonlinear Dynamics of Electronic Systems (NDES 2004)*, Évora, Portugal, p. 336.
Tereshko, V.; Chacón, R. & Preciado, V. (2004b). Controlling chaotic oscillators by altering their energy. *Phys. Lett. A* 320, 408–416.
Tereshko, V. & Shchekinova, E. (1998). Resonant control of the Rossler system. *Phys. Rev. E* 58, 423–426.
Ueda, Y. (1992). *The Road to Chaos*, Aerial Press, Santa Cruz.
Wu, S. (1987). Chua's circuit family. *Proc. IEEE* 75, 1022–1032.

7

Adaptive Control of Chaos

Hassan Salarieh and Mohammad Shahrokhi
Sharif University of Technology
IRAN

1. Introduction

Since Ott et al. (1990) presented a feedback control technique for stabilizing unstable fixed points of chaotic maps, many linear and nonlinear control techniques based on feedback were introduced for chaos control of continuous and discrete dynamical systems (Fradkov and Evans 2005) . Consider the following dynamical systems:

$$\dot{x} = f(x,u) \tag{1}$$

$$x[n+1] = f(x[n],u[n]) \tag{2}$$

where $x \in \Re^n$ is the state vector, $u \in \Re^m$ is the control vector and $f : \Re^n \times \Re^m \to \Re^n$ is a sufficiently smooth function. The first equation presents a continuous time dynamical system and the second one a discrete dynamical system. It is assumed that both equations show chaotic behavior. The techniques of chaos control can be categorized based on different view points.

a) open-loop and closed-loop control

If the control action u has the following form:

$$\begin{aligned} &u = u(t) \;\; \textit{for continuous time system} \\ &u = u[n] \;\; \textit{for discrete time system} \end{aligned} \tag{3}$$

then the control strategy is called open loop. There are some works on chaos control in an open loop format (Fradkov and Evans 2005, Kiss et al. 2000, Parmanada and Eiswirth 1999). If the control action u has the following form:

$$\begin{aligned} &u = u(x(t)) \;\; \textit{for continuous time system} \\ &u = u(x[n]) \;\; \textit{for discrete time system} \end{aligned} \tag{4}$$

then it is called closed loop or feedback control. Feedback control has been frequently used in chaos control. The OGY control method and the delayed feedback control presented by Pyragas (1992, 2006) are the early works on controlling chaos via feedback. Recently, linear feedback control methods based on linearization and dynamic programming (Vincent and Yu 1991, Merat et al. 2009), nonlinear feedback control methods based on Lyapunov stability theory (Alasty and Salarieh 2007, Salarieh et al. 2009), sliding mode control (Konishi et al. 1998, Arjmand et al. 2008), backstepping method (Wu and Lu 2003, Yongguang and

Suochun 2003, Yassen 2006) and some geometrical techniques (Tian and Yu 2000) have been widely used for chaos control in closed loop format.
b) Model based and mode free control:
If the control action u is calculated based on the information obtained from dynamical model of the system, the control technique is called model based method. There are many control methods applied to chaotic systems which are designed based on the system model. When the control action is calculated without using the system model, the control technique is called model free control method. The minimum entropy control of chaos (Salarieh and Alasty 2009, 2009) and controlling chaos on a Poincare section presented by Bonakdar et al. (2008) are two model free control techniques.
c) Adaptive and Non-adaptive control:
When a dynamical system has some unknown parameters in its describing equations, usually an identification algorithm is coupled with the control algorithm to provide an adaptive control system. In adaptive control, parameter estimation and control are performed simultaneously. Usually the following dynamical equations are used for adaptive control applications:

$$\dot{x} = F(x,u)\Theta + g(x,u) \tag{5}$$

$$x[n+1] = F(x[n],u[n])\Theta + g(x[n],u[n]) \tag{6}$$

where $F(x,u)$ and $g(x,u)$ are two known functions and Θ is a vector of unknown parameters which must be estimated for control application. Adaptive control is divided into two categories; indirect and direct methods (Astrom and Wittenmark 1994). When the system parameters are estimated and control action is calculated based on the estimated parameters, the adaptive control scheme is called indirect adaptive control. In direct adaptive control, controller parameters are directly updated using an adaptive law. Adaptive control has been used widely for controlling chaos in discrete and continuous time systems (Hua and Guan 2004). Salarieh and Shahrokhi (2007) have proposed an indirect adaptive control scheme for chaotic maps to stabilize their unstable fixed points when there are some unknown parameters in the model of system. Direct adaptive control of a modified Chua's circuit has been considered by Yassen (2003). Adaptive control of delayed continuous time chaotic systems has been considered by Tian and Gao (1998). Zeng and Singh (1997), Liao and Lin (1999) and Pishkenari et al. (2007) have presented some direct and indirect adaptive controls for the Lorenz system. Adaptive control of the Chua circuit and the Lorenz system has been presented by Ge and Wang (2000) and Pyragas et al. (2004), respectively.
Sometimes in addition to the system parameters, the functions $F(x,u)$ and $g(x,u)$ in Eqs. (5) and (6) are also unknown. In these cases the unknown functions are substituted by a series or a finite summation of other known functions which are called the base functions:

$$\begin{aligned} F(x,u) &= \sum_k \Phi_k^F(x,u)\Gamma_k^F \\ g(x,u) &= \sum_k \Phi_k^g(x,u)\Gamma_k^g \end{aligned} \tag{7}$$

where Φ_k^F and Φ_k^g are base functions which can be selected from neuro, fuzzy or neuro-fuzzy base functions or form polynomial functions. Γ_k^F and Γ_k^g are the unknown parameters which are estimated adaptively. Fuzzy adaptive control of chaos has been used by many authors to

stabilize unstable fixed points and periodic orbits (Chen et al. 1999). An indirect adaptive fuzzy control of chaos based on the sliding mode control has been presented by Layeghi et al. (2008). A fuzzy adaptive control of discrete time chaotic systems based on the Takagi Sugeno Kang fuzzy model has been proposed by Feng and Chen (2005). Adaptive fuzzy model based control of chaos with application to the Lorenz system has been investigated by Park et al. (2002). Guan and Chen (2003) have studied adaptive fuzzy control of chaos in presence of disturbance.
Sometimes an adaptive algorithm is used to update the parameters of the fuzzy IF-THEN rules during control procedures. Wang (1993) proposed a direct fuzzy adaptive control and applied to chaotic systems based on updating the parameters of IF-THEN fuzzy rules of the inference engine.

2. Controlling a class of discrete-time chaotic systems

In this section an adaptive control technique applicable to a class of discrete chaotic systems for stabilizing their unstable fixed points is presented. The method is an indirect adaptive control scheme which is proposed originally by Salarieh and Shahrokhi (2007).

2.1 Problem statement

Consider a discrete chaotic system given below:

$$x_j[k+1] = f_j^T(\underline{x}[k])\theta_j^f + (g_j^T(\underline{x}[k])\theta_j^g)u_j[k], \quad j = 1,...,N \tag{8}$$

where $f_j(.)$ and $g_j(.)$ $j = 1,...,N$ are known smooth functions, and θ_j^f and θ_j^g, $j = 1,...,N$ are unknown constant coefficients. By successive substitution (d times) the following delayed discrete time system is obtained:

$$\begin{aligned} x_j[k+d] &= F_j^T(\underline{x}[k], \underline{u}[k], \ldots, \underline{u}[k+d-2])\Theta_j^F \\ &\quad + (G_{j,1}^T(\underline{x}[k], \underline{u}[k], \ldots, \underline{u}[k+d-2])\Theta_{j.1}^G)u_j[k+d-1] + \cdots + (G_{j,d}^T(\underline{x}[k])\Theta_{j,d}^G)u_j[k] \\ j &= 1, \ldots, N \end{aligned} \tag{9}$$

where $F_j(.)$ and $G_{j,i}(.)$, $i = 1,...,d$, $j = 1,...,N$ are known smooth functions, $\Theta_{j,i}^F$ and $\Theta_{j,i}^G$, $i = 1,...,d$, $j = 1,...,N$ are unknown constant coefficients and $\underline{u} = [u_1\ u_2\ ...\ u_N]^T$. Equation (9) is a general delayed form of the discrete system (8) and can be used for stabilizing a d-cycle unstable fixed point of a discrete time chaotic system. It is assumed that the nonlinear coefficient of $u_j[k+d-1]$ is invertible, all of the nonlinear functions are sufficiently smooth and the state variables are available. The main goal is to stabilize the given fixed points of system (9). Note that by using some numerical techniques, the fixed points of a chaotic system whose states are accessible can be calculated without using its dynamic equation (Ramesh and Narayanan 2001, Schmelcher and Diakonos, 1997) hence it is assumed that the fixed points of the system are obtained by a numerical algorithm without using the system parameters.

2.2 Identification method

To identify the unknown parameters of system (9), it is written in the following form:

$$x_j[k+d]=\left[F_j^T(.)\;\; G_{j,1}^T(.)u_j[k+d-1]\;\ldots\; G_{j,d}^T(.)u_j[k]\right]\begin{bmatrix}\Theta_j^F\\ \Theta_{j,1}^G\\ \vdots\\ \Theta_{j,d}^G\end{bmatrix} \quad (10)$$

Now define,

$$\eta_j[k]=x_j[k+d] \quad (11)$$

$$\Phi_j[k]=\left[F_j^T(.)\;\; G_{j,1}^T(.)u_j[k+d-1]\;\ldots\; G_{j,d}^T(.)u_j[k]\right]^T \quad (12)$$

$$\Theta_j=\left[\left(\Theta_j^F\right)^T\;\left(\Theta_{j,1}^G\right)^T\ldots\left(\Theta_{j,d}^G\right)^T\right]^T \quad (13)$$

Using the above definitions Eq. (11) can be written as:

$$\eta_j[k]=\Phi_j^T[k]\Theta_j \quad (14)$$

$\hat{\Theta}_j[k]$ denotes the estimate of Θ_j and it is defined as:

$$\hat{\Theta}_j[k]=\left[\left(\hat{\Theta}_j^F[k]\right)^T\;\left(\hat{\Theta}_{j,1}^G[k]\right)^T\ldots\left(\hat{\Theta}_{j,d}^G[k]\right)^T\right]^T \quad (15)$$

The error vector can be written as:

$$\varepsilon_j[k]=\eta_j[k]-\Phi_j^T[k]\hat{\Theta}_j[k-1] \quad (16)$$

To obtain the estimated parameters, $\hat{\Theta}_j[k]$, the least squares technique is used. Consider the following objective functions:

$$J_k=\sum_{n=1}^{k}(\eta_j[n]-\Phi_j^T[n]\hat{\Theta}_j[k])^2 \quad (17)$$

By differentiating Eq. (17) with respect to $\hat{\Theta}$ and set it to zero we have:

$$\hat{\Theta}_j[k]=\left(\left[\Phi_j[1]\;\cdots\;\Phi_j[k]\right]\begin{bmatrix}\Phi_j^T[1]\\ \vdots\\ \Phi_j^T[k]\end{bmatrix}\right)^{-1}\left[\Phi_j[1]\;\cdots\;\Phi_j[k]\right]\begin{bmatrix}\eta_j[1]\\ \vdots\\ \eta_j[k]\end{bmatrix} \quad (18)$$

Let:

$$P_j[k]=\left(\left[\Phi_j[1]\;\cdots\;\Phi_j[k]\right]\begin{bmatrix}\Phi_j^T[1]\\ \vdots\\ \Phi_j^T[k]\end{bmatrix}\right)^{-1} \quad (19)$$

Substituting Eq. (19) into Eq. (18) yields:

$$\begin{aligned}\hat{\Theta}_j[k] &= P_j[k]\textstyle\sum_{n=1}^{k}\Phi_j[n]\eta_j[n] \\ &= P_j[k]\left(\textstyle\sum_{n=1}^{k-1}\Phi_j[n]\eta_j[n] + \Phi_j[k]\eta_j[k]\right) \\ &= P_j[k]P_j^{-1}[k-1]\hat{\Theta}_j[k-1] + P_j[k]\Phi_j[k]\eta_j[k]\end{aligned} \tag{20}$$

Using Eq. (19) one can write:

$$P_j^{-1}[k-1] = P_j^{-1}[k] - \Phi_j[k]\Phi_j^T[k] \tag{21}$$

Substituting Eq. (21) into Eq. (20) results in:

$$\hat{\Theta}_j[k] = \hat{\Theta}_j[k-1] + P_j[k]\Phi_j[k]\varepsilon_j[k] \tag{22}$$

After some matrix manipulations, Eqs. (21) and (22) can be rewritten as:

$$P_j[k] = P_j[k-1] - \frac{P_j[k-1]\Phi_j[k]\Phi_j^T[k]P_j[k-1]}{1+\Phi_j^T[k]P_j[k-1]\Phi_j[k]} \tag{23}$$

$$\hat{\Theta}_j[k] = \hat{\Theta}_j[k-1] + \frac{P_j[k-1]\Phi_j[k]\varepsilon_j[k]}{1+\Phi_j^T[k]P_j[k-1]\Phi_j[k]} \tag{24}$$

The above recursive equations can be solved using a positive definite initial matrix for $P_j[0]$ and an arbitrary initial vector for $\hat{\Theta}_j[0]$.
The identification method given by Eqs. (23) and (24) implies that:

$$\Phi_j^T[k]\hat{\Theta}_j[k-1] \to \Phi_j^T[k]\Theta_j \quad as\ k \to \infty \tag{25}$$

To show the property (25), note Eq. (19) implies that $P[k]$ is a positive definite matrix. Define:

$$\delta_j[k] = \hat{\Theta}_j[k] - \Theta_j \tag{26}$$

Consider the following Lyapunov function:

$$V_j[k] = \delta_j^T[k]P_j^{-1}[k]\delta_j[k] \tag{27}$$

Using Eq. (24), we have:

$$\delta_j[k] = P_j[k]P_j^{-1}[k-1]\delta_j[k-1] \tag{28}$$

$\Delta V_j[k]$ can be obtained as follows:

$$\begin{aligned} V_j[k]-V_j[k-1] &= \delta_j^T[k]P_j^{-1}[k]\delta_j[k]-\delta_j^T[k-1]P_j^{-1}[k-1]\delta_j[k-1] \\ &= \delta_j^T[k]P_j^{-1}[k-1]\delta_j[k-1]-\delta_j^T[k-1]P_j^{-1}[k-1]\delta_j[k-1] \\ &= (\hat{\Theta}_j^T[k]-\hat{\Theta}_j^T[k-1])P_j^{-1}[k-1](\hat{\Theta}_j[k-1]-\Theta_j) \\ &= -\frac{(\eta_j[k]-\Phi_j^T[k]\hat{\Theta}_j[k-1])^2}{1+\Phi_j^T[k]P_j[k-1]\Phi_j[k]} = -\frac{\varepsilon_j^2[k]}{1+\Phi_j^T[k]P_j[k-1]\Phi_j[k]} \end{aligned} \tag{29}$$

Equation (29) shows that $V_j[k]$ is a decreasing sequence, and consequently:

$$\sum_{k=1}^{n}\frac{\varepsilon_j^2[k]}{1+\Phi_j^T[k]P_j[k-1]\Phi_j[k]} = V_j[0]-V_j[n]<\infty \tag{30}$$

Hence,

$$\lim_{k\to\infty}\frac{\varepsilon_j^2[k]}{1+\Phi_j^T[k]P_j[k-1]\Phi_j[k]}=0 \quad \text{or} \quad \lim_{k\to\infty}\varepsilon_j[k]=0 \tag{31}$$

and consequently:

$$\Phi_j^T[k]\hat{\Theta}_j[k-1]\to\eta_j[k]=\Phi_j^T[k]\Theta_j,\ as\ k\to\infty \tag{32}$$

2.3 Indirect adaptive control of chaos

Assume that $\underline{x}_j^F=\left(x_j^F[0],x_j^F[1],...,x_j^F[d-1]\right)$ is the fixed point of Eq. (9) when $u[k]\equiv 0$, i.e.

$$\begin{gathered} x_j^F[0]=x_j^F[d]=F_j^T\left(\underline{x}^F[0],0,...,0\right)\Theta_j^F \\ \text{or} \\ x_j^F[k+d]=x_j^F[k] \end{gathered} \tag{33}$$

The main goal is stabilizing the fixed point x_j^F. Let,

$$\begin{aligned} \rho_j[k]=\Big[&-F_j^T\left(\underline{x}[k],\underline{u}[k],...,\underline{u}[k+d-2]\right)\Theta_j^F \\ &-\left(G_{j,2}^T\left(\underline{x}[k],\underline{u}[k],...,\underline{u}[k+d-3]\right)\Theta_{j,2}^F\right)u\left[k+d-2\right]-\cdots \\ &-\left(G_{j,d}^T\left(\underline{x}[k]\right)\Theta_{j,d}^G+x_j^F[k+d]-\sum_{j=1}^{d}\lambda_j\left(x_j[k+d-j]-x_j^F[k+d-j]\right)\right)\Big] \end{aligned} \tag{34}$$

$$\begin{aligned} \hat{\rho}_j[k]=\Big[&-F_j^T\left(\underline{x}[k],\underline{u}[k],...,\underline{u}[k+d-2]\right)\hat{\Theta}_j^F[k-1] \\ &-\left(G_{j,2}^T\left(\underline{x}[k],\underline{u}[k],...,\underline{u}[k+d-3]\right)\Theta_{j,2}^F[k-1]\right)u\left[k+d-2\right]-\cdots \\ &-\left(G_{j,d}^T\left(\underline{x}[k]\right)\Theta_{j,d}^G[k-1]+x_j^F[k+d]-\sum_{j=1}^{d}\lambda_j\left(x_j[k+d-j]-x_j^F[k+d-j]\right)\right)\Big] \end{aligned} \tag{35}$$

where λ_i 's are chosen such that all roots of the following polynomial lie inside the unit circle.

$$z^d + \lambda_1 z^{d-1} + \cdots + \lambda_d = 0 \tag{36}$$

Assume that $G_{j,1}^T(x[k],u[k],...,u[k+d-2])\Theta_{j,1}^G[k-1] \neq 0$ and consider the conrol law as given below:

$$u_j[k+d-1] = \frac{\hat{\rho}_j[k]}{G_{j,1}^T(x[k],u[k],...,u[k+d-2])\Theta_{j,1}^G[k-1]} \tag{37}$$

To show that the above controller can stabilize the fixed point of Eq. (9), note that from Eq. (25) we have:

$$\begin{aligned}\lim_{k\to\infty} F_j^T(.)\hat{\Theta}_j^F[k-1] + \sum_{j=1}^{d} G_{j,i}^T(.)\hat{\Theta}_{j,i}^G[k-1]u[k+d-i] \\ = F_j^T(.)\Theta_j^F + \sum_{j=1}^{d} G_{j,i}^T(.)\Theta_{j,i}^G u[k+d-i]\end{aligned} \tag{38}$$

One can write the above equation in the following form:

$$\begin{aligned}&\varepsilon_j[k] = F_j^T(.)\left(\hat{\Theta}_j^F[k-1] - \Theta_j^F\right) + \sum_{i=1}^{d} G_{j,i}^T(.)\left(\hat{\Theta}_{j,i}^G[k-1] - \Theta_{j,i}^G\right)u[k+d-i] \\ &\lim_{k\to\infty} \varepsilon_j[k] = 0\end{aligned} \tag{39}$$

From Eqs. (34), (35) and (39) one can obtain:

$$\hat{\rho}_j[k] - \rho_j[k] = \varepsilon_j[k] + G_{j,1}^T(.)\left(\hat{\Theta}_{j,1}^G[k-1] - \Theta_{j,1}^G\right) + u[k+d-1] \tag{40}$$

Using Eqs. (9), (34), (35) and (37) the controlled system can be written as:

$$\begin{aligned}x_j[k+d] = -\rho[k] + x_j^F[k+d] - \sum_{i=1}^{d} \lambda_i\left(x_j[k+d-i] - x_j^F[k+d-i]\right) \\ + \frac{G_{j,1}^T(\underline{x}[k],\underline{u}[k],...,\underline{u}[k+d-2])\Theta_{j,1}^G}{G_{j,1}^T(\underline{x}[k],\underline{u}[k],...,\underline{u}[k+d-2])\hat{\Theta}_{j,1}^G[k-1]}\hat{\rho}[k]\end{aligned} \tag{41}$$

Using Eq. (40) in Eq. (41), we have:

$$\begin{aligned}x_j[k+d] = -\hat{\rho}[k] + \varepsilon_j[k] + x_j^F[k+d] - \sum_{i=1}^{d} \lambda_i\left(x_j[k+d-i] - x_j^F[k+d-i]\right) \\ + \frac{G_{j,1}^T(\underline{x}[k],\underline{u}[k],...,\underline{u}[k+d-2])\Theta_{j,1}^G}{G_{j,1}^T(\underline{x}[k],\underline{u}[k],...,\underline{u}[k+d-2])\hat{\Theta}_{j,1}^G[k-1]}\hat{\rho}[k]\end{aligned} \tag{42}$$

After some manipulations we get:

$$x_j[k+d] = x_j^F[k+d] - \sum_{i=1}^{d} \lambda_i(x_j[k+d-i] - x_j^F[k+d-i]) + \varepsilon_j[k] \tag{43}$$

or,

$$(x_j[k+d] - x_j^F[k+d]) + \sum_{i=1}^{d} \lambda_i(x_j[k+d-i] - x_j^F[k+d-i]) = \varepsilon_j[k] \tag{44}$$

Define,

$$y_1[k] = x_j[k] - x_j^F[k],\ y_2[k] = x_j[k+1] - x_j^F[k+1],\ \ldots,\ y_d[k] = x_j[k+d-1] - x_j^F[k+d-1], \quad (45)$$

Eq. (44) can be re-written as:

$$\begin{bmatrix} y_1[k+1] \\ y_2[k+1] \\ \vdots \\ y_d[k+1] \end{bmatrix} = \begin{bmatrix} 0 & & & \\ 0 & & I_{(d-1)\times(d-1)} & \\ 0 & & & \\ -\lambda_1 & -\lambda_2 & \cdots & -\lambda_d \end{bmatrix} \begin{bmatrix} y_1[k] \\ y_2[k] \\ \vdots \\ y_d[k] \end{bmatrix} + \begin{bmatrix} 0 \\ \vdots \\ 0 \\ 1 \end{bmatrix} \varepsilon_j[k] \quad (46)$$

Let:

$$G = \begin{bmatrix} 0 & & & \\ 0 & & I_{(d-1)\times(d-1)} & \\ 0 & & & \\ -\lambda_1 & -\lambda_2 & \cdots & -\lambda_d \end{bmatrix},\ H = \begin{bmatrix} 0 \\ \vdots \\ 0 \\ -1 \end{bmatrix} \quad (47)$$

Equation (45) can be written as:

$$Y[k+1] = GY[k] + H\varepsilon_j[k] \quad (48)$$

Taking z-transform from both sides of Eq. (48) we get:

$$Y(z) = (zI - G)^{-1} zY(0) + (zI - G)^{-1} H\varepsilon_j(z) \quad (49)$$

Taking inverse yields:

$$Y(k) = G^k Y[0] + z^{-1}[(zI - G)^{-1} H\varepsilon_j(z)] \quad (50)$$

Note that $\lim G^k Y[0] = 0$ as $k \to \infty$ (because all eigen-values of G lie inside the unit circle), besides $\lim \varepsilon_j[k] = 0$ as $k \to \infty$ and G is a stable matrix therefore:

$$\lim_{k\to\infty} z^{-1}[(zI - G)^{-1} H\varepsilon_j(z)] = 0 \quad (51)$$

Consequently we have:

$$\lim_{k\to\infty} Y[k] = 0 \Rightarrow x_j[k] \to x_j^F[k], \ldots, x_j[k+d-1] \to x_j^F[k+d-1] \quad (52)$$

From Eq. (52) the stability of the proposed controller is established.

Remark 1

In practice, control law (37) works well but theoretically there is the remote possibility of division by zero in calculating $u[.]$. This can be easily avoided. For example $u[.]$ can be calculated as follows:

$$u_j[k+d-1]=\begin{cases}\dfrac{\hat{\rho}_j[k]}{\mu_j[k]}, & |\mu_j[k]|\neq 0\\ \dfrac{\hat{\rho}_j[k]}{m_\varepsilon} & |\mu_j[k]|=0\end{cases} \tag{53}$$

where

$$\mu_j[k]=G_{j,1}^T\left(\underline{x}[k],\underline{u}[k],\ldots,\underline{u}[k+d-2]\right)\hat{\Theta}_{j,1}^G[k-1] \tag{54}$$

and $m_\varepsilon>0$ is a small positive real number.

Remark 2

For the time varying systems, least squares algorithm with variable forgetting factor can be used. The corresponding updating rule is given below (Fortescue et al. 1981):

$$\begin{aligned}P_j[k]&=\frac{1}{v[k]}\left[P_j[k-1]-\frac{P_j[k-1]\Phi_j[k]\Phi_j^T[k]P[k-1]}{v_j[k]+\Phi_j^T[k]P_j[k-1]\Phi_j[k]}\right]\\ \hat{\Theta}_j[k]&=\hat{\Theta}_j[k-1]+\frac{P_j[k-1]\Phi_j[k]\varepsilon_j[k]}{v_j[k]+\Phi_j^T[k]P_j[k-1]\Phi_j[k]}\end{aligned} \tag{55}$$

where,

$$v_j[k]=\max\left\{1-\frac{\varepsilon_j^2[k]}{1+\varepsilon_j^2[k]},\ \lambda_{\min}\right\} \tag{56}$$

and $0<\lambda_{\min}<1$ usually set to 0.95.

2.4. Simulation results

In this section through simulation, the performance of the proposed adaptive controller is evaluated.

Example 1:

Consider the logistic map given below:

$$x[k+1]=\mu\, x[k](1-x[k])+u[k] \tag{57}$$

For $\mu\geq 3.567$ and $u[k]=0$ the behavior of the system is chaotic. In this example stabilization of the 2-cycle fixed point of the following logistic map is considered. In this case the governing equation is:

$$\begin{aligned}x[k+2]&=\mu^2x[k]-(\mu^2+\mu^3)x^2[k]+2\mu^3x^3[k]-\mu^3x^4[k]\\ &+\mu u[k]-2\mu^2x[k]u[k]+2\mu^2x^2[k]u[k]-\mu u^2[k]+u[k+1]\end{aligned} \tag{58}$$

and the system fixed points for $\mu=3.6$ are $x_F[1]=0.8696$, $x_F[2]=0.4081$ and for $\mu=3.9$ are $x_F[1]=0.8974$, $x_F[2]=0.3590$. Equation (58) can be written in the following form:

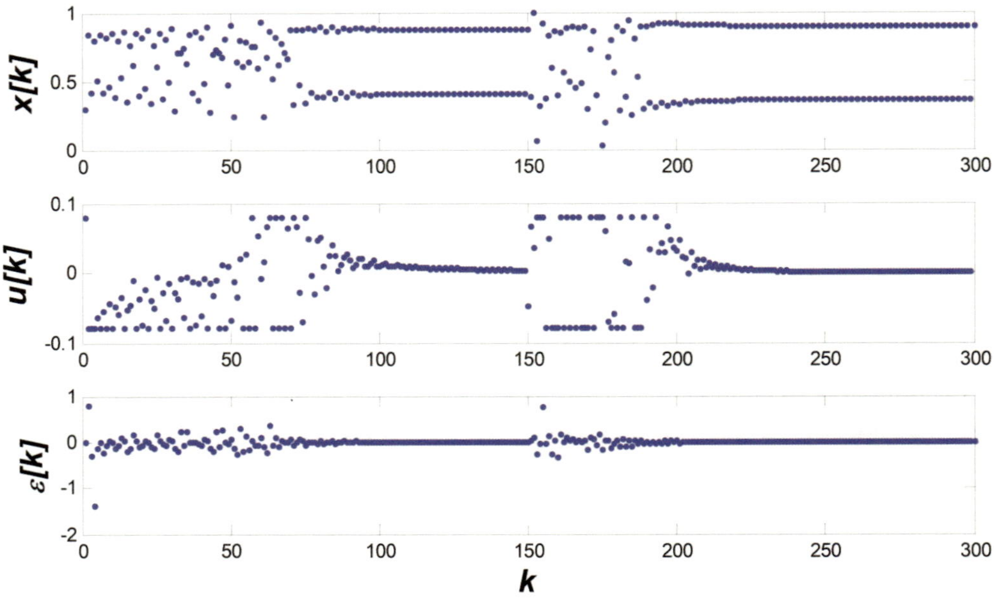

Fig. 1. Closed-loop response of the logistic map (59), for stabilizing the 2-cycle fixed point, when the parameter μ changes from $\mu = 3.6$ to $\mu = 3.9$ at $k = 150$.

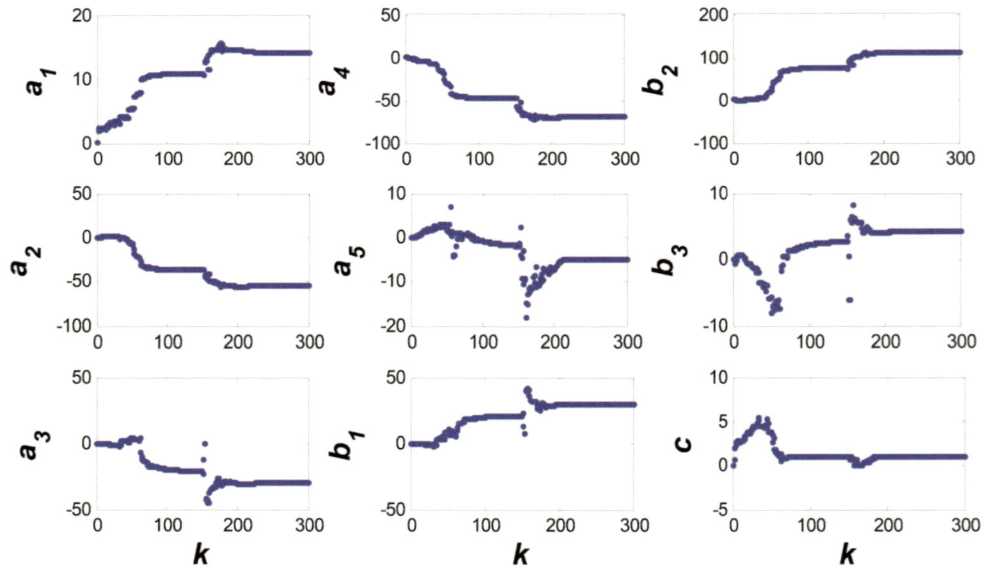

Fig. 2. Parameter estimates for the logistic map (59), when the parameter μ changes from $\mu = 3.6$ to $\mu = 3.9$ at $k = 150$.

$$x[k+2]=\begin{bmatrix}x[k] & x^2[k] & x^3[k] & x^4[k] & u^2[k]\end{bmatrix}\begin{bmatrix}a_1\\a_2\\a_3\\a_4\\a_5\end{bmatrix}+\begin{bmatrix}1 & x[k] & x^2[k]\end{bmatrix}\begin{bmatrix}b_1\\b_2\\b_3\end{bmatrix}u[k]+cu[k+1] \tag{59}$$

It is assumed that the system parameter μ changes from $\mu=3.6$ to $\mu=3.9$ at $k=150$.
The results are shown in Figs. (1) and (2). As can be seen the 2-cycle fixed point of the system is stabilized and the tracking error tends to zero, although the parameter estimates are not converged to their actual values.

Example 2:

For the second example, the Henon map is considered,

$$\begin{aligned}x_1[k+1]&=1-ax_1^2[k]+x_2[k]+u_1[k]\\x_2[k+1]&=bx_1[k]+u_2[k]\end{aligned} \tag{60}$$

where for $a=1.4$, $b=0.3$ and $u_1[k]=u_2[k]=0$ the behavior of the system is chaotic. The 1-cycle fixed point is regarded for stabilization. Equation (60) can be written in the following form:

$$\begin{aligned}x_1[k+1]&=f_1^T\left(x_1[k],x_2[k]\right)\Theta_1^f+g_1^T\left(x_1[k],x_2[k]\right)\Theta_1^g u_1[k]\\x_2[k+1]&=f_2^T\left(x_1[k],x_2[k]\right)\Theta_2^f+g_2^T\left(x_1[k],x_2[k]\right)\Theta_2^g u_2[k]\end{aligned} \tag{61}$$

where,

$$\begin{aligned}&f_1\left(x_1[k],x_2[k]\right)=\begin{bmatrix}1 & x_2[k] & x_1^2[k]\end{bmatrix}^T, && f_2\left(x_1[k],x_2[k]\right)=1\\&G_1\left(x_1[k],x_2[k]\right)=1, && G_2\left(x_1[k],x_2[k]\right)=1\end{aligned} \tag{62}$$

and

$$\Theta_1^f=\begin{bmatrix}\theta_{1,1}^f & \theta_{1,2}^f & \theta_{1,3}^f\end{bmatrix}^T,\qquad \Theta_1^f=\theta_1^f,\qquad \Theta_i^g=\theta_i^g,\ i=1,2 \tag{63}$$

Again the 1-cycle fixed point is obtained, using numerical methods, $(x_1^F=0.6314,\ x_2^F=0.1894)$. Figures (3) and (4) show the results of applying the proposed adaptive controller to the Henon map. It is observed that the 1-cycle fixed point of the system is stabilized.
It must be noted that if in the system model the exact functionality is not know, a more general form with additional parameters can be considered. For example system (61) can be modeled as follows:

$$\begin{aligned}f_i\left(x_1[k],x_2[k]\right)&=g_i\left(x_1[k],x_2[k]\right)\\&=\begin{bmatrix}1 & x_1[k] & x_2[k] & x_1^2[k] & x_1[k]x_2[k] & x_2^2[k]\end{bmatrix}^T\end{aligned} \tag{64}$$

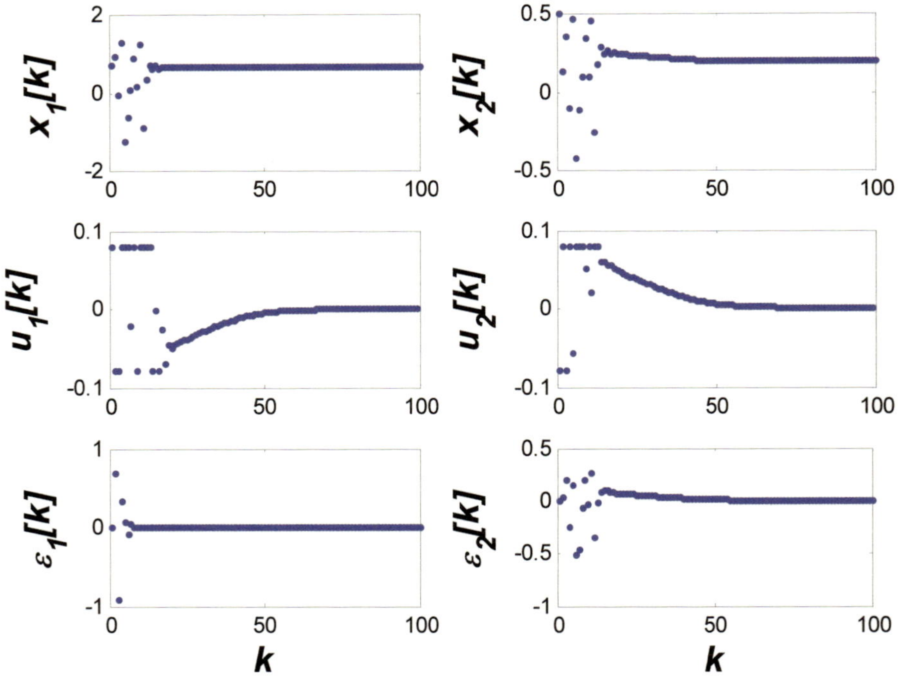

Fig. 3. Closed-loop response of the Henon map (61), for stabilizing the 1-cycle fixed point.

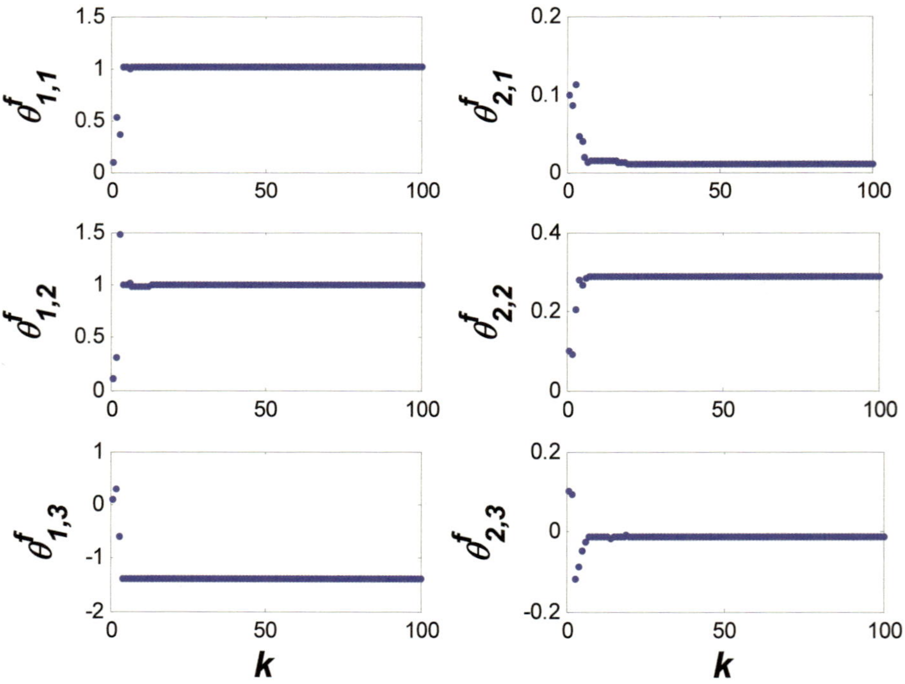

Fig. 4. Parameter estimates of the Henon map (61).

and

$$\Theta_i^f = \begin{bmatrix} \theta_{i,1}^f & \theta_{i,2}^f & \theta_{i,3}^f & \theta_{i,4}^f & \theta_{i,5}^f & \theta_{i,6}^f \end{bmatrix}^T$$
$$\Theta_i^g = \begin{bmatrix} \theta_{i,1}^g & \theta_{i,2}^g & \theta_{i,3}^g & \theta_{i,4}^g & \theta_{i,5}^g & \theta_{i,6}^g \end{bmatrix}^T \tag{65}$$

As it is illustrated in Fig. (5), the 1-cycle fixed point is stabilized successfully. It shows that in cases where the system dynamics is not known completely, the proposed method can be applied successfully using the over-parameterized model.

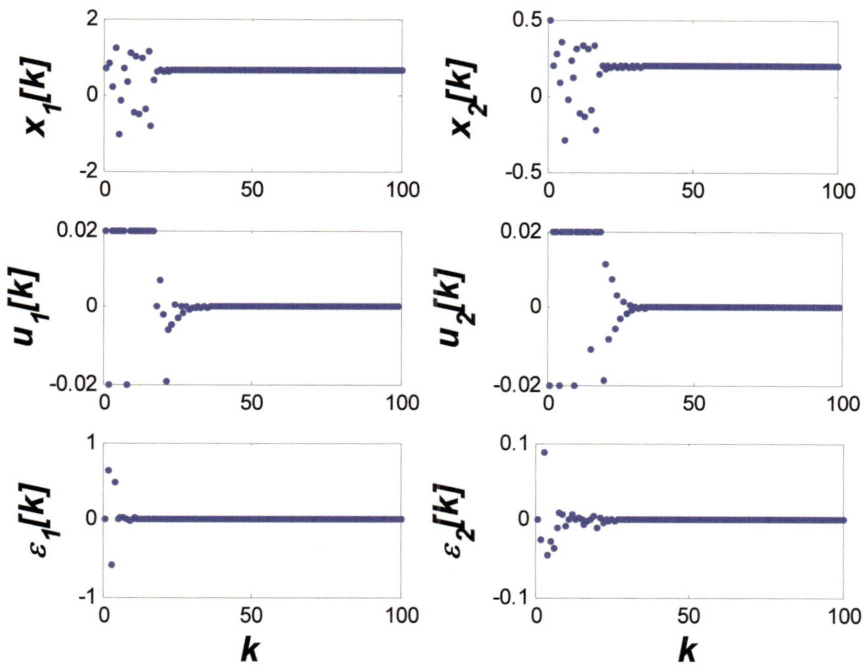

Fig. 5. Closed-loop response of the Henon map (61), for stabilizing the 1-cycle fixed point, using over-parameterized model.

3. Controlling a class of continuous-time chaotic systems

In this section a direct adaptive control scheme for controlling chaos in a class of continuous-time dynamical system is presented. The method is based on the proposed adaptive technique by Salarieh and Alasty (2008) in which the unstable periodic orbits of a stochastic chaotic system with unknown parameters are stabilized via adaptive control. The method is simplified and applied to a non-stochastic chaotic system.

3.1 Problem statement

It is assumed that the dynamics of the under study chaotic system is given by:

$$\dot{x} = f(x) + F(x)\theta + G(x)u \tag{66}$$

where $x \in \Re^n$ is the state vector of the system, $\theta \in \Re^m$ is the vector of the system parameters, $u \in \Re^n$ is the control vector, $f \in C^1(\Re^n, \Re^n)$, $F \in C^1(\Re^n, \Re^{n\times m})$ and for all x $\|F(x)\|_2 < M$, where M is a positive constant, i.e. F is bounded, and $G \in C^1(\Re^n, \Re^{n\times n})$. The Unstable Periodic Orbit (UPO) of chaotic system (66) with $u = 0$ is denoted by $\bar{x}$, and consequently we have:

$$\dot{\bar{x}} = f(\bar{x}) + F(\bar{x})\theta \tag{67}$$

It is assumed that all states of the chaotic system are available, G is invertible, functions f, F and G are known, and the system parameters, θ, are unknown. The main objective is designing a feedback direct adaptive controller for stabilizing the unstable periodic orbit, $\bar{x}$ such that:

$$\|x - \bar{x}\| \to 0, \text{ as } t \to \infty \tag{68}$$

3.2 Direct adaptive control of chaos

By using the following theorem, a direct adaptive controller can be designed which fulfills the above objective:

Theorem

Let $e = x - \bar{x}$ and $k > 0$, than the control and adaptation laws given by:

$$u = -G^{-1}(x)[f(x) - f(\bar{x}) + (F(x) - F(\bar{x}))\alpha + \eta sign(e) + k\ e] \tag{69}$$

$$\dot{\alpha} = [F(x) - F(\bar{x})]^T e \tag{70}$$

make the UPO defined by Eq. (67) asymptotically stable.

■

Note that the *sign* function in Eq. (69), acts on each elements of the $x - \bar{x}$ vector.

Proof:

To design a control and adaptation law, a Lyapunov function is defined as:

$$V = \frac{1}{2}\|x(t) - \bar{x}(t)\|^2 + \frac{1}{2}\|\alpha(t) - \theta\|^2 \tag{71}$$

where α is the estimate of θ obtained from the adaptive law (71). Differentiating both sides of Eq. (70) yields:

$$\dot{V} = \left(x(t) - \bar{x}(t)\right)^T \left(\dot{x}(t) - \dot{\bar{x}}(t)\right) + \left(\alpha(t) - \theta\right)^T \dot{\alpha} \tag{72}$$

Using Eqs. (66), (67) and (69), Eq. (72) can be written as:

$$\begin{aligned}\dot{V} &= \left(x - \bar{x}\right)^T \left(-\left(F(x) - F(\bar{x})\right)\left(\alpha - \theta\right) - \eta sign(x - \bar{x}) - k(x - \bar{x})\right) + \left(\alpha(t) - \theta\right)^T [F(x) - F(\bar{x})]^T (x - \bar{x}) \\ &= -k\|e\|^2 - \eta|e|\end{aligned} \tag{73}$$

Since $\dot{V}$ is negative semi-definite, so the closed-loop system is stable, and $e = x - \bar{x}$ and x are bounded. In addition $\dot{e}$ is bounded too, because it satisfies the following equation:

$$\dot{e} = \dot{x} - \dot{\bar{x}} = F(x)\theta + f(\bar{x}) - \left(F(x) - F(\bar{x})\right)\alpha - \eta sign\left(e\right) - k\ e - \dot{\bar{x}} \tag{74}$$

in which $f(.)$ and $F(.)$ are continuous functions. From Eq. (73) we have

$$-\int_{t_0}^{\infty} \dot{V}(t)dt = \int_{t_0}^{\infty} \left(k\|e\|^2 + \eta|e|\right)dt = V(0) - V(\infty) < \infty \tag{75}$$

Since $e \in L^2 \cap L^\infty$ and $\dot{e} \in L^\infty$, due to Barbalat's Lemma (Sastry, Bodson 1994) we have

$$\lim_{t\to\infty} e(t) = 0 \ \Rightarrow \ \lim_{t\to\infty} x(t) = \bar{x}(t) \tag{76}$$

■

3.3 Simulation results

In this section the presented controller has been used for stabilizing the UPOs of the Lorenz, and the Rossler dynamical systems.

Example 1: Stabilizing a UPO of the Lorenz system:

The Lorenz system has the following governing equations:

$$\begin{bmatrix} \dot{x}_1 \\ \dot{x}_2 \\ \dot{x}_3 \end{bmatrix} = \begin{bmatrix} 0 \\ -x_2 - x_1x_3 \\ x_1x_2 \end{bmatrix} + \begin{bmatrix} x_2 - x_1 & 0 & 0 \\ 0 & x_1 & 0 \\ 0 & 0 & -x_3 \end{bmatrix} \begin{bmatrix} \theta_1 \\ \theta_2 \\ \theta_3 \end{bmatrix} + \begin{bmatrix} 1 & 0 & 0 \\ 0 & 1 & 0 \\ 0 & 0 & 1 \end{bmatrix} \begin{bmatrix} u_1 \\ u_2 \\ u_3 \end{bmatrix} \tag{77}$$

where x_1, x_2 and x_3 are the state variables, θ_1, θ_2 and θ_3 are unknown parameters. For $\theta_1 = 16$, $\theta_2 = 45.92$, $\theta_3 = 4$ and $u_i = 0$, the Lorenz system shows chaotic behavior, and one of its UPOs is initiated from $x_1(0) = 19.926$, $x_2(0) = 30.109$ and $x_3(0) = 40$ with the period of $T = 0.941$, as shown in Fig. (6). The presented adaptive control is applied to the Lorenz dynamical system. Figure (7) shows the states dynamics in the time-domain and in the phase space. The control actions are shown in Fig. (8).

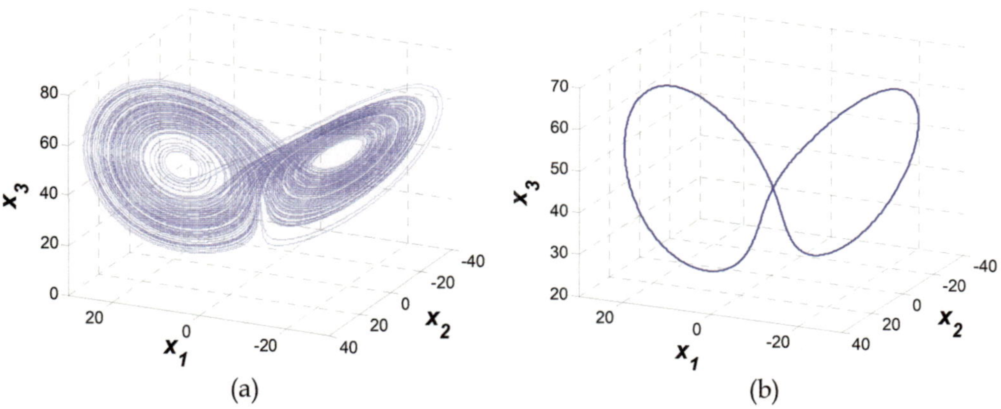

Fig. 6. (a) Chaotic attractor of the Lorenz system, (b) the UPO with the period of $T = 0.941$ and the initial conditions of: $x_1(0) = 19.926$, $x_2(0) = 30.109$ and $x_3(0) = 40$ (Salarieh and Alasty, 2008).

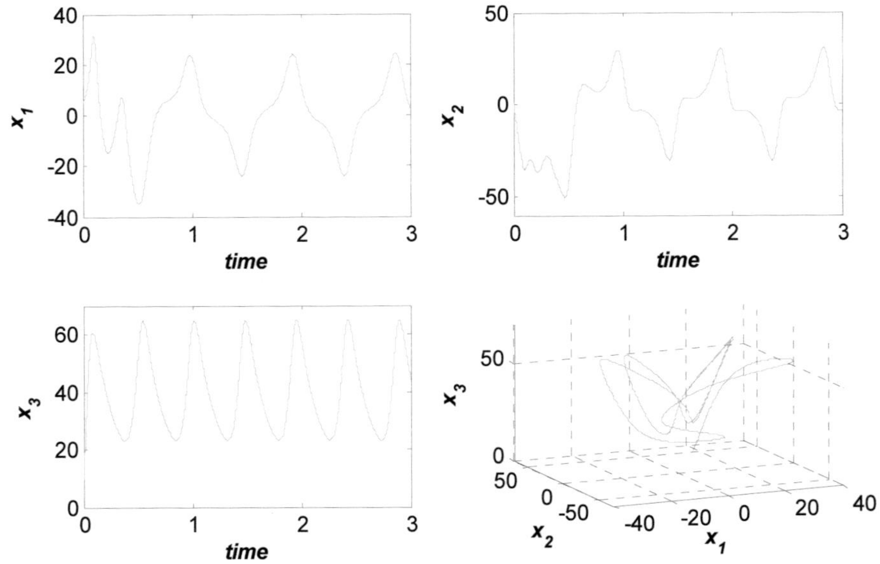

Fig. 7. The trajectory of the Lorenz system after applying the adaptive control law (69).

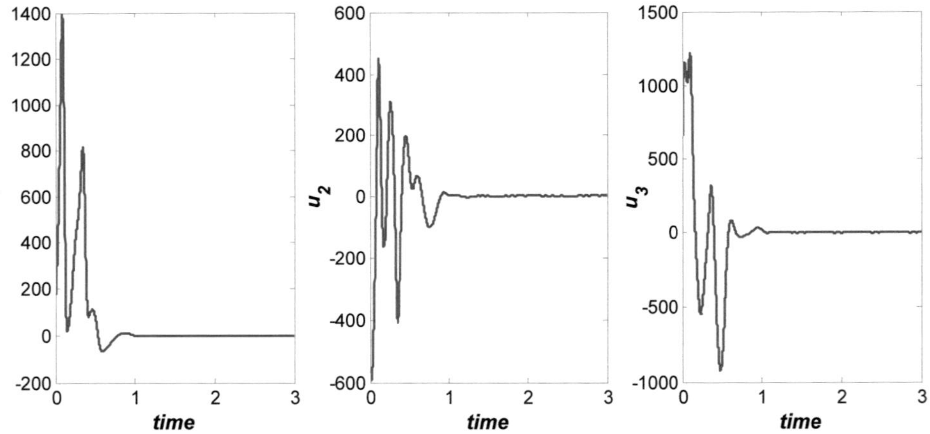

Fig. 8. Corresponding control actions.

Example 2: Stabilizing a UPO of the Rossler system:

The Rossler dynamical system is described by the following equation:

$$\begin{bmatrix} \dot{x}_1 \\ \dot{x}_2 \\ \dot{x}_3 \end{bmatrix} = \begin{bmatrix} -(x_2 + x_3) \\ x_1 \\ x_1 x_3 \end{bmatrix} + \begin{bmatrix} 0 & 0 & 0 \\ x_2 & 0 & 0 \\ 0 & 1 & -x_3 \end{bmatrix} \begin{bmatrix} \theta_1 \\ \theta_2 \\ \theta_3 \end{bmatrix} + \begin{bmatrix} 1 & 0 & 0 \\ 0 & 1 & 0 \\ 0 & 0 & 1 \end{bmatrix} \begin{bmatrix} u_1 \\ u_2 \\ u_3 \end{bmatrix} \tag{78}$$

For $\theta_1 = 0.2$, $\theta_2 = 0.2$, $\theta_3 = 5.7$ and $u_i = 0$, the system trajectories are chaotic. The system behavior in the phase space and one UPO of the system are shown in Fig. (9). In this case the UPO has the period of $T = 5.882$ which is obtained from the initial condition $x_1(0) = 0$,

$x_2(0) = 6.089$ and $x_3(0) = 1.301$. The presented adaptive control scheme is applied to the system for stabilizing the UPO shown in Fig. (9). Simulation results are shown in Figs. (10) and (11). Figure (10) shows that the system trajectories converge to the desired UPO.

4. Fuzzy adaptive control of chaos

In this section an adaptive fuzzy control scheme for chaotic systems with unknown dynamics is presented.

4.1 Problem statement

It is assumed that the dynamics of the chaotic system is given by:

$$x^{(n)} = f(X) + g(X)u \tag{79}$$

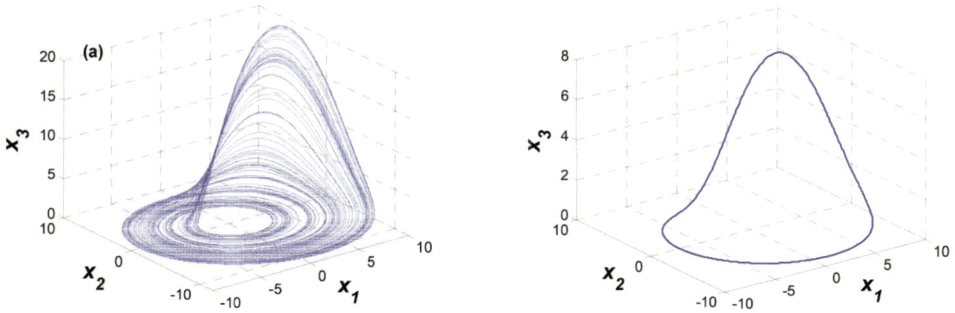

(a) (b)

Fig. 9. (a) Chaotic attractor of the Rossler system, (b) the UPO with the period of $T = 5.882$ and the initial conditions of: $x_1(0) = 0$, $x_2(0) = 6.089$ and $x_3(0) = 1.301$ (Salarieh and Alasty, 2008).

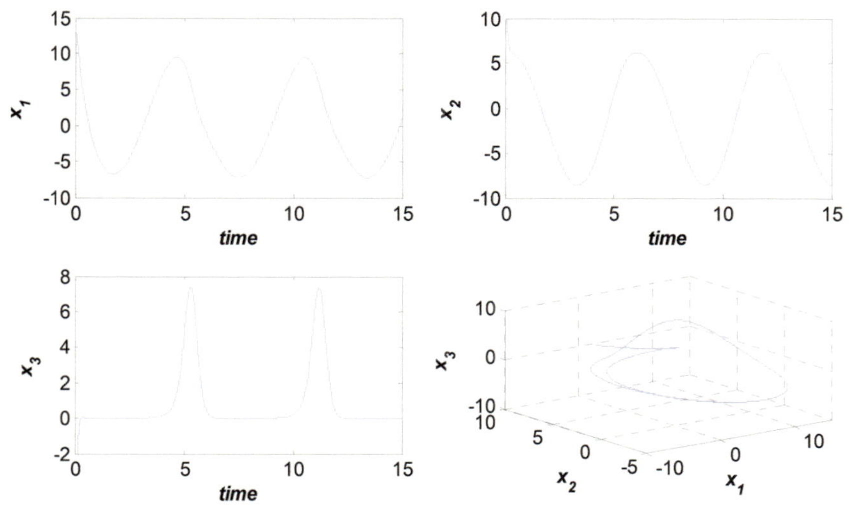

Fig. 10. The trajectory of the Rossler system after applying the adaptive control law (69).

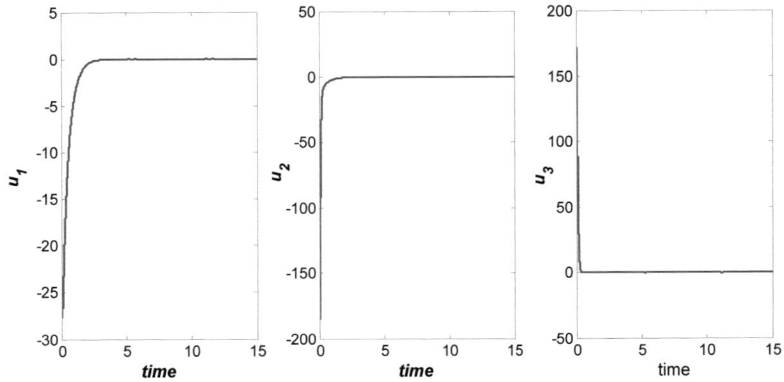

Fig. 11. Corresponding control actions.

where $X=[x_1, x_2,..., x_n]^T=[x,\dot{x},...,x^{(n-1)}]^T$ is the system state vector, $u\in\Re$ is the control vector, $f\in C^1(\Re^n,\Re)$ and $g\in C^1(\Re^n,\Re)$. It is also assumed that $f(.)$ is an unknown function but $g(.)$ is a known function.

The Unstable Periodic Orbit (UPO) of chaotic system (79) with $u=0$ is denoted by $\overline{X}$, therefore:

$$\bar{x}^{(n)}=f(\bar{X}) \tag{80}$$

The main objective is to design a feedback direct adaptive controller for stabilizing the unstable periodic orbit, $\overline{X}$. It is also assumed that all state variables are available for controller design.

4.2 Fuzzy estimation of *f* (*X*)

Since $f(.)$ is not known, a fuzzy system is used to estimate it. $f(.)$ can be estimated as:

$$\hat{f}(X)=\sum_{k=1}^{N}\theta_k\phi_k(X)=\Theta^T\Phi(X) \tag{81}$$

where $\hat{f}(.)$ is the fuzzy estimation of $f(.)$ and

$$\begin{aligned}\Phi(X)&=[\phi_1(X),...,\phi_N(X)]^T\\ \Theta&=\left[\theta_1,\theta_2,\ldots,\theta_N\right]^T\end{aligned} \tag{82}$$

$\phi_k(.)$ functions have the following form:

$$\phi_k(X)=\frac{\prod_{i=1}^{n}\mu_k(x_i)}{\sum_{k=1}^{N}\prod_{i=1}^{n}\mu_k(x_i)} \tag{83}$$

where $\mu_k(x_i)$ is the output of fuzzy membership function for i^{th} input argument. Fuzzy systems (81) and (83) are obtained using singleton fuzzifier and product inference engine (PIE) and center average defuzzifier. According to the universal approximation theorem of

Fuzzy systems, for sufficiently large N, i.e. the number of fuzzy rules, one can estimate $f(.)$ such that for every $\varepsilon_f > 0$ the following inequality holds:

$$\left\| f(X) - \hat{f}(X) \right\|_\infty < \varepsilon_f \tag{84}$$

The optimum vector parameter Θ which satisfies Eq. (84) is denoted by Θ_o, and its corresponding estimated $f(.)$ is denoted by $\hat{f}_o(.)$.

4.3 Direct fuzzy adaptive control scheme

The following theorem provides an adaptive control law for system (79).

Theorem 2

Let $E = X - \overline{X}$ and select $\mu_i, i = 0,1,...,n-1$ such that all roots of equation $s^n + \mu_0 s^{n-1} + \cdots + \mu_{n-1} = 0$ have negative real parts. Consider the control and adaptation laws:

$$u = -\frac{1}{g(X)}\left[\hat{f}(X) - \overline{x}^{(n)} + \sum_{i=0}^{n-1} \mu_{n-1-i}\left(x^{(i)} - \overline{x}^{(i)}\right)\right] \tag{85}$$

$$\dot{\Theta} = \Phi(X) B^T PE \tag{86}$$

where $B^T = [0\ 0 \ldots 0\ 1]$ and P is a positive definite symmetric matrix that satisfies the Lyapunov equation $A^T P + PA = -Q$ with any arbitrary positive definite and symmetric matrix Q and Hurwitz matrix A given below:

$$A = \begin{bmatrix} 0 & 1 & 0 & \cdots & 0 \\ 0 & 0 & 1 & \cdots & 0 \\ \vdots & \vdots & \vdots & \ddots & \vdots \\ 0 & 0 & 0 & \cdots & 1 \\ -\mu_{n-1} & -\mu_{n-2} & -\mu_{n-3} & \cdots & -\mu_0 \end{bmatrix} \tag{87}$$

Applying the control and adaptation laws given by Eqs. (85) and (86) to the system (79) results in the following tracking error bound:

$$\|E\| \le \frac{2\varepsilon_f \lambda_{\max}(P)}{\lambda_{\min}(Q)} \tag{88}$$

in which $\lambda(.)$ is the eigen-value and $\|...\|$ is the Euclidian norm.

■

Proof:

To achieve the control and adaptation laws given by Eq. (85) and (86) consider the following Lyapunov function:

$$V = E^T PE + \frac{1}{2}\left\|\Theta - \Theta_o\right\|^2 \tag{89}$$

Differentiating both sides of Eq. (89) yields:

$$\dot{V} = \dot{E}^T PE + E^T P\dot{E} + (\Theta - \Theta_o)^T \dot{\Theta} \tag{90}$$

By subtracting Eq. (80) from Eqs. (79) and using the control law (85) we have:

$$\begin{aligned} x^{(n)} - \overline{x}^{(n)} &= f(X) - f(\overline{X}) - g(X)\left(\frac{1}{g(X)}\left[\hat{f}(X) - \overline{x}^{(n)} + \sum_{i=0}^{n-1} \lambda_i (x^{(i)} - \overline{x}^{(i)})\right]\right) \\ &= f(X) - f(\overline{X}) - \sum_{i=0}^{n-1} \mu_{n-1-i}(x^{(i)} - \overline{x}^{(i)}) \end{aligned} \tag{91}$$

Using Eq. (87), Eq (91) can be rewritten as:

$$\dot{E} = AE + B\left(f(X) - \hat{f}(X)\right) \tag{92}$$

Substituting Eq. (92) and the adaptation law (86) into Eq. (90) get:

$$\begin{aligned} \dot{V} &= \left[E^T A^T + \left(f(X) - \hat{f}(X)\right)B^T\right]PE + E^T P\left[AE + B\left(f(X) - \hat{f}(X)\right)\right] + (\Theta - \Theta_o)^T \Phi(X) B^T PE \\ &= E^T\left(A^T P + PA\right)E + 2\left(f(X) - \hat{f}(X)\right)B^T PE + (\Theta - \Theta_o)^T \Phi(X) B^T PE \end{aligned} \tag{93}$$

Adding and subtracting an $\hat{f}_o(.)$ in the above equation results in

$$\begin{aligned} \dot{V} &= E^T\left(A^T P + PA\right)E + 2\left(f(X) - \hat{f}_o(X) + \hat{f}_o(X) - \hat{f}(X)\right)B^T PE + (\Theta - \Theta_o)^T \Phi(X) B^T PE \\ &= E^T\left(A^T P + PA\right)E + 2\left(\Delta f - (\Theta - \Theta_o)^T \Phi(X)\right)B^T PE + (\Theta - \Theta_o)^T \Phi(X) B^T PE \end{aligned} \tag{94}$$

where $\Delta f = f(.) - \hat{f}_o(.)$. Using inequality (84) in Eq. (94) yields:

$$\dot{V} \le -E^T QE + 2\varepsilon_f B^T PE \tag{95}$$

Since $Q - \lambda_{\min}(Q)I$ and $\lambda_{\max}(P)I - P$ are positive semi-definite (I is the identity matrix), we have:

$$\dot{V} \le -\lambda_{\min}(Q)\|E\|^2 + 2\varepsilon_f \lambda_{\max}(P)\|E\| \tag{96}$$

From the above inequality it is concluded that:

$$\|E(t)\| \le \frac{2\varepsilon_f \lambda_{\max}(P)}{\lambda_{\min}(Q)} \quad as \quad t \to \infty \tag{97}$$

because for $\|E\| > {2\varepsilon_f \lambda_{\max}(P)}/{\lambda_{\min}(Q)}$, we have $\dot{V} < 0$ and consequently the region defined by (97) is an attracting set for the error trajectories.

Remark

From Eq. (97) it is concluded that if $\varepsilon_f \in L^1$, E converges to zero as t approaches to infinity.

Proof:

From inequality (95) we have:

$$\lambda_{\min}(Q)\int_0^\infty \|E\|^2\,dt \le -\int_0^\infty \dot{V}dt + 2\lambda_{\max}(P)\int_0^\infty \varepsilon_f\,\|E\|\,dt \tag{98}$$

Or

$$\lambda_{\min}(Q)\int_0^\infty \|E\|^2\,dt \le V(0)-V(\infty) + 2\lambda_{\max}(P)\int_0^\infty \varepsilon_f\,\|E\|\,dt \tag{99}$$

If $\varepsilon_f \in L^1$, then from the above equation, it is concluded that $E \in L^2$. Besides, $\dot{E}$ satisfies Eq. (92) which consists of continuously differentiable functions implying that $\dot{E} \in L^\infty$. Since $E \in L^2 \cap L^\infty$ and $\dot{E} \in L^\infty$, due to Barbalat's Lemma (Sastry and Bodson, 1994), the E converges to zero as t approaches to infinity.

4.4 Simulation results

The above described control scheme is used to control states of the modified Duffing system. Consider the following modified Duffing system:

$$\begin{aligned}\dot{x}_1 &= x_2\\ \dot{x}_2 &= \alpha x_1 + \beta x_1^{\,3} + \delta x_2 + f_0\cos t + (3+\cos x_1)u\end{aligned} \tag{100}$$

The system shows chaotic behavior for $\alpha = 1$, $\beta = -1$, $\delta = -0.15$, $f_0 = 0.3$ and $u = 0$. For this system $g(X) = 3 + \cos x_1$. The objective is to force the state variables to track the desired trajectory using adaptive control scheme described in the previous section. For $\alpha = 1$, $\beta = -1$, $\delta = -0.15$, $f_0 = 0.3$, the Duffing system (100) has periodic orbits with 2π-period (Fig. (12)) which is selected as desired trajectory in simulation study.

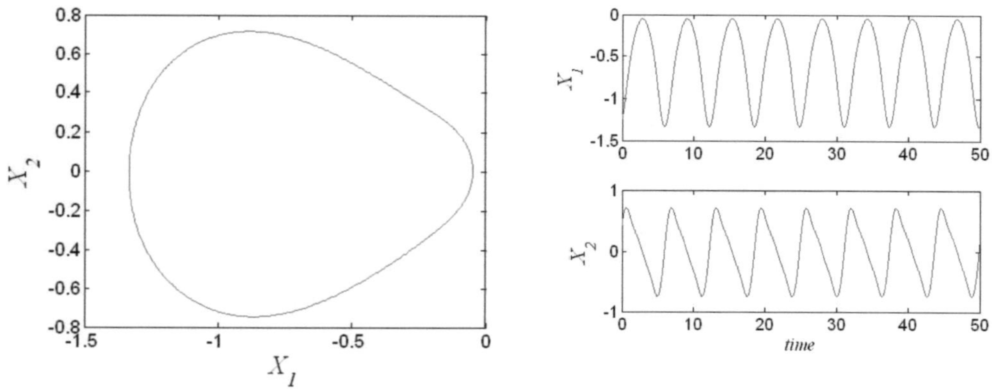

Fig. 12. 2π periodic solution of the Duffing system (Layeghi et al. 2008).

The variation ranges of x_1 and x_2 are partitioned into 3 fuzzy sets with Gaussian membership functions, $\mu(x) = \exp\left[-\left(\frac{x-\bar{x}}{\sigma}\right)^2\right]$, whose centers are at $\{-2,-1,0,1,2\}$. The range of t is partitioned to 4 fuzzy sets with Gaussian membership functions and centers at $\{0,2,4,6\}$. Note that t in Eq.(100) can be always considered in the interval $(0,2\pi)$. The parameter σ is chosen such that the summation of membership values at the intersection of any two neighboring membership functions be equal to 1. Simulation is performed for $Q = 2I$.

Simulation results of the presented method are shown in Fig. (13).

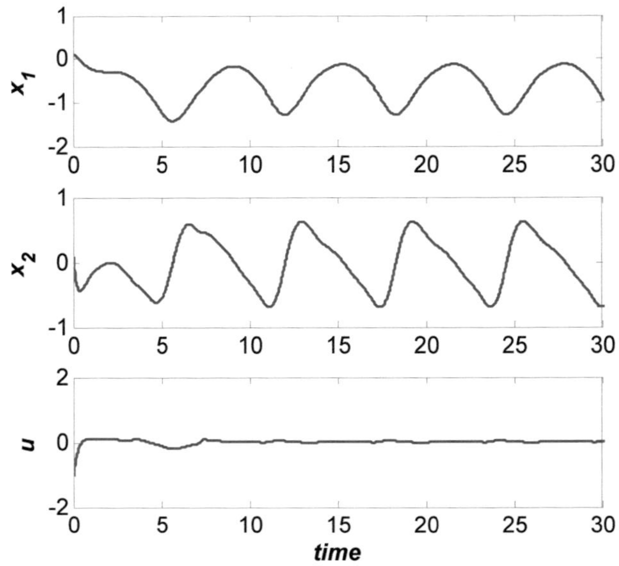

Fig. 13. (a) Trajectory of x_1, x_2 and control action u for fuzzy adaptive control of Duffing system.

As can be seen from Figs. (13), stability of unstable periodic orbits is completely achieved and the tracking errors vanish.

5. Conclusion

In this chapter adaptive control of chaos has been studied. Indirect and direct adaptive control techniques have been presented, and their applications for chaos control of two classes of discrete time and continuous time systems have been considered. The presented methods have been applied to some chaotic systems to investigate the effectiveness and performance of the controllers. In addition a fuzzy adaptive control method has been introduced and it has been utilized for control of a chaotic system.

6. References

Alasty, A. & Salarieh, H. (2007). Nonlinear feedback control of chaotic pendulum in presence of saturation effect, *Chaos Solitons and Fractals,* Vol. 31, No. 2, 292-304.

Arjmand, M.T., Sadeghian, H., Salarieh, H. & Alasty, A. (2008) Chaos control in AFM systems using nonlinear delayed feedback via sliding mode control, *Nonlinear Analysis: Hybrid Systems,* Vol. 2, No. 3, 993-1001.

Astrom, K.J. & Wittenmark, B. (1994). *Adaptive Control*, 2nd edition, Prentice Hall, 1994.

Bonakdar, M., Samadi, M., Salarieh, H. & Alasty, A. (2008). Stabilizing periodic orbits of chaotic systems using fuzzy control of Poincaré map, *Chaos Solitons and Fractals*, Vol. 36, No. 3, 682-693.

Chen, L., Chen, G. & Lee, Y.-W. (1999). Fuzzy modeling and adaptive control of uncertain chaotic systems, *Information Sciences*, Vol. 121, 27-37.

Feng, G. & Chen, G. (2005). Adaptive control of discrete time chaotic systems: a fuzzy control approach, *Chaos Solitons Fractals*, Vol. 23, 459-467.

Fortescue, T.R., Kershenbaum, L.S. & Ydstie B.E. (1981). Implementation of self-tuning regulators with variable forgetting factors, *Automatica*, Vol. 17, 831-835.

Fradkov, A.L. & Evans, R. (2005). Control of Chaos: Methods and Applications in Engineering. Annual Reviews in Control, Vol. 29, 33-56.

Ge, S.S. & Wang, C. (2000). Adaptive control of uncertain Chua's circuit, *IEEE Transactions on Circuits and Systems I: Fundamental Theory and Applications* Vol. 47, No. 9, 1397-1402.

Guan, X. & Chen, C. (2003). Adaptive fuzzy control for chaotic systems with H_∞ tracking performance, *Fuzzy Sets and Systems*, Vol. 139, 81-93.

Hua, C. & Guan, X. (2004). Adaptive control for chaotic systems, *Chaos Solitons and Fractals* Vol. 22, 55-60.

Kiss, I.Z. & Gaspar, V., and Hudson, J.L. (2000). Experiments on Synchronization and Control of Chaos on Coupled Electrochemical Oscillators, *J. Phys. Chem. B*, Vol. 104, 7554-7560.

Konishi, K., Hirai, M. & Kokame, H. (1998). Sliding mode control for a class of chaotic systems, *Physics Letters A*, Vol. 245, No. 6, 511-517.

Layeghi, H., Arjmand, M.T., Salarieh, H. & Alasty, A. (2008). Stabilizing periodic orbits of chaotic systems using fuzzy adaptive sliding mode control, *Chaos Solitons and Fractals*, Vol. 37, No. 4, 1125-1135.

Liao, T.-L. & Lin, S.-H. (1999). Adaptive control and synchronization of Lorenz system, *Journal of the Franklin Institute*, Vol. 336, 925-937.

Merat, K., Salarieh, H. & Alasty, A. (2009). Implementation of dynamic programming for chaos control in discrete systems, *Journal of Computational and Applied Mathematics*, Vol . 232, No. 2, 531-544.

Ott, E.; Grebogi, C. & Yorke, J.A. (1990). Controlling chaos, *Physics Review Letters*, Vol. 64, 1196-1199.

Park, C.-W., Lee, C.-H. & Park, M. (2002). Design of an adaptive fuzzy model based controller for chaotic dynamics in Lorenz systems with uncertainty, *Information Sciences*, Vol. 147 245-266.

Parmananda, P. & Eiswirth, M. (1999). Suppression of Chemical Turbulence Using Feedbacks and Forcing, *J. Phys. Chem. A*, Vol. 103, 5510-5514.

Pishkenari, H.N., Shahrokhi, M. & Mahboobi, S.H. (2007). Adaptive regulation and set point tracking of the Lorenz attractor, *Chaos Solitons and Fractals*, Vol. 32, 832-846.

Pyragas, K. (1992). Continuous control of chaos by self-controlling feedback. *Physics Letters A*, Vol. 170, No. 6, 421-428.

Pyragas, K., Pyragas, V., Kiss, I.Z. & Hudson, J.L. (2004). Adaptive control of unknown unstable steady states of dynamical systems, *Physical Review E*, Vol. 70, 026215 1-12.

Pyragas, K. (2006), Delayed feedback control of chaos, *Philosophical Transactions of The Royal Society A* Vol. 364(1846), 2309-2334.

Ramesh, M. & Narayanan, S. (2001). Chaos control of Bonhoeffer–van der Pol oscillator using neural networks. *Chaos Solitons and Fractals,* Vol. 12, 2395–2405.

Salarieh, H. & Sharhrokhi, M. (2007). Indirect adaptive control of discrete chaotic systems, *Chaos Solitons and Fractals,* Vol. 34, No. 4, 1188-1201.

Salarieh, H. & Alasty, A. (2008). Stabilizing unstable fixed points of chaotic maps via minimum entropy control, *Chaos Solitons and Fractals,* Vol. 37, No. 3, 763-769.

Salarieh, H. & Alasty, A. (2008). Delayed feedback control of chaotic spinning disk via minimum entropy approach, *Nonlinear Analysis: Theory, Methods and Applications,* Vol. 69, No. 10, 3273-3280.

Salarieh, H. & Alasty, A. (2008). Adaptive control of chaotic systems with stochastic unknown parameters, *Chaos Solitons and Fractals,* Vol. 38, 168-177.

Salarieh, H. & Alasty, A. (2009). Control of chaos in atomic force microscopes using delayed feedback based on entropy minimization, *Communications in Nonlinear Science and Numerical Simulation,* Vol. 14, No. 3, 637-644.

Salarieh, H., Sadeghian, H. & Merat, K. (2009). Chaos control in lateral oscillations of spinning disks via nonlinear feedback, *Nonlinear Analysis: Real World Applications,* Vol. 10, No. 5, 2864-2872.

Sastry, S. & Bodson, M. (1994). *Adaptive control: Stability, Convergence and Robustness,* Prentice Hall, ISBN 0-13-004326-5.

Schmelcher, P. & Diakonos, F.K. (1997). Detecting unstable periodic orbits of chaotic dynamical systems. *Physics Review Letters,* Vol. 78, No. 25, 4733-4736.

Tian, Y.-C. & Gao, F. (1998). Adaptive control of chaotic continuous-time systems with delay, Physica D, Vol. 117, 1-12

Tian, Y.-P. & Yu, X. (2000). Adaptive control of chaotic dynamical systems using invariant manifold approach, *IEEE Transactions on Circuits and Systems I: Fundamental Theory and Applications,* Vol. 47, No. 10, 1537-1542.

Vincent, T.L. & Yu, J. (1991). Control of a chaotic system, Dynamics and Control 1(1) 35-52.

Wang L.-X. (1993). Stable adaptive fuzzy control of nonlinear systems, *IEEE Transactions on Fuzzy Systems,* Vol. 1, No. 2.

Wu, X.-Q. & Lu, J.-A. (2003). Parameter identification and backstepping control of uncertain Lü system, *Chaos Solitons and Fractals,* Vol. 18, No. 4, 721-729.

Yassen, M.T. (2003). Adaptive control and synchronization of a modified Chua's circuit system, *Applied Mathematics and Computation,* Vol. 135, 113-128.

Yassen, M.T., (2006). Chaos control of chaotic dynamical systems using backstepping design, *Chaos Solitons and Fractals,* Vol. 27, No. 2, 537-548.

Yongguang, Y. & Suochun, Z. (2003). Controlling uncertain Lü system using backstepping design, *Chaos Solitons and Fractals,* Vol. 15, No. 5, 897-902.

Zeng, Y. & Singh, S. N. (1997). Adaptive control of chaos in Lorenz system, *Dynamics and Control,* Vol. 7, 143-154.

Part 3

Synchronization

8

Chaotic Clustering: Fragmentary Synchronization of Fractal Waves

Elena N. Benderskaya[1] and Sofya V. Zhukova[2]
[1]*St.Petersburg State Politechnical University*
[2]*Graduate School of Management, SPbSU*
Russia

1. Introduction

Chaotic neural networks seized attention of scientists from various points of view due to the amazing effects they produce. Phenomenology of structure formation in nature inspired scholars to mimic complex and with the same time quasi-optimal solutions to generate artificial systems with similar capabilities. One of the dominant ways to provide collective dynamics of previously unordered elements is self-synchronization that happens without any outside enforcement.

In theory of dynamic chaos and chaotic synchronization were discovered different types of synchronous behaviour of coupled dynamic systems: complete, lag, generalized, phase, time-scale, frequency, partial synchronizations (Pikovsky & Maistrenko, 2008; Anishchenko & et. al., 2007; Koronovskii & Maistrenko, 2009; Fujisaka & Shimada, 1997, Kapitaniak & Maistrenko 1996; Kurths & et. al., 1997). Most of the results were obtained by computer modelling and visualization techniques. Unpredictable and instable long time period behaviour stems from peculiarities of elements self-dynamics governed by deterministic function that predetermine chaotic behaviour (Lyapunov coefficients are positive). Research subject in numerous articles is collective dynamics of chaotic elements that somehow happens to be stable in terms of group oscillations, but vulnerable when individual trajectory is considered (Politi & Torcini, 2010; Liu & et. al., 2010 ; Pikovsky & et. al., 2003; Manrubia & Mikhailov, 1999). Strange attractors correspond to synchronous clusters (Benderskaya & Zhukova, 2008; Chen & et. al., 2006; Anishenko & et. al., 2002).

Extreme complexity of elements individual dynamics constrains the type of interconnection strength to be homogeneous in overwhelming majority of articles. Most of them consider dependence of synchronous regimes from strength of coupling equal for all elements. This limitation prevents from further generalization of results and makes them to be partial solutions. In most recent researches are considered heterogeneous couplings strength. Heterogeneous field of links between elements extends greatly the analysis complexity (especially mathematical analysis) but allows to reveal interesting effects (Inoue & Kaneko, 2010; Li & et. al., 2004; Popovych & et. al., 2000).

In this paper we consider the analysis of fragmentary synchronization of fractal waves generated by large dimension inhomogeneous chaotic neural network. In our previous papers fragmentary synchronization phenomenon was discovered and applied. Further research of new synchronization type shows that we can speak about fractal structure of synchronous clusters. We propose that the fact of fractal structure existence can settle the problem of finding out the end of transition period in order to reduce computation complexity of clustering method introduced in our previous papers (Benderskaya & Zhukova, 2008, 2009).

2. Chaotic oscillators

During the last decades, the emergence of collective dynamics in large networks of coupled units has been investigated in disciplines such as physics, chemistry, biology, and ecology (Yamapi et. al., 2010; Wang et. al., 2010; Vasconcelos et. al., 2004). In particular, the effect of synchronization in systems of coupled oscillators nowadays provides a unifying framework for different phenomena observed in nature. Complex networks have recently provided a challenging framework for synchronization studies on dynamic objects with main focus on the interplay between topology complexity and local dynamic properties of coupled elements. A key problem is to define conditions that guarantee the stability of neurons synchronous behavior for this or that network topology.

The complexity of interconnected chaotic systems comes from different directions:

a. nonlinear dynamics of elements;
b. exponential dependence on initial conditions;
c. unpredictable result of the influence on nonlinear vulnerable system from other ones;
d. insufficient mathematical apparatus that help to describe multidimensional nonlinear systems;
e. computer modelling investigation methodology (the calculations precision starts to be critical in terms of forecasting the long term behaviour of nonlinear systems);

All this factors predetermines the research focus mainly on the analysis of interdependent pair of chaotic oscillators, or on the collective dynamics of oscillators ensemble, but with homogeneous type of linkage (Li et. al., 2004; Popovych et. al., 2000).

As it is hard to find formal mathematical solution for a system of multidimensional difference equations we can try to obtain solution by means of computer programming and visualizing of the results. Rapid development of computer technology extended the abilities of scientist to find answers with computer modeling techniques. We use different visualization techniques.

2.1 Synchronization phenomenon

Synchronization as a universal concept is thoroughly discussed in literature (Pykovski & et. al., 2003). One of the most important generalization of inner synchronization effects are the conditions that cause inner synchronous motions among groups of nonlinear elements:

a. large amount of globally coupled nonlinear elements;
b. weak coupling strength to exclude the possibility of several elements to suppress
c. individual dynamics of all others;
d. instability dynamics of each nonlinear element;
e. feedbacks to provide own element's dynamics tuning to the neighbors' fluctuations.

Primary results on modeling high dimensional chaotic map lattices were published by K. Kaneko (Kaneko, 1987, 1989). His works showed up the fact that globally coupled chaotic map lattices exhibit formation of ensembles synchronously oscillating elements. These ensembles were called clusters serving as system's attractors. If there appear to be several clusters then the system is characterized by multistability, when several attractors coexist in the phase space at the same parameters values. The main focus of research in terms of synchronization is on the combination of systems parameters that predetermine the appearance of different synchronization types corresponding to functioning regimes.

2.2 Clustering

The fundamental research provides the basis for various applications of chaotic networks (Fang et. al., 2009; Herrera Martín, 2009; Hammami et. al., 2009, Mosekilde et. al., 2002). In this paper we apply chaotic neural network to 2D and 3D clustering problem. L. Angelini introduced to correspond dataset groups to dynamical oscillatory clusters by means of neural network parametrization (Angelini & et. al., 2000, 2001, 2003). In our previous papers we introduced modifications of chaotic neural network (CNN) clustering method, proposed by Angelini, in order to ensure better clusterization quality (Benderskaya & Zhukova, 2008, 2009). In this paper we give the description of modified CNN model.

3. Chaotic neural network model

Let us consider chaotic neural network model simultaneously from several angels mentioned above as its complexity has many dimensions.

3.1 Structure complexity

CNN does not have classical inputs - it is recurrent neural network with one layer of N neurons. Each neuron is responsible for one object in the dataset, but the image itself is not given to inputs. Instead input dataset is given to logistic map network by means of inhomogeneous weights assignment.

$$W = \{w_{ij}\} = \exp\left(-\frac{d_{ij}^{\ 2}}{2a}\right),\ d_{ij} = | x_i - x_j |,\ i,j = \overline{1,N}, \tag{1}$$

where N - number of elements, w_{ij} - strength of link between elements i and j, d_{ij} - Euclidean distance between neurons i and j, a - local scale, depending on k-nearest neighbors. Influence of linkage mean field on the dynamics of CNN is demonstrated on Fig. 1.

The value of a is fixed as the average distance of k-nearest neighbor pairs of points in the whole system. To define nearest neighbors taking into account image topology we use Delaunay triangulation. Delaunay triangulation (Preparata & Shamos, 1993) gives us all the nearest neighbors of each point from all directions. The value of a is now fixed as the average distance of Delaunay-nearest neighbor pairs of points in the whole system. Thus we form the proper mean field that contributes greatly to convergence of CNN dynamics to macroscopic attractor.

Evolution of each neuron is governed by

$$f(y(t) = 1 - \lambda y^2(t) \tag{2}$$

$$y_i(t+1) = \frac{1}{C_i} \sum_{i \neq j}^{N} w_{ij} f(y_i(t)),\ t = 1 \ldots T, \tag{3}$$

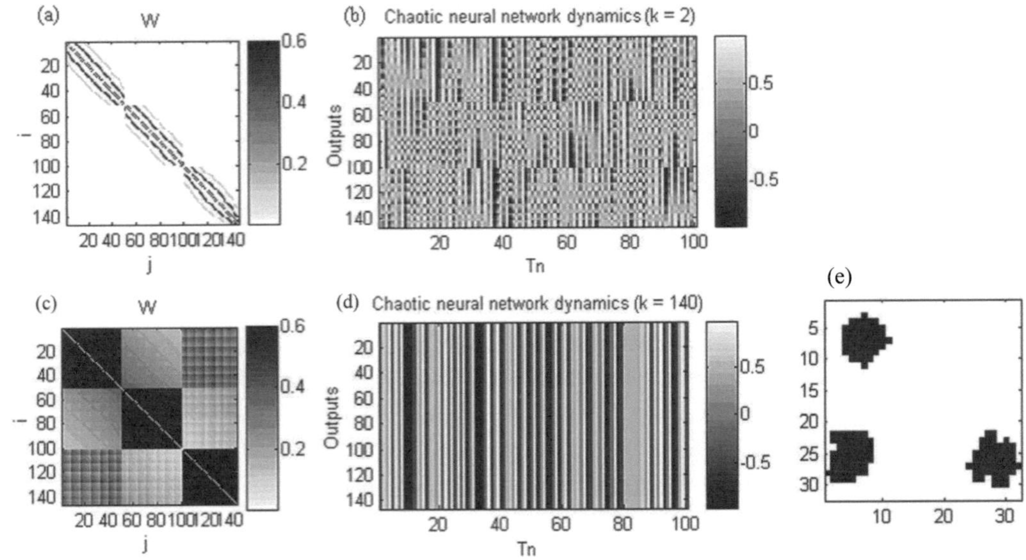

Fig. 1. Example of improper field of weight coefficients and the corresponding dynamics of the CNN for the image (e) that is clustered: (a, b) – the number of nearest neighbors $k = 2$ (cluster synchronization is absent); (c, d) – the number of nearest neighbors $k = 140$ - all the neurons oscillate synchronously and division into clusters is impossible. The values of the weight coefficients are represented by concrete colours in correspondence with the nearby given colorbars).

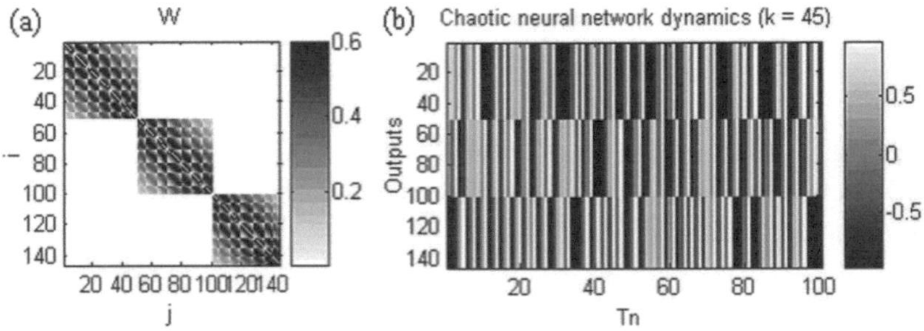

Fig. 2. The inhomogeneous field of weight coefficients within one cluster (distinctly pronounced oscillation clusters when $a = 2.2$, calculated on the average distance of Delaunay neighbours: (a) – visual map of the weight coefficient matrix; (b) – the change of the CNN output values in time.

where $C_i = \sum_{i \neq j} w_{ij}, i, j = \overline{1,N}$, T - time interval, N - number of elements, λ - logistic map parameter. Neurons state is dependent on the state of all other elements. The logistic map with parameter $\lambda = 2$ predetermines the chaotic behaviour of each neuron.

The structure of chaotic neural network (number of neurons, field of weight coefficients) and dynamics depends on the image size and topology. It happens to be very difficult to find out formal measures to forecast oscillators behaviour especially because of chaotic nature of each neuron. Thus we deal with N-dimensional inhomogeneous system of chaotic oscillators that evolves in discrete time and generates continuous outputs. The main research method: computer modelling.

3.2 Extreme instability of each neuron

One of the basic models of chaotic nonlinear systems is logistic map (Peitgen, 2004). If the parameter is set as $\lambda=2$, then strange attractor can be detected in the phase space (Fig. 3).

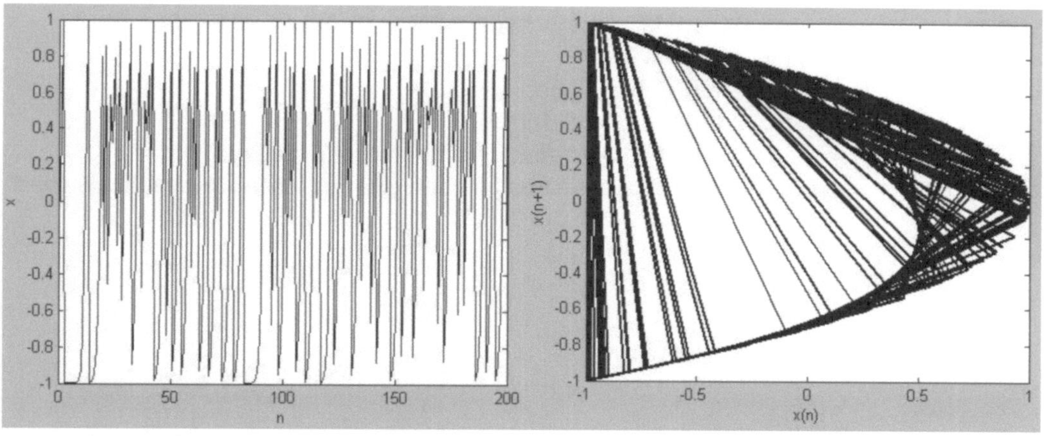

Fig. 3. One neuron dynamics analysis: strange attractor is constructed when $\lambda=2$.

One of the main characteristic is exponential instability to initial conditions. The logistic map fully demonstrates this quality (Fig. 4). As we can see even small delta of 0.0000001 leads to the serious trajectories' changes after 24 iterations.

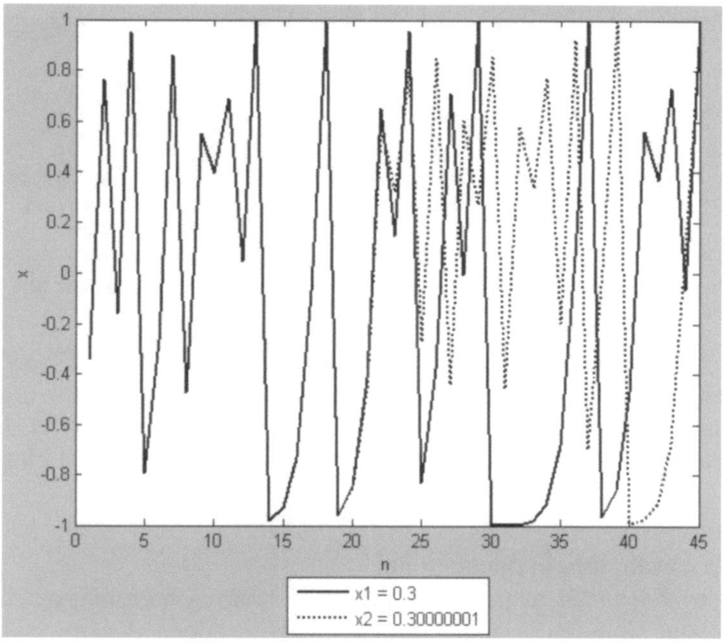

Fig. 4. Trajectories, starting from very close initial conditions with difference of 0.0000001.

Clusterization phenomenon stems from the chaotic oscillations of each neuron. The logistic map parameter $\lambda=2$ guarantees chaotic dynamics of each neuron, as the eldest Lyapunov indicator is positive.

3.3 Dynamical clusters and synchronization types

In accordance with (Pykovski et al., 2003; Peitgen et al. 2004) in the ensembles of poorly connected identical neurons emerge synchronization of various types, depending on the system's parameter combination. We introduce these types on the example of CNN:

a. complete synchronization (Fig. 5.a);
b. imphase synchronization (Fig. 5.b);
c. phase synchronization (Fig. 5.c, Fig. 5.d);
d. lag synchronization (time series coincide but with some delay in time);
e. generalized synchronization (there is some functional dependence between time series).

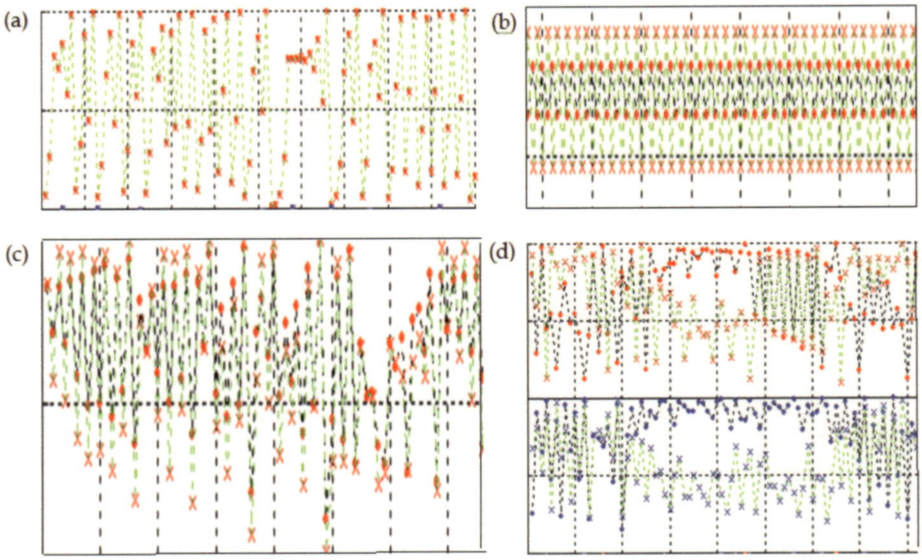

Fig. 5. Synchronization types of chaotic time series: (a) - complete; (b)-imphase; (c) - phase synchronization with slight amplitude deviations; (d) - phase synchronization of neurons pairs within two clusters reveal the outputs changes in the same direction but with significantly different amplitudes.

Besides these well-known synchronization types we found out CNN to produce new synchronization type - we named it fragmentary synchronization. It is characterized by different oscillatory melodies-fragments (Fig 6.e, 6.f). Synchronization is no more about comparing separate trajectories, but about integrative consideration of cluster's music of fragments.

3.4 Macroscopic attractors in oscillations

The dynamics of a separate neuron output highly depends on initial conditions, but the most fruitful about CNN is its ability to form stable (independent of initial conditions) synchronous clusters in terms of joint dynamics of neurons. Stable mutual synchronization of neurons (points) within each cluster in terms of CNN corresponds to the macroscopic attractor, when we receive indifferent to initial conditions oscillatory clusters, though instant outputs of neurons differ greatly (Fig. 6). The complexity of mutual oscillations depends on the complexity of input image. Simple image comprised by 146 points (Fig 5.a) organized in compact groups located far from each other predetermines almost complete synchronization of oscillations within clusters (Fig. 6.b, 6.c). But if the image of 158 points with less compact topology and inter cluster distance more complex synchronization take place - fragmentary synchronization (Fig. 6.e, 6.f) .

The system is stable in terms of mutual synchronous dynamics of outputs within time but not in terms of instant values of separate neurons.

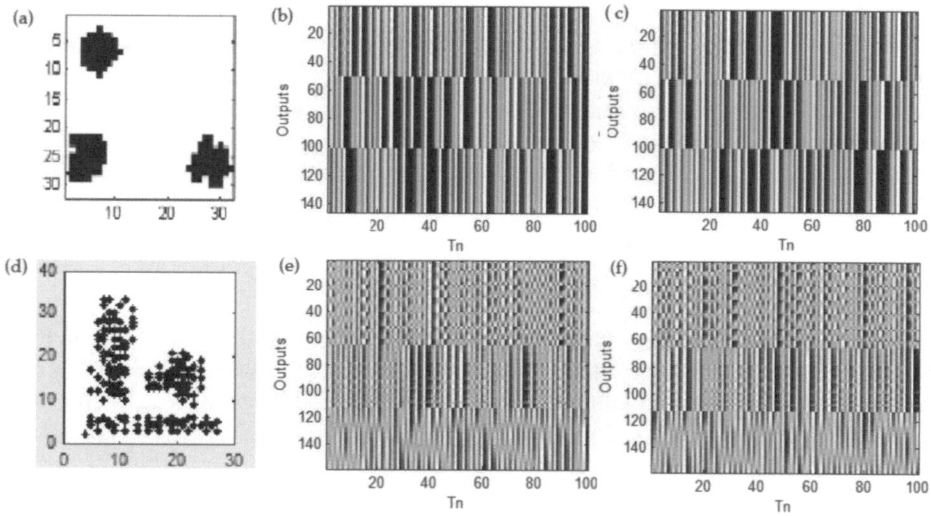

Fig. 6. Visualization of CNN outputs: in stationary regime trajectories being chaotic form the three different oscillatory clusters from absolutely different initial conditions: (a) - simple input dataset to be clustered ; (b), (c) - 146 outputs of CNN completely synchronous within clusters evolving during observation period Tn=100 from different initial conditions; (d) - complex input dataset to be clustered; (e), (f) - 158 fragmentary synchronized outputs of CNN evolving during observation period Tn=100 from different initial conditions.

3.5 Clustering technique drawback

All the figures above demonstrate CNN dynamics statistics gathered after some transition period. One of the unsolved problems at the moment is finding out some formal way to state that transition period is over and it is time of macroscopic attractor to govern trajectories. We introduced some indirect approach that consists in CNN output statistics processing. At different level of resolution due to the theory of hierarchical data mining (Han, 2005) are generated dozens of clusterizations, then they are compared and the variant that repeats more often wins (is considered to be the answer). After that we repeat the procedure all over again to be sure that with the cause of time mutual synchronization remains to be the same. This approach is desperately resource consuming and takes dozens more time than generating CNN oscillatory clusters. Thus it prevents from wide application of CNN clustering technique especially with the growth of objects number in the input

image (it does not matter 2D, 3D or N-dimensional), though it has a wide set of advantages in compare to other clustering methods.
The novelty of this paper consists in discovering fractal structures in fragmentary synchronized outputs. This phenomenon encourages us to shift our focus on the direct analysis of outputs value and not on their desensitization with the main aim to reduce clustering method complexity.

4. In pursuit of strange attractor

The captivating interplay of oscillations within dynamical clusters that we call fragmentary synchronization could hardly be interpreted somehow in a numerical way. Other problem that seemed to have no answer is that the dependence between clustering quality and the size of outputs statistics is not obvious. The extensive growth of CNN states to be analysed sometimes was not successful in terms of clustering problem and predetermined even worse results than those obtained on a smaller dataset. Such observations forced us to focus mainly on synchronization of time-series once more in order to reveal some order in the macroscopic attractor, comprised by temporal sequences. The indication of macroscopic attractor existence is the coincidence of clustering results (synchronous dynamical clusters) obtained for different initial conditions.

4.1 Fractal waves

Under the notion of fractal coexists a wide set of structures, both of spatial and temporal nature that demonstrate self-similarity. The very word fractal is formed from latin fractus which means to consist of fragments. Broad definition tells that fractal is the structure consisted of the parts which are similar the whole (Mandelbrot, 1983). In the case of CNN it is more applicable to say that fractals are signals that display scale-invariant or self-similar behaviour. Fractals reflect nature as inherently complex and nonlinear according to Dardik (Dardic, 1995). Smaller rhythms are imbedded within larger rhythms, and those within larger still. The short biochemical cycles of cells of the human heart waves are embedded within the circadian rhythm of the whole body, and they are all embedded within the larger waves of weeks, months and years. Fractal superwaves spiral in all directions as an inherent continuum of waves nested within other waves. Thus everything is affecting everything else simultaneously and casually, while everything is changing, throughout all scales. In terms of recurrent behaviour of CNN outputs we consider the joint dynamics of neurons as waves of complex form. What does it mean - self-similarity in CNN?
We started with careful consideration of fragmentary synchronized neurons dynamics (Fig. 7). The dynamics statistics was gathered during Tn = 2000 (Fig. 7.a). Then we focused on first counts (states of CNN represented on the figure by vertical lines) and visualized them in a more and more detailed way (Fig. 7.b-e).
After careful consideration we noticed that there exist quasi similar fragments not only in terms of horizontal lines that comprise melodies, but repeating waves in the overall chaotic neural network (Fig. 7b., Fig. 7c). This temporal similarity leads us to the hypothesis of oscillations fractal structure.

4.2 CNN fractals

Temporal fractals as well as space fractals are characterized by self-similarity at different scales of consideration. But in case of CNN we deal not with geometric object, but with

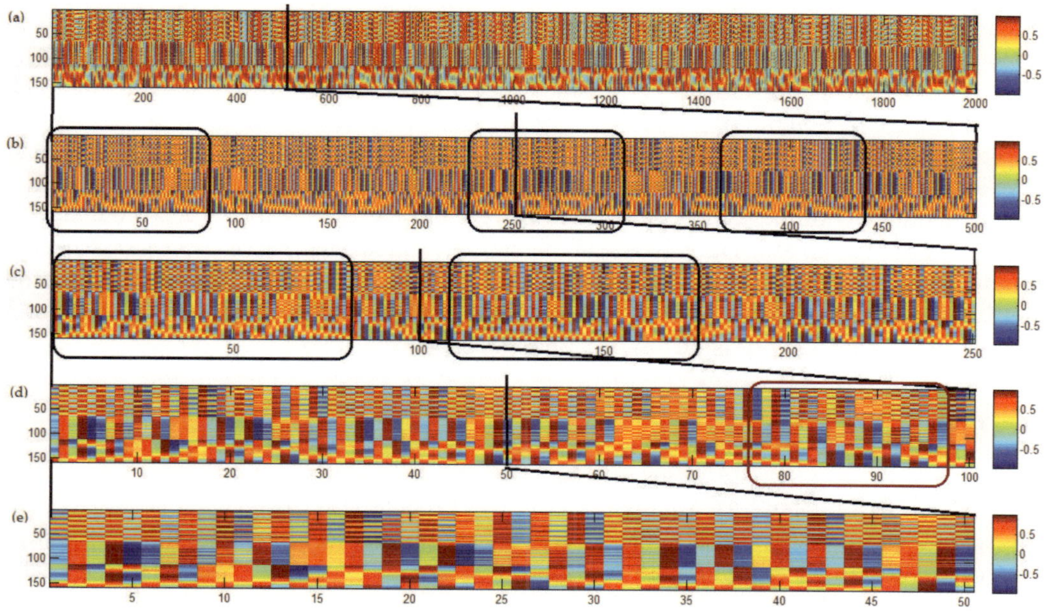

Fig. 7. Fragmentary synchronization with detailed consideration of first counts: (a) - CNN outputs dynamics during 2000 iterations; (b) - bunch of 500 first counts; (c) - bunch of 250 first counts; (d) - bunch of 100 first counts; (e) - bunch of 50 first counts.

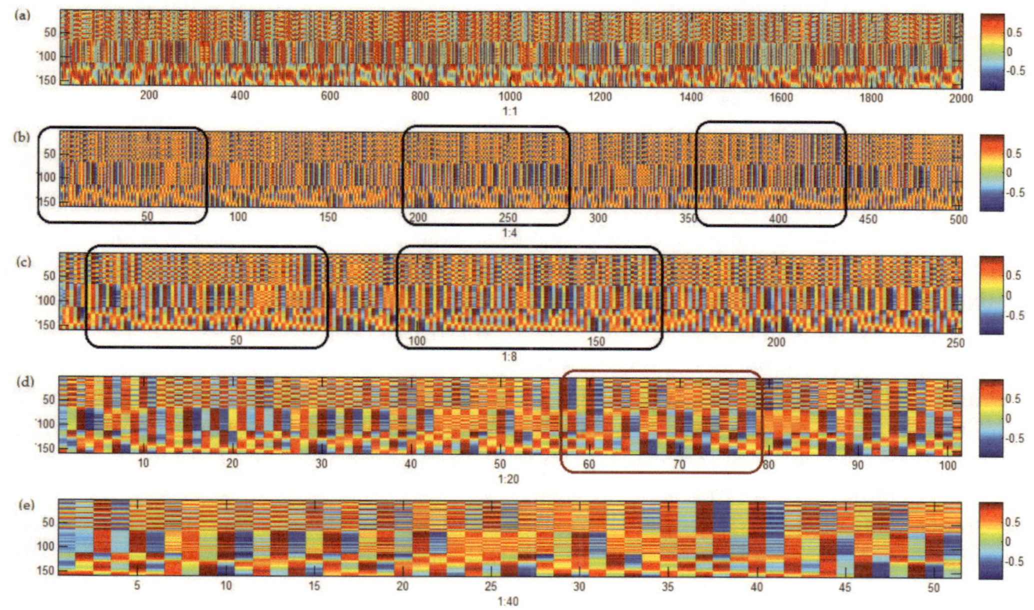

Fig. 8. Scaling of CNN dynamics by means of decimation: (a) - original dynamics; (b) - scale 1:4 (every 4th count out of 2000 original counts); (c) - scale 1:8 (every 8th count out of 2000 original ones); (d) - scale 1:20 (every 20th count out of 2000 original counts); (e) - scale 1:40 (every 20th count out of 2000 original counts).

fractal structure of multidimensional time-series, comprised by CNN counts. The scaling is done by means of time-series decimation (bolting) with different coefficient in order to observe CNN dynamics at various detail levels (this is similar to CNN modeling with different discretization time).

Representation of CNN time-series at different scales is shown on Fig. 8. Interested in less detailed temporal picture we gradually decrease the scale.

Amazing thing about the scaling on Fig. 8 is that it looks like almost the same in comparison to Fig. 7. On Fig. 7.b and Fig. 8.b as well as on Fig. 7.c and Fig. 8.c one can see the same fragments though they are viewed absolutely from different perspectives. More over the similarity is observed not only on small scales (1:4, 1:8) but on rather huge ones (1:20, 1:40) with several counts lag precision (Fig. 7.d and Fig. 8.d).

4.3 Fractal visualization

One of the common ways to reveal fractals is construction of phase portraits. In case of CNN we observe almost the same phase portrait like on Fig. 3, as individual trajectory is forced by logistic map to be chaotic. To investigate recurrent behaviour of complex multidimensional time-series recurrent analysis is applied. In case of CNN we propose to visualize trajectories by means of recurrence plots (RP) introduced by J.P. Eckmann (Eckmann et al., 1987, Romano et al., 2005). Recurrence plots visualize the recurrence of states in a phase space. Usually, a phase space does not have enough dimension (two or three) to be pictured. Higher-dimensional phase spaces can only be visualized by projection into the two or three-dimensional sub-spaces. However, Eckmann's tool enables us to investigate the *m*-dimensional phase space trajectories through a two-dimensional representation of its recurrences. Such recurrence of a state at time *i* at a different time *j* is pictured within a two-dimensional squared matrix with black and white dots, where black dots mark a recurrence, and both axes are time axes. This representation is called recurrence plot. Such an RP can be mathematically expressed as

$$R(i, j) = Q(Eps - ||x(i)-x(j)||), \; i, j = 1, \dots, N \tag{4}$$

where N is the number of states $x(i)$ (counts of CNN dynamics) , Eps is a threshold distance, $||*||$ - a Euclidean norm and Q the Heaviside step function. Recurrence plot contains typical small-scale structures, as single dots, diagonal lines and vertical/horizontal lines (or a mixture of those). The large-scale structure, also called texture, can be visually characterised by homogenous, periodic, drift or disrupted. The visual appearance of an RP gives hints about the dynamics of the system.

If recurrence behaviour occurs in two different time-series then synchronization takes place. If self-recurrent pieces are detected or similar dynamics is revealed between original time-series and their scaled copy then we can speak about application of RP to the analysis of CNN fractal temporal structure (self-similarity).

Recurrence plots of CNN dynamics temporal structure is introduced on Fig. 9 in two ways: self-reflection of first counts bunches 500, 250, 100, 50 correspondingly represented on Fig. 9.a, Fig. 9.c, Fig. 9.e, Fig. 9.h and self-reflection of scaled bunches 1:4, 1:8, 1:20, 1:40 represented on Fig. 9.b, Fig. 9.d, Fig. 9.f, Fig. 9.h. We can see that recurrence plots of first bunches and scaled bunches have much in common (partly just the copy of each other). It happens to have no difference whether to observe first 500 counts or picture, comprised by decimated counts with four times magnification (every 4th count out of 2000). This is the evidence for fractal structure of time-series, generated by CNN. The indicator of oscillations

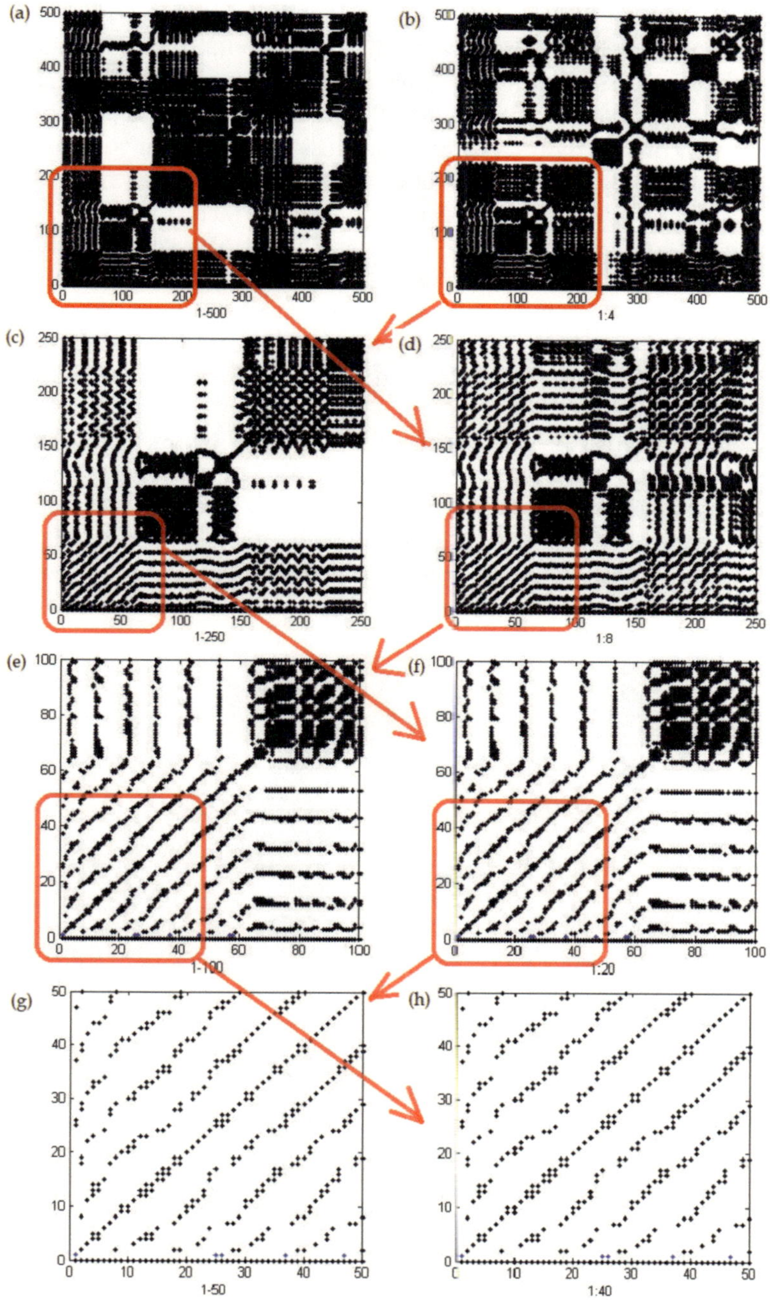

Fig. 9. Recurrence plots of CNN dynamics: (a) - self-reflection of 500 first counts bunch; (b) - self-reflection of scaled dynamics with 1:4 magnification level; (c) - self-reflection of 250 first counts bunch ; (d) – self-reflection of scaled dynamics with 1:8 magnification level; (e) - self-reflection of 100 first counts bunch ; (f) – self-reflection of scaled dynamics with 1:20 magnification level; (g) - self-reflection of 50 first counts bunch ; (h) – self-reflection of scaled dynamics with 1:8 magnification level.

periodical dynamics is the presence of diagonal lines and patterns arranged in staggered order. Irregular fragments speak about chaotic synchronization and quasi periodical character of oscillations. Dissimilar pieces of recurrence plots can also be the consequence of coincidence precision demands, predetermined by (4) (it is well-known practise to use tolerance discrepancy when analysis of multidimensional nonlinear systems with chaotic dynamics is conducted). By means of arrows we note the nesting similarity of different recurrent plots (both first and scale bunches) - evidence for fractal structure.

Further investigation leads us to cross-recurrence analysis. The comparison of first count bunches and scaled count bunches is provided (Fig. 10). And again one can see self-similarity of results: the same as in case of recurrence plots the mutual correspondence among plots is detected in spite of different scaling of original CNN statistics: Fig. 10.a is similar to Fig. 9.b; Fig. 10.c is similar to Fig. 9.d; Fig. 10.b is similar to Fig. 9.f; Fig. 10.d is similar to Fig. 9.h.

To be careful with conclusions we checked the existence of fractal nesting depth and compared the reflection of scaled bunch of counts into each other (Fig. 11). As for recurrence plots on Fig. 9 and Fig. 10 on Fig. 11 the same structure is observed accurate within small fragments. This verifies the importance of discrepancy thresholds not only for absolute values of CNN outputs coincidence but also for comparison of fragments when fragmentary synchronization is analyzed.

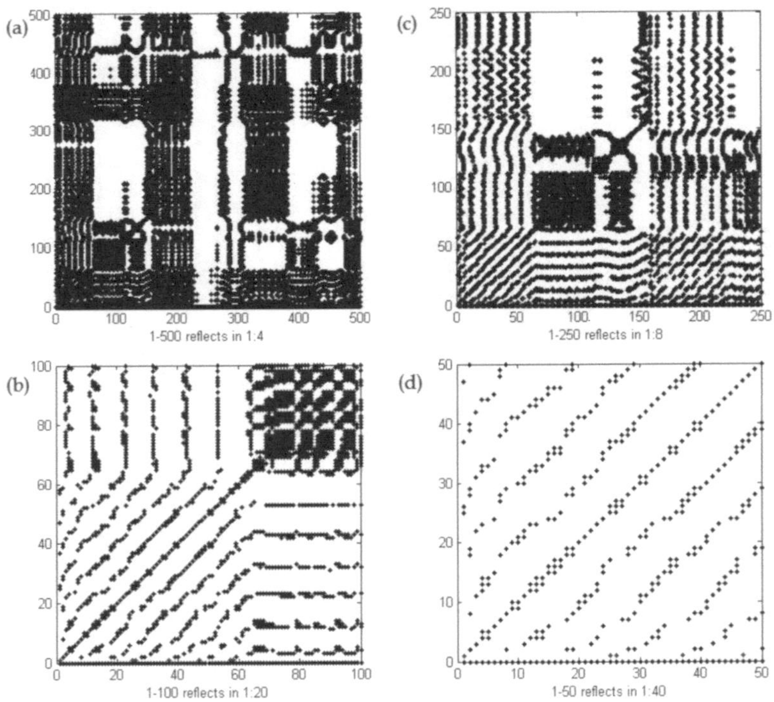

Fig. 10. Cross recurrence plots of CNN dynamics: (a) - reflection of 500 first counts bunch into scaled 1:4 bunch of counts; (b) – reflection of 250 first counts bunch into scaled 1:8 bunch of counts; (c) - reflection of 100 first counts bunch into scaled 1:20 bunch of counts; (d) – reflection of 100 first counts bunch into scaled 1:40 bunch of counts.

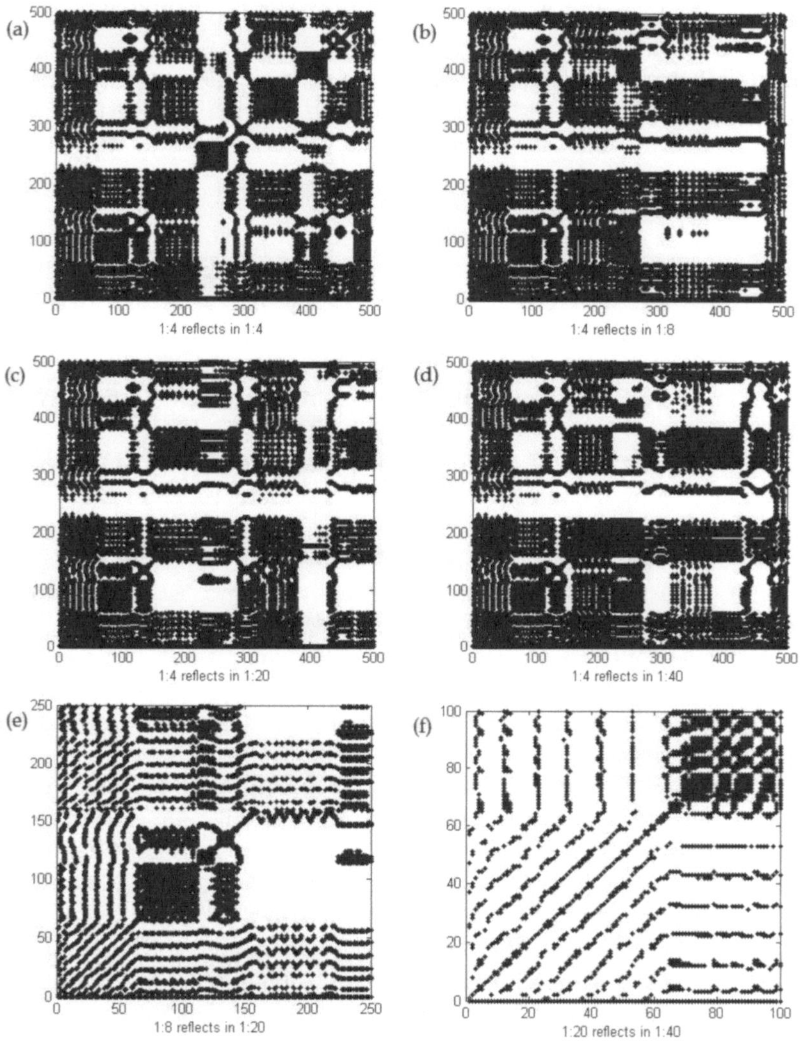

Fig. 11. Cross-recurrent plots of scaled count bunches: (a) - self-reflection of 1:4 dynamics scale; (b) - reflection of 1:4 scaled bunch into 1:8 scaled bunch; (c) - reflection of 1:4 scaled bunch into 1:20 scaled bunch; (d) - reflection of 1:4 scaled bunch into 1:40 scaled bunch; (e) - reflection of 1:8 scaled bunch into 1:20 scaled bunch; (f) - reflection of 1:20 scaled bunch into 1:40 scaled bunch.

5. Conclusion

In this paper fractal structure of fragmentary synchronization is discovered. The structure of fragment's and overall dynamics of CNN was investigated by means of recurrence and cross-recurrence plots visualization techniques. Understanding the mechanism of fragments interplay (periodical vertical similarity) along with oscillatory clusters interplay (horizontal dissimilarity of cluster's melodies) is vital for discovering the low resource consuming algorithm of CNN outputs processing in order to translate nonlinear language of oscillation

into the language of images in data mining field (important to solve general clustering problem).
Analogous fractal effects were obtained for a wide set of well-known clustering datasets. Further research will follow in the direction of fractal structures measurement. This is important to formalize the analysis of inner phase space patterns by means of automatic techniques for recurrence plots analysis.

6. References

Angelini, L. (2003). Antiferromagnetic effects in chaotic map lattices with a conservation law, *Physics Letters A* 307(1), pp.41–49

Angelini, L.; Carlo, F.; Marangi, C.; Pellicoro, M.; Nardullia, M. & Stramaglia, S. (2001). Clustering by inhomogeneous chaotic maps in landmine detection, *Phys. Rev. Lett.* 86, pp.89–132

Angelini, L.; Carlo, F.; Marangi, C.; Pellicoro, M.; Nardullia, M. & Stramaglia, S. (2000). Clustering data by inhomogeneous chaotic map lattices, *Phys. Rev. Lett.* 85, pp.78–102

Anishchenko, V.; Astakhov, V.; Neiman, A.; Vadivasova, T. & Schimansky-Geier, L. (2007). *Nonlinear Dynamics of Chaotic and Stochastic Systems: Tutorial and Modern Developments*, Springer-Verlag, New York, ISBN 3540381643

Anishchenko, V. S.; Sosnovtseva, O. V. ; Kopejkin, A. S.; Matujshkin, D. D. & Klimshin, A. V. (2002). Synchronization effects in networks of stochastic bistable oscillators, *Mathematics and Computers in Simulation*, Volume 58, Issue 4-6 (Mar. 2002), pp. 469-476, Elsevier Science Publishers B. V., Amsterdam

Benderskaya, Elena N. & Zhukova, Sofya V. (2008). Clustering by chaotic neural networks with mean field calculated via Delaunay triangulation, *Proceedings of Third international workshop on Hybrid artificial intelligence systems*, pp. 408-416, ISBN 978-3-540-87655-7, Burgos, Spain, September 24-26, 2008, Lecture Notes in Computer Science, vol. 5271, Springer-Verlag, Berlin-Heidelberg

Benderskaya, Elena N. & Zhukova, Sofya V. (2009). Fragmentary synchronization in chaotic neural network and data mining, *Proceedings of 4th international conference on Hybrid artificial intelligence systems*, pp. 319-326, ISBN 978-3-642-02318-7, Salamanca, Spain, June 10-12, 2009, Lecture Notes in Computer Science, vol. 5572, Springer-Verlag, Berlin-Heidelberg

Chen, Y. ; Rangarajan, G. & Ding, M. (2006). Stability of synchronized dynamics and pattern formation in coupled systems:Review of some recent results, *Communications in Nonlinear Science and Numerical Simulation,* 11 (2006) pp.934–960

Dardik, I. (1995). The law of waves, *Cycles*, Vo. 45, pp. 49-60

Eckman, J.-P.; Kamphorst S.O. & Ruelle, D. (1987). Recurrence Plots of Dynamical Systems, *Europhys. Lett.*, 4 (9), pp. 973-977

Fang, X.; Yu, H. & Jiang, Z.(2009). Chaotic synchronization of nearest-neighbor divusive coupling Hindmarsh–Roseneural networks in noisy environments, *Chaos, Solitonsand Fractals* 39 (2009) pp. 2426–2441

Fujisaka H. & Shimada T. (1997). Phase synchronization and nonlinearity decision in the network of chaotic flows, *Phys. Rev. E*, 55(3), pp. 2426-2433, 1997.

Hammami, S.; BenSaad, K. & Benrejeb, M. (2009). On the synchronization of identical and non-identical 4-D chaotic systems using arrow form matrix, *Chaos, Solitons and Fractals,* 42 (2009), pp. 101–112

Han, J.; Kamber, M. & Pei, J. (2005). *Data Mining: Concepts and Techniques,* The Morgan Kaufmann Series in Data Management Systems

Herrera, D. & Martín, J. (2009). Ananalytical study in coupled map lattices of synchronized states and traveling waves, and of their period-doubling cascades, *Chaos, Solitonsand Fractals* 42 (2009) pp. 901–910

Inoue, M. & Kaneko, K. (2010). Dynamics of Coupled Adaptive Elements: Bursting and Intermitteny Oscillations Generated by Frustration in the Network, *Phys. Rev. E,* 81, pp. 126-203

Kaneko, K. (1987). Phenomenology of spatio-temporal chaos, In *Directions in chaos.* - World Scientific Publishing Co., pp. 272-353, Singapore

Kaneko, K. (1989). Chaotic but regular posi-nega switch among coded attractors by cluster-size variations, *Phys. Rev. Lett.,* 63(14), pp. 219-223

Kapitaniak, T. & Maistrenko, Y. (1996). Different types of chaos synchronization in coupled chaotic oscillators, *Phys. Rev. E,* 54(4) pp. 3285-3292

Koronovskii, A. A.; Moskalenko, O. I. & Hramov, A. E. (2009). On the use of chaotic synchronization for secure communication, *Phys. Usp.* 52, pp.1213–1238

Kurths, J.; Pikovsky, A. & Rosenblum M. (1997). From phase to lag synchronization in coupled chaotic oscillators, *Phys. Rev. Lett.* 78, pp. 4193-4196

Li, S.; Liao, X. & Yu, J. (2004). Synchronization in coupled map lattices with small-world delayed interactions, *Physica A* 335, pp. 365–370

Liu, H.; Chen, J.; Lu, J. & Ming Cao (2010). Generalized synchronization in complex dynamical networks via adaptive couplings, *Physica A: Statistical Mechanics and its Applications,* Vol. 389, Issue 8, April 2010, pp. 1759-1770

Mandelbrot, B. (1983). *The Fractal Geometry of Nature,* W. H. Freeman and Co., ISBN 0-7167-1186-9, New York

Manrubia, S. & Mikhailov, A. (1999). Mutual synchronization and clustering in randomly coupled chaotic dynamical networks, *Phys. Rev. E* 60, pp. 1579–1589

Mosekilde, E.; Maistrenko, Yu. & Postnov, D. (2002). *Chaotic synchronization,* World Scientific Series on Nonlinear Science, Series A, Vol. 42

Marwan, N.; Romano, M. C.; Thiel, M. & Kurths, J. (2007). Recurrence Plots for the Analysis of Complex Systems, *Physics Reports,* 438(5-6), pp. 237-329

Peitgen, H.; Jürgens, H. & Dietmar S. (2004). *Chaos and Fractals. New Frontiers of Science,* Springer-Verlag, ISBN 978-0-387-20229-7, New York

Pikovsky, A. & Maistrenko, Y. (2008). *Synchronization: Theory and Application,* NATO Science Series II: Mathematics, Physics and Chemistry, Springer, ISBN 9781402014178

Pikovsky, A.; Rosenblum, M. & Kurths, J. (2003). *Synchronization: A Universal Concept in Nonlinear Sciences* (Cambridge Nonlinear Science Series) ISBN 978-0521533522, Cambridge University Press

Politi, A. & Torcini, A. (2010). Stable chaos in Nonlinear Dynamics and Chaos: Advances and Perspectives, *In Understanding Complex Systems,* 2010, pp. 103-129, DOI: 10.1007/978-3-642-04629-2_6

Popovych, O.; Maistrenko, Ya.; Mosekildec, E.; Pikovsky, A. & Kurths, J. (2000). Transcritical loss of synchronization in coupled chaotic systems, *Physics Letters A* 275, pp.401–406

Preparata, F. R. & Shamos, M. I. (1993). *Computational Geometry.* An Introduction, Monographs in Computer Science, Springer

Romano, M.C.; Thiel, M.; Kurths, J. ; Kiss, I.Z. & Hudson, J.L.(2005) . *Europhys. Lett.* 2005. V. 71 (3). P. 466.

Vasconcelos, D .; Viana, R .; Lopes, S.; Batista, A. & Pinto, S. (2004) Spatial correlations and synchronization in coupled map lattices with long-rangeinteractions, *Physica A* 343 (2004) pp.201–218

Wang, C .; Li, S.; Ma, J. & Jin, W. (2010). Synchronization transition in degenerate optical parametric oscillators induced by nonlinear coupling, *Applied Mathematics and Computation* 216 (2010), pp. 647–654

Yamapi, R ; Kadji, E. ; Filatrella G. (2010). Stability of the synchronization manifold in nearest neighbor nonidentical van der Pollike oscillators, *Nonlinear Dynamics,* Volume 61, Numbers 1-2, pp. 275-294

9

Coexistence of Synchronization and Anti-Synchronization for Chaotic Systems via Feedback Control

Hammami Sonia and Benrejeb Mohamed
UR LARA Automatique, École Nationale d'Ingénieurs de Tunis
BP 37, Tunis le Belvédère 1002
Tunisia

1. Introduction

The study of chaos can be introduced in several applications as: medical field, fractal theory, electrical circuits and secure communication, essentially based on synchronization techniques.

The synchronization for chaotic systems has been extended to the scope, such as generalized synchronization, phase synchronization, lag synchronization, and even anti-synchronization (Pecora & Carroll, 1990; Wu & Chua, 1993; Michael et al., 1996; Bai & Lonngsen, 1997; Yang & Duan, 1998; Taherion & Lai, 1999; Zhang & Sun, 2004; Li, 2005; Yassen, 2005; Hammami et al., 2009; Juhn et al., 2009; Hammami et al., 2010b).

For an n master chaotic system coupled to an n slave one, described respectively by $\dot{x}_m(t) = f(x_m(t))$ and by $\dot{x}_s(t) = g(x_s(t))$, where x_m and x_s are phase space variables, and $f(.)$ and $g(.)$ the corresponding nonlinear functions, the synchronization in a direct sense implies that $|x_s(t) - x_m(t)| \rightarrow 0$ as $t \rightarrow +\infty$.

The property of anti-synchronization constitutes a prevailing phenomenon in symmetrical oscillators, in which the state vectors have the same absolute values but opposite signs, which implies that $|x_s(t) + x_m(t)| \rightarrow 0$ as $t \rightarrow +\infty$.

When synchronization and anti-synchronization coexist, simultaneously, in chaotic systems, the synchronization is called hybrid synchronization (Juhn et al., 2009).

2. Chaotic hybrid synchronization and stability study

Let consider the chaotic master system (S_m) described, in the state space, by:

$$\dot{x}_m(t) = A\big(x_m(t)\big)x_m(t) \tag{1}$$

coupled with the following forced slave system (S_s):

$$\dot{x}_s(t) = A\big(x_s(t)\big)x_s(t) + B\big(x_s(t)\big)u(t) \tag{2}$$

where x_m and x_s are the n state vectors of the considered systems (S_m) and (S_s), respectively, $x_m = \left[x_{m1} \;\; \cdots \;\; x_{mn}\right]^T$, $x_s = \left[x_{s1} \;\; \cdots \;\; x_{sn}\right]^T$, u the h control vector, $u = \left[u_1 \;\; \cdots \;\; u_h\right]^T$, $A(.)$ an $n \times n$ instantaneous characteristic matrix, and $B(.)$ an $n \times h$ instantaneous control matrix.

Let denote by e_S the state synchronous error:

$$e_S(t) = x_s(t) - x_m(t) \tag{3}$$

and e_{AS} the anti-synchronous one:

$$e_{AS}(t) = x_s(t) + x_m(t) \tag{4}$$

$e_S = \left[e_{S1} \;\; \cdots \;\; e_{Sn}\right]^T$, $e_{AS} = \left[e_{AS1} \;\; \cdots \;\; e_{ASn}\right]^T$, and consider that the hybrid synchronization of the two chaotic systems, (S_m) and (S_s), is achieved if the following conditions hold (Juhn et al., 2009):

$$\begin{cases} \lim\limits_{t \to +\infty} \left|e_{Si}(t)\right| = \lim\limits_{t \to +\infty} \left|x_{si}(t) - x_{mi}(t)\right| = 0, \; \forall i = 1,2,\ldots,p, \; p < n \\ \lim\limits_{t \to +\infty} \left|e_{ASj}(t)\right| = \lim\limits_{t \to +\infty} \left|x_{sj}(t) + x_{mj}(t)\right| = 0, \; \forall j = p+1,\ldots,n \end{cases} \tag{5}$$

The satisfaction of the first relations of conditions (5) means that the synchronization property as far as p states of the error vector are concerned is satisfied. Nevertheless, the fulfilment of the second relations of the same system (5) guarantees the anti-synchronism relatively to the $(n - p)$ remaining states.

Then, the problem consisting in studying the convergence of both synchronous and anti-synchronous errors is equivalent to a stability study problem.

To force this property to the error system characterizing the evolution of the error vector of the coupled chaotic systems, one solution is to design a suitable feedback control law $u(t)$ of the slave system which can be chosen in the form, Fig. 1. (Kapitanialc, 2000):

$$u(t) = -K\left(x_s(t), x_m(t)\right)\left(x_s(t) \; \Delta \; x_m(t)\right) \tag{6}$$

such that, the operator Δ is replaced by the sign $(-)$ in the synchronization case and by the sign $(+)$ in the anti-synchronization one; $K(.)$ is an $h \times n$ nonlinear gain matrix.

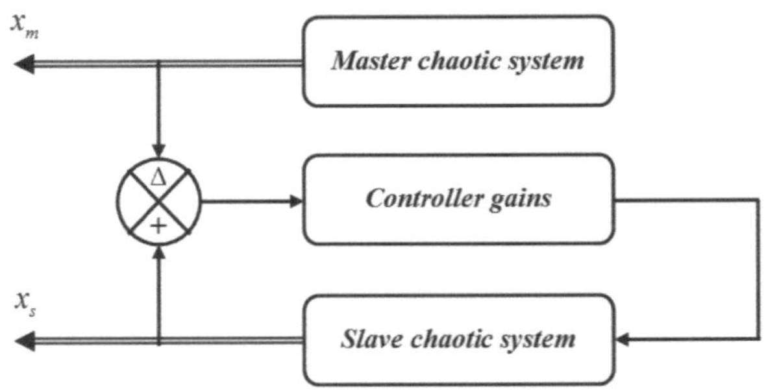

Fig. 1. Schematic representation of two chaotic systems synchronized in hybrid manner

The determination of the controller's gains, intended for the hybrid synchronization of the dynamic coupled master-slave chaotic system, is considered in the following section.

3. Analytic synchronization conditions of chaotic systems (Benrejeb & Hammami, 2008; Hammami, 2009; Hammami et al., 2010a)

To guarantee the synchronization as well as the anti-synchronization of chaotic systems, proposed approaches are based on the choice of both adapted stability method and of system description.

3.1 Case of nonlinear monovariable systems

Let consider the error dynamic system described by (7) in the monovariable case:

$$\dot{e}(t) = \hat{A}\left(x_s(t), x_m(t)\right)e(t) + \hat{B}\left(x_s(t), x_m(t)\right)u(t) \quad (7)$$

$$u(t) = -K\left(x_s(t), x_m(t)\right)e(t) \quad (8)$$

with $u \in \mathbb{R}$, $\hat{A}(.) = \left\{\hat{a}_{ij}(.)\right\}$, $\hat{B}(.) = \left\{\hat{b}_i(.)\right\}$, and $K(.) = \left\{k_j(.)\right\}$, $\forall i, j = 1,\ldots,n$, and the characteristic matrix of the closed-loop system $\tilde{A}(.)$, defined by:

$$\tilde{A}(.) = \hat{A}(.) - \hat{B}(.)K(.) \quad (9)$$

Theorem 1. *The system described by (7) and (8) and verifying (10):*

$$\hat{a}_{ij}(.) - \hat{b}_i(.)k_j(.) = 0 \;\; \forall i, j = 1,\ldots,n-1 \text{ for } i \neq j \quad (10)$$

such that:

i. the nonlinear elements are located in either one row or one column of the matrix $\tilde{A}(.)$,

ii. the diagonal elements $\left(\hat{a}_{ii}(.) - \hat{b}_i(.)k_i(.)\right)$ *of the matrix* $\tilde{A}(.)$ *are such that:*

$$\left(\hat{a}_{ii}(.) - \hat{b}_i(.)k_i(.)\right) < 0 \;\; \forall i = 1,\ldots,n-1 \quad (11)$$

is asymptotically stable, if there exist $\varepsilon > 0$ *such that:*

$$\left(\hat{a}_{nn}(.) - \hat{b}_n(.)k_n(.)\right) - \sum_{i=1}^{n-1}\left[\left|\left(\hat{a}_{ni}(.) - \hat{b}_n(.)k_i(.)\right)\left(\hat{a}_{in}(.) - \hat{b}_i(.)k_n(.)\right)\right|\left(\hat{a}_{ii}(.) - \hat{b}_i(.)k_i(.)\right)^{-1}\right] \leq -\varepsilon \quad (12)$$

Proof. Conditions (10) lead to an arrow form closed-loop characteristic matrix $\tilde{A}(.)$ (Benrejeb, 1980), called Benrejeb matrix (Borne et al., 2007):

$$\tilde{A}(.) = \begin{bmatrix} \times & & & & \times \\ & \times & & & \times \\ & & \ddots & & \vdots \\ & & & \times & \times \\ \times & \times & \ldots & \times & \times \end{bmatrix} \quad (13)$$

The choice of a comparison system having a characteristic matrix $\tilde{M}\left(\tilde{A}(.)\right)$, relatively to the vectorial norm $p(z)=\left[|z_1| \ \ldots \ |z_n|\right]^T$, $z=\left[z_1 \ \ldots \ z_n\right]^T$, leads, when the nonlinearities are isolated in either one row or one column, to the following sufficient conditions, by the use of Borne-Gentina practical stability criterion (Borne & Benrejeb, 2008):

$$(-1)^i \tilde{M}\left(\tilde{A}(.)\right)\begin{pmatrix} 1 & 2 & \ldots & i \\ 1 & 2 & \ldots & i \end{pmatrix} > 0 \ \forall i = 1,2,\ldots,n \tag{14}$$

This criterion, useful for the stability study of complex and large scale systems generalizes the Kotelyanski lemma for nonlinear systems and defines large classes of systems for which the linear conjecture can be verified, either for the initial system or for its comparison system.

The comparison system associated to the previous vectorial norm $p(z)$, is defined, in this case, by the following differential equations:

$$\dot{z}(t) = \tilde{M}\left(\tilde{A}(.)\right)z(t) \tag{15}$$

such that the elements $\tilde{m}_{ij}(.)$ of $\tilde{M}\left(\tilde{A}(.)\right)$ are deduced from the ones of the matrix $\tilde{A}(.)$ by substituting the off-diagonal elements by their absolute values, which can be written as:

$$\begin{cases} \tilde{m}_{ii}(.) = \tilde{a}_{ii}(.) \quad \forall i = 1,\ldots,n \\ \tilde{m}_{ij}(.) = \left|\hat{a}_{ij}(.) - \hat{b}_i(.)k_j(.)\right| \ \forall i,j = 1,\ldots,n, \ i \neq j \end{cases} \tag{16}$$

The system (7) is then stabilized by (8) if the matrix $\tilde{M}\left(\tilde{A}(.)\right)$ is the opposite of an $M-$ matrix, or equivalently, by application of the practical Borne-Gentina criterion:

$$\begin{cases} \tilde{a}_{ii}(.) < 0 \ \forall i = 1,2,\ldots,n-1 \\ (-1)^n \det\left(\tilde{M}\left(\tilde{A}(.)\right)\right) > 0 \end{cases} \tag{17}$$

The development of the first member of the last inequality of (17):

$$(-1)^n \det\left(\tilde{M}\left(\tilde{A}(.)\right)\right) = (-1)\left(\tilde{a}_{nn}(.) - \sum_{i=1}^{n-1}\left(\left|\tilde{a}_{ni}(.)\tilde{a}_{in}(.)\right|\right)\tilde{a}_{ii}^{-1}(.)\right)(-1)^{n-1}\prod_{j=1}^{n-1}\tilde{a}_{jj}(.) \tag{18}$$

achieves easily the proof of theorem 1.

Corollary 1. *The system described by (7) and (8) and verifying (10) such that:*

i. *the nonlinear elements are located in either one row or one column of the matrix* $\tilde{A}(.)$,

ii. *the diagonal elements* $\left(\hat{a}_{ii}(.) - \hat{b}_i(.)k_i(.)\right)$, $\forall i = 1,\ldots,n-1$, *of the matrix* $\tilde{A}(.)$ *are strictly negative,*

iii. *the products of the off-diagonal elements of the matrix* $\tilde{A}(.)$ *are such that:*

$$\left(\hat{a}_{ni}(.) - \hat{b}_n(.)k_i(.)\right)\left(\hat{a}_{in}(.) - \hat{b}_i(.)k_n(.)\right) \geq 0 \ \forall i = 1,\ldots,n-1 \tag{19}$$

is asymptotically stable if there exist $\varepsilon > 0$ *for which the instantaneous characteristic polynomial* $P_{\tilde{A}(.)}(.,\lambda)$ *of* $\tilde{A}(.)$ *satisfies the condition:*

$$P_{\tilde{A}(.)}(.,0) = (-1)^n \det\left(M\left(\tilde{A}(.)\right)\right) \geq \varepsilon \tag{20}$$

Proof. The proof of corollary 1 is inferred of theorem 1 by taking into account the new added iii. conditions, which guarantee, through a simple transformation, the identity of the matrix $\tilde{A}(.)$ and its overvaluing matrix $\tilde{M}\left(\tilde{A}(.)\right)$.
These conditions, associated to aggregation techniques based on the use of vector norms, have led to stability domains for a class of Lur'e Postnikov systems whereas, for example, Popov stability criterion use failed (Benrejeb, 1980).

3.2 Nonlinear multivariable systems case

In the case of nonlinear multivariable systems, let us consider the closed-loop error system described by:

$$\dot{e}(t) = \hat{A}(.)e(t) + \hat{B}(.)u(t) \tag{21}$$

$$u(t) = -K(.)e(t) \tag{22}$$

then by:

$$\dot{e}(t) = \tilde{A}(.)e(t) \tag{23}$$

$$\tilde{A}(.) = \hat{A}(.) - \hat{B}(.)K(.) \tag{24}$$

with $u \in \mathbb{R}^h$ the control vector, $\hat{A}(.)$ the $n \times n$ instantaneous characteristic matrix, $\hat{A}(.) = \left\{\hat{a}_{ij}(.)\right\}$, $\hat{B}(.)$ the $n \times h$ control matrix, $\hat{B}(.) = \left\{\hat{b}_{ij}(.)\right\}$ and $K(.)$ the $h \times n$ instantaneous gain matrix, $K(.) = \left\{k_{ij}(.)\right\}$.
The conditions allowing to put $\tilde{A}(.)$ under arrow form, are expressed as follows:

$$\hat{a}_{ij}(.) - \sum_{l=1}^{h} \hat{b}_{il}(.)k_{lj}(.) = 0 \ \forall i,j = 1,\ldots,n-1,\ i \neq j \tag{25}$$

Then, a necessary condition leading to the existence of a control law is that the number of equations to solve, $(n-1)(n-2)$, must be less than or equal to the number of unknown parameters, $n \times h$, then:

$$h \geq n-2 \tag{26}$$

Remark 1. If there exist $i,\ i<n,$ such that $\hat{b}_{il}(.),\ \forall l = 1,\ldots,h,$ is equal to zero and by considering the conditions (25) allowing to put the matrix $\tilde{A}(.)$ under the arrow form, the system (21) must be such that:

$$\hat{a}_{ij}(.) = 0 \ \forall j = 1,\ldots,n-1 \text{ for } i \neq j \tag{27}$$

Remark 2. If all the elements $\hat{b}_{il}(.)$, $\forall i=1,\ldots,n-1$, $\forall l=1,\ldots,h$, are equal to zero, then the equations (25) cannot be satisfied only in the particular case where the matrix $\hat{A}(.)$ is under the arrow form; that is to say, that all the elements $\hat{a}_{ij}(.)$, $\forall i,j=1,\ldots,n-1$, for $i \neq j$, are equal to zero, due to:

$$\sum_{l=1}^{h} \hat{b}_{il}(.)k_{lj}(.)=0 \ \forall i,j=1,\ldots,n-1,\ i\neq j \tag{28}$$

Theorem 2. *The system described by (21) and (22) and verifying (25) and (26), is stabilized by the control law (22) if the instantaneous characteristic matrix $\tilde{A}(.)$, defined by (24), is such that:*

i. *the nonlinear elements are located in either one row or one column of the matrix $\tilde{A}(.)$,*

ii. *the first $(n-1)$ diagonal elements of the matrix $\tilde{A}(.)$ are such that:*

$$\left(\hat{a}_{ii}(.)-\sum_{l=1}^{h}\hat{b}_{il}(.)k_{li}(.)\right)<0 \ \forall i=1,2,\ldots,n-1 \tag{29}$$

iii. *there exist $\varepsilon>0$, such that:*

$$\left(\hat{a}_{nn}(.)-\sum_{l=1}^{h}\hat{b}_{nl}(.)k_{ln}(.)\right)-\sum_{i=1}^{n-1}\left[\begin{array}{c}\left|\left(\hat{a}_{ni}(.)-\sum_{l=1}^{h}\hat{b}_{nl}(.)k_{li}(.)\right)\left(\hat{a}_{in}(.)-\sum_{l=1}^{h}\hat{b}_{il}(.)k_{ln}(.)\right)\right| \\ \times\left(\hat{a}_{ii}(.)-\sum_{l=1}^{h}\hat{b}_{il}(.)k_{li}(.)\right)^{-1}\end{array}\right]\leq-\varepsilon \tag{30}$$

Proof. The proof of theorem 2 is similar to the theorem 1 relatively to the dynamic nonlinear monovariable continuous system; the conditions (29) and (30) are inferred from the conditions (11) and (12), by replacing the elements $\tilde{a}_{ij}(.)$ by their expressions according to the elements of $\hat{A}(.)$, $\hat{B}(.)$ and $K(.)$ matrices.

Remark 3. The previous results, well adapted for multivariable systems, can be applied only for monovariable ones which are, at most, of third order, by respect to the above-mentioned necessary condition (26).

Although, according to the class of systems described by differential scalar equation, the arrow form matrix can be advantageously used in a different way.

In such a view, let us consider the closed-loop nonlinear system assumed to be described by the following differential scalar equation:

$$s^{(n)}(t)+\sum_{i=0}^{n-1}a_i\left(s(t),\ s'(t),\ \ldots,\ s^{(n-1)}(t)\right)s^{(i)}(t)=0 \tag{31}$$

s is the output, $s\in\mathbb{R}$, y the state vector $y=\left[s\ \ s'\ \ \ldots\ \ s^{(n-1)}\right]^T$, $y\in\mathbb{R}^n$, and $a_i(.)$, $\forall i=0,1,\ldots,n-1$, coefficients of the instantaneous characteristic polynomial $P_{A(.)}(.,\lambda)$ of the matrix $A(.)$, such that:

$$P_{A(.)}(.,\lambda)=\det(\lambda\mathbb{I}-A(.))=\lambda^n+\sum_{i=0}^{n-1}a_i(.)\lambda^i \tag{32}$$

The system (31) can be rewritten as:

$$\dot{y}(t) = A(.)y(t) \tag{33}$$

$$A(.) = \begin{bmatrix} 0 & 1 & 0 & \dots & 0 \\ \vdots & \ddots & \ddots & \ddots & \vdots \\ 0 & & & & 0 \\ 0 & & \dots & 0 & 1 \\ -a_0(.) & & \dots & & -a_{n-1}(.) \end{bmatrix} \tag{34}$$

The change of base defined by (Benrejeb, 1980):

$$y = Px \tag{35}$$

$$P = \begin{bmatrix} 1 & 1 & \dots & 1 & 0 \\ \alpha_1 & \alpha_2 & \dots & \alpha_{n-1} & \vdots \\ \vdots & \vdots & & \vdots & \vdots \\ \alpha_1^{n-2} & \alpha_2^{n-2} & \dots & \alpha_{n-1}^{n-2} & 0 \\ \alpha_1^{n-1} & \alpha_2^{n-1} & \dots & \alpha_{n-1}^{n-1} & 1 \end{bmatrix} \tag{36}$$

with α_i, $\forall i = 1,2,\dots,n-1$, distinct arbitrary constant parameters, $\alpha_i \neq \alpha_j$, $\forall i \neq j$, leads to the following description:

$$\dot{x}(t) = \breve{A}(.)x(t) \tag{37}$$

where the new instantaneous characteristic matrix, denoted by $\breve{A}(.)$ is in the Benrejeb arrow form:

$$\breve{A}(.) = P^{-1}A(.)P \tag{38}$$

$$\breve{A}(.) = \begin{bmatrix} \alpha_1 & & & \beta_1 \\ & \ddots & & \vdots \\ & & \alpha_{n-1} & \beta_{n-1} \\ \gamma_1(.) & \dots & \gamma_{n-1}(.) & \gamma_n(.) \end{bmatrix} \tag{39}$$

with:

$$\beta_i = \prod_{\substack{i,j=1 \\ i \neq j}}^{n-1} \left(\alpha_i - \alpha_j\right)^{-1} \tag{40}$$

$$\gamma_i(.) = -P_{\breve{A}(.)}\left(.,\alpha_i\right) \ \forall i = 1,2,\dots,n-1 \tag{41}$$

$$\gamma_n(.) = -a_{n-1}(.) - \sum_{i=1}^{n-1} \alpha_i \tag{42}$$

For the system described by (37) and (39), the application of Borne-Gentina criterion can lead to the stability conditions of the studied nonlinear system as shown in the following.

The equilibrium state of the nonlinear system (37) is asymptotically stable if the conditions:

i. $$\alpha_i < 0,\ i = 1,\ldots,n-1,\ \alpha_i \neq \alpha_j,\ \forall i \neq j \tag{43}$$

ii. there exist a positive parameter ε, such that:

$$\gamma_n(.) - \sum_{i=0}^{n-1} \left|\beta_i \gamma_i(.)\right| \alpha_i^{-1} \leq -\varepsilon \tag{44}$$

are satisfied.

When the $(n-1)$ products $\beta_i \gamma_i(.)$, $\forall i = 1,\ldots,n-1$, are non-negative, the condition (44) can be reduced and stated, by means of the instantaneous characteristic polynomial of the matrix $\breve{A}(.)$, in the following manner:

$$P_{\breve{A}(.)}(.,0) \geq \varepsilon \tag{45}$$

which constitutes a verification case of the validity of the linear Aizerman conjecture.

4. Synchronization and anti-synchronization cases

4.1 Synchronization of two identical coupled chaotic Chen systems

In this part, let focus on the problem of synchronization process of two identical coupled chaotic Chen dynamical systems.

The studied system is described by the following differential equations (Fallahi et al., 2008):

$$\begin{bmatrix} \dot{x}_1(t) \\ \dot{x}_2(t) \\ \dot{x}_3(t) \end{bmatrix} = \begin{bmatrix} -\alpha & \alpha & 0 \\ \gamma - \alpha & \gamma & 0 \\ 0 & 0 & -\beta \end{bmatrix} \begin{bmatrix} x_1(t) \\ x_2(t) \\ x_3(t) \end{bmatrix} + \begin{bmatrix} 0 \\ -x_1(t)x_3(t) \\ x_1(t)x_2(t) \end{bmatrix} \tag{46}$$

where α, β and γ are three positive parameters.

The system (46) exhibits a chaotic attractor at the parameter values: $\alpha = 35$, $\beta = 3$ and $\gamma = 28$, starting at the initial value of the state vector $x(0) = \begin{bmatrix} 1 & 1 & 0.5 \end{bmatrix}^T$, Fig. 2.

Obviously, the Chen nonlinear model can also be presented by respect to the following model:

$$\dot{x}(t) = A(.)x(t) \tag{47}$$

where $x(t) = \begin{bmatrix} x_1(t) & x_2(t) & x_3(t) \end{bmatrix}^T$ is the state vector and $A(.)$ the instantaneous characteristic matrix such that:

$$A(.) = \begin{bmatrix} -\alpha & \alpha & 0 \\ \gamma - \alpha & \gamma & -x_1(t) \\ 0 & x_1(t) & -\beta \end{bmatrix} \tag{48}$$

At this stage, we choose a master Chen system given by:

$$\begin{cases} \dot{x}_{m1}(t) = \alpha\left(x_{m2}(t) - x_{m1}(t)\right) \\ \dot{x}_{m2}(t) = \left(\gamma - \alpha - x_{m3}(t)\right)x_{m1}(t) + \gamma x_{m2}(t) \\ \dot{x}_{m3}(t) = x_{m1}(t)x_{m2}(t) - \beta x_{m3}(t) \end{cases} \tag{49}$$

which drives a slave Chen system described by:

$$\begin{cases} \dot{x}_{s1}(t) = \alpha\left(x_{s2}(t) - x_{s1}(t)\right) \\ \dot{x}_{s2}(t) = \left(\gamma - \alpha - x_{s3}(t)\right)x_{s1}(t) + \gamma x_{s2}(t) + u_1(t) \\ \dot{x}_{s3}(t) = x_{s1}(t)x_{s2}(t) - \beta x_{s3}(t) + u_2(t) \end{cases} \tag{50}$$

$u_i(t)$, $i = 1,2$, are the appropriate control functions to be determined.
It comes the error dynamics equations below:

$$\begin{cases} \dot{e}_{S1}(t) = \alpha\left(e_{S2}(t) - e_{S1}(t)\right) \\ \dot{e}_{S2}(t) = \left(\gamma - \alpha\right)e_{S1}(t) + \gamma e_{S2}(t) + \left(x_{m1}(t)x_{m3}(t) - x_{s1}(t)x_{s3}(t)\right) + u_1(t) \\ \dot{e}_{S3}(t) = -\beta e_{S3}(t) - \left(x_{m1}(t)x_{m2}(t) - x_{s1}(t)x_{s2}(t)\right) + u_2(t) \end{cases} \tag{51}$$

which can be rewritten in the form:

$$\begin{bmatrix} \dot{e}_{S1}(t) \\ \dot{e}_{S2}(t) \\ \dot{e}_{S3}(t) \end{bmatrix} = \begin{bmatrix} \alpha\left(e_{S2}(t) - e_{S1}(t)\right) \\ \left(\gamma - \alpha\right)e_{S1}(t) + \gamma e_{S2}(t) + \left(x_{m1}(t)x_{m3}(t) - x_{s1}(t)x_{s3}(t)\right) \\ -\beta e_{S3}(t) - \left(x_{m1}(t)x_{m2}(t) - x_{s1}(t)x_{s2}(t)\right) \end{bmatrix} + Bu(t) \tag{52}$$

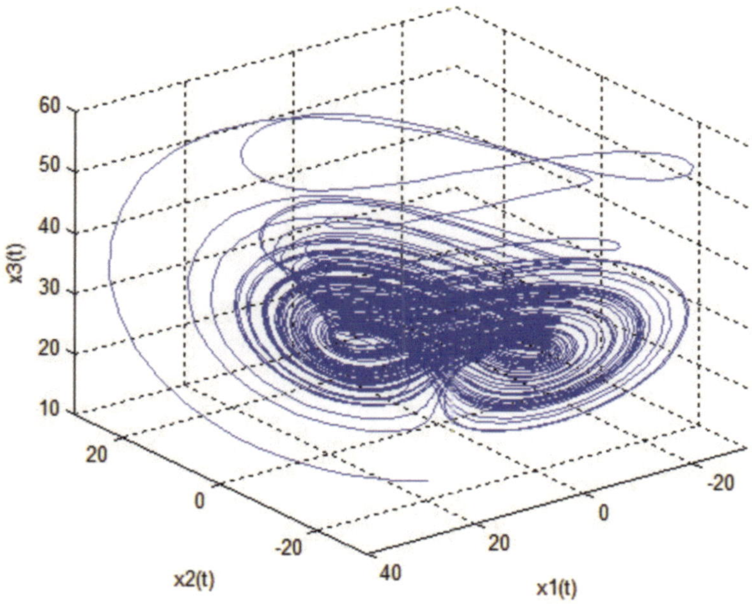

Fig. 2. Three-dimensional attractor of Chen dynamical chaotic system

with:

$$B=\begin{bmatrix}0 & 0\\ 1 & 0\\ 0 & 1\end{bmatrix} \tag{53}$$

The synchronization problem for coupled Chen chaotic dynamical systems is to achieve the asymptotic stability of this error system (52), with the following active control functions $u_i(t),\ i=1,2,$ defined by:

$$u_i(t)=-\sum_{j=1}^{2}k_{ij}(.)x_j(t)-f_i(.)\ \forall i=1,2 \tag{54}$$

Then, for an instantaneous 2×2 gain matrix $K(.)$, $K(.)=\{k_{ij}(.)\}$, we obtain:

$$\begin{cases}\dot{e}_{S1}(t)=\alpha\left(e_{S2}(t)-e_{S1}(t)\right)\\ \dot{e}_{S2}(t)=\left(\gamma-\alpha-k_{11}(.)\right)e_{S1}(t)+\left(\gamma-k_{12}(.)\right)e_{S2}(t)+\left(x_{m1}(t)x_{m3}(t)-x_{s1}(t)x_{s3}(t)\right)-f_1(.)\\ \dot{e}_{S3}(t)=-k_{21}(.)e_{S1}(t)-k_{22}(.)e_{S2}(t)-\beta e_{S3}(t)-\left(x_{m1}(t)x_{m2}(t)-x_{s1}(t)x_{s2}(t)\right)-f_2(.)\end{cases} \tag{55}$$

The characterization of the closed-loop system by an arrow form matrix is easily checked, by choosing the correction parameter $k_{22}(.)$ such that:

$$k_{22}=0 \tag{56}$$

Then, to satisfy the constraints (29) as well as the condition (30) of the theorem 2, the two following inequalities must be, respectively, fulfilled:

$$\gamma-k_{12}(.)<0 \tag{57}$$

$$-\alpha-\left(\left|\alpha\left(\gamma-\alpha-k_{11}(.)\right)\right|\left(\gamma-k_{12}(.)\right)^{-1}\right)<0 \tag{58}$$

So, $\forall\ k_{21}(.)$, possible choices of the other parameters are given by:

$$\begin{cases}k_{12}=\alpha\\ k_{11}=\gamma-\alpha\end{cases} \tag{59}$$

Finally, it remains to study the stability of a linear controlled system, in the case where the following possible choices are adopted:

$$\begin{cases}f_1(.)=x_{m1}(t)x_{m3}(t)-x_{s1}(t)x_{s3}(t)\\ f_2(.)=-x_{m1}(t)x_{m2}(t)+x_{s1}(t)x_{s2}(t)\end{cases} \tag{60}$$

Then, the constant gain matrix K, can be chosen as:

$$K=\begin{bmatrix}\gamma-\alpha & \alpha\\ 2 & 0\end{bmatrix} \tag{61}$$

Thus, when stabilized by the above-mentioned feedback $u_i(t)$, $i=1,2,$ the error system (55) will converge to zero as $t \to +\infty$ implying that system (50) will globally synchronize with system (49).

Fig. 3. shows the error dynamics in the uncontrolled state, while both Fig. 4. and Fig. 5. illustrate the error dynamics when controller is switched on. Obviously, the two chaotic Chen systems evolve in the same direction as well as the same amplitude; they are globally asymptotically synchronized by means of the proposed controller.

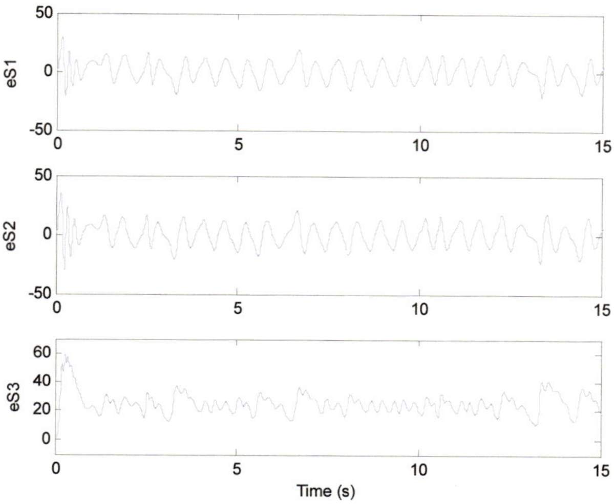

Fig. 3. Error dynamics of the coupled master-slave Chen system when controller is deactivated

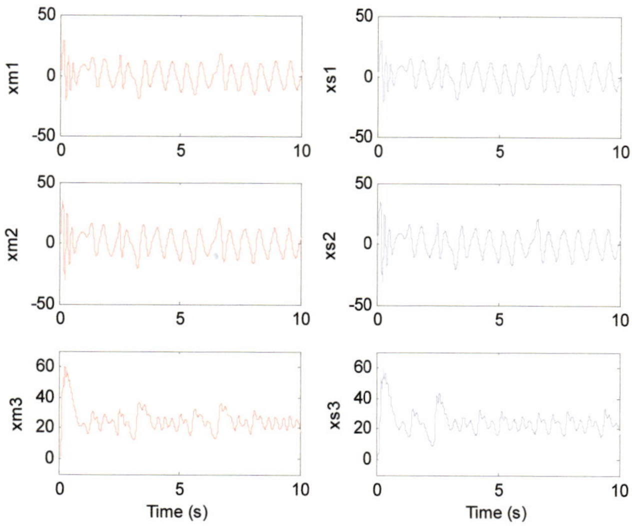

Fig. 4. Synchronization dynamics between the coupled master-slave Chen system when controller is activated

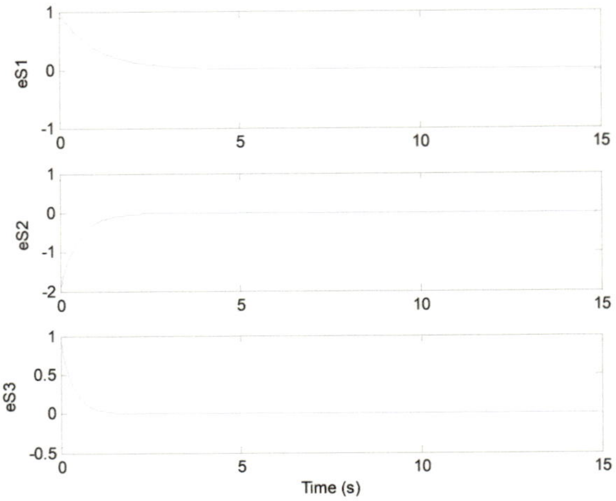

Fig. 5. Error dynamics of the coupled master-slave Chen system when controller is switched on

4.2 Anti-synchronization of two identical coupled chaotic Lee systems

The studied chaotic Lee system is described by the following differential equations (Juhn et al., 2009):

$$\begin{bmatrix} \dot{x}_1(t) \\ \dot{x}_2(t) \\ \dot{x}_3(t) \end{bmatrix} = \begin{bmatrix} -10 & 10 & 0 \\ 40 & 0 & -x_1(t) \\ 4x_1(t) & 0 & -2.5 \end{bmatrix} \begin{bmatrix} x_1(t) \\ x_2(t) \\ x_3(t) \end{bmatrix} \tag{62}$$

It exhibits a chaotic attractor, starting at the initial value of the state vector $x(0) = \begin{bmatrix} 2 & 3 & 2 \end{bmatrix}^T$, Fig. 6.

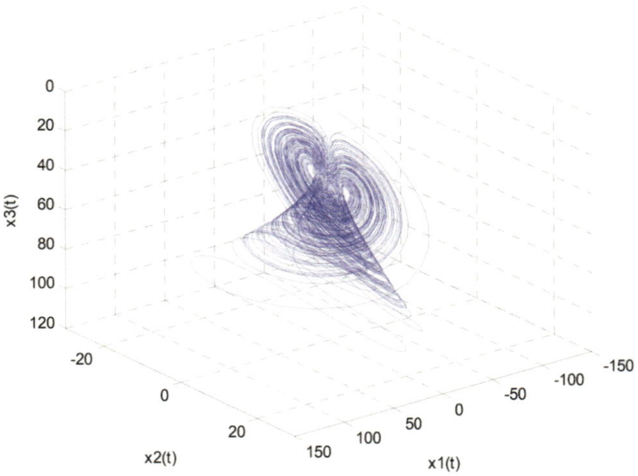

Fig. 6. Three-dimensional view of the Lee chaotic attractor

Let us consider the master Lee system (S_m) given by (63):

$$\begin{bmatrix} \dot{x}_{m1}(t) \\ \dot{x}_{m2}(t) \\ \dot{x}_{m3}(t) \end{bmatrix} = \begin{bmatrix} -10 & 10 & 0 \\ 40 & 0 & -x_{m1}(t) \\ 4x_{m1}(t) & 0 & -2.5 \end{bmatrix} \begin{bmatrix} x_{m1}(t) \\ x_{m2}(t) \\ x_{m3}(t) \end{bmatrix} \quad (63)$$

driving a similar controlled slave Lee system (S_s) described by (64):

$$\begin{bmatrix} \dot{x}_{s1}(t) \\ \dot{x}_{s2}(t) \\ \dot{x}_{s3}(t) \end{bmatrix} = \begin{bmatrix} -10 & 10 & 0 \\ 40 & 0 & -x_{s1}(t) \\ 4x_{s1}(t) & 0 & -2.5 \end{bmatrix} \begin{bmatrix} x_{s1}(t) \\ x_{s2}(t) \\ x_{s3}(t) \end{bmatrix} + \begin{bmatrix} 0 \\ 1 \\ 0 \end{bmatrix} u(t) \quad (64)$$

$u(t)$ is the scalar active control.

For the following state error vector components, defined relatively to anti-synchronization study:

$$\begin{cases} e_{AS1}(t) = x_{s1}(t) + x_{m1}(t) \\ e_{AS2}(t) = x_{s2}(t) + x_{m2}(t) \\ e_{AS3}(t) = x_{s3}(t) + x_{m3}(t) \end{cases} \quad (65)$$

the error system can be defined by the following differential equations:

$$\begin{cases} \dot{e}_{AS1}(t) = -10e_{AS1}(t) + 10e_{AS2}(t) \\ \dot{e}_{AS2}(t) = 40e_{AS1}(t) - \left(x_{s1}(t)x_{s3}(t) + x_{m1}(t)x_{m3}(t)\right) + u(t) \\ \dot{e}_{AS3}(t) = -2.5e_{AS3}(t) + 4\left(x_{s1}^2(t) - x_{m1}^2(t)\right) \end{cases} \quad (66)$$

The problem of chaos anti-synchronization between two identical Lee chaotic dynamical systems is solved here by the design of a state feedback structure $k_i(.)$, $\forall i = 1,2,3$, and the choice of nonlinear functions $f_i(.)$, $\forall i = 1,2,3$, such that:

$$u(t) = -\sum_{i=1}^{3} k_i(.)x_i(t) - f_j(.) \ \forall j = 1,2,3 \quad (67)$$

It comes the following closed-loop dynamical error system:

$$\begin{bmatrix} \dot{e}_{AS1}(t) \\ \dot{e}_{AS2}(t) \\ \dot{e}_{AS3}(t) \end{bmatrix} = \begin{bmatrix} -10 & 10 & 0 \\ 40 - k_1(.) & -k_2(.) & -k_3(.) \\ -2.5 & 0 & 0 \end{bmatrix} \begin{bmatrix} e_{AS1}(t) \\ e_{AS2}(t) \\ e_{AS3}(t) \end{bmatrix} - \begin{bmatrix} f_1(.) \\ \left(x_{s1}(t)x_{s3}(t) + x_{m1}(t)x_{m3}(t)\right) + f_2(.) \\ 4\left(x_{s1}^2(t) + x_{m1}^2(t)\right) + f_3(.) \end{bmatrix} \quad (68)$$

The nonlinear elements $f_i(.)$ and $k_i(.)$ have to be chosen to make the instantaneous characteristic matrix of the closed-loop system in the arrow form and the closed-loop error system asymptotically stable.

From the possible solutions, allowing to put the instantaneous characteristic matrix of (68) under the arrow form, let consider the following:

$$k_3 = 0 \tag{69}$$

and:

$$\begin{cases} f_1(.) = 0 \\ f_2(.) = -\left(x_{s1}(t)x_{s3}(t) + x_{m1}(t)x_{m3}(t)\right) \\ f_3(.) = e_{AS3}(t) - 4\left(x_{s1}^2(t) + x_{m1}^2(t)\right) \end{cases} \tag{70}$$

For the vector norm $p(e_{AS})$, $e_{AS} = \begin{bmatrix} e_{AS1} & e_{AS2} & e_{AS3} \end{bmatrix}^T$:

$$p(e_{AS}) = \begin{bmatrix} |e_{AS1}| & |e_{AS2}| & |e_{AS3}| \end{bmatrix}^T \tag{71}$$

the overvaluing matrix is in arrow form and has non negative off-diagonal elements and nonlinearities isolated in either one row or one column.
By the use of the proposed theorem 2, stability and anti-synchronization properties are satisfied for the both following sufficient conditions (72) and (73):

$$-k_2(.) < 0 \tag{72}$$

$$\left(-10 - \left(-10\left(40 - k_1(.)\right)k_2^{-1}(.)\right)\right) < 0 \tag{73}$$

Various choices of the gain vector $K(.)$, $K(.) = \begin{bmatrix} k_1(.) & k_2(.) & 0 \end{bmatrix}$, are possible, such as the following linear one:

$$K = \{k_i\} = \begin{bmatrix} 4 & 2 & 0 \end{bmatrix} \tag{74}$$

By considering the initial condition $e_{AS}(0) = \begin{bmatrix} 2 & 3 & 2 \end{bmatrix}^T$, for the Lee error system (66) when the active controller is deactivated, it is obvious that the error states grow with time chaotically, as shown in Fig. 7., and after activating the controller, Fig. 8. shows three parametrically harmonically excited 3D systems evolve in the opposite direction. The trajectories of error system (68) imply that the asymptotical anti-synchronization has been, successfully, achieved, Fig. 9.

5. Hybrid synchronization by a nonlinear state feedback controller – Application to the Chen–Lee chaotic system (Hammami, 2009)

Let consider two coupled chaotic Chen and Lee systems (Juhn et al., 2009). The following nonlinear differential equations, of the form (1), correspond to a master system (Tam & Si Tou, 2008):

$$\dot{x}_m(t) = A\left(x_m(t)\right)x_m(t)$$

with:

$$A(x_m(t)) = \begin{bmatrix} a & -x_{m3}(t) & 0 \\ 0 & b & x_{m1}(t) \\ cx_{m2}(t) & 0 & d \end{bmatrix} \tag{75}$$

x_{m1}, x_{m2} and x_{m3} are state variables, and a, b, c and d four system parameters.
For the following parameters $(a,b,c,d)=(5,-10,0.3,-3.8)$, and initial condition $\begin{bmatrix} x_{m1}(0) & x_{m2}(0) & x_{m3}(0) \end{bmatrix}^T = \begin{bmatrix} 1.5 & -32 & 13 \end{bmatrix}^T$, the drive system, described by (1) and (75) is a chaotic attractor, as shown in Fig. 10.

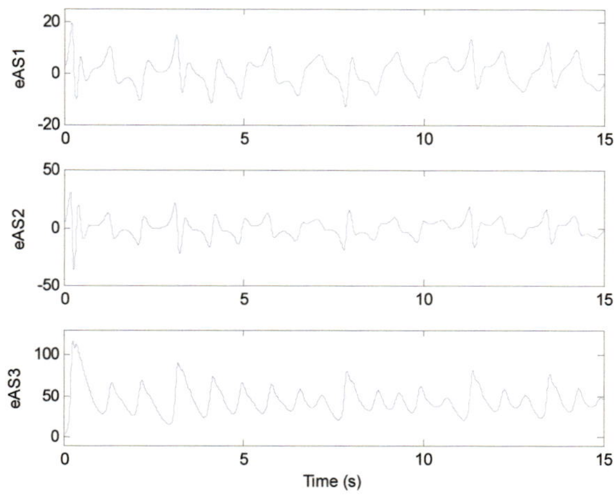

Fig. 7. Error dynamics $(e_{AS1}, e_{AS2}, e_{AS3})$ of the coupled master-slave Lee system when the active controller is deactivated

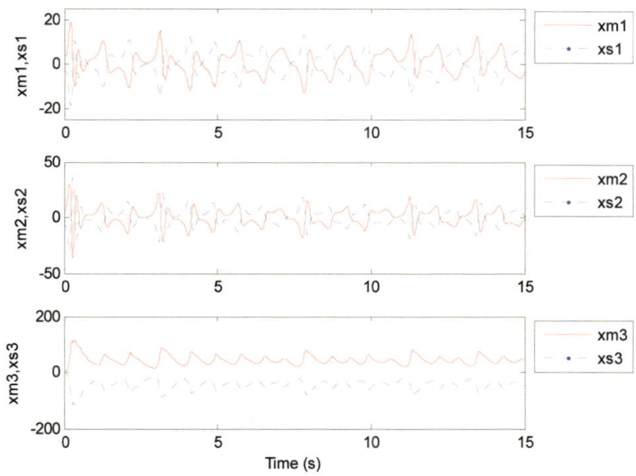

Fig. 8. Partial time series of anti-synchronization for Lee chaotic system when the active controller is switched on

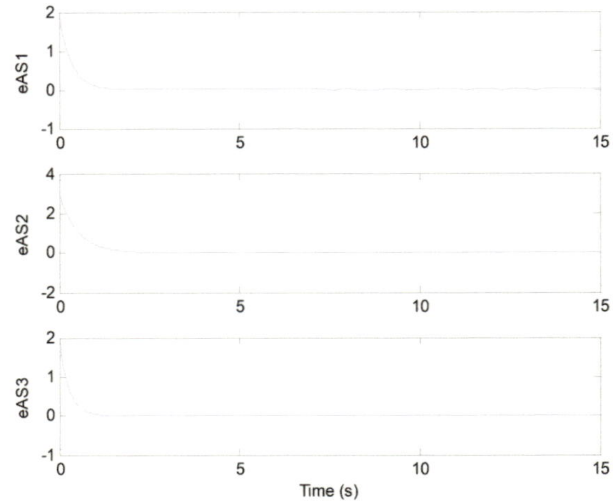

Fig. 9. Error dynamics of the coupled master-slave Lee system when control is activated

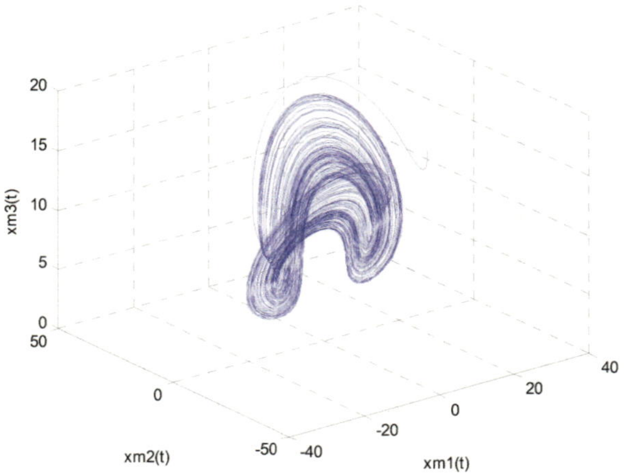

Fig. 10. The 3-dimensional strange attractor of the chaotic Chen–Lee master system

For the Chen–Lee slave system, described in the state space by:

$$\dot{x}_s(t) = A(x_s(t))x_s(t) + u(t) \tag{76}$$

with:

$$A(x_s(t)) = \begin{bmatrix} a & -x_{s3}(t) & 0 \\ 0 & b & x_{s1}(t) \\ cx_{s2}(t) & 0 & d \end{bmatrix} \tag{77}$$

we have selected the anti-synchronization state variables x_{m1} and x_{m3} facing to x_{s1} and x_{s3}, and the synchronization state variable x_{m2} facing to x_{s2}.
Then, the hybrid synchronization errors between the master and the slave systems $e(t) = \left[e_{AS1}(t) \quad e_{S2}(t) \quad e_{AS3}(t)\right]^T$, are such as:

$$\begin{cases} e_{AS1}(t) = x_{s1}(t) + x_{m1}(t) \\ e_{S2}(t) \ = x_{s2}(t) - x_{m2}(t) \\ e_{AS3}(t) = x_{s3}(t) + x_{m3}(t) \end{cases} \tag{78}$$

Let compute the following continuous state feedback controller's structure:

$$u(t) = -K\left(x_m(t), x_s(t)\right)e(t) \tag{79}$$

to guarantee the asymptotic stability of the error states defined by (78), $e = \begin{bmatrix} e_{AS1} & e_{S2} & e_{AS3} \end{bmatrix}^T$, so that the slave system, characterized by (76) and (77), synchronizes and anti-synchronizes, simultaneously, to the master one, described by (1) and (75), by assuring that the synchronization error e_{S2} and the anti-synchronization errors e_{AS1} and e_{AS3} decay to zero, within a finite time.

Thus, for a state feedback controller of the form (79), $K(.)$, $K(.) = \left\{k_{ij}(.)\right\}$, $\forall i,\ j = 1,2,3$, and by considering the differential systems (1), (75), (76), (77) and (78), we obtain the following state space description of the error resulting system:

$$\dot{e}(t) = A(.)e(t) \tag{80}$$

with:

$$A(.) = \begin{bmatrix} a - k_{11}(.) & -x_{m3}(t) - k_{12}(.) & -k_{13}(.) \\ -k_{21}(.) & b - k_{22}(.) & x_{m1}(t) - k_{23}(.) \\ cx_{m2}(t) - k_{31}(.) & -k_{32}(.) & d - k_{33}(.) \end{bmatrix} \tag{81}$$

By respect to the stabilisability conditions announced in the above-mentioned theorem 2, the dynamic error system (80) is first characterized by an instantaneous arrow form matrix $A(.)$, that is to say, the main requirements concerning the choice of the feedback gains $k_{12}(.)$ and $k_{21}(.)$ are given by:

$$\begin{cases} k_{12}(.) = -x_{m3}(t) \\ k_{21} = 0 \end{cases} \tag{82}$$

To satisfy that the two first diagonal elements of the characteristic matrix $A(.)$ are strictly negative:

$$\begin{cases} a - k_{11}(.) < 0 \\ b - k_{22}(.) < 0 \end{cases} \tag{83}$$

a possible solution is:

$$\begin{cases} k_{11} = 7 \\ k_{22} = -6 \end{cases} \tag{84}$$

Besides, to annihilate the nonlinearities in system (80), a solution is:

$$\begin{cases} k_{23}(.) = x_{m1}(t) \\ k_{31}(.) = c x_{m2}(t) \end{cases} \tag{85}$$

Finally, by considering the fixed values of k_{11}, $k_{12}(.)$, k_{21}, k_{22}, $k_{23}(.)$ and $k_{31}(.)$, it is relevant to denote that to satisfy the sufficient condition (30) of theorem 2, for any arbitrary chosen parameters of correction $k_{13}(.)$ and $k_{32}(.)$, it is necessary to tune the remaining design parameter $k_{33}(.)$, guaranteeing the hybrid synchronization of the coupled chaotic studied system such that:

$$d - k_{33}(.) < 0 \tag{86}$$

Then, for the following instantaneous gain matrix $K(.)$, easily obtained:

$$K(.) = \begin{bmatrix} 7 & -x_{m3}(t) & 0 \\ 0 & -6 & x_{m1}(t) \\ c x_{m2}(t) & 0 & -1 \end{bmatrix} \tag{87}$$

the studied dynamic error system (80) is asymptotically stable.
For the following initial master and slave systems conditions, $x_m(0) = \begin{bmatrix} 1.5 & -52 & 13 \end{bmatrix}^T$, $x_s(0) = \begin{bmatrix} -2 & 10 & -15 \end{bmatrix}^T$, and without activation of the designed controller, the numerical simulation results of the above master-slave system are shown in Fig. 11.
It is obvious, from Fig. 12., that the error states grow with time chaotically.
Therefore, by designing an adequate nonlinear controlled slave system and under mild conditions, the hybrid synchronization is achieved within a shorter time, as it is shown in Fig. 13., with an exponentially decaying error, Fig. 14.
The obtained phase trajectories of the Fig. 15., show that the Chen-Lee slave chaotic attractor is synchronized in a hybrid manner with the master one.

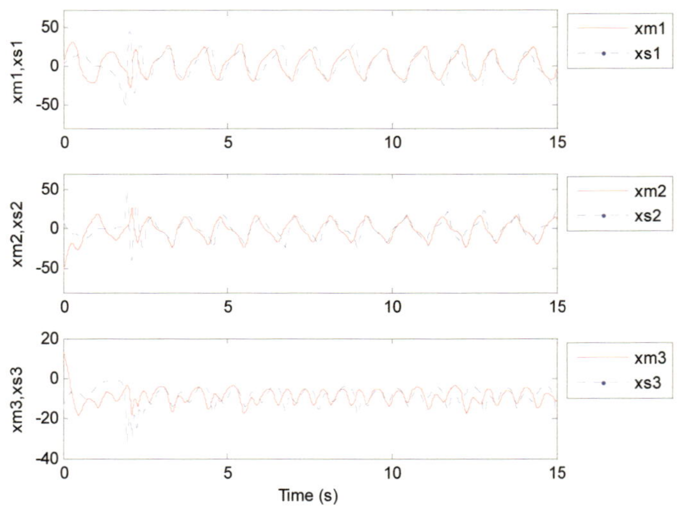

Fig. 11. Error dynamics between the master Chen-Lee system
and its corresponding slave system before their hybrid synchronization

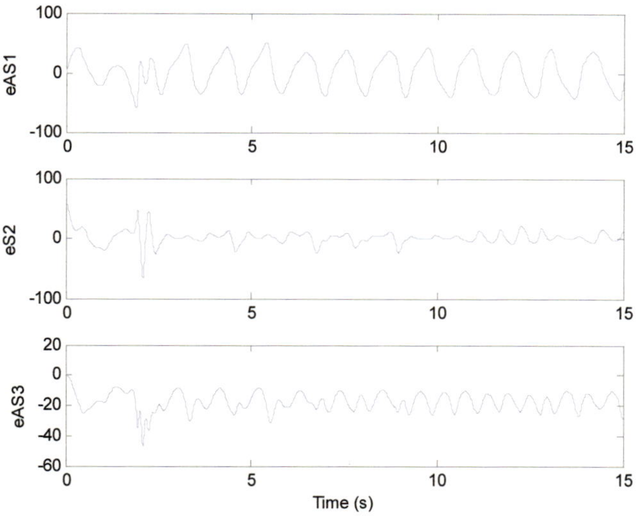

Fig. 12. Evolutions of the hybrid synchronization errors versus time when the proposed controller is turned off

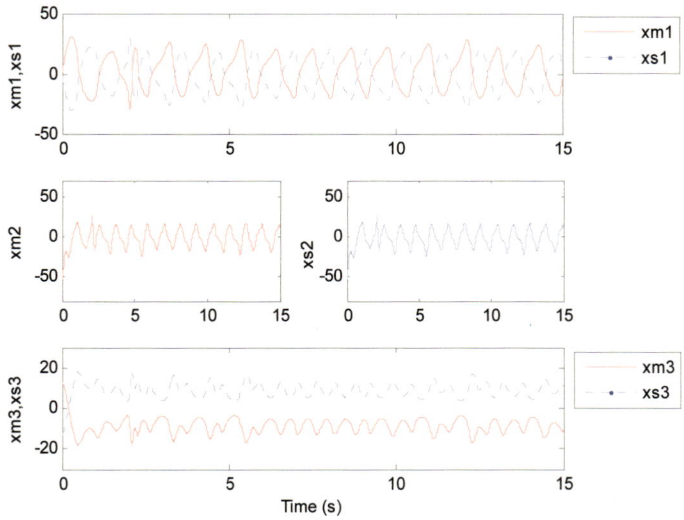

Fig. 13. Hybrid synchronization of the master-slave Chen–lee chaotic system

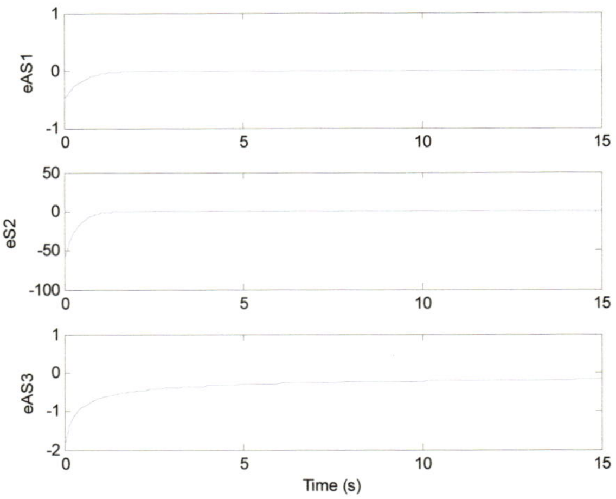

Fig. 14. Exponential convergence of the error dynamics

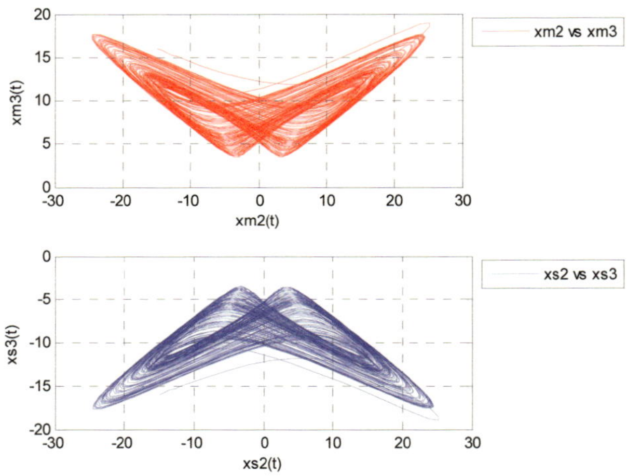

Fig. 15. 2-D projection of the hybrid synchronized attractors associated to the Chen-Lee chaotic system

6. Conclusion

Appropriate feedback controllers are designed, in this chapter, for the chosen slave system states to be synchronized, anti-synchronized as well as synchronized in a hybrid manner with the target master system states. It is shown that by applying a proposed control scheme, the variance of both synchronization and anti-synchronization errors can converge to zero. The synchronisation of two identical Chen chaotic systems, the anti-synchronization of two identical Lee chaotic systems and, finally, the coexistence of both synchronization and anti-synchronization for two identical Chen-Lee chaotic systems, considered as a coupled master-slave systems, are guaranteed by using the practical stability criterion of Borne and Gentina, associated to the specific matrix description, namely the arrow form matrix.

7. References

Bai, E.W. & lonngsen, K.E. (1997). Synchronization of two Lorenz systems using active control. *Chaos, Solitons and Fractals,* 8, 51–58, 0960-0779

Benrejeb, M. (1980). Sur l'analyse et la synthèse de processus complexes hiérarchisés. Application aux systèmes singulièrement perturbés. *Thèse de Doctorat ès Sciences Physiques,* Université des Sciences et Techniques de Lille, France

Benrejeb, M. (2010). Stability study of two level hierarchical nonlinear systems. *Plenary lecture, 12th International Federation of Automatic Control Large Scale Systems Symposium: Theory and Applications,* IFAC - LSS 2010, Lille, July 2010, France

Benrejeb, M. & Hammami, S. (2008). New approach of stabilization of nonlinear continuous monovariable processes characterized by an arrow form matrix. *1st International Conference Systems ENgineering Design and Applications,* SENDA 2008, Monastir, October 2008, Tunisia

Borne, P. & Benrejeb, M. (2008). On the representation and the stability study of large scale systems. *International Journal of Computers Communications and Control,* 3, 55–66, 1841-9836

Borne, P.; Vanheeghe, P. & Dufols, E. (2007). *Automatisation des processus dans l'espace d'état,* Editions Technip, 9782710808794, Paris

Fallahi, K.; Raoufi, R. & Khoshbin, H. (2008). An application of Chen system for secure chaotic communication based on extended Kalman filter and multi-shift cipher algorithm. *Communications in Nonlinear Science and Numerical Simulation,* 763–81, 1007-5704

Hammami, S. (2009). Sur la stabilisation de systèmes dynamiques continus non linéaires exploitant les matrices de formes en flèche. Application à la synchronisation de systèmes chaotiques. *Thèse de Doctorat,* École Nationale d'Ingénieurs de Tunis, Tunisia

Hammami, S.; Benrejeb, M. & Borne, P. (2010a). On nonlinear continuous systems stabilization using arrow form matrices. *International Review of Automatic Control,* 3, 106–114, 1974-6067

Hammami, S.; Ben saad, K. & Benrejeb, M. (2009). On the synchronization of identical and non-dentical 4-D chaotic systems using arrow form matrix. *Chaos, Solitons and Fractals,* 42, 101–112, 0960-0779

Hammami, S.; Benrejeb, M.; Feki, M. & Borne, P. (2010b). Feedback control design for Rössler and Chen chaotic systems anti-synchronization. *Phys. Lett. A,* 374, 2835–2840, 0375-9601

Juhn, H.C.; Hsien, K.C. & Yu, K.L. (2009). Synchronization and anti-synchronization coexist in Chen–Lee chaotic systems. *Chaos, Solitons and Fractals,* 39, 707–716, 0960-0779

Kapitanialc, T. (2000). *Chaos for Engineers: Theory, Applications and Control,* Second revised Springer edition, 3540665749, Berlin

Li, G.H. (2005). Synchronization and anti-synchronization of Colpitts oscillators using active control. *Chaos, Solitons and Fractals,* 26, 87–93, 0960-0779

Michael, G.R.; Arkady, S.P. & Jürgen, K. (1996). Phase synchronization of chaotic oscillators. *Phys. Rev. Lett.,* 76, 1804–1807, 0031-9007

Pecora, L.M. & Carroll, T.L. (1990). Synchronization in chaotic systems. *Phys. Rev. Lett.,* 64, 821-824, 0031-9007

Taherion, I.S. & Lai, Y.C. (1999). Observability of lag synchronization of coupled chaotic oscillators. *Phys. Rev. E,* 59, 6247–6250, 1539-3755

Tam, L.M. & Si Tou, W.M. (2008). Parametric study of the fractional order Chen–Lee System. *Chaos Solitons and Fractals,* 37, 817–826, 0960-0779

Wu, C.W. & Chua, L.O. (1993). A simple way to synchronize chaotic systems with applications to secure communication systems. *International Journal of Bifurcation and Chaos,* 3, 1619–1627, 1793-6551

Yang, S.S. & Duan, K. (1998). Generalized synchronization in chaotic systems. *Chaos, Solitons and Fractals,* 10, 1703–1707, 0960-0779

Yassen, M.T. (2005). Chaotic synchronization between two different chaotic systems using active control. *Chaos, Solitons and Fractals,* 131–140, 0960-0779

Zhang, Y. & Sun, J. (2004). Chaotic synchronization and anti-synchronization based on suitable separation. *Phys. Lett. A,* 330, 442–447, 0375-9601

Part 4

Applications

10

Design and Applications of Continuous-Time Chaos Generators

Carlos Sánchez-López[1], Jesus Manuel Muñoz-Pacheco[2], Victor Hugo Carbajal-Gómez[3], Rodolfo Trejo-Guerra[4], Cristopher Ramírez-Soto[5], Oscar S. Echeverria-Solis[6] and Esteban Tlelo-Cuautle[7]

[1]*UAT, CSIC and University of Sevilla*
[2]*Universidad Politécnica de Puebla*
[3]*INAOE*
[1,2,3,4,5,6,7]*México*
[1]*Spain*

1. Introduction

Chaos systems can be classified as one type of complex dynamical systems that possess special features such as being extremely sensitive to tiny variations of initial conditions. In general, for deterministic chaos to exists, a dynamical system must have a dense set of periodic orbits, it must be transitive and it has to be sensitive to initial conditions (Strogatz, 2001). Chaos systems have bounded trajectories in the phase space, and they have at least one positive maximum Lyapunov exponent (Dieci, 2002; Lu et al., 2005; Muñoz-Pacheco & Tlelo-Cuautle, 2010; Ramasubramanian & Sriram, 2000).

Nowadays, several chaos generators have been implemented with electronic devices and circuits in order to have a major impact on many novel applications, as the ones reported in (Cruz-Hernández et al., 2005; Ergun & Ozoguz, 2010; Gámez-Guzmán et al., 2008; Lin & Wang, 2010; Strogatz, 2001; Trejo-Guerra et al., 2009). Furthermore, this chapter is mainly devoted to highlight the design automation of continuous-time multi-scroll chaos generators, their implementations by using behavioral models of commercially available electronic devices, their experimental realizations and applications to secure communications. A review of the double-scroll Chua's circuit is also presented along with the generation of hyperchaos by Coupling Two Chua's circuits. Basically, we present the generation of multi-scroll attractors by using saturated nonlinear function series. We show their implementation by using traditional operational amplifiers (opamps) and current-feedback operational amplifiers (CFOAs) (Senani & Gupta, 1998). Besides, we summarize some performances of multi-scroll chaos generators by using opamps (Muñoz-Pacheco & Tlelo-Cuautle, 2010), CFOAs (Trejo-Guerra, Sánchez-López, Tlelo-Cuautle, Cruz-Hernández & Muñoz-Pacheco, 2010), current conveyors (CCs) (Sánchez-López et al., 2010) and unity-gain cells (UGCs) (Sánchez-López et al., 2008). However, not only the CC and the UGC can be taken from the commercially available CFOA AD844, but also they can be designed with standar integrated complementary metal-oxide-semiconductor (CMOS) technology (Trejo-Guerra, Tlelo-Cuautle, Muñoz-Pacheco, Cruz-Hernández & Sánchez-López, 2010).

The usefulness of the chaos generators is highlighted through the physical realization of a secure communication system by applying Hamiltonian forms and observer approach (Cruz-Hernández et al., 2005). This chapter finishes by listing several trends on the implementation of chaos generators by using integrated CMOS technology, which may open new lines for research covering the behavioral modeling, synthesis, design and simulation of integrated chaotic oscillators.

1.1 Description of a chaos system

In order to make any quantitative progress in understanding a system, a mathematical model is required. The model may be formulated in many ways, but their essential feature allows us to predict the behavior of the system, sometimes by given its initial conditions and a knowledge of the external forces which affect it. In electronics, the mathematical description for a dynamical system, most naturally adopted for behavioral modeling, is done by using the so-called state-space representation, which basically consists of a set of differential equations describing the evolution of the variables whose values at any given instant determine the current state of the system. These are known as the state variables and their values at any particular time are supposed to contain sufficient information for the future evolution of the system to be predicted, given that the external influences (or input variables) which act upon it are known.

In the state-space approach, the differential equations are of first order in the time-derivative, so that the initial values of the variables will suffice to determine the solution. In general, the state-space description is given in the form:

$$\begin{aligned} \dot{\mathbf{x}} &= \mathbf{f}(\mathbf{x}, \mathbf{u}, t) \\ \mathbf{y} &= \mathbf{h}(\mathbf{x}, \mathbf{u}, t) \end{aligned} \tag{1}$$

where the dot denotes differentiation with respect to time (t) and the functions **f** and **h** are in general nonlinear. In (1), the variety of possible nonlinearities is infinite, but it may nevertheless be worthwhile to classify them into some general categories. For example: There are simple analytic functions such as powers, sinusoids and exponentials of a single variable, or products of different variables. A significant feature of these functions is that they are smooth enough to possess convergent Taylor expansions at all points and consequently can be linearized (Strogatz, 2001). A type of nonlinear function frequently used in system modeling is the piecewise-linear (PWL) approximation, which consists of a set of linear relations valid in different regions (Elhadj & Sprott, 2010; Lin & Wang, 2010; Lü et al., 2004; Muñoz-Pacheco & Tlelo-Cuautle, 2009; Sánchez-López et al., 2010; Suykens et al., 1997; Trejo-Guerra, Sánchez-López, Tlelo-Cuautle, Cruz-Hernández & Muñoz-Pacheco, 2010; Yalçin et al., 2002). The use of PWL approximations have the advantage that the dynamical equations become linear or linearized in any particular region, and hence the solutions for different regions can be joined together at the boundaries.

When applying PWL approximation to a system described by (1), the resulting linearized system has finite dimensional state-space representation, as a result the equations describing a linear behavioral model become:

$$\begin{aligned} \dot{\mathbf{x}} &= \mathbf{A}\mathbf{x} + \mathbf{B}\mathbf{u} \\ \mathbf{y} &= \mathbf{C}\mathbf{x} + \mathbf{D}\mathbf{u} \end{aligned} \tag{2}$$

where **A, B, C,** and **D** are matrices (possibly time-dependent) of appropriate dimensions. The great advantage of linearity is that, even in the time dependent case, a formal solution can

immediately be constructed, which is moreover applicable for all initial conditions and all input functions.
An important point which must be kept in mind for a nonlinear dynamical system, is that the stability properties are essentially more complicated than in the linear case. For instance, when nonlinearities are present, several features can appear such as limit cycles or the phenomenon known as chaos (Chakraborty & Dana, 2010; Chua, 1975; Cook, 1994; Muñoz-Pacheco & Tlelo-Cuautle, 2010; Ott, 1994; Strogatz, 2001).

1.2 Autonomous systems

Although the equations describing a behavioral dynamical model will in general depend on the time, either explicitly or through the input function, or both, a large part of nonlinear system theory is concerned with cases where there is no time dependence at all (Ott, 1994). Such systems are said to be autonomous, and they arise quite naturally in practice when, for example, the input vector is held fixed. In any such case, the differential equation for the state vector become:

$$\dot{\mathbf{x}} = \mathbf{f}(\mathbf{x}, \hat{\mathbf{u}}) \tag{3}$$

where $\hat{\mathbf{u}}$ is a constant vector. Thus, the equilibrium points in the state-space are determined by $\mathbf{f}(\mathbf{x}, \hat{\mathbf{u}}) = 0$. Assuming that $\mathbf{f}(\mathbf{x}, \hat{\mathbf{u}})$ satisfies Lipschitz condition (Chua, 1975), the differential equation for $x(t)$ will have a unique solution, for any given initial state $x(0)$. The path traced out in the state-space by $x(t)$ is called a trajectory of the system and because of the uniqueness property, there will be one and only one trajectory passing through any given point. If it is suppressed the dependence on $\hat{\mathbf{u}}$, the state-space differential equations for an autonomous system can be written simply as:

$$\dot{\mathbf{x}} = \mathbf{f}(\mathbf{x}) \tag{4}$$

and the set of all trajectories of this equation provides a complete geometrical representation of the dynamical behavior of the system, under the specified conditions. As a result, it is possible to give an essentially complete classification of behavior in the phase plane, though not in higher-dimensional state-spaces. In general, the equations describing a nonlinear system cannot be solved analytically, so that, in order to construct the trajectories accurately, it is necessary to use numerical methods.

1.3 Strange attractors and chaos

Although singular points and closed curves constitute the only asymptotic terms of bounded trajectories for autonomous systems in the phase plane, this is no longer true in spaces of higher dimension (Cook, 1994). In general, the term for a limit set where all trajectories in its vicinity approach it as $t \to \infty$; is an attractor, since it asymptotically attracts nearby trajectories to itself. For second-order dynamical systems, the only types of limit set normally encountered are singular points and limit cycles. Consequently, a continuous-time autonomous system requires more than two dimensions to exhibit chaos (Cook, 1994; Ott, 1994; Strogatz, 2001). More complicated still are the so-called strange limit sets (Strogatz, 2001). They may or may not be asymptotically attractive to neighboring trajectories; if so, they are known as strange attractors, though even then, the trajectories they contain may be locally divergent from each other, within the attracting set. Such structures are associated with the quasi-random behavior of solutions called chaos (Cook, 1994).

2. Chua's circuit and Hyperchaos

Over the last two decades, theoretical design and circuit implementation of various chaos generators have been a focal subject of increasing interest due to their promising applications in various real-world chaos-based technologies and information systems (Cook, 1994; Cruz-Hernández et al., 2005; Ergun & Ozoguz, 2010; Gámez-Guzmán et al., 2008; Lin & Wang, 2010; Ott, 1994; Strogatz, 2001; Trejo-Guerra et al., 2009).
In electronics, among the currently available chaotic oscillators, Chua's circuit has been the most used one (Chakraborty & Dana, 2010; Elhadj & Sprott, 2010; Sánchez-López et al., 2008; Senani & Gupta, 1998; Suykens et al., 1997; Trejo-Guerra et al., 2009), because it can be easily built, simulated, and tractable mathematically. It consists of five circuit elements: one linear resistor, one inductor, two capacitors, and one nonlinear resistor known as Chua's diode (Tlelo-Cuautle et al., 2006).

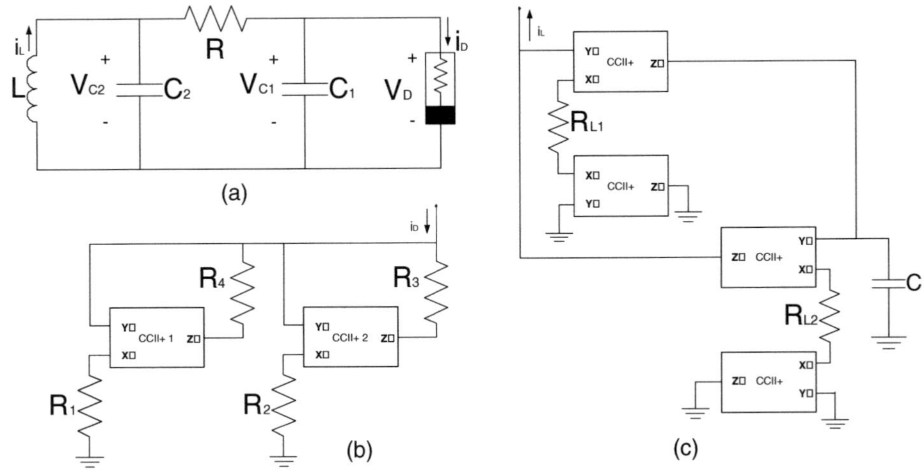

Fig. 1. (a) Chua's circuit, (b) Chua's diode and (c) Simulated inductance using CCII+s.

From the design point of view, there are many ways to realize the inductor and Chua's diode by using electronic devices, e.g. by using current-feedback operational amplifiers (CFOAs) (Senani & Gupta, 1998), positive-type second generation current conveyors (CCII+), and unity-gain cells (UGCs) (Sánchez-López et al., 2008). All these realizations can be made by using the commercially available CFOA AD844 from analog devices. In this subsection we show the realization using CCII+s, which is embedded into the CFOA AD844. It is worthy to mention that current conveyors present nonideal characteristics (Sánchez-López et al., 2010), and since its introduction in 1970 (Sedra & Smith, 1970), recently there exists other topologies (Tlelo-Cuautle & C. Sánchez-López, 2010). Among them, the CCII+ is a very useful building block (Trejo-Guerra et al., 2009).
In Chua's circuit the inductor can be implemented from the gyrator description (Sánchez-Sinencio & Silva-Martínez, 2000), and it can be designed using CCII+s. Chua's diode can also be implemented by using CCII+s as shown in Fig. 1, each CCII+ in Fig. 1(b) is biased with different voltage bias levels: CCII+1 is biased with +5V and CCII+2 with +12V. The values of the resistors are: R_1=6.76$k\Omega$, R_2=3.91$k\Omega$, R_3=470Ω, and R_4=10$k\Omega$. The CCII+ based simulated inductance is shown in Fig. 1(c), where for C=4.7nF, then $R_{L1}=R_{L2}$=2.36$k\Omega$.
By setting C_1=4.7nF and C_2=47nF in Chua's circuit, and by replacing Chua's diode and the inductor with the proposed circuits shown in Fig. 1(b) and Fig. 1(c), respectively, the sequence

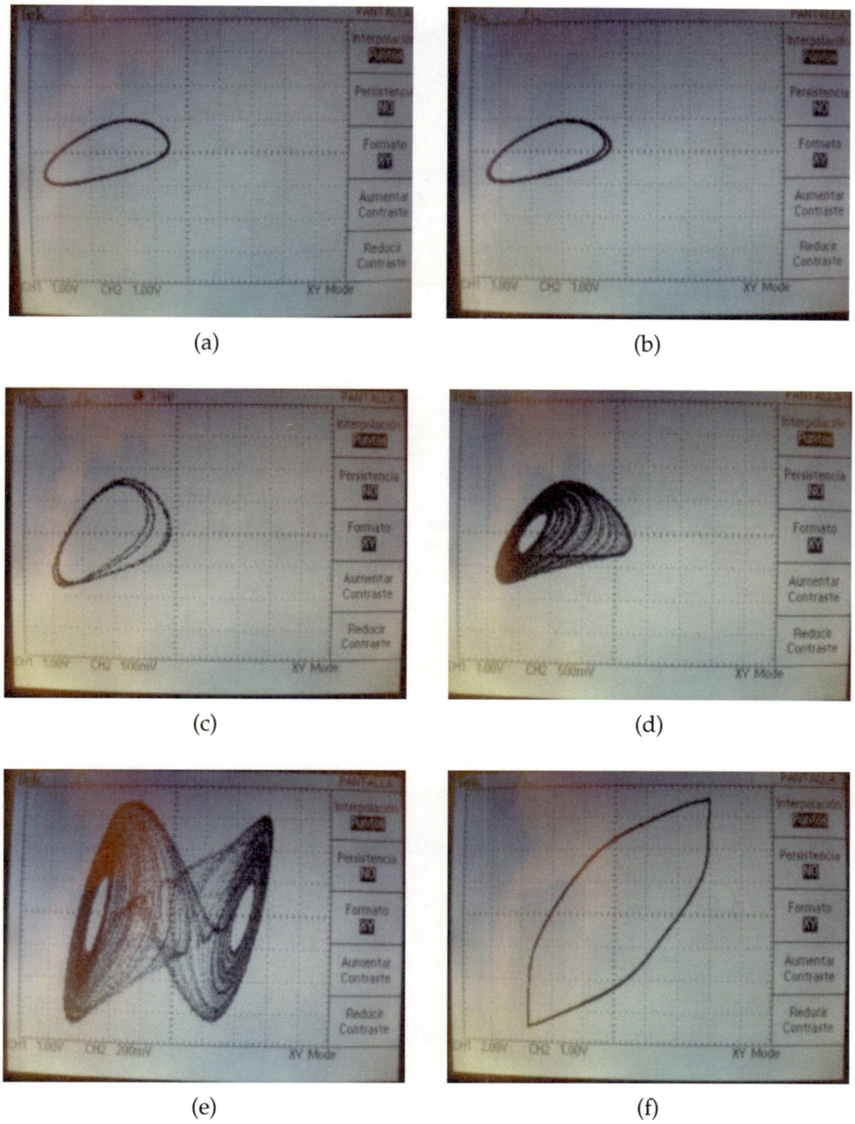

Fig. 2. Sequence of chaotic behaviors from the experimental realization of Chua's circuit

of chaotic behaviors (V_{C1} vs. V_{C2}) are shown in Fig. 2. When R=3490Ω one cycle is observed, with R=3466Ω two cycles, with R=3338Ω four cycles, with R=3261Ω one scroll and with R=2771Ω the double scroll is observed. Finally, the limit cycle is appreciated when R=2712Ω.

2.1 Hyperchaos

Hyperchaos can be generated by coupling two Chua's circuits as shown in Fig. 3. The Chua's circuit in the top of Fig. 3 is composed of RM, C1M, C2M, Chua's diode is implemented with the CCII+s 1DM and 2DM (including R1M to R4M), and the simulated inductance is implemented by C3M and two transconductors realized with two CCII+s (R5M connected between the CCII+s 3LM and 4LM, and R6M connected between the CCII+s 5LM and 6LM).

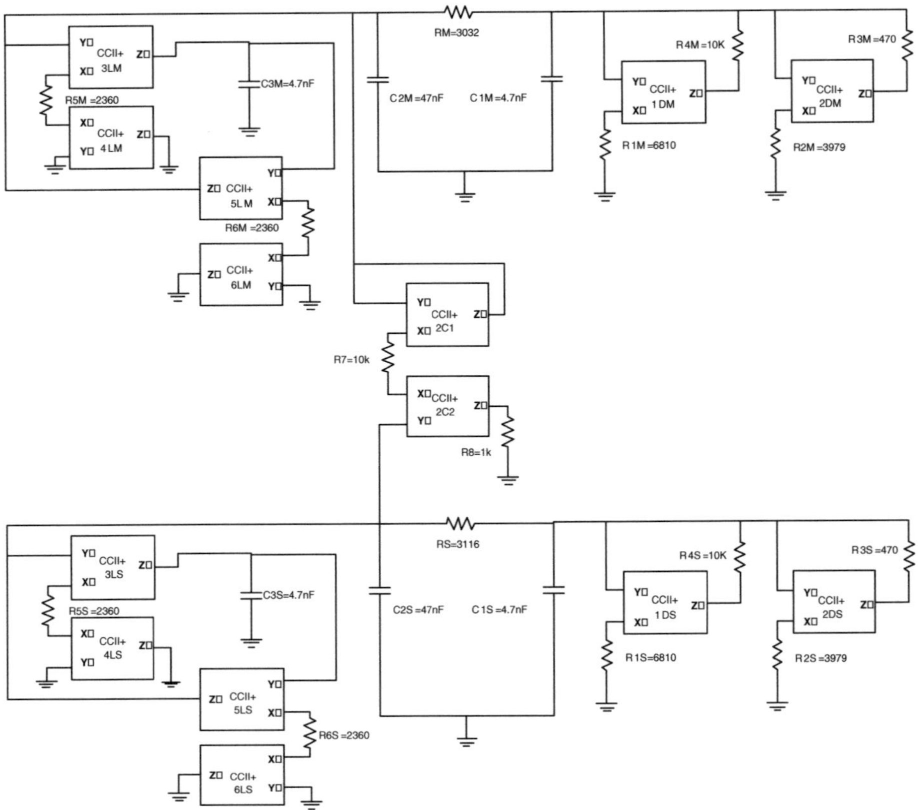

Fig. 3. Coupling two CCII+ based Chua's circuits

The second Chua's circuit (bottom of Fig. 3), is composed of RS, C1S, C2S, Chua's diode is implemented with the CCII+s 1DS and 2DS (including R1S to R4S), and the simulated inductance is implemented by C3S and two transconductors realized with two CCII+s (R5S connected between the CCII+s 3LS and 4LS, and R6S connected between the CCII+s 5LS and 6LS). Finally, the coupling is performed through R7 connected between two CCII+s (2C1 and 2C2). As one sees, RM=3032Ω in the first Chua's circuit has a different value compared to RS=3116Ω in the second Chua's circuit, the rest of the elements in both Chua's circuits have the same value. This difference is attributed to the coupling circuit, in which R7 establishes the gain and it can be varied.

The hyperchaotic behaviors can be appreciated by varying the gain, i.e. R7. In Fig. 4 are shown the hyperchatic behaviors by diminishing R7 without persistence, while in Fig. 5 are shown the same hyperchaotic behaviors provided in Fig. 4 but with persistence. It can be appreciated that hyperchaos is disappearing when R7 is diminished. However, we have a wide range of values for R7 to tune the hyperchaotic behavior for a specific application, e.g. secure communications.

3. Design automation of multi-scroll chaos generators

The design of multi-scroll chaotic attractors can be performed via PWL functions (Elhadj & Sprott, 2010; Lin & Wang, 2010; Lü et al., 2004; Muñoz-Pacheco & Tlelo-Cuautle, 2009; 2010;

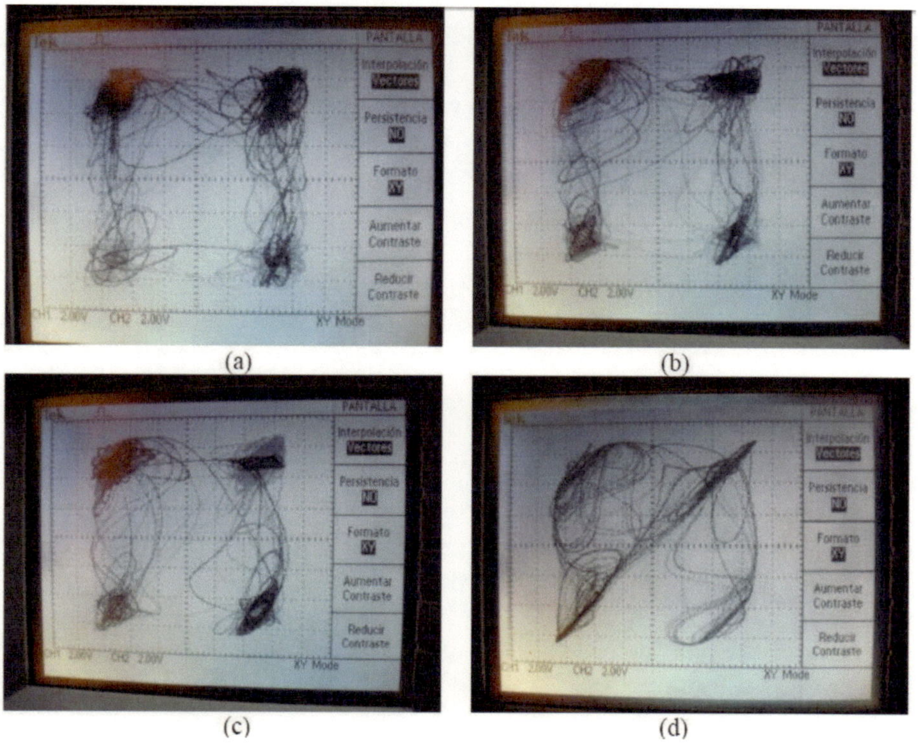

Fig. 4. Hyperchaos with: (a) R7=10kΩ, (b) R7=7kΩ, (c) R7=5kΩ, and (d) R7=500Ω without persistence.

Sánchez-López et al., 2010; Suykens et al., 1997; Trejo-Guerra, Sánchez-López, Tlelo-Cuautle, Cruz-Hernández & Muñoz-Pacheco, 2010; Trejo-Guerra, Tlelo-Cuautle, Jiménez-Fuentes & Sánchez-López, 2010; Yalçin et al., 2002). In the case of Chua's circuit based oscillators, the PWL function is designed by introducing additional breakpoints to Chua's diode (Trejo-Guerra, Sánchez-López, Tlelo-Cuautle, Cruz-Hernández & Muñoz-Pacheco, 2010), or by generalizing Chua's circuit as proposed in (Suykens et al., 1997; Yalcin et al., 2000).

When implementing multi-scroll chaos generators with electronic devices, it is necessary to remark that it is quite difficult to generate attractors with a large number of scrolls due to the limitation of the real dynamic range of the physical devices. Furthermore, among the basic circuits used to generate multi-scroll generators, the step circuit, hysteresis circuit and saturated circuit are the three most used ones. To generate multidimensional multi-scroll attractors, such as 1-D (Yalçin et al., 2002), 2-D (Muñoz-Pacheco & Tlelo-Cuautle, 2009), 3-D (Deng, 2007), and 4-D (Varrientos & Sanchez-Sinencio, 1998), the state equations of this family of systems depends on the number of nonlinear functions, for example: three nonlinear functions are needed to generate 3D-scrolls.

In (Lü et al., 2004) a saturated multi-scroll chaotic system based on saturated function series, is introduced. That system can produce three different types of attractors, as follows: 1-D saturated n-scroll chaotic attractors, 2-D saturated $n \times m$-grid scroll chaotic attractors and 3-D saturated $n \times m \times l$-grid scroll chaotic attractors, where n, m and l are integers and can have the same values. Since this multi-scroll system can be designed by using PWL functions, it is

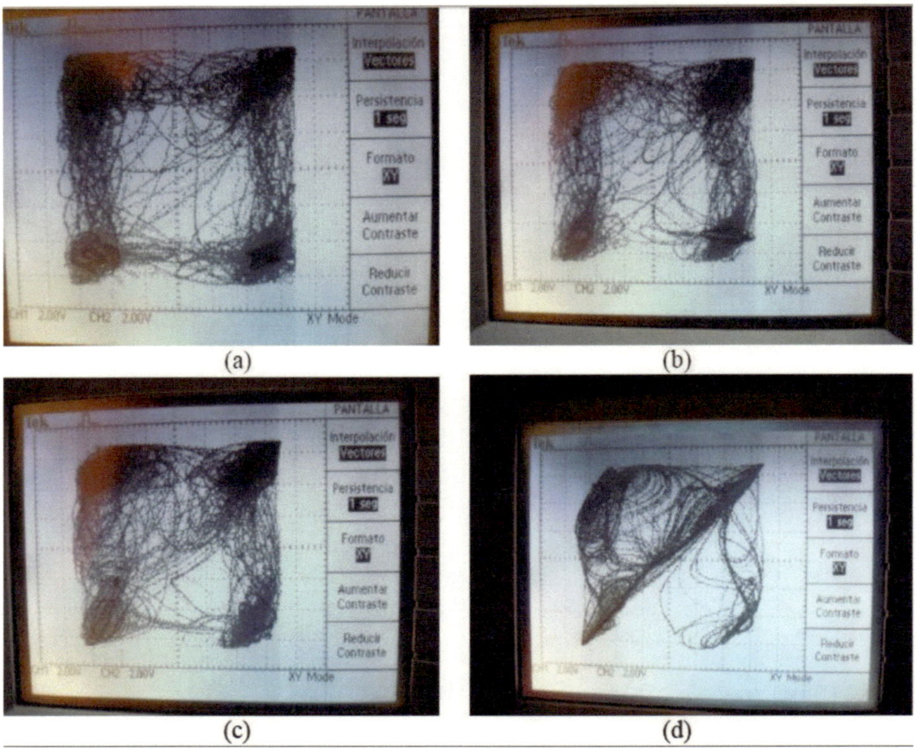

Fig. 5. Hyperchaos with: (a) R7=10kΩ, (b) R7=7kΩ, (c) R7=5kΩ, and (d) R7=500Ω with persistence.

a good chaos system suitable for the development of a systematic design automation process by applying behavioral modeling (Muñoz-Pacheco & Tlelo-Cuautle, 2010).

3.1 Design automation by behavioral modeling

Behavioral modeling can be a possible solution for successful development of analog electronic design automation (EDA) tools, because various types of systems that can be represented by means of an abstract model. The abstraction levels are an indication of the degree of detail specified about how the function is to be implemented. Therefore, behavioral models try to capture as much circuit functionality as possible with far less implementation details than the device-level description of the circuit (Kundert, 2004). However, it is difficult to make a strict distinction between different abstraction levels for analog systems, in contrast to common practice in digital synthesis methodologies (Castro-López et al., 2006). Instead, a division should be made between a description level and an abstraction level. A description level is a pair of two sets: a set of elementary elements and a set of interconnection types. The abstraction level of a description is the degree to which information about non-ideal effects or structure is neglected compared to the dominant behavior of the entire system.

In this manner, whereas a description level indicates how the analog system is represented; an abstraction level deals with the relation between the model of the system and its real behavior. Although it can be clear to consider the functional level at a high abstraction level and the physical level at a low abstraction level, it is not straightforward to compare the abstraction levels of different description levels. Besides, an electronic system can be designed by converting the functional specification at the highest abstraction level to a physical realization at the lowest abstraction level via operations between description and abstraction levels. Four fundamental types of such operations are distinguished: refinement, simplification, translation and transformation. Simplification is the reverse operation of refinement.

Model generation consists in applying multiple simplification operations to a system representation to obtain a model with less accuracy, but easier to interpret or to simulate. From this point of view, the design automation of an electronic system must indicate the kind and order of the operations to be applied during the design process and must include an appropriate modeling strategy to determine how a system is represented. In fact, the selection of a good modeling strategy makes easier to execute the design process. In (Muñoz-Pacheco & Tlelo-Cuautle, 2010) it is presented the analog design automation process of chaos systems which are modeled from the highest level of abstraction by applying state variables approach and PWL approximations.

For the design of autonomous chaos systems, their state variables approach are defined by (4), where the function **f** is nonlinear. However, the PWL approximation can be used to describe this nonlinear function, which consists of a set of linear relations valid in different regions. Such functions are not analytic at all points, since they contain discontinuities of value or gradient, but they have the advantage that the dynamical equations become linear (and hence soluble) in any particular region, and the solutions for different regions can then be joined together at the boundaries. Furthermore, (4) can be described by the linear state-space representation given in (2). The great advantage of linearity is that, even in the time dependent case, a formal solution can immediately be constructed, which is moreover applicable for all initial conditions and all input functions. A repertoire of the design automation of 1-D, 2-D and 3-D multi-scroll chaos generators by behavioral modeling and realized by using traditional operational amplifiers (opamps), is presented in Muñoz-Pacheco & Tlelo-Cuautle (2010). The chaos generators are based on saturated nonlinear function (SNLF) series, and realized with opamps working in the saturation regions, so that they can be modeled by PWL functions.

In Fig. 6 is shown a SNLF with 5 and 7 segments to generate 3 and 4 multi-scrolls, respectively. In (5) is described the PWL approximation called series of a SNLF, where $k \geq 2$ is the slope of the SNLF and multiplier factor to saturated plateaus, $plateau = \pm nk$, with n=integer odd to even-scrolls and n=integer even to odd-scrolls. h=saturated delay of the center of the slopes in Fig. 6, and must agree with $h_i = \pm mk$, where $i = 1, \ldots, [(scrolls - 2)/2]$ and $m = 2, 4, \ldots, (scrolls - 2)$ to even-scrolls; and $i = 1, \ldots, [(scrolls - 1)/2]$ and $m = 1, 3, \ldots, (scrolls - 2)$ to odd-scrolls; p and q are positive integers.

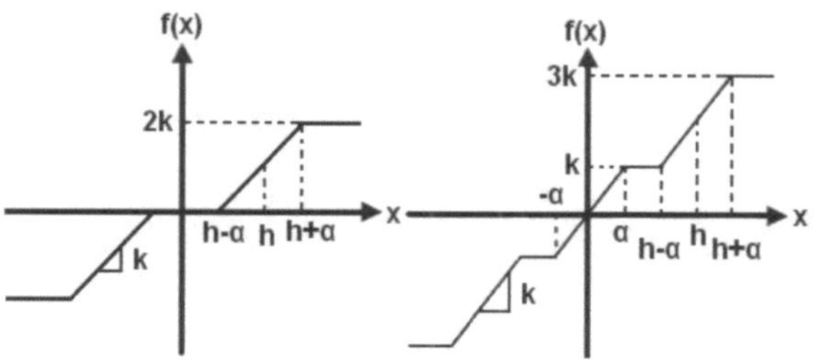

Fig. 6. PWL description of a SNLF with 5 and 7 segments

$$f(x;k,h,p,q) = \sum_{i=-p}^{q} f_i(x;h,k) \tag{5}$$

To generate multi-scrolls attractors a controller is added as shown in (6), where $f(x;k,h,p,q)$ is defined by (7), and a,b,c,d are positive constants and must be $0 < a,b,c,d < 1$ to accomplish chaos conditions (Lü et al., 2004).

$$\begin{aligned} \dot{x} &= y \\ \dot{y} &= z \\ \dot{z} &= -ax - by - cz - df(x;k,h,p,q) \end{aligned} \tag{6}$$

$$f(x;k,h,p,q) = \begin{cases} (2q+1)k & \text{if } x > qh+1 \\ k(x-ih)+2ik & \text{if } \mid x-ih \mid \leq 1 \\ & -p \leq i \leq q \\ (2i+1)k & \text{if } ih+1 < x < (i+1)h-1 \\ & -p \leq i \leq q-1 \\ -(2p+1)k & \text{if } x < -ph-1 \end{cases} \tag{7}$$

The simulation of multi-scrolls attractors modeled by (6) and (7), is executed using (Tlelo-Cuautle & Munoz-Pacheco, 2007). 6-scrolls attractors are generated with a=b=c=d=0.7, k=10, h=20, p=q=2, as shown in Fig. 7. As one sees, Fig. 7a shows that the dynamic ranges (DRs) are very large. Since real electronic devices cannot handle these DRs, (7) cannot be synthesized and it cannot have small DRs because $k \geq 2$ (Lü et al., 2004). Consequently, $h = 2k$ or $h = k$ for even or odd scrolls, respectively, to avoid superimposing of the slopes because the plateaus can disappear. This process has been automated in (Muñoz-Pacheco & Tlelo-Cuautle, 2010; Sánchez-López et al., 2010)

Henceforth, α is restricted to 1, so that to implement multi-scrolls attractors using practical opamps one needs to scale the DRs from the SNLF (Lü et al., 2004). Then, the SNLF series is redefined by (8), where α allows that $k < 1$ because the chaos-condition now applies on the new slope $s = \frac{k}{\alpha}$. In this manner, k and α can be selected to permit $k < 1$, so that the DRs in (7) can be scaled. As a result, 6-scrolls attractors are generated with $a = b = c = d = 0.7, k = 1, \alpha = 6.4e^{-3}, s = 156.25, h = 2, p = q = 2$, as shown in Fig. 7b. Now, the DRs of the attractors are within the DRs of the real behavior of the opamps. Besides, it is possible to have small DRs depending on the values of k and α.

$$f(x;k,h,p,q) = \begin{cases} (2q+1)k & \text{if } x > qh+\alpha \\ \frac{k}{\alpha}(x-ih)+2ik & \text{if } \mid x-ih \mid \leq \alpha \\ & -p \leq i \leq q \\ (2i+1)k & \text{if } ih+\alpha < x < (i+1)h-\alpha \\ & -p \leq i \leq q-1 \\ -(2p+1)k & \text{if } x < -ph-\alpha \end{cases} \tag{8}$$

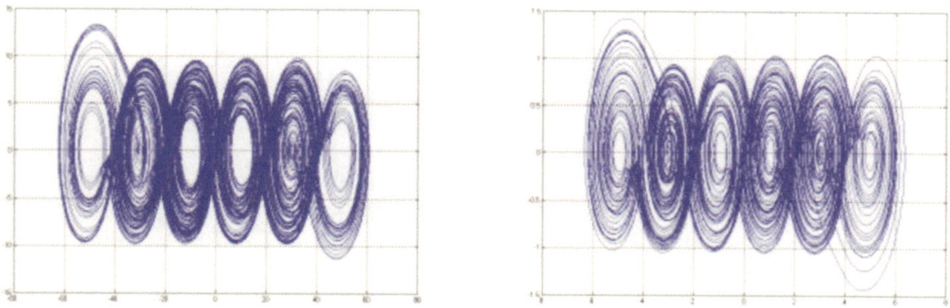

(a) (b)

Fig. 7. 6-scrolls attractors: (a) without DR scaling and (b) with DR scaling

3.2 Circuit realization

The dynamical system in (6) has the block diagram representation shown in Fig. 8, which is realized with 3 integrators and an adder. Each block can be realized with different kinds of active devices, namely: OpAmps, CFOAs, current conveyors (CC), unity-gain-cells (UGCs), and so on. The realization of the dynamical system in (6) using opamps is shown in Fig. 9 and by using CFOAs in Fig. 10.

By applying Kirchhoff's current-law in Fig. 10 one obtains (9), where $SNLF = i(x)R_{ix}$. The parameters are determined by (10).

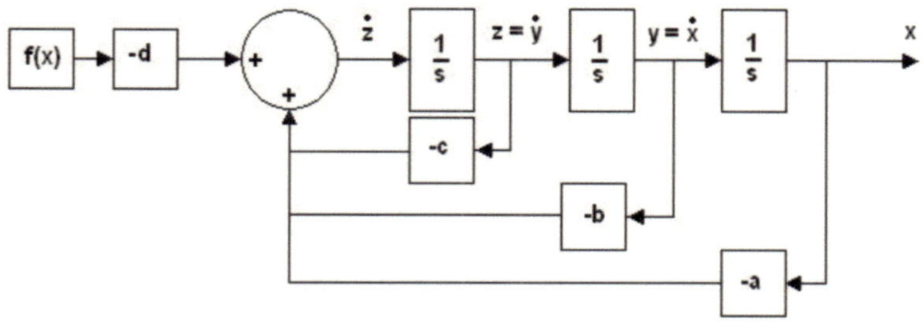

Fig. 8. Block diagram description of (6)

$$\begin{aligned} \frac{dx}{dt} &= \frac{y}{RC} \\ \frac{dy}{dt} &= \frac{z}{RC} \\ \frac{dz}{dt} &= -\frac{x}{R_x C} - \frac{y}{R_y C} - \frac{z}{R_{ix} C} + \frac{i(x)R_{ix}}{R_{ix} C} \end{aligned} \tag{9}$$

$$C = \frac{1}{0.7R_{ix}}, R_x = R_y = R_z = \frac{1}{0.7C}, R = \frac{1}{C} \tag{10}$$

The circuit realization of the SNLF in Fig. 9 and Fig. 10, can be implemented by using opamps and CFOAs, respectively working in the saturation region with shift bias-levels. For instance,

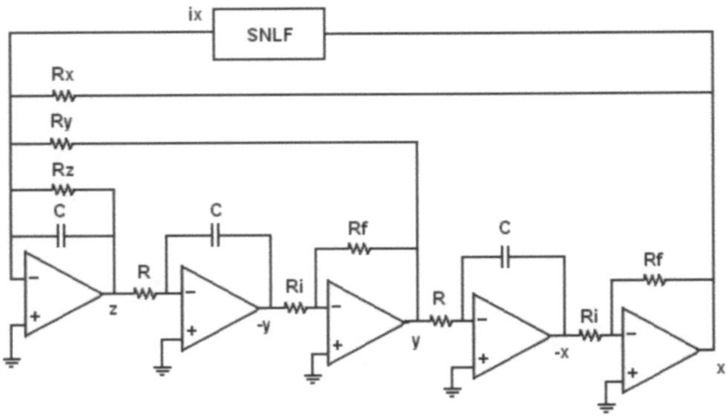

Fig. 9. OpAmp-based implementation of (6)

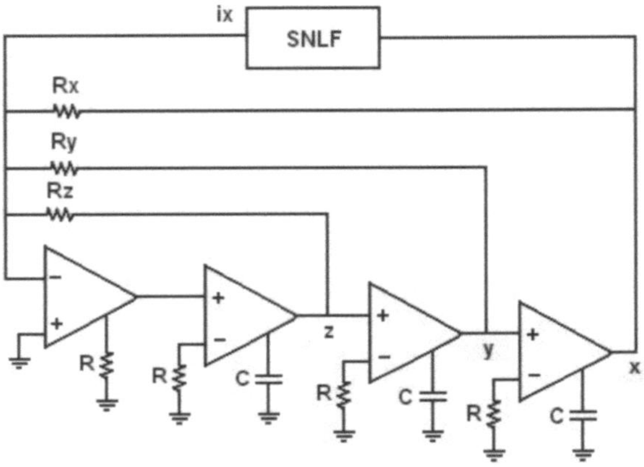

Fig. 10. CFOA-based implementation of (6)

the OpAmp and CFOA voltaje behaviors can be modeled by the opamp finite-gain model shown in Fig. 11 (Chen et al., 1995), so that a SNLF can be described by $V_o = \frac{A_v}{2}(\mid V_i + \frac{V_{sat}}{A_v} \mid - \mid V_i - \frac{V_{sat}}{A_v})$, and if a shift-voltage ($\pm E$) is added, as shown in Fig. 12, one gets the shifted-voltage SNLFs determined by (11) for positive and negative shifts, respectively. Now, $\alpha = V_{sat}/A_v$ are the breakpoints, $k = V_{sat}$ is the saturated plateau, and $s = V_{sat}/\alpha$ is the saturated slope. A resistor can be added to realize a current-to-voltage transformation, e.g. $i_o = V_o/R_c$.

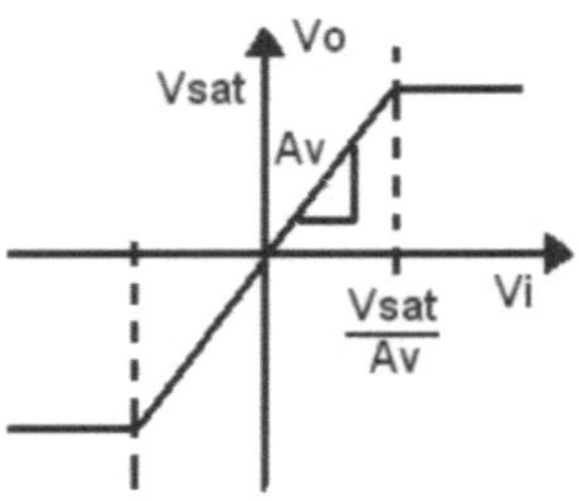

Fig. 11. OpAmp finite-gain model

To generate the SNLF (in Fig. 11), E takes different values in (11) to synthesize the required plateaus and slopes. The cell shown in Fig. 13a is used to realize voltage and current SNLFs from (11). The value of the plateaus k, in voltage and current modes, the breakpoints α, the slope and h are evaluated by (12) (Muñoz-Pacheco & Tlelo-Cuautle, 2008).

$$V_o = \frac{A_v}{2}(\mid V_i + \frac{V_{sat}}{A_v} - E \mid - \mid V_i - \frac{V_{sat}}{A_v} - E) \qquad V_o = \frac{A_v}{2}(\mid V_i + \frac{V_{sat}}{A_v} + E \mid - \mid V_i - \frac{V_{sat}}{A_v} + E) \tag{11}$$

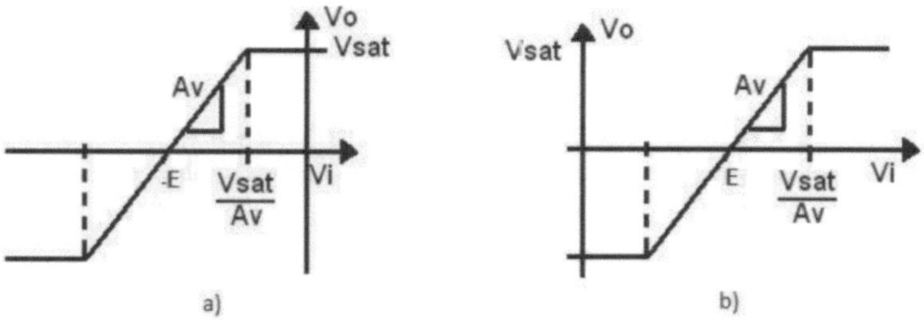

Fig. 12. SNLF shift-voltage (a) negative shift (b) positive shift

$$k = R_{ix} I_{sat}, \qquad I_{sat} = \frac{V_{sat}}{R_C}, \qquad \alpha = \frac{R_{iz} \mid V_{sat} \mid}{R_{fz}}, \qquad S = \frac{h}{\alpha}, \qquad h = \frac{E_i}{(1 + \frac{R_{iz}}{R_{fz}})} \tag{12}$$

For instance, the cell in Fig. 13 can realize the SNLF from (8), and the number of basic cells (BC) is determined by BC=(number of scrolls)-1, which are parallel-connected as shown in Fig. 14 (Muñoz-Pacheco & Tlelo-Cuautle, 2008).

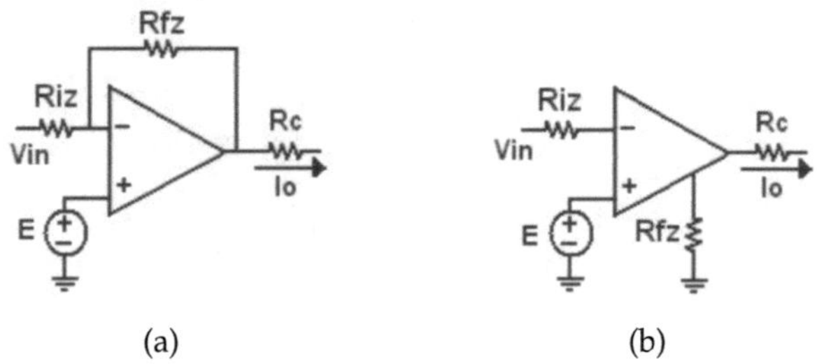

Fig. 13. Basic cell to generate SNLFs: (a) OpAmp implementation, (b) CFOA implementation

3.3 Multi-scroll attractors generation

The design automation of multi-scroll chaos generators for 1-3 dimensions can be found in (Muñoz-Pacheco & Tlelo-Cuautle, 2010). In this subsection we show the simulation using opamps. Experimental results using CFOAs and current conveyors can be found in (Trejo-Guerra, Sánchez-López, Tlelo-Cuautle, Cruz-Hernández & Muñoz-Pacheco, 2010) and (Sánchez-López et al., 2010), respectively.

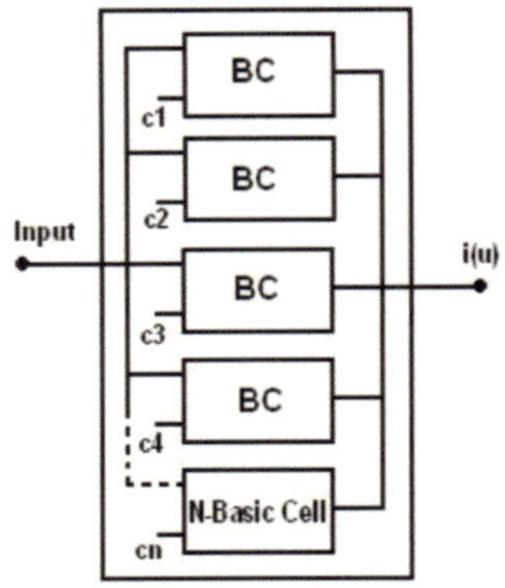

Fig. 14. Structure to synthesize SNLFs

By selecting funtional specifications: N=5-scrolls, F=10Khz and $EL = \pm 5V$, if $V_{sat} = \pm 6.4V$ (typical value for the commercially available OpAmp TL081 with $Vdd = \pm 8V$), the circuit synthesis result for 5 and 6- scrolls attractors are shown in Fig. 15 and Fig. 16. By setting $E_1 = \pm 1V, E_2 = \pm 3V, h_1 \cong 1, h_2 \cong 3$ to generate 5-scrolls; and $E_1 = \pm 2V, E_2 = \pm 4V, h_1 \cong 2, h_2 \cong 4$ to generate 6-scrolls; and $a = b = c = d = 0.7, k = 1, \alpha = 6.4e^{-3}, s = 156.25$, the circuit elements are: $R_{ix} = 10K\Omega, C = 2.2nf, R = 7K\Omega, R_x = R_y = R_z = 10K\Omega, R_f = 10K\Omega, R_i = 10K\Omega$ in (10) and $R_{ix} = 10K\Omega, R_c = 64K\Omega, R_{iz} = 1K\Omega, R_{fz} = 1M\Omega$ in (12).

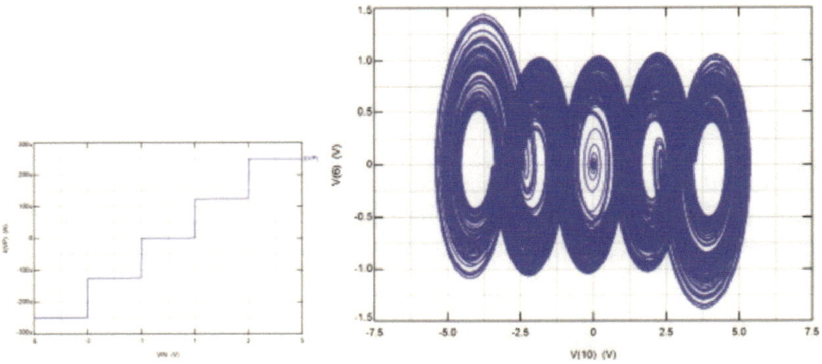

(a) SNLF (b) 5-scrolls attractor

Fig. 15. Generation of SNLF for 5-scrolls using opamps.

4. Realization of chaotic oscillators using current-feedback operational amplifiers

This section shows the simulation results for the SNLF based multi-scroll chaos generatos using CFOAs. Basically, from the results provided in the previos section, we can realize the circuit using CFOAs, instead of opamps. In this manner, by selecting funtional specifications: N=5-scrolls, F=10Khz and $EL = \pm 5V$, if $V_{sat} = \pm 6.4V$ (typical value for the coomercially available CFOA AD844 with $Vdd = \pm 10V$), the circuit simulation results for generating 5 and 6-scrolls attractors are shown in Fig. 17 and Fig. 18. Where $E_1 = \pm 1V, E_2 = \pm 3V, h_1 \cong 1, h_2 \cong 3$ to generate 5-scrolls; and $E_1 = \pm 2V, E_2 = \pm 4V, h_1 \cong 2, h_2 \cong 4$ to generate 6-scrolls; and $a = b = c = d = 0.7, k = 1, \alpha = 6.4e^{-3}, s = 156.25$, to calculate the circuit element values:

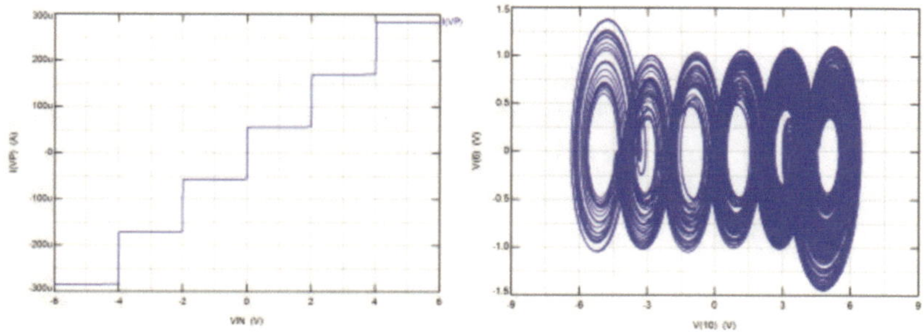

(a) SNLF (b) 6-scrolls attractor

Fig. 16. Generation of SNLF for 6-scrolls using opamps.

$R_{ix} = 10K\Omega, C = 2.2nf, R = 7K\Omega, R_x = R_y = R_z = 10K\Omega, R_f = 10K\Omega, R_i = 10K\Omega$ in (10), and $R_{ix} = 10K\Omega, R_c = 64K\Omega, R_{iz} = 1K\Omega, R_{fz} = 1M\Omega$ in (12).

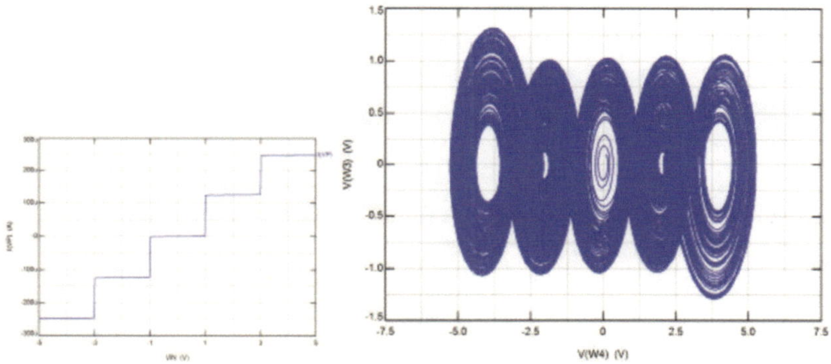

(a) SNLF (b) 5-scrolls attractor

Fig. 17. Generation of SNLF for 5-scrolls using CFOAs.

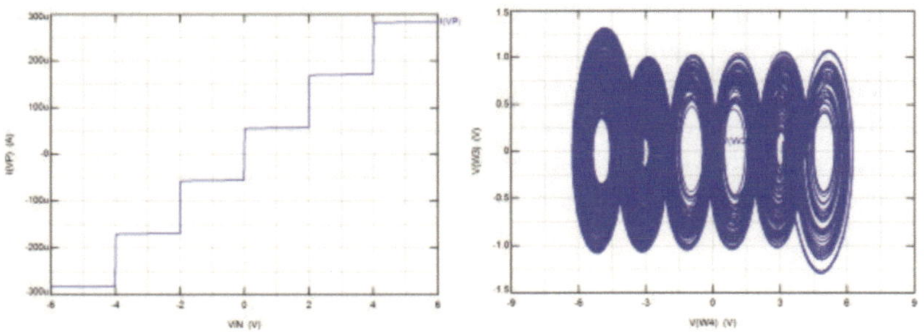

(a) SNLF (b) 6-scrolls attractor

Fig. 18. Generation of SNLF for 6-scrolls using CFOAs.

As one sees, the simulation results using CFOAs are quite similar to that using opamps. However, the electrical characteristics of the CFOA enhance the performance of the chaos generator, compared to opamp based circuit realizations. This advantage of the CFOA compared to the opamp is shown in the following section for the implementation of a secure communication system using multi-scroll chaos generators.

5. Synchronization of multi-scroll attractors

This section presents the synchronization using Hamiltonian forms and an observer approach (Sira-Ramírez & Cruz-Hernández, 2001). Let's consider the dynamical system described by the master circuit in (13). An slave system is a copy of the master and can be described by (14).

$$\dot{x} = F(x) \qquad \forall x \in \mathbb{R}^n \tag{13}$$

$$\dot{\xi} = F(\xi) \qquad \forall x \in \mathbb{R}^n \tag{14}$$

Definition: Two chaotic systems described by a set of states $x_1, x_2 \ldots x_n$ (13) and $\xi_1, \xi_2 \ldots \xi_n$ (14) will synchronize if the following limit fulfills (Shuh-Chuan et al., 2005; Sira-Ramírez & Cruz-Hernández, 2001):

$$\lim_{t \to \infty} \mid x(t) - \xi(t) \mid \equiv 0 \tag{15}$$

For any initial conditions $x(0) \neq \xi(0)$. Due to the real limitations of electronic devices, a tolerance value is used in practical applications, where there are some other agents like noise, distortion, component mismatching, etc.

$$\mid x(t) - \xi(t) \mid \leq \epsilon_t \qquad \forall t \geq t_f. \tag{16}$$

Where ϵ is the allowed tolerance value and a time $t_f < \infty$ is assumed. Equations (15) and (16) assume the synchronization error defined as

$$e(t) = x(t) - \xi(t) \tag{17}$$

5.1 Hamiltonian Synchronization Approach

To satisfy the condition in (15) and (17) between two systems, it is necessary to establish a physical coupling between them through which energy flows. If the energy flows in one direction between the systems, it is one-way coupling, known as master-slave configuration. This section is based on the work of (Sira-Ramírez & Cruz-Hernández, 2001). To synchronize two systems by applying Hamiltonian approach, their equations must be placed in the Generalized Hamiltonian Canonical form. Most of the well knew systems can fulfill this requirement, thus, the reconstruction of the state vector from a defined output signal will be possible attending to the observability or detectability of a pair of constant matrices.
Consider a class of Hamiltonian Forms with destabilizing vector field $F(y)$ and lineal output $y(t)$ of the form (18).

$$\dot{x} = J(y)\frac{\partial H}{\partial x} + (I + S)\frac{\partial H}{\partial x} + F(y), \qquad \forall x \in \Re^n; \qquad y = C\frac{\partial H}{\partial x}, \qquad \forall y \in \Re^n \tag{18}$$

Where I denotes a constant antisymmetric matrix; S denotes a symmetric matrix; the vector $y(t)$ is the system output and C is a constant matrix. The described system has an observer if one first considers $\xi(t)$ as the vector of the estimated states $x(t)$,when $H(\xi)$ is the observer's energy function. In addition $n(t)$ is the estimated output calculated from $\xi(t)$ and the gradient vector $\frac{\partial H(\xi)}{\partial \xi}$ is equal to $M\xi$ with M being a symmetric constant matrix positive definited. Then, for (18) a nonlinear observer with gain K is (19).

$$\dot{\xi} = J(y)\frac{\partial H}{\partial \xi} + (I+S)\frac{\partial H}{\partial \xi} + F(y) + K(y-\eta), \qquad \eta = C\frac{\partial H}{\partial \xi} \tag{19}$$

Where the state estimation error is naturally $e(t) = x(t) - \xi(t)$ and the system estimated error output is $e_y = y(t) - \eta(t)$, both described by the dynamical system (20).

$$\dot{e} = J(y)\frac{\partial H}{\partial e} + (I+S-KC)\frac{\partial H}{\partial e}, \qquad e \in \Re^n; \qquad e_y = C\frac{\partial H}{\partial e}, \qquad e_y \in \Re^m. \tag{20}$$

The following assumption has been made with some abuse of notation $\frac{\partial H(e)}{\partial e} = \frac{\partial H}{\partial x} - \frac{\partial H}{\partial \xi} = M(x-\xi) = Me$. Also, the equivalence $I + S = W$ will be assumed. To maintain stability and to guarantee the synchronization error convergence to zero, two theorems are taken into account.

THEOREM **1.** *(Sira-Ramírez & Cruz-Hernández, 2001). The state $x(t)$ of the system in the form (18) can be globally, asymptotically and exponentially estimated by the state $\xi(t)$ of an observer in the form (19), if the pair of matrix (C,W) or (C, S), are observable or at least detectable.*

THEOREM **2.** *(Sira-Ramírez & Cruz-Hernández, 2001). The state $x(t)$ of the system in the form (18) can be globally, asymptotically and exponentially estimated by the state $\xi(t)$ of an observer in the form (19), if and only if, a constant matrix K can be found to form the matrix $[W-KC]+[W-KC]^T = [S-K]+[S-KC]^T = 2[S-\frac{1}{2}(KC+C^TK^T)]$ which must be negative de□nite.*

In the successive, to find an observer for a system in the Hamiltonian form (18), the system will be arranged in the form (19), keeping observability or at least detectability and proposing a matrix $y(t)$ such that a gain matrix K can be found to achieve the conditions of Theorem 2.

5.2 Synchronization circuit implementation

Our proposed schemes for the synchronization of multi-scroll chaos systems of the form (19), by using CFOAs and OpAmps are shown in Fig.19 and Fig.20, respectively. The vector K in (19) is the observer gain and it is adjusted according to the sufficiency conditions for synchronization (Sira-Ramírez & Cruz-Hernández, 2001).
By selecting $R_{io} = 10k\Omega, R_{fo} = 3.9M\Omega$ and $R_{ko} = 22\Omega$ in Fig. 19 and Fig. 20, HSPICE simulation of the response of the synchronization whit OpAmps and CFOAs is shown in Fig. 21 and Fig. 24, respectively.
The synchronization error is shown in Fig. 22 and Fig. 25, which can be adjusted with the gain of the observer. The coincidence of the states is represented by a straight line with a unity-slope (identity function) in the phase plane of each state as shown in Fig. 23 and Fig. 26.

6. Experimental Synchronization results using CFOAs

The realization of Fig. 20 was done by using the commercially available CFOA AD844.

6.1 Generation of a 5-scrolls attractor

Figure 27 shows the experimental mesurement for the implementation of the 5-scrolls SNLF. By selecting $R_{ix} = 10K\Omega, C = 2.2nf, R = 7K\Omega, R_x = R_y = R_z = 10K\Omega, R_f = 10K\Omega, R_i = 10K\Omega$ in Fig. 20 and $R_{ix} = 10K\Omega, R_c = 64K\Omega, R_{iz} = 1K\Omega, R_{fz} = 1M\Omega, E_1 = \pm 1V$ and $E_2 = \pm 3V$ with $V_{sat} = +7.24V$ and $-7.28V$ in the BC (SNLF), the result is N=5-scrolls, F=10Khz, $EL = \pm 5V$ as shown in Fig. 28.

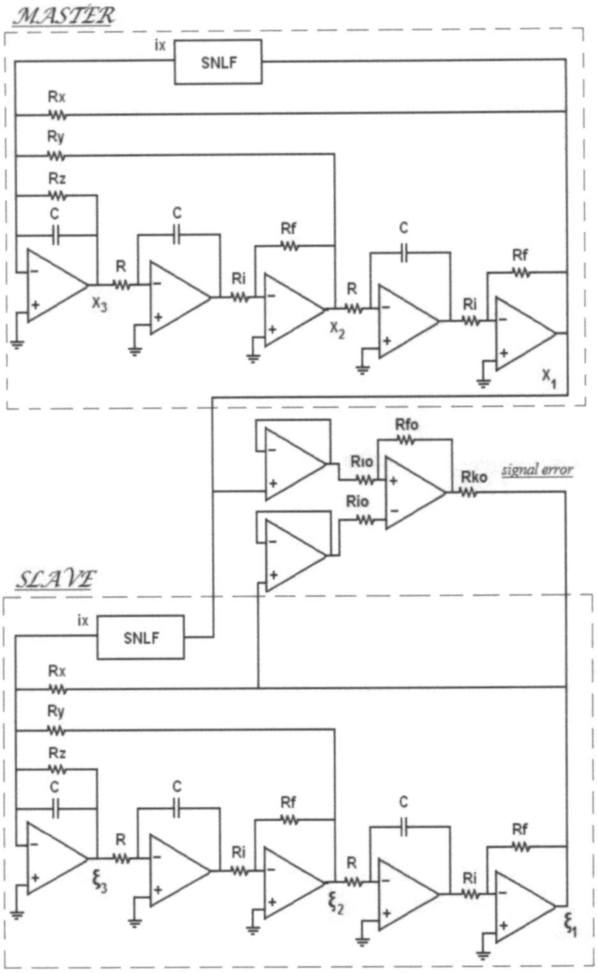

Fig. 19. Circuit realization for the synchronization using OpAmps

The synchronization result of Fig. 20 by selecting $R_{io} = 10k\Omega, R_{fo} = 3.9M\Omega$ and $R_{ko} = 3\Omega$ is shown in Fig. 29, the coincidence of the states is represented by a straight line with slope equal to unity in the phase plane for each state.

6.2 Chaotic system whit 6-scrolls attractor

Figure 30 shows the implementation of the 6-scrolls SNLF.
The synchronization result of Fig. 31 by selecting $R_{io} = 10k\Omega, R_{fo} = 3.9M\Omega$ and $R_{ko} = 3\Omega$ is shown in Fig. 32, the coincidence of the states is represented by a straight line with slope equal to unity in the phase plane for each state.

7. Chaos systems applied to secure communications

A communication system can be realized by using chaotic signals (Cruz-Hernández et al., 2005; Kocarev et al., 1992). Chaos masking systems are based on using the chaotic signal, broadband and look like noise to mask the real information signal to be transmitted, which

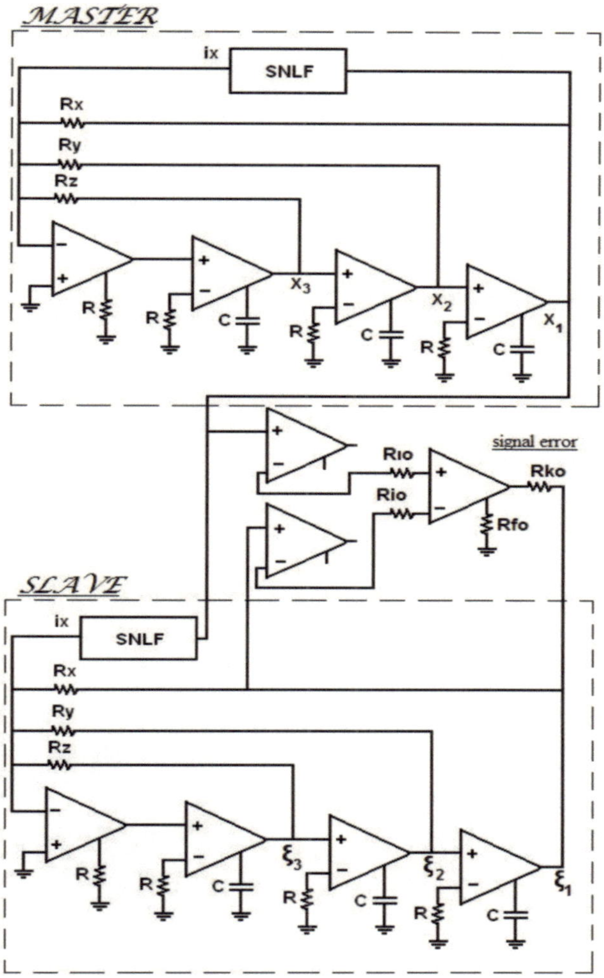

Fig. 20. Circuit realization for the synchronization using CFOAs

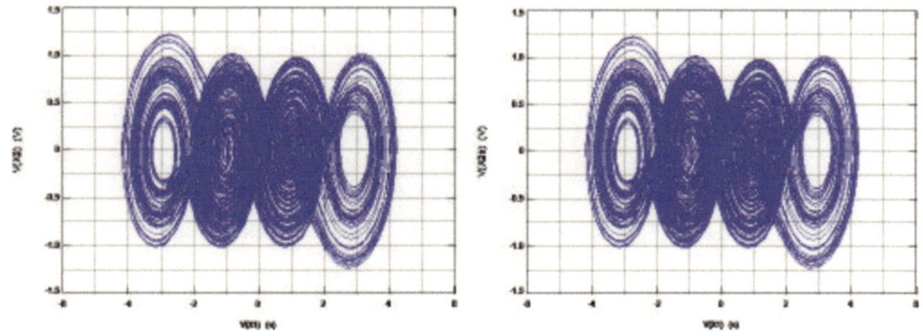

(a) master circuit (b) slave circuit

Fig. 21. Chaotic 4-scrolls atractor realized with OpAmps

may be analog or digital. One way to realize a chaos masking system is to add the information

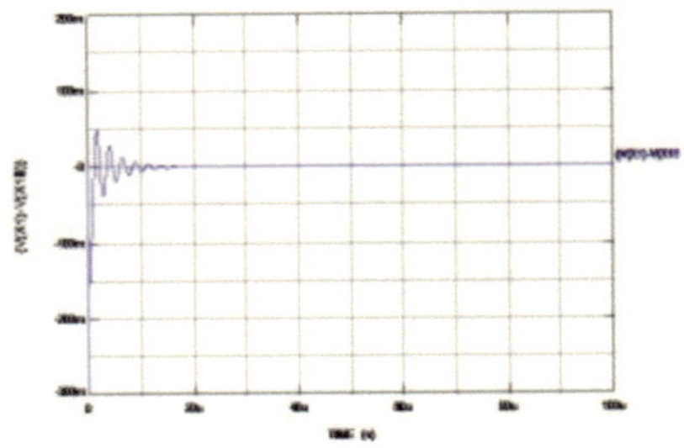

Fig. 22. Synchronization Error when using OpAmps

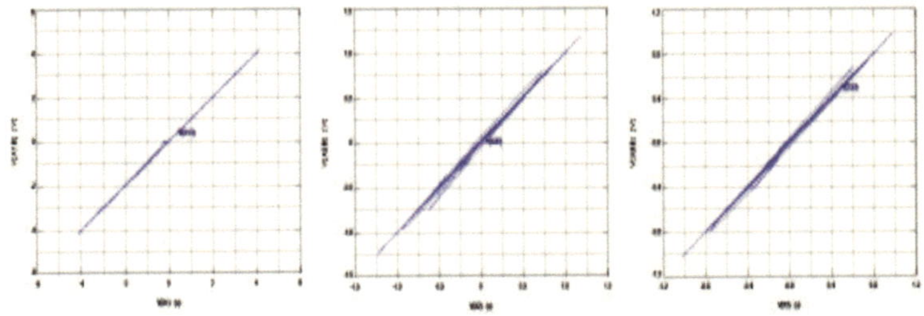

(a) (b) (c)

Fig. 23. Error phase-plane when using OpAmps

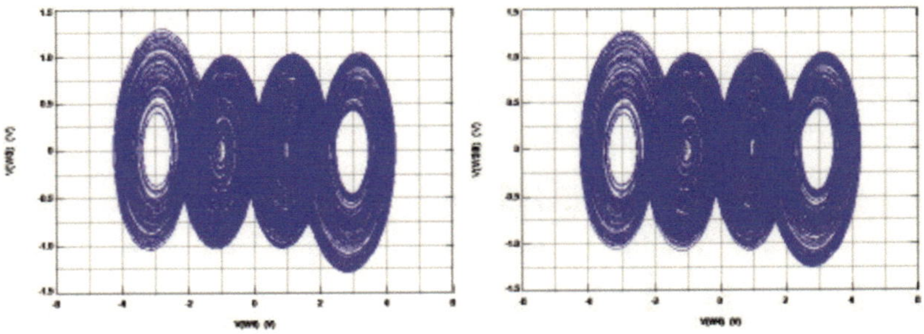

(a) master circuit (b) slave circuit

Fig. 24. Chaotic 4-scrolls atractor using CFOAs

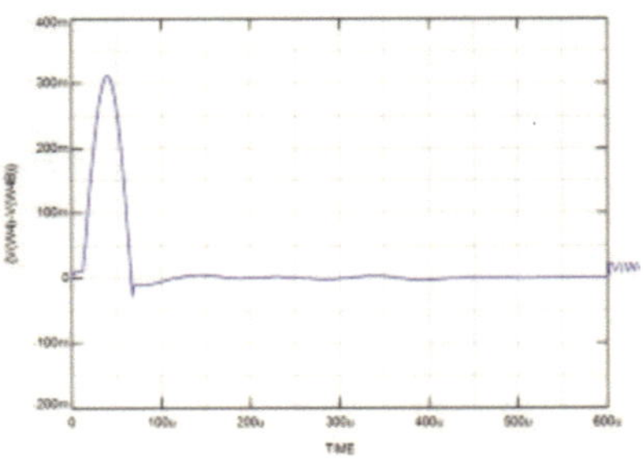

Fig. 25. Synchronization Error when using CFOAs

signal to the chaotic signal generated by an autonomous chaos system, as shown in Figure 33. The transmitted signal in this case is:

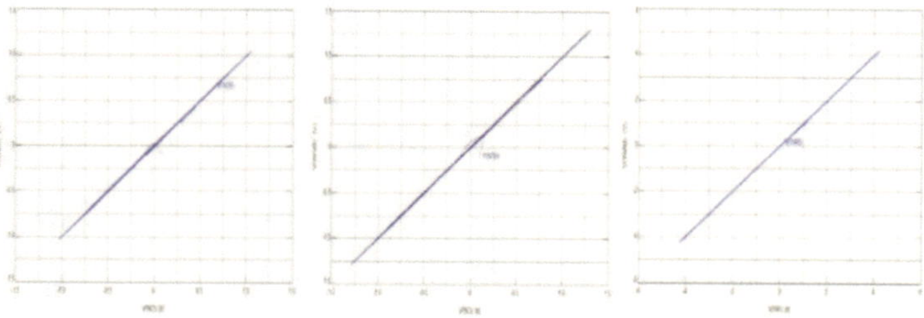

(a) (b) (c)

Fig. 26. Error phase plane when using CFOAs

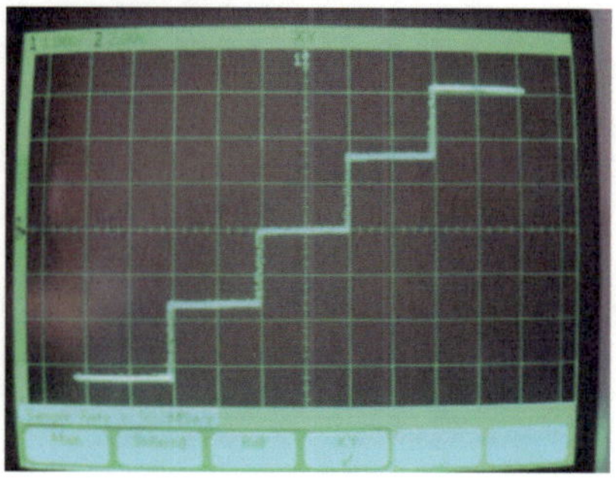

Fig. 27. 5-scrolls SNLF

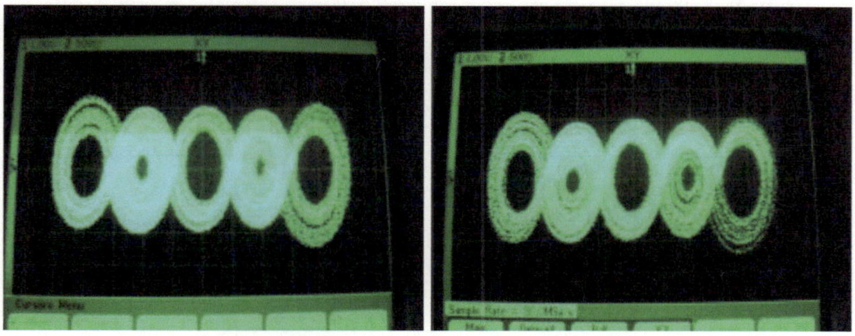

(a) master circuit (b) slave circuit

Fig. 28. Chaotic 5-scrolls attractor

$$\bar{y}(t) = y(t) + m(t) \tag{21}$$

where $m(t)$ is the signal information to be conveyed (the message) and $y(t)$ is the output signal of the chaotic system.

7.1 Two transmission channels

As illustrated in Fig. 34, this method is to synchronize the systems in master-slave configuration by a chaotic signal, $x_1(t)$, transmitted exclusively on a single channel, while to transmit a confidential message $m(t)$, it is encrypted with another chaotic signal, $x_2(t)$ by an additive process, this signal can be send through a second transmission channel.

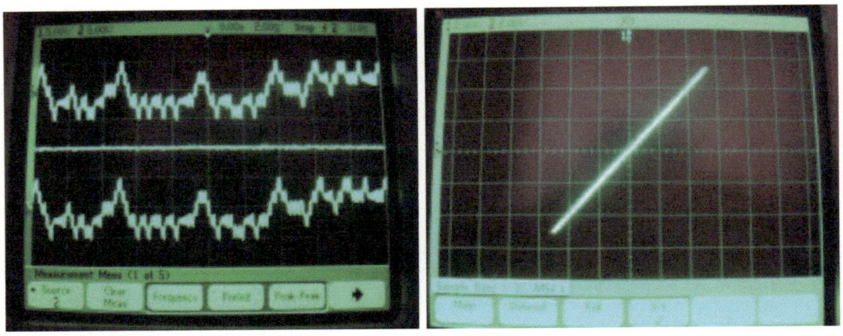

(a)

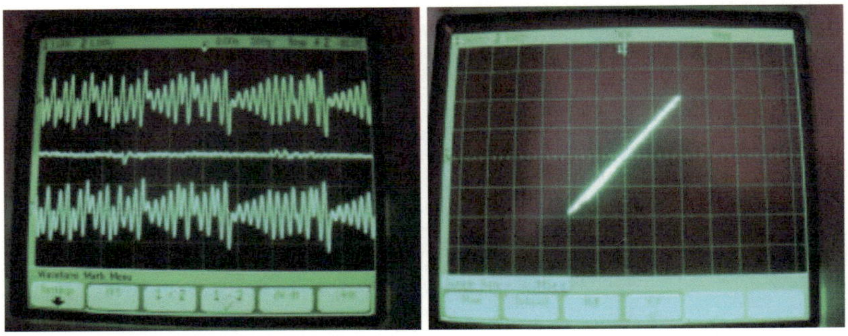

(b)

Fig. 29. Diagram in the phase plane and time signal (a) X_1vs ξ_1, (b) X_2 vs ξ_2

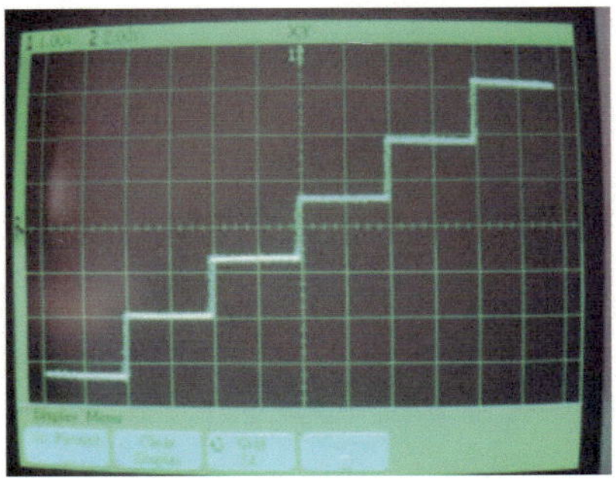

Fig. 30. 6-scrolls SNLF

Message recovery is performed by a reverse process, in this case, a subtraction to the signal received $\bar{y}(t) = x_2(t) + m(t)$, it is obvious that ywe want to subtract a chaotic signal identical to $x_2(t)$ for faithful recovery of the original message. It is important to note that there exists an error in synchrony given by $e_1(t) = x_1(t) - \hat{x}_1(t) = 0$, thus, $\hat{m}(t) = m(t)$.

7.2 Experimental results

We implemented an additive chaotic masking system using two transmission channels of the form (18), synchronized by Hamiltonian forms the receiver chaotic system is given by (19) , using the scenario of unidirectional master-slave coupling, as shown in Fig. 35.
The message to convey is a sine wave of frequency f = 10Khz and 500mV amplitude. Figures 36 and 37 show the experimental result of the secure transmission using chaos generators

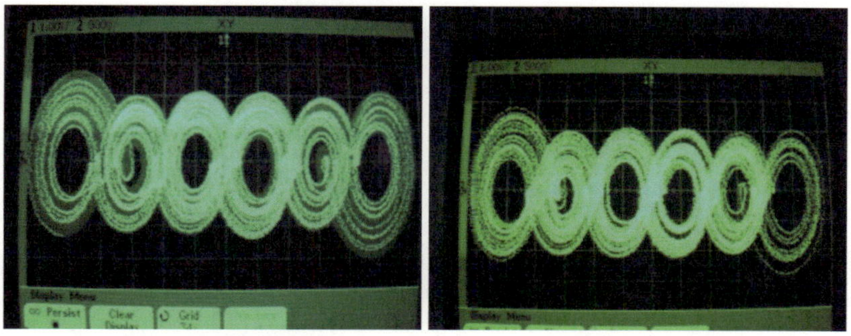

(a) master circuit (b) slave circuit

Fig. 31. Chaotic 6-scrolls attractor

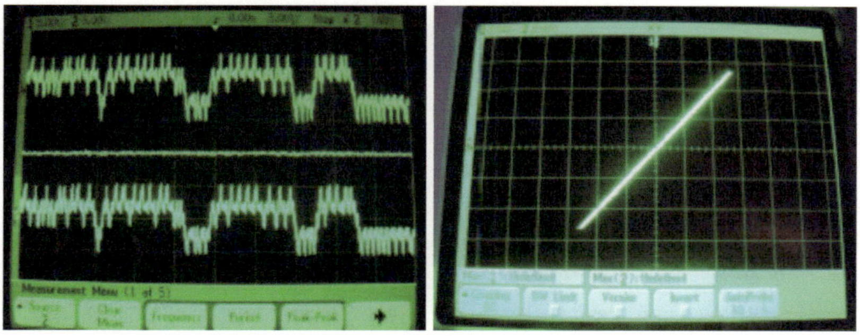

(a)

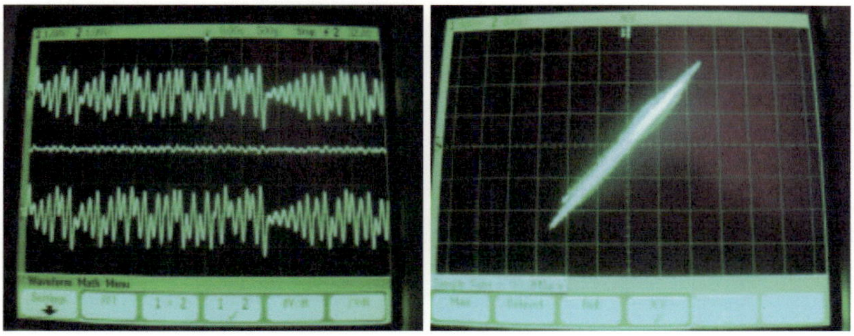

(b)

Fig. 32. Diagram in the phase plane and time signal (a) X_1vs ξ_1, (b) X_2 vs ξ_2

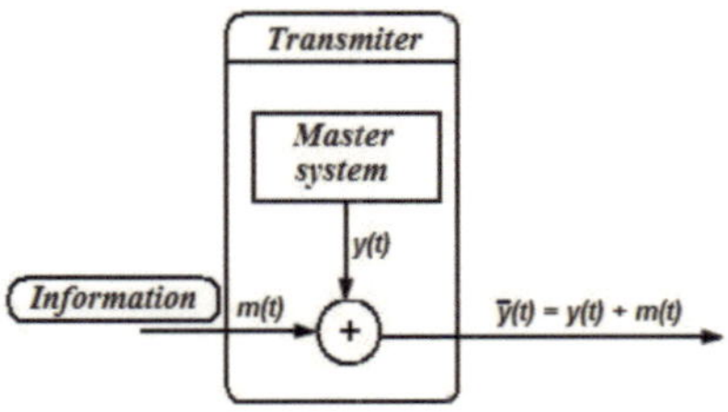

Fig. 33. Chaotic masking scheme

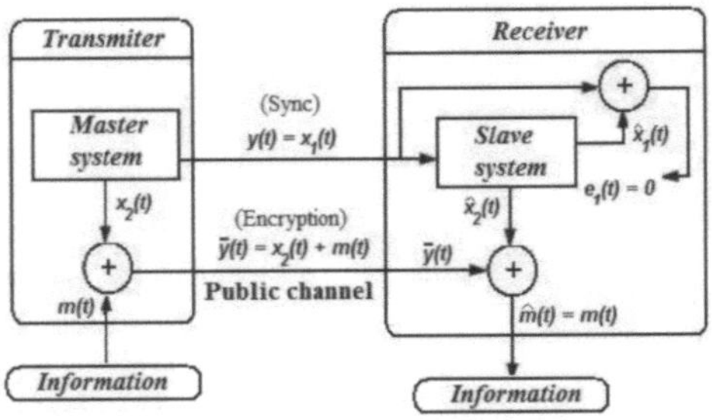

Fig. 34. Additive chaotic encryption scheme using two transmission channels

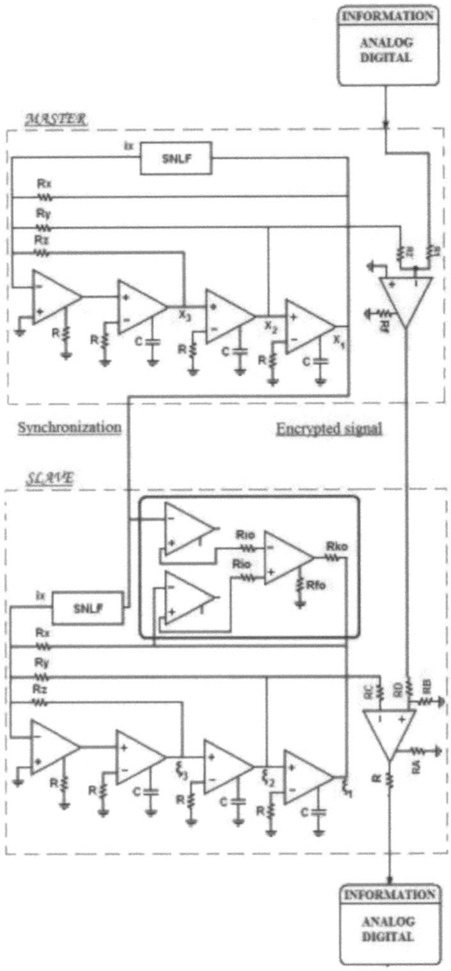

Fig. 35. Chaotic transmission system using CFOAs

of 5 and 6-scrolls, respectively. $m(t)$: confidential signal, $x_2(t) + m(t)$: encrypted signal transmitted by the public channel and $\hat{m}(t)$: reconstructed signal by the receiver.

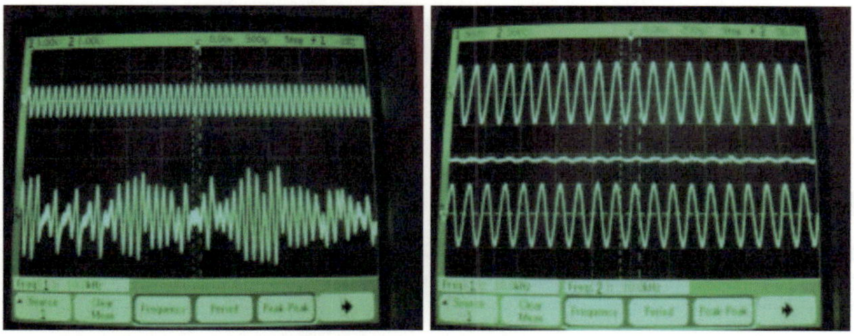

(a) (Ch1:1V/div; Ch2:1V/div).$Ch1$: $m(t), Ch2 : x_2(t) + m(t)$

(b) (Ch1:500mV/div; Ch2:500mV/div; Center:500mV/div

Fig. 36. (a) Encryption of information, (b) Information retrieval

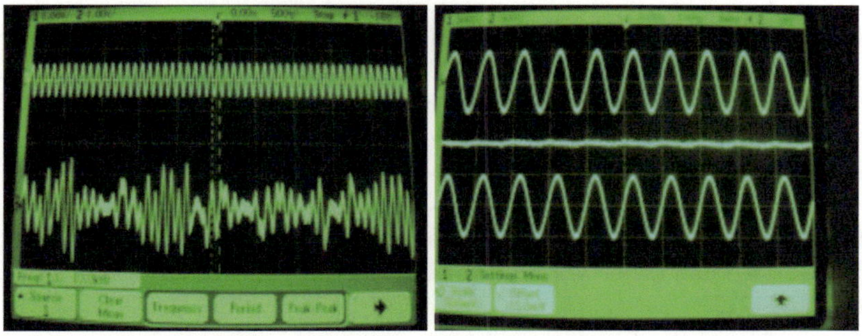

(a) (Ch1:1V/div; Ch2:1V/div) $Ch1$: $m(t), Ch2 : x2_(t) + m(t)$

(b) (Ch1:500mV/div; Ch2:500mV/div; Center:500mV/div

Fig. 37. (a) Encryption of information, (b) Information retrieval

8. Conclusion

Chaos systems can be realized with almost every commercially available electronic device, and they can be designed with integrated circuit technology, for which there are many open problems regarding the number of scrolls to be generated, the bias levels to reduce power consumption, the increment in frequency response, tolerance to process and environment variations, and so on. Furthermore, the performances of the chaos systems will depend on the electrical characteristics of the devices. In this chapter we presented the design of chaos systems using commercially available devices such as the opamp and CFOA AD844.

We described how to generate multi-scroll attractors and how to realize the circuitry for the chaotic oscillator based on SNLFs.

The application of the designed chaos generators to a communication system was highlighted through experimental results using CFOAs. Open problems can also be related to the development of applications by using chaos systems with different number of scrolls and dimensions and with different kinds of chaos system topologies.

Acknowledgment

The first author thanks the support of the JAE-Doc program of CSIC, co-funded by FSE, of Promep-México under the project UATLX-PTC-088, and by Consejeria de Innovacion Ciencia y Empresa, Junta de Andalucia, Spain, under the project number TIC-2532. The second author thanks the support from Promep-México under the project UPPUE-PTC-033. The last author thanks the CONACyT grant for his sabbatical stay at University of California at Riverside, during 2009-2010.

9. References

Castro-López, R., Fernández, F., Guerra-Vinuesa, O. & Rodriguez-Vazquez, A. (2006). *Reuse-Based Methodologies and Tools in the Design of Analog and Mixed-Signal Integrated Circuits*, Springer Publishers.

Chakraborty, S. & Dana, S. (2010). Shil'nikov chaos and mixed-mode oscillation in chua circuit, *Chaos* 20(2): 023107.

Chen, W., Vandewalle, J. & Vandenberghe, L. (1995). Piecewise-linear circuits and piecewiselinear analysis: Circuits and filters handbook, *CRC Press/IEEE Press* .

Chua, L. (1975). *Computer-Aided Analysis of Electronic Circuits: Algorithms and Computational Techniques*, Prentice Hall.

Cook, P. (1994). *Nonlinear Dynamical Systems*, Prentice Hall.

Cruz-Hernández, C., López-Mancilla, D., García-Gradilla, V., Serrano-Guerrero, H. & nez Pérez, R. N. (2005). Experimental realization of binary signals transmission using chaos, *J. Circuits Syst. Comput.* 14: 453–468.

Deng, W. (2007). Generating 3-D scroll grid attractors of fractional differential systems via stair function, *International Journal of Bifurcations and Chaos* 17(11): 3965–3983.

Dieci, L. (2002). Jacobian free computation of lyapunov exponents, *J. Dynam. Differ. Equat.* 14(3): 697–717.

Elhadj, Z. & Sprott, J. (2010). Generating 3-scroll attractors from one chua circuit, *International Journal of Bifurcations and Chaos* 20(1): 135–144.

Ergun, S. & Ozoguz, S. (2010). Truly random number generators based on non-autonomous continuous-time chaos, *International Journal of Circuit Theory and Applications* 38: 1–24.

Gámez-Guzmán, L., Cruz-Hernández, C., López-Gutiérrez, R. & García-Guerrero, E. (2008). Synchronization of multi-scroll chaos generators: Application to private communication, *Rev. Mexicana Fís.* 54(4): 299–305.

Kocarev, L., Halle, K. S., Eckert, K., Chua, L. O. & Parlitz, U. (1992). Experimental demonstration of secure communications via chaotic synchronization, *International Journal of Bifurcations and Chaos* 2(3): 709–713.

Kundert, K. (2004). *The Designer's Guide to Verilog-AMS*, Kluwer Academic Publishers.

Lin, Z. H. & Wang, H. X. (2010). Efficient image encryption using a chaos-based PWL memristor, *IETE Technical Review* 27(4): 318–325.

Lü, J., Chen, G., Yu, X. & Leung, H. (2004). Design and analysis of multiscroll chaotic attractors from saturated function series, *IEEE Trans. Circuits Syst. I* 51(12): 2476–2490.

Lu, J., Yang, G., Oh, H. & Luo, A. (2005). Chaos computing lyapunov exponents of continuous dynamical systems: method of lyapunov vectors, *Chaos, Solitons & Fractals* 23: 1879–1892.

Muñoz-Pacheco, J. & Tlelo-Cuautle, E. (2008). Synthesis of n-scroll attractors using saturated functions from high-level simulation, *Journal of Physics-Conference Series* (2nd Int. Symposium on Nonlinear Dynamics).

Muñoz-Pacheco, J. & Tlelo-Cuautle, E. (2009). Automatic synthesis of 2D-n-scrolls chaotic systems by behavioral modeling, *Journal of Applied Research and Technology* 7(1): 5–14.

Muñoz-Pacheco, J. & Tlelo-Cuautle, E. (2010). *Electronic design automation of multi-scroll chaos generators*, Bentham Sciences Publishers Ltd.

Ott, E. (1994). *Chaos in Dynamical systems*, Cambridge University Press.

Ramasubramanian, K. & Sriram, M. (2000). A comparative study of computation of lyapunov spectra with different algorithms, *Phys. Nonlinear Phenom.* 139: 72–86.

Sánchez-López, C., Castro-López, A. & Pérez-Trejo, A. (2008). Experimental verification of the Chua's circuit designed with UGCs, *IEICE Electron. Express* 5: 657–661.

Sánchez-López, C., Trejo-Guerra, R., Muñoz-Pacheco, J. & Tlelo-Cuautle, E. (2010). N-scroll chaotic attractors from saturated functions employing CCII+s, *Nonlinear Dynamics* 61(1-2): 331–341.

Sánchez-Sinencio, E. & Silva-Martínez, J. (2000). Cmos transconductance amplifiers, architectures and active filters: a tutorial, *IEE Proceedings- Circuits, Devices and Systems* 147(1): 3–12.

Sedra, A. & Smith, K. (1970). A second-generation current conveyor and its applications, *IEEE Trans. Circuit Th.* 17: 132–134.

Senani, R. & Gupta, S. (1998). Implementation of Chua's chaotic circuit using current feedback opamps, *Electron. Lett.* 34: 829–830.

Shuh-Chuan, T., Chuan-Kuei, H., Wan-Tai, C. & Yu-Ren, W. (2005). Synchronization of chua chaotic circuits with application to the bidirectional secure communication systems, *International Journal of Bifurcations and Chaos* 15(2): 605–616.

Sira-Ramírez, H. & Cruz-Hernández, C. (2001). Synchronization of chaotic systems: A generalized hamiltonian systems approach, *International Journal of Bifurcations and Chaos* 11(5): 1381–1395.

Strogatz, S. H. (2001). *Nonlinear Dynamics And Chaos: With Applications To Physics, Biology, Chemistry, And Engineering*, Westview Press.

Suykens, J., Huang, A. & Chua, L. (1997). A family of n-scroll attractors from a generalized chua's circuit, *International Journal of Electronics and Communications* 51(3): 131–138.

Tlelo-Cuautle, E. & C. Sánchez-López, D. M.-F. (2010). Symbolic analysis of (MO)(I)CCI(II)(III)-based analog circuits, *International Journal of Circuit Theory and Applications* 38(6): 649–659.

Tlelo-Cuautle, E., Gaona-Hernández, A. & Garcia-Delgado, J. (2006). Implementation of a chaotic oscillator by designing chua's diode with CMOS CFOAs, *Analog Integrated Circuits and Signal Processing* 48(2): 159–162.

Tlelo-Cuautle, E. & Munoz-Pacheco, J. (2007). Numerical simulation of chua's circuit oriented to circuit synthesis, *International Journal of Nonlinear Sciences and Numerical Simulation* 8(2): 249–256.

Trejo-Guerra, R., Sánchez-López, C., Tlelo-Cuautle, E., Cruz-Hernández, C. & Muñoz-Pacheco, J. (2010). Realization of multiscroll chaotic attractors by using current-feedback operational amplifiers, *Revista Mexicana de Física* 56(4): 268–274.

Trejo-Guerra, R., Tlelo-Cuautle, E., Cruz-Hernández, C. & Sánchez-López, C. (2009). Chaotic communication system using chua's oscillators realized with CCII+s, *Int. J. Bifurc. Chaos* 19(12): 4217–4226.

Trejo-Guerra, R., Tlelo-Cuautle, E., Jiménez-Fuentes, M. & Sánchez-López, C. (2010). Multiscroll oscillator based on floating gate cmos inverter, *Proceedings of the International Conference on Electrical Engineering, Computing Science and Automatic Control*, IEEE, Tuxtla Gutiérrez, pp. 541 – 545.

Trejo-Guerra, R., Tlelo-Cuautle, E., Muñoz-Pacheco, J., Cruz-Hernández, C. & Sánchez-López, C. (2010). Operating characteristics of mosfets in chaotic oscillators, *in* B. M. Fitzgerald (ed.), *Transistors: Types, Materials and Applications*, NOVA Science Publishers Inc.

Varrientos, J. & Sanchez-Sinencio, E. (1998). A 4-D chaotic oscillator based on a differential hysteresis comparator, *IEEE Trans. on Circuits and Systems I* 45(1): 3–10.

Yalçin, M., Suykens, J. & Vandewalle, J. (2002). Families of scroll grid attractors, *International Journal of Bifurcation and Chaos* 12(1): 23–41.

Yalcin, M., Suykens, J. & Vandewalle, J. (2000). Experimental confirmation of 3- and 5-scroll attractors from a generalized chua's circuit, *IEEE Trans. Circuits Syst.-I* 47: 425–429.

11

Applying Estimation Techniques to Chaos-based Digital Communications

Marcio Eisencraft[1] and Luiz Antonio Baccalá[2]
[1]*Centro de Eng., Modelagem e Ciências Sociais Aplicadas, Universidade Federal do ABC*
[2]*Escola Politécnica da Universidade de São Paulo*
Brazil

1. Introduction

Chaotic signal applications have been considered in a variety of areas, see e.g. (Strogatz, 2001). Signal Processing and Telecommunications are no exception specially after the seminal work by Pecora & Carroll (1990). Applications of chaos ranging from digital and analog modulation to cryptography, pseudorandom sequences generation and watermarking have been proposed (Kennedy & Kolumban, 2000; Kennedy, Setti & Rovatti, 2000; Stavroulakis, 2005; Tsekeridou et al., 2001). Chaos has also been shown in connection to devices used in signal processing such as nonlinear adaptive filters and phase-locked loop networks (Endo & Chua, 1988; Harb & Harb, 2004; Monteiro et al., 2009; Tavazoei & Haeri, 2009).

In particular, many recent works have described digital modulations using chaotic carriers (Kennedy & Kolumban, 2000; Kennedy, Setti & Rovatti, 2000; Kolumban et al., 1997; Kolumban, Kennedy & Chua, 1998; Lau & Tse, 2003) even though their performance proved below that of equivalent conventional systems under additive white gaussian noise channel (Kaddoum et al., 2009; Williams, 2001).

This chapter's first aim is to compare these chaos-based modulations to their conventional counterparts via their discrete-time low-pass equivalent models. Special attention is devoted to Chaos Shift Keying (CSK), Differential CSK and some of their variants in Section 3 as that analysis points out reasons for the low observed performance of chaotic modulation and thus paves the way for result improvement.

In fact, we show that the poor Bit Error Rate (BER) performance of many current modulations employing chaos is in part due to their systematic neglect of the details behind the chaos generation mechanisms. To overcome this we explicitly exploit chaos generating map information to estimate the received noise-embedded chaotic signal (Section 4) and show that it leads to improved BER performance. Two approaches to achieve that are considered and contrasted: (a) Maximum Likelihood Estimation and (b) the Modified Viterbi Algorithm (MVA) for discrete-time one-dimensional chaotic maps.

In the context of MVA, we further examine two digital modulation schemes: the Modified Maximum Likelihood Chaos Shift Keying using (a) one and (b) two maps both of which have better BER characteristics than previous noncoherent chaos communication schemes (Section 5).

Before proceeding we start reviewing basic definitions and the discrete-time low-pass equivalent models.

2. Preliminary notions

For our present purposes we take a limited signal to be chaotic if it is deterministic, aperiodic and exhibits sensitive dependence on initial conditions (Alligood et al., 1997), i.e. when its generating system is initialized in a slightly different initial condition, the resulting signal very quickly diverges from that with the original unperturbed initial conditions.

Due to these properties, chaotic signals occupy a large bandwidth, their autocorrelations are impulsive and the cross-correlations between signals generated by different initial conditions present low values (Djurovic & Rubezic, 2008; Kennedy & Kolumban, 2000; Kennedy, Setti & Rovatti, 2000; Stavroulakis, 2005). These characteristics have been behind the rationale for using chaotic signals as candidates for spreading signal information. When chaotic signals modulate independent narrowband sources increased bandwidths result with lower power spectral density levels in a fashion similar to what happens in Spread Spectrum (SS) systems (Lathi, 1998). Consequently, chaos-based and SS systems share several properties namely (i) they are difficult to intercept by any unauthorized user; (ii) they are easily hidden, i.e. from any unauthorized receiver, it is difficult to even detect their presence in many cases; (iii) they are resistant to jamming; and (iv) they provide a measure of immunity to distortion due to multipath propagation.

The unified low pass representation used here is based on (Kolumban et al., 1997; Kolumban, Kennedy & Chua, 1998) in the discrete time context which is more suitable to treating signals generated by chaotic maps.

In the following, only the transmission of isolated symbols is considered, i.e. intersymbol interference is assumed absent.

2.1 Equivalent low-pass discrete-time models

To facilitate simulation and analysis of digital modulations it is usual to work with discrete-time baseband equivalent models, whose results are valid for the original ones (Lathi, 1998). This modeling allows us to represent the transmitted signals by means of finite length sequences.

In the conventional case, a baseband signal, supposed to have a bandwidth B, is used to modify the sinusoidal carrier with frequency $f_0 \gg B$.

As any bandpass signal can be described by (Lathi, 1998)

$$x(t) = x_c(t)\cos(2\pi f_0 t) - x_s(t)\sin(2\pi f_0 t), \tag{1}$$

its low-pass representation denoted by $x_l(t)$ turns out to be a complex function with real and imaginary parts $x_c(t)$ and $x_s(t)$ respectively, so that:

$$x_l(t) = x_c(t) + jx_s(t), \tag{2}$$

where both $x_c(t)$ and $x_s(t)$ are low-pass signals termed *in-phase* and *quadrature* components respectively (Haykin, 2000).

The discrete-time version of the baseband model is obtained sampling $x_l(t)$ at a convenient sampling rate $1/T_A$ (Lathi, 1998). To simplify the notation, we denote $x_l(nT_a)$ as $x(n)$.

The set of equivalent waveform sequences used in a given system using M symbols is represented by $x_m(n)$, $m = 1, 2, \ldots, M$, where $x_m(n) \neq 0$ only for $0 \leq n \leq N-1$. To transmit the m-th symbol, the signal represented in discrete-time by $x_m(n)$ is sent through the analog channel.

To simplify demodulation, it is convenient to define a set with fewer signals, called *basis functions*, so that the signals represented by $x_m(n)$ are weighted sums of the elements of this basis (Wozencraft & Jacobs, 1987).
Let $s_i(n), i = 1, 2, \ldots, N_b, n = 0, 1, \ldots, N-1$ be an orthonormal basis sequence, i.e.,

$$\sum_{n=0}^{N-1} s_i(n)s_j(n) = \begin{cases} 1, & \text{if } i = j \\ 0, & \text{if } i \neq j \end{cases}, 1 \leq i, j \leq N_b. \tag{3}$$

Thus, each of the M signals $x_m(n)$ is represented as a linear combination of the N_b sequences $s_i(n)$, with $N_b \leq M$:

$$x_m(n) = \sum_{i=1}^{N_b} x_{mi} s_i(n), \; m = 1, 2, \ldots, M. \tag{4}$$

The coefficients x_{mi} in Eq.(4) can be interpreted as the components of an N_b-dimensional column vector $\mathbf{x}_m$.
Since the basis sequences are orthonormal, the $\mathbf{x}_m$ signal vector can be recovered from the transmitted signal if all basis signals $s_i(n)$ are known:

$$x_{mi} = \sum_{n=0}^{N-1} x_m(n) s_i(n), \; i = 1, 2, \ldots, N_b. \tag{5}$$

Interestingly, this notation applies to both conventional and chaotic modulations. The difference between them lies in the nature of the chosen basis.
The chaotic sequences in the next section are assumed to be composed of N points derived from the tent map $f_T(.)$ defined by

$$s(n+1) = f_T(s(n)) = 1 - 2|s(n)|, \; 0 \leq n \leq N-1, \tag{6}$$

with initial conditions $s(0)$ uniformly distributed over the $(-1, 1)$ interval. To achieve unit mean energy the latter sequences are then multiplied by $\sqrt{3/N}$ (Eisencraft et al., 2010).

3. Digital modulations using chaotic carriers

We focus on Chaos Shift Keying (CSK) and its variants based on noncoherent or differential demodulation because of their promise in proposed practical applications (Kennedy, Kolumbán, Kis & Jákó, 2000; Kennedy, Setti & Rovatti, 2000; Kolumban et al., 1997; Kolumban, Kennedy & Chua, 1998; Lau & Tse, 2003; Stavroulakis, 2005). In fact, researchers from the Optical Communications Laboratory of the Athens University in Greece, implemented an 120km optical fiber link in metropolitan Athens and managed to transmit at gigabit rates using CSK (Argyris et al., 2005; Syvridis, 2009).

3.1 The CSK and the DCSK

CSK is a digital modulation where each symbol to be transmitted is encoded as the coefficients of a linear combination of signals generated by different chaotic attractors (Kolumban et al., 1997).
Using the previously defined notation, the required basis sequences must be chosen as segments of the chaotic signals generated by N_b different attractors. As a result of the chaos related non-periodicity, the sequences $s_i(n)$ and therefore the signals $x_m(n)$ are different for each subsequent transmitted symbol.

We impose that the chaotic basis sequences are orthonormal *in the mean*, i.e.

$$E\left[\sum_{n=0}^{N-1} s_i(n)s_j(n)\right] = \begin{cases} 1, \text{ if } i = j \\ 0, \text{ if } i \neq j \end{cases}, \quad 1 \leq i,j \leq N_b, \tag{7}$$

where $E[.]$ denotes the expectation operator. Eq.(7) identifies an important characteristic of digital chaotic modulation schemes: the orthonormality of the basis signals can be defined only in terms of expected values.
Using Eq. (5), the coefficients x_{mi} can be recovered from the transmitted signal by correlation with locally generated copies of the basis sequences $\hat{s}_i(n)$ as shown in Figure 1(a) for the case $N_b = 1$.

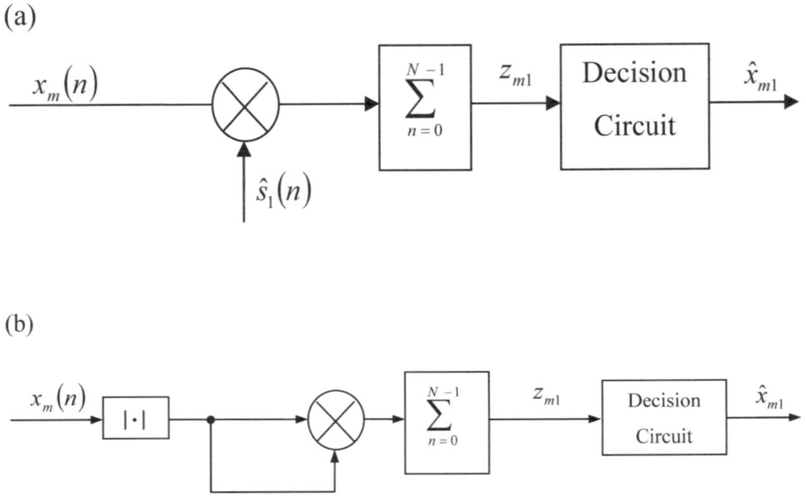

Fig. 1. Receiver (a) coherent and (b) non-coherent case with $N_b = 1$.

If the coefficients x_{mi} generate signals with different energies for each m, demodulation can also be done by estimating the energy of the received signal. In this case, copies of the basis sequences are unnecessary. A block diagram of the non-coherent demodulator for $N_b = 1$ is shown in Figure 1(b).
In the special case of binary CSK with one basis function, the symbols are transmitted using the signals $x_1(n) = x_{11}s_1(n)$ and $x_2(n) = x_{21}s_1(n)$. Three possibilities are highlighted in the literature:

i. **Unipodal CSK** (Kennedy, Setti & Rovatti, 2000), where x_{11} and x_{21} are positive and different;

ii. **Chaotic On-Off Keying (COOK)** (Kolumban, Kennedy & Chua, 1998), where x_{11} is positive and $x_{21} = 0$ and

iii. **Antipodal CSK**(Kennedy, Setti & Rovatti, 2000), where $x_{21} = -x_{11} \neq 0$.

Figure 2 shows examples of transmitted signals $x(n)$ for the sequence of symbols $\{1,1,0,1,0,0,1,0\}$ using each type of CSK above, with $N = 50$ and mean energy per symbol $E_b = 1$. The $s_1(n)$ sequence is obtained by iterating the tent map of Eq. (6). The symbols "1" and "0" are transmitted using $x_1(n) = x_{11}s_1(n)$ and $x_2(n) = x_{21}s_1(n)$ respectively.

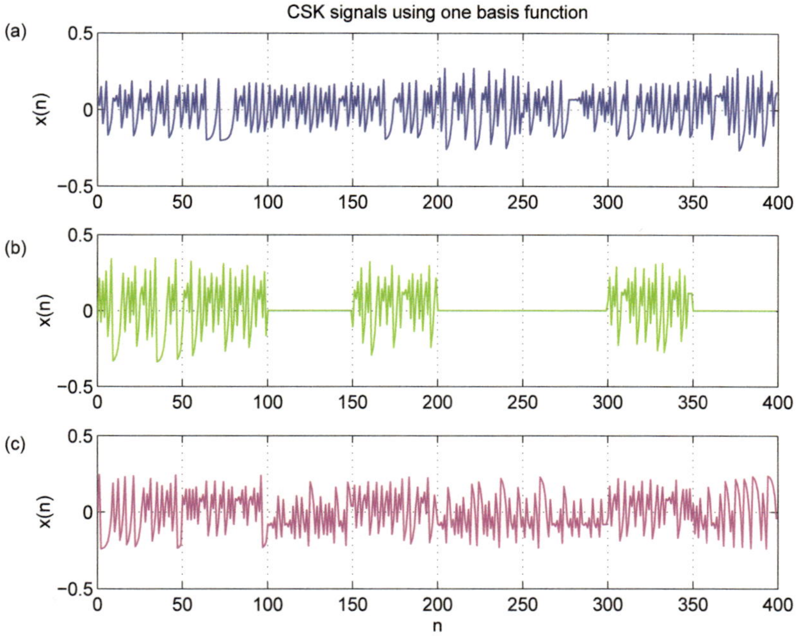

Fig. 2. CSK transmitted signals for the sequence $\{1, 1, 0, 1, 0, 0, 1, 0\}$: (a) unipodal CSK; (b) COOK; (c) antipodal CSK. In each case, $N = 50$ samples and $E_b = 1$.

Differential CSK (DCSK) is a variant of CSK with two maps whose basis sequences consist of repeated segments of chaotic waveforms. For DCSK the two basis signals are chosen as:

$$s_i(n) = \begin{cases} s(n), & 0 \leq n < \frac{N}{2} \\ (-1)^{i+1} s\left(n - \frac{N}{2}\right), & \frac{N}{2} \leq n < N \end{cases}, \tag{8}$$

where $i = 1, 2$, $s(n)$ is a chip of a chaotic signal and N is even.
A typical binary DCSK signal $x(n)$ corresponding to the symbol sequence $\{1, 1, 0, 1, 0, 0, 1, 0\}$ using the tent map $f_T(.)$ from Eq. (6) as the chaotic generator is shown in Figure 3. Symbols "1" and "0" are transmitted using $x_1(n) = \sqrt{E_b} s_1(n)$ and $x_2(n) = \sqrt{E_b} s_2(n)$ respectively. The number of samples per symbol is $N = 50$ and $E_b = 1$.

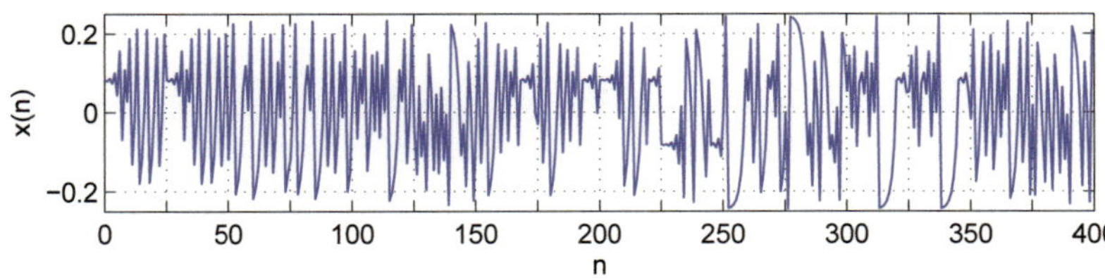

Fig. 3. DCSK signal transmitted for the data sequence $\{1, 1, 0, 1, 0, 0, 1, 0\}$ with $N = 50$ samples and $E_b = 1$.

In the DCSK signal, information is mapped on the correlation between the *reference chip* $(0 \leq n < N/2)$ and the *information-bearing chip* $(N/2 \leq n < N)$. Thus, one may demodulate the signal with a differential receiver, besides the coherent correlation receiver (Lathi, 1998).

The block diagram of a differential DCSK receiver is shown in Figure 4. The received signal is delayed by $N/2$, half of its duration and the correlation between the received signal and its delayed version is determined. The observation variable z_{m1} is obtained by sampling the output of the correlator at time $(N-1)$.

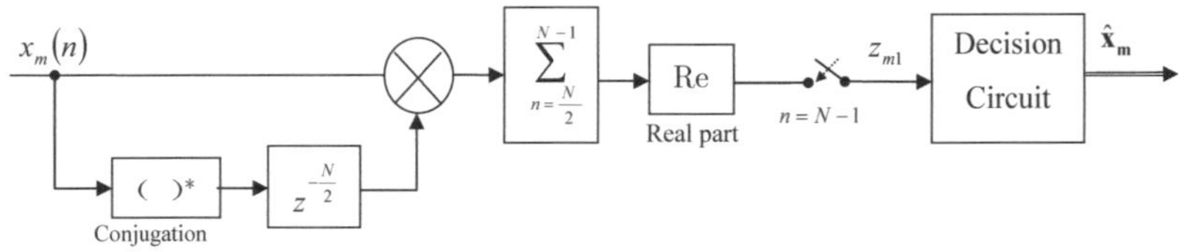

Fig. 4. Block diagram of a differential DCSK receiver.

3.2 The energy per symbol variability problem and FM-DCSK

For a conventional modulation scheme using only one periodic basis function $s_1(n)$ composed of N samples per symbol as an integer multiple of the period of $s_1(n)$, the energy per symbol is given by

$$E_{bm} = x_{m1}^2 \sum_{n=0}^{N-1} s_1^2(n) \tag{9}$$

and is constant for each distinct symbol. In contrast, chaotic signals are by definition aperiodic. Thus, when using a chaotic basis, $s_1(n)$ is different at each interval and

$$E_{s1} = \sum_{n=0}^{N-1} s_1^2(n) \tag{10}$$

is different for each transmitted symbol.

In the periodic case, all values of E_{s1} are equal to $\sum_{n=0}^{N-1} s_1^2(n)$ with zero variance. In the chaotic case, the values of E_{s1} are centered at $E\left[\sum_{n=0}^{N-1} s_1^2(n)\right]$ with non-zero variance.

Compared to conventional systems, the fact that the energy per symbol is not constant is a major disadvantage of the communication systems using chaotic signals discussed so far. For them, errors in reception can occur even in ideal noiseless channels, which is undesirable in practice. Increasing the number of points N does not solve the problem as the standard deviation in the estimate of E_{s1} falls slowly with N (Kennedy, Setti & Rovatti, 2000). Furthermore increasing the number of transmitted points per symbol also limits the maximum transmission rate.

An alternative solution is to modify the modulation scheme so that the transmitted energy for each symbol is kept constant. That is the aim of Frequency Modulated DCSK (FM-DCSK) (Kolumbán, Kennedy, Kis & Jákó, 1998).

The FM-DCSK transmitter generates a DCSK signal with constant energy per symbol. The idea is to take advantage of the fact that the power of a frequency modulated signal is independent of the signal, as long as it is slowly-varying compared to the carrier (Lathi, 1998). Thus, the chaotic signal is fed into a frequency modulator. If the output of this modulator is used in implementing DCSK, then the output of the correlator at the receiver will be a constant in the absence of noise and the problem of energy variability disappears.

For its simulation and analysis, the equivalent discrete time low-pass model of the FM-DCSK may be obtained by considering a reference chip described by

$$x_m(t) = A\cos\left[2\pi\left(f_0 + K_f s(t)\right)t\right],\ 0 \le t < \frac{T}{2}, \tag{11}$$

where T is the symbol period, f_0 is the carrier frequency, A and K_f are constants (Lathi, 1998). The constant K_f that defines the modulation intensity is heretofore taken as 1. Hence, one can rewrite Eq. (11) as

$$x_m(t) = A\left[\cos(2\pi s(t)t)\cos(2\pi f_0 t) - \sin(2\pi s(t)t)\sin(2\pi f_0 t)\right], \tag{12}$$

with $0 \le t \le T/2$. Thus, according to Eq. (2), the discrete-time low-pass equivalent of this chip of $x_m(t)$ becomes

$$x_m(n) = A\left[\cos(2\pi s(n)n) + j\sin(2\pi s(n)n)\right] = Ae^{j2\pi n s(n)} \tag{13}$$

with $0 \le n < N/2$, N even.

Note that $|x_m(n)| = A$ for any n. We adopt $A = \sqrt{\frac{E_b}{N}}$ so that each symbol is represented as a signal with energy E_b and

$$x_m(n) = \sqrt{\frac{E_b}{N}}e^{j2\pi n s(n)},\ 0 \le n < N/2. \tag{14}$$

The information-bearing chip occupies the time slot $N/2 \le n < N$ and repeats the reference chip for $m = 1$ or is equal to its opposite for $m = 2$.
A block diagram of a low-pass equivalent FM-DCSK signals generator is shown in Figure 5.

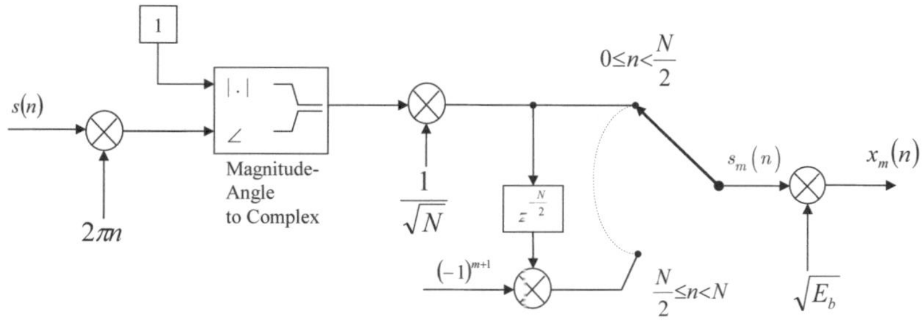

Fig. 5. Block diagram of a discrete-time FM-DCSK signals generator, $m = 1, 2$.

Figure 6 shows the real and imaginary part of the low-pass equivalent $x(n)$ of an FM-DCSK signal for the symbol sequence $\{1, 1, 0, 1, 0, 0, 1, 0\}$ using $N = 50$ samples per symbol and $E_b = 1$. Again symbol "1" and "0" are transmitted using $x_1(n)$ and $x_2(n)$ respectively using iterations of Eq. (6) to generate $s(n)$.

3.3 Comparison of performance in AWGN channel

Next we consider the Additive White Gaussian Noise (AWGN) channel performance of the afore mentioned modulations. For simplicity, only binary transmission systems using a single basis sequence $s_1(n)$ are examined. As such the transmitted signals are $x_m(n) = x_{m1}s_1(n)$, $m = 1, 2$. We denote by $\hat{s}_1(n)$ the reference signal and by $x'_m(n)$ the noisy signal that arrives at the receiver:

$$x'_m(n) = x_m(n) + r(n) = x_{m1}s_1(n) + r(n), \tag{15}$$

where $r(n)$ is zero mean AWGN with power σ^2.

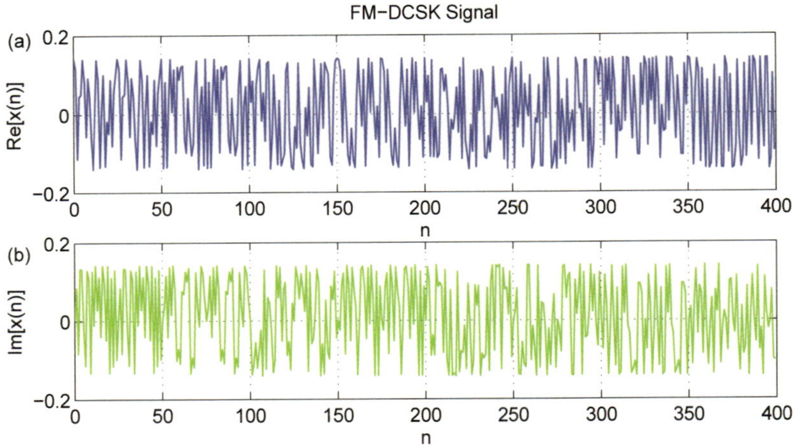

Fig. 6. (a) Real and (b) imaginary part of an FM-DCSK signal for the data sequence $\{1, 1, 0, 1, 0, 0, 1, 0\}$ using $N = 50$ samples and $E_b = 1$.

3.3.1 Non-coherent correlation receiver

In a non-coherent correlation receiver, as shown in Figure 1(b), the reference signal $\hat{s}_1(n)$ is equal to the signal that reaches the receiver $x'_m(n) = x_m(n) + r(n)$ and the observed component can be expressed as

$$z_{m1} = \sum_{n=0}^{N-1} (x_m(n) + r(n))^2 = \sum_{n=0}^{N-1} x_m^2(n) + 2\sum_{n=0}^{N-1} x_m(n)r(n) + \sum_{n=0}^{N-1} r^2(n). \tag{16}$$

In the noiseless case, $r(n) = 0$ and the expected value of the observed component is equal to the mean energy of the transmitted symbol, x_{m1}^2.

The presence of noise in the channel causes the expected value of the random variable z_{m1} to differ from x_{m1}^2. The expected value of z_{m1} depends on the chaotic signal and on the noise power as expressed by the first and third terms of the right member of Eq. (16), respectively.

In this case, z_{m1} *is a biased estimator of the energy of* $x_m(n)$ *and the threshold used at the comparator decision circuit explicitly depends on the noise level.* The way to produce an unbiased estimator with larger distance between the observed component symbols is to use coherent CSK or DCSK.

3.3.2 Coherent correlation receiver with chaotic synchronization

Let $\hat{s}_1(n)$ be the chaotic basis function recovered so that $\hat{s}_1(n) \approx s_1(n)$ for $n \geq N_{Sync}$ in Figure 1(a).

One drawback of the coherent CSK receiver is that synchronization is lost and recovered each time a new symbol is transmitted (Kennedy, Setti & Rovatti, 2000). Thus, N_{Sync} samples of each symbol are required for synchronization. In other words synchronization time imposes an upper bound on the symbol rate and thus on the data rate.

As the synchronization transient can not be used to transmit information, the observed component is obtained by correlation only in the interval $N_{Sync} \leq n < N - 1$. Let $x_m(n)$, $m = 1, 2$, be the transmitted signals for the CSK binary modulation with a single basis sequence $s_1(n)$. Then, the observed component is given by

$$z_{m1} = \sum_{n=N_{Sync}}^{N-1} [x_m(n) + r(n)] \hat{s}_1(n) = \sum_{n=N_{Sync}}^{N-1} [x_{m1} s_1(n) + r(n)] \hat{s}_1(n) =$$
$$= x_{m1} \sum_{n=N_{Sync}}^{N-1} s_1(n)\hat{s}_1(n) + \sum_{n=N_{Sync}}^{N-1} r(n)\hat{s}_1(n). \quad (17)$$

Assuming that $r(n)$ and $\hat{s}_1(n)$ are uncorrelated, the mean value of z_{m1} is independent of noise; thus, the receiver becomes an *unbiased estimator* of x_{m1}; in particular, the decision level in the comparator does not depend on the noise level in the channel.
As with conventional coherent receivers that use periodic basis functions, the performance of coherent receivers that use chaotic basis functions under AWGN is theoretically optimal (Lathi, 1998). However, the BER also depends on synchronization quality, i.e., the closeness between the reference signal $\hat{s}_1(n)$ and the original chaotic basis function $s_1(n)$. Any synchronization error, especially the loss of synchronization, leads to large performance degradation (Kennedy, Setti & Rovatti, 2000).
Chaos synchronization techniques published to date are very sensitive to noise. In particular, the basis functions $s_i(n)$ can not be recovered exactly when $x'_m(n) \neq x_m(n)$ (Kennedy, Setti & Rovatti, 2000; Williams, 2001). This makes receivers based on chaotic synchronization unsuitable for propagation environments with low SNR.
The number of samples N_{Sync} needed for synchronization is another factor that degrades the performance of these systems under noise. As no information can be transmitted during the synchronization transient, the energy corresponding to that signal section is lost implying BER degradation.
Thus, even though coherent correlation CSK receivers outperform non-coherent ones by providing an unbiased transmitted symbol estimator, its performance depends critically on the ability to regenerate the basis functions at the receiver. The existing chaotic synchronization techniques are insufficiently robust for practical wireless communication systems (Williams, 2001).

3.3.3 Differential receiver

In a differential receiver for DCSK or FM-DCSK, the reference signal $\hat{s}(n)$ is a delayed version of the noisy signal that reaches the receiver, as was shown in Figure 4. Note that different noise samples corrupt the correlator entries. The observed component is given by

$$z_{m1} = \sum_{n=\frac{N}{2}}^{N-1} [x_m(n) + r(n)] \left[x_m \left(n - \frac{N}{2}\right) + r\left(n - \frac{N}{2}\right)\right]. \quad (18)$$

Substituting Eqs.(4) and (8) in Eq.(18) gives the observed component for DCSK as

$$z_{m1} = (-1)^{m+1} E_b \sum_{n=\frac{N}{2}}^{N-1} s^2(n) + \sqrt{E_b} \sum_{n=\frac{N}{2}}^{N-1} r(n) s\left(n - \frac{N}{2}\right) + (-1)^{m+1}\sqrt{E_b} \sum_{n=\frac{N}{2}}^{N-1} s(n) r\left(n - \frac{N}{2}\right) +$$
$$\sum_{n=\frac{N}{2}}^{N-1} r(n) r\left(n - \frac{N}{2}\right), \quad (19)$$

assuming $s(n) = s\left(n - \frac{N}{2}\right)$ for $N/2 \leq n < N$.
For DCSK, the mean value of the first term is $E_b/2$ or $-E_b/2$. In the equivalent FM-DCSK case, the transmitted symbol energy value is constant and equal to $E_b/2$ or $-E_b/2$. The other three terms containing the AWGN sequence are zero mean. This shows that z_{m1} is an unbiased estimator of $\pm E_b/2$ in this case. The decision level is zero and independent of the noise level in the channel.
In the DCSK case, the variance of z_{m1} is determined by the statistical variability of the energy per symbol of the chaotic signal and by the noise power in the channel. Therefore, the uncertainty in the energy estimation also influences the performance of DCSK.
For the FM-DCSK, the first term of Eq.(19) equals $\pm E_b/2$ and the uncertainty in the energy estimation does not appear, also the decision threshold is fixed and there is no need for chaotic synchronization. This makes FM-DCSK superior to the other previous chaotic modulations schemes in terms of performance in AWGN channel.
In Figure 7 we numerically evaluate the performance of the analyzed systems in terms of BER as a function of E_b/N_0 for $N = 10$. The white noise power spectral density in the channel is $N_0/2$. As expected, it is clear that the FM-DCSK is the one that has the best performance among them. This is so basically because the energy per symbol is kept constant in this system. Still, its performance is below that of its counterpart using sinusoidal carriers, the Differential Phase Shift Keying (DPSK). In DPSK the knowledge of the basis functions by the receiver, allows the use of matched filters or correlation which improves its BER for a given E_b/N_0 (Lathi, 1998).

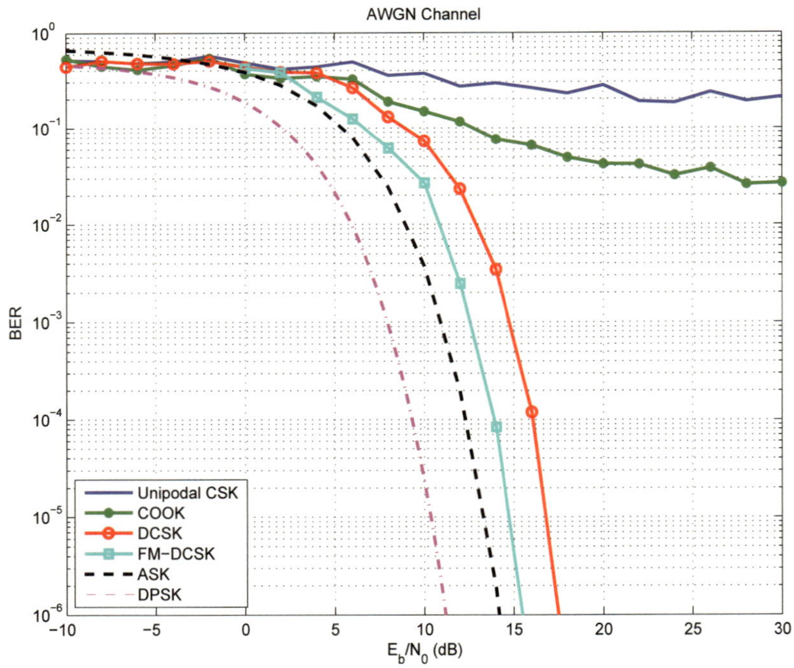

Fig. 7. Symbol error rates in AWGN channel of digital communication systems using chaotic signals for $N = 10$. The curves for conventional Amplitude Shift Keying (ASK) and DPSK are shown for comparison.

Though FM-DCSK has the best features among the analyzed chaotic systems, it is important to note that no information concerning the dynamics of the chaotic map is used in its demodulation. Its performance would be essentially the same in case random sequences were used instead of chaotic ones.
If knowledge of the dynamics of the generator map were used in demodulation process, certainly better results could be obtained, as in conventional systems that use matched filters.

3.4 Chaotic modulations summary

Thus far we presented some of the most studied modulation systems using chaotic signals. Their performance in AWGN channel was qualitatively and quantitatively analyzed.
The discrete-time notation used here is a contribution of this chapter as it is consistent with the maps used in the generation of chaotic signals and also simplifies computational simulations.
Table 1 summarizes the problems encountered in the main digital modulations described. The column **Threshold** concerns the problem of dependence of the decision threshold on the noise power in the channel. The column **Energy** represents the problem of variability of energy per symbol. The column **Sync.** means the need for recovery of basis chaotic functions at the receiver and the last column, **Map Info** when signaled means that the system does not use properties of the chaotic attractor in the estimation of the transmitted symbol.

System	Threshold	Energy	Sync.	Map Info
Coherent CSK		X	X	
Noncoherent CSK	X	X		X
DCSK		X		X
FM-DCSK				X

Table 1. Problems of chaotic modulations studied in the section.

Among the modulations studied, FM-DCSK has the best results because it does not depend on chaotic synchronization, its decision level threshold is independent of noise and it has constant mean energy per symbol.
The analyzed non-coherent and differential receivers have a common feature: they do not use any characteristic of the dynamics of the systems that generate the chaotic signals to process the demodulation. These techniques are limited to estimating characteristics of the received signal and to comparing them to an adequate decision threshold.
A priori knowledge of generating maps by the receiver can be used in two ways:

i. via chaotic synchronization using coherent demodulation or

ii. via improving signal to noise ratio or by distinguishing them through techniques to estimate the chaotic signals arriving at the receiver.

The presence of noise and distortion in the channel brings unsatisfactory results when using chaotic synchronization due to the sensitive dependence on initial conditions that characterize chaotic signals (Kennedy, Setti & Rovatti, 2000; Lau & Tse, 2003; Williams, 2001). Hence the only remaining option is to examine the second alternative.
Some estimation techniques for orbits and initial conditions based on maximizing likelihood functions (Eisencraft et al., 2009; Kisel et al., 2001) have been proposed recently, yielding results better than those presented in this section. The rest of the chapter is devoted to these techniques.

4. Chaotic signal estimation

Assume that an N-point sequence $s'(n)$ is observed whose model is given by

$$s'(n) = s(n) + r(n),\ 0 \leq n \leq N-1, \tag{20}$$

where $s(n)$ is an orbit of the known one-dimensional system

$$s(n) = f(s(n-1)) \tag{21}$$

and $r(n)$ is zero mean AWGN with variance σ^2. The $f(.)$ map is defined over the interval U. The problem is to obtain an estimate $\hat{s}(n)$ of the orbit $s(n)$.
The Cramer-Rao Lower Bound (CRLB), the minimum mean square error that an estimator of the initial condition $s(0)$ can attain, was derived by Eisencraft & Baccalá (2006; 2008).
Let the *estimation gain* G_{dB} in decibels be given by

$$G_{dB} = 10 \log \left(\frac{\sigma^2}{e} \right), \tag{22}$$

be the figure of merit, where $e = \overline{(\hat{s}(n) - s(n))^2}$ is the mean square estimation error.
We succinctly review two estimation techniques for noise-embedded chaotic signals: the Maximum Likelihood (ML) Estimator and the Modified Viterbi algorithm (MVA).

4.1 Maximum likelihood estimator

The ML estimator of some scalar parameter θ is the value that maximizes the likelihood function $p(\mathbf{x};\theta)$ for the observation vector $\mathbf{x}$ (Kay, 1993). What motivates this definition is that $p(\mathbf{x};\theta)d\mathbf{x}$ represents the probability of observing $\mathbf{x}$ within a neighborhood given by $d\mathbf{x}$ for some value of θ. In the present context, it was first used by Papadopoulos & Wornell (1993) who show that the estimation gain for an N-point orbit generated by a map with uniform invariant density (Lasota & Mackey, 1985) is limited by

$$G_{dB} \leq 10 \log(N+1). \tag{23}$$

which asymptotically corresponds to the Cramer-Rao performance bound.

4.2 Modified Viterbi algorithm

This algorithm is based on that proposed by Dedieu & Kisel (1999) and was generalized for maps with nonuniform invariant density by Eisencraft & do Amaral (2009).
Consider the domain U as the union of disjoint intervals U_j, $j = 1, 2, \ldots, N_S$. At a given instant n, let the signal *state* be $q(n) = j$ if $s(n) \in U_j$. A $(k+1)$-length state sequence is represented by

$$\mathbf{q}_k = [q(0), q(1), \ldots, q(k)]^T \tag{24}$$

and the first $k+1$ observed samples by

$$\mathbf{s}'_k = \left[s'(0), s'(1), \ldots, s'(k)\right]^T. \tag{25}$$

To simplify notation, consider the N-length sequences $\mathbf{q}_{N-1} \equiv \mathbf{q}$ and $\mathbf{s}'_{N-1} \equiv \mathbf{s}'$. Furthermore, the center of interval U_j is denoted by $B(j)$.

Given $\mathbf{s}'$, an estimated state sequence $\hat{\mathbf{q}}$ is sought that maximizes the posterior probability

$$P(\hat{\mathbf{q}}|\mathbf{s}') = \max_{\mathbf{q}} P(\mathbf{q}|\mathbf{s}'). \tag{26}$$

Using Bayes' theorem,

$$P(\mathbf{q}|\mathbf{s}') = \frac{p(\mathbf{s}'|\mathbf{q})P(\mathbf{q})}{p(\mathbf{s}')}, \tag{27}$$

where $p(\mathbf{s}')$ and $p(\mathbf{s}'|\mathbf{q})$ are, respectively, the Probability Density Function (PDF) of $\mathbf{s}'$ and the PDF of $\mathbf{s}'$ given that the state sequence of the signal is $\mathbf{q}$. The probability $P(\mathbf{q})$ is the chance of obtaining the state sequence $\mathbf{q}$ when $f(.)$ is iterated.
Thus, the argument $\hat{\mathbf{q}}$ is such that

$$\hat{\mathbf{q}} = \arg\max_{\mathbf{q}} P(\mathbf{q}|\mathbf{s}') = \arg\max_{\mathbf{q}} p(\mathbf{s}'|\mathbf{q})P(\mathbf{q}). \tag{28}$$

It is important to note that because of the AWGN model and of how signals are generated, $\mathbf{q}_k$ is a first order Markov process where k is the time variable. Thus

$$P(\mathbf{q}_k) = P(q(k)|q(k-1))\, P(\mathbf{q}_{k-1}), \tag{29}$$

where $P(q(k)|q(k-1))$ is the transition probability from the state $q(k-1)$ to $q(k)$.
Furthermore, taking into account the independence between the noise samples,

$$p(\mathbf{s}'_k|\mathbf{q}_k) = \prod_{n=0}^{k} p\left(s'(n)|q(n)\right) = \prod_{n=0}^{k} p_r(s'(n) - s(n)) \approx \prod_{n=0}^{k} p_r\left(s'(n) - B\left(q(n)\right)\right), \tag{30}$$

with $p_r(.)$ standing for the noise PDF. The approximation in Eq. (30) holds only for sufficiently large N_S.
Using Eqs. (28-30), one can express $P(\mathbf{q}|\mathbf{s}')$ as a product of state transition probabilities by conditional observation probabilities. Hence $\hat{\mathbf{q}}$ is the sequence that maximizes

$$\left(\prod_{n=1}^{N-1} P\left(q(n)|q(n-1)\right) p\left(s'(n)|q(n)\right)\right) P\left(q(0)\right). \tag{31}$$

Choosing the partition $U_j, j = 1, 2, \ldots, N_S$ so that the probability of each possible state $q(n) = j$ is the same for all j, the last term in Eq. (31), $P(q(0))$, can be eliminated leading to

$$\hat{\mathbf{q}} = \arg\max_{\mathbf{q}} \prod_{n=1}^{N-1} P\left(q(n)|q(n-1)\right) p\left(s'(n)|q(n)\right), \tag{32}$$

as in (Kisel et al., 2001). Note, however, the central role played by the choice of the partition in obtaining this result as recently pointed out by Eisencraft et al. (2009).
Finding $\mathbf{q}$ that maximizes the product in Eq. (32) is a classic problem whose efficient solution is given by the Viterbi Algorithm (Forney, 1973; Viterbi, 1967), which was first applied to the estimation of chaotic signals by Marteau & Abarbanel (1991). The main advantage in its use lies in dispensing with exhaustive search on the $(N_S)^N$ possible state sequences for an N-point signal.
Let $\gamma(n, j)$ be the probability of the most probable state sequence, in the maximum likelihood sense, that ends in state j, at instant $n \geq 1$, given the observed sequence $\mathbf{s}'$, or

$$\gamma(n, j) = \max_{\mathbf{q}_n} P(\mathbf{q}_{n-1}, q(n) = j|\mathbf{s}'). \tag{33}$$

Using Eqs. (29-30), $\gamma(n,j)$ can be calculated recursively

$$\gamma(n,j) = \max_{i} \left[\gamma(n-1,i)a_{ij}\right] b_j\left(s'(n)\right), \tag{34}$$

for $n > 1$ where

$$a_{ij} = P\left(q(n) = j | q(n-1) = i\right) \tag{35}$$

and

$$b_j\left(s'(n)\right) = p\left(s'(n) | q(n) = j\right). \tag{36}$$

The coefficients a_{ij} are the state transition probabilities that depend on the map $f(.)$ and on the partition. Let the transition probability matrix be given by

$$\mathbf{A}_{N_S \times N_S} = a_{ij}, 1 \leq i,j \leq N_S. \tag{37}$$

The $b_j(.)$ coefficients represent the observation conditional probabilities that depend only on the noise PDF $p_r(.)$.
The Viterbi algorithm proceeds in two passes, the forward one and the backward one:

- **Forward pass**: for each instant $1 \leq n \leq N-1$, Eqs. (33 - 34) are used to calculate $\gamma(n,j)$ for the N_S states. Among the N_S paths that can link states $j = 1,\ldots,N_S$ at instant $n-1$ to state j at instant n, only the most probable one is maintained. The matrix $\varphi(n,j)$, $n = 1,\ldots,N-1, j = 1,\ldots,N_S$, stores the state at instant $n-1$ that takes to state j with maximal probability. In the end of this step, at instant $n = N-1$, we select the most probable state as $\hat{q}(N-1)$.
- **Backward pass**: for obtaining the most probable sequence, it is necessary to consider the argument i that maximizes Eq. (34) for each n and j. This is done defining

$$\hat{q}(n) = \varphi\left(n+1, \hat{q}(n+1)\right), \; n = N-2,\ldots,0. \tag{38}$$

Once obtained $\hat{q}(n)$, the estimated orbit is given by the centers of the subintervals related to the most probable state sequence,

$$\hat{s}(n) = B\left(\hat{q}(n)\right), \; n = 0,\ldots,N-1. \tag{39}$$

4.2.1 Partition of the state space

To apply the algorithm one must choose a partition so that the probability of an orbit point to be in any state is the same, to eliminate $P\left(q(0)\right)$ in Eq. (31). This means that if a given map has invariant density $p(s)$ (Lasota & Mackey, 1985), one should take N_S intervals $U_j = [u_j; u_{j+1}]$ so that, for every $j = 1,\ldots,N_S$,

$$\int_{u_j}^{u_{j+1}} p(s)ds = \frac{1}{N_S}. \tag{40}$$

Using the ergodicity of chaotic orbits (Lasota & Mackey, 1985), it is possible to estimate $p(s)$ for a given $f(.)$ and thereby obtain the correct partition.
The maps taken as examples by Xiaofeng et al. (2004) and Kisel et al. (2001) have uniform invariant density and the authors proposed using equal length subintervals. However, this choice is not applicable to arbitrary one-dimensional maps. When using Viterbi algorithm with the correct partition, it is called here *Modified Viterbi Algorithm* (MVA) (Eisencraft et al., 2009).

As illustrative examples, consider the uniform invariant density tent map defined in $U = (-1,1)$ as Eq.(6) and the nonuniform invariant density quadratic map

$$f_Q(s) = 1 - 2s^2, \tag{41}$$

defined over the same U (Eisencraft & Baccalá, 2008). It can be shown (Lasota & Mackey, 1985) that, the invariant density of these maps are

$$p_T(s) = 1/2 \tag{42}$$

and

$$p_Q(s) = \frac{1}{\pi\sqrt{1-s^2}}, \tag{43}$$

respectively.
An example of orbit for each of these maps and their respective invariant densities are shown in Figures 8 and 9. The partition satisfying Eq. (40) for each case is also indicated when $N_S = 5$.

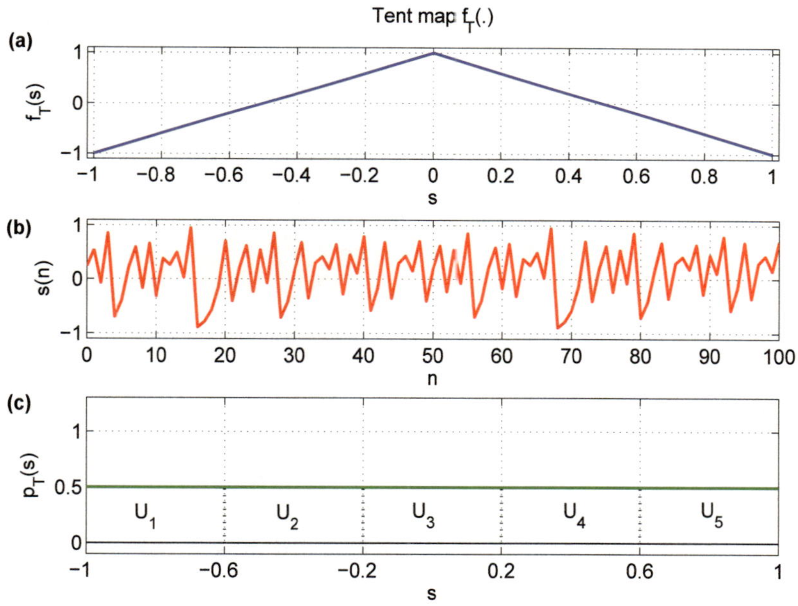

Fig. 8. (a) Tent map $f_T(.)$; (b) example of a 100-point signal generated by $f_T(.)$; (c) invariant density along with the partition satisfying Eq. (40) for $N_S = 5$.

Figures 10 and 11 present how the performance of MVA varies for different values of N_S and $N = 10$. In Figure 10 the generating map is $f_T(.)$ whereas $f_Q(.)$ is used in Figure 11. To illustrate the importance of the correct partition choice, Figure 11(a) displays the results of mistakenly using a uniform partition whereas Figure 11(b) displays the results of using the correct partition according to Eq. (40). The input and output SNR are defined as

$$\mathrm{SNR_{in}} = \frac{\sum_{n=0}^{N-1} s^2(n)}{N\sigma^2} \tag{44}$$

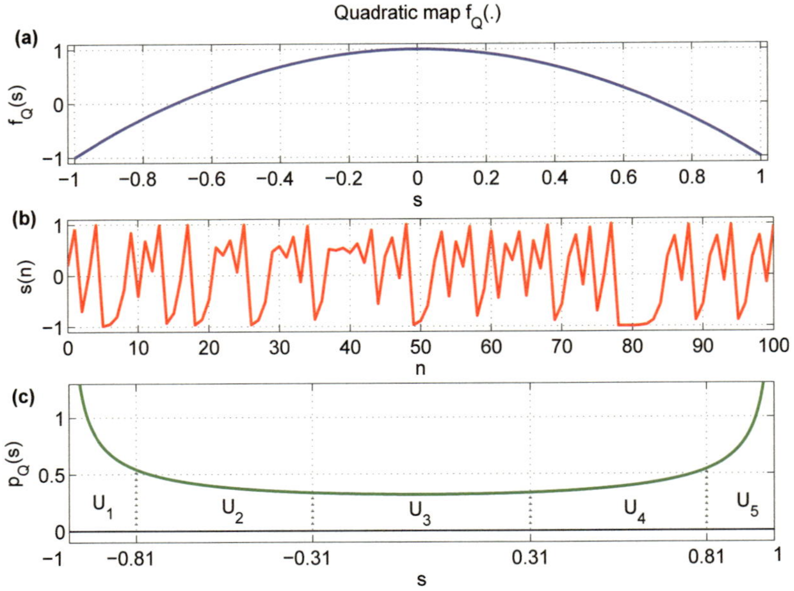

Fig. 9. (a) Quadratic map $f_Q(.)$; (b) example of a 100-point signal generated by $f_Q(.)$; (c) invariant density along with the partition satisfying Eq. (40) for $N_S = 5$.

and

$$\mathrm{SNR_{out}} = \frac{\sum_{n=0}^{N-1} s^2(n)}{\sum_{n=0}^{N-1} (s(n) - \hat{s}(n))^2}. \tag{45}$$

For each $\mathrm{SNR_{in}}$ of the input sequence, the average $\mathrm{SNR_{out}}$ of 1000 estimates is shown. Choosing the right partition, the estimation algorithm has an increasing performance as a function of $\mathrm{SNR_{in}}$ until $\mathrm{SNR_{out}}$ attains a limit value which depends on N_S. This limiting value can be calculated assuming that, in the best possible case, the estimation error is caused by domain quantization alone. As such, for an uniform partition, the estimation error is an uniformly distributed random variable in the interval $[-1/N_S, 1/N_S]$. Therefore the mean squared value of $s(n) - \hat{s}(n)$ is limited by $1/\left(3N_S^2\right)$. Additionally, $s(n)$ is uniformly distributed in $[-1,1]$ and, consequently, has a mean squared value of 1/3. Hence if all the points are in the correct subintervals, the expected value of $\mathrm{SNR_{out}}$, $E[\mathrm{SNR_{out}}]$ in dB is

$$E\left[\mathrm{SNR_{out}}\right] = E\left[10\log\frac{\sum_{n=0}^{N-1} s^2(n)}{\sum_{n=0}^{N-1}(s(n) - \hat{s}(n))^2}\right] = 10\log\frac{N/3}{N/(3N_S^2)} = 20\log N_S. \tag{46}$$

These limits, which are exact only in the uniform partition case, are indicated with dashed lines for each N_S value in Figures 10 and 11.

Comparing Figures 11(a) and (b) reveals the critical role played by the partition choice. Clearly the uniform partition of Xiaofeng et al. (2004) and Kisel et al. (2001) cannot attain the best possible $\mathrm{SNR_{out}}$ for the quadratic map whose invariant density is not uniform.

Figures 10 and 11(b) show that the algorithm has slightly better performance for the quadratic map. This result confirms the importance of map choice.

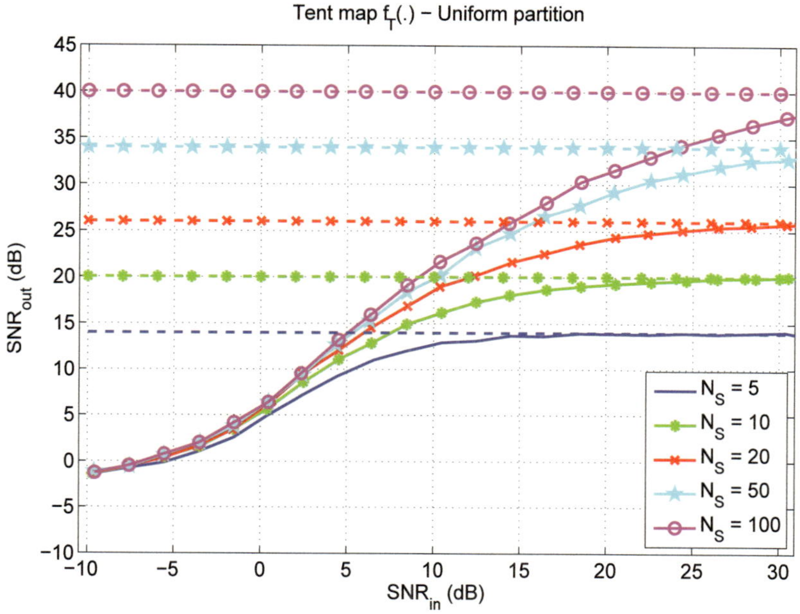

Fig. 10. SNR_{out} of MVA for an orbit of length $N = 10$ using different numbers of partition intervals N_S . The generating map is $f_T(.)$. Performance limits of Eq. (46) are indicated by dashed lines.

4.3 Comparing MVA and MLE

MLE's performance is strongly influenced by the length of the estimated orbit N, as shown by inequality (23). MVA is more sensitive to the number of subsets N_S used in the partition. Simulations show that the gain obtained via MLE monotonically increases with Signal to Noise Ratio (SNR) being bounded by the CRLB. Using MVA, the gain attains a maximum value and decays and even becomes negative (in dB) due to quantization error. So the N_S choice is a very important concern for MVA and it is a function of the expected SNR.
The estimation gain for both methods on tent map orbits from Eq. (6) corrupted by AWGN is shown in Figure 12. For the MVA only the $N = 20$ result is depicted as simulations show little improvement for larger N.
From Figure 12 one can see that for SNR $\leq$ 20dB, which is the usual operating range, MVA's performance is superior.
These results, plus the fact that MVA can be simply applied to broader map classes have induced the choice of MVA in the communication applications described next.

5. Chaotic signal estimation applied to communication

In this section we propose two binary digital modulation using chaotic system identification. They are the *Modified Maximum Likelihood Chaos Shift Keying* (MMLCSK) using one and two maps. Both are based on the ones proposed by Kisel et al. (2001). We have modified them using nonuniform partitions for the MVA as discussed in the previous section. In this way, it is possible to test the performance of nonuniform invariant density maps.

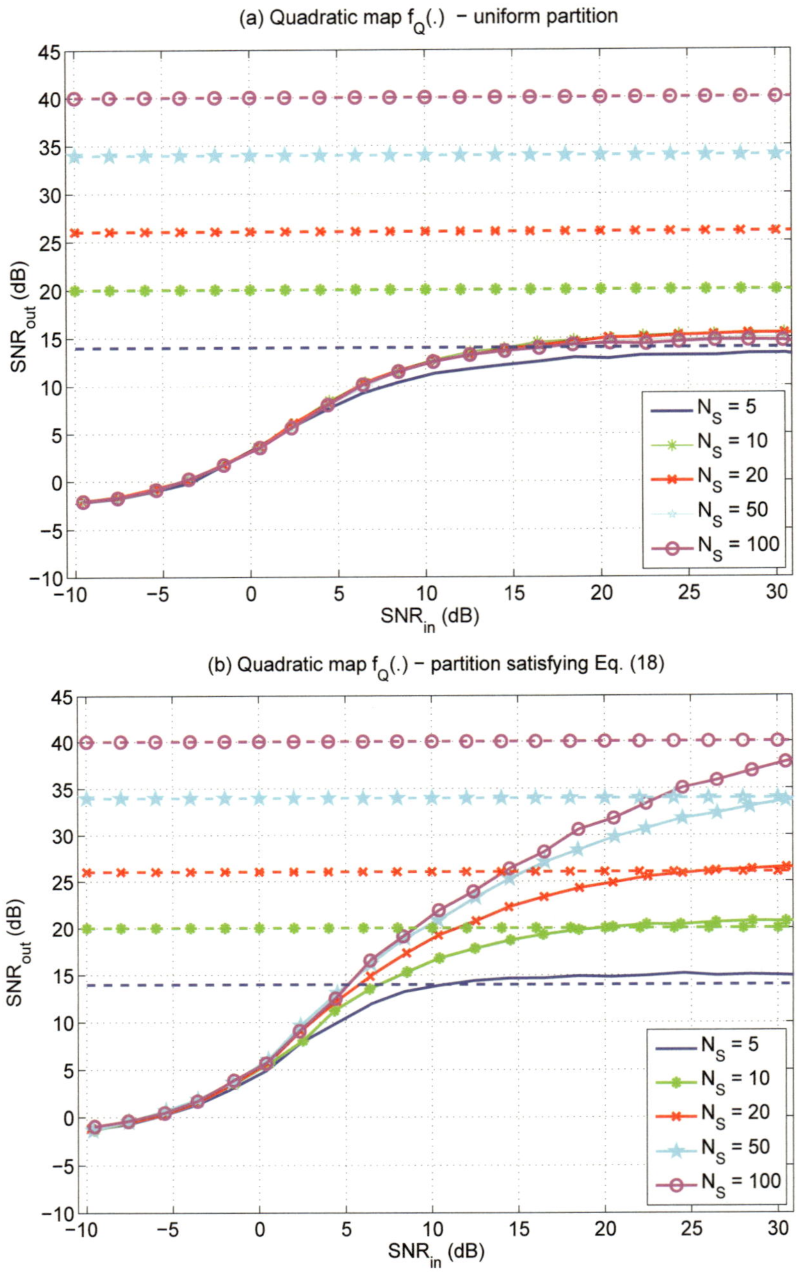

Fig. 11. SNR_{out} of the MVA for an orbit of length $N = 10$ using different number of partition intervals N_S. The generating map is $f_Q(.)$. Results for an uniform partition (a) are contrasted to the improved values in (b) using a partition satisfying Eq. (40). Limits of Eq. (46) are indicated by dashed lines.

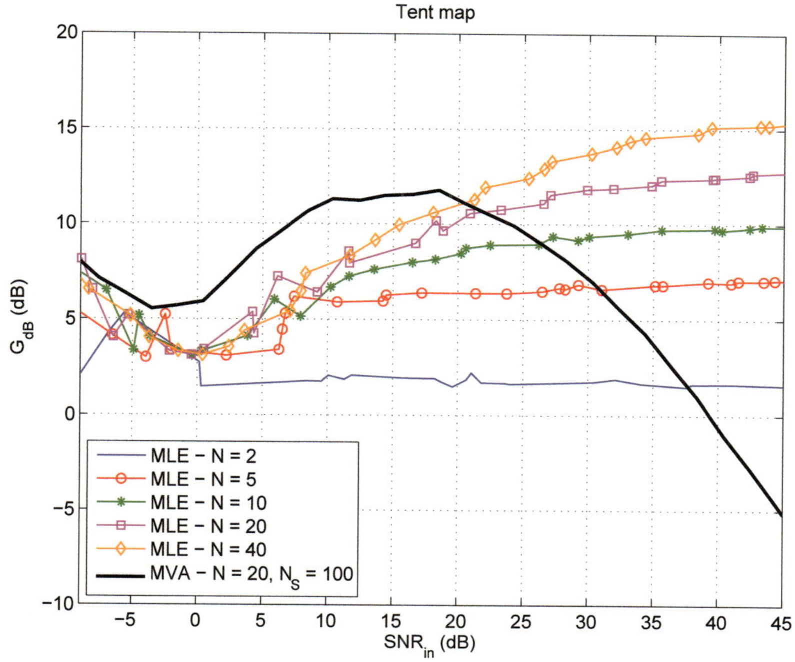

Fig. 12. Estimation gain for MLE and MVA for tent map Eq. (6).

5.1 MMLCSK using two maps

In this case, each symbol is associated with a different map, $f_1(.)$ or $f_2(.)$. To transmit a "0", the transmitter sends an N-point orbit $s_1(.)$ of $f_1(.)$ and to transmit a "1" it sends an N-point orbit $s_2(.)$ of $f_2(.)$.

Maps must be chosen so that their state transition probabilities matrix (Eq. (37)) $\mathbf{A}_1$ and $\mathbf{A}_2$ are different. Estimating $s_1(n)$ using MVA with $\mathbf{A}_2$ must produce a small estimation gain or even a negative (in dB) one. The same must happen when we try to estimate $s_2(n)$ using $\mathbf{A}_1$.

The receiver for MMLCSK using two maps is shown in Figure 13. The Viterbi decoders try to estimate the original $s(n)$ using $\mathbf{A}_1$ or $\mathbf{A}_2$. For each symbol, the estimated state sequences are $\hat{\mathbf{q}}_1$ and $\hat{\mathbf{q}}_2$.

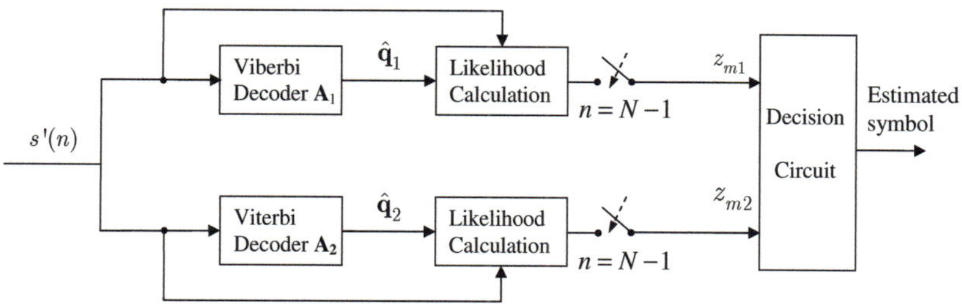

Fig. 13. Receiver for MMLCSK using two maps.

Given the observed samples, z_{m1} e z_{m2} are proportional to the probability of obtaining $\hat{\mathbf{q}}_1$ and $\hat{\mathbf{q}}_2$ respectively. More precisely,

$$z_{m1} = \prod_{n=1}^{N-1} P(\hat{q_1}(n)|\hat{q}_1(n-1), \mathbf{A}_1)p(s'(n)|\hat{q_1}(n)), \tag{47}$$

$$z_{m2} = \prod_{n=1}^{N-1} P(\hat{q_2}(n)|\hat{q}_2(n-1), \mathbf{A}_2)p(s'(n)|\hat{q_2}(n)). \tag{48}$$

In these equations the likelihood measure of Eq. (32) was used. The probability $P(\hat{q}(n)|\hat{q}(n-1), \mathbf{A}_i)$ can be read directly from $\mathbf{A}_i$ and $p(x'(n)|\hat{q}(n))$ depends only on the noise and can be approximated as described by Dedieu & Kisel (1999).
Choosing the largest between z_{m1} e z_{m2} allows *identifying* the map used in the transmitter with maximum likelihood and thereby decode the transmitted symbol.
Given some $f_1(.)$ map, an important problem is to find the matching $f_2(.)$ map so that its probability transition matrix $\mathbf{A}_2$ permits optimal discrimination between the likelihood measures of Eqs. (47) and (48). For piecewise linear maps on the interval $U = [-1, 1]$ we can use the following rule adapted from (Kisel et al., 2001):

$$f_2(s) = \begin{cases} f_1(s) + 1, \ f_1(s) < 0 \\ f_1(s) - 1, \ f_1(s) \geq 0 \end{cases}. \tag{49}$$

Figure 14(a) shows the construction of map $f_2(.)$ from $f_1(.) = f_T(.)$. This way, $f_1(s)$ and $f_2(s)$ map a point s a unity away.
In this case, using an uniform partition for $N_S = 5$ we have

$$\mathbf{A}_1 = \begin{bmatrix} 1/2 & 1/2 & 0 & 0 & 0 \\ 0 & 0 & 1/2 & 1/2 & 0 \\ 0 & 0 & 0 & 0 & 1 \\ 0 & 0 & 1/2 & 1/2 & 0 \\ 1/2 & 1/2 & 0 & 0 & 0 \end{bmatrix}, \mathbf{A}_2 = \begin{bmatrix} 0 & 0 & 1/3 & 1/3 & 1/3 \\ 1/3 & 1/3 & 0 & 0 & 1/3 \\ 0 & 1/2 & 1/2 & 0 & 0 \\ 1/3 & 1/3 & 0 & 0 & 1/3 \\ 0 & 0 & 1/3 & 1/3 & 1/3 \end{bmatrix}. \tag{50}$$

It can be shown that almost every orbit generated by $f_2(.)$ is in fact chaotic (Kisel et al., 2001). Note however that this method is not necessarily optimal and must be used prudently. There is no guarantee that the orbits of $f_2(.)$ given by Eq. (49) are chaotic in general.
For instance, if we apply the same strategy for the quadratic map $f_1(s) = f_Q(s)$ from Eq. (41), we obtain $f_2(s)$ show in Figure 14(b). All the orbits of $f_2(.)$ converge to a stable fixed point at $s = 0$ and hence are not chaotic at all (Alligood et al., 1997).
In the simulations presented here $f_2(.) = -f_Q(.)$ as shown in Figure 14(c). This map is possibly not optimum because points next to the roots of $f_1(.)$ and $f_2(.)$ are mapped near to each other by both functions. The transition matrix for these two maps for $N_S = 5$ using the partition obeying Eq. (40) are

$$\mathbf{A}_1 = \begin{bmatrix} 1/2 & 1/2 & 0 & 0 & 0 \\ 0 & 0 & 1/2 & 1/2 & 0 \\ 0 & 0 & 0 & 0 & 1 \\ 0 & 0 & 1/2 & 1/2 & 0 \\ 1/2 & 1/2 & 0 & 0 & 0 \end{bmatrix}, \mathbf{A}_2 = \begin{bmatrix} 0 & 0 & 0 & 1/2 & 1/2 \\ 0 & 0 & 1 & 0 & 0 \\ 1 & 0 & 0 & 0 & 0 \\ 0 & 0 & 1 & 0 & 0 \\ 0 & 0 & 0 & 1/2 & 1/2 \end{bmatrix}. \tag{51}$$

In this case, it can be shown that $f_2(.)$ generates chaotic orbits (Alligood et al., 1997). However, note that a_{23} and a_{43} exhibit nonzero probabilities in both matrices that will probably generate

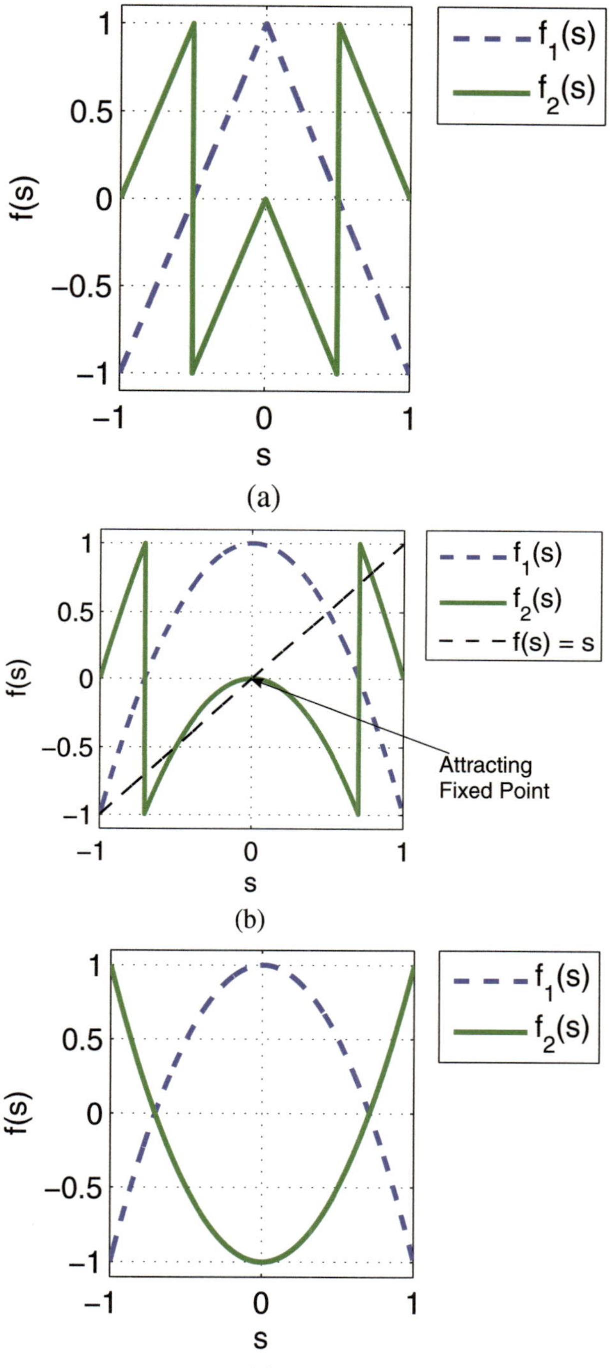

Fig. 14. (a) Construction of map $f_2(.)$ for $f_1(.) = f_T(.)$ using Eq. (49); (b) construction of $f_2(.)$ for $f_1(.) = f_Q(.)$ using Eq. (49). Note the attracting fixed point; (c) construction of $f_2(.)$ for $f_1(.) = f_Q(.)$ used in simulations.

errors in the MMLCSK receiver. As such this pair of maps is expected to have worse performance when compared to the one with matrices given by Eq. (50).
To find $f_2(.)$ given a map $f_1(.)$ that presents optimal properties when it comes to identification through matrices $\mathbf{A}_1$ and $\mathbf{A}_2$ is an open problem. As shown by the last example, it is necessary to impose that $f_2(.)$ generates chaotic orbits.
Figure 15 shows examples of transmitted MMLCSK using two maps for $f_1(.) = f_T(.)$ and $f_1(.) = f_Q(.)$.

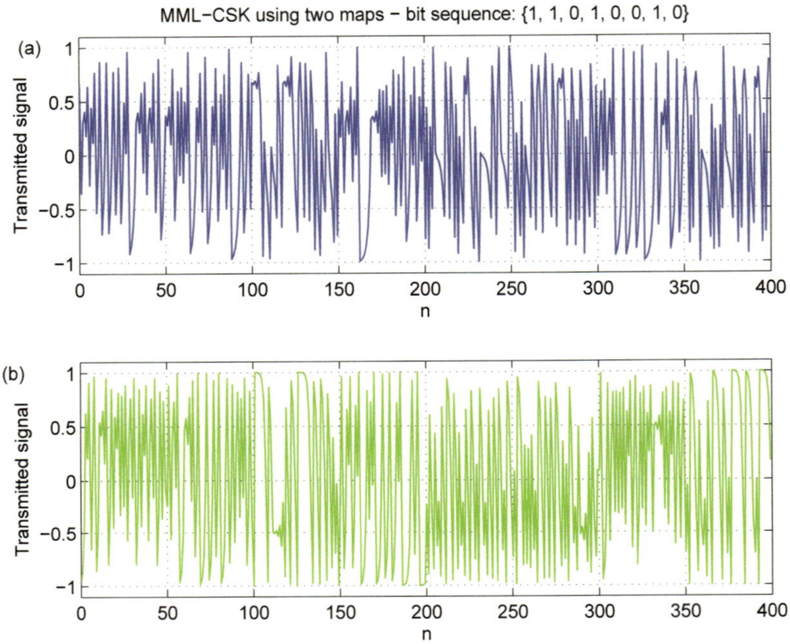

Fig. 15. MML-CSK signals using two maps for the bit sequence $\{1, 1, 0, 1, 0, 0, 1, 0\}$: (a) $f_T(.)$; (b) $f_Q(.)$. In both cases, 50 samples per bit are used.

5.2 MMLCK using one map

As an alternative, it is possible to construct a communication system based on MVA estimation using just one map. In this case, according to the symbol that is intended to be communicated, the chaotic signal is directly transmitted or an invertible transformation is applied on the sequence. This operation must modify the sequence so that it is no longer a valid orbit of the map which dispenses with finding an $f_2(.)$ map.
In the binary case, for maps that are not odd, this transformation can be, for instance, $T(s) = -s$ which can be undone by multiplying the sequence by -1. To transmit a **0**, an N-point orbit $s_1(.)$ of $f_1(.)$ is sent. To transmit a **1** is sent $-s_1(.)$.
The receiver for this system is shown in Figure 16. The variables z_{m1} and z_{m2} are calculated by Eq. (47). However, when calculating z_{m2}, $s'(n)$ is substituted by $-s'(n)$. So, when a **0** is received, the likelihood expressed by z_{m1} must be greater than z_{m2} because $-s_1(n)$ is not an orbit of $f_1(.)$. The opposite is true when a **1** is received.
It is relevant to note that this scheme can be easily generalized to M-ary modulation, $M > 2$. For this all that is needed is to consider other invertible transformations.

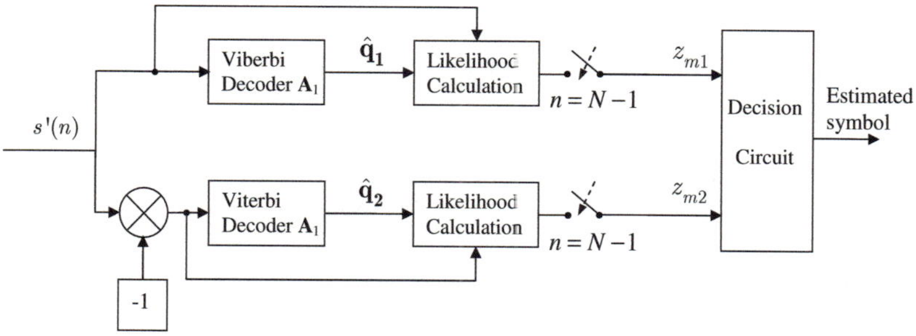

Fig. 16. Receiver for MMLCSK using one maps.

Figure 17 shows examples of modulated signals using one map for $f_1(.) = f_T(.)$ and $f_1(.) = f_Q(.)$.

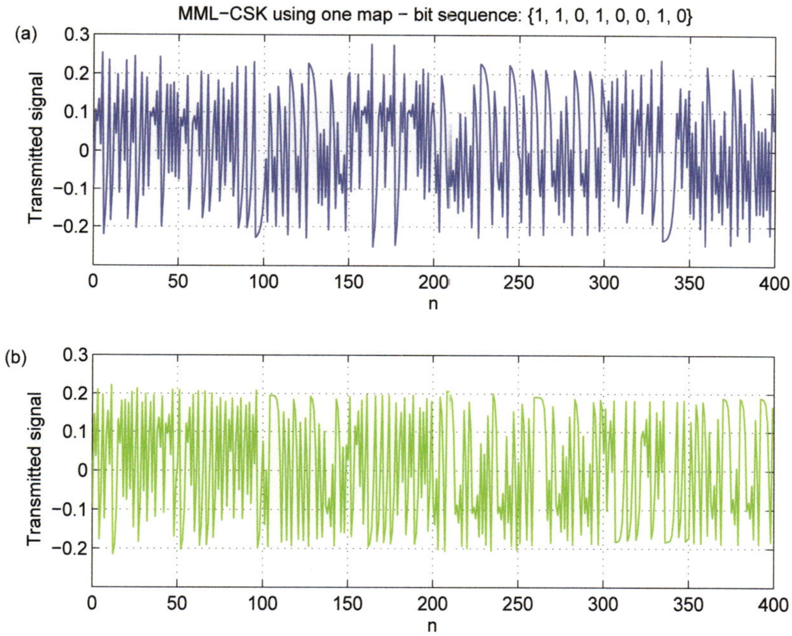

Fig. 17. MML-CSK signals using one map for the bit sequence $\{1,1,0,1,0,0,1,0\}$: (a) $f_T(.)$; (b) $f_Q(.)$. In both cases, 50 samples per bit are used.

5.3 Numerical simulations

Figure 18 shows the BER as a function of the bit energy per power spectral density of the AWGN (E_b/N_0) for the MMLCSK using one and two maps. In the estimation and identification process $N_S = 100$ subsets and $N = 50$ samples per bit were used. For the sake of comparison, the performance of Chaos On-Off Keying (COOK) (the best performing non-coherent chaos communication system that does not use estimation) is also shown (Kolumban, Kennedy & Chua, 1998). COOK uses only bit energy estimation to decode the signal. MMLCSK performs much better than COOK. The attained BER, however, is still far from that of conventional Amplitude Shift Keying (ASK).

Our simulations show that MMLCSK using one map has slightly better performance than MMLCSK using two maps. Besides $f_T(.)$ performs better than $f_Q(.)$. This last results confirms the importance of both map choice and transformation.

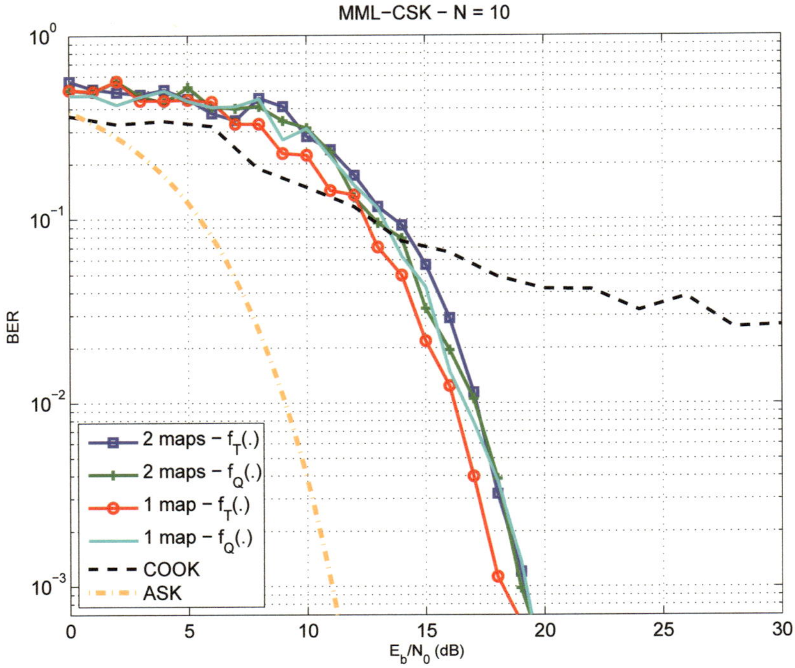

Fig. 18. Bit Error Rate (BER) for the tested MMLCSK modulations. Each bit was represented by $N = 10$ samples.

6. Conclusions

In this chapter we reviewed some chaos-based digital communication systems and studied their performance in a noisy environment.

In Section 3 we described CSK, DCSK and FM-DCSK using a discrete-time low-pass unifying notation. We concluded that FM-DCSK has the best performance among them. However the BER it attains in an AWGN channel is still unsatisfactory compared to conventional systems. This occurs mainly because FM-DCSK does not use any characteristic of the system that generate the chaotic signals to process the demodulation.

One possible way for improvement is to use estimation techniques to increase the SNR at the receiver. We review two such estimation techniques in Section 4, MLE and MVA. Due to its superior characteristics, we used the latter to propose two binary digital modulation schemes using chaotic signal estimation. Despite presenting better BER performance than the previous proposals, chaos based modulations still have a long way to go before they can attain the same performance level of conventional systems and so become practical options in noisy environments.

7. References

Alligood, K. T., Sauer, T. D. & Yorke, J. A. (1997). *Chaos: An Introduction to Dynamical Systems*, Textbooks In Mathematical Sciences, Springer-Verlag, New York.

Argyris, A., Syvridis, D., Larger, L., Annovazzi-Lodi, V., Colet, P., Fischer, I., Garcia-Ojalvo, J., Mirasso, C., Pesquera, L. & Shore, K. (2005). Chaos-based communications at high bit rates using commercial fibre-optic links, *Nature* 438(7066): 343–346.

Dedieu, H. & Kisel, A. (1999). Communications with chaotic time series: probabilistic methods for noise reduction, *International Journal of Circuit Theory and Applications* 27(6): 577–587.

Djurovic, I. & Rubezic, V. (2008). Chaos detection in chaotic systems with large number of components in spectral domain, *Signal Processing* 88(9): 2357 – 2362.

Eisencraft, M. & Baccalá, L. A. (2006). Estimating the initial conditions of chaotic orbits: performance bounds, *Proc. 1st IFAC Conference on Analysis and Control of Chaotic Systems*, Reims, France, pp. 291–295.

Eisencraft, M. & Baccalá, L. A. (2008). The Cramer-Rao Bound for initial conditions estimation of chaotic orbits, *Chaos Solitons & Fractals* 38(1): 132–139.

Eisencraft, M. & do Amaral, M. A. (2009). Estimation of nonuniform invariant density chaotic signals with applications in communications, *Second IFAC meeting related to analysis and control of chaotic systems*, London, England, pp. 1–6.

Eisencraft, M., do Amaral, M. A. & Lima, C. A. M. (2009). Estimation of chaotic signals with applications in communications, *Proc. 15th IFAC Symposium on System Identification*, Saint-Malo, France, pp. 1–6.

Eisencraft, M., Kato, D. M. & Monteiro, L. H. A. (2010). Spectral properties of chaotic signals generated by the skew tent map

Endo, T. & Chua, L. (1988). Chaos from phase-locked loops, *IEEE Transactions on Circuits and Systems* 35(8): 987–1003.

Forney, G. D. (1973). Forney, G. D. (1973). The Viterbi algorithm, *IProceedings of the IEEE* 61(3): 268 - 278.

Harb, B. A. & Harb, A. M. (2004). Chaos and bifurcation in a third-order phase locked loop, *Chaos, Solitons & Fractals* 19(3): 667 – 672.

Haykin, S. S. (2000). *Communication systems*, fourth edn, Wiley, New York.

Kaddoum, G., Charge, P., Roviras, D. & Fournier-Prunaret, D. (2009). A Methodology for Bit Error Rate Prediction in Chaos-based Communication Systems, *Circuits Systems and Signal Processing* 28(6): 925–944.

Kay, S. M. (1993). *Fundamentals of statistical signal processing: estimation theory*, Prentice-Hall, Inc., Upper Saddle River, NJ, USA.

Kennedy, M. & Kolumban, G. (2000). Digital communications using chaos, *Signal Processing* 80(7): 1307–1320.

Kennedy, M. P., Kolumbán, G., Kis, G. & Jákó, Z. (2000). Performance evaluation of FM-DCSK modulation in multipath enviromnments, 47(12): 1702–1711.

Kennedy, M. P., Setti, G. & Rovatti, R. (eds) (2000). *Chaotic Electronics in Telecommunications*, CRC Press, Inc., Boca Raton, FL, USA.

Kisel, A., Dedieu, H. & Schimming, T. (2001). Maximum likelihood approaches for noncoherent communications with chaotic carriers, *Circuits and Systems I: Fundamental Theory and Applications, IEEE Transactions on* 48(5): 533–542.

Kolumban, G., Kennedy, M. & Chua, L. (1997). The role of synchronization in digital communications using chaos. I . fundamentals of digital communications, 44(10): 927–936.

Kolumban, G., Kennedy, M. & Chua, L. (1998). The role of synchronization in digital communications using chaos. II. chaotic modulation and chaotic synchronization, 45(11): 1129–1140.

Kolumbán, G., P.Kennedy, M., Kis, G. & Jákó, Z. (1998). FM-DCSK: a novel method for chaotic communications, *Proc. ISCAS'98*, Vol. 4, Monterey, USA, pp. 477–480.

Lasota, A. & Mackey, M. (1985). *Probabilistic Properties of Deterministic Systems*, Cambridge University Press, Cambridge.

Lathi, B. P. (1998). *Modern Digital and Analog Communication Systems*, 3.ed edn, Oxford University Press, Inc., New York, NY, USA.

Lau, F. C. M. & Tse, C. K. (2003). *Chaos-based digital communication systems*, Springer, Berlin.

Marteau, F. F. & Abarbanel, H. D. I. (1991). Noise reduction in chaotic time series using scaled probabilistic method, *Jornal of Nonlinear Science* 1(3): 313–343.

Monteiro, L. H. A., Lisboa, A. C. & Eisencraft, M. (2009). Route to chaos in a third-order phase-locked loop network, *Signal Processing* 89(8): 1678–1682.

Papadopoulos, H. & Wornell, G. (1993). Optimal detection of a class of chaotic signals, *Acoustics, Speech, and Signal Processing, 1993. ICASSP-93., 1993 IEEE International Conference on* 3: 117–120 vol.3.

Pecora, L. & Carroll, T. (1990). Synchronization in chaotic systems, *Physical Review Letters* 64(8): 821–824.

Stavroulakis, P. (ed.) (2005). *Chaos Applications in Telecommunications*, CRC Press, Inc., Boca Raton, FL, USA.

Strogatz, S. H. (2001). *Nonlinear Dynamics and Chaos: with Applications to Physics, Biology, Chemistry and Engineering*, Perseus Books Group.

Syvridis, D. (2009). Optical Chaos Encoded Communications: Solutions for Today and Tomorrow, *2009 IEEE LEOS Annual Meeting Conference Proceedings, Vols 1and 2*, IEEE Lasers and Electro-Optics Society (LEOS) Annual Meeting, IEEE Photon Soc, IEEE, pp. 759–760.

Tavazoei, M. S. & Haeri, M. (2009). Chaos in the APFM nonlinear adaptive filter, *Signal Processing* 89(5): 697 – 702.

Tsekeridou, S., Solachidis, V., Nikolaidis, N., Nikolaidis, A., Tefas, A. & Pitas, I. (2001). Statistical analysis of a watermarking system based on Bernoulli chaotic sequences, *Signal Processing* 81(6): 1273–1293.

Viterbi, A. J. (1967). Error bounds for convolutional codes and an asymptotically optimum decoding algorithm, *Information Theory, IEEE Transactions on* 13(2): 260–269.

Williams, C. (2001). Chaotic communications over radio channels, *Circuits and Systems I: Fundamental Theory and Applications, IEEE Transactions on* 48(12): 1394 –1404.

Wozencraft, J. M. & Jacobs, I. M. (1987). *Principles of Communication Engineering*, Wiley, New York, NY, USA.

Xiaofeng, G., Xingang, W. & Meng, Z. (2004). Chaotic digital communication by encoding initial conditions, *Chaos* 14(2): 358–363.

12

Emergence of Matured Chaos During, Network Growth, Place for Adaptive Evolution and More of Equally Probable Signal Variants as an Alternative to Bias p

Andrzej Gecow
Centre for Ecological Research PAS
Poland

1. Introduction

This introduction describes contemporary investigations and interpretations of Kauffman networks, especially in the context of the 'life on the edge of chaos' hypothesis. The Kauffman networks are known as Boolean networks. They were introduced by Kauffman (1969), and later investigated and developed by many authors. These networks take various forms, e.g. cellular automata which stress the spatial order of their nearest neighbours as connection pattern. I will not consider such specific forms. Generally, this approach for the description of living systems, or a system designed by humans, using dynamical directed networks is now one of the most attractive and promising tools. His 'The Origins of Order' (Kauffman, 1993) is a large summary of first period Boolean network investigations and a base for the usually agreed on 'life on the edge of chaos' hypothesis. Later this hypothesis was 'experimentally verified' using the Gene Regulatory Network model (Rämö et al., 2006; Serra et al., 2004; 2007; Shmulevich et al., 2005; Wagner, 2001) but in this paper I call into question this verification. My explanation is based on an interpretation where stability and chaos play the main role. This introduction is designed as a description of Kauffman networks and their variants and extensions, in order to make my arguments comprehensible. No previous knowledge about the Kauffman network is assumed.

1.1 Elements, structure, functions and parameters of Boolean networks

In Fig. 1 the depicted Boolean network is small. It consists of $N = 5$ nodes named G, E, A, P and S. I show here a simple, imagined gene regulatory network of a plant. Node G describes the decision: 'to grow, or not to grow'. It depends on two detected parameters of the environment: w - warm - temperature sufficient for growth; and l - sufficient day length. In the winter it is not warm ($w = 0$ means: false) and days are short ($l = 0$) which is the environment state at time 0 shown in the Table on the left. For the decision 'to grow' ($g = 1$) both warmth ($w = 1$) and spring ($l = 1$) are needed which is calculated using Boolean function AND ($g := l$ AND w) performed by node G. Input signals l and w are taken as they are at time step t but a result g appears in the next ($t + 1$) time step. Such an updating scheme is called 'synchronous mode'. There are a few updating schemes, but for the main questions this fact it is not very important (Gershenson, 2004). The result g of node function calculation is called 'state of node' G. It also is an output signal of node G which is sent to other nodes as their input signals through output links of node G. There is $k = 2$ of output links (also called outputs) of node G. Number k for a particular node of network can be any, it is called 'node degree'. Distribution of node degree k for a particular network defines the network type. It will be discussed later. It is easy to add or remove an output link of node in Boolean network because it does no change node function. The input signals l and w come to node G through its input links. Arrows show direction of signal movement through the link, therefore the network is 'directed'.

Consecutive states (columns) of network

time	0	1	2	3	4	5	6	7	8	9	10	11	12
w	0	0	1	1	1	1	1	1	1	1	1	1	1
l	0	1	1	1	1	1	1	1	1	1	1	1	1
f	1	1	1	0	0	0	0	0	0	0	0	0	0
r	1	1	1	1	1	1	1	1	1	1	1	0	0
s	1	1	1	1	0	0	0	1	1	1	0	0	0
g	0	0	0	1	1	1	1	1	1	1	1	1	1
e	0	0	0	0	1	0	0	0	1	1	1	0	0
a	0	0	0	0	0	1	1	1	0	0	0	1	1
p	0	0	0	0	0	0	1	1	1	0	0	0	0

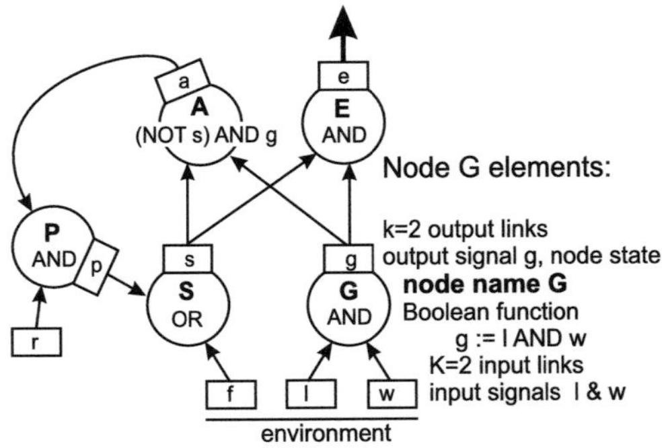

Fig. 1. Example of Boolean network, its basic elements (on the right) and function (on the left).

Node G has $K = 2$ input links (also called inputs). Usualy is assumed that each node of the network has the same fixed number K of input links. It is a useful approximation and I use it also, but more recently flexible K in one particular network is often used. It is not so easy to add or remove node input while simulation of the Boolean network is being processed because it changes the number of function variables and in effect it changes the node function. Fortunately, Serra et al. (2007) prove that distribution of damage size depends upon the distribution of k only, and does not depend upon the topology of the inputs.
The environment also can contains substrate f. This substrate is present in the plant (s) if it is present in the environment ($f = 1$) OR produced by the plant (p) using its internal reserve (r). As can be seen in the table, substrate f is present in the environment at the beginning and the plant also has a reserve r for the production of p. An effect e of the 'to grow' (g) decision can occur if substrate s is present in the plant which depicts node E. However, if the decision g is taken but substrate s is absent ($s = 0$) which happen at time step 4, then alarm a happens in the next time step. If alarm a occurs, then the plant can use its reserve r and produce substitute substrate p which is ready at time step 6. But because of the restriction taken before (e.g. $K = 2$ for all nodes) and rules it can be available for E and A only at time step 7 as s signal (the result of OR operation which takes a time). Effect e which disappeared at step 5 next appears at time 8. Check the table of network states - it is defined by state in time 0 and network structure with node functions. Such network is deterministic. The annealed approximation model discussed in Ch.2.2.3 is not deterministic (Derrida & Weisbuch, 1986).

1.2 Attractors, damage and chaos-order boundary

1.2.1 Attractors and their basins

A network contains a finite number N of nodes. The space of states of such a finite Boolean network also is finite and the network (system) must meet some previously left state in the finite number of time steps. In a deterministic network, from this time step the sequence of

states must repeat ad infinitum. This repeated sequence of network states is called 'attractor'. It can be 'point attractor' if it is one stable state, otherwise it is circular attractor. One system (network) typically has lot of attractors. Not all of the system (network) states are elements of any attractor, but starting from any system state the network always reaches some attractor. The set of states leading to a particular attractor is called 'basin of attraction'.
Kauffman (1969) has proposed that different types of cells in the animal body are an effect of different attractors of its common gene regulatory network (see also (Serra et al., 2010)). Therefore number and length of attractors for a network with a particular set of parameters is one of the main investigated themes.

1.2.2 Damage spreading in chaotic and ordered systems

If we start two identical deterministic systems A and B from the same state, then they will always have identical states. However, if a small disturbance is introduced in one of them (B), e.g. a changed state of one node, then some difference in node states between two such previously identical systems appears as an effect. These differences are called 'damage' (Jan & Arcangelis, 1994) (or 'perturbations' (Rämö et al., 2006; Serra et al., 2004)). The damage is measured as a fraction of all N nodes which have a different state than in the not disturbed network and in this article are denotet by d. Note, $0 < d < 1$. I will also use damage measured on $m = 64$ network external outputs in number L of changed output signals.
Damage can take various forms, e.g. it describes typically: epidemic spreading (Grabowski & Kosiński, 2004), opinion formation (Fortunato, 2005; Grabowski & Kosiński, 2006; Sousa, 2005) and attack or error effects (Crucitti et al., 2004; Gallos et al., 2004). However, these networks are not usually directed networks, and their important aspect is the spatial description which uses a particular lattice shape in the form of 'cellular automata'.
The main characteristic of the chaotic (term: 'pseudochaotic' can be also found (Serra et al., 2010)) behaviour of dynamical systems is high sensitivity to initial conditions. For chaotic systems (I use the term 'chaos' as Kauffman (1993) does) a small initiation of damage typically causes a large avalanche of damage which spreads onto a big part of the finite system and ends at an equilibrium level. The existence of this limitation is the main difference between this 'chaos' and the more commonly taken definition (Schuster, 1984) used for continuous arguments of a function. Levels of damage equilibrium are discussed in Ch.2.2.3 on a base of annealed approximation (Derrida & Pomeau, 1986; Kauffman, 1993).
High stability of ordered systems does not allow for damage to evolve into a large avalanche. There could be a very small avalanche in 'small unfrozen lakes of activity' which I do not call 'avalanche', especially not a 'large avalanche'. However, it is only statistical law, and theoretically large avalanche can happen but not practically for randomly constructed networks. Unfortunately, Serra et al. (2004) have introduced on credit term 'avalanche' which is consequently used later (Rämö et al., 2006; Serra et al., 2010; Shmulevich et al., 2005), for damage size in range especially small 'avalanches', e.g. 0 to 6 damaged nodes. This credit can be paid by damage in range of chaotic behaviour. I will come back to the view of 'frozen' areas, for the time being I want to introduce (fully in Ch.2.2.1 and in (Gecow, 1975; Gecow & Hoffman, 1983; Gecow, 2008) see also (Aldana et al., 2003; Serra et al., 2004)) 'coefficient of change multiplication on one node' also called 'coefficient of damage propagation' which simply shows why and when damage should grow. If a node has k outputs and on one input damage appears (changed input signal comparatively to undisturbed system), then on the average, $w = k/2$ outputs will be changed (damaged). Note that for $k = 2$ $w = 1$ which means that damage does not grow. For this coefficient a random function is assumed. Equal

probability of both signals in Boolean network is also assumed. For completion 'internal homogeneity' P (Kauffman, 1993) should be kept minimal. The internal homogeneity P of a Boolean function is defined as the fraction of the 2^K positions with 1 values or with 0 values depending on which fraction is higher, (P always is greater than 50 %) (Kauffman, 1993). If these assumptions are not true, then typically $w < k/2$. If K is fixed for an autonomous network (without external links from and to environment), then the average k is equal to K ($\langle k \rangle = K$). For such a network $K = 2$ is a boundary of the radically different behaviour, which Derrida & Pomeau (1986) has found. This is called 'phase transition' - for $K > 2$ it is the chaotic phase where damage typically grows and for $K < 2$ it is an ordered phase where even large damage typically fades out.
"Harris et al. (2002) pointed out that most biological systems tend to make use of a regulatory systems which, in the Boolean approximation, is described by canalising functions. ... A Boolean function is said to be canalising if at least one value of one of its inputs uniquely determines its output, no matter what the other input values are. Real gene networks show a proportion of canalising functions much higher than the one corresponding to a uniform choice"(Serra et al., 2004) (i.e. for K=2 without XOR and NOT XOR).
An assumption of equal probability of both signals is too strong and from the beginning bias p - probability of one signal variant is considered. This method of description however, is not universal and I introduce an alternative which differs in interpretation and results. It is more than two equally probable signal variants which is one of the main themes of this article.

1.2.3 Stability types, spontaneous order and negative feedbacks

There are four similar terms used in the Kauffman approach which should be clearly separated: 'structural stability', 'homeostatic stability', 'ultrastability' and 'spontaneous order'.
The 'structurally stable systems'(Kauffman, 1993) evolve in correlated landscape (e.g. of fitness) which typically allows the small initial change to give a small change as its effect. This landscape is considered on a space of system parameters where the nearest neighbours vary by the smallest change of connection, function or state. It means that such neighbours are similar and they function similarly. Chaotic systems are not 'structurally stable'. They evolve in uncorrelated landscape where small change typically causes crossing many 'walls of bifurcation', radically changing the system's properties (e.g. adding a new basin of attraction). Functions of neighbours typically are not similar (large damage avalanche means just this).
Adaptive evolution needs small changes. Large change usually lost collected aptness (fitness). Kauffman's approach, therefore, looks for such a 'structurally stable' area and found that it occurs between the chaotic and ordered phase. For this reason in Kauffman's approach, the phase transition between chaos and order is one of the most important themes of the investigation. Kauffman isolates this area on the basis of effects for the evolvability and structure of fitness landscape as a third region called 'liquid'. This region lies between 'solid' (because frozen, i.e. constant states of nodes) ordered region and 'gas' - a chaotic region. "Landscape is very rugged in the chaotic regime. This ruggedness is a direct consequence of the fact that damage spreads widely in networks in the chaotic regime. Almost any single mutation will dramatically alter landscape structure" (Kauffman, 1993). Note - though not all mutation will cause a large alteration. A liquid region lies on formally ordered and chaotic regions and its boundaries are smooth and not well defined. John Holland (1998) named this region 'the edge-of-chaos membrane' but Serra et al. (2007) - the 'critical' state, zone or regime.

After a small initiation of damage the effected damage (perturbation, change) can be large or small. Minimizing of initiation's effect defines a homeostatic feature. Typical homeostatic mechanisms based on negative feedbacks are named 'ultrastability' in Kauffman's approach. Kauffman following Ashby (1960) uses 'essential variable' to describe them: "In the context of Boolean networks, keeping the essential variables in bounds corresponds most simply to holding them fixed" (page 211 in (Kauffman, 1993)). Therefore, later Kauffman looks for systems with 'frozen' areas and finds them near the phase transition. In the ordered phase, frozen areas 'percolate' (i.e. connect into one space) leaving small isolated lakes of activity inside which leads to 'homeostatic stability'. In the chaotic phase there are isolated islands of frozen areas. As can be seen in Fig. 3 (state of $T = a, b, c$), to model the regulation (mechanism of stability) using negative feedbacks, all variables (including essential ones) must be flexible. They cannot be 'frozen' because it is only a substitute for the regulations by their effects ($T = b$).
Kauffman uses the term 'homeostatic stability' for the general resistance of the system to disturbance. This resistance refers mainly to stability which emerges spontaneously together with spontaneous order. Due to practical rejection of ultrastability from this research (more in (Gecow, 2010)), homeostatic stability contains the only aspect of spontaneous resistance to disturbance which in effect leads to overestimation of spontaneous order.
The ordered area and its near vicinity, where maximum spontaneous order occurs, also exhibit the highest 'structural stability'. This is useful for adaptive evolution and 'homeostatic stability' which should be an effect of evolution. The maximum of spontaneous order is one of the most important features of this area. For Boolean networks (with equal probability of signal versions) it is the case of $K = 2$: "If the stability of each state cycle attractor is probed by transient reversing of the activity of each element in each state of the state cycle, then 80-90% of all such perturbations, the system flows back to the same state cycle. Thus state cycles are inherently stable to most minimal transient perturbations" (Kauffman, 1993).

1.2.4 Hypothesis of 'life on the edge of chaos'

Evolution using random walk in the space of network parameters should lean towards this ordered area because changes are smaller there; the system is more stable and the effects of evolution may be larger. This expectation is known as 'life on the edge of chaos'. Kauffman even expects living systems in solid regime in his "bold hypothesis: Living systems exist in solid regime near the edge of chaos, and natural selection achieves and sustains such a poised state" - page 232 in (Kauffman, 1993). I question the use of 'natural selection' as a typical Darwinian meaning. It needs elimination which is based on death. On the edge of chaos there is not anything which models death. Such a model of death can be found in the chaotic phase as large damage avalanche. Above Kauffman's view as useful approximation for certain purpose is correct if description is limited to live period without death possibility and Darwinian mechanisms. However, in such a case natural selection (working outside) cannot 'achieve' but only 'sustain' the state which is connected to reproduction ability.
A large change; large damage avalanche in chaotic systems, is obviously taken as improbable in adaptive evolution but the conclusion that adaptive evolution is improbable in chaotic systems would be too hasty. As noted above (in the description of the liquid region) in chaotic systems, small change only typically causes large effective change. Small effective changes can also take place. They may be used by adaptive evolution. It happens more frequently if parameters of a network are nearer the phase transition between order and chaos. This possibility is discussed in Ch.2.3 in Fig.6 as degrees of order r and chaos c ($r + c = 1$) of

different particular networks and it is one of more important themes of this paper. See also Fig.7 for $sf3,4$ in the middle on the right (typical case) where left peak of $P(d|N)$ of very small damage is present for chaotic systems. This peak contains initiation cases which in effect manifest 'ordered' behaviour and can be used for adaptive evolution. Small networks where $N = 50$, behave like at the edge of chaos and order. This dependency remains as the left peak for larger N. Its distribution is near power law, like for the avalanches in the pile of sand which Per Bak's self-organized criticality (Bak, 1996) controls. But living systems have a method against such control - it is self-multiplying. In effect, some systems usually avoid large avalanche which for living systems means death, i.e. elimination. It cannot be a new evolutionary change (compare to (Farmer et al., 1986)). It is much more than even Lysenko proposed. Can you imagine that more than half (see Fig.5) of all the mechanisms of living organism have been changed and the organism survived? Replication allows living systems to grow (in N meaning) and this way they enter chaotic regime and can stay there. Above r (degree of order in Fig.6) is a fraction of all initiation cases which contain cases building the left peak (of very small effective changes). The right peak contains cases of chaotic behaviour which must be eliminated during adaptive evolution by Darwinian elimination; they model death. This death is necessary for typical natural selection but in an ordered regime it is absent. (Theoretically Darwinian mechanism can work without death, but for this infinite capacities of environment are necessary.)

1.2.5 Kauffman's model of gene regulatory network and its comparison to real life

The model of gene regulatory network was proposed by Kauffman (1969; 1971), it is based on the Kauffman (Boolean) network. Boolean states of gene are interpreted as active or inactive. All general expectations for the Boolean network described above concern this gene regulatory network, including the nearest of chaos-order phase transition as an effect of evolution.

Hughes et al. (2000) in real genome of *Saccaromices cerevisiae* containing $N = 6312$ genes, knocked out 227 genes, one at a time and they measured the effects of such disturbance. Next, the authors of Refs. (Rämö et al., 2006; Serra et al., 2004; 2007; Wagner, 2001) compared obtained stability to theoretical stability for different parameters. They conclude that similar stability appears for the Boolean network with fixed K=2, i.e. really near phase transition. Shmulevich et al. (2005) compare the amount of information stored in the time sequence of gene expression of HeLa cells with the results of simulated RBNs and they conclude that eukaryotic cells are dynamically ordered or critical but not chaotic. These results are taken as an experimental base for the 'life on the edge of chaos' hypothesis.

Nevertheless, I dispute the interpretation of this result. First of all in both these experiments data are captured from practically living cells. Theoretical homeostatic stability underestimates ultrastability as its part, i.e. regulators based on negative feedbacks which are the base of stability for living systems. Ultrastability is commonly observed as an extremely high concentration of negative feedbacks in living systems which is even used for a life definition (Korzeniewski, 2001; 2005) as its specific property. Creation of these mechanisms is an effect of Darwinian selection (in which death, as mentioned above is needed; large avalanche of damage models this death). Because cells are alive, homeostasis was not broken and stability was kept. This means there was no large avalanche, i.e. death. But it does not mean that such large avalanche cannot appear and such cells are immortal. It is obvious true that living systems behave like ordered systems and it is expected result that description of these behaviours is similar to ordered systems build randomly. It is interesting result that similarity is so deep. But it does not imply that source of such stability is similar. In Kauffman's approach negative feedbacks are considered only on a random normal average level of appearance without any preferences. This is a very large simplification (Gecow, 2010) leading to a non-realistic modelling of stability causes of living systems. Obtained similarity has, however, simple explanation given by Kauffman - it is mentioned above simplification of ultrastability using fixed (frozen) essential variable. This move rejects out of consideration right source of stability together with its cause - Darwinian elimination but remains their effect. This is why, 'homeostatic stability' based on 'spontaneous order', i.e. typically 'structural stability', is taken as an explanation of stability of gene regulatory network (Kauffman, 1971; Rämö et al., 2006; Serra et al., 2004; 2007; Wagner, 2001) instead of the neglected homeostasis based on negative feedbacks which realize the regulation. This is the above mentioned (Ch.1.2.3) overestimation of spontaneous order.

Homeostasis built by Darwinian selection leads to stability for a certain set of initial changes. Such changes may randomly occur but they are 'known' to the system, i.e. the system reacts to them in a non-random way. E.g. small defects in DNA copying are 'known' and a certain set of repair or other safety mechanisms are prepared. The remaining changes can be treated as 'fully random'. When these changes occur, the system can behave in a chaotic or ordered way. The investigation should be focused on this set of 'fully random' changes but with stability of system in mind, it is important not to neglect 'known' changes. Current living things 'know' most of the typical changes and therefore exhibit high stability. This is true even though for fully random (unknown) changes these living systems are chaotic. Life is a continuous maintenance of equilibrium at a high level, which is a semi-unstable equilibrium - it will collapse into a large damage avalanche after a single false move. This view correctly describes a chaotic state but not an ordered one. Therefore, observed stability cannot be spontaneous, but it must be carefully collected. Only Darwinian selection can find observed stability and not in the form suggested by Kauffman (place near the ordered phase) but in the form of active regulation which are usually negative feedbacks. Kauffman, and I, do not model these homeostatic answers (based typically on negative feedbacks) which are effects of 'known type initialisations' of the system. This large simplification, however, must be taken into consideration when stability of living systems is discussed.

Currently Kauffman's model of the gene regulatory network is taken as 'early' and more attention is given to the GRN based on the Banzhaf model (Banzhaf, 2003; Knabe et al., 2006). Also 2 signal variants are taken as too strong a simplification. Nonetheless, Kauffman's model was a first approximation needed to open the way for more exact models.

1.3 Networks variants

1.3.1 Currently investigated network types in the range RBN

Kauffman (1969) introduced Boolean networks. For statistical investigation, a method of a random creation of such a network was needed. That time the obvious candidate was Erdős-Rényi pattern (Erdős & Rényi, 1960) where, for given node number N connections are chosen randomly. The number of inputs K was usually fixed and the above rule considers outputs k. This type of network was named 'Random Boolean Network' (RBN).

Barabási et al. (1999) have discovered the famous, scale free network and its importance, therefore it is known as the BA (Barabási-Albert) network. It is constructed using 'preferential attachment', i.e. new added node links to a node in the current network with a probability proportional to its node degree k. BA networks typically are not directed and k is a number of all the links of the node. Using this formula for Boolean networks it is necessary to separately consider the number of inputs K and outputs k. Usually an easier fixed K was used (see Ch.1.1) but currently both of them are often flexible. The dynamics of Boolean networks with scale free topology were studied e.g. by Aldana (2003), Kauffman et al. (2004), Serra et al. (2004a) and Iguchi et al. (2007). They named the network SFRBN (Scale-Free RBN). Iguchi et al. (2007) also used for comparison 'directed Exponential-Fluctuation networks EFRBN' known also as a 'single scale' network where new node links to node in current network with equal probability. The old Classic RBN which Serra et al. (2004a) proposed to rename to CRBN is also used for comparison. All of these network types differ in $P(k)$ - distribution of node degree: CRBN has Poisson distribution without hubs (nodes with extremely high node degree k), $P(k)$ of SFRBN is a straight line in log-log diagram and contains many hubs, EFRBN gives a straight line in the log diagram and contain less hubs.

Most authors stay with Boolean networks due to 'life on the edge of chaos' idea. For this reason, they investigate the point of phase transition between order and chaos. There are lots of different attempts to introduce a new type of Boolean network. E.g. in opposition to the deterministic case Shmulevich et al. (2002) introduced the Probabilistic Boolean Network (PBN). The PBN is used to model gene regulatory network where transition rules are considered as random variables. Such an idea in a slightly different form appears in "a Dynamical Boolean Network (DBN), which is a Virtual Boolean Network (VBN) In this network, the set of nodes is fixed but the transition matrix can change from one time step to another" (Ito, 2008).

1.3.2 Extension of the Kauffman networks over Boolean networks - RNS, RWN and my RSN

Applying the Boolean networks to describe living things, e.g. for gene regulatory network, suggests that only two signal variants is a large simplifications - a first approximation only, and more variants should be used. I will come back to this problem later in Ch.2. As second approximation Luque & Solé (1997) introduced RNS (Random Network with multiple States) (Sole et al., 2000). In RNS, in order to reach edge of chaos a bias p is used for one signal variant making it different from the other signal variants. Later Luque & Ballesteros (2004) introduced another construction - RWN (Random Walk Network) (Ballesteros & Luque, 2005) which contains memory in its nodes' states. Functions of node perform a shift of node state which resemble differential regulations. This shifting reaches upper or lower boundaries and the result is random but in a complicated way. Construction of RWN also is an effect of the assumption that point of phase transition is important.

To these two ideas I add (Gecow, 2010) another one, but now I await living systems in chaotic regime, so the point of phase transition is not so important. My network allows for more than two equally probable variants of signal values which is an exclusive alternative based on the interpretation to bias p. I introduce s - number of equally probable variants of signal values. I call (Gecow, 2010) such a network 'Random Signal Network' (RSN). (The full name: 'Random equally probable Signal variants Network' is too long.) Note, using parameter s in the range of RSN we know that these s variants are equally probable and in range $s \geq 2$. In the Boolean network there are only two variants e.g. 1 and 0 but they must not to be equally probable.

RSN, together with known RNS and RWN, expand the notion of the 'Kauffman network'. Up till now 'the Kauffman-' and 'the Boolean network' were synonymous, but they should not be anymore. The term 'Boolean' must be limited to two variants of a signal but the 'Kauffman network' can and should contain more signal variants as is used in the RSN, RWN or in RNS models. One output signal taken as a state of node which is transmitted through all output links should be characteristic of the Kauffman network.

1.3.3 Network types and their rules of growth used in simulation of RSN

RSN is a directed functioning network. The main characteristic of the RSN, is that all signal value variants are equally probable and *s*; the number of these variants can be more than two $s \geq 2$. RSN type was performed for statistical analysis (typically using simulation) of general features of networks and their dependency on different parameters like K, k, s, N and growth rules. The basic formula of RSN emerged from an important overlooked cause of probability difference in Boolean's two signals (Ch.2.1.2) described using bias *p*. Such a description leads to wrong results in this case. So, RSN becomes the exclusive alternative to bias *p*.

RSN term contains the Kauffman networks with two, and more than two equally probable signal variants. RSN also contains 'aggregates of automata' which I have introduced in (Gecow, 1975; Gecow & Hoffman, 1983; Gecow et al., 2005; Gecow, 2005a; 2008), with the same range of signals and which are not the Kauffman networks as they are defined above. The aggregate of automata has as a state of a node a *k*-dimensional vector of independent output signals transmitted each by another output link. It also has fixed $K = k$ for all nodes of network. This type of network has a secondary meaning - some simple examples (like *lw* and *lx* networks, Ch.3.3) do not simply work in the Kauffman mode; the coefficient of damage propagation has for aggregate of automata simple intuitive meaning (Ch.2.2.1). I have made the first investigation of structural tendencies using such simple network parameters and they gave strong effects. For the Kauffman networks this effect is weaker and comparison to aggregate of automata with the same parameters can indicate causes of observed effects.

Structural tendencies are the main goal of my approach. They model regularities of ontogeny evolution observed in classical evolutionary biology such as Weismann's 'terminal additions', Naef's 'terminal modifications' or the most controversial - Haeckel's recapitulation. These tendencies are also typically detected in any complex human activity like computer programming, technical projects or maintenance. Knowledge of their rules should give important prediction. Structural tendencies, however, occur in complex systems, but the term 'complex' is wide and vague with a lot of different meanings. Complexity needed for structural tendencies is connected to the chaos phenomena, therefore when investigating their mechanisms, chaotic systems should be well known. I investigate them using simulation of different network types in the range of RSN. In this article, simulation of ten network types will be discussed. For such a number of network types short names and a system for arranging them are needed. Therefore, I do not repeat in each name 'RSN', but I use two letters for network type name. In the Figures where there is limited space, I use only one second letter.

The general type of aggregate of automata is indicated as *aa*, its versions without feedbacks: genelal - *an*, extremely ordered in levels of fixed node number - *lw* and *lx*.

Similar to *aa* network but following Kauffman's rule (one output signal but fixed $K = k$) is named *ak*. For the old classical Erdős & Rényi (1960) pattern used in RBN (CRBN) '*er*' is used. Note, in range of RSN it must not be a Boolean network. For scale-free network (BA - Barabási-Albert (Barabási et al., 1999; 2003)) I use '*sf*'. It corresponds to SFRBN. Single-scale (Albert & Barabási, 2002) corresponding to EFRBN, I denote as '*ss*'. For all simulated networks I use fixed *K* which in addition differentiate these two types from SFRBN and EFRBN.

The main structural tendencies need removing of nodes; only addition is insufficient. But for *sf* and *ss* network types removing includes a significant new feature of the network - it generates $k = 0$ for some nodes. Such networks are different than the typical *sf* and *ss* because removals change node degree distribution. Therefore networks built with a 30% of removals of nodes and 70% of additions get other names - *sh* for modified *sf* and *si* for *ss* with removals. In simulations of structural tendencies Gecow (2008; 2009a) I use parameter of

removal participation instead. A problem of significant change of distribution of node degree emerges which leads to some modification of growth pattern of sf network in different ways (Gecow, 2009b) with different network names - *se* and *sg*. As can be seen, a network type should be treated as parameter with a lot of particular values (denoted by two-letter name). This parameter covers different other parameters used sporadically in different options.
Damage investigation in dependency on network size N has two stages: construction of the network and damage investigation in the constant network. Construction of the network depends on the chosen network type. Except the type '*er*', all networks have a rule of growth. Aggregate of automata '*aa*' and Kauffman network '*ak*' need to draw K links in order to add a new node (links g and h for $K = 2$ in Fig.2 on the left). These links are broken and their beginning parts become inputs to the new node and their ending parts become its outputs.
For all types whose name starts with 's' (sf, *sh*, *ss* and *si* denoted later as *s*?) we draw first one link (g in Fig.2 on the right) and we break it like for: *aa* and *ak* to define one output and input. For sf and *sh* types at least one such output is necessary to participate in further network growth. Later, the remaining inputs are drawn according to the rules described above: for *ss* and *si* by directly drawing the node (B in Fig.2 on the right); for sf and *sh* by drawing a link (h in Fig.2 on the right) and using its source node (B in Fig.2 on the right).

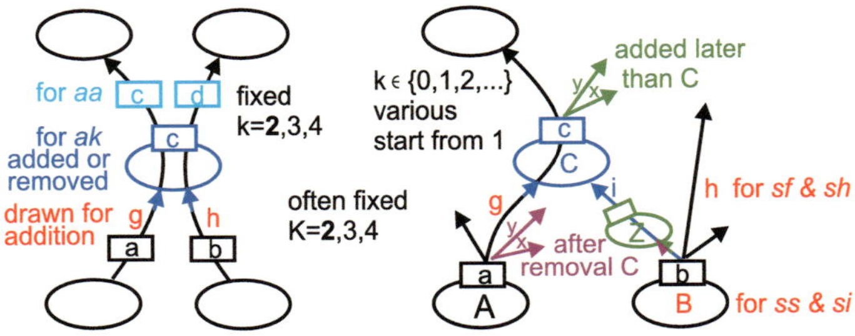

Fig. 2. Changeability patterns for *aa* and *ak* (left), *sh*, sf, *si* and *ss* network (right) depicted for $K = 2$. For addition of a new node to the network, links g and h are drawn. Node B is drawn instead of link h for *ss* and *si*. For $K > 2$ additional inputs are constructed like the ones on the right. The *ak* network is maintained as *aa* but there is only one, common output signal c. For removal of node, only a drawing of the node to remove is needed. Main moves are the same as for addition, but in an opposite sequence, however, for *s*?, events which occur after the addition change the situation. Removal can create $k = 0$: node Z added on link i can remain a $k = 0$ node while removing node C because part of link i from Z to removed C disappears. The outgoing links x, y, which were added to C after adding this node to the network, are moved to node A where link g starts. This lack of symmetry causes changes in distributions $P(k)$ and other features of a network. For this reason, networks sf and *ss* with removals of node are different than without removal of node and are named *sh* and *si* respectively.

Random removal of a node needs to draw a node only. Each node should have equal probability to be chosen. The pattern of node disconnection should be the same but in the opposite direction to connection while adding. However, if removing happens not directly after addition, the situation can change and such a simple assumption will be insufficient. Such a case appears for *s*? networks when k of the removed node can be ($k > 1$, x, y links in Fig.2 right) different than just after addition ($k = 1$) and interestingly, when on the right input link a new node (Z in Fig.2 right) was added. During the removal (of C node), this new (Z) node loses its output link and may become a $k = 0$ node. Nodes with $k = 0$ and other nodes connected to them, which have not further way for their output signals (e.g. to external outputs) are called 'blind' nodes. The existence of 'blind' nodes in the network is one of the biggest and the most interesting problems especially for the modelling of adaptation. The importance and complexity of this problem is similar to the problem of feedbacks.

1.3.4 Connection to environment: L damaged of m outputs

Following ref. (Kauffman, 1993) the size of damage $d \in \langle 0, 1 \rangle$ is measured as the fraction of nodes with damaged output state in the all nodes of system. Serra et al. (2004) measure size of damage in number of damaged nodes and call such parameter the 'Avalanche', see Fig.7. However, this parameter is usually hard to observe for real systems (Hughes et al. (2000) done it, see Ch.1.2.5). The adaptation process concerns interactions between the system and its environment. If such a process is to be described, then damage should be observed outside the system, on its external outputs. However, network with outputs is no longer an autonomous network like the ones considered from Ref. (Kauffman, 1969) up to (Iguchi et al., 2007) and (Serra et al., 2010). Some links are special as they are connected to environment. Environment is another, special 'node' which does not transmit damage (in the first approximation), unlike all the remaining ones. Damage fades out on the outputs like on a node with $k = 0$. This is why the dynamics of damage d should be a little bit different depending on the proportion of output size m and network size N (compare sf 3,4 in Fig7). Environment as an objectively special node can be used for the indication of the nodes' place in a network, which without such special node generally have no objective point of reference. The main task of this special node in the adaptation process is a fitness calculation and Darwinian elimination of some network changes.

The simplest definition of damage size on system outputs is: the number L of damaged output signals. For large networks with feedbacks it is applicable using only a simplified algorithm described in Ch.3.1, and e.g. Ref. (Gecow, 2010). It omits the problem of circular attractors. Formally, L is a Hamming distance of system output signal vectors between a control system and a damaged one. Practically, using my algorithm, it is the distance between system output before and after damage simulation. For simulations, the system has a fixed number $m = 64$ of output signals which means that $L \in \langle 0, m \rangle$. We can expect, that distributions $P(d)$ and $P(L)$ will be similar. In fact, asymptotic values (for 'matured systems'): dmx of d and Lmx of L are simply connected: $dmx = Lmx/m$. But such a connection is not true for smaller systems and L is smaller than expected. Note, that the number of output signals m is constant and much smaller than the growing number N of nodes in the network, which must influence the statistical parameters and their precision.

2. RSN - More of equally probable signal variants as alternative to bias p

RSN is not a version of a known network type or a second approximation describing the same phenomena. Although RSN can be formally treated as a version of RNS (see Ch.1.3.2) with bias p equal to the probability of the remaining signal variants. It is an important, overlooked, simple and basic case of described reality, competitive to bias p and to the not so simple RWN formula. As will be shown, RSN leads to different results than when using bias p. Bias p has been used for all cases up till now.

2.1 Why more equally probable signal variants should be considered

2.1.1 Boolean networks are not generally adequate

It is commonly assumed, that Boolean networks are always adequate in any case. A simple example (Fig.3) shows that this is false and it leads to wrong effects, especially for statistical

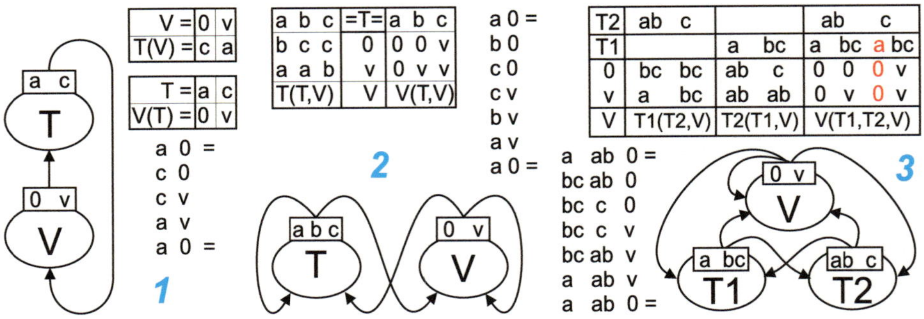

Fig. 3. Thermostat of fridge described using Kauffman networks as an example of regulation based on negative feedbacks and the inadequateness of the Boolean networks. Case (2) describes thermostat just as it is in reality - temperature T is split into three sections a - too cold, b - accurate, c - too hot, but this case is not then Boolean. To hold signal in Boolean range we can neglect temperature state b - case (1) or split node T into two nodes with separate states - case (3) which together describe all temperature states, but using this way a dummy variant $(a + c)$ of temperature state is introduced. Node V decides power for aggregate: v - on, 0 - off. Tables of functions for nodes and for consecutive system states are attached.

expectation. Normally, more than two signal variants are needed for an adequate description. If a fridge leaves the proper temperature range b as a result of environment influence and enters too high a temperature in the range c, then power supply for the aggregate is turned on and temperature inside the fridge goes down. It passes range b and reaches the too-cold range a, then power is turned off and the temperature slowly grows through b section. Case (2) in Fig.3 this regulation mechanism is properly described in Kauffman network terms. However, there are three states of temperature a, b, c which are described by three variants of node T and therefore, this case of the Kauffman network is not a Boolean network.
To hold signal describing temperature in Boolean range (two variants only) we can neglect temperature state b. This is case (1) but here, the most important, proper temperature state, which is the state the fridge stays in most of the time, is missing. Almost any time we check the state of a real fridge this state is not present in such a description. Reading such a description we find that wrong temperature a; meaning too cold occurs directly after wrong temperature c; too hot and vice versa. Splitting node T into two nodes $T1$ and $T2$ with separate states - case (3) is the second method to hold Boolean signals. Two separate Boolean signals together create four variants but temperature takes only three of them. A new dummy state emerges: a - too cold and c - too hot simultaneously. It has no sense and never appears in reality but a function should be defined for such a state. In the Table, the functions values for such dummy input state are marked by red. For statistical investigation, it is taken as a real proper state. Such groundless procedure produces incorrect results.
Cases (1) and (3) describe reality inadequately. It is because Boolean networks are not generally adequate. We can describe everything we need using Boolean networks but in many cases we will introduce dummy states or we will simplify something which we do not want to simplify. In both cases the statistical investigation will be false. The only way is to use a real number of signal variants and not limit ourselves to only two Boolean alternatives.

2.1.2 Two variants are often subjective

Two alternatives used in Boolean networks may be an effect of two different situations: first - there are really two alternatives and they have different or similar probabilities; and second

- there are lots of real alternatives, but we are watching one of them and all the remaining we collect into the second one (as is done for *T*1 and *T*2 in Fig.3). If in this second case, all of real alternatives have similar probability, then the watched one has this small probability which is usually described using bias *p*. The collection of the remaining ones then, have large probability. Characteristically, the watched alternative event is 'the important event' as far as systems which adapt are concerned. Note 1: such adapting systems are normally investigated. Note 2: for system which adapt, the notions: 'important', 'proper' and 'correct' are defined using fitness but it has nothing to do with the statistical mechanism and such simplification remains subjective. This is the main, yet simple and important cause of introducing more than two alternatives. It is used to be objective and obtain adequate results

If the long process leading from gene mutations to certain properties assessed directly using fitness has to be described, then more than two signal alternatives seem much more adequate. It should be remarked that there are 4 nucleotides, 20 amino acids (similarly probable in the first approximation) and other unclear spectra of similarly probable alternatives. In this set of the spectra of alternatives, the case of as few as two alternatives seems to be an exception, however, for gene regulatory network it seems to be adequate in the first approximation (active or inactive gene). Investigators of real gene networks suggest: "While the segment polarity gene network was successfully modelled by a simple synchronous binary Boolean model, other networks might require more detailed models incorporating asynchronous updating and/or multi-level variables (especially relevant for systems incorporating long-range diffusion)."(Albert & Othmer, 2003) In second approximations which are RNS (Luque & Solé, 1997; Sole et al., 2000) and RWN (Ballesteros & Luque, 2005; Luque & Ballesteros, 2004), more than two variants are used but in a different way than here (RSN).

2.1.3 Equal probability of signal variants as typical approximation

For a first approximation using equal probability of alternatives from the set of possibilities is a typical method and a simplification necessary for prediction and calculation. In this way we obtain s (which can be more than two) equally probable signal variants ($s \geq 2$) (Gecow, 1975; Gecow & Hoffman, 1983; Gecow et al., 2005; Gecow, 2008; 2010). This is a similar simplification as collections of remaining alternatives to one signal variant, but seems to be less different to the usually described real cases.

2.2 Differences of results for descriptions using bias p and $s \geq 2$

At this point an important example should be shown which leads to very different results for the above two basic variants of description - the old using bias p and my new using s. I do not suggest that using bias p is always an incorrect description but that for the meaning part of the cases it is a very wrong simplification and other ones with $s > 2$ should be used.

2.2.1 w^t describes the first critical period of damage spreading and simply shows that case $s = 2$ is extreme

Returning to coefficient of damage propagation introduced in Ch.1.2.2 I now define it using s and K. This is $w = \langle k \rangle (s-1)/s$. It can be treated as damage multiplication coefficient on one element of system if only one input signal is changed. w indicates how many output signals of a node will be changed on the average (for the random function used by nodes to calculate outputs from the inputs). (I assume minimal P - internal homogeneity (Kauffman, 1993) in this whole paper and approach.) I have introduced it in Refs. (Gecow, 1975; Gecow & Hoffman,

1983; Gecow, 2005a) as a simple intuitive indicator of the ability of damage to explode (rate of change propagation) which can be treated as a chaos-order indicator.
Coefficient w is interesting for the whole network or for part of the network, not for a single particular node. However, it is easier to discuss it on a single, average node. Therefore I have started my approach using aggregate of automata (Gecow, 1975; Gecow & Hoffman, 1983; Gecow et al., 2005) (Ch.1.3.3 - *aa*, Fig.2) where $K = k$ and each outgoing link of node has its own signal. It differs to Kauffman network where all outgoing links transmit the same signal. In this paper I consider networks with fixed K and $\langle k \rangle = K$, i.e. all nodes in the particular network have the same number of inputs. If so, I can write $w = K(s-1)/s$.
If $w > 1$ then the damage should statistically grow and spread onto a large part of a system. It is similar to the coefficient of neutron multiplication in a nuclear chain reaction. It is less than one in a nuclear power station, for values greater than one an atomic bomb explodes. Note that $w = 1$ appears only if $K = 2$ and $s = 2$. Both these parameters appear here in their smallest, extreme values. The case $k < 2$ is sensible for a particular node but not as an average in a whole, typical, randomly built network, however, it is possible to find the case $K = 1$ in Fig.3.1 and Fig.4 or in Refs. (Iguchi et al., 2007; Kauffman, 1993; Wagner, 2001). For all other cases where $s > 2$ or $K > 2$ it is $w > 1$.
In the Ref. (Aldana et al., 2003) similar equation (6.2): $K_c(s-1)/s = 1$ is given which is a case for the condition $w = 1$. K_c is a critical connectivity between an ordered and chaotic phase. They state: "The critical connectivity decreases monotonically when $s > 2$, approaching 1 as $s \to \infty$ The moral is that for this kind of multi-state networks to be in the ordered phase, the connectivity has to be very small, contrary to what is observed in real genetic networks." However, as I am going to show in this paper, that the assumption that such networks should be in ordered phase is false.
The critical connectivity was searched by Derrida & Pomeau (1986) and they found for bias p that $2K_cp(1-p) = 1$. (See also (Aldana, 2003; Fronczak et al., 2008). Shmulevich et al. (2005) use 'expected network sensitivity' defined as $2Kp(1-p)$ which Rämö et al. (2006) call the 'order parameter'. Serra et al. (2007) use (4.9) $\langle k \rangle q$ where q is the probability that node change its state if one of its inputs is changed. This value "coincides with 'Derrida exponent' which has been often used to characterize the dynamics of RBN".) The meaning of these equations is similar to that above (6.2) equation in the (Aldana et al., 2003). See Fig. 4. But putting $p = 1/s$ it takes the form: $2K_c(s-1)/s^2 = 1$ which only for $s = 2$ is the same as above.
For coefficient w it is assumed that only one input signal is damaged. This assumption is valid in a large network, only at the beginning of damage spreading. But this period is crucial for the choice: a small initiation either converts into a large avalanche or it does not - damage fades out at the beginning. In this period each time step damage is multiplied by w and if $w > 1$, then it grows quickly. When damage becomes so large that probability of more than one damaged input signal is meaning, then already the choice of large avalanche was done (i.e. early fade out of damage is practically impossible). See Fig. 5. in Ch 2.2.3.

2.2.2 Area of order

For $s \geq 2$ (and $K \geq 2$) damage should statistically always grow if it does not fade out at the beginning when fluctuations work on a small number of damaged signals, and whenever it has room to grow. That damage should statistically always grow is shown in my 'coefficient of damage propagation', and chaos should always be obtained. Only case $s = 2, K = 2$ is an exception. However, (see Fig. 4) if we take a particular case with larger s (e.g. 6) and small $K > 2$ (e.g. $K = 3$), and we use the old description based on bias p, then we obtain an extreme

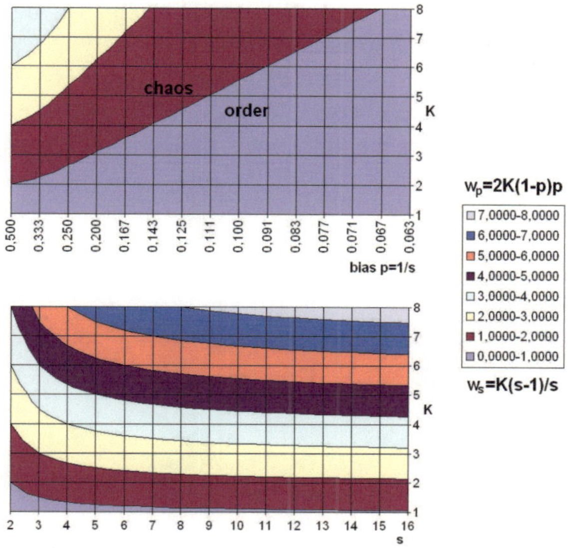

Fig. 4. Values of coefficient of damage propagation w_s for s and K and phase transition between order and chaos also for bias p. If the case where s equally probable variants is described using the bias p method ($s-1$ variants as the second Boolean signal variant), then instead the lower diagram, the upper one is used, but it is very different.

bias $p = 1/6$ for which order is expected (upper diagram in Fig. 4). In the lower diagram the coefficient w is shown for description case with all signal variants, but for simplicity they are taken as equally probable. These two dependences are very different, but for $s = 2$ they give identical predictions. This means, that we cannot substitute more than two similarly probable signal variants for an 'interesting' one and all remaining as a second one and use 'bias p description', because it leads to an incorrect conclusion.

In RNS signal variants are not equally probable. In RNS bias p plays an important role allowing investigation of phase transition to chaos as in the whole Kauffman approach. It is not a mechanism which substitutes bias p, although using $p = 1/s$ the RNS formally contains my RSN. Typically the case of more than two variants which is taken as interpretatively better (Aldana et al., 2003), is rejected (Aldana et al., 2003) (see above Ch.2.2.1) or not developed as contradictory with the expectation of 'life at the edge of chaos' which I question here.

2.2.3 Damage equilibrium levels for $s > 2$ are significantly higher

Dependences of new damage size on current damage size after the one synchronous time step depicted in Fig. 5 on the right, are calculated in a theoretical way based on annealed approximation (Derrida & Pomeau, 1986) described in Kauffman (1993) book (p.199 and Fig.5.8 for $s = 2$). Such a diagram is known as 'Derrida plot', here it is expanded to case $s > 2$ and for *aa* - aggregate of automata.

If a denotes a part of damaged system B with the same states of nodes as an undisturbed system A, then a^K is the probability that the node has all its K inputs with the same signals in both systems. Such nodes will have the same state in the next time point $t+1$. The remaining $1 - a^K$ part of nodes will have a random state, which will be the same as in system A with probability $1/s$. The part of system B which does not differ with A in $t+1$ is therefore

$a^K + (1 - a^K)/s$. It is the same as for RNS (Sole et al., 2000). The damage $d = 1 - a$. For $K = 2$ we obtain $d_2 = wd_1 - wd_1^2/2$ where for small d_1 we can neglect the second element. For aggregate of automata (*aa*) if $K = 2$ then $d_2 = d_1 * w - d_1^2 * (s-1)^2/(s+1)/s$ which is obtained in a similar way as the above. Here also for small d_1 we can neglect element with d_1^2 which allows us to use simple w^t for the first crucial period of damage spreading.

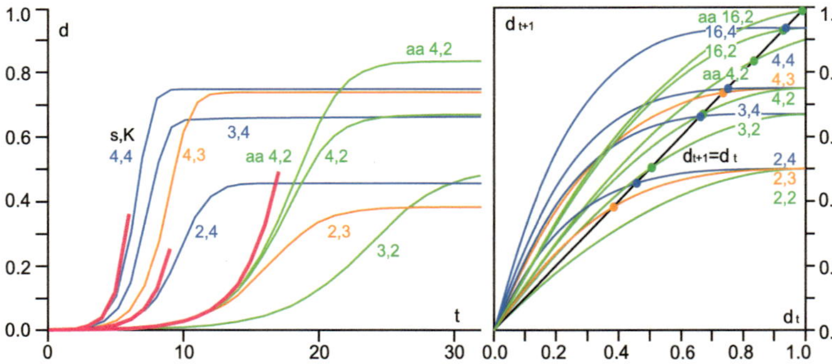

Fig. 5. Theoretical damage spreading calculated using an annealed approximation. On the right - damage change at one time step in synchronous calculation known as the 'Derrida plot', extended for the case $s > 2$ and for *aa* network type. The crossing of curves $d_{t+1}(d_t, s, K)$ with line $d_{t+1} = d_t$ shows equilibrium levels dmx up to which damage can grow. Case $s, K = 2, 2$ has a damage equilibrium level in $d = 0$. These levels are reached on the left which shows damage size in time dependency. For $s > 2$ they are significantly higher than for Boolean networks and for *aa* than for the Kauffman network. All cases with the same K have the same colour to show s influence. A simplified expectation $d(t) = d_0 w^t$ using coefficient w is shown (three short curves to the left of the longer reaching equilibrium). This approximation is good for the first critical period when d is still small.

These figures show that the level of damage equilibrium for aggregate of automata is much higher than for the Kauffman networks. To expect $a_{aa,t+1}$ - the part of the nodes in *aa* network which does not differ at $t + 1$ in systems A and B, we can use expectation for the Kauffman networks shown above. Such $a_{Kauff,t+1}$ describes signals on links of *aa*, not the node states of *aa* network which contain K signals: $a_{aa,t+1} = a^K_{Kauff,t} + (1 - a^K_{Kauff,t})/s^K$

2.3 Importance of parameter s from simulation

The results of simulations show other important influences of parameter s, especially for its lower values, on the behaviour of different network types. The annealed approximation does not see those phenomena. It is shown in Fig.6. However, to understand this result I should first describe model and its interpretation. The puzzles of such a complex view of a complex system are not a linear chain but, as a described system, a non-linear network with a lot of feedbacks resembling tautology. Therefore, some credit for a later explanation is needed. For now it can build helpful intuition for a later description.

To describe Fig.6 I must start from Fig.7 which is later discussed in detail. Now, please focus on the right distributions in first row of Fig.7. It is $P(d|N)$ for autonomous sf network type with $s, K = 3, 4$. It is the usual view of damage size distribution when a network grows, here from $N = 50$ to $N = 4000$. What is important? - That for larger N there are two peaks and a deep pass between them, which reaches zero frequency (blue bye) and therefore clearly separates events belonging to particular peaks. These two peaks have different interpretations. The

right peak, under which there is a black line, contains cases of large avalanches which reach equilibrium level (as annealed model expects) and never fade out. Size of damage can be understand as the effect of its measure in lots of particular points during its fluctuation around equilibrium level. It is chaotic behaviour. The left peak is depicted on the left in A - number of damaged nodes, i.e. 'Avalanche'(Serra et al., 2004), because in this parameter it is approximately constant. It contains cases of damage initiation after which damage spreading really fades out. But because initiation is a permanent change (in interpretation, see Ch.3.1), a certain set of damaged nodes remains and this is a damage size, which is small. This is an ordered behaviour. Autonomous case was investigated in simulation described in Fig.6 and by the Kauffman approach. In Fig.6 the fractions of ordered (r) and chaotic (c) cases are depicted. Together, they are all cases of damage initiation ($r + c = 1$). Parameters r and c have an important interpretation: r is a 'degree of order' , and c is a degree of chaos of a network. Real fadeout described by r only occurs in a random way which does not consider negative feedbacks collected by adaptive evolution of living systems. Assuming essential variable fixed we can move effects of negative feedbacks into left peak and add them into r.
For comparison I choose five cases described as s, K: 2,3; 2,4; 3,2; 4,2; 4,3 for the five network types: er, ss, sf, ak, aa. In this set there are: $K = 3$ and $K = 4$ for $s = 2$, next: $s = 3$ and $s = 4$ for $K = 2$. Similarly for $K = 3$ and $s = 4$ the second parameter has two variants. The coefficient w is the smallest for case 3,2 ($w = 1.33$) and the largest in the shown set for 4,3 ($w = 2.25$). Cases 2,3 and 4,2 have the same $w = 1.5$ and for er they have the same value r.
Each simulation consists of 600 000 damage initiations in 100 different networks which grow randomly up to a particular N. After that each node output state was changed 3 times (2 times). Types of fadeout (real or pseudo) were separated using threshold $d = 250/N$ where zero frequency is clear for all cases. The shown in Fig.6 results have 3 decimal digits of precision, therefore the visible differences are not statistical fluctuations. Simulations were made for $N = 2000$ and $N = 3000$ nodes in the networks but result are practically the same.
As can be seen, using higher $s = 4$ for $K = 2$ causes damage spreading to behave differently than for $s = 2$ and $K = 3$, despite the same value of coefficient $w = 1.5$, except for er network type. Therefore, both these parameters cannot substitute for each other, i.e. we cannot limit ourselves to one of them or to the coefficient w. In the Kauffman approach, chaotic regime was investigated mainly for two equally probable signal variants, i.e. $s = 2$ and different K parameter only, but dimension of s is also not trivial and different than dimension K.
The ss and ak networks exhibit symmetrical dependency in s and K but for the most interesting sf and er network types there is no symmetry (see (Gecow, 2009)). For sf the dependency on s is stronger but for er it is weaker than the dependency on K. These differences are not big but may be important. The scale-free network, due to the concentration of many links in a few hubs, has a much lower local coefficient of damage spreading w for most of its area than coefficient for the whole network. The significantly lower damage size for sf network is known (Crucitti et al., 2004; Gallos et al., 2004) as the higher tolerance of a scale-free network of attack. Also Iguchi et al. (2007) state: "It is important to note that the SFRBN is more ordered than the RBN compared with the cases with $K = \langle k \rangle$". The er network, however, contains blind nodes of $k = 0$ which are the main cause for the different behaviour of this network type. Networks types create directed axis used in Fig. 6 where degrees of order and chaos are monotonic except $K = 2$ for er.
Ending agitation for $s \geq 2$ I would like to warn that the assumption of two variants is also used in a wide range of similar models e.g. cellular automata, Ising model or spin glasses (Jan & Arcangelis, 1994). It is typically applied as a safe, useful simplification which should be used

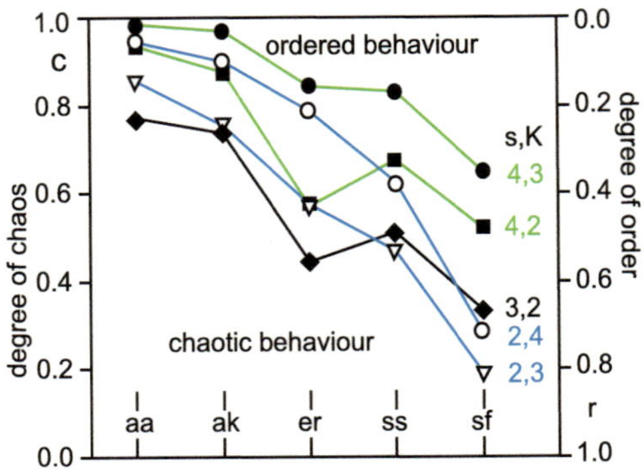

Fig. 6. Degrees of order and chaos as fractions of ordered (real fade out) and chaotic (pseudo fade out - large damage avalanche up to equilibrium level) behaviour of damage after small disturbance for five different network types and small values of parameters s and K. For $N = 2000$ and $N = 3000$ the results are practically the same. The points have 3 decimal digits of precision. Cases of parameters s and K are selected for easy comparison. Note that for $s, K = 4{,}2$ and 2,3 the coefficient $w = 1.5$.

for preliminary recognition. But, just as in the case of Boolean networks, this assumption may not be so safe and should be checked carefully. In the original application of Ising model and spin glasses to physical spin it is obviously correct, but these models are nowadays applied to a wide range of problems, from social (e.g. opinion formation) to biological ones, where such an assumption is typically a simplification.

3. Emergence of matured chaos during network growth

3.1 Model of a complex system, its interpretation and algorithm

3.1.1 Tasks of the model

This model is performed to capture the mechanisms leading to the emergence of regularities of ontogeny evolution observed in old, classical evolutionary biology. For example, 'terminal addition' which means that ontogeny changes accepted by evolution typically are an addition of new transformation which takes place close to the end of ontogeny, i.e. in the form similar to adult. (Ontogeny is a process of body development from zygote to adult form.) 'Terminal modification' is a second such regularity, typically taken as competitive to first one. It states, that additions and removals of transformation are equally probable, but these changes happen much more frequently in later stages. I define such regularities as 'structural tendencies' which are the by-product of adaptive conditions during adaptive evolution of complex networks. Structural tendencies are differences between changeability distribution before and after elimination of non-adaptive changes. Structural tendencies are easily visible in human activity as well. This is wide and important theme.

This main task of a model indicates the range and scale of the modelled process. It is not a system answer for particular stimuli that will be modelled, but a statistical effect of adaptive changes of a large general functioning network over a very long time period. Maybe, mathematical methods can be implemented, but the preferred method for such a non-linear model is a computer simulation which to be real, model and algorithm must be strongly simplified. As was described in Ch.1.2 typical behaviour of network activity is looping in circular attractor. This view was developed for autonomous networks, i.e. without links from- and to the external environment. However, interaction with the environment is intensive for living systems, crucial for adaptive evolution mechanism, and very complex. It includes two main elements which in first approximation can be separated. The first is: influence of the environment on network function which can be described using external inputs of network. The second is: elimination based on network features which can be described using external output signals of network (through define fitness). Fitness is actually an effect of a large number of events where a particular environment sends particular stimuli, and the system answers on the stimuli. In the effect of such a long conversation, large avalanche of damage in the system happens or does not happen. Many such events and similar systems, after averaging, define fitness. This whole process can be omitted using similarity of network output to arbitrary defined requirements. But this method is easy to do in simple models where such particular output exists. Even if environment is constant, circular attractors instead are expected. Constant environment may describe statistically stable environment over a long time period. In this period the stable function of a system with a particular output signal vector should be described (for the fitness definition). Evolutionary change of network structure changes network function and gives new fitness. This fitness is used to decide whether this change should be accepted or eliminated.

3.1.2 Starting model of a stably functioning system without feedbacks

To obtain such a description of stable function of system which can give correct statistical results it is easier to start from the simple case of network without feedbacks. This starting model is lack of simplifications and has simple interpretation. Later, when feedbacks will be added, some necessary simplifications, or a neglecting of the interpretational restrictions which do not change the results, will be introduced.

Let each node-state of this network equal the value of the current signals function on the node inputs. It is not a typical system state - in the next time step (e.g. in the synchronous mode) nothing will be changed. Now a disturbance which permanently changes (change remains constant) one node function is introduced and this node is calculated. To obtain a new stable state of the system function, only nodes with at least one input signal which had changed (as a result of damage) are calculated. For this calculation the old signals on the remaining inputs can be used if for a given node they do not depend on the remaining nodes waiting for calculation. Such a node will always exist because a node does not depend on itself (above it is assumed that the network is without feedbacks). After a finite number of node calculations the process of damage spreading will stop (fade out) - it reaches outputs of the network or 'blind nodes' without outputs or it simple fades out. Now all the node states are again equal to the function value of the current node inputs as was the case at the beginning. However, despite this fade out of damage spreading, lots of node states are different than at the beginning, i.e. - damaged. Only the size of damage is important here. The damaged part of the network is a clear tree which grows inside the 'cone of influence' of the first damaged node (Fig.9 Ch.3.3.1) It is necessary to emphasize that the dynamical process of damage spreading really fades out - i.e. in the next time steps there are no new nodes whose states become different than in a not disturbed system. But in effect, the nodes which function in other ways remain in the new stably functioning system because initiating change is permanent. To control damage spreading only the disturbed system and only nodes with damaged input are calculated.

This paper is limited to damage spreading; I will not use fitness and discuss adaptive evolution. For statistical investigation of damage size, particular functions do not need to be used. Therefore, it is not necessary to check a dependency, and a waiting; node in any sequence can be calculated, i.e. its new state can be drawn. In such a case, the assumption that all node states are equal to the value of the function of the current input signal is not necessary.

3.1.3 Including feedbacks

The process of damage spreading must fade out, because there are no feedbacks, although feedbacks are usual in modelled systems and cannot be neglected. In the case of feedbacks, sometimes an already calculated node gets a damaged input signal for a second time. For measuring the statistical damage size only, it is not necessary to examine its initiation for the second time. If such a second initiation will be processed, then the process virtually never stops. In one large simulated network there are a few decades of such feedbacks with lots of common points and probability, then all of them will simultaneously fade out when coefficient $w > 1$ is very small. Therefore, damage can really fade out only in the first few steps, when the probability that the loop of feedback is reached and closes is still very small. 'Loop closes' means that some already calculated (damaged) nodes get damaged input the second time. Because the already calculated node is not calculated a second time, then damage must also fade out. But it is 'pseudo fade out' which substitutes infinite damage spreading on an equilibrium level. Obtained damage size is statistically identical to distribution of damage size checked in lots of points when damage size fluctuates around equilibrium level.
Such assumptions of model, define simple and useful algorithm described in Ref.(Gecow, 2010) which I use in my investigation. Existence of damage initiation cases with effective middle damage size is a limitation of parameters of this model. In these cases it is not clear if there is pseudo- or real fade out. In such a range of network parameters, the result may be not exact. It is more or less exact depending on fraction of the middle damage cases. This model and algorithm are therefore prepared for chaotic networks where they are exact. As was mentioned in Ch.2.3 and will be discussed below, on chaotic area the cases of real- and pseudo fade out are clearly separated in two peaks of damage size distribution.

3.2 Simulation of networks growth and damage spreading

In opposition to Kauffman's approach and simulation described above in Ch.2.3, now I examine networks with external outputs and inputs. For all simulation I assume $m = 64$ external output signals which are watched for damage and the same number of input signals which are constant. Therefore networks are not autonomous but similar. The main task of this experiment is to get a view of how chaos emerges during network growth and when it can be treated as matured. This task can be translated to obtain and analyse distributions of damage size inside different networks and on their outputs in a large range of network sizes and for other different parameters like $type, s, K$.
This theme was interesting because structural tendencies clearly occur in a range of 'complex' networks. Such complexity was connected to clear separation of right peak from the left one in damage size distribution. These dependency was observed from the beginning of the structural tendencies investigation. Similar in effects three criterion of such 'complexity' threshold are shown in (Gecow, 2008) in Table 1. I.e. 90% of dmx (equilibrium level, see Fig.5), 80% of Lmx and zero occurrence in frequency between peaks even for large statistics. These investigations, however, were a first. Much wider data are analysed in (Gecow, 2009) in Fig.10 (unfortunately, not with the latest version of the description). The upper diagrams (10.1 and 10.2) show the position of the right peak maximum in $P(d)$ distribution in dependency on N up till 4000, and the lower ones (10.3 and 10.4) analogue for $P(L)$. In the left diagrams (10.1 and 10.3) all 5 network types (sf, ss, er, ak, aa) are shown for $s, K = 4, 2$ but for right diagrams,

only extreme sf and ak for s = 4, 16, 64 with K = 2 and only K = 3 with s = 4. In the effect the previous suggestion of very similar results of the above three criterions has not been confirmed. Therefore, in (Gecow, 2010a) a simulation experiment investigating the whole interesting range of parameters was performed. As in Fig.7 is shown, criterions based on distance to dmx or Lmx are an effect of existence in the network special node - 'environment' and its parameter m, but it is an important element of described reality, e.g. living systems.

3.2.1 Description of the experiment

Fig.7 shows the main results of simulations: distributions $P(d|N)$ of damage size d (a fraction of all N nodes which have different state than in the non-disturbed network); and distributions $P(L|N)$ damage size of network external output signals in number of damaged signals L. Each of these distributions are shown for 20 particular points of N = 50, 70, 100, 130, 160, 200, 240, 300, 400, 500, 600, 800, 1000, 1200, 1400, 1600, 2000, 2400, 3000, 4000 shown in log-scale. In Fig.7, only three cases of network types and their particular parameters s and K are shown but all combinations of 7 network types $(sh, sf, si, ss, er, ak, aa)$, $s = 2, 3, 4, 16$ and $K = 2, 3, 4$ except cases s, K = 2,2 and 16,4 were simulated. This is together $7 * (4 * 3 - 2) = 70$ cases(Gecow, 2010a). As in Ref. (Gecow, 2010;a) these parameters are denoted in the form: two (or one, second only) letters of network $type$, followed by s and K parameters in number separated by a comma.
Networks grow during the simulation (except er which is drawn each time). At the particular levels of N damage is simulated as in Ch.2.3 where all remaining variants of state of each node are used in turn as damage initiation. When they all are used, the network grows to the next level of N. Results of a few networks with the same parameters are summarised. For each level of N the same number of events is assumed (near 300 thousands, for s? 2,3 - 800 000), therefore for larger N less networks are sufficient. When s=16, then there are 15 remaining states and to obtain 300 000 events for a network containing N=4000 nodes it is enough to build 5 networks. As it will be shown later, it is a relatively small number and a large but interesting fluctuation was obtained (see Ch.3.2.3 and Fig.8). Distribution $P(d|N)$ has a discrete number of points, it is N. For all N in Fig.7 there are a fixed 200 points used to make comparison available, but such an operation must cause some visible discontinuities in the beginning of the first, left peak.
In Fig.7 only 3 cases are shown, but they depict all the basic phenomena well. One autonomous case is added for comparison. This is the main view of the evolution process of distribution of damage size d and L during network growth. In the details of this process a threshold of matured chaos is searched for. In the plane parallel to the paper, a distribution $P(d)$ or $P(L)$ is shown for the particular network size N. N grows depicted in logarithmic scale in depth behind the paper. For non-zero values of P (as frequency obtained as simulation results) red colour is used, for zero value - blue. The vertical lines are blue if both connected values of frequency (P) are zero and green otherwise. This useful method easily depicts the dynamics of chaos appearance as nice landscape with the important area of blue 'bay' where exact zero between peaks occurs.
The right peak (for networks with external connections) emerges from the tail of the left peak in the part of small damage (for autonomous network it appears faster and near dmx). In the first period of network growth it moves to the right, but later it turns smoothly and its position becomes stable, drawing an asymptotical line (black one) to the parallel line to the N axis. It is a vertical projection of the maximum of right peak on 'sea level' ($P = 0$). These lines from all simulation cases are collected and analysed in details in (Gecow, 2010a). In addition, the

degree of chaos c and similarity of d and L (as $L/m/d$, i.e. departure of $L = d * m$ expectation) are analysed. There are searched criteria of chaotic features where a small network effect can be neglected. The results have a short description in the next chapter. The main conclusion is that there is no critical point which can be used for such criterion. But matured chaos appears, and some threshold (but smooth and little bit different in different phenomena) objectively exist. In such a case, any particular criterion must contain arbitrary defined value.

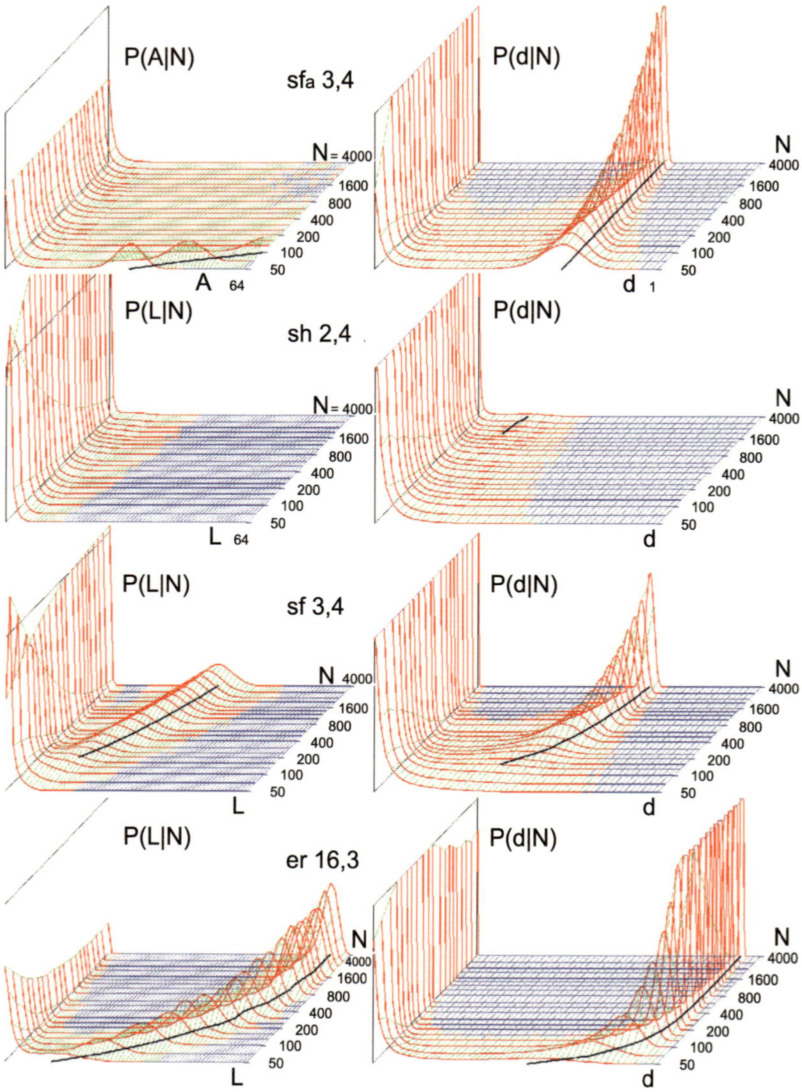

Fig. 7. Evolution of damage sizes L (left) and d (right) distributions during network growth for different $type, s, K$. In the first row autonomous case is shown, first part of left peak (left) in 'avalanche' A . 3 of 70 simulated cases show the full spectrum of main features: from the least- to the most chaotic. Blue indicates zero frequency. Vertical projection (black line) of the right peak maximum on the 'sea level' plane (P=0) is the equilibrium level of damage.

Small network ($N = 50$) typically behaves as it does on the edge of chaos and order (near power law as for percolation point). This dependency approximately remains as the left peak in the chaotic area and there is a place for life evolution. Length of d axis is constant for different N, those suppresses its shape for larger N even if it is the same for the number of damaged nodes (see Fig.7 'avalanche' distribution $P(A|N)$ for autonomous network). Right peak emerges where black line starts. For extremely ordered *sh* 2,4 (the least chaotic is *sh* 2,3) shown in the second row in Fig.7, right peak does not appear for $P(L|N)$ even for $N = 4000$ but for $P(d|N)$ it just starts to appear. For extremely chaotic network *er* 16,3 right peak is present already for $N = 50$. (The most chaotic are *ak* and *aa* 16,3.) Between peaks the pass forms whose minimum goes down and reaches zero frequency (forms the blue bay). Note, that only where this bay appears the reversed annealed algorithm used for these simulations becomes surely exact. For all sections of N up to this point, the algorithm gives only approximate results, but they sufficiently show the qualitative properties of the growth process and the emergence of the chaotic features.

3.2.2 Results

The term 'matured chaos' in the context of network size N has two main aspects, they are: 1- high level of chaos; and 2- small influence of 'finite size effects'. The first one splits itself into: a- high value of equilibrium level of damage (influence of environment can be neglected); and b - high value of degree of chaos c (Ch.2.3, Fig.6). The height of equilibrium level of damage (1.a) for the very large networks (infinite N), i.e. dmx and Lmx, are expected by annealed approximation (Ch.2.2.3, Fig.5) and depend first of all on s and secondly on K. Dependency on N is searched, therefore not the absolute values of dmx or Lmx, but departures of these values are interesting. These departures are in the range of point 2, i.e. 'finite size effects'. However, absolute value for particular N also influences peaks separation (2.d). Degree of chaos c (1.b) also have asymptotic value for infinite N for particular case of network *type* and parameters s, K. In such a case maturation of chaos is mainly a domain of aspect 2 - disappearance of finite size effect. In its range exist qualitative aspects of shape and clarity of separation of both peaks from which should be taken more measurable phenomenon - appearance of zero frequency (blue bay) between peaks. Its existence does not depend on connection to environment (upper row in Fig.7).

Each of analysed relations seems to be dependent in a different way on the observed parameters in detail, but generally they give similar conclusions. Differences in these relations' behaviour suggest that they are at least three or four different mechanisms. Each of them seems to be near 'scale free' and therefore there is no critical points in them which means that for a particular threshold, an arbitrary value must be chosen depending on our intention and needs (when properties of small network can be neglected). The last criterion (i.e. appearance of zero frequency between peaks) seems to be the most 'correct' and useful. It shifts very slowly with the growth of statistics (event number). This shift needs more investigation. This criterion works correctly only for networks with feedbacks. For a network without feedbacks (which in described reality is a strange case) it can be used with approximation. This theme will be discussed in Ch.3.3.

3.2.3 Two causes of dispersion, reversed-annealed simulation

Separation level of the left and right peaks depends on the wideness of the right one but what are the sources of this wideness? Two of them can be expected:

1- Necessary effects of taken parameters m for L and N for d, when it is described by a binomial

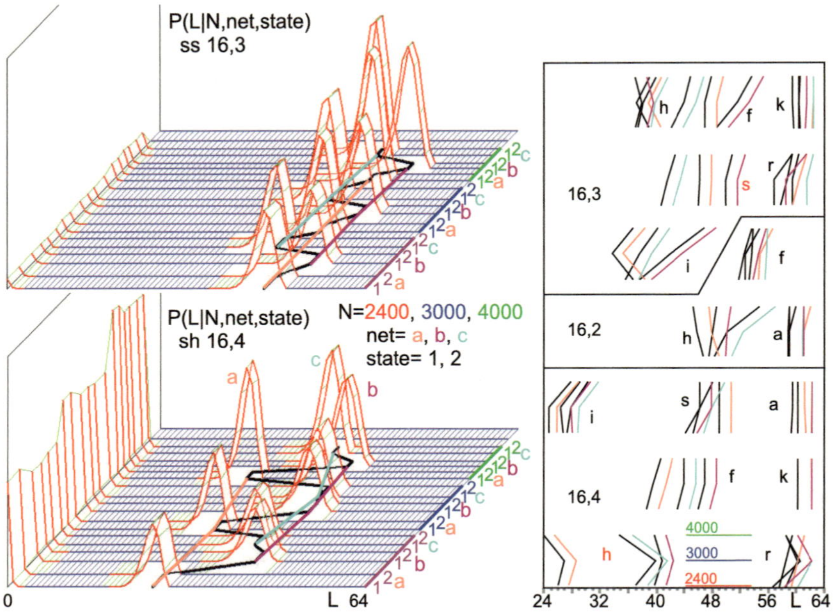

Fig. 8. Individual structure influence on the right peak width. Extreme examples of differences in 3 particular networks (a, b, c) on N=2400, 3000, 4000 measured two times, the second time after a random change of all node states, while keeping the structure stable. Value of shift is larger (s=16) than the width of peak which is exactly repeatable (two consecutive cases 1 and 2). The stable character of deviation for a particular network during its three steps of growth is visible, especially in the right diagram. Compare to *er* which doesn't growth. This diagram contains all the simulated cases depicted only as points of maximum (colour lines) and its standard deviation (black lines).

distribution if each node or output signal has equal probability to be damaged. Such a simple model works too well. For L $K = 2$ the comparison theoretical standard deviation to the experimental data are in the range of error (10%) but for $K = 3$ and $K = 4$ the obtained standard deviation is a little bit lower than theoretical which needs correction of assumption. It also approximately explains well the shapes for *d* and *ak* network, however, for $K < 4$ experimental standard deviations are greater than the theoretical ones; up to two times for s, K=4,2. This discrepancy has unknown source, it grows for more chaotic networks and reaches a 4 times higher value for *sh* 4,2. This study of dispersion sources is only a preliminary investigation.

2- Each particular network has its own particular individual structure which should cause a deviation from the average behaviour. Above I remark (Ch.3.2.1) that for s=16 where only 5 networks were used for the last N=4000, large fluctuations are observed. To confirm that the fluctuation source is the structure, and to get a scale of this phenomenon three networks were simulated for N=2400, 3000 and 4000. For each N level two damage measurements were performed: one with node states as they were obtained during network growth and the second one with new random states of all nodes. Fig.8 shows two of the most extreme examples (*ss* 16,3 and *sh* 16,4) of the effects of this experiment in the form of full distributions. All results in the form of three points of the right peak's maximum, connected by line in the according colour accomplished by black line showing standard deviation are also shown.

As was expected, effects of changing node states and original states are identical. This method resembles the annealed model Derrida & Pomeau (1986); Kauffman (1993) but reversed: in the original annealed model, the states are kept and the structure is changed. This is the source of the algorithm name: 'reversed annealed'. Please note that for these simulations it is not necessary to use particular functions for nodes. Such functions are used (Gecow, 2009a) for certain structural tendencies simulation. As can be seen in Fig.8 in the right diagram, deviations are typically stable during the next levels N of network growth and the distances of peak maxims are larger than the standard deviation of peaks for one network. It is probably an effect of hubs and blind nodes as more chaotic networks (aa, ak, er) exhibit the effect in a much smaller way. For ss, si, sf and sh the wideness of total and individual peaks, and their absolute differences consecutively grow and are relatively and absolutely the biggest for sh, but it depend on K and s parameters.

3.3 Explanation of two peaks

Two separated peaks, one for real fade out and the second for pseudo fade out are an assumption of the simplified algorithm ('reversed annealed') used for simulation. Using this algorithm I investigated these two peaks and the appearance of the right one. Is it a tautology? No, however, in the area where the second peak emerges, this algorithm is not clear and may produce effects which are not exactly correct. Such effects have no clear interpretation. Thus, it is desirable to model this area in another way to understand why we should expect two peaks and why they are not present from the beginning. Percolation theory is a known theory which explain these two peaks. Another way for intuition for a different point of view and different aspects will be shown here.

3.3.1 Extremely simple lw network and cone of influence

A good place to begin is the extremely simple network depicted in Fig.9 upper row on the right. Imagine that there are 32 nodes in each level. Each node has two inputs and two outputs like aa network for $K = 2$. Nodes from one level are connected to higher level nodes in an extremely ordered way depicted in the figure. To eliminate boundaries on the left and right a cylinder is created. Network ends at the top in external outputs of network which send signals to the environment as a result of network function. I, however, will consider network outputs in a more complicated way. I name this network 'lw' - 'l' because it has clear levels and 'w' because this letter is similar to the connection pattern.

The lw network does not contain feedbacks, it is probably the most ordered one in the sense of simplicity of connection pattern which requires an extremely small amount of information for its description. Only for a similarly simple network can one draw on paper a 'cone of influence' for a given node. The cone contains in its 'later' part, all nodes which can be damaged if the given one (in the vertex of cone) is damaged. Outputs are the base of the cone. Arrows depict the direction of signal flow which means that lw is a directed and functioning network like all the networks of our interest (RSN) Gecow (2010). In such a case, information in the form of signals flows up from the bottom (if cylinders stand up); this is functional order (or sequence) which defines terms 'early', 'later' and 'terminal' (closely near outputs, at the end of signal path). A similar phenomenon named 'supremacy' is investigated in Holyst et al. (2004) in a more theoretical way for directed scale-free network.

Levels can be numbered by number H (height) starting from an indicated node, however, nodes are similar and such a method is not stable. It can be substituted by a numbering which starts from the stable outputs therefore, such numbering is a depth D measure. The depth

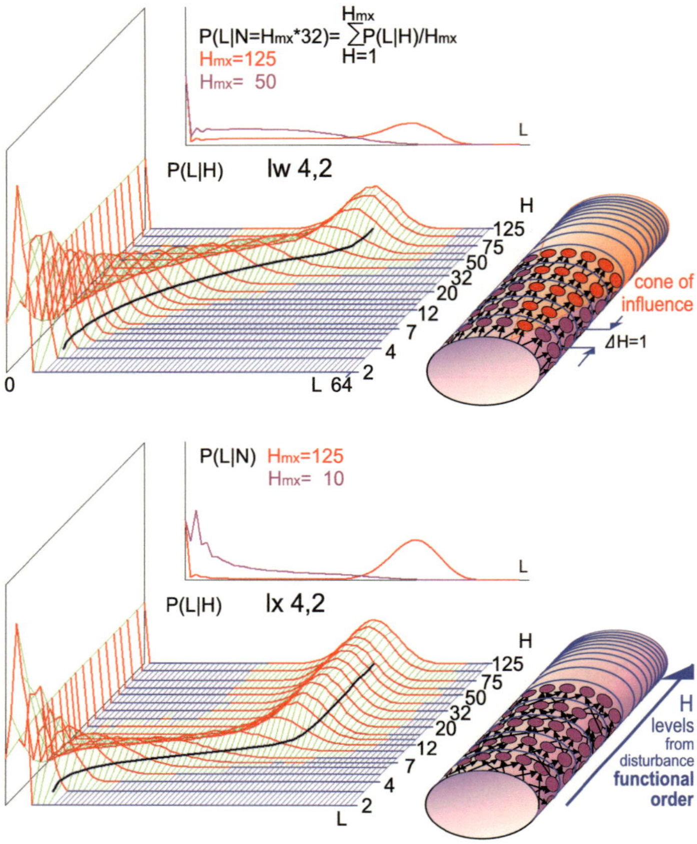

Fig. 9. Definitions of: lw and lx networks, cone of influence, functional order and levels. $P(L|H)$ - damage size distribution for consecutive levels H (if initiation was made in depth $D = H$), and $P(L|N)$ - damage size L distribution for networks which are Hmx high (all depth D are equally probable, $N = Hmx * 32$)

D is a useful structural substitution of the functional sequence. For a cone of influence it is the height of it, which indicates the number of outputs which can be reached by damage initialised in the vertex of the cone. Not all of the later nodes and network outputs will be damaged. The density of filling the cone by damage depends on the coefficient w of damage propagation described in Ch.2.2.1 and Ref. Gecow (2010). If $w > 1$ and damage does not fade out in the first few steps, then it also becomes a cone and is greater for greater cone height.

3.3.2 Damage on outputs and damage path through network without feedbacks, complexity

Next, the distribution of number L of damaged output signals in dependency on depth D will be examined. As an equivalent of using the depth D for the real network outputs, the sets of node outputs in consecutive higher levels (numbered by H) from initiation of damage can be watched. In Fig.9 this process is shown for $s = 4$. The levels are numbered with H but for comparison to the old known term, it can be calculated $N = H * 32$ which is the number of nodes in levels from initiation of damage. As in Fig.7 there are two peaks, zero in-between and the process of emergence of the right peak, however, it does not yet correspond with Fig.7.

To obtain the same meaning as in Fig.7 the height of the full network (which we can assume to be equal to Hmx) must be defined. Distributions from all equally probable levels (from the beginning to the shown one $= Hmx$) must also be summarized. The result is also shown in Fig.9, but only for two heights Hmx of network (for $Hmx, N = 10,320$ for lx or 50,1600 for lw and 125,4000 for both). Now we also find two peaks, but in-between there cannot be zero because middle levels exist and were summarized.
Let a part of 'order' from the description of structure be removed using random connection between neighbouring levels. Much more information for the description of such a particular network is necessary those it is more complex. I use the name 'lx' for this network (Fig.9 lower row in the right). In the left it depicts the damage propagation for lx in consecutive distributions of damage size for growing distance from the initiation point as above for lw. For lx the right peak reaches its stable position much faster and the transitional stages contribute much less to the sum between peaks, which is visible in $P(L|N)$ (here N is used to distinguish $P(L|H)$ for particular level and summarized case for all levels from initiation point to Hmx). When s grows, e.g. two times; from 4 to 8, then the effect is similar to an increase of complexity. Much more is necessary to know in order to describe such a particular network with states, and the right peak reaches a stable position two times faster.

3.3.3 Damage path through network with feedbacks

It is now necessary to discuss the network case with feedbacks. This question crops up: how deep is a particular place of damage initiation in such a network? This question can be translated into a question about the length of path from initiation point to outputs, however, in opposite to networks lw and lx such paths typically are very different and the clear answer is not defined. They are different for two reasons. First, because clear levels used in lw and lx are a strong assumption which must not be taken even for network without feedbacks, e.g. for *an* network described in Ref. Gecow (2008). The second reason is because feedbacks make such a measure undefined.
Feedbacks are the loops in which signals and damage can loop many times even up to infinity therefore there is no longest path, but the shortest path, which is only defined, is not very adequate. This theme is discussed more widely in Ref. (Gecow, 2009b). In a typical randomly constructed network there are a lot of feedbacks, they are a cause of the equilibrium state of damage which should remain stable to infinity. If damage passes the first period when it is small and has real probability of fade out, then it reaches the feedbacks loops and its path through network will be infinite. It corresponds to an infinite depth of initiation, still, outputs may also be reached fast. Therefore in a network with feedbacks there are no middle paths and middle damage sizes placed between peaks. Then in this area zero frequency occurs. This zero means that the network is so large that feedbacks are reached quickly (after a short way, frequently) enough that middle ways cannot happen.
For a network without feedbacks there remains the criterion (of matured chaos) based on the stable position of the right peak and for practice some arbitrary percent of asymptotical level should be used. A large flat area between peaks of small value of probability in comparison to the right peak may be taken as a good approximation of zero occurrence.

4. Conclusion

In comparison to the main stream of investigation of transition to chaos which concerns the exact 'edge of chaos' ($K \leq 2$, $s = 2$) on the K axis, my approach expands s dimension (more equally probable signal variants) and moves attention into the area known as chaotic ($K \geq 2$,

$s \geq 2$ without the case $s, K = 2, 2$) and large networks. When network is small, it typically is not chaotic, then (matured) chaos emerges during its growth. Investigation of this emerging reaches much higher network sizes ($N = 4000$ even for $s, K = 4, 4$ and 16,3). In this area another transition to 'matured' chaos and its threshold is investigated, now on the N axis which is another, independent dimension of searched space.
The 'matured chaos' in context of network size N is an effect of the disappearance of finite size effect during network growth. Important part of causes the effect is constant special node - connection to environment. Three or four independent mechanisms can be seen. Each of them seems to be near 'scale free' and therefore there are no critical points in them which means that for particular threshold an arbitrary value must be chosen depending on our needs. Appearance of zero frequency between peaks in damage size distribution seems to be the most 'correct' and useful criterion of matured chaos.
Living systems are shifted following Ref. Gecow (2010) to 'matured chaos' onto the opposite shore of Kauffman's liquid region near the 'edge of chaos'. Evolution of living systems needing small changes is placed in the left peak of damage size distribution which was underestimated up till now. An other-than-zero limitation of order degree r (fraction of damage initiation which do not convert into large avalanche and create the left peak) found in the described experiment takes up the importance of this place.

5. References

R. Albert, A.-L. Barabási, 2002. Statistical mechanics of complex networks. Rev. Mod. Phys., 74,1, 47–97

R. Albert, H.G. Othmer, 2003. The topology of the regulatory interactions predicts the expression pattern of the segment polarity genes in Drosophila melanogaster. J. Theor. Biol. 223. 1–18

M. Aldana, 2003. Dynamics of Boolean Networks with Scale Free Topology. Physica D 185, 45-66

M. Aldana, S. Coppersmith, L. P. Kadanoff, 2003. Boolean Dynamics with Random Couplings. in *Perspectives and Problems in Nonlinear Science*, Applied Mathematical Sciences Series, ed. E. Kaplan, J. E. Marsden, K. R. Sreenivasan (Springer-Verleg, Berlin).

W. R. Ashby, 1960. *Design for a Brain* 2nd edn. (Wiley, New York)

P. Bak, 1996. *How Nature Works: The Science of Self-Organized Criticality*, New York: Copernicus.

F. J. Ballesteros, B. Luque, 2005. Phase transitions in random networks: Simple analytic determination of critical points. Phys. Rev. E 71, 031104

W. Banzhaf, 2003. On the Dynamics of an Artificial Regulatory Network. In *Advances in Arti□cial Life, 7th European Conference, ECAL'03, LNAI Springer* , 2801, 217–227

A.-L. Barabási, R. Albert, H. Jeong, 1999. Mean-field theory for scale-free random networks. Physica A 272, 173–187

A.-L. Barabási, E. Bonabeau, 2003. Scale-Free Networks. Scientific American 50–59

P. Crucitti, V. Latora, M. Marchiori, A. Rapisarda, 2004. Error and attacktolerance of complex networks Physica A 340 388–394

B. Derrida, Y. Pomeau, 1986. Random Networks of Automata: A Simple Annealed Approximation. Europhys. Lett., 1(2), 45–49

B. Derrida, G.Weisbuch, 1986. Evolution of Overlaps Between Configurations in Random Boolean Networks. Journal De Physique 47, 1297– 1303.

P. Erdős and A. Rényi, 1960. Random graphs. Publication of the Mathematical Institute of the Hungarian Academy of Science, 5, 17–61

J. D. Farmer, S. Kauffman, N. H. Packard, 1986. Autocatalytic Replication of Polymers. Physica D 22(1-3), 50–67.

S. Fortunato, 2005. Damage spreading and opinion dynamics on scale-free networks. Physica A 348, 683–690

P. Fronczak, A. Fronczak, J.A. Holyst, 2008. Kauffman Boolean model in undirected scale-free networks. Phys. Rev. E 77, 036119

L.K. Gallos, P. Argyrakis, A. Bunde, R. Cohen, S. Havlin, 2004. Tolerance of scale-free networks: from friendly to intentional attack strategies. Physica A 344, 504 - 509

A. Gecow, 1975. A cybernetic model of improving and its application to the evolution and ontogenesis description. In: *Fifth International Congress of Biomathematics* Paris

A. Gecow, A. Hoffman, 1983. Self-improvement in a complex cybernetic system and its implication for biology. Acta Biotheoretica 32, 61–71

A. Gecow, M. Nowostawski, M. Purvis, 2005. Structural tendencies in complex systems development and their implication for software systems. J.UCS, 11,2 327–356

A. Gecow, 2005a. From a "Fossil" Problem of Recapitulation Existence to Computer Simulation and Answer. Neural Network World. Acad. Sci. Czech Rep.3/2005, 189–201

A. Gecow, 2008. Structural Tendencies - effects of adaptive evolution of complex (chaotic) systems. Int.J Mod.Phys.C, 19, 4, 647–664.

A. Gecow, 2009. Emergence of Chaos and Complexity During System Growth. In *From System Complexity to Emergent Properties*. M.A. Aziz-Alaoui & Cyrille Bertelle (eds), Springer, Understanding Complex Systems Series, 115–154

A. Gecow, 2009a. Emergence of Growth and Structural Tendencies During Adaptive Evolution of System. In as above, 211–241

A. Gecow, 2009b. The conditions of structural tendencies. In *Modelling and Analysis of Complex Interacting Systems*. M.A. Aziz-Alaoui & Cyrille Bertelle (eds), DCDIS-B, 551–572

A. Gecow, 2010. More Than Two Equally Probable Variants of Signal in Kauffman Networks as an Important Overlooked Case, Negative Feedbacks Allow Life in the Chaos. arXiv:1003.1988v1

A. Gecow, 2010a. Complexity Threshold for Functioning Directed Networks in Damage Size Distribution. arXiv:1004.3795v1

C. Gershenson, 2004. Updating Schemes in Random Boolean Networks: Do They Really Matter? arXiv:nlin/0402006v3

A. Grabowski, R.A. Kosiński, 2004. Epidemic spreading in a hierarchical social network. Phys.Rev.E, 70, 031908

A. Grabowski, R.A. Kosiński, 2006. Ising-based model of opinion formation in a complex network of nterpersonal interactions. Physica A, 361, 651-664

S. E.Harris, B.K. Sawhill, A. Wuensche, S.A. Kauffman, 2002. A model of transcriptional regulatory networks based on biases in the observed regulation rules. Complexity 7, 23

G. Ito, 2008. A Dynamical Boolean Network. arXiv:0804.1179v3

J. H. Holland, 1998. *Emergence: from chaos to order*. Oxford University Press

J.A. Holyst, A.Fronczak, and P.Fronczak, 2004. Supremacy distribution in evolving networks. Phys. Rev. E 70, 046119

T. R. Hughes et al., 2000. Functional discovery via a compendium of expression profiles. Cell textbf102, 109–126.

K. Iguchi, S.-i. Kinoshita, H. Yamada, 2007. Boolean dynamics of Kauffman models with a scale-free network. J. Theor. Biol. 247, 138–151

N. Jan, L. de Arcangelis, 1994. Computational Aspects of Damage Spreading. In: *Annual Reviews of Computational Physics I*, ed by D. Stauffer (World Scientific, Singapore) 1–16

S.A. Kauffman, 1969. Metabolic stability and epigenesis in randomly constructed genetic nets. J. Theor. Biol. 22, 437-467

S.A. Kauffman, 1971. Gene regulation networks: a theory for their global structure and behaviour. Current topics in dev. biol. 6, 145.

S.A. Kauffman, 1993. *The Origins of Order: Self-Organization and Selection in Evolution* (Oxford University Press New York)

S.A. Kauffman, C. Peterson, B. Samuelsson, C. Troein, 2004. Genetic networks with canalyzing Boolean rules are always stable. PNAS 101,49, 17102–17107

J. F. Knabe, C. L. Nehaniv, M. J. Schilstra, T. Quick, 2006. Evolving Biological Clocks using Genetic Regulatory Networks. In *Proceedings of the Arti□cial Life X Conference (Alife 10)*, 15–21, MIT Press

B. Korzeniewski, 2001. Cybernetic formulation of the definition of life. J.Theor.Biol. 209, 275

B. Korzeniewski, 2005. Confrontation of the cybernetic definition of living individual with the real word. Acta Biotheoretica 53, 1–28

B. Luque, R.V. Solé, 1997. Phase transitions in random networks: Simple analytic determination of critical points. Phys. Rev. E 55(1), 257–260

B. Luque, F.J. Ballesteros, 2004. Random walk networks. Physica A 342 207–213

P. Rämö, J. Kesseli, O. Yli-Harja, 2006. Perturbation avalanches and criticality in gene regulatory networks. J. Theor. Biol. 242 164–170

H. Schuster, 1984. Deterministic Chaos: An Introduction. Physik-Verlag

R. Serra, M. Villani, A. Semeria, 2004. Genetic network models and statistical properties of gene expression data in knock-out experiments. J. Theor. Biol. 227, 149–157

R. Serra, M. Villani, L. Agostini, 2004a. On the dynamics of random Boolean networks with scale-free outgoing connections. Physica A 339 665 – 673

R. Serra, M. Villani, A. Graudenzi, S. A. Kauffman, 2007. Why a simple model of genetic regulatory networks describes the distribution of avalanches in gene expression data. J. Theor. Biol. 246 449–460

R. Serra, M. Villani, A. Barbieri, S. A. Kauffman, A. Colacci, 2010. On the dynamics of random Boolean networks subject to noise: attractors, ergodic sets and cell types. J. Theor. Biol. 265, 185–193

I. Shmulevich, E.R. Dougherty, W. Zhang, 2002. From Boolean to Probabilistic Boolean Networks as Models of Genetic Regulatory Networks. Proc. IEEE, 90(11), 1778–1792

I. Shmulevich, S. A. Kauffman, M. Aldana, 2005. Eukaryotic cells are dynamically ordered or critical but not chaotic. PNAS 102 (38), 13439–13444

R.V. Sole, B. Luque, S. Kauffman, 2000. Phase transitions in random networks with multiple states. Technical Report 00-02-011, Santa Fe Institute

A.O. Sousa, 2005. Consensus formation on a triad scale-free network. Physica A 348 701–710

A. Wagner, 2001. Estimating coarse gene network structure from large-scale gene perturbation data. Santa Fe Institute Working Paper, 01-09-051.